CW01652270

[LO]CAL [GO]VERNMENT [CO]MMISSION FOR ENGLAND

FINAL RECOMMENDATIONS ON THE FUTURE LOCAL GOVERNMENT OF:

BASILDON & THURROCK

BLACKBURN & BLACKPOOL

BROXTOWE, GEDLING & RUSHCLIFFE

DARTFORD & GRAVESHAM, GILLINGHAM & ROCHESTER upon MEDWAY

EXETER

GLOUCESTER

HALTON & WARRINGTON

HUNTINGDONSHIRE & PETERBOROUGH

NORTHAMPTON

NORWICH

SPELTHORNE

THE WREKIN

Report to the Secretary of State for Environment
Volume II The Evidence

December 1995

HMSO: LONDON

LOCAL GOVERNMENT COMMISSION FOR ENGLAND

This report summarises the views expressed to the Commission arising from its draft recommendations published on 26 September 1995. These have been taken into account by the Commission in reaching its final recommendations for the future local government of the 21 districts referred to it by the Secretary of State on 29 June 1995. The final recommendations, and the Commission's reasoning, are set out in Volume I.

Members of the Commission are:

Sir David Cooksey (Chairman)

Professor Malcolm Grant (Deputy Chairman)

Peter Brokenshire

Professor Michael Clarke

Ken Ennals CB

Bob Scruton*

Helena Shovelton

David Thomas

Norman Warner

Dr Bob Chilton (Chief Executive)

* As a serving parish councillor in Kent, and a member of the Executive Committee of the Kent Association of Parish Councils, Mr Scruton declared an interest and did not participate in the Commission's deliberations on the four districts in Kent.

First published 1995
ISBN 0-11-780127-5

CONTENTS

INTRODUCTION

The Secretary of State for the Environment issued a Direction to the Local Government Commission for England (the Commission) on 29 June 1995 to undertake 21 district-based structural reviews in 12 counties. On 26 September 1995 the Commission published its draft recommendations in separate reports, which are available from HMSO, for each of the 12 county areas affected by the review. These reports also contain a summary of the evidence from the Stage One consultation period, 5 July 1995 to 10 August 1995, and the findings of opinion surveys on community identity that were undertaken by MORI (Market & Opinion Research International Ltd) during the earlier county-wide reviews. The Commission set out the reasoning behind its draft recommendations in *The 1995 Review of 21 Districts in England, Overview Report*, which is also available from HMSO. A list of the Commission's publications, relating to the 21 district-based structural reviews is in the Appendix to this volume.

In its deliberations, the Commission took into account all the material submitted to it in respect of each review area during the Stage Three consultation period, which lasted from the publication of the draft recommendations until 8 November 1995, and also reflected further on the evidence received during Stage One.

Volume I of this report sets out the reasoning behind the Commission's final recommendations. This volume summarises the representations received, reflecting the range of views expressed. These summaries do not purport to be an exhaustive précis of the evidence received by the Commission, but seek to reflect respondents' main areas of concern or interest. Copies of all representations are available for inspection by appointment at the Commission's offices. A list of respondents is available on request.

For each review area, this volume first sets out the Commission's draft recommendations, then summarises the representations received on them together with tabulations classifying the responses, prepared by the NOP Research Group Limited (NOP). Finally the results of opinion surveys carried out by MORI during Stage Three of the review process are presented.

During both the Stage One and Stage Three the Commission also received representations that addressed issues of general concern, not specific to particular review areas. These national representations are summarised separately in this volume.

"The Commission is most grateful to all concerned for their co-operation and assistance, and to all those - both individuals and organisations - who submitted written representations."

During Stage Three of the review, Commission members and staff visited the review areas and met local authority members and officers, interest groups and business organisations. The Commission is most grateful to all concerned for their co-operation and assistance, and to all those - both individuals and organisations - who submitted written representations.

CHAPTER 1

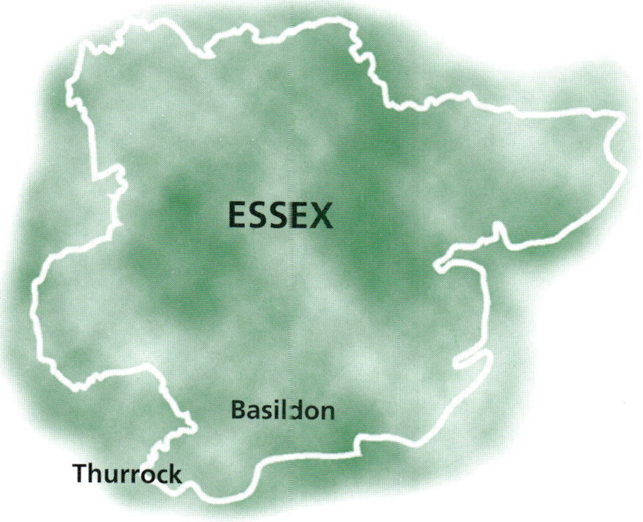

BASILDON AND THURROCK IN THE COUNTY OF ESSEX

Draft Recommendations

1.1 The Commission's report *Draft Recommendations on the Future Local Government of Basildon and Thurrock in the County of Essex* summarised the evidence taken into account by the Commission in reaching its draft recommendations.

Figure 1.1
Draft Recommendations for Basildon and Thurrock in the County of Essex

Structure

- There should be no change to the current two-tier structure of local government in Basildon. However, Billericay (the existing district wards of Billericay East, Billericay West and Burstead) should cease to form part of Basildon and should join with the existing administrative area of Brentwood to form a new Brentwood and Billericay District Council. Wickford (the existing district wards of Wickford North and Wickford South) should also cease to form part of Basildon and should join with the existing administrative area of Rochford to form a new Rochford and Wickford District Council. A new Basildon District Council should be established based on the remaining nine Basildon district wards.

- The existing two-tier structure of local government in Thurrock should be replaced. Thurrock should become a unitary authority responsible for the broad range of local government functions currently carried out by both county and district councils.

Ceremonial Arrangements

- The county of Essex should be retained for ceremonial and related purposes, and Thurrock should be associated with the county for such purposes.

Public Protection

- There should be a combined authority established in the present county area for the fire service, on which the representatives of the new unitary authority for Thurrock should serve. Similarly, representatives of the new unitary authority should also serve on a joint committee with representatives of the County Council to select the local authority membership of the Essex Police Authority. No changes are proposed to the area covered by the Essex Police Authority, or to the probation and magistrates' court services.

Strategic Planning

- The new unitary authority for Thurrock should prepare a unitary development plan for its area, within the framework of the Secretary of State's strategic planning guidance for the Thames Gateway. The new authority should also be a minerals and waste planning authority and exercise development control functions for its area for all purposes.

Electoral Arrangements

- The unitary authority for Thurrock should initially comprise 41 members, serving the existing 15 wards, including an additional member in each of the West Thurrock and East Tilbury wards, giving twelve three-member wards, two double-member wards and one single-member ward. Elections should be held by thirds.

- The continuing Essex County Council should have 79 members, with one member being returned from each of the county divisions outside the current local government administrative areas of Thurrock and Southend-on-Sea.

Views Expressed to the Commission

1.2 The Commission received a wide range of direct representations on its draft recommendations, from local authorities, residents, Members of Parliament, business and voluntary groups, parish and town councils, and from other public and private sector organisations. Over 900 representations were received from individuals and organisations, including over 700 from respondents within the two review districts (Figures 1.2, 1.3 and 1.4).

The Commission also received over 8,800 representations in the form of standard letters, response slips and petitions which were recorded separately (Figure 1.5). Over 6,700 of these were response slips from a letter circulated by the Billericay Town Council Steering Committee in support of the draft recommendation for a new Brentwood and Billericay District Council. Figures 1.2, 1.3 and 1.4 exclude representations from the local authorities; these are summarised separately (Figure 1.6).

Figure 1.2
Views of Respondents Within Basildon

Preferred structure	Individuals	Organisations
Unitary Basildon New Town	31	12
Unitary Basildon (on existing boundaries)	43	3
No change	95	4
Billericay and Wickford removed from Basildon (two-tier)	30	1
Billericay with Brentwood (two-tier)	68	5
Wickford with Rochford (two-tier)	21	1
Wickford to join another area (i.e. not Rochford)	7	0
Billericay and Wickford removed and a unitary Basildon New Town established	15	4
Opposition to structural options (no positive preference stated)	22	0
Other/no preference	26	3

Source: Local Government Commission for England and NOP

Figure 1.3
Views of Respondents Within Thurrock

Preferred structure	Individuals	Organisations
Unitary Thurrock	132	9
Opposition to structural options (no positive preference stated)	60	9
No change	112	6
Other/no preference	8	3

Source: Local Government Commission for England and NOP

Figure 1.4
Views of Respondents From Outside The Review Districts

Preferred structure	Individuals	Organisations
Unitary Thurrock	1	1
Billericay with Brentwood (two-tier)	23	8
Wickford with Rochford (two-tier)	18	5
Opposition to structural options (no positive preference stated)	19	6
No change	59	12
Other/no preference	20	6

Source: Local Government Commission for England and NOP
Note: Excludes out of county representations

Figure 1.5
Views of Respondents: Standard Letters and Petition Signatures

Preferred structure	Thurrock residents	Basildon residents	Billericay/Brentwood residents	Residents of other areas
Billericay with Brentwood (two-tier)	0	7,380	864	184
Billericay and Wickford removed and a unitary Basildon New Town established	0	71	0	0
Unitary Thurrock	64	0	0	0
No change	0	258	2	0
Opposition to structural options	0	6	5	0
Other option	0	5	0	0

Source: Local Government Commission for England
Note:550 residents of Billericay and Brentwood, who supported the merger of their two areas, stated that the A127 should form the new authority's southern boundary

1.3 In addition, 16 representations were received from outside the county, of which five preferred no change, five preferred a unitary Thurrock, with the rest either favouring other options or expressing no preference. A more detailed tabulation of the written representations from individuals and interest groups, produced by the NOP on behalf of the Commission, can be found towards the end of this Chapter.

1.4 In publicising its views, Basildon District Council conducted its own survey through a leaflet delivered to all households in the district. There was a high response (25 per cent), which reflected support in the district for the Commission's recommendation to split the area: 59 per cent overall. Support was highest in the Billericay area (82 per cent), followed by 71 per cent in Wickford and 39 per cent in the New Town. On the basis of the district being split, residents were also asked whether they would support a unitary authority for the New Town: support was highest among New Town residents (47 per cent), although lower overall: 31 per cent.

The Views of Local Authorities

1.5 The Commission received submissions from six of the 15 principal local authorities in Essex during Stage Three (Figure 1.6).

Figure 1.6
Preferences of Essex Local Authorities at Stage Three

Authority	Preference
Basildon District Council	Unitary authority for Basildon New Town. Rest of the district to remain two-tier with Billericay joining Brentwood and Wickford joining Rochford. Alternative electoral arrangements proposed for Billericay and Wickford wards.
Braintree District Council	Continued support for the principle of creating unitary local authorities.
Brentwood Borough Council	Approved of the draft recommendations. Continued to support Brentwood being linked with Billericay, subject to not inheriting part of Basildon's general fund deferred purchase debt.
Castle Point Borough Council	No views received.
Chelmsford Borough Council	No views received.
Colchester Borough Council	No views received.
Epping Forest District Council	No views received.
Harlow District Council	No views received.
Maldon District Council	No views received.
Rochford District Council	Could not support link with Wickford unless it was clear that the majority of Wickford residents had a strong sense of belonging to Rochford and the Government would fully fund any additional costs. If the merger were to be pursued, the Council would be supportive of Basildon's proposed electoral arrangements for the Wickford wards.
Southend-on-Sea Borough Council	No views received.
Tendring District Council	No views received.
Thurrock Borough Council	Unitary Thurrock.
Uttlesford District Council	No views received.
Essex County Council	Split of Basildon as proposed in draft recommendations. No change in Thurrock.

Source: Local authorities' submissions

1.6 Basildon District Council and Thurrock Borough Council maintained their preferences throughout the present reviews. Some other local authority views, however, have changed. Brentwood Borough Council, during the initial stage, expressed concern that local people should be consulted if the Commission decided to propose linking Billericay with Brentwood. Having considered the draft recommendations, the Council now supports a link with Billericay, subject to it not being obliged to inherit part of Basildon's general fund deferred purchase debt for facilities in the New Town.

1.7 Rochford District Council was also initially concerned about the possibility of bearing some of Basildon's general fund deferred purchase debt. At Stage Three, it expressed concern that Wickford residents had a desire to leave Basildon but did not feel a particularly close affinity with Rochford. The Council, in its submission, concluded: "If the Commission can provide incontrovertible evidence that the majority of Wickford residents have a strong sense of belonging to Rochford district and the Government is prepared to fully fund any additional costs to the residents of the Rochford district, the Council would be happy to be merged with Wickford. Otherwise, the Council cannot support the Commission's draft recommendation and remains wholly committed to the mandate from its residents to stand on its own boundaries in the two-tier county".

1.8 The Leader of Thurrock Borough Council wrote in support of a unitary authority for Basildon New Town. Although the issue had not been debated again during the present review, the comments reflected the Council's position during the county-wide review, which was generally that "...unitary authorities are the best form of local government to meet the needs of urban areas".

1.9 Essex County Council maintained its view that the case for change in Thurrock had not been made. However, it agreed with and supported the draft recommendation to split Basildon, and accepted the Commission's invitation to undertake, in association with Basildon District Council, a full audit of the economic and social needs of the district and its urban fabric. The County Council stated that it was "...willing to discuss with the District Council the best way of doing this".

1.10 The Essex Branch of the Association of District Councils did not make representations; the Association of District Councils' national submission is referred to in the Summary of National Representations. The Association of County Councils expressed support for the proposals for Basildon district but believed that the interests of Thurrock would best be served by a continuation of the two-tier structure.

The Views of Others

1.11 A range of other interest groups, albeit a small number, made representations on the Commission's draft recommendations, as summarised in the following paragraphs. These are in addition to those made in Stage One.

Businesses and Business Groups

1.12 The Essex Training and Enterprise Council (TEC) considered that the two-tier structure in both Basildon and Thurrock should remain. The TEC Board, in commenting on the possibility of a unitary Thurrock, was concerned about losing the strategic capability of the County Council. It also felt that a unitary Thurrock "...would incur considerable costs over and above those already identified. In simple terms, the pay back period is too long and in our view does not make economic sense".

1.13 Thurrock Chamber of Trade and Commerce wrote in support of a unitary authority for the borough. It commented that there was "...very strong support for Thurrock becoming a unitary authority amongst the business community". It added that one council "...should enable us to build up better informal as well as formal contact with the council and its officers". With regard to economic development, the Chamber felt that the new authority would provide "...an excellent opportunity for businesses to get involved in new developments, particularly in view of Thurrock's involvement in the Thames Gateway and [the Commission's] recommendation that it become the strategic planning authority for the area".

1.14 With regard to the proposal to split the present Basildon District Council area, letters of support were received from the Brentwood Enterprise Agency and the Brentwood Chamber of Commerce, the latter commenting that it saw "...benefits for the commercial and industrial businesses in the two towns if the merger were to take place. There are good transport links and a very similar business structure". The Business Association of the Basildon District felt that "...the interests of the local business community would be best served by accepting the proposal" for a unitary Basildon.

County, Regional and National Interests (including the Voluntary Sector)

1.15 The Commission for the New Towns commented that it would "... look favourably on a proposal for a unitary authority in Basildon if [the Commission] were to conclude that such an authority could be a viable and efficient arrangement".

1.16 A variety of interests expressed concern over the provision of strategic services on a county-wide basis. These included the Rural Community Council of Essex, the Essex Deaf Children's Society and the Royal Commission on the Historical Monuments of England. Age Concern (Essex) commented that many changes "...have taken place over the last few years in health, social services and education [which] have caused confusion and have carried costs". It added: "The time has come for a period of consolidation and reflection. Further changes, such as those proposed by the boundary changes, can only add to the confusion". While Age Concern (Essex) was not against unitary authorities in principle, it did not feel that the time was right to put such major changes in place.

1.17 The Port of London Authority felt that "...the greater good of the region can be met by retention of strategic authorities, who can take a more regional view than local authorities, who are, of necessity, responsible to a relatively limited community". It advocated the retention of the responsibilities of Essex County Council across the whole of the county.

1.18 The Museums and Galleries Commission indicated that in the event of the proposal for a unitary authority for Thurrock being accepted, it would "...be necessary to ensure adequate funding for Thurrock Museum and the development of a museum policy for the area. Membership of the Museums in Essex Committee should be continued in the case of Thurrock", and Basildon should be "...encouraged to join to ensure networking arrangements during and after reorganisation".

1.19 The Association of County Archaeological Officers considered that local knowledge and adequately maintained information systems were crucial to archaeological work. It hoped that were a unitary authority for Thurrock to be created, the Department of National Heritage's guidance would be followed by the new authority, and the appropriate arrangements put in place to ensure the continued provision of archaeological services.

1.20 The Town and Country Planning Association supported no change for Basildon and the establishment of a unitary authority for Thurrock. The Library Association and the Rural Community Council of Essex, however, preferred the two-tier structure.

1.21 The Essex Physically Handicapped Association expressed its concern at the prospect of breaking up the county into unitary authorities, thus resulting in it having to deal with more departments and adding to the cost of local government.

Education Groups

1.22 The Essex division of the National Union of Teachers opposed a unitary authority for Thurrock. The Union argued that the proposal was doing nothing to support teaching morale or provide confidence and considered that early indications from members in Thurrock "...confirms concerns about an uncertain future". Basildon College supported a unitary authority for the new town area.

Health Interests

1.23 The Thurrock Family Service Unit supported the proposal for a unitary Thurrock as did the Thameside Community Healthcare NHS Trust which also supported a unitary Basildon New Town. The Family Service Unit felt that a unitary structure for Thurrock would reduce public confusion and time-wasting often experienced with the present two-tier structure. It felt that the division "...has also manifested itself in terms of an unwillingness to work together on issues, and an unproductive rivalry between Essex Council and Thurrock Council. The result of which has been inaction, with local communities suffering". The Unit considered that both residents and community groups would be better served by a unitary authority.

1.24 The Chief Inspector of the Social Services Inspectorate (Department of Health) commented that, under the Commission's draft recommendations, Essex would remain as a viable county area, but added: "Care will be necessary to ensure that personal social services are adequately resourced should [Thurrock] become unitary".

Law, Order and Emergency Services

1.25 The Essex Police Authority considered that, for reasons to do with accountability and working relationships, no further unitary authorities should be established in the county.

Local Groups

1.26 A variety of organisations in Thurrock supported the proposal that there should be a unitary authority for the borough. These included the Thurrock West Community Group, the Thurrock Arts Council and the Thurrock Local History Society.

1.27 Thurrock Council for Voluntary Service commented that: "Thurrock has a strong voluntary sector and would be able to address local issues and heighten awareness to service providers much more effectively and efficiently if they were local". It went on to say "...we recognise that a lot of work has to be done in order to ensure that appropriate structures are put in place and maintained to ensure a successful and meaningful working relationship is continued and developed".

1.28 The proposal to split the present Basildon district was supported by various local groups including the Billericay Society and the Billericay District Residents' Association. The Billericay Town Council Steering Committee supported the proposal for a merger of Billericay with Brentwood. There were various comments in respect of specific boundary issues, including that Noak Bridge and Steepleview should be incorporated within the new district of Brentwood and Billericay, rather than Basildon. The Wickford District Residents' Association suggested that the Parish of Runwell (in the Borough of Chelmsford) should also join the new Rochford and Wickford District Council. Some concerns were expressed from the Wickford area about differences in the level of service provision between Basildon and its neighbouring authorities, the Wickford District Old People's Welfare Committee commenting on bus passes, day centre support and transport for the housebound.

Parliamentary Interests

1.29 Mr Andrew MacKinlay, MP for Thurrock, and Mr Richard Howitt, MEP for Essex South, both favoured a unitary authority for Thurrock, welcoming in particular the proposal that the unitary authority should take on responsibilities through a unitary development plan for strategic planning and waste regulation. Mr Hugh Kerr, MEP for Essex West and Hertfordshire East, supported the merger of Brentwood with Billericay.

Parish And Town Councils

1.30 There are currently no parish councils in Basildon or Thurrock. Only 13 representations were received from parish and town councils in other parts of the county. Of these, seven supported the merger of Wickford with Rochford, two supported the Commission's draft recommendations, one was opposed to change, one supported the merger of Billericay with Brentwood, one supported retaining Rochford district's current boundary and the other voiced concerns about the ability of a reduced county council to take a strategic overview.

NOP Tabulations of Written Representations

1 The following tabulations summarise the views expressed by members of the public and other interested parties during the consultation on the Local Government Commission's draft recommendations for Basildon and Thurrock.

2 The tabulations include only letters sent directly to NOP at its Chelmsford offices and to the Commission's offices in London. Where more than one person's view has been expressed in a letter, the comments from each individual have been recorded separately. Staff from the Commission and NOP have worked closely in ensuring that care has been taken in the interpretation of comments, and that a consistent approach has been adopted.

3 While many people expressed support for one or other of the draft options presented by the Commission, other responses were coded by NOP after further discussion. The pattern of views expressed has been carefully examined, and where a number of respondents supported an option not included in those put forward by the Commission, those views have been separately coded and reported by NOP.

4 The Commission has advertised through the local media, encouraging people to make their views known. All responses received up to two days after the end of the Stage Three consultation period have been included. Returns from campaigns organised by local authorities or other groups (for example, standardised postcards and letters, questionnaires and petitions) have not been included in the tabulations. These, and submissions written and dated before the commencement of the consultation process, have been considered separately by the Commission.

The following definitions have been applied by NOP in compiling the tabulations:

(i) Type of Respondent

Individuals:	includes individual members of the public, local councillors and Members of the Westminster and European Parliaments.
Businesses and Business Groups:	includes organisations which represent businesses, such as local Chambers of Commerce.
County, Regional and National Interests:	any organisation which covers an area which is the size of a county or larger is included here, for example, a county-wide voluntary organisation or a regional association. This classification includes most of the statutory consultees.
Education (and Church) Groups:	this group includes schools, religious organisations and teaching unions.
Local Groups:	this includes organisations smaller than a county area, for example, a district-level voluntary sector body. The group could be voluntary, sporting, political or cultural but does not include organisations from the education or religious sectors (included above). It also includes constituency parties and political groups on local authorities.
Parish and Town Councils:	this also includes district-level associations of town and parish councils. County level associations are classified as County, Regional and National interests.

(ii) Structural Options (Reports A, D and H)

No change in own district:	this code is used where there is more than one review district in the county. It indicates where respondents from a review district have expressed support for no change for that district and have not made reference to the other review district(s) in that county.
District/county-level authorities:	represents support for either a district or county-level authority although it is not clear whether this is for a unitary or a two-tier structure.
Opposition to structural preferences:	represents responses where a negative, but unspecified, structural preference has been expressed.
Rejects:	rejects are those responses with unclear comments/interpretation.

(iii) Other

Other issues (Reports B and I):	these illustrate preferences in relation to boundary and electoral changes and (where applicable) the restoration of historic counties.
Parishing issues (Report C):	these illustrate preferences in relation to parishing issues, for example, the creation of new parishes or the enhancement of the role of parish and town councils.
Services (Report E):	these illustrate concerns expressed about the impact of proposed changes on particular service areas where the respondent has not additionally expressed a positive structural preference.

(iv) Ward/Area Level (Reports H and I)

Tabulations by local authority wards or specified areas are designed to examine whether structural preferences vary across a particular local authority area. These areas broadly correspond to those parts of the district of Basildon defined in the proposed split of the district (Billericay, Wickford and Basildon New Town):

Area	Comprising district wards of
Billericay and Burstead	Billericay East Billericay West Burstead
Wickford	Wickford North Wickford South
Basildon New Town	Chapel North Fryerns East Fryerns Central Laindon Langdon Hills Nethermayne Pitsea East Pitsea West Vange

NOP Analysis of Responses to Local Government Commission Draft Recommendations - ESSEX

Report A: Opinions on the structural options, by authority of respondent
Base: all

	Review districts		Other districts in county														
	Basildon	Thurrock	Brain-tree	Brent-wood	Castle Point	Chelms-ford	Col-chester	Epping Forest	Harlow	Maldon	Rochford	Southend-on-Sea	Tendring	Uttles-ford	Rest of county total	County total	Out of county total
Status quo/two-tier	54 *14%*	78 *23%*	3 *100%*	4 *10%*	1 *50%*	10 *42%*	2 *67%*	- -	- -	1 *50%*	4 *4%*	1 *33%*	- -	- -	26 *14%*	158 *17%*	5 *29%*
Unitary Thurrock with Basildon split (two-tier)	- -	3 *1%*	- -	- -	-	- -	-	- -	-	- -	- -	- -	- -	- -	- -	3 *	1 *6%*
Unitary Thurrock	1 *	138 *41%*	- -	-	- -	1 *4%*	- -	- -	- -	- -	- -	1 *33%*	- -	- -	2 *1%*	141 *15%*	4 *24%*
Unitary Basildon New Town	43 *11%*	1 *	- -	- -	- -	- -	- -	- -	- -	- -	- -	- --	- -	- -	- -	44 *5%*	1 *6%*
Unitary Basildon (on existing boundaries)	46 *12%*	1 *	- -	1 *3%*	- -	- -	- -	- -	- -	- -	- -	- -	- -	- -	1 *1%*	48 *5%*	- -
Billericay and Wickford removed from Basildon (in two-tier)	31 *8%*	- -	- -	- -	- -	2 *8%*	- -	- -	- -	- -	1 *1%*	- -	- -	- -	3 *2%*	34 *4%*	1 *6%*
Billericay with Brentwood (no reference to Wickford) in two-tier	73 *19%*	- -	- -	24 *62%*	1 *50%*	3 *13%*	- -	- -	1 *100%*	1 *50%*	- -	- -	- -	1 *100%*	31 *17%*	104 *11%*	1 *6%*
Wickford with Rochford (no reference to Billericay) in two-tier	22 *6%*	- -	- -	- -	- -	4 *17%*	- -	- -	-	- -	18 *18%*	1 *33%*	- -	- -	23 *13%*	45 *5%*	- -
Wickford to join alternative area (i.e. not Rochford)	7 *2%*	- -	- -	- -	- -	- -	- -	- -	- -	- -	4 *4%*	- -	- -	- -	4 *2%*	11 *1%*	- -
Billericay and Wickford split from Basildon New Town and unitary authority for Basildon New Town	19 *5%*	1 *	- -	- -	- -	- -	- -	- -	- -	- -	- -	- -	- -	- -	- -	20 *2%*	- -
No change in own district	45 *12%*	40 *12%*	- -	4 *10%*	- -	- -	- -	- -	- -	- -	43 *43%*	- -	- -	- -	47 *26%*	132 *15%*	- -
County-level authority (either two-tier or unitary)	1 *	- -	- -	- -	- -	- -	- -	- -	- -	- -	- -	- -	- -	- -	- -	1 *	- -
District-level authority (either two-tier or unitary)	2 *1%*	- -	- -	- -	- -	- -	- -	- -	- -	- -	- -	- -	- -	- -	- -	2 *	- -
Opposition to structural options (where no positive preference is stated)	22 *6%*	69 *20%*	- -	5 *13%*	- -	4 *17%*	- -	- -	- -	- -	15 *15%*	- -	1 *100%*	- -	25 *14%*	116 *13%*	- -
Other specified	5 *1%*	- -	- -	- -	- -	- -	1 *33%*	- -	- -	-	1 *1%*	- -	- -	- -	2 *1%*	7 *1%*	1 *6%*
No preference expressed/option defined	20 *5%*	8 *2%*	- -	1 *3%*	- -	- -	- -	- -	- -	- -	15 *15%*	- -	- -	- -	16 *9%*	44 *5%*	3 *18%*
BASE TOTAL	391	339	3	39	2	24	3	-	1	2	101	3	1	1	180	910	17

* *Less than ½%*

NOP Analysis of Responses to Local Government Commission Draft Recommendations - ESSEX

Report B: Opinions on other issues, by authority of respondent
Base: all

	Review districts		Other districts in county														
	Basildon	Thurrock	Brain -tree	Brent -wood	Castle Point	Chelms -ford	Col- chester	Epping Forest	Harlow	Maldon	Rochford	Southend -on-Sea	Tendring	Uttles -ford	Rest of county total	County total	Out of county total
Electoral issues	2 1%	- -	- -	- -	- -	- -	- -	- -	- -	- -	- -	- -	- -	- -	- -	2 *	- -
Opposition to a unitary Thurrock	1 *	65 19%	- -	- -	- -	5 21%	- -	- -	- -	- -	- -	- -	1 100%	1 100%	7 4%	73 8%	1 6%
Opposition to a unitary Basildon	4 1%	1 *	- -	- -	- -	1 4%	- -	- -	- -	- -	- -	- -	- -	 -	1 1%	6 1%	- -
Opposition to Billericay joining Brentwood	12 3%	- -	- -	5 13%	- -	- -	- -	- -	- -	- -	- -	- -	- -	- -	5 3%	17 2%	- -
Opposition to Wickford joining Rochford	7 2%	- -	- -	- -	1 50%	- -	- -	- -	- -	- -	17 17%	- -	- -	- -	18 10%	25 3%	- -
Support for Steeple View and Noak Bridge joining Billericay (as opposed to Basildon New Town)	12 3%	- -	- -	- -	- -	- -	- -	- -	- -	- -	- -	- -	- -	- -	- -	12 1%	- -
Objection to paying Basildon debt	- -	- -	- -	4 10%	- -	- -	- -	- -	- -	- -	34 34%	1 33%	- -	- -	39 22%	39 4%	- -
BASE TOTAL	391	339	3	39	2	24	3	-	1	2	101	3	1	1	180	910	17

The figures in the table above do not sum to the base total/100% because undefined fields are not included, except as part of the base total.

** Less than ½%*

NOP Analysis of Responses to Local Government Commission Draft Recommendations - ESSEX

Report C: Opinions on parishing issues, by authority of respondent
Base: all

	Review districts		Other districts in county														
	Basildon	Thurrock	Brain -tree	Brent -wood	Castle Point	Chelms -ford	Col- chester	Epping Forest	Harlow	Maldon	Rochford	Southend -on-Sea	Tendring	Uttles -ford	Rest of county total	County total	Out of county total
Create new parish council	2 1%	- -	- -	- -	- -	- -	- -	- -	- -	- -	1 1%	- -	- -	- -	1 1%	3 *	- -
BASE TOTAL	391	339	3	39	2	24	3	-	1	2	101	3	1	1	180	910	17

The figures in the table above do not sum to the base total/100% because undefined fields are not included, except as part of the base total.

** Less than ½%*

Basildon & Thurrock

NOP Analysis of Responses to Local Government Commission Draft Recommendations - ESSEX

Report D1: Opinions on the structural options, by respondent type (all respondents)
Base: all

	Respondent Type					
	Indiv-iduals	Business groups	County, regional & national interests	Education (& church) groups	Local groups	Parish and town councils
Status quo/two-tier	141 *17%*	1 *4%*	9 *43%*	10 *42%*	-	2 *15%*
Unitary Thurrock with Basildon split (two-tier)	3 *	-	1 *5%*	-	-	-
Unitary Thurrock	135 *17%*	1 *4%*	-	2 *8%*	6 *22%*	1 *8%*
Unitary Basildon New Town	31 *4%*	10 *42%*	-	1 *4%*	3 *11%*	-
Unitary Basildon (on existing boundaries)	44 *5%*	2 *8%*	-	-	2 *7%*	-
Billericay and Wickford removed from Basildon (in two-tier)	31 *4%*	-	3 *14%*	-	1 *4%*	-
Billericay with Brentwood (no reference to Wickford) in two-tier	92 *11%*	3 *13%*	-	1 *4%*	7 *26%*	2 *15%*
Wickford with Rochford (no reference to Billericay) in two-tier	39 *5%*	-	-	-	1 *4%*	5 *38%*
Wickford to join alternative area (i.e. not Rochford)	11 *1%*	-	-	-	-	-
Billericay and Wickford split from Basildon New Town and unitary authority for Basildon New Town	15 *2%*	3 *13%*	-	-	2 *7%*	-
No change in own district	128 *16%*	-	-	1 *4%*	2 *7%*	1 *8%*
County-level authority (either two-tier or unitary)	1 *	-	-	-	-	-
District-level authority (either two-tier or unitary)	2 *	-	-	-	-	-
Opposition to structural options (where no positive preference is stated)	101 *12%*	4 *17%*	3 *14%*	7 *29%*	1 *4%*	-
Other specified	7 *1%*	-	1 *5%*	-	-	-
No preference expressed/option defined	37 *5%*	-	4 *19%*	2 *8%*	2 *7%*	2 *15%*
BASE TOTAL	818	24	21	24	27	13

* *Less than ½%*

NOP Analysis of Responses to Local Government Commission Draft Recommendations - ESSEX

Report D2: Opinions on the structural options, by respondent type
Base: respondents in Basildon only

	Respondent Type					
	Indiv-iduals	Business groups	County, regional & national interests	Education (& church) groups	Local groups	Parish and town councils
Status quo/two-tier	51 *14%*	-	-	3 *50%*	-	-
Unitary Thurrock	1 *	-	-	-	-	-
Unitary Basildon New Town	31 *9%*	9 *64%*	-	1 *17%*	2 *17%*	-
Unitary Basildon (on existing boundaries)	43 *12%*	2 *14%*	-	-	1 *8%*	-
Billericay and Wickford removed from Basildon (in two-tier)	30 *8%*	-	-	-	1 *8%*	-
Billericay with Brentwood (no reference to Wickford) in two-tier	68 *19%*	-	-	-	5 *42%*	-
Wickford with Rochford (no reference to Billericay) in two-tier	21 *6%*	-	-	-	1 *8%*	-
Wickford to join alternative area (i.e. not Rochford)	7 *2%*	-	-	-	-	-
Billericay and Wickford split from Basildon New Town and unitary authority for Basildon New Town	15 *4%*	3 *21%*	-	-	1 *8%*	-
No change in own district	44 *12%*	-	-	1 *17%*	-	-
County-level authority (either two-tier or unitary)	1 *	-	-	-	-	-
District-level authority (either two-tier or unitary)	2 *1%*	-	-	-	-	-
Opposition to structural options (where no positive preference is stated)	22 *6%*	-	-	-	-	-
Other specified	5 *1%*	-	-	-	-	-
No preference expressed/option defined	17 *5%*	-	1 *100%*	1 *17%*	1 *8%*	-
BASE TOTAL	358	14	1	6	12	-

* *Less than ½%*

NOP Analysis of Responses to Local Government Commission Draft Recommendations - ESSEX

Report D3: Opinions on the structural options, by respondent type
Base: respondents in Thurrock only

	Respondent Type					
	Indiv-iduals	Business groups	County, regional & national interests	Education (& church) groups	Local groups	Parish and town councils
Status quo/two-tier	73 23%	- -	- -	5 36%	- -	- -
Unitary Thurrock with Basildon split (two-tier)	3 1%	- -	- -	- -	- -	- -
Unitary Thurrock	129 41%	1 50%	- -	2 14%	6 67%	- -
Unitary Basildon New Town	- -	- -	- -	- -	1 11%	- -
Unitary Basildon (on existing boundaries)	1 *	- -	- -	- -	- -	- -
Billericay and Wickford split from Basildon New Town and unitary authority for Basildon New Town	- -	- -	- -	- -	1 11%	- -
No change in own district	39 13%	- -	- -	- -	1 11%	- -
Opposition to structural options (where no positive preference is stated)	60 19%	1 50%	2 100%	6 43%	- -	- -
No preference expressed/option defined	7 2%	- -	- -	1 7%	- -	- -
BASE TOTAL	312	2	2	14	9	-

* *Less than ½%*

NOP Analysis of Responses to Local Government Commission Draft Recommendations - ESSEX

Report D4: Opinions on the structural options, by respondent type
Base: respondents in rest of county only

	Respondent Type					
	Indiv-iduals	Business groups	County, regional & national interests	Education (& church) groups	Local groups	Parish and town councils
Status quo/two-tier	16 11%	- -	6 67%	2 50%	-	2 15%
Unitary Thurrock	1 1%	- -	- -	- -	- -	1 8%
Unitary Basildon (on existing boundaries)	- -	- -	- -	- -	1 17%	- -
Billericay and Wickford removed from Basildon (in two-tier)	1 1%	- -	2 22%	- -	- -	- -
Billericay with Brentwood (no reference to Wickford) in two-tier	23 16%	3 50%	- -	1 25%	2 33%	2 15%
Wickford with Rochford (no reference to Billericay) in two-tier	18 13%	- -	- -	- -	- -	5 38%
Wickford to join alternative area (i.e. not Rochford)	4 3%	- -	- -	- -	- -	- -
No change in own district	45 32%	- -	- -	- -	1 17%	1 8%
Opposition to structural options (where no positive preference is stated)	19 13%	3 50%	1 11%	1 25%	1 17%	- -
Other specified	2 1%	- -	- -	- -	- -	- -
No preference expressed/option defined	13 9%	- -	- -	- -	1 17%	2 15%
BASE TOTAL	142	6	9	4	6	13

Basildon & Thurrock

NOP Analysis of Responses to Local Government Commission Draft Recommendations - ESSEX

Report E: Views on services, by authority of respondent
Base: all

	Review districts		Other districts in county														
	Basildon	Thurrock	Brain -tree	Brent -wood	Castle Point	Chelms -ford	Col- chester	Epping Forest	Harlow	Maldon	Rochford	Southend -on-Sea	Tendring	Uttles -ford	Rest of county total	County total	Out of county total
Archives	1	-	-	-	-	-	-	-	-	-	-	-	-	-	-	1	1
	*	-	-	-	-	-	-	-		-	-	-	-	-	-	*	*6%*
Education	3	14	-	-	-	1	-	-	-	-	-	-	-	-	1	18	-
	1%	*4%*	-	-	-	*4%*	-	-	-	-	-	-	-	-	*1%*	*2%*	-
Other specified services (or multiples of)	6	1	-	-	-	-	-	-	-	-	-	-	-	-	-	7	2
	2%	*	-	-	-	-	-	-	-	-	-	-	-	-	-	*1%*	*12%*
BASE TOTAL	391	339	3	39	2	24	3	-	1	2	101	3	1	1	180	910	17

The figures in the table above do not sum to the base total/100% because undefined fields are not included, except as part of the base total.

NOP Analysis of Responses to Local Government Commission Draft Recommendations - ESSEX

Report F: Views on services, by respondent type
Base: all

	Respondent Type					
	Indiv- iduals	Business groups	County, regional & national interests	Education (& church) groups	Local groups	Parish and town councils
Archives	-	-	2	-	-	-
	-	-	*10%*	-	-	-
Education	9	-	-	9	-	-
	1%	-	-	*38%*	-	-
Other specified services (or multiples of)	6	-	2	-	1	-
	1%	-	*10%*	-	*4%*	-
BASE TOTAL	818	24	21	24	27	13

The figures in the table above do not sum to the base total/100% because undefined fields are not included, except as part of the base total.

* *Less than ½%*

NOP Analysis of Responses to Local Government Commission Draft Recommendations - ESSEX

Report G: Type of respondent, by authority of respondent
Base: all

	Review districts		Other districts in county														
	Basildon	Thurrock	Brain -tree	Brent -wood	Castle Point	Chelms -ford	Col- chester	Epping Forest	Harlow	Maldon	Rochford	Southend -on-Sea	Tendring	Uttles -ford	Rest of county total	County total	Out of county total
Individuals	358	312	-	31	1	13	3	-	1	2	89	1	-	1	142	812	6
	92%	*92%*	-	*79%*	*50%*	*54%*	*100%*	-	*100%*	*100%*	*88%*	*33%*	-	*100%*	*79%*	*89%*	*35%*
Business groups	14	2	-	3	-	1	-	-	-	-	2	-	-	-	6	22	2
	4%	*1%*	-	*8%*	-	*4%*	-	-	-	-	*2%*	-	-	-	*3%*	*2%*	*12%*
County, regional and national interests	1	2	-	-	-	7	-	-	-	-	1	1	-	-	9	12	9
	*	*1%*	-	-	-	*29%*	-	-	-	-	*1%*	*33%*	-		*5%*	*1%*	*53%*
Education (and church) groups	6	14	1	1	1	1	-	-	-	-	-	-	-	-	4	24	-
	2%	*4%*	*33%*	*3%*	*50%*	*4%*	-	-	-	-	-	-	-	-	*2%*	*3%*	-
Local Groups	12	9	-	3	-	-	-	-	-	-	2	-	1	-	6	27	-
	3%	*3%*	-	*8%*	-	-	-	-	-	-	*2%*	-	*100%*	-	*3%*	*3%*	-
Parish and town councils	-	-	2	1	-	2	-	-	-	-	7	1	-	-	13	13	-
	-	-	*67%*	*3%*	-	*8%*	-	-	-	-	*7%*	*33%*	-	-	*7%*	*1%*	-
BASE TOTAL	391	339	3	39	2	24	3	-	1	2	101	3	1	1	180	910	17

* *Less than ½%*

NOP Analysis of Responses to Local Government Commission Draft Recommendations - ESSEX

Report H: Opinions on the structural options, by ward/area of respondent
Base: respondents in Basildon only

	Basildon			
	Billericay	Burstead	Wickford	Basildon New Town
Status quo/two-tier	7 *8%*	6 *18%*	7 *8%*	34 *19%*
Unitary Thurrock	- -	- -	- -	1 *1%*
Unitary Basildon New Town	- -	- -	1 *1%*	42 *23%*
Unitary Basildon (on existing boundaries)	3 *3%*	- -	3 *3%*	40 *22%*
Billericay & Wickford removed from Basildon (in two-tier)	6 *7%*	1 *3%*	15 *17%*	9 *5%*
Billericay with Brentwood (no reference to Wickford) in two-tier	57 *62%*	10 *30%*	- -	6 *3%*
Wickford with Rochford (no reference to Billericay) in two-tier	- -	- -	21 *24%*	1 *1%*
Wickford to join alternative area (i.e. not Rochford)	- -	- -	7 *8%*	- -
Billericay and Wickford split from Basildon New Town and unitary authority for Basildon New Town	- -	- -	2 *2%*	17 *9%*
No change in own district	6 *7%*	9 *27%*	19 *22%*	11 *6%*
County-level authority (either two-tier or unitary)	- -	- -	- -	1 *1%*
District-level authority (either two-tier or unitary)	- -	- -	- -	2 *1%*
Opposition to structural options (where no positive preference is stated)	9 *10%*	5 *15%*	6 *7%*	2 *1%*
Other specified	2 *2%*	- -	1 *1%*	2 *1%*
No preference expressed/option defined	2 *2%*	2 *6%*	5 *6%*	11 *6%*
BASE TOTAL	92	33	87	179

* *Less than ½%*

NOP Analysis of Responses to Local Government Commission Draft Recommendations - ESSEX

Report I: Opinions on other issues, by ward/area of respondent
Base: respondents in Basildon only

	Basildon			
	Billericay	Burstead	Wickford	Basildon New Town
Electoral issues	1 *1%*	- -	- -	1 *1%*
Opposition to a unitary Thurrock	1 *1%*	- -	- -	-
Opposition to a unitary Basildon	2 *2%*	- -	- -	2 *1%*
Opposition to Billericay joining Brentwood	6 *7%*	6 *18%*	-	- -
Opposition to Wickford joining Rochford	- -	- -	7 *8%*	- -
Support for Steeple View and Noak Bridge joining Billericay (as opposed to Basildon New Town)	1 *1%*	1 *3%*	1 *1%*	9 *5%*
BASE TOTAL	92	33	87	179

The figures in the table above do not sum to the base total/100% because undefined fields are not included, except as part of the base total.

MORI Research Study for the Local Government Commission

Introduction

Background

1 This summary report highlights the key findings from a survey of public opinion conducted in the District of Basildon, the Borough of Thurrock and across the County of Essex on behalf of the Local Government Commission for England. A copy of each of the marked-up questionnaires is appended. The computer tabulations are contained in a separate volume, which is available from MORI (32 Old Queen Street, London SW1H 9HP. Telephone 0171-222 0232. Price £15)

2 The survey was designed in close consultation with the Commission, following extensive qualitative research and pilot testing. All sampling, interviewing and analysis have been carried out independently by MORI, within the guidelines of the profession laid out by the Market Research Society.

3 In Basildon and in Thurrock, all Census Enumeration Districts (EDs) were sorted by ward, and stratified according to social class. EDs were then sampled (32 in total in each of Basildon and Thurrock) in proportion to the population size of each, and quotas set for sex, age and work status. In Basildon, a total of 324 interviews with adults aged 18+, conducted face-to-face and in-home, were carried out between 5 and 29 October 1995. Two special booster samples were conducted in the wards comprising Wickford (to produce a total of 108 interviews) and Billericay (124 interviews) to allow separate analysis of these areas. These data are excluded from the main analysis in Basildon. In Thurrock, 306 interviews were conducted. Data were weighted to match the population profile of each District/Borough.

4 In the remaining districts of Essex, all EDs were sorted into wards, and again were stratified according to social class. A total of 32 EDs across the whole area (that is, Essex excluding Basildon and Thurrock) were sampled, with quotas set by sex, age and work status. Face-to-face interviews, conducted in-home, were carried out with 315 adults aged 18+ between 5 and 29 October 1995. Data were weighted to match the population profile of the County excluding Basildon and Thurrock.

Publication of the Results

5 As with all our studies, these findings are subject to our Standard Terms and Conditions of Contract. Any press release or publication of the findings of this survey require the advance approval of MORI. Such approval will only be refused on the grounds of inaccuracy or misinterpretation.

Objectives

6 This survey took place during Stage Three, the consultation period on the Commission's draft recommendations. It measures public preferences for the organisation of local government in the area currently comprising the District of Basildon and the Borough of Thurrock, as well as exploring strength of feeling, levels of knowledge about the review, involvement in, and broader perceptions of, local government in the area.

Statistical Reliability of the Data

7 Because we have interviewed a sample of residents, rather than the whole population, the results are subject to statistical tolerance limits, or "margins of error". These are expressed as our confidence that the true figure for the whole population falls within a given range. By convention this is expressed as a percentage, so our 95% confidence level means that in 95 times out of 100 the true figure would lie within this range.

8 The table below shows ranges of the 95% confidence level for a range of sample sizes. For each sample size, the table shows the tolerance limits for sample results close to 10%, 30% and 50%. Take, for example, the results of a survey of 300 residents showing that 50% are aware of the review. In 95 times out of 100 the true figure would lie between 44% and 56% (ie between 50% ±6%).

Sample size	Sampling tolerances applicable to results at or near these percentages (based on 95% confidence level)		
	10/90% ±%	30/70% ±%	50% ±%
300	3	5	6
200	4	6	7
150	5	7	8
100	6	9	10
50	8	13	14

9 Clearly, 10% or 30% of the sample being aware of the review equate to 90% or 70% not being aware of it. So this table shows the ranges of 95% confidence for responses close to 10%, 30%, 50%, 70% and 90% of our sample. The figures for responses between can be obtained by extrapolation.

10 The true figure would only be known if all the residents of the area had been interviewed. It can be seen in the table, however, that large increases in the sample size do not greatly reduce the sampling tolerance. In addition, the true figure is more likely to lie at the midpoint of the range, rather than at either extreme.

11 When comparing results from separate groups within a sample we need to be sure that the differences are statistically significant. This would be important in comparing views expressed by different parts of a county. The table below shows how the statistical significance of the difference is determined by the size of the groups and the percentage result from the sample.

12 Assuming a 95% confidence level, the table shows the size of the differences required if different results are to be regarded as statistically significant. It can be seen that if 50% of a group of 300 were aware of the review, the result from another group of 300 would not become statistically significant until it became less than 42% or more than 58%.

Sample sizes	Differences required for significance at or near these percentage levels		
	10/90% ±	30/70% ±	50% ±
300 and 300	5	7	8
300 and 200	5	8	9
300 and 100	7	10	11
200 and 100	7	11	12
100 and 100	8	13	14

Survey Findings

Knowledge and Awareness

13 Residents in Basildon and Thurrock profess broadly similar levels of knowledge and interest in local government as those living in the rest of the County of Essex. A majority in each area likes to know what their council is doing, but want no greater involvement. Around one in five (20%) in Basildon, one in four in Thurrock (26%), and three in ten in the rest of the County (28%) say that they want a higher level of involvement.

14 There is no real difference between residents' professed levels of knowledge - 39% in Basildon, 38% in Thurrock and 36% in the rest of Essex say that they know at least a fair amount about local councils and services. In all areas, a clear majority admit not knowing very much at all.

15 This is reflected in the number of residents who incorrectly ascribe services between the two tiers of local government. Thus, although between four and six in ten recognise libraries as a county council service, as many as one in three allocate responsibility to their district/borough council. And although around seven in ten realise that refuse collection is a district/borough service, around one in ten thinks it is a county council service.

16 Awareness of the review itself is higher in Basildon (where 83% have heard of it) than in Thurrock (63%), or the rest of Essex (63%). The proportions who say they know a fair amount or more are also higher in Basildon (21%) than in Thurrock and the rest of Essex (10% and 9% respectively).

Sources of Information

17 Local newspapers are the most common source of information about the review in all three areas. Of those who have at least heard of the review, 44% name the local press as a recent source in the areas of the County outside the review districts, 57% do so in Basildon, and 59% in Thurrock.

18 It would appear that both the County and District councils have been fairly active in providing information to residents in Basildon, 61% name a Borough source (including 49% who specify Borough Council household leaflets), and 53% name a County Council source (including 41% specifying household leaflets from the County Council). By comparison, the figures are 21% and 30% respectively in Thurrock and 9% and 18% in the rest of the County. An advertisement from the County Council in the local press has also gained the attention of some 30% in Basildon and 24% in Thurrock. Very few have heard about the review from Local Government Commission information, although 10% in Basildon, say they saw an advertisement from the Commission in the local press.

19 Although most of those aware of the review recognise one or more recent sources of information, relatively few (around a quarter) claim that this has influenced their opinion.

20 Furthermore, in spite of a relatively low level of knowledge of, and engagement with, their local authority, most people in Basildon and Thurrock say that the outcome of the review is either very important to them (27% and 32% respectively) or fairly important (39% and 41% respectively). As one might expect, people in the rest of Essex perceive a lower level of importance (19% very important and 29% fairly important).

The Preferred Option

21 In both Basildon and Thurrock, opinion is divided. In Basildon district, more people prefer no change (36%) than either of the two options for change. However, splitting the District to form a new district council for Basildon New Town, with Billericay joining Brentwood Borough, and Wickford joining Rochford District (all areas retaining the two tier structure) is preferred by 30%, and the same divide of the District (but with a unitary Basildon New Town) gains the support of 25%. Thus, a total of 55% throughout the district supports the proposed split, with either a district council or a unitary authority for the New Town Basildon; the proportions favouring the split are higher in Billericay (79%) and Wickford (60%) than in the new town (47%). However, the proportions favouring a unitary authority for the new town are fairly consistent between the three areas: 22% in Billericay and Wickford, and 27% in the new town. Reflecting on the options for Thurrock, the people of Basildon prefer no change for Thurrock, rather than a unitary borough, by 28% to 14% respectively.

22 In Thurrock, marginally more opt for a unitary borough (43%) than no change (39%), although this difference is not statistically significant.

Those expressing a view about the outcome for Basildon say they would prefer no change (34%) rather than either of the other options.

23 In the rest of the County, only 56% express a positive preference for a particular structural option in Basildon. Three in ten (30%) favour the proposed split (of which slightly fewer than half favour a unitary new town) and 25% favour no change. Half (53%) express a preference for a particular option in Thurrock, 19% preferring a unitary authority and 33% preferring no change.

24 People in Basildon and Thurrock feel more strongly about the preference they express than do those living elsewhere in the County. In Basildon, two thirds say they feel at least fairly strongly (including 22% very strongly) and in Thurrock, three-quarters say the same (26% very strongly). On the other hand, in the rest of the County, only four in ten feel strongly (10% very strongly).

25 In the County as a whole, it is people who prefer no change for Basildon who feel most strongly about the issue. The option selected has little influence, however, on how strongly they say they feel about Thurrock. In both Basildon and Thurrock themselves, however, the pattern of strength of feeling and options preferred is less clear, and it is not possible to say which option has the most dedicated supporters.

Factors in Expressing a Preference

26 In questions 13 to 23, residents were asked to say to what extent they agreed or disagreed with a range of statements which related to a change to unitary local government. The statements were designed to cover the main issues raised by residents during the qualitative phase of research, and others that formed a part of the Commission's brief to take into consideration in making its recommendations.

27 The following charts summarise the results from these questions, with the full question wording presented in the questionnaires in the appendices. Values have been ascribed to the five attitudinal positions that people were offered (+2 for strongly agree, +1 for tend to agree, 0 for neither agree nor disagree, -1 for tend to disagree, and -2 for strongly disagree) and mean scores calculated across all respondents expressing a view. This has the combined benefit of distilling the range of opinion into one summary figure, while incorporating the varying intensity of feeling by ascribing values. Bars to the right indicate that the mean score value is positive, and thus that there is a balance of agreement with the statement. Bars to the left, conversely, indicate a balance of disagreement.

28 The first chart, therefore, shows how the views of people living in Basildon and Thurrock differ from those across the rest of Essex. In doing so, it illustrates the attitudes or perceptions that are, in relative terms, shared by both groups of residents (where the bars project in the same direction), and those where views differ markedly. Thus there is broad agreement on the positive aspects of change, although the balance of opinion tends to be more marked in Basildon and Thurrock than in the rest of the County. On the other hand, there is broad agreement that a County Council is needed for national representation and, in Basildon and the rest of Essex (but less so in Thurrock) that services would suffer. On the need for national representation, it is again in Basildon and the rest of Essex that the balance of opinion is most marked. The only issue on which there is a clear divergence of opinion is on whether people feel that they will be affected by change; Basildon and Thurrock residents disagree, on balance, that they would not be affected. Residents of the two review districts are also more likely to want more information before making up their minds than are those in the rest of the County.

29 The subsequent charts take the results, separately, from Basildon (where there are three bars because of the three options presented), Thurrock and the rest of Essex, and illustrate the difference in views between those within each area whose preference is for change, and those who prefer no change. The perceived impact on efficiency is clearly a key determinant of opinion in Basildon and Thurrock, as this is the statement on which there is most differentiation between the two groups.

Attitudes to Change
(All respondents)

Q To what extent do you agree or disagree that...?
(Figures represent 'mean scores' with *strong agreement* given a value of +2 through to *strong disagreement* given -2)

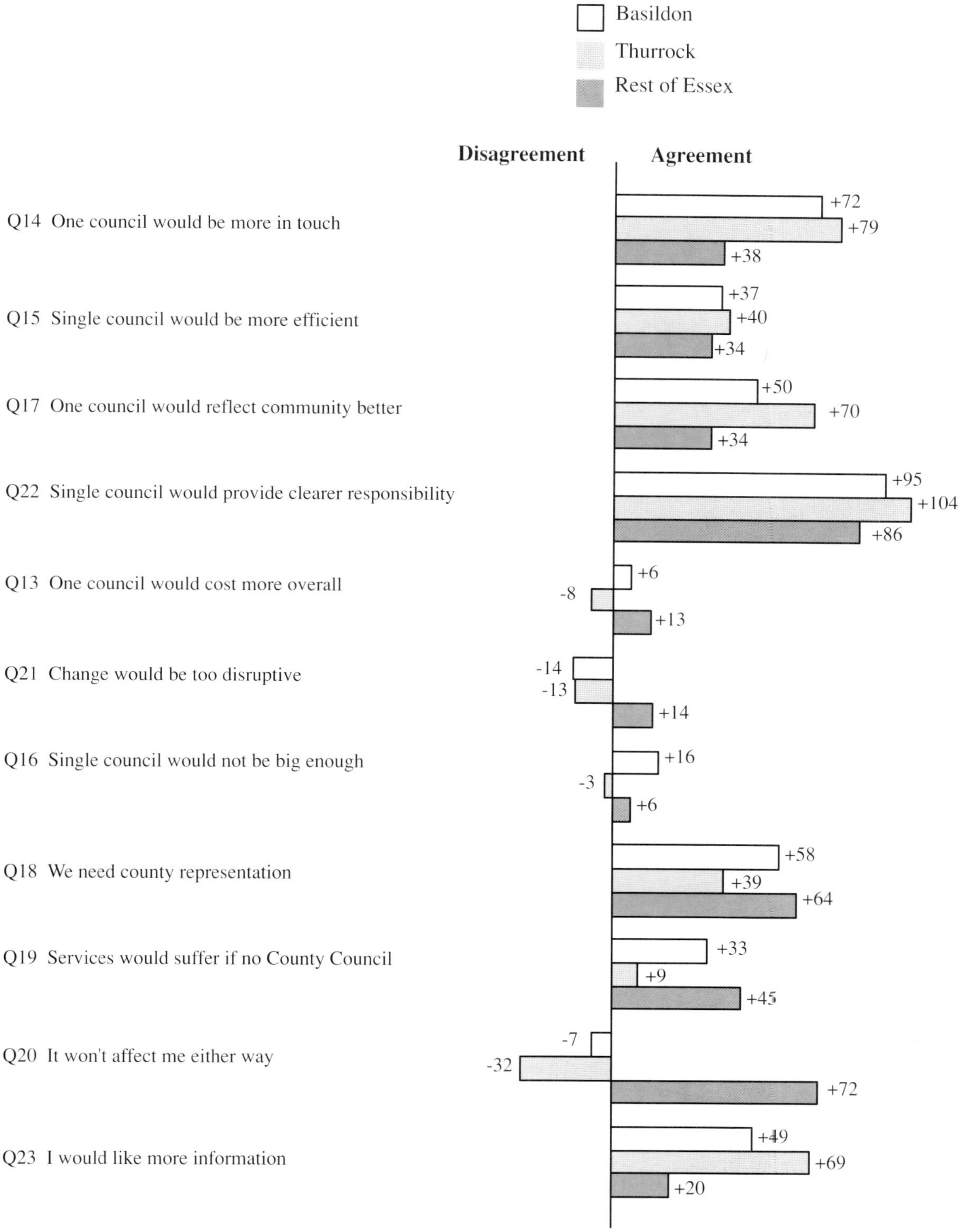

Attitudes to Change
(Respondents in Basildon)

Q To what extent do you agree or disagree that...?
(Figures represent 'mean scores' with *strong agreement* given a value of +2 through to *strong disagreement* given -2)

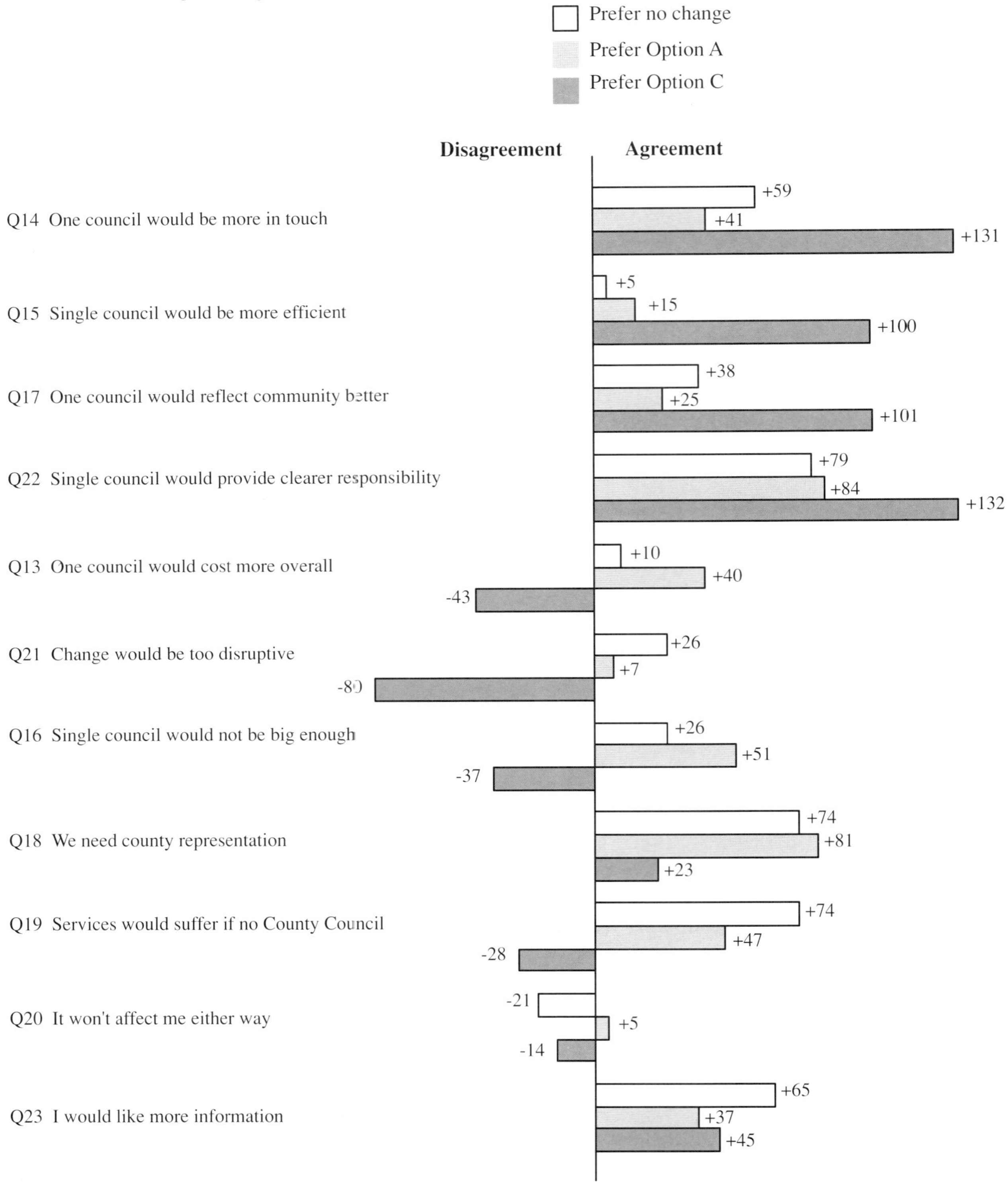

Attitudes to Change (Respondents in Thurrock)

Q To what extent do you agree or disagree that...?
(Figures represent 'mean scores' with *strong agreement* given a value of +2 through to *strong disagreement* given -2)

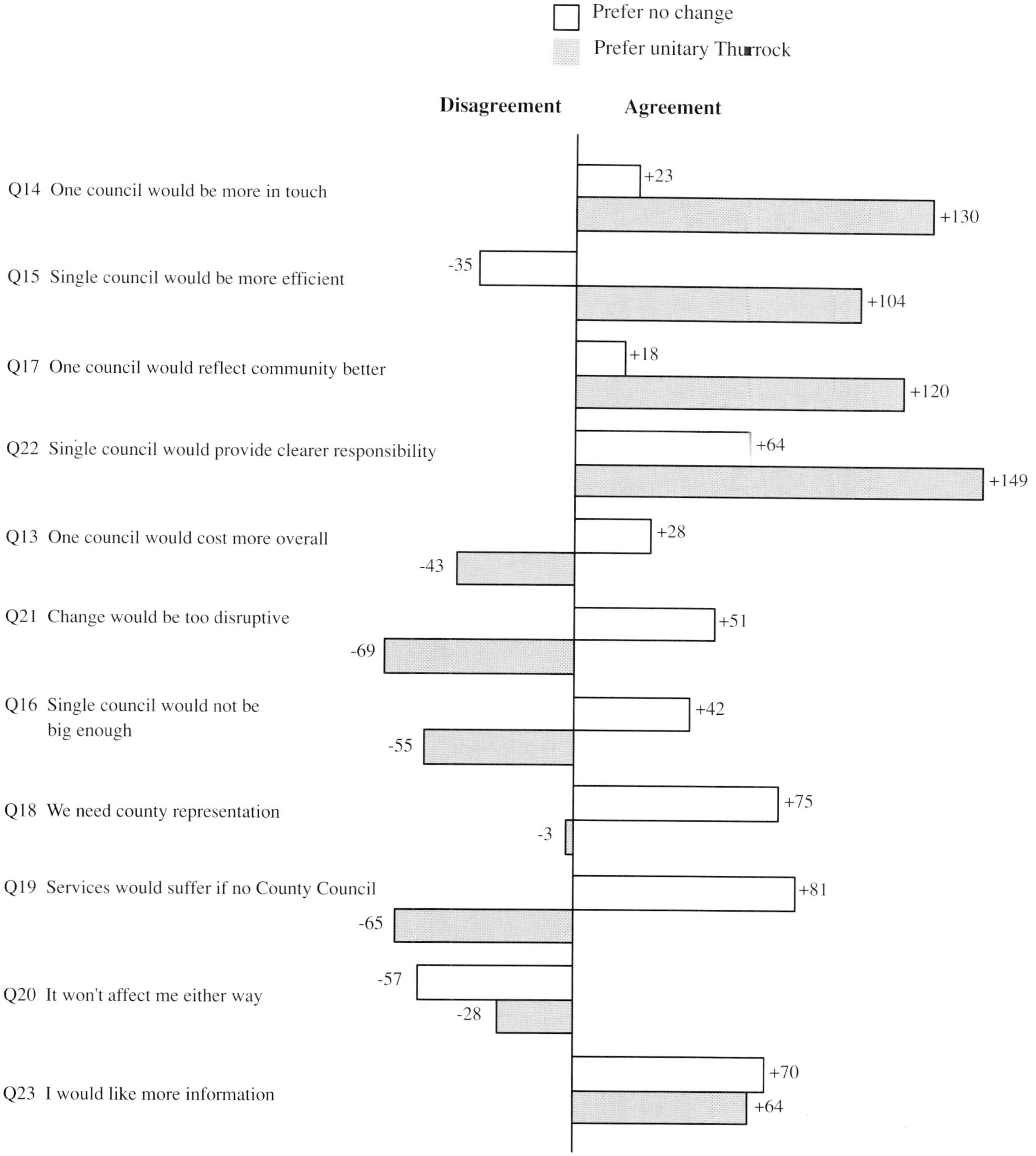

Attitudes to Change
(Respondents in the rest of Essex)

Q To what extent do you agree or disagree that...?
(Figures represent 'mean scores' with *strong agreement* given a value of +2 through to *strong disagreement* given -2)

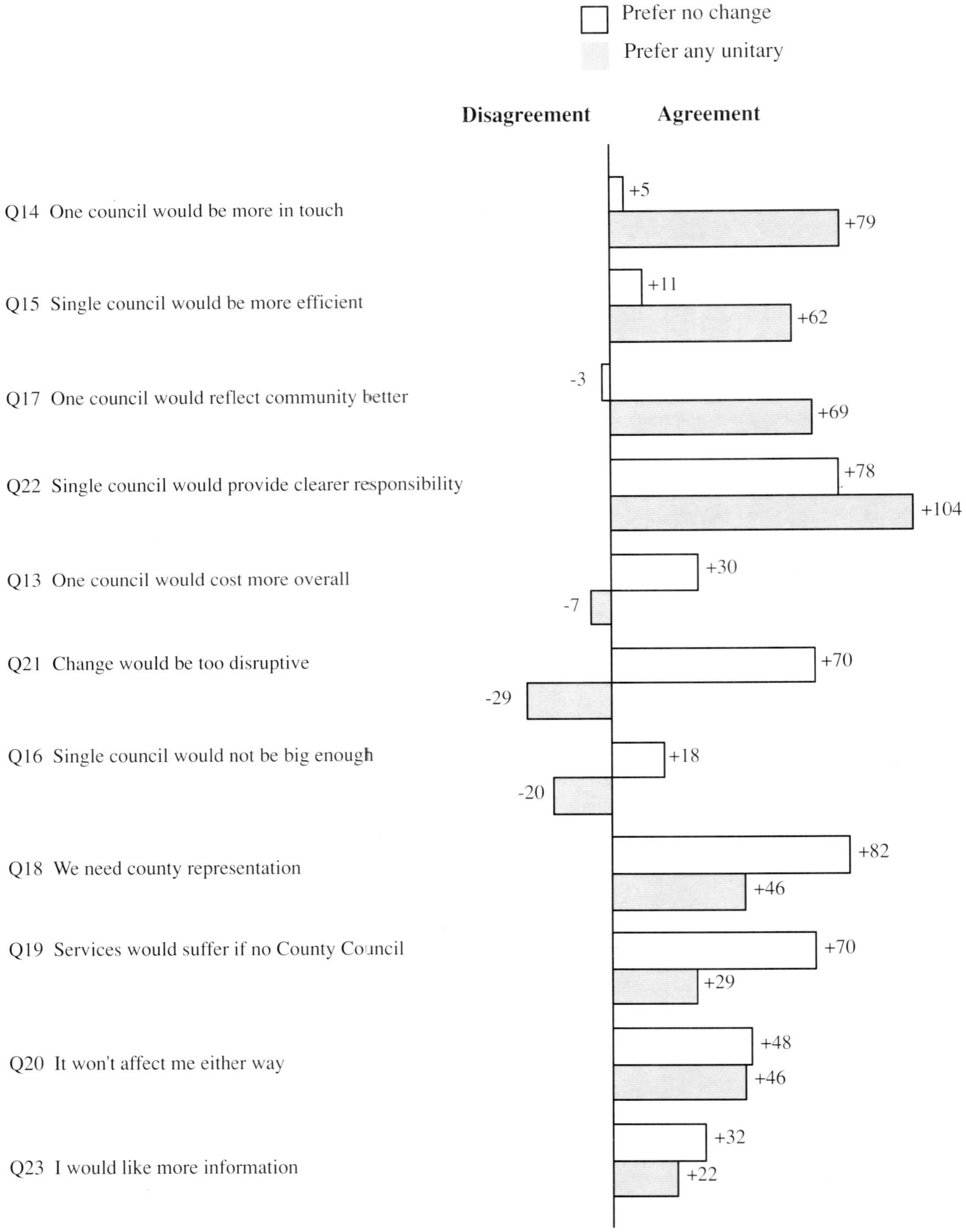

MORI/9101/04
(1-6)

ESSEX
REVIEW - REST OF COUNTY

Serial No ....
OUO (7-10)

Name/Initials/Title ....

Address ....

.... **Postcode**.......................................

Telephone: Yes...................................... 1 (11)

Number (inc STD code)

No 2

Sample Point

(12) (13) (14) (15) (16)

Gender %
Male 48
Female 52

Age %
18-24 13
25-34 18
35-44 19
45-54 16
55-64 13
65-74 16
75+... 5

WRITE IN AGE

Work Status %
Full-time (30 hrs/wk+) 47
Part-time (8-29 hrs/wk) 10
Not working (under 8 hrs) 2
Looking after home/children............. 7
Retired 24
Registered unemployed.................. 4
Unemployed but not registered 1
Student... 2
Other 1

Occupation of Chief Income Earner (CIE)
Position/rank/grade

....
Industry/type of company

....
Qualifications/degrees/apprenticeship

....
No of Staff Responsible for

....
PROBE FOR PENSION

	%
AB	19
C1	31
C2	26
D	14
E	10

* Less than $1/2$%

Number in Household
Adults aged 18+ (inc. respondent)

1 2 3 4 5+

Children (17 or under)

0 1 2 3 4+

QA **Are you or other members of your household employed by a council?** IF YES: **Is this a Borough/District Council or a County Council?**
CODE FOR BOTH RESPONDENT AND OTHER HOUSEHOLD MEMBERS

	Respondent %	Other %
Yes:		
Borough/District	2	2
County	4	4
Don't know which	0	0
No	94	83
Don't know	1	11

Tenure %
Owned outright.. 27
Buying on mortgage 48
Rented from Council 15
Rented from Housing Association 2
Rented from private landlord 6
Other 3

QB **Is this your main permanent home, or is it a second or holiday home?**
%
Main/permanent.................................... 99
Second/holiday 1

Car in Household
CIRCLE NUMBER

0 1 2 3+

Showcard Version
A-K ....
A1-K ....

THIS FORM IS THE PROPERTY OF MARKET & OPINION RESEARCH INTERNATIONAL (MORI)
32 OLD QUEEN STREET, LONDON, SW1H 9HP

INTERVIEWER DECLARATION: I confirm that I have conducted this interview face-to-face with the above named person and that I have asked all the relevant questions fully and recorded the answers in conformance with the survey specification and the MRS Code of Conduct.

Interviewer Name .... Signature ....

Interviewer Number					/	

	Month		Date	
DATE OF INTERVIEW				
	(29)	(30)	(31)	(32)

NB INTERVIEWER: ALL SHOWCARDS HAVE BEEN REVERSED. PLEASE BE CAREFUL TO CODE THE CORRECT RESPONSE.

Good morning/afternoon/evening. I'm from MORI, the market research and polling organisation. We are doing a survey about local issues, and I would like to ask you a few questions.

ASK ALL

Q1 **Firstly, how long have you lived in this area?** (WITHIN FIVE MILES)

	%
Less than 1 year	4
1-2 years	6
3-5 years	11
6-10 years	17
11-20 years	25
Over 20 years/all my life	37
Don't know/can't remember	*

Q2 SHOWCARD A (R) **From this card, how much would you say you know about local councils and the services they provide?**

	%
A great deal	2
A fair amount	34
Not very much	56
Nothing at all	7
Don't know	1

Q3 SHOWCARD B (R) **Which of the statements on this card comes closest to your own view of the Councils in this area?**

		%
A)	I'm not interested in what the Council does, or whether they do their job	1
B)	I'm not interested in what the Council does, as long as they do their job	17
C)	I like to know what the Council is doing, but I'm happy to let them get on with their job	52
D)	I would like to have more of a say in what the Council does and the services it provides	28
E)	I already work for, or am involved with the Council and the services it provides	2
	Don't know	*

Q4 **From what you know, how many councils provide the main services in this neighbourhood?** (INTERVIEWER - NOT INCLUDING PARISH COUNCILS)

	%
One	36
Two	31
Three+	6
Don't know	27

In fact there are two main councils that provide, or are responsible for most services in this area:. . .district/borough and Essex County Council.

ROTATE ORDER OF Q5/6

☐ Q5 SHOWCARD C (R) **From this list, what services do you think are the responsibility of... district/borough council? Just read out the letter(s) that apply**

☐ Q6 SHOWCARD C AGAIN (R) **And which services on this list do you think are the responsibility of Essex County Council? Again, just read out the letters that apply.**

Q7 SHOWCARD D (R) **Which, if any, of these services do you or members of your family use?** INCLUDE ONLY LOCAL USE

		Q5 "Borough" %	Q6 County %	Q7 Use %
A	Bus Services	47	27	43
B	Car Parks	67	20	73
C	Council Housing	65	24	12
D	Council Tax Benefit/Housing benefit	63	26	22
E	Fire service	20	68	31
F	Food safety	31	40	14
G	Household waste sites/dumps	63	25	56
H	Libraries	31	59	65
I	Parks, playgrounds and open spaces	63	26	58
J	Planning service	56	36	13
K	Public conveniences	67	18	44
L	Recycling/bottle banks	65	16	54
M	Refuse collection	76	16	76
N	Road maintenance	34	56	33
O	Schools/education	20	70	38
P	Social services	30	59	16
Q	Street sweeping	74	15	40
R	Swimming pools/sports facilities	63	24	55
	Other	2	3	2
	None of these	*	1	*
	Don't know	4	6	5

Q8 SHOWCARD E (R) **As you may know, there is currently a review being undertaken by the Local Government Commission on the future local government structure in the county. How much, if anything, would you say you know about this?**

	%
A great deal	1
A fair amount	8
Just a little	30
Heard of but know nothing about	24
Never heard of	38

PREFERENCES

HAND OVER MAP SHOWING AREAS UNDER REVIEW AND "CURRENT SERVICES" CARD
The Local Government Commission is considering options for the future structure of local government in parts of Essex. Could you please read through this card, (SHOW OPTIONS CARD) **which outlines the options.**

Q9 **Please tell me which of the options, if any, you would prefer for each of Basildon and Thurrock?**
CODE ONE ONLY FOR EACH DISTRICT

For Basildon

	%
Option A (Billericay to join Brentwood Borough; Wickford to join Rochford District, Basildon New Town to have its own district council, all three to keep Essex County services too)	16
Option B (Basildon District to remain unchanged/ status quo)	25
Option C (Billericay join Brentwood Borough; Wickford join Rochford; both keep Essex County services; but single new all purpose council for Basildon New Town	14
Some other option	1
Neither of these	*
Either of these/don't mind	19
Don't care	11
Don't know	14

For Thurrock

	%
Option A (single new all purpose council)	19
Option B (remain the same/status quo)	33
Some other option	1
Neither of these	-
Either of these/don't mind	20
Don't care	10
Don't know	17

ASK IF "OTHER" NAMED AT Q9 (CODE 3)

Q10 **What other option is that?**
PROBE FULLY - DO NOT PROMPT.

....

....

....

....

ASK ALL PREFERRING AN OPTION (1, 2 OR 3 AT Q9). OTHERS GO TO Q13

Q11 SHOWCARD F (R) **You say that the option you would prefer is .....** (INSERT OPTION PREFERRED). **How strongly would you say you feel about this?**

	%
Very strongly	10
Fairly strongly	32
Not very strongly	43
Not at all strongly	11
Don't know	4

Q12 **What do you think would be the main advantages of . . .**(OPTION PREFERRED)
PROBE FULLY FOR DETAILS

....

....

....

....

Nothing..
Don't know/can't think of anything...

ATTITUDES TO PROPOSALS

SHOWCARD G (R) **Imagine that there was one council in either or both of Basildon New Town and Thurrock providing <u>all</u> services. I am going to read out some statements that people have made about this proposal. To what extent do you agree or disagree that . . .?** READ OUT, ROTATE ORDER OF ASKING Q13-22. TICK START

	READ OUT:	Strongly agree %	Tend to agree %	Neither/ Nor %	Tend to disagree %	Strongly disagree %	Don't know %
☐	Q13 **It would cost more overall**	7	34	13	28	4	14
	Q14 **It would be more in touch with local people's needs**	10	47	10	21	6	6
	Q15 **The single Council would be more efficient than the current system of two Councils**	10	41	18	21	4	7
☐	Q16 **The single council would not be big enough to manage services such as Education and Social Services effectively**	9	29	18	33	4	7
	Q17 **It would better reflect the sense of community in those areas**	5	49	15	18	5	8
	Q18 **We need a County Council to represent us nationally**	14	50	14	15	1	5
☐	Q19 **Services would suffer if the County Council no longer provides services in those areas**	13	40	16	20	2	9
	Q20 **It won't affect me whether there is a single Council in those areas or not**	30	33	10	16	5	5
	Q21 **The change to a single Council for those areas would be too disruptive**	8	34	16	29	4	10
☐	Q22 **With a single Council it would be clearer who is responsible for local services**	17	59	8	10	1	5
	ASK LAST Q23 **I would like to have more information on the proposals before making up my mind**	13	32	20	16	12	6

Q24 **On balance, which would you say is more in touch with local people and issues, ...** (ROTATE ORDER OF "DISTRICT" AND COUNTY) (INSERT NAME OF "DISTRICT COUNCIL)**..district/borough council, or Essex County Council,** or **would you say that they are both about the same?**

	%
District/borough/city council	71
Essex County Council	5
Both about the same	17
Don't know	7

REFER BACK TO Q8. ASK ALL WHO HAVE HEARD OF REVIEW AT Q8 (IE CODES 1/2/3/4). OTHERS TO Q28

Q25 SHOWCARD H **Earlier in the interview, you said that you had heard of the Review of local government structure. From which, if any, of the sources shown on this card have you recently heard about the Review?** INTERVIEWER NOTE: "RECENTLY" = IN PAST 3 MONTHS

		%
A	Leaflet from County Council delivered to your door	18
B	Leaflet from County Council in library/ offices, etc	1
C	Advertisement from County Council in local newspaper	9
D	Advertisement from County Council on local radio/TV	1
E	Leaflet from Borough Council delivered to your door	9
F	Leaflet from Borough Council in library/ offices, etc	1
G	Borough Council newspaper	7
H	County Council newspaper	2
I	Advertisement from Borough Council in local newspaper	8
J	Advertisement from Borough Council on local radio/TV	3
K	Advertisement by the Commission on local radio	*
L	Local Government Commission advertisement in local newspaper	2
M	Local newspaper	44
N	National newspaper	8
O	TV	13
P	Local radio	12
Q	National radio	3
R	Friends/neighbours/family	8
S	Conversation with Borough Councillor	3
T	Conversation with County Councillor	2
U	Conversation with Borough Council staff	3
V	Conversation with County Council staff	2
W	Parish/community council	3
X	Residents' Association	2
	Other	5
	None of these	13
	Don't know	6

ASK ALL NAMING A SOURCE AT Q25. OTHERS GO TO Q28

Q26 **Would you say that the information you have received has influenced your opinion, or not?**

	%
Yes	25
No	71
Don't know	5

Q27 **What information in particular has influenced your opinion?**

....

....

....

....

ASK ALL

Q28 SHOWCARD I (R) **Assuming you receive the same level of services, how important is it to you, if at all, what the final decision is on the future local government structure in the areas under review?**

	%
Very important	19
Fairly important	29
Not very important	30
Not at all important	20
Don't know	3

ACTIVISM

Q29 SHOWCARD J **Which of the things on this list, if any, have you done in the last three years? Just read out the letter(s) that apply.**

		%
A	Voted in Local Council elections	77
B	Spoken or written to a local Councillor	33
C	Responded to the earlier Review of local government	9
D	Been to a meeting of a local committee or organisation	15
E	Spoken on a radio phone-in about a local issue	4
F	Written to a local newspaper about a local issue	6
G	Been to a meeting of a local branch of a political party	5
H	Written to your MP about a local issue	9
I	Been to a Council Committee meeting	5
J	Been to a Council meeting	5
K	Attended a public meeting run by the Council	8
	None of these	17
	Don't know/refused	2

Q30 SHOWCARD K **Which, if any, of these apply to you? Just read out the letter(s) that apply.**

		%
I am a member of a:		
A	Residents' Association	7
B	Community Association	4
C	Tenants' Association	2
D	Neighbourhood Watch	23
E	PTA/school governors	3
I do unpaid work for:		
F	A school	8
G	Citizens Advice Bureau	*
H	Volunteer Bureau	3
I	Scouts/Guides/Cubs/Brownies	5
J	Church group	8
	Other	6
	None of these	56
	Don't know	1

THANK RESPONDENT. GO TO DEMOGRAPHICS

- 9 -

MORI/9101/04 (1-6)

ESSEX
REVIEW - BASILDON

Serial No.........
OUO (7-10)

Name/Initials/Title ....

Address ....

.... **Postcode**..............................

Telephone: Yes.............................. 1 (11)

Number (inc STD code)

No 2

Sample Point

(12) (13) (14) (15) (16)

Gender %

	%
Male	48
Female	52

Age

	%
18-24	14
25-34	21
35-44	21
45-54	14
55-64	12
65-74	11
75+	7

WRITE IN AGE

Work Status

	%
Full-time (30 hrs/wk+)	49
Part-time (8-29 hrs/wk)	7
Not working (under 8 hrs)	3
Looking after home/children	14
Retired	22
Registered unemployed	3
Unemployed but not registered	0
Student	1
Other	*

Occupation of Chief Income Earner (CIE)
Position/rank/grade

....

Industry/type of company

....

Qualifications/degrees/apprenticeship

....

No of Staff Responsible for

....

PROBE FOR PENSION

	%
AB	19
C1	28
C2	26
D	9
E	17

Number in Household
Adults aged 18+ (inc. respondent)

1 2 3 4 5+

Children (17 or under)

0 1 2 3 4+

QA **Are you or other members of your household employed by a council ?** IF YES: **Is this a Borough/District Council or a County Council?**
CODE FOR BOTH RESPONDENT AND OTHER HOUSEHOLD MEMBERS

	Respondent %	Other %
Yes:		
Borough/District	3	1
County	3	3
Don't know which	0	0
No	94	78
Don't know	*	17

Tenure

	%
Owned outright	17
Buying on mortgage	50
Rented from Council	27
Rented from Housing Association	1
Rented from private landlord	1
Other	1

QB **Is this your main permanent home, or is it a second or holiday home?**

Main/permanent..............................
Second/holiday..............................

Car in Household
CIRCLE NUMBER

0 1 2 3+

Showcard Version
A-K ....
A1-K ....

THIS FORM IS THE PROPERTY OF MARKET & OPINION RESEARCH INTERNATIONAL (MORI)
32 OLD QUEEN STREET, LONDON, SW1H 9HP

- 10 -

INTERVIEWER DECLARATION: I confirm that I have conducted this interview face-to-face with the above named person and that I have asked all the relevant questions fully and recorded the answers in conformance with the survey specification and the MRS Code of Conduct.

Interviewer Name .... Signature ....

Interviewer Number				/	

	Month		Date	
DATE OF INTERVIEW				
	(29)	(30)	(31)	(32)

NB INTERVIEWER: ALL SHOWCARDS HAVE BEEN REVERSED. PLEASE BE CAREFUL TO CODE THE CORRECT RESPONSE.

Good morning/afternoon/evening. I'm from MORI, the market research and polling organisation. We are doing a survey about local issues, and I would like to ask you a few questions.

ASK ALL

Q1 **Firstly, how long have you lived in this area?** (WITHIN FIVE MILES)

	%
Less than 1 year	8
1-2 years	5
3-5 years	8
6-10 years	15
11-20 years	24
Over 20 years/all my life	41
Don't know/can't remember	0

Q2 SHOWCARD A (R) **From this card, how much would you say you know about local councils and the services they provide?**

	%
A great deal	3
A fair amount	36
Not very much	54
Nothing at all	7
Don't know	*

Q3 SHOWCARD B (R) **Which of the statements on this card comes closest to your own view of the Councils in this area?**

		%
A)	I'm not interested in what the Council does, or whether they do their job	*
B)	I'm not interested in what the Council does, as long as they do their job	19
C)	I like to know what the Council is doing, but I'm happy to let them get on with their job	56
D)	I would like to have more of a say in what the Council does and the services it provides	20
E)	I already work for, or am involved with the Council and the services it provides	3
	Don't know	1

Q4 **From what you know, how many councils provide the main services in this neighbourhood?** (INTERVIEWER - NOT INCLUDING PARISH COUNCILS)

	%
One	38
Two	36
Three+	4
Don't know	22

In fact there are two main councils that provide, or are responsible for most services in this area: Basildon District Council and Essex County Council.

ROTATE ORDER OF Q5/6

☐ Q5 SHOWCARD C (R) **From this list, what services do you think are the responsibility of Basildon District council? Just read out the letter(s) that apply**

☐ Q6 SHOWCARD C AGAIN (R) **And which services on this list do you think are the responsibility of Essex County Council? Again, just read out the letters that apply.**

Q7 SHOWCARD D (R) **Which, if any, of these services do you or members of your family use?** INCLUDE ONLY LOCAL USE

		Q5 "Borough" %	Q6 County %	Q7 Use %
A	Bus Services	37	32	39
B	Car Parks	64	12	62
C	Council Housing	71	15	19
D	Council Tax Benefit/Housing benefit	57	21	22
E	Fire service	18	62	24
F	Food safety	27	32	12
G	Household waste sites/dumps	49	28	43
H	Libraries	28	51	61
I	Parks, playgrounds and open spaces	61	21	53
J	Planning service	44	30	8
K	Public conveniences	61	11	35
L	Recycling/bottle banks	54	16	44
M	Refuse collection	73	9	75
N	Road maintenance	37	49	35
O	Schools/education	24	61	42
P	Social services	35	39	13
Q	Street sweeping	71	9	40
R	Swimming pools/sports facilities	64	15	54
	Other	1	1	2
	None of these	0	3	1
	Don't know	4	10	4

Q8 SHOWCARD E (R) **As you may know, there is currently a review being undertaken by the Local Government Commission on the future local government structure in the county. How much, if anything, would you say you know about this?**

	%
A great deal	2
A fair amount	19
Just a little	41
Heard of but know nothing about	21
Never heard of	17

PREFERENCES

HAND OVER MAP SHOWING AREAS UNDER REVIEW AND "CURRENT SERVICES" CARD
The Local Government Commission is considering options for the future structure of local government in parts of Essex. Could you please read through this card, (SHOW OPTIONS CARD) **which outlines the options.**

Q9 **Please tell me which of the options, if either, you would prefer for <u>each of</u> Basildon and Thurrock?**
CODE ONE ONLY FOR <u>EACH</u> DISTRICT

For Basildon	%
Option A (Billericay to join Brentwood Borough; Wickford to join Rochford District, Basildon New Town to have its own district council, all three to keep Essex County services too)	30
Option B (Basildon District to remain unchanged/ status quo)	36
Option C (Billericay join Brentwood Borough; Wickford join Rochford; both keep Essex County services; but single new all purpose council for Basildon New Town	25
Some other option	3
Neither of these	0
Either of these/don't mind	1
Don't care	3
Don't know	3

For Thurrock	%
Option A (single new all purpose council)	14
Option B (remain the same/status quo)	28
Some other option	*
Neither of these	1
Either of these/don't mind	6
Don't care	16
Don't know	35

<u>ASK IF "OTHER" NAMED FOR BASILDON AT Q9 (CODE 3)</u>
Q10 **What other option for Basildon is that?**
PROBE FULLY - DO NOT PROMPT.

....

....

....

....

<u>ASK ALL PREFERRING AN OPTION (1, 2 OR 3 AT Q9). OTHERS GO TO Q13</u>
Q11 SHOWCARD F (R) **You say that the option you would prefer for Basildon is . . . . .** (INSERT OPTION PREFERRED). **How strongly would you say you feel about this?**

	%
Very strongly	22
Fairly strongly	46
Not very strongly	22
Not at all strongly	4
Don't know	6

Q12 **What do you think would be the main advantages of . . .**(OPTION PREFERRED)
PROBE FULLY FOR DETAILS

....

....

....

....

Nothing..
Don't know/can't think of anything..................................

ATTITUDES TO PROPOSALS

SHOWCARD G (R) **Imagine that there was one council in Basildon New Town providing <u>all</u> services. I am going to read out some statements that people have made about this proposal. To what extent do you agree or disagree that . . . .?** READ OUT, ROTATE ORDER OF ASKING Q13-22. TICK START

READ OUT:	Strongly agree %	Tend to agree %	Neither/ Nor %	Tend to disagree %	Strongly disagree %	Don't know %
☐ Q13 **It would cost more overall**	7	30	18	30	4	12
Q14 **It would be more in touch with local people's needs**	21	51	6	13	6	4
Q15 **The single Council would be more efficient than the current system of two Councils**	14	40	11	24	5	6
☐ Q16 **The single council would not be big enough to manage services such as Education and Social Services effectively**	11	33	14	25	8	9
Q17 **It would better reflect the sense of community in Basildon New Town**	12	45	16	16	3	8
Q18 **We need a County Council to represent us nationally**	17	48	11	15	5	4
☐ Q19 **Services would suffer if the County Council no longer provides services in Basildon New Town**	14	37	10	23	6	9
Q20 **It won't affect me whether there is a single Council in Basildon New Town or not**	6	33	15	27	12	7
Q21 **The change to a single Council for Basildon New Town would be too disruptive**	7	26	19	34	9	6
☐ Q22 **With a single Council it would be clearer who is responsible for local services**	23	58	7	7	2	3
ASK LAST Q23 **I would like to have more information on the proposals before making up my mind**	24	36	11	20	8	1

Q24 **On balance, which would you say is more in touch with local people and issues, ...** (ROTATE ORDER OF "DISTRICT" AND COUNTY)
Basildon district council, or
Essex County Council, or would you say that they are both about the same?

	%
Basildon District council	46
Essex County Council	4
Both about the same	39
Don't know	11

REFER BACK TO Q8. ASK ALL WHO HAVE HEARD OF REVIEW AT Q8 (IE CODES 1/2/3/4). OTHERS TO Q28

Q25 SHOWCARD H **Earlier in the interview, you said that you had heard of the Review of local government structure. From which, if any, of the sources shown on this card have you recently heard about the Review?** INTERVIEWER NOTE: "RECENTLY" = IN PAST 3 MONTHS

		%
A	Leaflet from County Council delivered to your door	41
B	Leaflet from County Council in library/ offices, etc	9
C	Advertisement from County Council in local newspaper	30
D	Advertisement from County Council on local radio/TV	5
E	Leaflet from district Council delivered to your door	49
F	Leaflet from district Council in library/ offices, etc	7
G	District Council newspaper	13
H	County Council newspaper	3
I	Advertisement from District Council in local newspaper	17
J	Advertisement from District Council on local radio/TV	2
K	Advertisement by the Commission on local radio	2
L	Local Government Commission advertisement in local newspaper	10
M	Local newspaper	57
N	National newspaper	4
O	TV	6
P	Local radio	10
Q	National radio	3
R	Friends/neighbours/family	14
S	Conversation with District Councillor	2
T	Conversation with County Councillor	1
U	Conversation with District Council staff	3
V	Conversation with County Council staff	1
W	Parish/community council	1
X	Residents' Association	9
	Other	3
	None of these	*
	Don't know	4

ASK ALL NAMING A SOURCE AT Q25. OTHERS GO TO Q28

Q26 **Would you say that the information you have received has influenced your opinion, or not?**

	%
Yes	21
No	75
Don't know	4

Q27 **What information in particular has influenced your opinion?**

....

....

....

....

ASK ALL

Q28 SHOWCARD I (R) **Assuming you receive the same level of services, how important is it to you, if at all, what the final decision is on the future local government structure in Basildon?**

	%
Very important	27
Fairly important	39
Not very important	25
Not at all important	8
Don't know	2

ACTIVISM

Q29 SHOWCARD J **Which of the things on this list, if any, have you done in the last three years? Just read out the letter(s) that apply.**

		%
A	Voted in Local Council elections	82
B	Spoken or written to a local Councillor	23
C	Responded to the earlier Review of local government	17
D	Been to a meeting of a local committee or organisation	8
E	Spoken on a radio phone-in about a local issue	1
F	Written to a local newspaper about a local issue	3
G	Been to a meeting of a local branch of a political party	3
H	Written to your MP about a local issue	8
I	Been to a Council Committee meeting	4
J	Been to a Council meeting	3
K	Attended a public meeting run by the Council	9
	None of these	15
	Don't know/refused	*

Q30 SHOWCARD K **Which, if any, of these apply to you? Just read out the letter(s) that apply.**

		%
	I am a member of a:	
A	Residents' Association	12
B	Community Association	2
C	Tenants' Association	4
D	Neighbourhood Watch	18
E	PTA/school governors	4
	I do unpaid work for:	
F	A school	7
G	Citizens Advice Bureau	2
H	Volunteer Bureau	3
I	Scouts/Guides/Cubs/Brownies	3
J	Church group	8
	Other	3
	None of these	59
	Don't know	*

THANK RESPONDENT. GO TO DEMOGRAPHICS.

- 16 -

MORI/9101/04
(1-6)

ESSEX
REVIEW - THURROCK

Serial No ....
OUO (7-10)

Name/Initials/Title ....

Address ....

.... **Postcode**..

(11)
Telephone: Yes..1
Number (inc STD code)
No 2

Sample Point
(12) (13) (14) (15) (16)

Gender %
Male 49
Female 51

Age %
18-24 15
25-34 22
35-44 20
45-54 14
55-64 13
65-74 13
75+... 4

WRITE IN AGE

Work Status %
Full-time (30 hrs/wk+) 48
Part-time (8-29 hrs/wk) 9
Not working (under 8 hrs) 2
Looking after home/children........... 15
Retired 20
Registered unemployed.................. 4
Unemployed but not registered 1
Student.. 1
Other .... -

Occupation of Chief Income Earner (CIE)
Position/rank/grade

....

Industry/type of company

....

Qualifications/degrees/apprenticeship

....

No of Staff Responsible for

....

PROBE FOR PENSION
%
AB 9
C1... 25
C2... 27
D... 22
E... 17

Number in Household
Adults aged 18+ (inc. respondent)

1 2 3 4 5+

Children (17 or under)

0 1 2 3 4+

QA **Are you or other members of your household employed by a council?** IF YES: **Is this a Borough/District Council or a County Council?** CODE FOR BOTH RESPONDENT AND OTHER HOUSEHOLD MEMBERS

	Respondent %	Other %
Yes:		
Borough/District	2	2
County	4	3
Don't know which	-	-
No	93	85
Don't know	*	9

Tenure %
Owned outright.................................... 18
Buying on mortgage 51
Rented from Council 27
Rented from Housing Association ....-
Rented from private landlord 4
Other ....-

QB **Is this your main permanent home, or is it a second or holiday home?**

Main/permanent.......................................
Second/holiday ....

Car in Household
CIRCLE NUMBER

0 1 2 3+

Showcard Version
A-K ....
A1-K ....

THIS FORM IS THE PROPERTY OF MARKET & OPINION RESEARCH INTERNATIONAL (MORI)
32 OLD QUEEN STREET, LONDON, SW1H 9HP

INTERVIEWER DECLARATION: I confirm that I have conducted this interview face-to-face with the above named person and that I have asked all the relevant questions fully and recorded the answers in conformance with the survey specification and the MRS Code of Conduct.

Interviewer Name .... Signature ....

Interviewer Number				/	

	Month		Date	
DATE OF INTERVIEW				
	(29)	(30)	(31)	(32)

NB INTERVIEWER: ALL SHOWCARDS HAVE BEEN REVERSED. PLEASE BE CAREFUL TO CODE THE CORRECT RESPONSE.

Good morning/afternoon/evening. I'm from MORI, the market research and polling organisation. We are doing a survey about local issues, and I would like to ask you a few questions.

<u>ASK ALL</u>

Q1 **Firstly, how long have you lived in this area?** (WITHIN FIVE MILES)

	%
Less than 1 year	3
1-2 years	5
3-5 years	7
6-10 years	12
11-20 years	17
Over 20 years/all my life	56
Don't know/can't remember	-

Q2 SHOWCARD A (R) **From this card, how much would you say you know about local councils and the services they provide?**

	%
A great deal	4
A fair amount	34
Not very much	51
Nothing at all	10
Don't know	*

Q3 SHOWCARD B (R) **Which of the statements on this card comes closest to your own view of the Councils in this area?**

		%
A)	I'm not interested in what the Council does, or whether they do their job	2
B)	I'm not interested in what the Council does, as long as they do their job	16
C)	I like to know what the Council is doing, but I'm happy to let them get on with their job	53
D)	I would like to have more of a say in what the Council does and the services it provides	26
E)	I already work for, or am involved with the Council and the services it provides	2
	Don't know	1

Q4 **From what you know, how many councils provide the main services in this neighbourhood?** (INTERVIEWER - NOT INCLUDING PARISH COUNCILS)

	%
One	37
Two	30
Three+	2
Don't know	31

In fact there are two main councils that provide, or are responsible for most services in this area: Thurrock Borough Council and Essex County Council.

ROTATE ORDER OF Q5/6

☐ Q5 SHOWCARD C (R) **From this list, what services do you think are the responsibility of Thurrock Borough council? Just read out the letter(s) that apply**

☐ Q6 SHOWCARD C AGAIN (R) **And which services on this list do you think are the responsibility of Essex County Council? Again, just read out the letters that apply.**

Q7 SHOWCARD D (R) **Which, if any, of these services do you or members of your family use?** INCLUDE ONLY LOCAL USE

		Q5 "Borough" %	Q6 County %	Q7 Use %
A	Bus Services	32	32	36
B	Car Parks	61	12	63
C	Council Housing	70	16	15
D	Council Tax Benefit/Housing benefit	58	22	25
E	Fire service	23	55	29
F	Food safety	30	24	16
G	Household waste sites/dumps	54	19	55
H	Libraries	37	45	59
I	Parks, playgrounds and open spaces	64	18	54
J	Planning service	47	23	10
K	Public conveniences	55	12	29
L	Recycling/bottle banks	55	12	42
M	Refuse collection	71	12	76
N	Road maintenance	42	45	32
O	Schools/education	24	60	39
P	Social services	37	38	16
Q	Street sweeping	71	15	34
R	Swimming pools/sports facilities	63	16	56
	Other	1	2	*
	None of these	*	1	*
	Don't know	7	19	3

Q8 SHOWCARD E (R) **As you may know, there is currently a review being undertaken by the Local Government Commission on the future local government structure in the county. How much, if anything, would you say you know about this?**

	%
A great deal	1
A fair amount	9
Just a little	37
Heard of but know nothing about	16
Never heard of	37

PREFERENCES

HAND OVER MAP SHOWING AREAS UNDER REVIEW AND "CURRENT SERVICES" CARD
The Local Government Commission is considering options for the future structure of local government in parts of Essex. Could you please read through this card, (SHOW OPTIONS CARD) **which outlines the options.**

Q9 **Please tell me which of the options, if either, you would prefer for each of Basildon and Thurrock?**
CODE ONE ONLY FOR EACH DISTRICT

For Basildon

	%
Option A (Billericay to join Brentwood Borough; Wickford to join Rochford District, Basildon New Town to have its own district council, all three to keep Essex County services too)	10
Option B (Basildon District to remain unchanged/ status quo)	34
Option C (Billericay join Brentwood Borough; Wickford join Rochford; both keep Essex County services; but single new all purpose council for Basildon New Town	6
Some other option	*
Neither of these	2
Either of these/don't mind	6
Don't care	19
Don't know	23

For Thurrock

	%
Option A (single new all purpose council)	43
Option B (remain the same/status quo)	39
Some other option	3
Neither of these	*
Either of these/don't mind	2
Don't care	3
Don't know	10

ASK IF "OTHER" NAMED FOR THURROCK AT Q9 (CODE 3)

Q10 **What other option for Thurrock is that?**
PROBE FULLY - DO NOT PROMPT.

....

....

....

....

ASK ALL PREFERRING AN OPTION (1, 2 OR 3 AT Q9). OTHERS GO TO Q13

Q11 SHOWCARD F (R) **You say that the option you would prefer for Thurrock is . . . .** (INSERT OPTION PREFERRED). **How strongly would you say you feel about this?**

	%
Very strongly	26
Fairly strongly	53
Not very strongly	16
Not at all strongly	2
Don't know	3

PREFERENCES

HAND OVER MAP SHOWING AREAS UNDER REVIEW AND "CURRENT SERVICES" CARD
The Local Government Commission is considering options for the future structure of local government in parts of Essex. Could you please read through this card, (SHOW OPTIONS CARD) **which outlines the options.**

Q9 **Please tell me which of the options, if either, you would prefer for each of Basildon and Thurrock?**
CODE ONE ONLY FOR EACH DISTRICT

For Basildon

	%
Option A (Billericay to join Brentwood Borough; Wickford to join Rochford District, Basildon New Town to have its own district council, all three to keep Essex County services too)	10
Option B (Basildon District to remain unchanged/ status quo)	34
Option C (Billericay join Brentwood Borough; Wickford join Rochford; both keep Essex County services; but single new all purpose council for Basildon New Town	6
Some other option	*
Neither of these	2
Either of these/don't mind	6
Don't care	19
Don't know	23

For Thurrock

	%
Option A (single new all purpose council)	43
Option B (remain the same/status quo)	39
Some other option	3
Neither of these	*
Either of these/don't mind	2
Don't care	3
Don't know	10

ASK IF "OTHER" NAMED FOR THURROCK AT Q9 (CODE 3)
Q10 **What other option for Thurrock is that?**
PROBE FULLY - DO NOT PROMPT.

....

....

....

....

ASK ALL PREFERRING AN OPTION (1, 2 OR 3 AT Q9). OTHERS GO TO Q13
Q11 SHOWCARD F (R) **You say that the option you would prefer for Thurrock is . . . .** (INSERT OPTION PREFERRED). **How strongly would you say you feel about this?**

	%
Very strongly	26
Fairly strongly	53
Not very strongly	16
Not at all strongly	2
Don't know	3

Q24 **On balance, which would you say is more in touch with local people and issues,** .... (ROTATE ORDER OF "DISTRICT" AND COUNTY)
Thurrock Borough council, or
Essex County Council, or would you say that they are both about the same?

	%
Thurrock Borough council	55
Essex County Council	3
Both about the same	32
Don't know	10

REFER BACK TO Q8. ASK ALL WHO HAVE HEARD OF REVIEW AT Q8 IE CODES 1/2/3/4). OTHERS TO Q28

Q25 SHOWCARD H **Earlier in the interview, you said that you had heard of the Review of local government structure. From which, if any, of the sources shown on this card have you recently heard about the Review?** INTERVIEWER NOTE: "RECENTLY" = IN PAST 3 MONTHS

Base: 198

		%
A	Leaflet from County Council delivered to your door	30
B	Leaflet from County Council in library/ offices, etc	4
C	Advertisement from County Council in local newspaper	24
D	Advertisement from County Council on local radio/TV	1
E	Leaflet from Borough Council delivered to your door	21
F	Leaflet from Borough Council in library/ offices, etc	2
G	Borough Council newspaper	17
H	County Council newspaper	2
I	Advertisement from Borough Council in local newspaper	16
J	Advertisement from Borough Council on local radio/TV	3
K	Advertisement by the Commission on local radio	1
L	Local Government Commission advertisement in local newspaper	1
M	Local newspaper	59
N	National newspaper	7
O	TV	11
P	Local radio	6
Q	National radio	2
R	Friends/neighbours/family	16
S	Conversation with Borough Councillor	1
T	Conversation with County Councillor	1
U	Conversation with Borough Council staff	1
V	Conversation with County Council staff	2
W	Parish/community council	-
X	Residents' Association	2
	Other	3
	None of these	4
	Don't know	1

ASK ALL NAMING A SOURCE AT Q25. OTHERS GO TO Q28

Q26 **Would you say that the information you have received has influenced your opinion, or not?**

Base: 170

	%
Yes	26
No	70
Don't know	4

Q27 **What information in particular has influenced your opinion?**

....

....

....

....

ASK ALL

Q28 SHOWCARD I (R) **Assuming you receive the same level of services, how important is it to you, if at all, what the final decision is on the future local government structure in Thurrock?**

	%
Very important	32
Fairly important	41
Not very important	16
Not at all important	8
Don't know	3

ACTIVISM

Q29 SHOWCARD J **Which of the things on this list, if any, have you done in the last three years? Just read out the letter(s) that apply.**

		%
A	Voted in Local Council elections	79
B	Spoken or written to a local Councillor	20
C	Responded to the earlier Review of local government	4
D	Been to a meeting of a local committee or organisation	7
E	Spoken on a radio phone-in about a local issue	1
F	Written to a local newspaper about a local issue	2
G	Been to a meeting of a local branch of a political party	4
H	Written to your MP about a local issue	9
I	Been to a Council Committee meeting	2
J	Been to a Council meeting	3
K	Attended a public meeting run by the Council	7
	None of these	16
	Don't know/refused	2

Q30 SHOWCARD K **Which, if any, of these apply to you? Just reac out the letter(s) that apply.**

		%
	I am a member of a:	
A	Residents' Association	5
B	Community Association	2
C	Tenants' Association	3
D	Neighbourhood Watch	25
E	PTA/school governors	5
	I do unpaid work for:	
F	A school	6
G	Citizens Advice Bureau	1
H	Volunteer Bureau	2
I	Scouts/Guides/Cubs/Brownies	2
J	Church group	6
	Other	1
	None of these	59
	Don't know	11

THANK RESPONDENT. GO TO DEMOGRAPHICS

CHAPTER 2

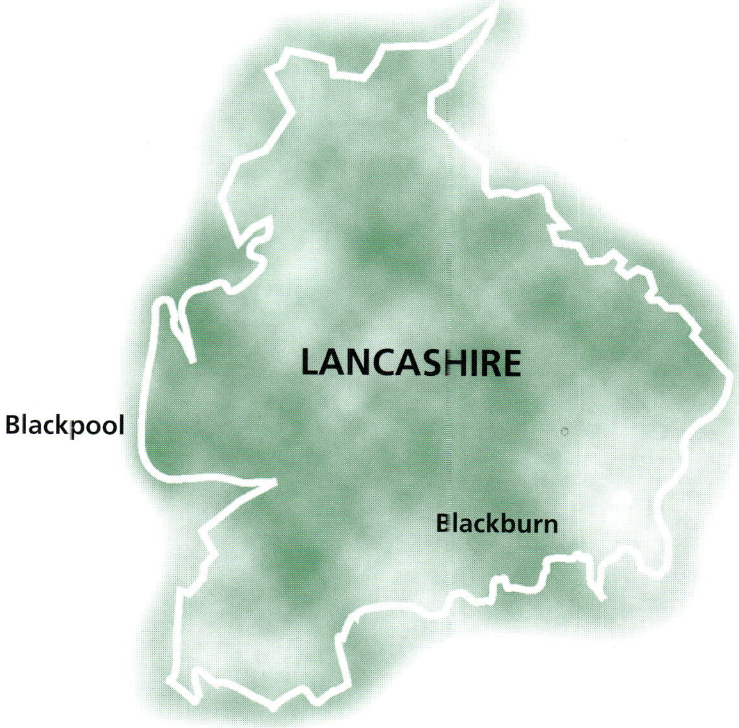

BLACKBURN AND BLACKPOOL IN THE COUNTY OF LANCASHIRE

Draft Recommendations

2.1 The Commission's report *Draft Recommendations on the Future Local Government of Blackburn and Blackpool in the County of Lancashire* summarised the evidence taken into account by the Commission in reaching its draft recommendations.

Figure 2.1
Draft Recommendations for Blackburn and Blackpool in the County of Lancashire

Structure

- The existing two-tier structure of local government in Blackburn should be replaced. Blackburn should become a unitary authority, responsible in its area for the broad range of local government functions currently carried out by both county and district councils.

- The existing two-tier structure of local government in Blackpool should be replaced. Blackpool should become a unitary authority, responsible in its area for the broad range of local government functions currently carried out by both county and district councils.

Ceremonial Arrangements

- The county of Lancashire should be retained for ceremonial and related purposes, and the district areas of Blackburn and Blackpool should be associated with the county for such purposes.

Public Protection

- There should be a combined authority established in the present county area for the fire service, on which the representatives of the new unitary authorities should serve. Similarly, representatives of the new unitary authorities should also serve on a joint committee with representatives of the county council to select the local authority membership of the Lancashire Police Authority. No changes are proposed to the area covered by the Lancashire Police Authority, or to the probation and magistrates' courts services.

Strategic Planning

- For strategic planning, the new unitary authorities and the remaining county council should assume joint responsibility for structure planning for the whole of their combined areas. Where the existing two-tier structure is retained, there would be no change to existing arrangements for minerals and waste polices and the exercise of development control functions. In Blackburn and Blackpool, the new unitary authorities should also be separate minerals and waste planning authorities with strategic minerals and waste policies being included in the joint structure plan. The unitary authorities should have the responsibility for formulating detailed minerals and waste policies for their areas in general conformity with the policy framework established by the structure plan, and they should be authorised to include such policies in their local plans. Responsibility for local plans should rest with the new unitary authorities in their areas and they should also exercise development control functions in their areas for all purposes.

Electoral Arrangements

- The Blackburn unitary authority should retain the existing Blackburn Borough Council electoral arrangements. The council should therefore have a total of 60 members with 19 three-member wards, one two-member ward and one single-member ward. Elections should be by thirds.

- The Blackpool unitary authority should retain the existing Blackpool Borough Council electoral arrangements. The council should therefore have a total of 44 members with 22 two-member wards. Elections should be held for the whole council every four years.

- The continuing Lancashire County Council should have 78 members with one member for each of the existing 78 county divisions outside the boroughs of Blackburn and Blackpool.

Views Expressed to the Commission

2.2 The Commission received a wide range of direct representations on its draft recommendations, from local authorities, residents, Members of Parliament, business and voluntary groups, parish and town councils, and from other public and private sector organisations. Just over 4,000 representations were received from individuals and organisations, including around 1,800 from respondents within the two review districts. The Commission also received nearly 2,400 representations in the form of standard letters, completed questionnaires, pre-printed postcards and petitions (Figures 2.2, 2.3 and 2.4). Figures 2.2, 2.3 and 2.4 exclude representations from the local authorities which are summarised separately (Figure 2.5).

Figure 2.2
Views of Respondents Within Blackburn

Preferred structure	Individuals	Organisations	Standard letters and petition signatures
Unitary Blackburn	389	101	11
Unitary Blackburn and Blackpool	13	0	0
No change	282	21	244
Other	11	0	0
No preference	6	1	0

Source: Local Government Commission for England and NOP

Figure 2.3
Views of Respondents Within Blackpool

Preferred structure	Individuals	Organisations	Standard letters and petition signatures
Unitary Blackpool	570	17	29
Unitary Blackburn	4	0	0
Unitary Blackburn and Blackpool	4	1	0
No change	338	33	400
Other	19	1	0
No preference	21	5	0

Source: Local Government Commission for England and NOP

Figure 2.4
Views of Respondents from Outside the Review Districts

Preferred structure	Individuals	Organisations	Standard letters and petition signatures
Unitary Blackburn	101	10	0
Unitary Blackpool	20	0	0
Unitary Blackburn and Blackpool	24	6	0
No change	1,784	233	1,708
Other	15	3	0
No preference	31	12	0

Source: Local Government Commission for England and NOP
Note: Excludes out of county representations

2.3 In addition, 182 representations were received from outside the county, of which just under a quarter supported a unitary authority for Blackburn and around two-thirds supported the retention of the two-tier structure. A more detailed tabulation of the written representations from individuals and interest groups, produced by NOP on behalf of the Commission, can be found towards the end of this Chapter.

The Views of Local Authorities

2.4 The Commission received submissions from 13 of the 15 principal local authorities in Lancashire during Stage Three (Figure 2.5).

Figure 2.5

Preferences of Lancashire Local Authorities at Stage Three

Authority	Preference
Blackburn Borough Council	Restated its support for unitary Blackburn and Blackpool authorities. It considered unitary status for Blackburn would ensure more convenient and effective local government and would create a single authority which reflected the local identities and interests of the people of the borough.
Blackpool Borough Council	Restated its support for unitary Blackpool and Blackburn authorities. It considered unitary status for Blackpool would provide a stable structure of local government without adversely affecting the rest of Lancashire. It also believed that unitary status would assist the Council in addressing Blackpool's socio-economic problems.
Burnley Borough Council	Believed that there is a very real possibility that the creation of unitary authorities in Blackburn and Blackpool would weaken the existing County Council, both financially and politically. Therefore it supported the status quo.
Chorley Borough Council	Expressed no views in Stage Three.
Fylde Borough Council	Concluded that the bids submitted by Blackburn and Blackpool should be supported provided that no additional costs were passed on to local taxpayers in Fylde and that the Blackpool boundary remained unaltered.
Hyndburn Borough Council	Believed that the hybrid solution proposed would lead to great confusion amongst the public and would give rise to a widespread perception of the structure as an inequitable and divisive one.
Lancaster City Council	Expressed no views in Stage Three.
Pendle Borough Council	Opposed to granting Blackburn and Blackpool unitary status as it could jeopardise the viability of specialist county services such as education, social services and planning.

continued/

/continued

Authority	Preference
Preston Borough Council	Supported the present two-tier structure as the financial assessments carried out by the Audit Commission showed potential ongoing costs and that some of the ongoing costs would fall on the remaining county.
Ribble Valley Borough Council	The Council supported the principle of unitary authorities, but in the absence of such a system for the whole county, it considered that the way forward should be by improvements to the existing two-tier system
Rossendale Borough Council	Reaffirmed its concerns that the draft recommendations would adversely affect people in the borough.
South Ribble Borough Council	Believed that because of the uncertainties and inconsistencies and all the arguments against change, that the present local government arrangements in Lancashire should not be changed.
West Lancashire District Council	Supported the existing pattern of local government in Lancashire in order not to diminish the scale of activity of the County Council, especially in areas such as environmental protection and economic development.
Wyre Borough Council	Considered that improvements to the present two-tier system would provide a far more accountable mechanism as compared with the creation of a hybrid system which may prove to be costly and overly bureaucratic.
Lancashire County Council	Restated its support for the two-tier structure in its current form, or modified to recognise the strategic role of the County Council and local service delivery of District Councils, with as much devolution as possible, without incurring additional costs. It considered this would ensure the provision of cost effective, accountable and high quality services both locally and strategically.

Source: Local authorities' submissions

2.5 The local authorities confirmed their preferences expressed at Stage One of the review other than Chorley Borough and Lancaster City Councils, which previously supported the unitary principle, and Hyndburn and Preston Borough Councils, which preferred no change at Stage Three. Ribble Valley Borough Council did not respond at Stage One of the review.

2.6 The Lancashire Branch of the Association of District Councils did not make representations; the Association of District Councils' national submission is referred to in the Summary of National Representations. The Association of County Councils preferred no change to the current structure of local government in Lancashire. It believed that: "Blackburn and Blackpool as unitary authorities would be too small in terms of their resource bases and strategic capacities to tackle effectively the significant social and economic problems each of the two boroughs faces...".

The Views of Others

2.7 A range of other interest groups made representations on the Commission's draft recommendations as summarised in the following paragraphs. These are in addition to those made in Stage One.

Businesses and Business Groups

2.8 There was overwhelming support for a unitary authority for Blackburn from the business community of the borough. The Blackburn Partnership indicated that it would prefer unitary status for the borough as this would simplify local government organisation and eliminate unnecessary levels of bureaucracy. The East Lancashire Chamber of Commerce and Industry, with a membership of 838 companies, also preferred a unitary Blackburn, commenting that it had been impressed by the existing Borough Council's determination and commitment to economic development. It stated that while the prospect of a mixed unitary and two-tier structure in Lancashire was not ideal, unitary status for Blackburn was supported by most companies in the borough.

2.9 The majority of business respondents from Blackpool supported unitary status for the borough. The Director and Company Secretary for The Blackpool Pleasure Beach Limited wrote that he was satisfied that the existing Council, with its private sector partners, would thrive under unitary status. Blackpool Transport Services preferred a unitary Blackpool authority and supported the need for a joint approach to strategic planning and for continued co-operation with the County Council over highway and public transport issues.

2.10 Support for the retention of the two-tier structure was stronger in the rest of the county. Lancashire Enterprises plc stated that the proposed unitary authorities would be too small, would not have the existing infrastructure necessary to enable them to compete on an equal basis with other local authorities in the north west, and would result in a loss of specialist services and strategic capacity. The Lancashire Business Consultation Team expressed concerns that unitary status for Blackburn and Blackpool would be an expensive exercise of little benefit to business, commerce or its employees across Lancashire.

County, Regional and National Interests (including the Voluntary Sector)

2.11 There was a majority opposing unitary status for Blackburn and Blackpool from those interest groups that wrote to the Commission. Several respondents did not express a structural preference but drew attention to certain service-related issues that they wished the Commission to take into account. Concern was expressed about the delivery of some services currently employing small teams of specialist staff.

2.12 The North Western Regional Library System, for example, indicated that it would prefer the retention of the two-tier structure across Lancashire, and expressed concern about the effects change would have on library services in the North West and on the existing co-operative arrangements. The Lancashire Council for Voluntary Youth Services also supported no change, stating that having painstakingly established such good relations with the County Council over many years, it felt that it was overwhelmingly in the best interests of the young people in Lancashire to retain the present two-tier structure in its entirety. The Royal Commission on the Historical Monuments of England believed there was an "...opportunity for more effective organisational support for the existing conservation service to emerge from the present review" but did not express a structural preference.

Education Groups

2.13 The majority of education groups across Lancashire indicated that they would prefer the retention of the two-tier structure. There was particular concern that funding might be reduced and that specialist services could suffer if Blackburn and Blackpool become unitary authorities. The Lancashire Federation of the National Association of Schoolmasters and Union of Women Teachers feared that creating unitary authorities would be expensive, reduce the level of funding to all schools, and give rise to a reduction in school support services. The Very Reverend Canon A J Cochrane, who has an interest in the Aided Sector of Maintained Education, preferred education to be left unaltered and allowed to "...get on with a job that is difficult enough at the present time and does not need any alteration to make that work far more difficult, expensive and less efficient". The Lancashire Association of Severe Learning Difficulties Schools'

Headteachers also preferred no change, stating that the need for very specialist input with children with severe learning difficulties is paramount, and stressed that, in its view, smaller authorities would not be able to provide the wide range of professionally trained specialists and advisers that Lancashire County Council presently provides.

2.14 The Corporation Board of Blackburn College expressed support for a unitary Blackburn, as it considered a county-wide strategy was unable to operate in a responsive way to meet the needs of widely differing local areas. The College argued that the development of appropriate facilities and policies to cater for the multi-cultural needs of the borough was central in Blackburn thinking but could not be regarded as a central feature in a county-wide strategy. It also argued that there was a particular need for education and training provision to correspond to identified employment trends and to respond to skill gaps and that these would be best achieved in partnership with a unitary Blackburn authority.

Health Interests

2.15 The health interests that responded to the Commission's draft recommendations were divided as to a preferred structure. The Lancashire Care Association, for example, preferred unitary status for Blackburn and Blackpool, on the grounds that they would be more likely to provide a mixed economy of care, with quality and cost being important criteria. Likewise the Blackburn, Hyndburn and Ribble Valley Healthcare NHS Trust supported unitary status for Blackburn and believed, particularly in the area of community care, that it would improve communications, open up new areas for co-operation and enhance the effectiveness of joint working. The Lancaster Priority Services NHS Trust considered unitary authorities could improve links with social services, as they would not be subject to centralised policies.

2.16 The East Lancashire Health Authority stated that there were "...good arguments both for keeping the two-tier structure and for Blackburn to be given unitary status". However, the Authority was marginally inclined towards the retention of the existing two-tier structure. The Blackpool, Wyre and Fylde Community Health Services NHS Trust expressed concern about the effect of too many strategic authorities with potentially different policies, which could cause additional strain on the service. The Director of Public Health of North West Lancashire Health, writing in a personal capacity, supported no change, stating his concerns regarding the proposed hybrid structure.

Law, Order and Emergency Services

2.17 The Lancashire Chief Fire Officer, the Fire Brigades Union and the Fire Officers Association all supported no change. The Chief Fire Officer believed that there would be funding difficulties for a combined fire authority and that the Lancashire Brigade needed the support of elected members who are able to communicate a Lancashire perspective to issues raised within the community.

Local Groups

2.18 Nearly 90 per cent of the 42 local groups that wrote from within Blackburn supported the establishment of a unitary authority. Fewer Blackpool groups responded, with the majority of those that did favouring no change. Around 90 per cent of groups in the rest of the county also preferred the retention of the two-tier structure.

2.19 Blackburn, Hyndburn and Ribble Valley Council for Voluntary Service wrote to express support for a unitary authority for Blackburn. The Provost of Blackburn also wrote to state a preference for a unitary authority for the borough. He said: "I believe that strengthened civic pride and resolve, together with the local delivery of more services, will give the opportunity to maximise the potential of Blackburn as a sub-regional and cathedral town for the ultimate benefit of Lancashire and of the Diocese". Several groups with members drawn from ethnic minority communities of Blackburn responded, the majority preferring a unitary authority for the borough, which they believed would be better able to address the specific needs of the communities.

2.20 The Blackpool Pensioners' Pressure Group supported unitary status for the borough. The Blackpool Youth Workers' Forum, however, preferred no change as it worked successfully in partnership with the two principal authorities at present.

Parliamentary Interests

2.21 Blackburn's bid for unitary status received support from the two Members of Parliament whose constituencies cover the borough. Mr Jack Straw, MP for Blackburn, argued that there was considerable overlap and duplication and that services previously delivered on a district basis in Blackburn had now been broken up and replaced by arrangements that were incomprehensible. Mrs Janet Anderson, MP for Rossendale and Darwen, supported a unitary Blackburn and argued that the people of Darwen now regarded themselves as an integral part of the wider borough. Mr Nigel Evans, MP for Ribble Valley, supported the establishment of unitary authorities for Blackburn and Blackpool. Support for unitary Blackburn also came from Baroness Castle and Lord Taylor. Mr Michael Hindley, MEP for Lancashire South, also expressed support for a Blackburn unitary authority.

2.22 Support for Blackpool's bid for unitary status was divided. Mr Harold Elletson, MP for Blackpool North, preferred the retention of the two-tier structure as he believed the unitary authority proposed for Blackpool would not be able to provide adequate specialist support for services such as education and social services. However, Mr Nicholas Hawkins, MP for Blackpool South, supported the Commission's draft recommendation. Of those who wrote to the Commission, most Members of Parliament outside the review districts were opposed to unitary status for Blackburn and Blackpool. Mr Peter Pike, MP for Burnley, saw unitary status for Blackburn and Blackpool on their own being detrimental to service levels and cost for the rest of Lancashire, and considered that unitary local government based on districts should be considered alongside the creation of regional government. Mr Gordon Prentice, MP for Pendle, opposed unitary status for the review districts, stating that he was bemused that: "Blackburn and Blackpool should be given unitary status when Preston, Lancaster, Burnley and other districts are to remain in the two-tier system". Lord Clitheroe wrote to support the retention of the existing two-tier system.

Parish And Town Councils

2.23 Blackpool has no parish or town councils. Within Blackburn, North Turton Parish Council supported the retention of the two-tier structure, as it considered that a unitary Blackburn would lack sufficient population, financial resources and community cohesion to be an effective all-purpose authority. Eccleshill Parish Council supported unitary status for Blackburn.

2.24 Of the 46 parish and town councils in the rest of Lancashire that responded, over 80 per cent opposed any change in Blackburn or Blackpool. The Lancashire Association of Parish and Town Councils wrote of its concerns about the financial impact which structural change might have on the remainder of the county and, in particular, that the hinterlands of Blackburn and Blackpool would, in its view, be disadvantaged.

NOP Tabulations of Written Representations

1 The following tabulations summarise the views expressed by members of the public and other interested parties during the consultation on the Local Government Commission's draft recommendations for Blackburn and Blackpool.

2 The tabulations include only letters sent directly to NOP at its Chelmsford offices and to the Commission's offices in London. Where more than one person's view has been expressed in a letter, the comments from each individual have been recorded separately. Staff from the Commission and NOP have worked closely in ensuring that care has been taken in the interpretation of comments, and that a consistent approach has been adopted.

3 While many people expressed support for one or other of the draft options presented by the Commission, other responses were coded by NOP after further discussion. The pattern of views expressed has been carefully examined, and where a number of respondents supported an option not included in those put forward by the Commission, those views have been separately coded and reported by NOP.

4 The Commission has advertised through the local media, encouraging people to make their views known. All responses received up to two days after the end of the Stage Three consultation period have been included. Returns from campaigns organised by local authorities or other groups (for example, standardised postcards and letters, questionnaires and petitions) have not been included in the tabulations. These, and submissions written and dated before the commencement of the consultation process, have been considered separately by the Commission.

The following definitions have been applied by NOP in compiling the tabulations:

(i) Type of Respondent

Individuals:	includes individual members of the public, local councillors and Members of the Westminster and European Parliaments.
Businesses and Business Groups:	includes organisations which represent businesses, such as local Chambers of Commerce.
County, Regional and National Interests:	any organisation which covers an area which is the size of a county or larger is included here, for example, a county-wide voluntary organisation or a regional association. This classification includes most of the statutory consultees.
Education (and Church) Groups:	this group includes schools, religious organisations and teaching unions.
Local Groups:	this includes organisations smaller than a county area, for example, a district-level voluntary sector body. The group could be voluntary, sporting, political or cultural but does not include organisations from the education or religious sectors (included above). It also includes constituency parties and political groups on local authorities.
Parish and Town Councils:	this also includes district-level associations of town and parish councils. County level associations are classified as County, Regional and National interests.

(ii) Structural Options (Reports A and D)

No change in own district:	this code is used where there is more than one review district in the county. It indicates where respondents from a review district have expressed support for no change for that district and have not made reference to the other review district(s) in that county.
District/county-level authorities:	represents support for either a district or county-level authority although it is not clear whether this is for a unitary or a two-tier structure.
Opposition to structural preferences:	represents responses where a negative, but unspecified, structural preference has been expressed.
Rejects:	rejects are those responses with unclear comments/interpretation.

(iii) Other

Other issues (Report B):	these illustrate preferences in relation to boundary and electoral changes and (where applicable) the restoration of historic counties.
Parishing issues (Report C):	these illustrate preferences in relation to parishing issues, for example, the creation of new parishes or the enhancement of the role of parish and town councils.
Services (Report E):	these illustrate concerns expressed about the impact of proposed changes on particular service areas where the respondent has not additionally expressed a positive structural preference.

NOP Analysis of Responses to Local Government Commission Draft Recommendations - LANCASHIRE

Report A: Opinions on the structural options, by authority of respondent
Base: all

	Review districts		Other districts in county														
	Blackburn	Blackpool	Burnley	Chorley	Fylde	Hynd -burn	Lan- caster	Pendle	Preston	Ribble Valley	Rossen -dale	South Ribble	West Lanca- shire	Wyre	Rest of county total	County total	Out of county total
Status quo/two-tier	153	102	85	137	133	93	151	77	405	92	43	484	90	221	2011	2266	113
	19%	*10%*	*90%*	*87%*	*86%*	*68%*	*92%*	*89%*	*97%*	*71%*	*84%*	*96%*	*91%*	*89%*	*90%*	*56%*	*62%*
Unitary Blackburn	490	4	3	14	3	38	1	6	4	23	7	8	2	2	111	605	43
	59%	*	*3%*	*9%*	*2%*	*28%*	*1%*	*7%*	*1%*	*18%*	*14%*	*2%*	*2%*	*1%*	*5%*	*15%*	*24%*
Unitary Blackpool	-	587	-	-	10	-	-	-	1	-	-	-	-	9	20	607	2
	-	*58%*	-	-	*6%*	-	-	-	*	-	-	-	-	*4%*	*1%*	*15%*	*1%*
Two Unitary Districts (Blackburn and Blackpool)	13	5	3	2	4	-	4	3	2	4	-	3	-	5	30	48	5
	2%	*	*3%*	*1%*	*3%*	-	*2%*	*3%*	*	*3%*	-	*1%*	-	*2%*	*1%*	*1%*	*3%*
No change in own district	150	269	-	-	-	1	-	-	-	2	-	-	-	3	6	425	1
	18%	*27%*	-	-	-	*1%*	-	-	-	*2%*	-	-	-	*1%*	*	*10%*	*1%*
County-level authority (either two-tier or unitary)	1	2	-	-	-	2	1	1	1	2	-	-	-	-	7	10	2
	*	*	-	-	-	*1%*	*1%*	*1%*	*	*2%*	-	-	-	-	*	*	*1%*
District-level authority (either two-tier or unitary)	9	13	-	-	-	-	-	-	-	-	-	-	-	-	-	22	-
	1%	*1%*	-	-	-	-	-	-	-	-	-	-	-	-	-	*1%*	-
Pre-1974 structure	-	2	-	-	-	-	-	-	-	-	-	-	-	-	-	2	-
	-	*	-	-	-	-	-	-	-	-	-	-	-	-	-	*	-
County-wide unitary structure	-	1	1	1	2	-	-	-	-	1	-	-	-	-	5	6	-
	-	*	*1%*	*1%*	*1%*	-	-	-	-	*1%*	-	-	-	-	*	*	-
Opposition to structural options (where no positive preference is stated)	-	-	1	-	-	-		-	-	-	-	-	-	-	1	1	-
	-	-	*1%*	-	-	-	-	-	-	-	-	-	-	-	*	*	-
Reject	-	1	-	-	-	-	-	-	-	-	-	-	-	-	-	1	1
	-	*	-	-	-	-	-	-	-	-	-	-	-	-	-	*	*1%*
Other specified	1	1	-	-	-	1	-	-	1	-	-	3	-	-	5	7	-
	*	*	-	-	-	*1%*	-	-	*	-	-	*1%*	-	-	*	*	-
No preference expressed/option defined	7	26	1	3	3	2	7	-	2	6	1	4	7	7	43	76	15
	1%	*3%*	*1%*	*2%*	*2%*	*1%*	*4%*	-	*	*5%*	*2%*	*1%*	*7%*	*3%*	*2%*	*2%*	*8%*
BASE TOTAL	824	1013	94	157	155	137	164	87	416	130	51	502	99	247	2239	4076	182

* *Less than ½%*

Blackburn & Blackpool

NOP Analysis of Responses to Local Government Commission Draft Recommendations - LANCASHIRE

Report B: Opinions on other issues, by authority of respondent
Base: all

	Review districts		Other districts in county														
	Blackburn	Blackpool	Burnley	Chorley	Fylde	Hynd -burn	Lan-caster	Pendle	Preston	Ribble Valley	Rossen -dale	South Ribble	West Lanca-shire	Wyre	Rest of county total	County total	Out of county total
Historic Lancashire	-	2	-	-	-	-	-	-	-	1	-	-	-	-	1	3	1
	-	*	-	-	-	-	-	-	-	*1%*	-	-	-	-	*	*	*1%*
BASE TOTAL	824	1013	94	157	155	137	164	87	416	130	51	502	99	247	2239	4076	182

The figures in the table above do not sum to the base total/100% because undefined fields are not included, except as part of the base total.
* *Less than ½%*

NOP Analysis of Responses to Local Government Commission Draft Recommendations - LANCASHIRE

Report C: Opinions on parishing issues, by authority of respondent
Base: all

	Review districts		Other districts in county														
	Blackburn	Blackpool	Burnley	Chorley	Fylde	Hynd -burn	Lan-caster	Pendle	Preston	Ribble Valley	Rossen -dale	South Ribble	West Lanca-shire	Wyre	Rest of county total	County total	Out of county total
BASE TOTAL	824	1013	94	157	155	137	164	87	416	130	51	502	99	247	2239	4076	182

The figures in the table above do not sum to the base total/100% because undefined fields are not included, except as part of the base total.
* *Less than ½%*

NOP Analysis of Responses to Local Government Commission Draft Recommendations - LANCASHIRE

Report D1: Opinions on the structural options, by respondent type (all respondents)
Base: all

	Respondent Type					
	Indiv-iduals	Business groups	County, regional & national interests	Education (& church) groups	Local groups	Parish and town councils
Status quo/two-tier	2079 *56%*	57 *39%*	27 *56%*	149 *79%*	29 *34%*	38 *79%*
Unitary Blackburn	525 *14%*	72 *50%*	5 *10%*	7 *4%*	38 *45%*	1 *2%*
Unitary Blackpool	591 *16%*	11 *8%*	1 *2%*	3 *2%*	3 *4%*	- -
Two Unitary Districts (Blackburn and Blackpool)	45 *1%*	- -	4 *8%*	- -	- -	4 *8%*
No change in own district	394 *11%*	3 *2%*	1 *2%*	18 *10%*	9 *11%*	1 *2%*
County-level authority (either two-tier or unitary)	10 *	1 *1%*	- -	1 *1%*	- -	- -
District-level authority (either two-tier or unitary)	22 *1%*	- -	- -	- -	- -	- -
Pre-1974 structure	2 *	- -	- -	- -	- -	- -
County-wide unitary structure	5 *	1 *1%*	- -	- -	- -	- -
Opposition to structural options (where no positive preference is stated)	1 *	- -	- -	- -	- -	- -
Reject	2 *	- -	- -	- -	- -	- -
Other specified	5 *	- -	1 *2%*	1 *1%*	- -	- -
No preference expressed/option defined	63 *2%*	- -	9 *19%*	9 *5%*	6 *7%*	4 *8%*
BASE TOTAL	3744	145	48	188	85	48

* *Less than ½%*

NOP Analysis of Responses to Local Government Commission Draft Recommendations - LANCASHIRE

Report D2: Opinions on the structural options, by respondent type
Base: respondents in Blackburn only

	Respondent Type					
	Indiv-iduals	Business groups	County, regional & national interests	Education (& church) groups	Local groups	Parish and town councils
Status quo/two-tier	140 *20%*	1 *2%*	1 *20%*	8 *40%*	3 *7%*	- -
Unitary Blackburn	389 *55%*	53 *98%*	3 *60%*	7 *35%*	37 *88%*	1 *50%*
Two Unitary Districts (Blackburn and Blackpool)	13 *2%*	- -	- -	- -	- -	- -
No change in own district	142 *20%*	- -	- -	5 *25%*	2 *5%*	1 *50%*
County-level authority (either two-tier or unitary)	1 *	- -	- -	- -	- -	- -
District-level authority (either two-tier or unitary)	9 *1%*	- -	- -	- -	- -	- -
Other specified	1 *	- -	- -	- -	- -	- -
No preference expressed/option defined	6 *1%*	- -	1 *20%*	- -	- -	- -
BASE TOTAL	701	54	5	20	42	2

* *Less than ½%*

Blackburn & Blackpool

NOP Analysis of Responses to Local Government Commission Draft Recommendations - LANCASHIRE

Report D3: Opinions on the structural options, by respondent type
Base: respondents in Blackpool only

	Respondent Type					
	Indiv-iduals	Business groups	County, regional & national interests	Education (& church) groups	Local groups	Parish and town councils
Status quo/two-tier	93 *10%*	2 *13%*	- -	4 *16%*	3 *23%*	- -
Unitary Blackburn	4 *	- -	- -	- -	- -	- -
Unitary Blackpool	570 *60%*	11 *69%*	- -	3 *12%*	3 *23%*	- -
Two Unitary Districts (Blackburn and Blackpool)	4 *	- -	1 *33%*	- -	- -	- -
No change in own district	245 *26%*	3 *19%*	1 *33%*	13 *52%*	7 *54%*	- -
County-level authority (either two-tier or unitary)	1 *	- -	- -	1 *4%*	- -	- -
District-level authority (either two-tier or unitary)	13 *1%*	- -	- -	- -	- -	- -
Pre-1974 structure	2 *	- -	- -	- -	- -	- -
County-wide unitary structure	1 *	- -	- -	- -	- -	- -
Reject	1 *	- -	- -	- -	- -	- -
Other specified	1 *	- -	- -	- -	- -	- -
No preference expressed/option defined	21 *2%*	- -	1 *33%*	4 *16%*	- -	- -
BASE TOTAL	956	16	3	25	13	-

* *Less than ½%*

NOP Analysis of Responses to Local Government Commission Draft Recommendations - LANCASHIRE

Report D4: Opinions on the structural options, by respondent type
Base: respondents in rest of county only

	Respondent Type					
	Indiv-iduals	Business groups	County, regional & national interests	Education (& church) groups	Local groups	Parish and town councils
Status quo/two-tier	1778 *90%*	21 *68%*	19 *83%*	135 *96%*	20 *87%*	38 *83%*
Unitary Blackburn	101 *5%*	9 *29%*	- -	- -	1 *4%*	- -
Unitary Blackpool	20 *1%*	- -	- -	- -	- -	- -
Two Unitary Districts (Blackburn and Blackpool)	24 *1%*	- -	2 *9%*	- -	- -	4 *9%*
No change in own district	6 *	- -	- -	- -	- -	- -
County-level authority (either two-tier or unitary)	7 *	- -	- -	- -	- -	- -
County-wide unitary structure	4 *	1 *3%*	- -	- -	- -	-
Opposition to structural options (where no positive preference is stated)	1 *	- -	- -	- -	- -	- -
Other specified	3 *	- -	1 *4%*	1 *1%*	- -	- -
No preference expressed/option defined	31 *2%*	- -	1 *4%*	5 *4%*	2 *9%*	4 *9%*
BASE TOTAL	1975	31	23	141	23	46

* *Less than ½%*

NOP Analysis of Responses to Local Government Commission Draft Recommendations - LANCASHIRE

Report E: Views on services, by authority of respondent
Base: all

	Review districts		Other districts in county														
	Blackburn	Blackpool	Burnley	Chorley	Fylde	Hynd -burn	Lan- caster	Pendle	Preston	Ribble Valley	Rossen -dale	South Ribble	West Lanca- shire	Wyre	Rest of county total	County total	Out of county total
Archives	1	-	-	2	3	-	1	-	2	3	-	3	1	3	18	19	6
	*	-	-	1%	2%	-	1%	-	*	2%	-	1%	1%	1%	1%	*	3%
Education	3	13	-	-	-	1	2	-	-	-	1	-	6	2	12	28	-
	*	1%	-	-	-	1%	1%	-	-	-	2%	-	6%	1%	1%	1%	-
Libraries	-	-	-	-	-	-	-	-	-	-	-	-	-	-	-	-	1
	-	-	-	-	-	-	-	-	-	-	-	-	-	-	-	-	1%
Trading standards	-	-	-	-	-	-	-	-	-	-	-	-	-	-	-	-	1
	-	-	-	-	-	-	-	-	-	-	-	-	-	-	-	-	1%
Other specified services (or multiples of)	-	-	-	-	-	-	-	-	-	-	-	-	-	-	-	-	-
	-	-	-	-	-	-	-	-	-	-	-	-	-	-	-	-	1%
BASE TOTAL	824	1013	94	157	155	137	164	87	416	130	51	502	99	247	2239	4076	182

The figures in the table above do not sum to the base total/100% because undefined fields are not included, except as part of the base total.
* *Less than ½%*

NOP Analysis of Responses to Local Government Commission Draft Recommendations - LANCASHIRE

Report F: Views on services, by respondent type
Base: all

	Respondent Type					
	Indiv-iduals	Business groups	County, regional & national interests	Education (& church) groups	Local groups	Parish and town councils
Archives	20	-	2	-	3	-
	1%	-	*4%*	-	*4%*	-
Education	18	-	-	10	-	-
	*	-	-	*5%*	-	-
Libraries	-	-	1	-	-	-
	-	-	*2%*	-	-	-
Trading standards	-	-	1	-	-	-
	-	-	*2%*	-	-	-
Other specified services (or multiples of)	-	-	1	-	-	-
	-	-	2%	-	-	-
BASE TOTAL	3744	145	48	188	85	48

The figures in the table above do not sum to the base total/100% because undefined fields are not included, except as part of the base total.
* *Less than ½%*

NOP Analysis of Responses to Local Government Commission Draft Recommendations - LANCASHIRE

Report G: Type of respondent, by authority of respondent
Base: all

	Review districts		Other districts in county														
	Blackburn	Blackpool	Burnley	Chorley	Fylde	Hynd-burn	Lan-caster	Pendle	Preston	Ribble Valley	Rossen-dale	South Ribble	West Lanca-shire	Wyre	Rest of county total	County total	Out of county total
Individuals	701 *85%*	956 *94%*	76 *81%*	138 *88%*	139 *90%*	119 *87%*	129 *79%*	74 *85%*	379 *91%*	110 *85%*	39 *76%*	483 *96%*	84 *85%*	205 *83%*	1975 *88%*	3632 *89%*	112 *62%*
Business groups	54 *7%*	16 *2%*	2 *2%*	1 *1%*	1 *1%*	4 *3%*	3 *2%*	3 *3%*	8 *2%*	1 *1%*	4 *8%*	2 *	1 *1%*	1 *	31 *1%*	101 *2%*	44 *24%*
County, regional and national interests	5 *1%*	3 *	1 *1%*	2 *1%*	2 *1%*	- -	5 *3%*	1 *1%*	8 *2%*	1 *1%*	- -	2 *	- -	1 *	23 *1%*	31 *1%*	17 *9%*
Education (and church) groups	20 *2%*	25 *2%*	13 *14%*	11 *7%*	7 *5%*	12 *9%*	21 *13%*	4 *5%*	13 *3%*	5 *4%*	6 *12%*	12 *2%*	11 *11%*	26 *11%*	141 *6%*	186 *5%*	2 *1%*
Local Groups	42 *5%*	13 *1%*	1 *1%*	2 *1%*	2 *1%*	2 *1%*	- -	1 *1%*	2 *	2 *2%*	2 *4%*	1 *	2 *2%*	6 *2%*	23 *1%*	78 *2%*	7 *4%*
Parish and town councils	2 *	- -	1 *1%*	3 *2%*	4 *3%*	- -	6 *4%*	4 *5%*	6 *1%*	11 *8%*	- -	2 *	1 *1%*	8 *3%*	46 *2%*	48 *1%*	- -
BASE TOTAL	824	1013	94	157	155	137	164	87	416	130	51	502	99	247	2239	4076	182

* *Less than ½%*

Blackburn & Blackpool

MORI Research Study for the Local Government Commission

Introduction

Background

1 This summary report highlights the key findings from a survey of public opinion conducted in the Boroughs of Blackburn and Blackpool and across the County of Lancashire on behalf of the Local Government Commission for England. A copy of each of the marked-up questionnaires is appended. The computer tabulations are contained in a separate volume, which is available from MORI (32 Old Queen Street, London SW1H 9HP. Telephone 0171-222 0232. Price £15)

2 The survey was designed in close consultation with the Commission, following extensive qualitative research and pilot testing. All sampling, interviewing and analysis have been carried out independently by MORI, within the guidelines of the profession laid out by the Market Research Society.

3 In each of Blackburn and Blackpool, all Census Enumeration Districts (EDs) were sorted by ward, and stratified according to social class. EDs were then sampled (32 in total) in proportion to the population size of each, and quotas set for sex, age and work status. In Blackburn, a total of 314 interviews with adults aged 18+, conducted face-to-face and in-home, were carried out between 4-30 October 1995. In Blackpool, 306 interviews were conducted. Data were weighted to match the population profile in each of the two Boroughs.

4 In the remaining districts of Lancashire, all EDs were sorted into wards, and again were stratified according to social class. A total of 32 EDs across the whole area (that is, Lancashire excluding Blackburn and Blackpool) were sampled, with quotas set by sex, age and work status. Face-to-face interviews, conducted in-home, were carried out with 318 adults aged 18+ on 29 September-29 October 1995. Data were weighted to match the population profile of the County excluding Blackburn and Blackpool. In addition, booster interviews took place in both Fylde and Wyre districts. In both cases, a further five EDs were selected in proportion to population size, and quotas set; 50 interviews took place in each between 4-30 October 1995. Booster data is not included in the main analysis.

Publication of the Results

5 As with all our studies, these findings are subject to our Standard Terms and Conditions of Contract. Any press release or publication of the findings of this survey require the advance approval of MORI. Such approval will only be refused on the grounds of inaccuracy or misinterpretation.

Objectives

6 This survey took place during Stage Three, the consultation period on the Commission's draft recommendations. It measures public preferences for the organisation of local government in the areas currently comprising the Boroughs of Blackburn and Blackpool, as well as exploring strength of feeling, levels of knowledge about the review, involvement in, and broader perceptions of, local government in the area.

Statistical Reliability of the Data

7 Because we have interviewed a sample of residents, rather than the whole population, the results are subject to statistical tolerance limits, or "margins of error". These are expressed as our confidence that the true figure for the whole population falls within a given range. By convention this is expressed as a percentage, so our 95% confidence level means that in 95 times out of 100 the true figure would lie within this range.

8 The table below shows ranges of the 95% confidence level for a range of sample sizes. For each sample size, the table shows the tolerance limits for sample results close to 10%, 30% and 50%. Take, for example, the results of a survey of 300 residents showing that 50% are aware of the review. In 95 times out of 100 the true figure would lie between 44% and 56% (ie 50% ±6%).

Sample size	Sampling tolerances applicable to results at or near these percentages (based on 95% confidence level) 10/90% ±%	30/70% ±%	50% ±%
300	3	5	6
200	4	6	7
150	5	7	8
100	6	9	10
50	8	13	14

9 Clearly, 10% or 30% of the sample being aware of the review equate to 90% or 70% not being aware of it. So this table shows the ranges of 95% confidence for responses close to 10%, 30%, 50%, 70% and 90% of our sample. The figures for responses between can be obtained by extrapolation.

10 The true figure would only be known if all the residents of the area had been interviewed. It can be seen in the table, however, that large increases in the sample size do not greatly reduce the sampling tolerance. In addition, the true figure is more likely to lie at the midpoint of the range, rather than at either extreme.

11 When comparing results from separate groups within a sample we need to be sure that the differences are statistically significant. This would be important in comparing views expressed by different parts of a county. The table below shows how the statistical significance of the difference is determined by the size of the groups and the percentage result from the sample.

12 Assuming a 95% confidence level, the table shows the size of the differences required if different results are to be regarded as statistically significant. It can be seen that if 50% of a group of 300 were aware of the review, the result from another group of 300 would not become statistically significant until it became less than 42% or more than 58%.

Sample sizes	Differences required for significance at or near these percentage levels 10/90% ±	30/70% ±	50% ±
300 and 300	5	7	8
300 and 200	5	8	9
300 and 100	7	10	11
200 and 100	7	11	12
100 and 100	8	13	14

Survey Findings

Knowledge and Awareness

13 Over four in ten residents within the Boroughs of Blackburn and Blackpool say that they like to know what their council is doing, but want no further involvement, while around one in five want more involvement. In the rest of Lancashire, three in five want to know what the council is doing, with no further involvement. The proportion wanting greater involvement is the same, at one in five.

14 While around three in ten in Blackburn, Blackpool and the rest of the County say they know at least a fair amount about what their council does, around seven in ten admit to knowing not very much or nothing at all.

15 This is reflected in the number of residents who incorrectly ascribe services between the two tiers of local government. Thus, although around four in ten recognise libraries as a county council service, as many as one in three allocate responsibility to their district/borough/city council. And although between six and seven in ten realise that refuse collection is a district/ borough/city service, up to one in six thinks it is a county council service. There is little difference between the different groups of residents on being able to correctly allocate services across the two tiers.

16 Awareness of the review itself varies from 49% in the rest of the County to 74% in Blackpool. There is, however, little variation in the proportions who say that they know a fair amount or more about the review, from eight per cent in the rest of the County to 12% in Blackpool.

Sources of Information

17 Local newspapers are the most common source of information about the review, by a considerable margin. Of those who have at least heard of the review, around half name the local press as a recent source. Between two-thirds and three-quarters cite some media source as a recent source of information on the review.

18 Local authorities may have been more active in Blackpool than elsewhere. Here, 35% name a County Council source, and 34% a Borough source, compared with 29% and 26% respectively in Blackburn and 25% and 13% respectively in the rest of the County. Very few recognise receiving information directly from the Local Government Commission itself.

19 Although most of those aware of the review recognise one or more recent sources of information, few (one in five at most) say that this has influenced their opinion.

20 Furthermore, in spite of a relatively low level of knowledge and engagement with their local authority, most people say that the outcome of the review is important to them. The importance figures are remarkably consistent across the three areas surveyed: around one in four say that the outcome is very important, and another one in three say that it is fairly important.

The Preferred Option

21 Residents of Blackburn and Blackpool would prefer a unitary council to no change. The margins are, respectively, 39% to 32% and 43% to 32%. In the rest of the County, no change is favoured for both the review districts by a ratio of two-to-one (by 35% to 16% for Blackburn, and by 38% to 17% for Blackpool). However, in no area does a majority select any option. Almost all the rest had no views either way or were indifferent.

22 As is the case with the importance of the outcome of the review, there is a fair amount of consistency between the three areas surveyed on how strongly those expressing a preference say they feel about their preference. Between seven and eight in ten say they feel strongly. There is little difference in the strength of feeling expressed irrespective of which option is preferred.

Factors in Expressing a Preference

23 In questions 13 to 23, residents were asked to say to what extent they agreed or disagreed with a range of statements which related to a change to unitary local government. The statements were designed to cover the main issues raised by residents during the qualitative phase of research, and others that formed a part of the Commission's brief to take into consideration in making its recommendations.

24 The following charts summarise the results from these questions, with the full question wording presented in the questionnaires in the appendices. Values have been ascribed to the five

attitudinal positions that people were offered (+2 for strongly agree, +1 for tend to agree, 0 for neither agree nor disagree, -1 for tend to disagree, and -2 for strongly disagree) and mean scores calculated across all respondents expressing a view. This has the combined benefit of distilling the range of opinion into one summary figure, while incorporating the varying intensity of feeling by ascribing values. Bars to the right indicate that the mean score value is positive, and thus that there is a balance of agreement with the statement. Bars to the left, conversely, indicate a balance of disagreement.

25 The first chart, therefore, shows how the views of people living in the review Boroughs of Blackpool and Lancashire differ from those across the rest of Lancashire. In doing so, it illustrates the attitudes or perceptions that are, in relative terms, shared by both groups of residents (where the bars project in the same direction), and those where views differ markedly. Thus there is broad agreement on many of the positive aspects of change, most notably on the clarification of responsibilities, although the balance of opinion is more marked among residents in Blackpool and Blackburn than among those in the rest of Lancashire, as one might expect. There is some divergence when it comes to whether change would be too disruptive, or whether a unitary Blackpool or Blackburn would be too small to manage services like education and social services. There is also divergence on whether people feel that they will be affected by change. Those in the rest of the County are most likely to agree that they would like more information before making up their minds.

26 The subsequent charts take the results separately from Blackburn, Blackpool and the rest of the County, and illustrate the difference in views between those within each area whose preference is for unitary status, and those who prefer no change. The chart therefore illustrates those attitudinal statements that most, or least, differentiate residents expressing two opposing preferences.

Attitudes to Change
(All respondents)

Q To what extent do you agree or disagree that...?
(Figures represent 'mean scores' with *strong agreement* given a value of +2 through to *strong disagreement* given -2)

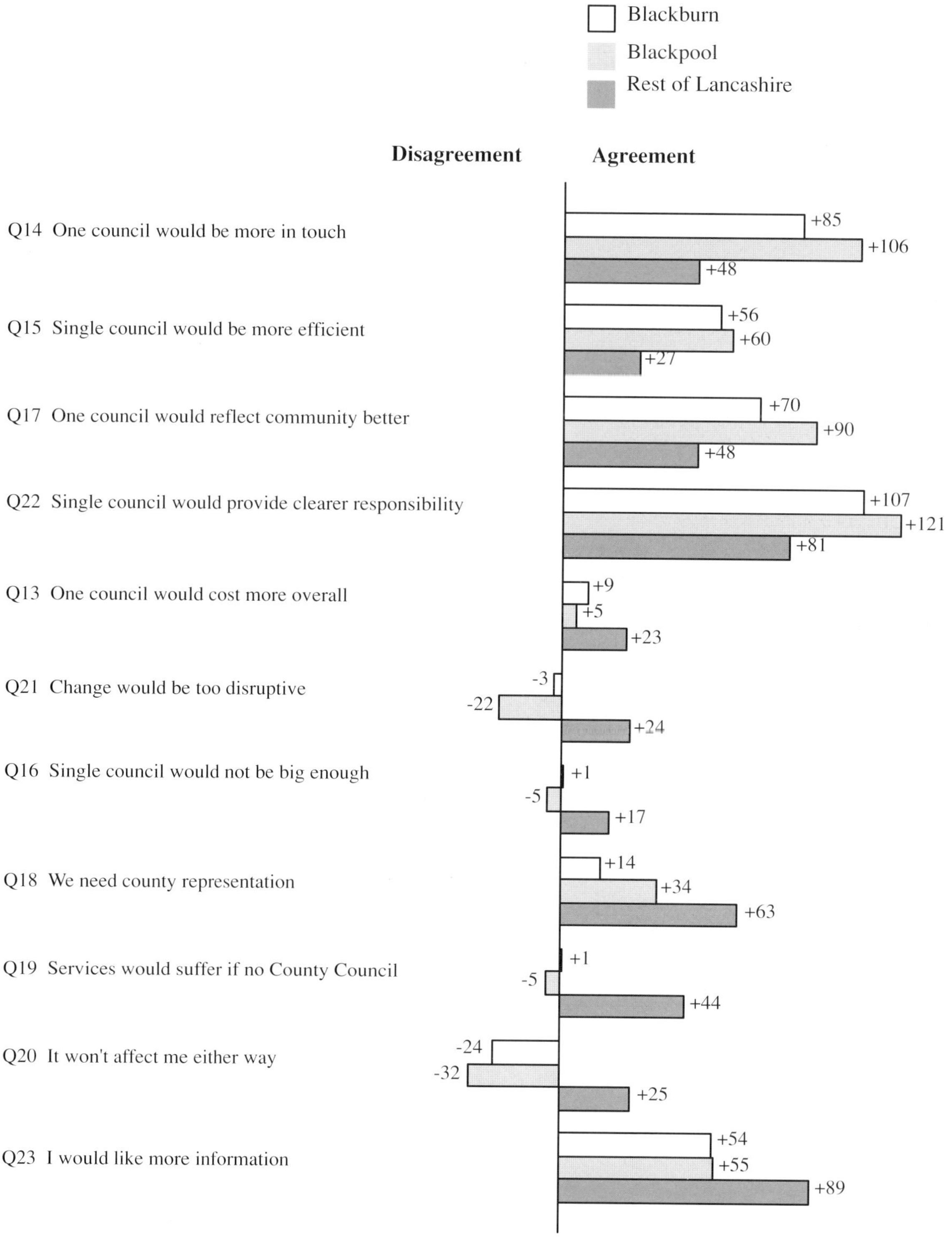

Attitudes to Change
(Respondents in Blackburn)

Q To what extent do you agree or disagree that...?
(Figures represent 'mean scores' with *strong agreement* given a value of +2 through to *strong disagreement* given -2)

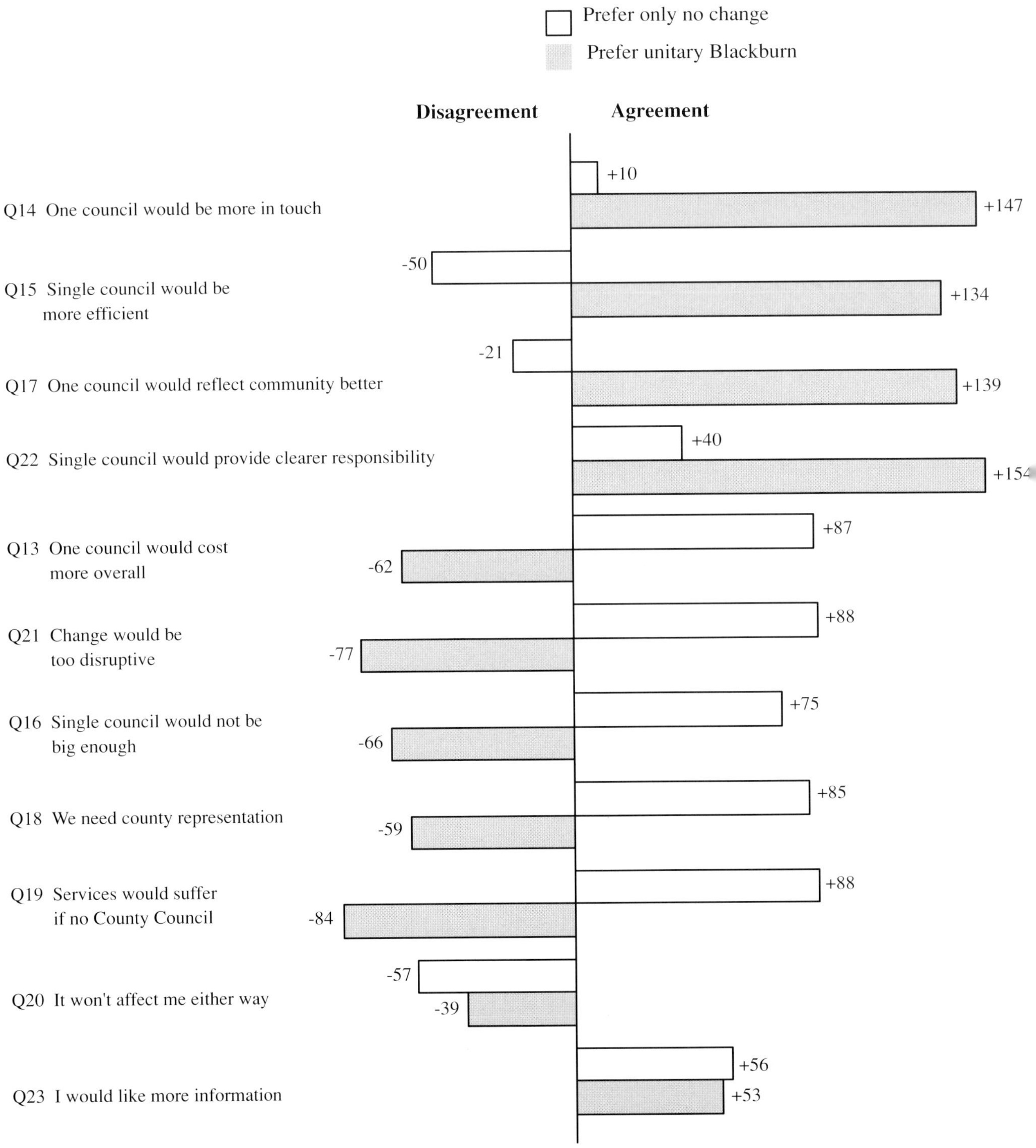

Attitudes to Change
(Respondents in Blackpool)

Q To what extent do you agree or disagree that...?
(Figures represent 'mean scores' with *strong agreement* given a value of +2 through to *strong disagreement* given -2)

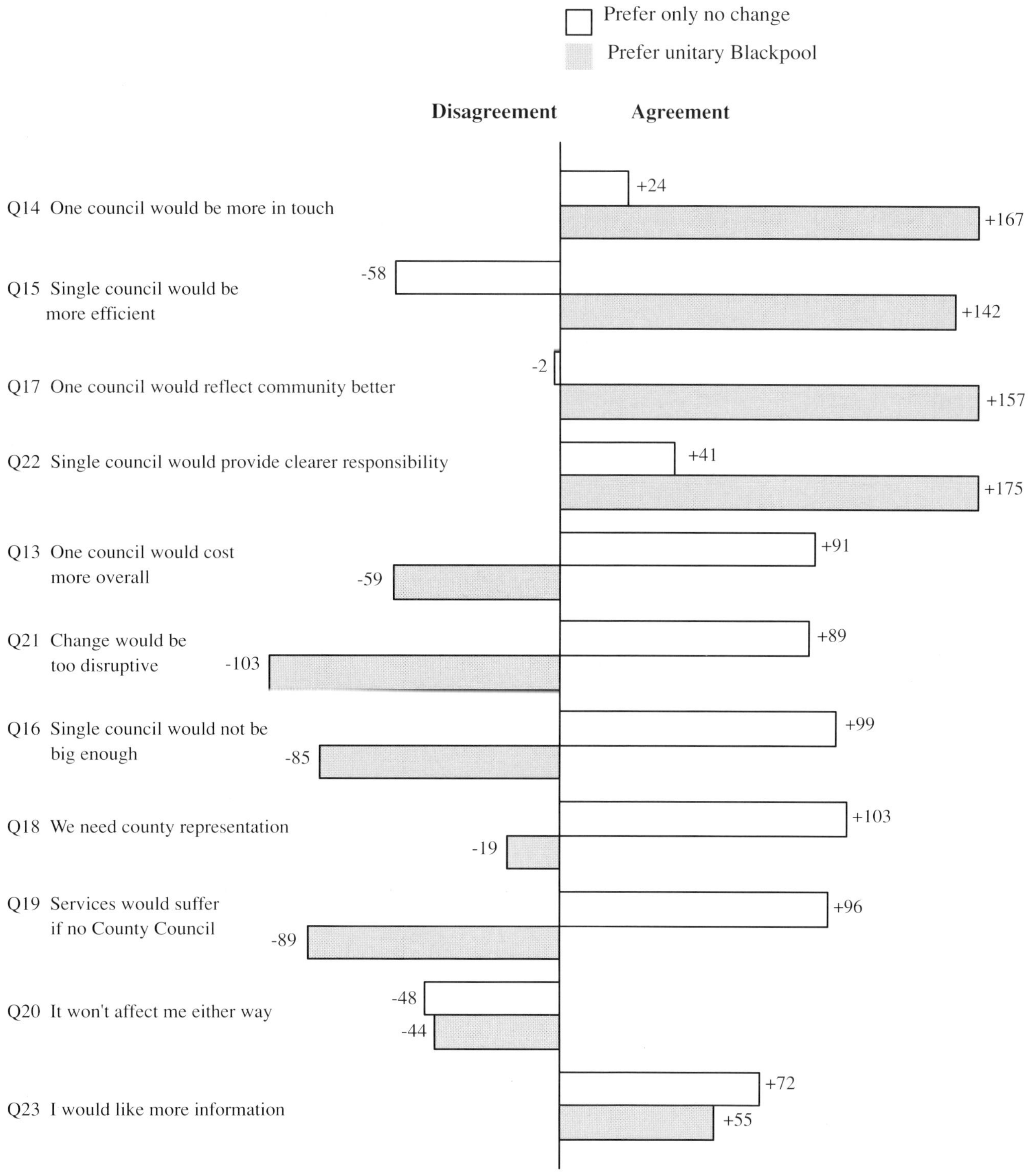

Attitudes to Change
(Respondents in the rest of Lancashire)

Q To what extent do you agree or disagree that...?
(Figures represent 'mean scores' with *strong agreement* given a value of +2 through to *strong disagreement* given -2)

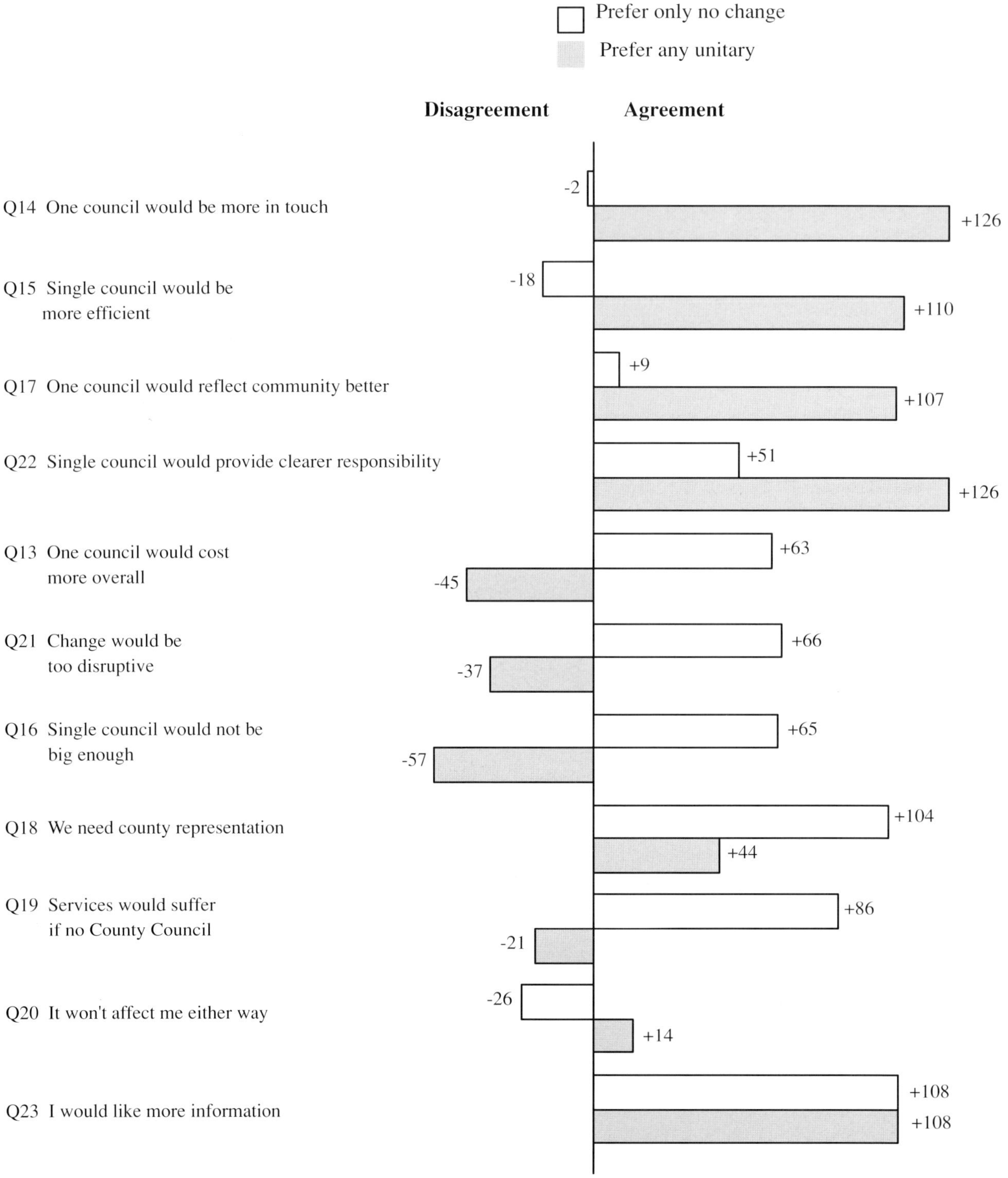

MORI/9101/07

LANCASHIRE
REVIEW - REST OF COUNTY
TOPLINE FINDINGS

Serial No ....

OUO (7-10)

N = 314
4 - 30 October 1995
Main sample data only
Base: All, unless stated

Gender	%
Male	48
Female	52

Age	%
18-24	13
25-34	18
35-44	16
45-54	17
55-64	16
65-74	12
75+	7

WRITE IN AGE

Work Status	%
Full-time (30 hrs/wk+)	45
Part-time (8-29 hrs/wk)	10
Not working (under 8 hrs)	2
Looking after home/children	8
Retired	25
Registered unemployed	5
Unemployed but not registered	1
Student	3
Other	1

Occupation of Chief Income Earner (CIE)

Position/rank/grade

....

Industry/type of company

....

Qualifications/degrees/apprenticeship

....

No of Staff Responsible for

....

PROBE FOR PENSION

	%
AB	10
C1	37
C2	25
D	15
E	14

* Less than 1/2%

Number in Household
Adults aged 18+ (inc. respondent)

22%	59%	15%	3%	1%
1	2	3	4	5+

Children (17 or under)

66%	15%	13%	4%	2%
0	1	2	3	4+

QA **Are you or other members of your household employed by a council?** IF YES: **Is this a Borough/District Council or a County Council?** CODE FOR BOTH RESPONDENT AND OTHER HOUSEHOLD MEMBERS

	Respondent %	Other %
Yes:		
Borough/District	1	3
County	4	2
Don't know which	-	1
No	95	83
Don't know	1	12

Tenure	%
Owned outright	31
Buying on mortgage	46
Rented from Council	11
Rented from Housing Association	2
Rented from private landlord	6
Other	4

QB **Is this your main permanent home, or is it a second or holiday home?**

	%
Main/permanent	97
Second/holiday	3

Car in Household
CIRCLE NUMBER

24%	48%	21%	5%
0	1	2	3+

INTERVIEWER DECLARATION: I confirm that I have conducted this interview face-to-face with the above named person and that I have asked all the relevant questions fully and recorded the answers in conformance with the survey specification and the MRS Code of Conduct.

Interviewer Name .... Signature ....

Interviewer Number					/	

	Month		Date	
DATE OF INTERVIEW				
	(29)	(30)	(31)	(32)

NB INTERVIEWER: ALL SHOWCARDS HAVE BEEN REVERSED. PLEASE BE CAREFUL TO CODE THE CORRECT RESPONSE.

Good morning/afternoon/evening. I'm from MORI, the market research and polling organisation. We are doing a survey about local issues, and I would like to ask you a few questions.

ASK ALL

Q1 **Firstly, how long have you lived in this area?** (WITHIN FIVE MILES)

	%
Less than 1 year	3
1-2 years	6
3-5 years	13
6-10 years	16
11-20 years	20
Over 20 years/all my life	43

Q2 SHOWCARD A (R) **From this card, how much would you say you know about local councils and the services they provide?**

	%
A great deal	2
A fair amount	27
Not very much	55
Nothing at all	14
Don't know	1

Q3 SHOWCARD B (R) **Which of the statements on this card comes closest to your own view of the Councils in this area?**

		%
A)	I'm not interested in what the Council does, or whether they do their job	2
B)	I'm not interested in what the Council does, as long as they do their job	19
C)	I like to know what the Council is doing, but I'm happy to let them get on with their job	58
D)	I would like to have more of a say in what the Council does and the services it provides	18
E)	I already work for, or am involved with the Council and the services it provides	2
	Don't know	2

Q4 **From what you know, how many councils provide the main services in this neighbourhood?** (INTERVIEWER - NOT INCLUDING PARISH COUNCILS)

	%
One	31
Two	27
Three+	4
Don't know	38

In fact there are two main councils that provide, or are responsible for, most services in this area:. . .district/borough/city and Lancashire County Council.

ROTATE ORDER OF Q5/6

☐ Q5 SHOWCARD C (R) **From this list, what services do you think are the responsibility of... district/borough/city council? Just read out the letter(s) that apply**

☐ Q6 SHOWCARD C AGAIN (R) **And which services on this list do you think are the responsibility of Lancashire County Council? Again, just read out the letters that apply.**

Q7 SHOWCARD D (R) **Which, if any, of these services do you or members of your family use?** INCLUDE ONLY LOCAL USE

		Q5 "Borough" %	Q6 County %	Q7 Use %
A	Bus Services	31	16	49
B	Car Parks	49	16	62
C	Council Housing	50	18	11
D	Council Tax Benefit/Housing benefit	45	22	19
E	Fire service	21	44	35
F	Food safety	29	25	13
G	Household waste sites/dumps	49	20	54
H	Libraries	32	36	57
I	Parks, playgrounds and open spaces	52	14	53
J	Planning service	41	23	9
K	Public conveniences	52	8	37
L	Recycling/bottle banks	43	15	41
M	Refuse collection	58	16	83
N	Road maintenance	32	41	43
O	Schools/education	26	49	36
P	Social services	28	40	14
Q	Street sweeping	55	15	44
R	Swimming pools/sports facilities	50	14	51
	Other 3	3	2	2
	None of these	*	2	1
	Don't know	29	32	2

Q8 SHOWCARD E (R) **As you may know, there is currently a review being undertaken by the Local Government Commission on the future local government structure in the county. How much, if anything, would you say you know about this?**

	%
A great deal	2
A fair amount	6
Just a little	22
Heard of but know nothing about	19
Never heard of	51
Don't know	*

PREFERENCES

HAND OVER MAP SHOWING AREAS UNDER REVIEW AND "CURRENT SERVICES" CARD
The Local Government Commission is considering options for the future structure of local government in parts of Lancashire. Could you please read through this card, (SHOW OPTIONS CARD) **which outlines the options.**

Q9 **Please tell me which of the options, if either, you would prefer for each of Blackpool and Blackburn?**
CODE ONE ONLY FOR EACH DISTRICT

For Blackpool

	%
Option A (single all purpose council)	17
Option B (stay the same/status quo)	38
Some other option	1
Neither of these	-
Either of these/don't mind	18
Don't care	11
Don't know	15

For Blackburn

	%
Option A (single all purpose council)	16
Option B (stay the same/status quo)	35
Some other option	1
Neither of these	*
Either of these/don't mind	19
Don't care	12
Don't know	17

ASK IF "OTHER" NAMED AT Q9 (CODE 3)
Q10 **What other option is that?**
PROBE FULLY - DO NOT PROMPT.

....

....

....

....

ASK ALL PREFERRING AN OPTION (1, 2 OR 3 AT Q9). OTHERS GO TO Q13
Q11 SHOWCARD F (R) **You say that the option you would prefer is . . . . .** (INSERT OPTION PREFERRED). **How strongly would you say you feel about this?**
Base: All preferring an option (172)

	%
Very strongly	21
Fairly strongly	51
Not very strongly	24
Not at all strongly	4
Don't know	*

Q12 **What do you think would be the main advantages of . . .**(OPTION PREFERRED)
PROBE FULLY FOR DETAILS

....

....

....

....

Nothing...
Don't know/can't think of anything.................................

ATTITUDES TO PROPOSALS

SHOWCARD G (R) **Imagine that there was one council in any or both of Blackpool and Blackburn, providing <u>all</u> services. I am going to read out some statements that people have made about this proposal. To what extent do you agree or disagree that . . . .?**
READ OUT, ROTATE ORDER OF ASKING Q13-22. TICK START

READ OUT:	Strongly agree %	Tend to agree %	Neither/ Nor %	Tend to disagree %	Strongly disagree %	Don't know %
☐ Q13 **It would cost more overall**	11	25	12	25	2	25
Q14 **It would be more in touch with local people's needs**	13	41	13	15	5	14
Q15 **The single Council would be more efficient than the current system of two Councils**	9	35	15	17	6	18
☐ Q16 **The single council would not be big enough to manage services such as Education and Social Services effectively**	11	24	16	22	5	21
Q17 **It would better reflect the sense of community in those areas**	10	40	15	17	2	16
Q18 **We need a County Council to represent us nationally**	20	29	23	10	3	15
☐ Q19 **Services would suffer if the County Council no longer provides services in those areas**	14	28	19	16	2	21
Q20 **It won't affect me whether there is a single Council in those areas or not**	9	36	16	19	6	14
Q21 **The change to a single Council for those areas would be too disruptive**	8	27	22	19	3	21
☐ Q22 **With a single Council it would be clearer who is responsible for local services**	15	52	12	7	2	13
ASK LAST Q23 **I would like to have more information on the proposals before making up my mind**	30	36	15	7	4	8

Q24 **On balance, which would you say is more in touch with local people and issues,** .... (ROTATE ORDER OF "DISTRICT" AND COUNTY) (INSERT NAME OF "DISTRICT COUNCIL)..**district/borough/city council, or Lancashire County Council, or would you say that they are both about the same?**

	%
District/borough/city council	44
Lancashire County Council	8
Both about the same	25
Don't know	23

<u>REFER BACK TO Q8. ASK ALL WHO HAVE HEARD OF REVIEW AT Q8 (IE CODES 1/2/3/4). OTHERS TO Q28</u>

Q25 SHOWCARD H **Earlier in the interview, you said that you had heard of the Review of local government structure. From which, if any, of the sources shown on this card have you recently heard about the Review?** INTERVIEWER NOTE: "RECENTLY" = IN PAST 3 MONTHS

Base: All heard of Review (156)

		%
A	Leaflet from County Council delivered to your door	16
B	Leaflet from County Council in library/ offices, etc	4
C	Advertisement from County Council in local newspaper	5
D	Advertisement from County Council on local radio/TV	2
E	Leaflet from Borough Council delivered to your door	7
F	Leaflet from Borough Council in library/ offices, etc	1
G	Borough Council newspaper	2
H	County Council newspaper	2
I	Advertisement from Borough Council in local newspaper	2
J	Advertisement from Borough Council on local radio/TV	1
K	Advertisement by the Commission on local radio	-
L	Local Government Commission advertisement in local newspaper	2
M	Local newspaper	49
N	National newspaper	4
O	TV	16
P	Local radio	21
Q	National radio	3
R	Friends/neighbours/family	10
S	Conversation with Borough Councillor	4
T	Conversation with County Councillor	1
U	Conversation with Borough Council staff	-
V	Conversation with County Council staff	1
W	Parish/community council	1
X	Residents' Association	*
	Other	13
	None of these	1
	Don't know	7

ASK ALL NAMING A SOURCE AT Q25. OTHERS GO TO Q28

Q26 **Would you say that the information you have received has influenced your opinion, or not?**

Base: All specifying source (134)

	%
Yes	14
No	77
Don't know	9

Q27 **What information in particular has influenced your opinion?**

....

....

....

....

ASK ALL

Q28 SHOWCARD I (R) **Assuming you receive the same level of services, how important is it to you, if at all, what the final decision is on the future local government structure in the areas under review?**

	%
Very important	23
Fairly important	35
Not very important	26
Not at all important	11
Don't know	5

ACTIVISM

Q29 SHOWCARD J **Which of the things on this list, if any, have you done in the last three years? Just read out the letter(s) that apply.**

		%
A	Voted in Local Council elections	76
B	Spoken or written to a local Councillor	19
C	Responded to the earlier Review of local government	2
D	Been to a meeting of a local committee or organisation (WRITE IN NAME OF ORGANISATION)	5
E	Spoken on a radio phone-in about a local issue	1
F	Written to a local newspaper about a local issue	3
G	Been to a meeting of a local branch of a political party	1
H	Written to your MP about a local issue	9
I	Been to a Council Committee meeting	1
J	Been to a Council meeting	1
K	Attended a public meeting run by the Council	5
	None of these	18
	Don't know/refused	2

Q30 SHOWCARD K **Which, if any, of these apply to you? Just read out the letter(s) that apply.**

		%
	I am a member of a:	
A	Residents' Association	3
B	Community Association	1
C	Tenants' Association	2
D	Neighbourhood Watch	19
E	PTA/school governors	5
	I do unpaid work for:	
F	A school	6
G	Citizens Advice Bureau	*
H	Volunteer Bureau	3
I	Scouts/Guides/Cubs/Brownies	3
J	Church group	5
	Other	3
	None of these	62
	Don't know	2

THANK RESPONDENT. GO TO DEMOGRAPHICS.

Length of interview [ ][ ] minutes

MORI

MORI/9101/07

Lancashire
REVIEW: BLACKBURN
TOPLINE FINDINGS

Serial No ....
OUO (7-10)

N = 314
4 - 30 October 1995
Main sample data only
Base: All, unless stated

Gender %
Male 48
Female 52

Age %
18-24 15
25-34 20
35-44 18
45-54 15
55-64 14
65-74 11
75+ 8

WRITE IN AGE [ ][ ]

Work Status %
Full-time (30 hrs/wk+) 44
Part-time (8-29 hrs/wk) 6
Not working (under 8 hrs) 2
Looking after home/children 14
Retired 23
Registered unemployed.................... 7
Unemployed but not registered 1
Student.. 2
Other 2

Occupation of Chief Income Earner (CIE)
Position/rank/grade

....
Industry/type of company

....
Qualifications/degrees/apprenticeship

....
No of Staff Responsible for

....
PROBE FOR PENSION

%
AB 9
C1... 21
C2... 24
D... 21
E... 25

Number in Household
Adults aged 18+ (inc. respondent)

22%	59%	15%	3%	1%
1	2	3	4	5+

Children (17 or under)

66%	15%	13%	4%	2%
0	1	2	3	4+

QA **Are you or other members of your household employed by a council?** IF YES: **Is this a Borough/District Council or a County Council?** CODE FOR BOTH RESPONDENT AND OTHER HOUSEHOLD MEMBERS

	Respondent %	Other %
Yes:		
Borough/District	1	1
County	3	2
Don't know which	-	-
No	95	79
Don't know	1	17

Tenure %
Owned outright.. 29
Buying on mortgage 40
Rented from Council 23
Rented from Housing Association 4
Rented from private landlord 4
Other .... -

QB **Is this your main permanent home, or is it a second or holiday home?**

%
Main/permanent................................ 100
Second/holiday 0

Car in Household
CIRCLE NUMBER

24%	48%	21%	5%
0	1	2	3+

INTERVIEWER DECLARATION: I confirm that I have conducted this interview face-to-face with the above named person and that I have asked all the relevant questions fully and recorded the answers in conformance with the survey specification and the MRS Code of Conduct.

Interviewer Name .... Signature ....

Interviewer Number					/	

	Month		Date	
DATE OF INTERVIEW				
	(29)	(30)	(31)	(32)

29/32

NB INTERVIEWER: ALL SHOWCARDS HAVE BEEN REVERSED. PLEASE BE CAREFUL TO CODE THE CORRECT RESPONSE.

Good morning/afternoon/evening. I'm from MORI, the market research and polling organisation. We are doing a survey about local issues, and I would like to ask you a few questions.

ASK ALL

Q1 **Firstly, how long have you lived in this area?** (WITHIN FIVE MILES)

	%
Less than 1 year	4
1-2 years	4
3-5 years	10
6-10 years	22
11-20 years	20
Over 20 years/all my life	39

Q2 SHOWCARD A (R) **From this card, how much would you say you know about local councils and the services they provide?**

	%
A great deal	3
A fair amount	24
Not very much	57
Nothing at all	15
Don't know	2

Q3 SHOWCARD B (R) **Which of the statements on this card comes closest to your own view of the Councils in this area?**

		%
A)	I'm not interested in what the Council does, or whether they do their job	2
B)	I'm not interested in what the Council does, as long as they do their job	26
C)	I like to know what the Council is doing, but I'm happy to let them get on with their job	45
D)	I would like to have more of a say in what the Council does and the services it provides	23
E)	I already work for, or am involved with the Council and the services it provides	2
	Don't know	3

Q4 **From what you know, how many councils provide the main services in this neighbourhood?** (INTERVIEWER - NOT INCLUDING PARISH COUNCILS)

	%
One	20
Two	31
Three+	2
Don't know	48

In fact there are two main councils that provide, or are responsible for most services in this area: Blackburn Borough and Lancashire County Council.

ROTATE ORDER OF Q5/6

☐ Q5 SHOWCARD C (R) **From this list, what services do you think are the responsibility of Blackburn Borough Council? Just read out the letter(s) that apply**

☐ Q6 SHOWCARD C AGAIN (R) **And which services on this list do you think are the responsibility of Lancashire County Council? Again, just read out the letters that apply.**

Q7 SHOWCARD D (R) **Which, if any, of these services do you or members of your family use?** INCLUDE ONLY LOCAL USE

		Q5 "Borough" %	Q6 County %	Q7 Use %
A	Bus Services	57	13	59
B	Car Parks	60	12	51
C	Council Housing	60	12	19
D	Council Tax Benefit/Housing benefit	51	16	27
E	Fire service	22	48	30
F	Food safety	28	24	8
G	Household waste sites/dumps	49	20	37
H	Libraries	33	41	56
I	Parks, playgrounds and open spaces	57	18	65
J	Planning service	41	28	7
K	Public conveniences	60	8	44
L	Recycling/bottle banks	45	13	28
M	Refuse collection	67	6	73
N	Road maintenance	42	34	33
O	Schools/education	22	55	37
P	Social services	23	47	14
Q	Street sweeping	62	9	38
R	Swimming pools/sports facilities	48	15	48
	Other	2	-	3
	None of these	-	1	-
	Don't know	20	27	4

Q8 SHOWCARD E (R) **As you may know, there is currently a review being undertaken by the Local Government Commission on the future local government structure in the county. How much, if anything, would you say you know about this?**

	%
A great deal	2
A fair amount	8
Just a little	29
Heard of but know nothing about	22
Never heard of	37

PREFERENCES

HAND OVER MAP SHOWING AREAS UNDER REVIEW AND "CURRENT SERVICES" CARD
The Local Government Commission is considering options for the future structure of local government in parts of Lancashire. Could you please read through this card, (SHOW OPTIONS CARD) **which outlines the options.**

Q9 **Please tell me which of the options, if either, you would prefer for each of Blackpool and Blackburn?**
CODE ONE ONLY FOR EACH DISTRICT

For Blackpool

	%
Option A (single all purpose council)	16
Option B (stay the same/status quo)	14
Some other option	*
Neither of these	1
Either of these/don't mind	14
Don't care	10
Don't know	44

For Blackburn

	%
Option A (single all purpose council)	39
Option B (stay the same/status quo)	32
Some other option	2
Neither of these	-
Either of these/don't mind	6
Don't care	3
Don't know	18

ASK IF "OTHER" NAMED FOR BLACKBURN AT Q9 (CODE 3)

Q10 **What other option is that for Blackburn?**
PROBE FULLY - DO NOT PROMPT.

....

....

....

....

ASK ALL PREFERRING AN OPTION (1, 2 OR 3 AT Q9). OTHERS GO TO Q13

Q11 SHOWCARD F (R) **You say that the option you would prefer for Blackburn is . . . .** (INSERT OPTION PREFERRED). **How strongly would you say you feel about this?**
Base: All preferring an option (237)

	%
Very strongly	27
Fairly strongly	45
Not very strongly	20
Not at all strongly	4
Don't know	5

- 13 -

Q12 **What do you think would be the main advantages of . . .**(OPTION PREFERRED)
PROBE FULLY FOR DETAILS

....

....

....

....

Nothing...
Don't know/can't think of anything..................................

ATTITUDES TO PROPOSALS

SHOWCARD G (R) **Imagine that there was one council in Blackburn, providing all services. I am going to read out some statements that people have made about this proposal. To what extent do you agree or disagree that . . . .?** READ OUT, ROTATE ORDER OF ASKING Q13-22. TICK START

READ OUT:	Strongly agree %	Tend to agree %	Neither/ Nor %	Tend to disagree %	Strongly disagree %	Don't know %
☐ Q13 **It would cost more overall**	7	26	4	28	4	30
Q14 **It would be more in touch with local people's needs**	25	42	5	15	1	12
Q15 **The single Council would be more efficient than the current system of two Councils**	16	37	4	19	3	21
☐ Q16 **The single council would not be big enough to manage services such as Education and Social Services effectively**	11	22	7	26	9	26
Q17 **It would better reflect the sense of community in Blackburn**	19	38	10	14	2	17
Q18 **We need a County Council to represent us nationally**	9	32	17	22	8	12
☐ Q19 **Services would suffer if the County Council no longer provides services in Blackburn**	8	27	5	29	7	24
Q20 **It won't affect me whether there is a single Council in Blackburn or not**	2	30	8	30	12	17
Q21 **The change to a single Council for Blackburn would be too disruptive**	7	24	9	36	3	22
☐ Q22 **With a single Council it would be clearer who is responsible for local services**	35	38	4	7	4	13
ASK LAST Q23 **I would like to have more information on the proposals before making up my mind**	23	37	11	21	5	3

Q24 **On balance, which would you say is more in touch with local people and issues, ...** (ROTATE ORDER OF "DISTRICT" AND COUNTY)
Blackburn Borough Council, or
Lancashire County Council, or would you say that they are both about the same?

	%
Blackburn Borough Council	47
Lancashire County Council	8
Both about the same	27
Don't know	18

REFER BACK TO Q8. ASK ALL WHO HAVE HEARD OF REVIEW AT Q8 (IE CODES 1/2/3/4). OTHERS TO Q28

Q25 SHOWCARD H **Earlier in the interview, you said that you had heard of the Review of local government structure. From which, if any, of the sources shown on this card have you recently heard about the Review?** INTERVIEWER NOTE: "RECENTLY" = IN PAST 3 MONTHS
Base: All heard of Review (198)

		%
A	Leaflet from County Council delivered to your door	28
B	Leaflet from County Council in library/ offices, etc	1
C	Advertisement from County Council in local newspaper	7
D	Advertisement from County Council on local radio/TV	2
E	Leaflet from Borough Council delivered to your door	16
F	Leaflet from Borough Council in library/ offices, etc	3
G	Borough Council newspaper	5
H	County Council newspaper	-
I	Advertisement from Borough Council in local newspaper	5
J	Advertisement from Borough Council on local radio/TV	-
K	Advertisement by the Commission on local radio	-
L	Local Government Commission advertisement in local newspaper	5
M	Local newspaper	53
N	National newspaper	5
O	TV	20
P	Local radio	19
Q	National radio	3
R	Friends/neighbours/family	19
S	Conversation with Borough Councillor	4
T	Conversation with County Councillor	1
U	Conversation with Borough Council staff	2
V	Conversation with County Council staff	2
W	Parish/community council	1
X	Residents' Association	1
	Other	4
	None of these	4
	Don't know	5

ASK ALL NAMING A SOURCE AT Q25. OTHERS GO TO Q28

Q26 **Would you say that the information you have received has influenced your opinion, or not?**
Base: All specifying source (188)

	%
Yes	21
No	66
Don't know	13

Q27 **What information in particular has influenced your opinion?**

....

....

....

....

ASK ALL

Q28 SHOWCARD I (R) **Assuming you receive the same level of services, how important is it to you, if at all, what the final decision is on the future local government structure in Blackburn?**

	%
Very important	25
Fairly important	32
Not very important	27
Not at all important	11
Don't know	4

ACTIVISM

Q29 SHOWCARD J **Which of the things on this list, if any, have you done in the last three years? Just read out the letter(s) that apply.**

		%
A	Voted in Local Council elections	73
B	Spoken or written to a local Councillor	19
C	Responded to the earlier Review of local government	7
D	Been to a meeting of a local committee or organisation (WRITE IN NAME OF ORGANISATION)	4
E	Spoken on a radio phone-in about a local issue	1
F	Written to a local newspaper about a local issue	2
G	Been to a meeting of a local branch of a political party	1
H	Written to your MP about a local issue	6
I	Been to a Council Committee meeting	2
J	Been to a Council meeting	3
K	Attended a public meeting run by the Council	2
	None of these	21
	Don't know/refused	3

Q30 SHOWCARD K **Which, if any, of these apply to you? Just read out the letter(s) that apply.**

		%
	I am a member of a:	
A	Residents' Association	1
B	Community Association	2
C	Tenants' Association	1
D	Neighbourhood Watch	11
E	PTA/school governors	6
	I do unpaid work for:	
F	A school	4
G	Citizens Advice Bureau	*
H	Volunteer Bureau	1
I	Scouts/Guides/Cubs/Brownies	2
J	Church group	6
	Other	4
	None of these	72
	Don't know	1

THANK RESPONDENT. GO TO DEMOGRAPHICS.

Length of interview ☐☐ minutes

- 17 -

MORI/9101/07

Lancashire
REVIEW: BLACKPOOL
TOPLINE FINDINGS

Serial No ....
OUO (7-10)

N = 306
4 - 30 October 1995
Main sample data only
Base: All, unless stated

Gender %

	%
Male	46
Female	54

Age

	%
18-24	12
25-34	17
35-44	17
45-54	14
55-64	18
65-74	17
75+	6

WRITE IN AGE [ ][ ]

Work Status

	%
Full-time (30 hrs/wk+)	41
Part-time (8-29 hrs/wk)	7
Not working (under 8 hrs)	1
Looking after home/children	13
Retired	29
Registered unemployed	4
Unemployed but not registered	-
Student	2
Other	3

Occupation of Chief Income Earner (CIE)
Position/rank/grade

....

Industry/type of company

....

Qualifications/degrees/apprenticeship

....

No of Staff Responsible for

....

PROBE FOR PENSION

	%
AB	10
C1	31
C2	20
D	20
E	19

Number in Household
Adults aged 18+ (inc. respondent)

22%	59%	15%	3%	1%
1	2	3	4	5+

Children (17 or under)

66%	15%	13%	4%	2%
0	1	2	3	4+

QA **Are you or other members of your household employed by a council?** IF YES: **Is this a Borough/District Council or a County Council?** CODE FOR BOTH RESPONDENT AND OTHER HOUSEHOLD MEMBERS

	Respondent %	Other %
Yes:		
Borough/District	2	1
County	2	4
Don't know which	-	-
No	97	80
Don't know	*	15

Tenure

	%
Owned outright	33
Buying on mortgage	42
Rented from Council	10
Rented from Housing Association	1
Rented from private landlord	12
Other	1

QB **Is this your main permanent home, or is it a second or holiday home?**

	%
Main/permanent	99
Second/holiday	1

Car in Household
CIRCLE NUMBER

24%	48%	21%	5%
0	1	2	3+

THIS FORM IS THE PROPERTY OF MARKET & OPINION RESEARCH INTERNATIONAL (MORI)
32 OLD QUEEN STREET, LONDON, SW1H 9HP

- 18 -

INTERVIEWER DECLARATION: I confirm that I have conducted this interview face-to-face with the above named person and that I have asked all the relevant questions fully and recorded the answers in conformance with the survey specification and the MRS Code of Conduct.

Interviewer Name .... Signature ....

Interviewer Number					/	

	Month		Date	
DATE OF INTERVIEW				
	(29)	(30)	(31)	(32)

29/32

NB INTERVIEWER: ALL SHOWCARDS HAVE BEEN REVERSED. PLEASE BE CAREFUL TO CODE THE CORRECT RESPONSE.

Good morning/afternoon/evening. I'm from MORI, the market research and polling organisation. We are doing a survey about local issues, and I would like to ask you a few questions.

ASK ALL

Q1 **Firstly, how long have you lived in this area?** (WITHIN FIVE MILES)

	%
Less than 1 year	4
1-2 years	6
3-5 years	9
6-10 years	18
11-20 years	18
Over 20 years/all my life	45
Don't know/can't remember	*

Q2 SHOWCARD A (R) **From this card, how much would you say you know about local councils and the services they provide?**

	%
A great deal	4
A fair amount	27
Not very much	49
Nothing at all	20
Don't know	*

Q3 SHOWCARD B (R) **Which of the statements on this card comes closest to your own view of the Councils in this area?**

		%
A)	I'm not interested in what the Council does, or whether they do their job	4
B)	I'm not interested in what the Council does, as long as they do their job	22
C)	I like to know what the Council is doing, but I'm happy to let them get on with their job	44
D)	I would like to have more of a say in what the Council does and the services it provides	20
E)	I already work for, or am involved with the Council and the services it provides	2
	Don't know	8

Q4 **From what you know, how many councils provide the main services in this neighbourhood?** (INTERVIEWER - NOT INCLUDING PARISH COUNCILS)

	%
One	17
Two	30
Three+	4
Don't know	48

In fact there are two main councils that provide, or are responsible for most services in this area: Blackpool Borough and Lancashire County Council.

ROTATE ORDER OF Q5/6

☐ Q5 SHOWCARD C (R) **From this list, what services do you think are the responsibility of Blackpool Borough Council? Just read out the letter(s) that apply**

☐ Q6 SHOWCARD C AGAIN (R) **And which services on this list do you think are the responsibility of Lancashire County Council? Again, just read out the letters that apply.**

Q7 SHOWCARD D (R) **Which, if any, of these services do you or members of your family use?** INCLUDE ONLY LOCAL USE

		Q5 Blackpool %	Q6 County %	Q7 Use %
A	Bus Services	57	16	59
B	Car Parks	60	11	48
C	Council Housing	56	18	9
D	Council Tax Benefit/Housing benefit	41	22	20
E	Fire service	23	48	27
F	Food safety	22	26	8
G	Household waste sites/dumps	39	22	36
H	Libraries	28	42	45
I	Parks, playgrounds and open spaces	55	20	54
J	Planning service	41	22	6
K	Public conveniences	60	10	30
L	Recycling/bottle banks	35	14	26
M	Refuse collection	59	14	77
N	Road maintenance	31	41	30
O	Schools/education	24	53	32
P	Social services	25	40	17
Q	Street sweeping	56	14	46
R	Swimming pools/sports facilities	52	16	42
	Other	4	2	3
	None of these	*	1	1
	Don't know	20	26	5

Q8 SHOWCARD E (R) **As you may know, there is currently a review being undertaken by the Local Government Commission on the future local government structure in the county. How much, if anything, would you say you know about this?**

	%
A great deal	3
A fair amount	9
Just a little	35
Heard of but know nothing about	27
Never heard of	25

PREFERENCES

HAND OVER MAP SHOWING AREAS UNDER REVIEW AND "CURRENT SERVICES" CARD
The Local Government Commission is considering options for the future structure of local government in parts of Lancashire. Could you please read through this card, (SHOW OPTIONS CARD) **which outlines the options.**

Q9 **Please tell me which of the options, if either, you would prefer for each of Blackpool and Blackburn?**
CODE ONE ONLY FOR EACH DISTRICT

For Blackpool

	%
Option A (single all purpose council)	43
Option B (stay the same/status quo)	32
Some other option	-
Neither of these	1
Either of these/don't mind	1
Don't care	1
Don't know	22

For Blackburn

	%
Option A (single all purpose council)	20
Option B (stay the same/status quo)	18
Some other option	*
Neither of these	*
Either of these/don't mind	6
Don't care	17
Don't know	40

ASK IF "OTHER" NAMED FOR BLACKPOOL AT Q9 (CODE 3)
Q10 **What other option is that for Blackpool?**
PROBE FULLY - DO NOT PROMPT.

....

....

....

....

ASK ALL PREFERRING AN OPTION (1, 2 OR 3 AT Q9). OTHERS GO TO Q13
Q11 SHOWCARD F (R) **You say that the option you would prefer for Blackpool is . . . .** (INSERT OPTION PREFERRED). **How strongly would you say you feel about this?**
Base: All preferring an option (231)

	%
Very strongly	25
Fairly strongly	52
Not very strongly	17
Not at all strongly	4
Don't know	1

Q12 **What do you think would be the main advantages of . . .**(OPTION PREFERRED) PROBE FULLY FOR DETAILS

....

....

....

....

Nothing..........

Don't know/can't think of anything..........

ATTITUDES TO PROPOSALS

SHOWCARD G (R) **Imagine that there was one council in Blackpool providing all services. I am going to read out some statements that people have made about this proposal. To what extent do you agree or disagree that . . . .?** READ OUT, ROTATE ORDER OF ASKING Q13-22. TICK START

READ OUT:		Strongly agree %	Tend to agree %	Neither/ Nor %	Tend to disagree %	Strongly disagree %	Don't know %
☐ Q13	**It would cost more overall**	12	19	14	24	8	22
Q14	**It would be more in touch with local people's needs**	36	37	9	9	1	7
Q15	**The single Council would be more efficient than the current system of two Councils**	23	27	14	14	4	17
☐ Q16	**The single council would not be big enough to manage services such as Education and Social Services effectively**	12	22	14	23	13	15
Q17	**It would better reflect the sense of community in Blackpool**	29	39	11	9	3	10
Q18	**We need a County Council to represent us nationally**	14	33	18	16	7	13
☐ Q19	**Services would suffer if the County Council no longer provides services in Blackpool**	10	23	16	24	11	16
Q20	**It won't affect me whether there is a single Council in Blackpool or not**	2	23	22	22	16	15
Q21	**The change to a single Council for Blackpool would be too disruptive**	10	16	13	27	14	20
☐ Q22	**With a single Council it would be clearer who is responsible for local services**	41	33	9	6	*	10
ASK LAST Q23	**I would like to have more information on the proposals before making up my mind**	24	34	14	14	8	6

Q24 **On balance, which would you say is more in touch with local people and issues, ...** (ROTATE ORDER OF "DISTRICT" AND COUNTY)
Blackpool Borough Council, or
Lancashire County Council, or would you say that they are both about the same?

	%
Blackpool Borough Council	45
Lancashire County Council	4
Both about the same	31
Don't know	20

REFER BACK TO Q8. ASK ALL WHO HAVE HEARD OF REVIEW AT Q8 (IE CODES 1/2/3/4). OTHERS TO Q28

Q25 SHOWCARD H **Earlier in the interview, you said that you had heard of the Review of local government structure. From which, if any, of the sources shown on this card have you recently heard about the Review?** INTERVIEWER NOTE: "RECENTLY" = IN PAST 3 MONTHS
Base: All heard of Review (242)

		%
A	Leaflet from County Council delivered to your door	29
B	Leaflet from County Council in library/ offices, etc	5
C	Advertisement from County Council in local newspaper	8
D	Advertisement from County Council on local radio/TV	3
E	Leaflet from Borough Council delivered to your door	27
F	Leaflet from Borough Council in library/ offices, etc	6
G	Borough Council newspaper	2
H	County Council newspaper	-
I	Advertisement from Borough Council in local newspaper	2
J	Advertisement from Borough Council on local radio/TV	2
K	Advertisement by the Commission on local radio	2
L	Local Government Commission advertisement in local newspaper	4
M	Local newspaper	45
N	National newspaper	5
O	TV	21
P	Local radio	20
Q	National radio	2
R	Friends/neighbours/family	11
S	Conversation with Borough Councillor	2
T	Conversation with County Councillor	*
U	Conversation with Borough Council staff	*
V	Conversation with County Council staff	*
W	Parish/community council	1
X	Residents' Association	*
	Other	5
	None of these	4
	Don't know	5

ASK ALL NAMING A SOURCE AT Q25. OTHERS GO TO Q28

Q26 **Would you say that the information you have received has influenced your opinion, or not?**
Base: All specifying source (218)

	%
Yes	11
No	81
Don't know	8

Q27 **What information in particular has influenced your opinion?**

....

....

....

....

ASK ALL

Q28 SHOWCARD I (R) **Assuming you receive the same level of services, how important is it to you, if at all, what the final decision is on the future local government structure in Blackpool?**

	%
Very important	23
Fairly important	33
Not very important	23
Not at all important	5
Don't know	16

ACTIVISM

Q29 SHOWCARD J **Which of the things on this list, if any, have you done in the last three years? Just read out the letter(s) that apply.**

		%
A	Voted in Local Council elections	80
B	Spoken or written to a local Councillor	16
C	Responded to the earlier Review of local government	5
D	Been to a meeting of a local committee or organisation (WRITE IN NAME OF ORGANISATION)	5
E	Spoken on a radio phone-in about a local issue	1
F	Written to a local newspaper about a local issue	2
G	Been to a meeting of a local branch of a political party	1
H	Written to your MP about a local issue	6
I	Been to a Council Committee meeting	1
J	Been to a Council meeting	2
K	Attended a public meeting run by the Council	1
	None of these	18
	Don't know/refused	1

Q30 SHOWCARD K **Which, if any, of these apply to you? Just read out the letter(s) that apply.**

		%
	I am a member of a:	
A	Residents' Association	2
B	Community Association	1
C	Tenants' Association	-
D	Neighbourhood Watch	17
E	PTA/school governors	3
	I do unpaid work for:	
F	A school	3
G	Citizens Advice Bureau	*
H	Volunteer Bureau	1
I	Scouts/Guides/Cubs/Brownies	2
J	Church group	3
	Other	1
	None of these	73
	Don't know	1

THANK RESPONDENT. GO TO DEMOGRAPHICS.

Length of interview [|] minutes

CHAPTER 3

BROXTOWE, GEDLING AND RUSHCLIFFE IN THE COUNTY OF NOTTINGHAMSHIRE

Draft Recommendations

3.1 The Commission's report, *Draft Recommendations on the Future Local Government of Broxtowe, Gedling and Rushcliffe in the County of Nottinghamshire* summarised the evidence taken into account by the Commission in reaching its draft recommendations

Figure 3.1
Draft Recommendations for Broxtowe, Gedling and Rushcliffe in the County of Nottinghamshire

Structure
- There should be no change to the existing two-tier structure of local government in Broxtowe, Gedling and Rushcliffe.

Views Expressed to the Commission

3.2 The Commission received a wide range of direct representations on its draft recommendations, from local authorities, residents, Members of Parliament, business and voluntary groups, parish and town councils, and from other public and private sector organisations. Over 900 representations were received from individuals and organisations, including over 800 from respondents within the three review districts. The Commission also received a small number of representations in the form of petitions (Figures 3.2, 3.3, 3.4 and 3.5). Figures 3.2, 3.3, 3.4 and 3.5 exclude representations from the local authorities; these are summarised separately (Figure 3.6).

Figure 3.2
Views of Respondents Within Broxtowe

Preferred structure	Individuals	Organisations	Standard letters and petition signatures
Unitary Broxtowe	9	0	0
Unitary Gedling	0	0	0
Unitary Rushcliffe	0	0	0
Three unitary authorities	0	0	0
No change in own district	8	5	0
No change outside Nottingham City	48	5	0
No preference	3	1	0
Other	3	0	0

Source: Local Government Commission for England and NOP

Figure 3.3
Views of Respondents Within Gedling

Preferred structure	Individuals	Organisations	Standard letters and petition signatures
Unitary Gedling	121	8	0
Unitary Broxtowe	1	0	0
Unitary Rushcliffe	0	0	0
Three unitary authorities	4	0	0
No change in own district	23	0	0
No change outside Nottingham City	96	9	0
No preference	5	1	0
Other	7	0	0

Source: Local Government Commission for England and NOP

Figure 3.4

Views of Respondents Within Rushcliffe

Preferred structure	Individuals	Organisations	Standard letters and petition signatures
Unitary Rushcliffe	136	12	0
Unitary Broxtowe	1	0	0
Unitary Gedling	0	0	0
Three unitary authorities	5	0	0
No change in own district	69	2	0
No change outside Nottingham City	209	19	55
No preference	2	0	0
Other	6	0	0

Source: Local Government Commission for England and NOP

Figure 3.5

Views of Respondents From Outside The Review Districts

Preferred structure	Individuals	Organisations	Standard letters and petition signatures
No change outside Nottingham City	49	32	102
Unitary Broxtowe	0	0	0
Unitary Gedling	1	0	0
Unitary Rushcliffe	0	0	0
Three unitaries for Broxtowe, Gedling and Rushcliffe	0	0	0
No preference	1	2	0
Other	2	0	0

Source: Local Government Commission for England and NOP
Note: Excludes out of county representations

3.3 In addition, 24 representations were received from outside the county, of which nearly three-quarters supported the Commission's draft recommendation. A more detailed tabulation of the written representations from individuals and interest groups, produced by NOP on behalf of the Commission, can be found towards the end of this Chapter.

The Views of Local Authorities

3.4 The Commission received submissions from all nine of the principal local authorities in Nottinghamshire during Stage Three (Figure 3.6).

Figure 3.6

Preferences of Nottinghamshire Local Authorities at Stage Three

Authority	Preference
Ashfield District Council	Supported the retention of the existing structure of local government outside Nottingham City.
Bassetlaw District Council	Continued to support the creation of a unitary authority for Bassetlaw. However, "In the absence of the consideration of this position within the further review...the only position (the Council) can take is to support the Commission's draft recommendations".
Broxtowe Borough Council	Reiterated the comments made during Stage One, stating that the Council "...supports the Local Government Commission's final recommendation for Nottinghamshire and very much regrets (the) decision to consider a further review...since it considers further expenditure of time, effort and expense on this issue inappropriate".
Gedling Borough Council	The Council accepted the Commission's draft recommendations for Gedling, Broxtowe and Rushcliffe, but refutes any suggestion that Gedling does not have sufficient size, resources or strength of community identity to enable it to function as a coherent and effective unitary authority.
Mansfield District Council	"A fully unitary arrangement based on existing district council boundaries" remained the Council's preferred option. However, given the "...limited scope of the current review, this Council supports the Commission's draft recommendations...".
Newark and Sherwood District Council	The Council formally noted the Commission's draft recommendations.
Nottingham City Council	The Council endorsed the Commission's draft recommendations, and believed that there was no case for unitary status for any of the three districts under review.
Rushcliffe Borough Council	Reaffirmed its support for the creation of a unitary authority for Rushcliffe. In particular, the Council considered that the Commission's arguments that the south Nottinghamshire authorities lacked a clear concept for the comprehensive management of the 'metropolitan' area were inaccurate in view of the Strategic Partnership for Nottingham and Districts, which was agreed between the three authorities under review and Nottingham City Council in September 1994.

continued/

Authority	Preference
/continued	
Nottinghamshire County Council	Reaffirmed its support for the retention of the existing two-tier structure outside Nottingham City.

Source: Local authorities' submissions

3.5 At Stage One Bassetlaw District Council had expressed no preference and Newark and Sherwood District Council had formally expressed concern over unitary status for the three districts under review.

3.6 Of the three district council areas under review, only Rushcliffe formally supported a unitary outcome for its area. The Council pursued its case for a unitary authority vigorously and drew attention to the Strategic Partnership for Nottingham and Districts (SPAN) document, prepared by and on behalf of Broxtowe, Gedling and Rushcliffe Borough Councils and the City of Nottingham in 1994, as providing a framework for co-operation of the unitary authorities in south Nottinghamshire. Rushcliffe Borough Council also drew the Commission's attention to a consultancy report, published by Price Waterhouse in March 1992, which provided an assessment of the changes that would be necessary at that time to provide effective service delivery if Broxtowe, Gedling and Rushcliffe were to become unitary authorities.

3.7 One of the participants, the City of Nottingham, expressed the view that while the SPAN document would form the basis of future arrangements if unitary status were to be granted to the three districts under review, no further planning had been done in connection with these proposals, and that "...it is no longer seen as being viable". Gedling Borough Council similarly commented that a Gedling unitary authority would "...inevitably require a strategic partnership arrangement as set out in the broad terms of the SPAN document". However, "...no further work of fleshing out such an agreement has taken place bearing in mind the stance the Borough Council has taken on the second review process".

3.8
The Gedling Borough Council Conservative Group wrote in support of a unitary Gedling. The Rushcliffe Borough Council Conservative Group, independently of the formal council submission, wrote in support of unitary status for Rushcliffe.

3.9 The Nottinghamshire Branch of the Association of District Councils did not make representations; the Association of District Councils' national submission is referred to in the Summary of National Representations. The Association of County Councils supported the retention of the existing two-tier structure in the districts under review.

The Views of Others

3.10 A range of other interest groups made representations on the Commission's draft recommendations as summarised in the following paragraphs. These are in addition to those made in Stage One.

Businesses and Business Groups

3.11 There was strong support for the Commission's draft recommendations for no change from regional business interests and larger businesses based in Nottinghamshire. However, a number of smaller businesses supported the creation of a unitary authority for Gedling. The Banking Insurance and Finance Union, the Boots Company plc, the East Midlands branch of the Chartered Institute of Transport, and the Sand and Gravel Association were among the business organisations that expressed support for the draft recommendations. Nottinghamshire Chamber of Commerce and Industry also supported the draft recommendations, stating that "...the needs of the business community would not be best served by small local authorities". The Greater Nottingham Training and Enterprise Council welcomed the draft recommendations, stating that granting of unitary status to any of the districts under review would cause unnecessary cost and disruption to existing partnership strategies and could diminish the amount of European funding made available to the area.

County, Regional and National Interests (including the Voluntary Sector)

3.12 Strong support was expressed for the draft recommendations from among voluntary organisations. The Nottinghamshire Association of Voluntary Organisations expressed the desire for stability in a "... rapidly changing local community" and believed that: "Local voluntary organisations will feel best able to play a part in this if the County Council remains to develop wider area strategies...". The Nottingham Council for Voluntary Service echoed this view, believing it "...important that the Commission swiftly moves to confirm its preliminary findings and establishes a secure basis on which the future can be built".

3.13 The Nottinghamshire Branch of the Council for the Protection of Rural England also supported the Commission's draft recommendations. It said that: "Notts CPRE finds it extremely difficult to see how strategic planning could be effectively achieved if the three districts in question became unitary authorities".

3.14 The East Midlands Arts Board strongly favoured the retention of the existing two-tier structure outside the City of Nottingham, stating that "...the further reduction in the resources available to the County Council, if unitary status for Broxtowe, Gedling and Rushcliffe were to go ahead, would effectively destroy nationally recognised services in the arts, education and libraries".

3.15 The Nottinghamshire Archives Users' Group expressed concerns that the creation of additional unitary authorities would "...result in very considerable management problems for a small county-wide archives service. Above all, it could pose a serious threat to the continuance of funding to existing levels and therefore to the viability of the service". Similar concerns were expressed in the national submission from the Royal Commission on Historical Manuscripts, which stated that: "...archive services, predominantly provided at a county level at present, are potentially extremely vulnerable in the event of a break-up of the present two-tier system".

Education Groups

3.16 There was unanimous support for no change to the existing local government arrangements among the schools and educational associations. The Nottinghamshire Branch of the National Association of Head Teachers expressed the view that "...a change to a number of smaller unitary authorities would be detrimental to the best interests of children, parents and all those who work in, or for, the education service". Similar concerns were expressed by the Nottinghamshire Federation of Parent-Teacher Associations, which stated that: "Any further divisions in the county of Nottinghamshire will create organisation and administration problems without any benefits".

Health Interests

3.17 The Nottingham Health Authority stated that: "We do not support any further fragmentation of the county as it would not be in the interests of health services to patients". The authority believed that the creation of further unitary authorities would lead to increased costs and to liaison difficulties between health care and social services staff. The Nottingham Community Health Council was pleased to note the Commission's draft recommendations because: "Liaison with two departments of social services will be simpler, cheaper and less bureaucratic than between what would have been five departments". These views were echoed in the submission made by the North Nottinghamshire Health Authority, which stated that "...it is essential to protect the services provided for the more vulnerable members in the county...The fewer agencies involved [in joint working arrangements] the greater is the probability that the relationships will be robust and effective".

Law, Order and Emergency Services

3.18 There was support for the Commission's draft recommendations from organisations involved in public protection functions. The Nottinghamshire Police Authority expressed its strong support for the retention of the two-tier structure in the districts under review. The Nottinghamshire Constabulary, while not expressing a view on the outcome, did express concern over the impact of any increase in the number of strategic authorities on consistent working practices, saying that the greater the number of authorities, "...the greater are the implications for our resources".

3.19 The Nottinghamshire Probation Service supported the draft recommendations and expressed concern that greater numbers of social services departments and education authorities in the county would create "...considerable problems of liaison and joint working". The Nottingham Magistrates' Courts Committee supported the draft recommendations, believing that the Committee's interests were best served by having a minimum number of primary authorities in the county.

Local Groups

3.20 The Commission received submissions from 13 local community groups based in Rushcliffe, and from a small number of local organisations based in Broxtowe and Gedling. In all three districts, the majority of these groups favoured the retention of the two-tier structure.

3.21 The Nottingham and District Racial Equality Council supported the Commission's initial conclusions, particularly those relating to community identity, stating that "...we are very often struck by the very wide differences that exist within the Boroughs that have been the subject of this review... We wholeheartedly concur with the Commission's view that the co-ordination of effort between Nottingham and Nottinghamshire County Council provides a more satisfactory framework than a number of unitary authorities".

Parliamentary Interests

3.22 The Commission received written submissions from six of the eleven Nottinghamshire Members of Parliament. Mr Kenneth Clarke, MP for Rushcliffe, and Mr Andrew Mitchell, MP for Gedling, both expressed strong support for unitary status for Broxtowe, Gedling and Rushcliffe, while Mr Jim Lester, MP for Broxtowe, expressed support for the creation of a unitary authority for Broxtowe.

3.23 Mr John Heppell, MP for Nottingham East, Mr Alan Simpson, MP for Nottingham South, and Mr Paddy Tipping, MP for Sherwood, all supported the Commission's draft recommendations for no change, as did Mr Ken Coates, MEP for Nottinghamshire North and Chesterfield, and Ms Arlene McCarthy, MEP for the Peak District constituency, which includes Broxtowe.

Parish And Town Councils

3.24 The Commission received 10 submissions from parish councils in Rushcliffe, seven of which favoured the creation of a unitary authority for the borough. The Parish Council of Linby in Gedling expressed support for the Commission's draft recommendations. Three submissions were received from parish councils in Broxtowe, two of which favoured the retention of the existing two-tier structure of local government in the borough.

NOP Tabulations of Written Representations

1 The following tabulations summarise the views expressed by members of the public and other interested parties during the consultation on the Local Government Commission's draft recommendations for Broxtowe, Gedling and Rushcliffe.

2 The tabulations include only letters sent directly to NOP at its Chelmsford offices and to the Commission's offices in London. Where more than one person's view has been expressed in a letter, the comments from each individual have been recorded separately. Staff from the Commission and NOP have worked closely in ensuring that care has been taken in the interpretation of comments, and that a consistent approach has been adopted.

3 While many people expressed support for one or other of the draft options presented by the Commission, other responses were coded by NOP after further discussion. The pattern of views expressed has been carefully examined, and where a number of respondents supported an option not included in those put forward by the Commission, those views have been separately coded and reported by NOP.

4 The Commission has advertised through the local media, encouraging people to make their views known. All responses received up to two days after the end of the Stage Three consultation period have been included. Returns from campaigns organised by local authorities or other groups (for example, standardised postcards and letters, questionnaires and petitions) have not been included in the tabulations. These, and submissions written and dated before the commencement of the consultation process, have been considered separately by the Commission.

The following definitions have been applied by NOP in compiling the tabulations:

(i) Type of Respondent

Individuals:	includes individual members of the public, local councillors and Members of the Westminster and European Parliaments.
Businesses and Business Groups:	includes organisations which represent businesses, such as local Chambers of Commerce.
County, Regional and National Interests:	any organisation which covers an area which is the size of a county or larger is included here, for example, a county-wide voluntary organisation or a regional association. This classification includes most of the statutory consultees.
Education (and Church) Groups:	this group includes schools, religious organisations and teaching unions.
Local Groups:	this includes organisations smaller than a county area, for example, a district-level voluntary sector body. The group could be voluntary, sporting, political or cultural but does not include organisations from the education or religious sectors (included above). It also includes constituency parties and political groups on local authorities.
Parish and Town Councils:	this also includes district-level associations of town and parish councils. County level associations are classified as County, Regional and National interests.

(ii) Structural Options (Reports A and D)

No change in own district:	this code is used where there is more than one review district in the county. It indicates where respondents from a review district have expressed support for no change for that district and have not made reference to the other review district(s) in that county.
District/county-level authorities:	represents support for either a district or county-level authority although it is not clear whether this is for a unitary or a two-tier structure.
Opposition to structural preferences:	represents responses where a negative, but unspecified, structural preference has been expressed.
Rejects:	rejects are those responses with unclear comments/interpretation.

(iii) Other

Other issues (Report B):	these illustrate preferences in relation to boundary and electoral changes and (where applicable) the restoration of historic counties.
Parishing issues (Report C):	these illustrate preferences in relation to parishing issues, for example, the creation of new parishes or the enhancement of the role of parish and town councils.
Services (Report E):	these illustrate concerns expressed about the impact of proposed changes on particular service areas where the respondent has not additionally expressed a positive structural preference.

NOP Analysis of Responses to Local Government Commission Draft Recommendations - NOTTINGHAMSHIRE

Report A: Opinions on the structural options, by authority of respondent
Base: all

	Review districts			Other districts in county							
	Broxtowe	Gedling	Rushcliffe	Ashfield	Bassetlaw	Mansfield	Newark & Sherwood	Nottingham	Rest of county total	County total	Out of county total
No change (outside Nottingham)	53 *65%*	105 *38%*	228 *49%*	1 *100%*	5 *100%*	5 *83%*	23 *96%*	47 *92%*	81 *93%*	467 *52%*	17 *71%*
Unitary Broxtowe	9 *11%*	1 *	1 *	- -	- -	- -	- -	- -	- -	11 *1%*	- -
Unitary Gedling	- -	129 *47%*	- -	- -	- -	- -	- -	1 *2%*	1 *1%*	130 *14%*	- -
Unitary Rushcliffe	- -	- -	148 *32%*	- -	- -	- -	- -	- -	- -	148 *16%*	1 *4%*
Three unitary authorities for Broxtowe, Gedling & Rushcliffe	- -	4 *1%*	5 *1%*	- -	- -	- -	- -	- -	- -	9 *1%*	2 *8%*
No change in own district	13 *16%*	23 *8%*	71 *15%*	- -	- -	- -	- -	- -	- -	107 *12%*	- -
District-level authority (either two-tier or unitary)	- -	1 *	2 *	- -	- -	- -	- -	- -	- -	3 *	- -
Opposition to structural options (where no positive preference is stated)	- -	1 *	- -	- -	- -	- -	- -	- -	- -	1 *	- -
Reject	1 *1%*	- -	- -	- -	- -	- -	- -	- -	- -	1 *	- -
Other specified	2 *2%*	2 *1%*	4 *1%*	- -	- -	- -	- -	2 *4%*	2 *2%*	10 *1%*	1 *4%*
Other unspecified	- -	3 *1%*	- -	- -	- -	- -	- -	- -	- -	3 *	- -
No preference expressed/option defined	4 *5%*	6 *2%*	2 *	- -	- -	1 *17%*	1 *4%*	1 *2%*	3 *3%*	15 *2%*	3 *13%*
BASE TOTAL	82	275	461	1	5	6	24	51	87	905	24

* *Less than ½%*

NOP Analysis of Responses to Local Government Commission Draft Recommendations - NOTTINGHAMSHIRE

Report B: Opinions on other issues, by authority of respondent
Base: all

	Review districts			Other districts in county							
	Broxtowe	Gedling	Rushcliffe	Ashfield	Bassetlaw	Mansfield	Newark & Sherwood	Nottingham	Rest of county total	County total	Out of county total
BASE TOTAL	82	275	461	1	5	6	24	51	87	905	24

The figures in the table above do not sum to the base total/100% because undefined fields are not included, except as part of the base total.

NOP Analysis of Responses to Local Government Commission Draft Recommendations - NOTTINGHAMSHIRE

Report C: Opinions on parishing issues, by authority of respondent
Base: all

	Review districts			Other districts in county							
	Broxtowe	Gedling	Rushcliffe	Ashfield	Bassetlaw	Mansfield	Newark & Sherwood	Nottingham	Rest of county total	County total	Out of county total
Other specified	1	-	-	-	-	-	-	-	-	1	-
	1%	-	-	-	-	-	-	-	-	*	-
BASE TOTAL	82	275	461	1	5	6	24	51	87	905	24

The figures in the table above do not sum to the base total/100% because undefined fields are not included, except as part of the base total.

* *Less than* $^1/_2$%

NOP Analysis of Responses to Local Government Commission Draft Recommendations - NOTTINGHAMSHIRE

Report D1: Opinions on the structural options, by respondent type (all respondents)
Base: all

	Respondent Type					
	Indiv-iduals	Business groups	County, regional & national interests	Education (& church) groups	Local groups	Parish and town councils
No change (outside Nottingham)	408 *50%*	11 *58%*	23 *79%*	20 *95%*	17 *63%*	5 *33%*
Unitary Broxtowe	11 *1%*	- -	- -	- -	- -	- -
Unitary Gedling	122 *15%*	7 *37%*	- -	- -	1 *4%*	- -
Unitary Rushcliffe	136 *17%*	1 *5%*	- -	- -	5 *19%*	7 *47%*
Three unitary authorities for Broxtowe, Gedling & Rushcliffe	11 *1%*	- -	- -	- -	- -	- -
No change in own district	100 *12%*	- -	- -	1 *5%*	3 *11%*	3 *20%*
District-level authority (either two-tier or unitary)	3 *	- -	- -	- -	- -	- -
Opposition to structural options (where no positive preference is stated)	1 *	- -	- -	- -	- -	- -
Reject	1 *	- -	- -	- -	- -	- -
Other specified	11 *1%*	- -	- -	- -	- -	- -
Other unspecified	3 *	- -	- -	- -	- -	- -
No preference expressed/option defined	11 *1%*	- -	6 *21%*	- -	1 *4%*	- -
BASE TOTAL	818	19	29	21	27	15

* *Less than ½%*

NOP Analysis of Responses to Local Government Commission Draft Recommendations - NOTTINGHAMSHIRE

Report D2: Opinions on the structural options, by respondent type
Base: respondents in Broxtowe only

	Respondent Type					
	Indiv-iduals	Business groups	County, regional & national interests	Education (& church) groups	Local groups	Parish and town councils
No change (outside Nottingham)	48 *68%*	1 *100%*	- -	1 *50%*	2 *40%*	1 *33%*
Unitary Broxtowe	9 *13%*	- -	- -	- -	- -	1 *33%*
No change in own district	8 *11%*	- -	- -	1 *50%*	2 *40%*	1 *33%*
Reject	1 *1%*	- -	- -	- -	- -	- -
Other specified	2 *3%*	- -	- -	- -	- -	- -
No preference expressed/option defined	3 *4%*	- -	- -	- -	1 *20%*	- -
BASE TOTAL	71	1	-	2	5	3

NOP Analysis of Responses to Local Government Commission Draft Recommendations - NOTTINGHAMSHIRE

Report D3: Opinions on the structural options, by respondent type
Base: respondents in Gedling only

	Respondent Type					
	Indiv-iduals	Business groups	County, regional & national interests	Education (& church) groups	Local groups	Parish and town councils
No change (outside Nottingham)	96 *37%*	- -	2 *67%*	4 *100%*	2 *67%*	1 *100%*
Unitary Broxtowe	1 *	- -	- -	- -	- -	- -
Unitary Gedling	121 *47%*	7 *100%*	- -	- -	1 *33%*	- -
Three unitary authorities for Broxtowe, Gedling & Rushcliffe	4 *2%*	- -	- -	- -	- -	- -
No change in own district	23 *9%*	- -	- -	- -	- -	- -
District-level authority (either two-tier or unitary)	1 *	- -	- -	- -	- -	- -
Opposition to structural options (where no positive preference is stated)	1 *	- -	- -	- -	- -	- -
Other specified	2 *1%*	- -	- -	- -	- -	- -
Other unspecified	3 *1%*	- -	- -	- -	- -	- -
No preference expressed/option defined	5 *2%*	- -	1 *33%*	- -	- -	- -
BASE TOTAL	257	7	3	4	3	1

* *Less than ½%*

NOP Analysis of Responses to Local Government Commission Draft Recommendations - NOTTINGHAMSHIRE

Report D4: Opinions on the structural options, by respondent type
Base: respondents in Rushcliffe only

	Respondent Type					
	Indiv-iduals	Business groups	County, regional & national interests	Education (& church) groups	Local groups	Parish and town councils
No change (outside Nottingham)	209 *49%*	1 *50%*	4 *100%*	5 *100%*	7 *54%*	2 *22%*
Unitary Broxtowe	1 *	- -	- -	- -	- -	- -
Unitary Rushcliffe	136 *32%*	1 *50%*	- -	- -	5 *38%*	6 *67%*
Three unitary authorities for Broxtowe, Gedling & Rushcliffe	5 *1%*	- -	- -	- -	- -	- -
No change in own district	69 *16%*	- -	- -	- -	1 *8%*	1 *11%*
District-level authority (either 2-tier or unitary)	2 *	- -	- -	- -	- -	- -
Other specified	4 *1%*	- -	- -	- -	- -	- -
No preference expressed/option defined	2 *	- -	- -	- -	- -	- -
BASE TOTAL	428	2	4	5	13	9

* *Less than ½%*

NOP Analysis of Responses to Local Government Commission Draft Recommendations - NOTTINGHAMSHIRE

Report D5: Opinions on the structural options, by respondent type
Base: respondents in rest of county only

	Respondent Type					
	Indiv-iduals	Business groups	County, regional & national interests	Education (& church) groups	Local groups	Parish and town councils
No change (outside Nottingham)	49 *92%*	5 *100%*	11 *85%*	9 *100%*	6 *100%*	1 *100%*
Unitary Gedling	1 *2%*	- -	- -	- -	- -	- -
Other specified	2 *4%*	- -	- -	- -	- -	- -
No preference expressed/option defined	1 *2%*	- -	2 *15%*	- -	- -	- -
BASE TOTAL	53	5	13	9	6	1

NOP Analysis of Responses to Local Government Commission Draft Recommendations - NOTTINGHAMSHIRE

Report E: Views on services, by authority of respondent
Base: all

	Review districts			Other districts in county							
	Broxtowe	Gedling	Rushcliffe	Ashfield	Bassetlaw	Mansfield	Newark & Sherwood	Nottingham	Rest of county total	County total	Out of county total
Archives	- -	- -	- -	- -	- -	- -	- -	1 *2%*	1 *1%*	2 *	2 *8%*
Trading standards	- -	- -	1 *	- -	- -	- -	- -	- -	- -	1 *	- -
Other specified services (or multiples of)	1 *1%*	2 *1%*	- -	- -	- -	1 *17%*	- -	- -	1 *1%*	5 *	3 *13%*
BASE TOTAL	82	275	461	1	5	6	24	51	87	905	24

The figures in the table above do not sum to the base total/100% because undefined fields are not included, except as part of the base total.

* *Less than ½%*

Broxtowe, Gedling & Rushcliffe

NOP Analysis of Responses to Local Government Commission Draft Recommendations - NOTTINGHAMSHIRE

Report F: Views on services, by respondent type
Base: all

	Respondent Type					
	Indiv-iduals	Business groups	County, regional & national interests	Education (& church) groups	Local groups	Parish and town councils
Archives	2 *	- -	2 7%	- -	- -	- -
Trading standards	1 *	- -	- -	- -	- -	- -
Other specified services (or multiples of)	1 *	- -	6 19%	- -	1 4%	- -
BASE TOTAL	818	19	29	21	27	15

The figures in the table above do not sum to the base total/100% because undefined fields are not included, except as part of the base total.

NOP Analysis of Responses to Local Government Commission Draft Recommendations - NOTTINGHAMSHIRE

Report G: Type of respondent, by authority of respondent
Base: all

	Review districts			Other districts in county							
	Broxtowe	Gedling	Rushcliffe	Ashfield	Bassetlaw	Mansfield	Newark & Sherwood	Nottingham	Rest of county total	County total	Out of county total
Individuals	71 87%	257 93%	428 93%	1 100%	4 80%	3 50%	15 63%	30 59%	53 61%	809 89%	9 38%
Business groups	1 1%	7 3%	2 *	- -	- -	- -	- -	5 10%	5 6%	15 2%	4 17%
County, regional and national interests	- -	3 1%	4 1%	- -	1 20%	2 33%	2 8%	8 16%	13 15%	20 2%	9 38%
Education (and church) groups	2 2%	4 1%	5 1%	- -	- -	1 17%	4 17%	4 8%	9 10%	20 2%	1 4%
Local Groups	5 6%	3 1%	13 3%	- -	- -	- -	2 8%	4 8%	6 7%	27 3%	- -
Parish and town councils	3 4%	1 *	9 2%	- -	- -	- -	1 4%	- -	1 1%	14 2%	1 4%
BASE TOTAL	82 100%	275 100%	461 100%	1 100%	5 100%	6 100%	24 100%	51 100%	87 100%	905 100%	24 100%

* *Less than ½%*

MORI Research Study for the Local Government Commission

Introduction

Background

1 This summary report highlights the key findings from a survey of public opinion conducted in the Boroughs of Broxtowe, Gedling and Rushcliffe, and across the County of Nottinghamshire on behalf of the Local Government Commission for England. A copy of each of the marked-up questionnaires is appended. The computer tabulations are contained in a separate volume, which is available from MORI (32 Old Queen Street, London SW1H 9HP. Telephone 0171-222 0232. Price £15)

2 The survey was designed in close consultation with the Commission, following extensive qualitative research and pilot testing. All sampling, interviewing and analysis have been carried out independently by MORI, within the guidelines of the profession laid out by the Market Research Society.

3 In Broxtowe, Gedling and Rushcliffe, all Census Enumeration Districts (EDs) were sorted by ward, and stratified according to social class. EDs were then sampled (32 in total in each of Broxtowe and Gedling and Rushcliffe) in proportion to the population size of each, and quotas set for sex, age and work status. In Broxtowe, a total of 319 interviews with adults aged 18+, conducted face-to-face and in-home, were carried out between 1 and 31 October 1995. In Gedling, 322 interviews were conducted, and in Rushcliffe 329 interviews. Data were weighted to match the population profile of each Borough.

4 In the remaining districts of Nottinghamshire, all EDs were sorted into wards, and again stratified according to social class. A total of 32 EDs across the whole area (that is, Nottinghamshire excluding Broxtowe, Gedling and Rushcliffe) were sampled, with quotas set by sex, age and work status. Face-to-face interviews, conducted in-home, were carried out with 318 adults aged 18+ between 1 and 31 October 1995. Data were weighted to match the population profile of the County excluding Broxtowe, Gedling and Rushcliffe.

Publication of the Results

5 As with all our studies, these findings are subject to our Standard Terms and Conditions of Contract. Any press release or publication of the findings of this survey require the advance approval of MORI. Such approval will only be refused on the grounds of inaccuracy or misinterpretation.

Objectives

6 The survey took place during Stage Three, the consultation period on the Commission's draft recommendations. It measures public preferences for the organisation of local government in the area currently comprising the Boroughs of Broxtowe, Gedling, and Rushcliffe, as well as exploring strength of feeling, levels of knowledge about the review, involvement in, and broader perceptions of, local government in the area.

Statistical Reliability of the Data

7 Because we have interviewed a sample of residents, rather than the whole population, the results are subject to statistical tolerance limits, or "margins of error". These are expressed as our confidence that the true figure for the whole population falls within a given range. By convention this is expressed as a percentage, so our 95% confidence level means that in 95 times out of 100 the true figure would lie within this range.

8 The table below shows ranges of the 95% confidence level for a range of sample sizes. For each sample size, the table shows the tolerance limits for sample results close to 10%, 30% and 50%. Take, for example, the results of a survey of 300 residents showing that 50% are aware of the review. In 95 times out of 100 the true figure would lie between 44% and 56% (ie between 50% ±6%).

	Sampling tolerances applicable to results at or near these percentages (based on 95% confidence level)		
Sample size	10/90% ±%	30/70% ±%	50% ±%
300	3	5	6
200	4	6	7
150	5	7	8
100	6	9	10
50	8	13	14

9 Clearly, 10% or 30% of the sample being aware of the review equate to 90% or 70% not being aware of it. So this table shows the ranges of 95% confidence for responses close to 10%, 30%, 50%, 70% and 90% of our sample. The figures for responses between can be obtained by extrapolation.

10 The true figure would only be known if all the residents of the area had been interviewed. It can be seen in the table, however, that large increases in the sample size do not greatly reduce the sampling tolerance. In addition, the true figure is more likely to lie at the midpoint of the range, rather than at either extreme.

11 When comparing results from separate groups within a sample we need to be sure that the differences are statistically significant. This would be important in comparing views expressed by different parts of a county. The table below shows how the statistical significance of the difference is determined by the size of the groups and the percentage result from the sample.

12 Assuming a 95% confidence level, the table shows the size of the differences required if different results are to be regarded as statistically significant. It can be seen that if 50% of a group of 300 were aware of the review, the result from another group of 300 would not become statistically significant until it became less than 42% or more than 58%.

	Differences required for significance at or near these percentage levels		
Sample sizes	10/90% ±	30/70% ±	50% ±
300 and 300	5	7	8
300 and 200	5	8	9
300 and 100	7	10	11
200 and 100	7	11	12
100 and 100	8	13	14

Survey Findings

Knowledge and Awareness

13 Residents in Broxtowe profess a lower level of knowledge of their local councils than do residents in Gedling and Rushcliffe, or indeed, the rest of the districts in the County. They are not, however, less interested in knowing what the council is doing. A majority in each area likes to know what their council is doing, but want no greater involvement. Around one in seven (14%) in Broxtowe, one in six in Gedling (16%), one in five in Rushcliffe (19%) and one in five in the rest of the County (19%) say that they want a higher level of involvement.

14 There is some variation in residents' professed levels of knowledge - 25% in Broxtowe, 35% in Gedling, 42% in Rushcliffe and 31% in the rest of Nottinghamshire say that they know at least a fair amount about local councils and services. In all areas, a clear majority admit not knowing very much at all.

15 This is reflected in the number of residents who incorrectly ascribe services between the two tiers of local government. Thus, although between four and six in ten recognise libraries as a county council service, between three and four in ten allocate responsibility to their borough council. And although between seven and eight in ten realise that refuse collection is a borough service, around one in ten thinks it is a county council service.

16 Awareness of the review itself is lower in Broxtowe (where just 43% have heard of it) than in Rushcliffe (70%) and Gedling (66%). However, as one might expect, it is lower in the rest of Nottinghamshire (34%). The proportions who say they know a fair amount or more are low throughout, but highest in Rushcliffe (18%), followed by Gedling (10%), Broxtowe (5%) and rest of Nottinghamshire (3%).

Sources of Information

17 Local newspapers appear to play a less significant role in providing information to residents in Nottinghamshire than is the case in most other review areas. Although in some boroughs it is high (40% of those who have at least heard of the review in Broxtowe cite local papers as recent source), they do not stand clearly ahead of other sources. Thus in Broxtowe, leaflets delivered from the County Council are mentioned by 26%, and leaflets from the Borough by 21%. In Gedling, while 33% mention local newspapers, 31% cite County leaflets, and 27% Borough leaflets. And in Rushcliffe, 31% name local newspapers, but as many as 36% cite County Council leaflets and 25% Borough leaflets.

18 Although most of those aware of the review recognise one or more recent sources of information, relatively few claim that this has influenced their opinion.

19 Furthermore, in spite of a relatively low level of knowledge of, and engagement with, their local authority, most people in Broxtowe, Gedling and Rushcliffe say that the outcome of the review is either very important to them (13%, 17% and 22% respectively) or fairly important (42%, 46% and 47% respectively). As one might expect, people in the rest of Nottinghamshire perceive a lower level of importance (11% very important and 24% fairly important).

The Preferred Option

20 In Broxtowe a clear majority of residents (60%) would prefer no change, with around one in four (27%) opting for a unitary council. In Gedling, however, opinion is more divided, with 48% prefering no change, but as many as 40% opting for a unitary council. A similar picture is found in Rushcliffe, where 45% prefer no change, and 39%, a unitary council.

21 In Broxtowe, it is the proponents of no change who also tend to feel most strongly about the issue (78% very or fairly strongly, compared with 65% of those who prefer the unitary option). In Gedling, there is little to choose, although the intensity of feeling is perhaps marginally greater among those who prefer the unitary option. In Rushcliffe, there is even less difference in the intesity of feeling between the two groups.

22 Residents in the rest of the County are more inclined to no change for each borough than any other single option, although there is not a majority view on the outcome for any of them.

Factors in Expressing a Preference

23 In questions 13 to 23, residents were asked to say to what extent they agreed or disagreed with a range of statements which related to a change to unitary local government. The statements were designed to cover the main issues raised by residents during the qualitative phase of research, and others that formed a part of the Commission's brief to take into consideration in making its recommendations.

24 The following charts summarise the results from these questions, with the full question wording presented in the questionnaire in the appendices. Values have been ascribed to the five attitudinal positions that people were offered (+2 for strongly agree, +1 for tend to agree, 0 for neither agree nor disagree, -1 for tend to disagree, and -2 for strongly disagree) and mean scores calculated across all respondents expressing a view. This has the combined benefit of distilling the range of opinion into one summary figure, while incorporating the varying intensity of feeling by ascribing values. Bars to the right indicate that the mean score value is positive, and thus that there is a balance of agreement with the statement. Bars to the left, conversely, indicate a balance of disagreement.

25 The first chart, therefore, shows how the views of people living in Broxtowe and Gedling differ from those across the rest of Nottinghamshire. On the following page is a chart comparing Rushcliffe with the rest of the County. The charts illustrate the attitudes or perceptions that are, in relative terms, shared by both groups of residents (where the bars project in the same direction), and those where views differ markedly. Thus there is broad agreement on both the positive aspects of change, and, indeed, the negative aspects. One feature stands out, and that is that the people in Gedling are rather more likely to agree with the positive, and disagree with the negative. The main issue on which there is a clear divergence of opinion is on whether people feel that they will be affected by change; Broxtowe and Gedling (and, overleaf, Rushcliffe) residents disagree, on balance, that they would not be affected. Residents of the three review boroughs are also more likely to want more information before making up their minds than are those in the rest of the County.

26 The subsequent charts take the results, separately, from Broxtowe, Gedling, Rushcliffe and the rest of Nottinghamshire, and illustrate the difference in views between those within each area whose preference is for change, and those who prefer no change. The perceived impact on efficiency, for example, is clearly a key determinant of opinion in all areas, as this tends to be the statement on which there is most differentiation between the two groups. In Gedling, even the proponents of no change are likely to agree that a unitary council would be more in touch with local people's needs.

Attitudes to Change
(Respondents in Broxtowe, Gedling and the rest of Nottinghamshire)

Q To what extent do you agree or disagree that...?
(Figures represent 'mean scores' with *strong agreement* given a value of +2 through to *strong disagreement* given -2)

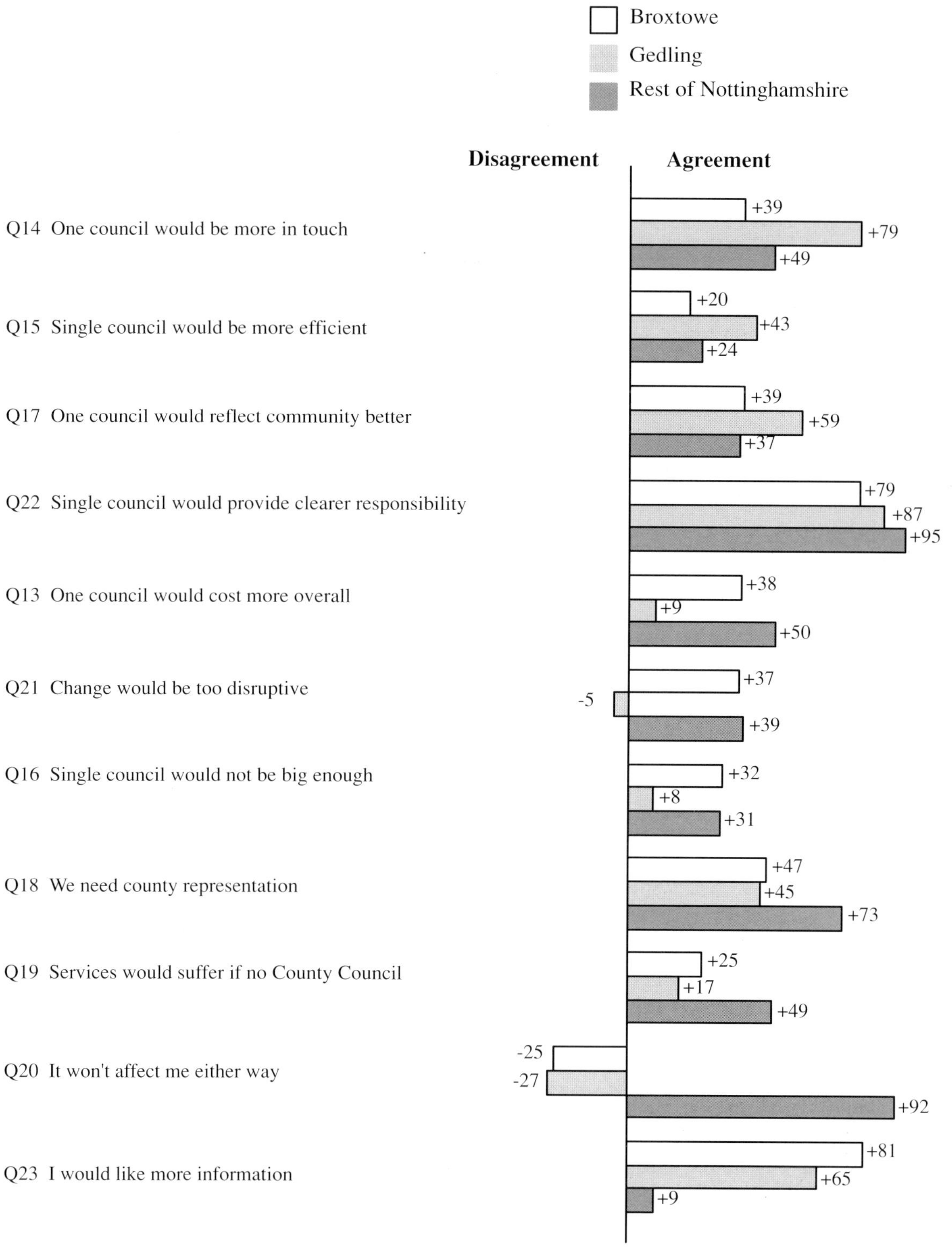

Attitudes to Change (Respondents in Rushcliffe and the rest of Nottinghamshire)

Q To what extent do you agree or disagree that...?
(Figures represent 'mean scores' with *strong agreement* given a value of +2 through to *strong disagreement* given -2)

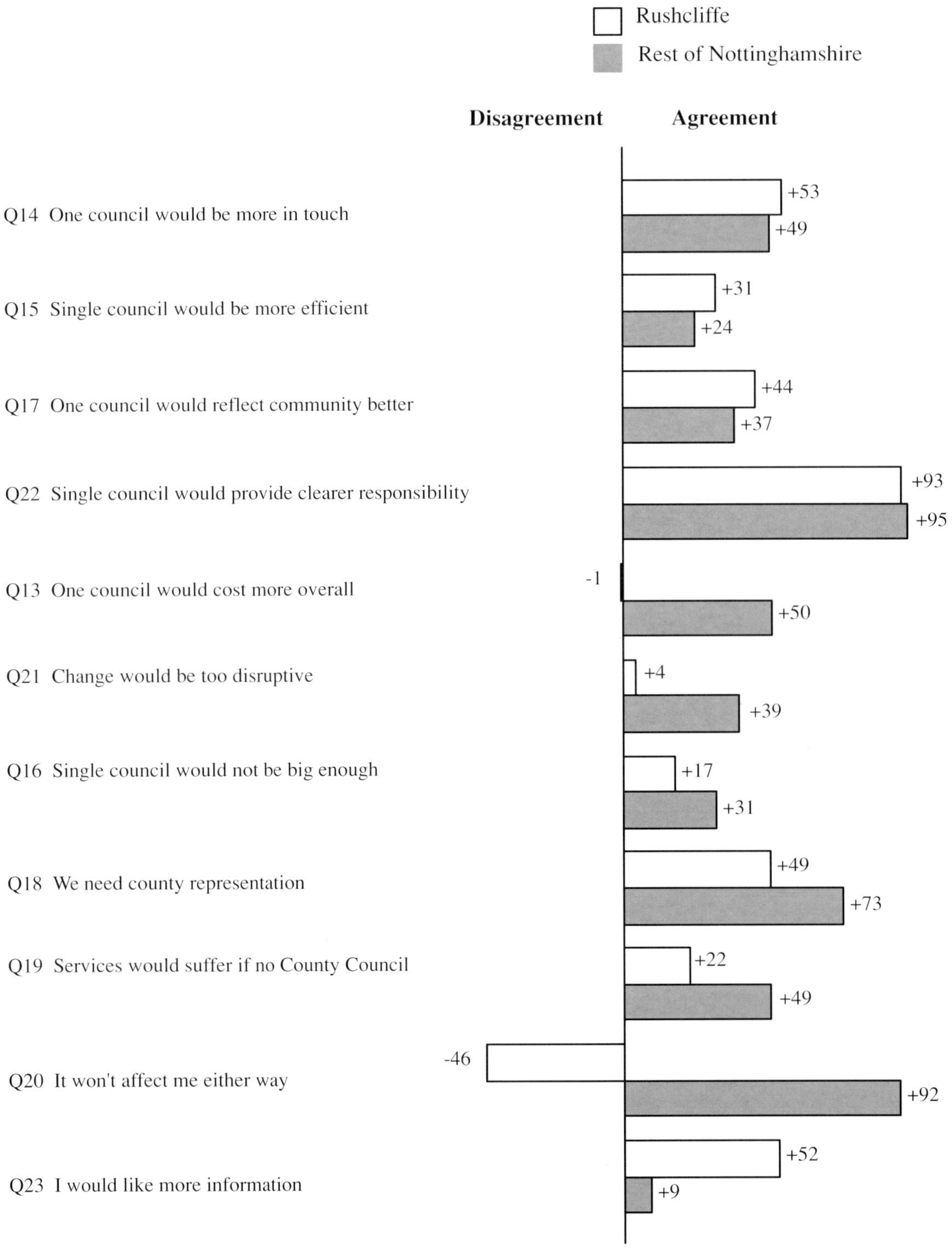

Attitudes to Change
(Respondents in Broxtowe)

Q To what extent do you agree or disagree that...?
(Figures represent 'mean scores' with *strong agreement* given a value of +2 through to *strong disagreement* given -2)

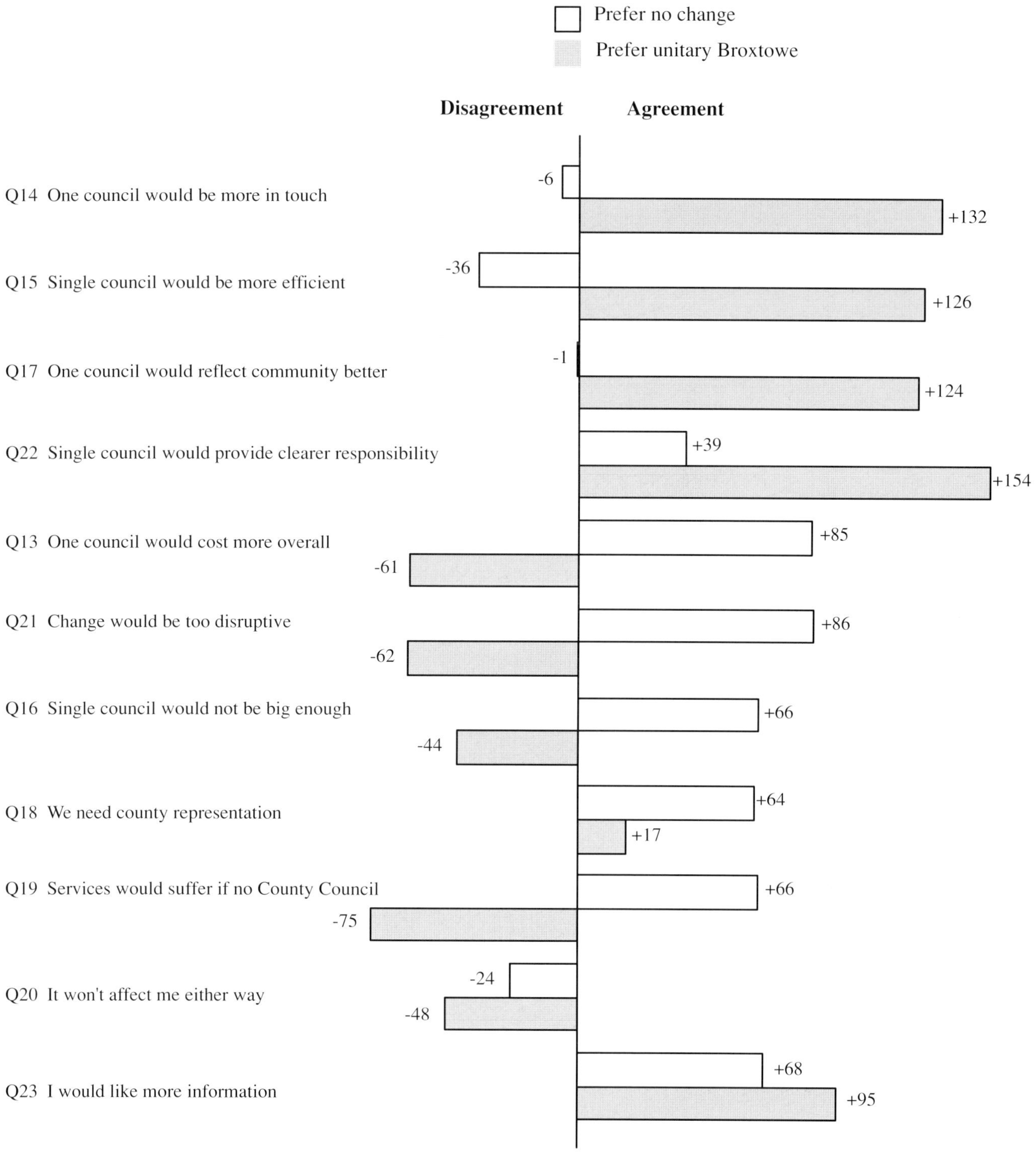

Broxtowe, Gedling & Rushcliffe

Attitudes to Change (Respondents in Gedling)

Q To what extent do you agree or disagree that...?
(Figures represent 'mean scores' with *strong agreement* given a value of +2 through to *strong disagreement* given -2)

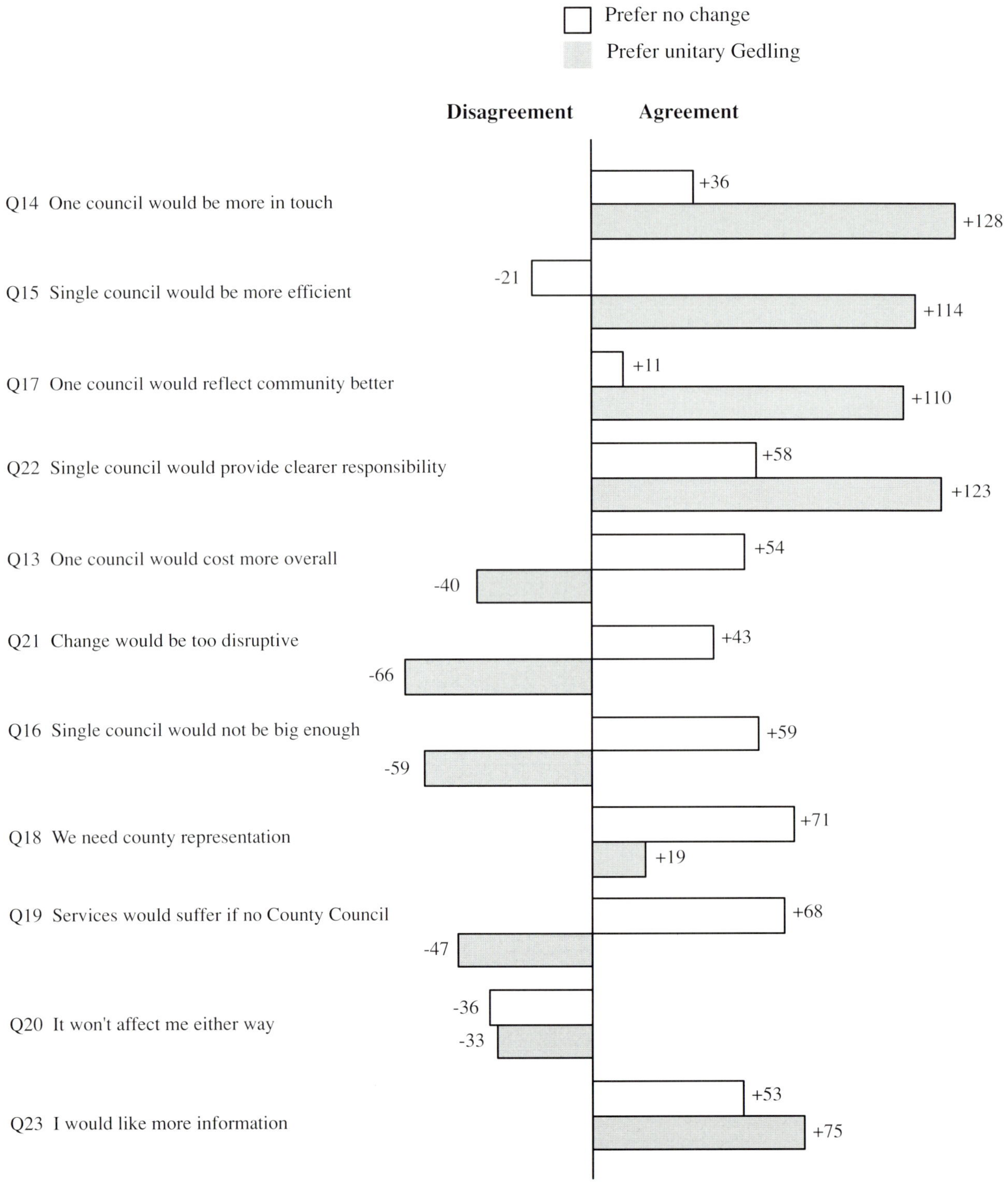

Attitudes to Change
(Respondents in Rushcliffe)

Q To what extent do you agree or disagree that...?
(Figures represent 'mean scores' with *strong agreement* given a value of +2 through to *strong disagreement* given -2)

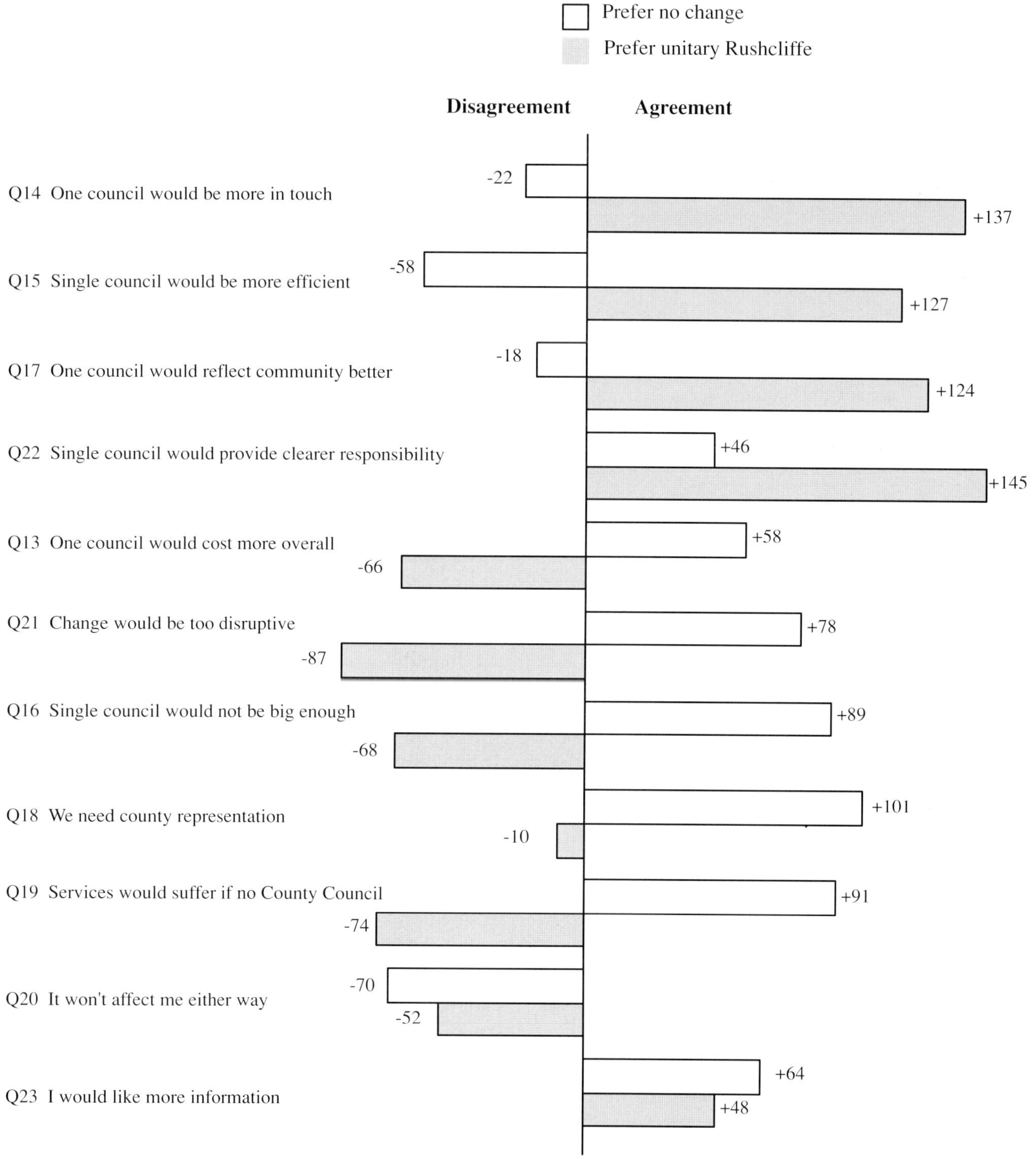

Attitudes to Change
(Respondents in the rest of Nottinghamshire)

Q To what extent do you agree or disagree that...?
(Figures represent 'mean scores' with *strong agreement* given a value of +2 through to *strong disagreement* given -2)

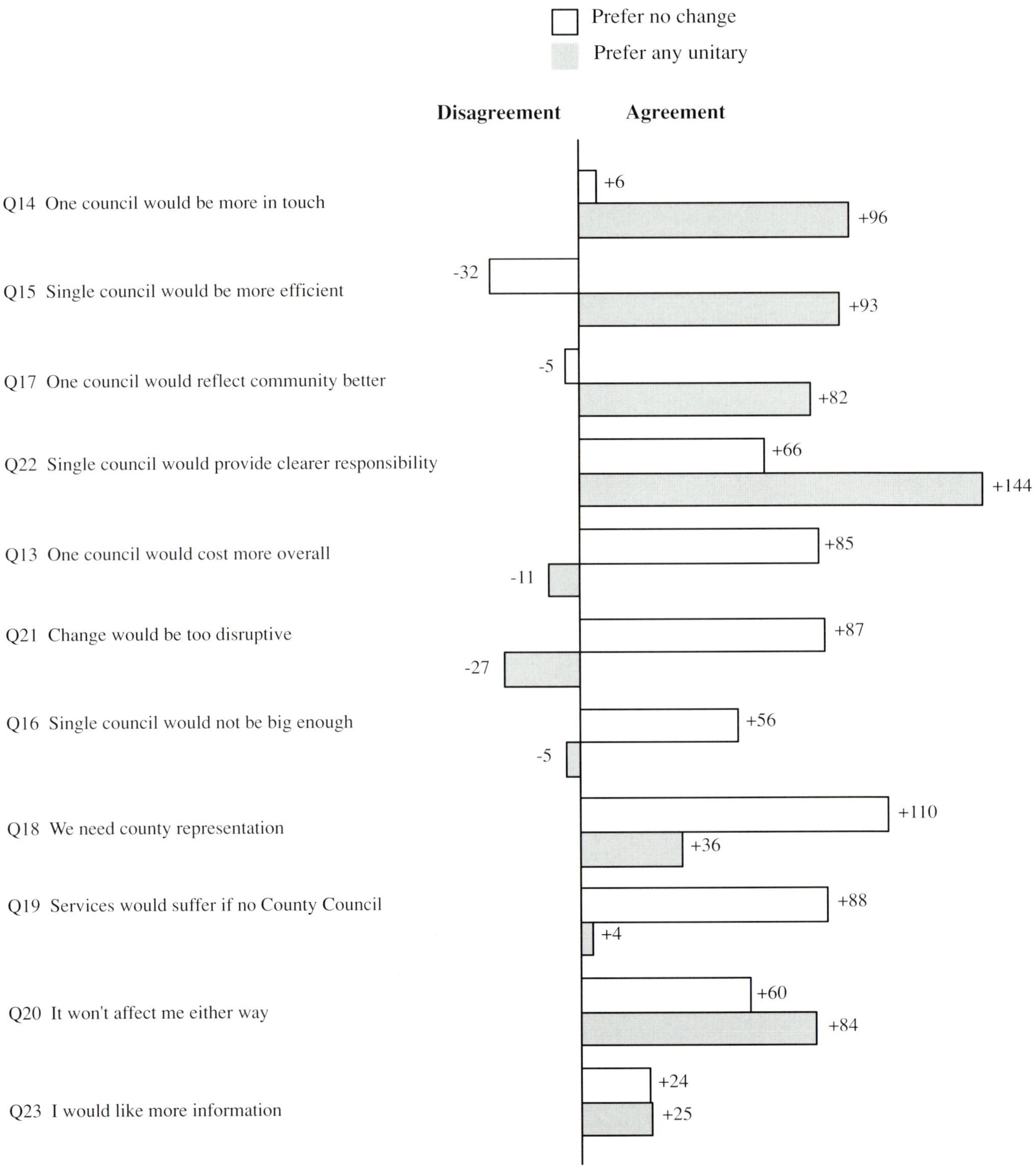

MORI/9101/10 (1-6)

NOTTINGHAMSHIRE

REVIEW - REST OF COUNTY

Serial No . . . .
OUO (7-10)

TOPLINE FINDINGS

Gender	%
Male	48
Female	52

Age	%
18-24	14
25-34	20
35-44	17
45-54	15
55-64	12
65-74	14
75+	8

WRITE IN AGE ☐☐

Work Status	%
Full-time (30 hrs/wk+)	42
Part-time (8-29 hrs/wk)	7
Not working (under 8 hrs)	2
Looking after home/children	14
Retired	24
Registered unemployed	5
Unemployed but not registered	1
Student	2
Other	2

Occupation of Chief Income Earner (CIE)

Position/rank/grade

....

Industry/type of company

....

Qualifications/degrees/apprenticeship

....

No of Staff Responsible for

....

PROBE FOR PENSION

	%
AB	9
C1	20
C2	22
D	26
E	23

* Less than 1/2%

Number in Household

Adults aged 18+ (inc. respondent)

1 2 3 4 5+

Children (17 or under)

0 1 2 3 4+

QA **Are you or other members of your household employed by a council?** IF YES: **Is this a Borough/District Council or a County Council?** CODE FOR BOTH RESPONDENT AND OTHER HOUSEHOLD MEMBERS

	Respondent %	Other %
Yes:		
Borough/District	2	2
County	4	5
Don't know which	0	0
No	93	87
Don't know	1	6

Tenure	%
Owned outright	22
Buying on mortgage	41
Rented from Council	25
Rented from Housing Association	3
Rented from private landlord	6
Other	2

QB **Is this your main permanent home, or is it a second or holiday home?**

	%
Main/permanent	99
Second/holiday	*

Car in Household

CIRCLE NUMBER

0 1 2 3+

Showcard Version	%
A-M	1
A1-M1	2

THIS FORM IS THE PROPERTY OF MARKET & OPINION RESEARCH INTERNATIONAL (MORI)
32 OLD QUEEN STREET, LONDON, SW1H 9HP

INTERVIEWER DECLARATION: I confirm that I have conducted this interview face-to-face with the above named person and that I have asked all the relevant questions fully and recorded the answers in conformance with the survey specification and the MRS Code of Conduct.

Interviewer Name .... Signature ....

Interviewer Number					/	

	Month		Date	
DATE OF INTERVIEW				

NB INTERVIEWER: ALL SHOWCARDS HAVE BEEN REVERSED. PLEASE BE CAREFUL TO CODE THE CORRECT RESPONSE.

Good morning/afternoon/evening. I'm from MORI, the market research and polling organisation. We are doing a survey about local issues, and I would like to ask you a few questions.

ASK ALL

Q1 **Firstly, how long have you lived in this area?** (WITHIN FIVE MILES)

	%
Less than 1 year	5
1-2 years	6
3-5 years	7
6-10 years	14
11-20 years	14
Over 20 years/all my life	54
Don't know/can't remember	0

Q2 SHOWCARD A (R) **From this card, how much would you say you know about local councils and the services they provide?**

	%
A great deal	3
A fair amount	28
Not very much	56
Nothing at all	12
Don't know	*

Q3 SHOWCARD B (R) **Which of the statements on this card comes closest to your own view of the Councils in this area?**

		%
A)	I'm not interested in what the Council does, or whether they do their job	3
B)	I'm not interested in what the Council does, as long as they do their job	19
C)	I like to know what the Council is doing, but I'm happy to let them get on with their job	54
D)	I would like to have more of a say in what the Council does and the services it provides	19
E)	I already work for, or am involved with the Council and the services it provides	4
	Don't know	2

Q4 **From what you know, how many councils provide the main services in this neighbourhood?** (INTERVIEWER - NOT INCLUDING PARISH COUNCILS)

	%
One	34
Two	22
Three+	4
Don't know	40

- 3 -

In fact there are two main councils that provide, or are responsible for, most services in this area:. . .district/borough/city and Lancashire County Council.

ROTATE ORDER OF Q5/6

☐ Q5 SHOWCARD C (R) **From this list, what services do you think are the responsibility of... district/borough/city council? Just read out the letter(s) that apply**

☐ Q6 SHOWCARD C AGAIN (R) **And which services on this list do you think are the responsibility of Lancashire County Council? Again, just read out the letters that apply.**

Q7 SHOWCARD D (R) **Which, if any, of these services do you or members of your family use?** INCLUDE ONLY LOCAL USE

		Q5 "Borough" %	Q6 County %	Q7 Use %
A	Bus Services	31	16	49
B	Car Parks	49	16	62
C	Council Housing	50	18	11
D	Council Tax Benefit/Housing benefit	45	22	19
E	Fire service	21	44	35
F	Food safety	29	25	13
G	Household waste sites/dumps	49	20	54
H	Libraries	32	36	57
I	Parks, playgrounds and open spaces	52	14	53
J	Planning service	41	23	9
K	Public conveniences	52	8	37
L	Recycling/bottle banks	43	15	41
M	Refuse collection	58	16	83
N	Road maintenance	32	41	43
O	Schools/education	26	49	36
P	Social services	28	40	14
Q	Street sweeping	55	15	44
R	Swimming pools/sports facilities	50	14	51
	Other	3	2	2
	None of these	*	2	1
	Don't know	29	32	2

Q8 SHOWCARD E (R) **As you may know, there is currently a review being undertaken by the Local Government Commission on the future local government structure in the county. How much, if anything, would you say you know about this?**

	%
A great deal	2
A fair amount	6
Just a little	22
Heard of but know nothing about	19
Never heard of	51
Don't know	*

PREFERENCES

HAND OVER MAP SHOWING AREAS UNDER REVIEW AND "CURRENT SERVICES" CARD
The Local Government Commission is considering options for the future structure of local government in parts of Nottinghamshire. Could you please read through this card, (SHOW OPTIONS CARD) **which outlines the options.**

Q9 **Please tell me which of the options, if either, you would prefer for <u>each of</u> Gedling, Broxtowe and Rushcliffe?**
CODE ONE ONLY FOR <u>EACH</u> DISTRICT

For Gedling	%
Option A (stay the same/status quo)	29
Option B (single all purpose council)	17
Some other option	1
Neither of these	0
Either of these/don't mind	8
Don't care	15
Don't know	30

For Broxtowe	%
Option A (stay the same/status quo)	30
Option B (single all purpose council)	17
Some other option	1
Neither of these	0
Either of these/don't mind	8
Don't care	13
Don't know	30

For Rushcliffe	%
Option A (stay the same/status quo)	28
Option B (single all purpose council)	17
Some other option	*
Neither of these	0
Either of these/don't mind	9
Don't care	14
Don't know	31

<u>ASK IF "OTHER" NAMED AT Q9 (CODE 3)</u>
Q10 **What other option is that?**
PROBE FULLY - DO NOT PROMPT.

....

....

....

....

<u>ASK ALL PREFERRING AN OPTION (1, 2 OR 3 AT Q9). OTHERS GO TO Q13</u>
Q11 SHOWCARD F (R) **You say that the option you would prefer is . . . . .** (INSERT OPTION PREFERRED). **How strongly would you say you feel about this?**
Base: 158

	%
Very strongly	20
Fairly strongly	45
Not very strongly	24
Not at all strongly	11
Don't know	1

Q12 **What do you think would be the main advantages of . . .**(OPTION PREFERRED) PROBE FULLY FOR DETAILS

Locally based/closer to people/local involvement 21%

....

....

....

Nothing...
Don't know/can't think of anything.................................

ATTITUDES TO PROPOSALS

SHOWCARD G (R) **Imagine that there was one council in any or all of Gedling, Broxtowe or Rushcliffe providing all services. I am going to read out some statements that people have made about this proposal. To what extent do you agree or disagree that . . .?** READ OUT, ROTATE ORDER OF ASKING Q13-22. TICK START

			Strongly agree	Tend to agree	Neither/ Nor	Tend to disagree	Strongly disagree	Don't know
READ OUT:								
☐ Q13	**It would cost more overall**	%	14	32	9	15	4	26
Q14	**It would be more in touch with local people's needs**	%	12	43	8	13	7	17
Q15	**The single Council would be more efficient than the current system of two Councils**	%	9	34	12	20	6	19
☐ Q16	**The single council would not be big enough to manage services such as Education and Social Services effectively**	%	11	32	10	20	5	22
Q17	**It would better reflect the sense of community in those areas**	%	6	42	10	14	6	22
Q18	**We need a County Council to represent us nationally**	%	19	42	11	10	4	14
☐ Q19	**Services would suffer if the County Council no longer provides services in those areas**	%	14	39	7	16	5	19
Q20	**It won't affect me whether there is a single Council in those areas or not**	%	37	29	6	12	5	11
Q21	**The change to a single Council for those areas would be too disruptive**	%	13	29	16	16	4	22
☐ Q22	**With a single Council it would be clearer who is responsible for local services**	%	21	52	6	7	2	12
ASK LAST								
Q23	**I would like to have more information on the proposals before making up my mind**	%	15	34	10	11	23	7

Broxtowe, Gedling & Rushcliffe

Q24 **On balance, which would you say is more in touch with local people and issues, ...** (ROTATE ORDER OF "DISTRICT" AND COUNTY) (INSERT NAME OF "DISTRICT COUNCIL)**..district/borough/city council, or Nottinghamshire County Council, or would you say that they are both about the same?**

	%
District/borough/city council	44
Nottinghamshire County Council	9
Both about the same	37
Don't know	11

REFER BACK TO Q8. ASK ALL WHO HAVE HEARD OF REVIEW AT Q8 (IE CODES 1/2/3/4). OTHERS TO Q28

Q25 SHOWCARD H **Earlier in the interview, you said that you had heard of the Review of local government structure. From which, if any, of the sources shown on this card have you recently heard about the Review?** INTERVIEWER NOTE: "RECENTLY" = IN PAST 3 MONTHS
Base: 105

		%
A	Leaflet from County Council delivered to your door	18
B	Leaflet from County Council in library/ offices, etc	1
C	Advertisement from County Council in local newspaper	7
D	Advertisement from County Council on local radio/TV	0
E	Leaflet from Borough Council delivered to your door	11
F	Leaflet from Borough Council in library/ offices, etc	0
G	Borough Council newspaper	4
H	County Council newspaper	4
I	Advertisement from Borough Council in local newspaper	0
J	Advertisement from Borough Council on local radio/TV	0
K	Advertisement by the Commission on local radio	0
L	Local Government Commission advertisement in local newspaper	2
M	Local newspaper	33
N	National newspaper	12
O	TV	10
P	Local radio	7
Q	National radio	2
R	Friends/neighbours/family	8
S	Conversation with Borough Councillor	2
T	Conversation with County Councillor	1
U	Conversation with Borough Council staff	0
V	Conversation with County Council staff	3
W	Parish/community council	0
X	Residents' Association	0
	Other	6
	None of these	12
	Don't know	18

ASK ALL NAMING A SOURCE AT Q25. OTHERS GO TO Q28

Q26 **Would you say that the information you have received has influenced your opinion, or not?**
Base: 71

	%
Yes	14
No	82
Don't know	4

Q27 **What information in particular has influenced your opinion?**

....

....

....

....

ASK ALL

Q28 SHOWCARD I (R) **Assuming you receive the same level of services, how important is it to you, if at all, what the final decision is on the future local government structure in the areas under review?**

	%
Very important	11
Fairly important	24
Not very important	21
Not at all important	36
Don't know	8

ACTIVISM

Q29 SHOWCARD J **Which of the things on this list, if any, have you done in the last three years? Just read out the letter(s) that apply.**

		%
A	Voted in Local Council elections	74
B	Spoken or written to a local Councillor	19
C	Responded to the earlier Review of local government	6
D	Been to a meeting of a local committee or organisation (WRITE IN NAME OF ORGANISATION)	5
E	Spoken on a radio phone-in about a local issue	1
F	Written to a local newspaper about a local issue	3
G	Been to a meeting of a local branch of a political party	2
H	Written to your MP about a local issue	5
I	Been to a Council Committee meeting	1
J	Been to a Council meeting	2
K	Attended a public meeting run by the Council	6
	None of these	21
	Don't know/refused	1

Q30 SHOWCARD K **Which, if any, of these apply to you? Just read out the letter(s) that apply.**

		%
	I am a member of a:	
A	Residents' Association	4
B	Community Association	1
C	Tenants' Association	3
D	Neighbourhood Watch	22
E	PTA/school governors	3
	I do unpaid work for:	
F	A school	5
G	Citizens Advice Bureau	0
H	Volunteer Bureau	2
I	Scouts/Guides/Cubs/Brownies	1
J	Church group	2
	Other	2
	None of these	66
	Don't know	1

THANK RESPONDENT. GO TO DEMOGRAPHICS.

MORI/9101/10 (1-6)

NOTTINGHAMSHIRE REVIEW: BROXTOWE

Serial No ....
OUO (7-10)

TOPLINE FINDINGS

Gender	%
Male	49
Female	51

Age	%
18-24	13
25-34	20
35-44	19
45-54	16
55-64	14
65-74	12
75+	7

WRITE IN AGE [|]

Work Status	%
Full-time (30 hrs/wk+)	48
Part-time (8-29 hrs/wk)	14
Not working (under 8 hrs)	1
Looking after home/children	9
Retired	21
Registered unemployed	3
Unemployed but not registered	1
Student	1
Other	1

Occupation of Chief Income Earner (CIE)
Position/rank/grade

....

Industry/type of company

....

Qualifications/degrees/apprenticeship

....

No of Staff Responsible for

....

PROBE FOR PENSION

	%
AB	18
C1	27
C2	29
D	18
E	8

Number in Household
Adults aged 18+ (inc. respondent)

1 2 3 4 5+

Children (17 or under)

0 1 2 3 4+

QA **Are you or other members of your household employed by a council?** IF YES: **Is this a Borough/District Council or a County Council?**
CODE FOR BOTH RESPONDENT AND OTHER HOUSEHOLD MEMBERS

	Respondent %	Other %
Yes:		
Borough/District	1	2
County	5	3
Don't know which	0	*
No	94	85
Don't know	0	0

Tenure	%
Owned outright	28
Buying on mortgage	50
Rented from Council	13
Rented from Housing Association	1
Rented from private landlord	7
Other	1

QB **Is this your main permanent home, or is it a second or holiday home?**

	%
Main/permanent	99
Second/holiday	*

Car in Household
CIRCLE NUMBER

0 1 2 3+

Showcard Version	%
A-M	1
A1-M1	2

THIS FORM IS THE PROPERTY OF MARKET & OPINION RESEARCH INTERNATIONAL (MORI)
32 OLD QUEEN STREET, LONDON, SW1H 9HP

INTERVIEWER DECLARATION: I confirm that I have conducted this interview face-to-face with the above named person and that I have asked all the relevant questions fully and recorded the answers in conformance with the survey specification and the MRS Code of Conduct.

Interviewer Name .... Signature ....

Interviewer Number					/	

	Month		Date		
DATE OF INTERVIEW					

NB INTERVIEWER: ALL SHOWCARDS HAVE BEEN REVERSED. PLEASE BE CAREFUL TO CODE THE CORRECT RESPONSE.

Good morning/afternoon/evening. I'm from MORI, the market research and polling organisation. We are doing a survey about local issues, and I would like to ask you a few questions.

ASK ALL

Q1 **Firstly, how long have you lived in this area?** (WITHIN FIVE MILES)

	%
Less than 1 year	5
1-2 years	6
3-5 years	9
6-10 years	12
11-20 years	21
Over 20 years/all my life	47
Don't know/can't remember	0

Q2 SHOWCARD A (R) **From this card, how much would you say you know about local councils and the services they provide?**

	%
A great deal	1
A fair amount	24
Not very much	52
Nothing at all	23
Don't know	0

Q3 SHOWCARD B (R) **Which of the statements on this card comes closest to your own view of the Councils in this area?**

		%
A)	I'm not interested in what the Council does, or whether they do their job	2
B)	I'm not interested in what the Council does, as long as they do their job	18
C)	I like to know what the Council is doing, but I'm happy to let them get on with their job	63
D)	I would like to have more of a say in what the Council does and the services it provides	14
E)	I already work for, or am involved with the Council and the services it provides	2
	Don't know	1

Q4 **From what you know, how many councils provide the main services in this neighbourhood?** (INTERVIEWER - NOT INCLUDING PARISH COUNCILS)

	%
One	30
Two	35
Three+	4
Don't know	31

In fact there are two main councils that provide, or are responsible for most services in this area: Broxtowe Borough and Nottinghamshire County Council.

ROTATE ORDER OF Q5/6

☐ Q5 SHOWCARD C (R) **From this list, what services do you think are the responsibility of Broxtowe Borough Council? Just read out the letter(s) that apply**

☐ Q6 SHOWCARD C AGAIN (R) **And which services on this list do you think are the responsibility of Nottinghamshire County Council? Again, just read out the letters that apply.**

Q7 SHOWCARD D (R) **Which, if any, of these services do you or members of your family use?** INCLUDE ONLY LOCAL USE

		Q5 "Borough" %	Q6 County %	Q7 Use %
A	Bus Services	24	30	44
B	Car Parks	57	19	63
C	Council Housing	56	21	8
D	Council Tax Benefit/Housing benefit	54	24	14
E	Fire service	20	57	8
F	Food safety	26	34	5
G	Household waste sites/dumps	54	15	42
H	Libraries	30	50	56
I	Parks, playgrounds and open spaces	55	20	45
J	Planning service	42	29	7
K	Public conveniences	58	11	29
L	Recycling/bottle banks	55	14	41
M	Refuse collection	76	9	75
N	Road maintenance	40	35	20
O	Schools/education	19	60	30
P	Social services	22	54	6
Q	Street sweeping	63	10	22
R	Swimming pools/sports facilities	48	24	49
	Other	1	1	1
	None of these	0	2	1
	Don't know	12	16	2

Q8 SHOWCARD E (R) **As you may know, there is currently a review being undertaken by the Local Government Commission on the future local government structure in the county. How much, if anything, would you say you know about this?**

	%
A great deal	1
A fair amount	4
Just a little	18
Heard of but know nothing about	19
Never heard of	57

PREFERENCES

HAND OVER MAP SHOWING AREAS UNDER REVIEW AND "CURRENT SERVICES" CARD
The Local Government Commission is considering options for the future structure of local government in parts of Nottinghamshire. Could you please read through this card, (SHOW OPTIONS CARD) **which outlines the options.**

Q9 **Please tell me which of the options, if either, you would prefer for each of Gedling, Broxtowe and Rushcliffe?**
CODE ONE ONLY FOR EACH DISTRICT

	%
For Gedling	
Option A (stay the same/status quo)	43
Option B (single all purpose council)	12
Some other option	0
Neither of these	1
Either of these/don't mind	18
Don't care	8
Don't know	18
For Broxtowe	
Option A (stay the same/status quo)	60
Option B (single all purpose council)	27
Some other option	*
Neither of these	1
Either of these/don't mind	3
Don't care	2
Don't know	7
For Rushcliffe	%
Option A (stay the same/status quo)	43
Option B (single all purpose council)	12
Some other option	0
Neither of these	1
Either of these/don't mind	17
Don't care	8
Don't know	18

ASK IF "OTHER" NAMED FOR BROXTOWE AT Q9 (CODE 3)

Q10 **What other option is that for Broxtowe?**
PROBE FULLY - DO NOT PROMPT.

....

....

....

....

ASK ALL PREFERRING AN OPTION (1, 2 OR 3 AT Q9). OTHERS GO TO Q13

Q11 SHOWCARD F (R) **You say that the option you would prefer for Broxtowe is . . . .** (INSERT OPTION PREFERRED). **How strongly would you say you feel about this?**

	%
Very strongly	13
Fairly strongly	61
Not very strongly	22
Not at all strongly	3
Don't know	1

- 13 -

Q12 **What do you think would be the main advantages of . . .**(OPTION PREFERRED)
PROBE FULLY FOR DETAILS

....

....

....

....

Nothing...

Don't know/can't think of anything.................................

ATTITUDES TO PROPOSALS

SHOWCARD G (R) **Imagine that there was one council in Broxtowe providing all services. I am going to read out some statements that people have made about this proposal. To what extent do you agree or disagree that . . . .?** READ OUT, ROTATE ORDER OF ASKING Q13-22. TICK START

READ OUT:

	Statement		Strongly agree	Tend to agree	Neither/ Nor	Tend to disagree	Strongly disagree	Don't know
☐ Q13	**It would cost more overall**	%	11	42	8	24	5	10
Q14	**It would be more in touch with local people's needs**	%	14	40	11	22	5	8
Q15	**The single Council would be more efficient than the current system of two Councils**	%	11	27	17	25	3	18
☐ Q16	**The single council would not be big enough to manage services such as Education and Social Services effectively**	%	9	38	14	24	1	14
Q17	**It would better reflect the sense of community in Broxtowe**	%	6	42	10	14	6	22
Q18	**We need a County Council to represent us nationally**	%	7	52	15	13	4	8
☐ Q19	**Services would suffer if the County Council no longer provides services in Broxtowe**	%	6	43	10	24	5	12
Q20	**It won't affect me whether there is a single Council in Broxtowe or not**	%	6	22	12	44	7	9
Q21	**The change to a single Council for Broxtowe would be too disruptive**	%	10	44	12	23	3	7
☐ Q22	**With a single Council it would be clearer who is responsible for local services**	%	21	49	9	15	1	5
ASK LAST Q23	**I would like to have more information on the .proposals before making up my mind**	%	27	46	7	15	3	1

Q24 **On balance, which would you say is more in touch with local people and issues, ...** (ROTATE ORDER OF "DISTRICT" AND COUNTY)
Broxtowe Borough Council, or
Nottinghamshire County Council, or would you say that they are both about the same?

	%
Broxtowe Borough Council	58
Nottinghamshire County Council	9
Both about the same	24
Don't know	9

REFER BACK TO Q8. ASK ALL WHO HAVE HEARD OF REVIEW AT Q8 (IE CODES 1/2/3/4). OTHERS TO Q28

Q25 SHOWCARD H **Earlier in the interview, you said that you had heard of the Review of local government structure. From which, if any, of the sources shown on this card have you recently heard about the Review?** INTERVIEWER NOTE: "RECENTLY" = IN PAST 3 MONTHS
Base: 141

		%
A	Leaflet from County Council delivered to your door	26
B	Leaflet from County Council in library/ offices, etc	1
C	Advertisement from County Council in local newspaper	4
D	Advertisement from County Council on local radio/TV	0
E	Leaflet from Borough Council delivered to your door	21
F	Leaflet from Borough Council in library/ offices, etc	2
G	Borough Council newspaper	3
H	County Council newspaper	1
I	Advertisement from Borough Council in local newspaper	3
J	Advertisement from Borough Council on local radio/TV	1
K	Advertisement by the Commission on local radio	0
L	Local Government Commission advertisement in local newspaper	1
M	Local newspaper	40
N	National newspaper	4
O	TV	5
P	Local radio	6
Q	National radio	0
R	Friends/neighbours/family	7
S	Conversation with Borough Councillor	2
T	Conversation with County Councillor	1
U	Conversation with Borough Council staff	4
V	Conversation with County Council staff	1
W	Parish/community council	2
X	Residents' Association	0
	Other	5
	None of these	11
	Don't know	5

ASK ALL NAMING A SOURCE AT Q25. OTHERS GO TO Q28

Q26 **Would you say that the information you have received has influenced your opinion, or not?**
Base: 121

	%
Yes	16
No	77
Don't know	7

Q27 **What information in particular has influenced your opinion?**

....

....

....

....

ASK ALL

Q28 SHOWCARD I (R) **Assuming you receive the same level of services, how important is it to you, if at all, what the final decision is on the future local government structure in Broxtowe?**

	%
Very important	13
Fairly important	42
Not very important	32
Not at all important	8
Don't know	5

ACTIVISM

Q29 SHOWCARD J **Which of the things on this list, if any, have you done in the last three years? Just read out the letter(s) that apply.**

		%
A	Voted in Local Council elections	74
B	Spoken or written to a local Councillor	19
C	Responded to the earlier Review of local government	6
D	Been to a meeting of a local committee or organisation (WRITE IN NAME OF ORGANISATION)	5
E	Spoken on a radio phone-in about a local issue	1
F	Written to a local newspaper about a local issue	3
G	Been to a meeting of a local branch of a political party	2
H	Written to your MP about a local issue	5
I	Been to a Council Committee meeting	1
J	Been to a Council meeting	2
K	Attended a public meeting run by the Council	6
	None of these	21
	Don't know/refused	1

Q30 SHOWCARD K **Which, if any, of these apply to you? Just read out the letter(s) that apply.**

		%
	I am a member of a:	
A	Residents' Association	1
B	Community Association	1
C	Tenants' Association	0
D	Neighbourhood Watch	21
E	PTA/school governors	3
	I do unpaid work for:	
F	A school	7
G	Citizens Advice Bureau	0
H	Volunteer Bureau	2
I	Scouts/Guides/Cubs/Brownies	4
J	Church group	5
	Other	3
	None of these	63
	Don't know	2

THANK RESPONDENT. GO TO DEMOGRAPHICS.

MORI/9101/10 (1-6)

NOTTINGHAMSHIRE
REVIEW: GEDLING

Serial No .... OUO (7-10)

TOPLINE FINDINGS

Gender %

	%
Male	48
Female	52

Age

	%
18-24	12
25-34	19
35-44	24
45-54	12
55-64	10
65-74	12
75+	11

WRITE IN AGE

Work Status

	%
Full-time (30 hrs/wk+)	49
Part-time (8-29 hrs/wk)	7
Not working (under 8 hrs)	2
Looking after home/children	8
Retired	28
Registered unemployed	2
Unemployed but not registered	1
Student	3
Other	1

Occupation of Chief Income Earner (CIE)
Position/rank/grade

....

Industry/type of company

....

Qualifications/degrees/apprenticeship

....

No of Staff Responsible for

....

PROBE FOR PENSION

	%
AB	20
C1	27
C2	29
D	13
E	11

Number in Household
Adults aged 18+ (inc. respondent)

1 2 3 4 5+

Children (17 or under)

0 1 2 3 4+

QA **Are you or other members of your household employed by a council?** IF YES: **Is this a Borough/District Council or a County Council?**
CODE FOR BOTH RESPONDENT AND OTHER HOUSEHOLD MEMBERS

	Respondent %	Other %
Yes:		
Borough/District	2	1
County	6	5
Don't know which	1	*
No	91	92
Don't know	0	2

Tenure

	%
Owned outright	28
Buying on mortgage	53
Rented from Council	11
Rented from Housing Association	2
Rented from private landlord	5
Other	1

QB **Is this your main permanent home, or is it a second or holiday home?**

	%
Main/permanent	98
Second/holiday	2

Car in Household
CIRCLE NUMBER

0 1 2 3+

Showcard Version

	%
A-M	1
A1-M1	2

INTERVIEWER DECLARATION: I confirm that I have conducted this interview face-to-face with the above named person and that I have asked all the relevant questions fully and recorded the answers in conformance with the survey specification and the MRS Code of Conduct.

Interviewer Name .... Signature ....

Interviewer Number					/	

	Month		Date	
DATE OF INTERVIEW				

NB INTERVIEWER: ALL SHOWCARDS HAVE BEEN REVERSED. PLEASE BE CAREFUL TO CODE THE CORRECT RESPONSE.

Good morning/afternoon/evening. I'm from MORI, the market research and polling organisation. We are doing a survey about local issues, and I would like to ask you a few questions.

ASK ALL

Q1 **Firstly, how long have you lived in this area?** (WITHIN FIVE MILES)

	%
Less than 1 year	4
1-2 years	6
3-5 years	9
6-10 years	12
11-20 years	27
Over 20 years/all my life	43
Don't know/can't remember	0

Q2 SHOWCARD A (R) **From this card, how much would you say you know about local councils and the services they provide?**

	%
A great deal	4
A fair amount	31
Not very much	56
Nothing at all	8
Don't know	1

Q3 SHOWCARD B (R) **Which of the statements on this card comes closest to your own view of the Councils in this area?**

		%
A)	I'm not interested in what the Council does, or whether they do their job	1
B)	I'm not interested in what the Council does, as long as they do their job	14
C)	I like to know what the Council is doing, but I'm happy to let them get on with their job	65
D)	I would like to have more of a say in what the Council does and the services it provides	16
E)	I already work for, or am involved with the Council and the services it provides	4
	Don't know	0

Q4 **From what you know, how many councils provide the main services in this neighbourhood?** (INTERVIEWER - NOT INCLUDING PARISH COUNCILS)

	%
One	30
Two	46
Three+	3
Don't know	21

In fact there are two main councils that provide, or are responsible for most services in this area: Gedling Borough and Nottinghamshire County Council.

ROTATE ORDER OF Q5/6

☐ Q5 SHOWCARD C (R) **From this list, what services do you think are the responsibility of Gedling Borough Council? Just read out the letter(s) that apply**

☐ Q6 SHOWCARD C AGAIN (R) **And which services on this list do you think are the responsibility of Nottinghamshire County Council? Again, just read out the letters that apply.**

Q7 SHOWCARD D (R) **Which, if any, of these services do you or members of your family use?** INCLUDE ONLY LOCAL USE

		Q5 "Borough" %	Q6 County %	Q7 Use %
A	Bus Services	15	61	43
B	Car Parks	51	35	65
C	Council Housing	65	25	6
D	Council Tax Benefit/Housing benefit	56	29	14
E	Fire service	17	68	25
F	Food safety	22	47	8
G	Household waste sites/dumps	60	25	40
H	Libraries	36	57	56
I	Parks, playgrounds and open spaces	64	24	46
J	Planning service	52	32	10
K	Public conveniences	60	23	25
L	Recycling/bottle banks	63	16	47
M	Refuse collection	79	14	84
N	Road maintenance	41	47	41
O	Schools/education	21	66	37
P	Social services	23	59	7
Q	Street sweeping	72	17	50
R	Swimming pools/sports facilities	59	28	48
	Other	1	4	1
	None of these	1	*	*
	Don't know	7	11	5

Q8 SHOWCARD E (R) **As you may know, there is currently a review being undertaken by the Local Government Commission on the future local government structure in the county. How much, if anything, would you say you know about this?**

	%
A great deal	2
A fair amount	8
Just a little	36
Heard of but know nothing about	19
Never heard of	34

PREFERENCES

HAND OVER MAP SHOWING AREAS UNDER REVIEW AND "CURRENT SERVICES" CARD
The Local Government Commission is considering options for the future structure of local government in parts of Nottinghamshire. Could you please read through this card, (SHOW OPTIONS CARD) **which outlines the options.**

Q9 **Please tell me which of the options, if either, you would prefer for <u>each of</u> Gedling, Broxtowe and Rushcliffe?**
CODE ONE ONLY FOR <u>EACH</u> DISTRICT

For Gedling	%
Option A (stay the same/status quo)	48
Option B (single all purpose council)	40
Some other option	1
Neither of these	0
Either of these/don't mind	5
Don't care	1
Don't know	6

For Broxtowe	%
Option A (stay the same/status quo)	36
Option B (single all purpose council)	23
Some other option	1
Neither of these	0
Either of these/don't mind	12
Don't care	14
Don't know	15

For Rushcliffe	%
Option A (stay the same/status quo)	35
Option B (single all purpose council)	24
Some other option	0
Neither of these	0
Either of these/don't mind	12
Don't care	14
Don't know	14

<u>ASK IF "OTHER" NAMED FOR GEDLING AT Q9 (CODE 3)</u>

Q10 **What other option is that for Gedling?**
PROBE FULLY - DO NOT PROMPT.

....

....

....

....

<u>ASK ALL PREFERRING AN OPTION (1, 2 OR 3 AT Q9). OTHERS GO TO Q13</u>

Q11 SHOWCARD F (R) **You say that the option you would prefer for Gedling is . . . . .** (INSERT OPTION PREFERRED). **How strongly would you say you feel about this?**

	%
Very strongly	19
Fairly strongly	47
Not very strongly	26
Not at all strongly	6
Don't know	3

Q12 **What do you think would be the main advantages of . . .**(OPTION PREFERRED)
PROBE FULLY FOR DETAILS

....

....

....

....

Nothing..
Don't know/can't think of anything..

ATTITUDES TO PROPOSALS

SHOWCARD G (R) **Imagine that there was one council in Gedling providing all services. I am going to read out some statements that people have made about this proposal. To what extent do you agree or disagree that . . . .?** READ OUT, ROTATE ORDER OF ASKING Q13-22. TICK START

READ OUT:		Strongly agree	Tend to agree	Neither/ Nor	Tend to disagree	Strongly disagree	Don't know
☐ Q13	**It would cost more overall** %	4	33	25	24	5	10
Q14	**It would be more in touch with local people's needs** %	17	59	8	13	1	2
Q15	**The single Council would be more efficient than the current system of two Councils** %	13	42	15	22	2	6
☐ Q16	**The single council would not be big enough to manage services such as Education and Social Services effectively** %	7	35	16	32	4	6
Q17	**It would better reflect the sense of community in Gedling** %	11	56	10	18	2	2
Q18	**We need a County Council to represent us nationally** %	9	48	20	16	3	5
☐ Q19	**Services would suffer if the County Council no longer provides services in Gedling** %	7	38	18	29	4	4
Q20	**It won't affect me whether there is a single Council in Gedling or not** %	2	24	23	42	6	3
Q21	**The change to a single Council for Gedling would be too disruptive** %	4	32	18	38	3	5
☐ Q22	**With a single Council it would be clearer who is responsible for local services** %	14	67	7	8	1	2
ASK LAST Q23	**I would like to have more information on the proposals before making up my mind** %	14	51	16	12	2	4

Q24 **On balance, which would you say is more in touch with local people and issues, ...** (ROTATE ORDER OF "DISTRICT" AND COUNTY)
Gedling Borough Council, or
Nottinghamshire County Council, or would you say that they are both about the same?

	%
Gedling Borough Council	55
Nottinghamshire County Council	2
Both about the same	38
Don't know	4

REFER BACK TO Q8. ASK ALL WHO HAVE HEARD OF REVIEW AT Q8 (IE CODES 1/2/3/4). OTHERS TO Q28

Q25 SHOWCARD H **Earlier in the interview, you said that you had heard of the Review of local government structure. From which, if any, of the sources shown on this card have you recently heard about the Review?** INTERVIEWER NOTE: "RECENTLY" = IN PAST 3 MONTHS
Base: 216

		%
A	Leaflet from County Council delivered to your door	31
B	Leaflet from County Council in library/ offices, etc	4
C	Advertisement from County Council in local newspaper	10
D	Advertisement from County Council on local radio/TV	3
E	Leaflet from Borough Council delivered to your door	27
F	Leaflet from Borough Council in library/ offices, etc	5
G	Borough Council newspaper	4
H	County Council newspaper	3
I	Advertisement from Borough Council in local newspaper	3
J	Advertisement from Borough Council on local radio/TV	3
K	Advertisement by the Commission on local radio	0
L	Local Government Commission advertisement in local newspaper	3
M	Local newspaper	33
N	National newspaper	10
O	TV	9
P	Local radio	19
Q	National radio	2
R	Friends/neighbours/family	11
S	Conversation with Borough Councillor	6
T	Conversation with County Councillor	2
U	Conversation with Borough Council staff	1
V	Conversation with County Council staff	3
W	Parish/community council	2
X	Residents' Association	2
	Other	5
	None of these	18
	Don't know	4

ASK ALL NAMING A SOURCE AT Q25. OTHERS GO TO Q28

Q26 **Would you say that the information you have received has influenced your opinion, or not?**
Base: 172

	%
Yes	13
No	84
Don't know	3

Q27 **What information in particular has influenced your opinion?**

....

....

....

....

ASK ALL

Q28 SHOWCARD I (R) **Assuming you receive the same level of services, how important is it to you, if at all, what the final decision is on the future local government structure in Gedling?**

	%
Very important	17
Fairly important	46
Not very important	25
Not at all important	6
Don't know	6

ACTIVISM

Q29 SHOWCARD J **Which of the things on this list, if any, have you done in the last three years? Just read out the letter(s) that apply.**

		%
A	Voted in Local Council elections	82
B	Spoken or written to a local Councillor	25
C	Responded to the earlier Review of local government	14
D	Been to a meeting of a local committee or organisation (WRITE IN NAME OF ORGANISATION)	6
E	Spoken on a radio phone-in about a local issue	2
F	Written to a local newspaper about a local issue	4
G	Been to a meeting of a local branch of a political party	3
H	Written to your MP about a local issue	12
I	Been to a Council Committee meeting	3
J	Been to a Council meeting	3
K	Attended a public meeting run by the Council	3
	None of these	14
	Don't know/refused	1

Q30 SHOWCARD K **Which, if any, of these apply to you? Just read out the letter(s) that apply.**

		%
	I am a member of a:	
A	Residents' Association	4
B	Community Association	2
C	Tenants' Association	2
D	Neighbourhood Watch	26
E	PTA/school governors	7
	I do unpaid work for:	
F	A school	7
G	Citizens Advice Bureau	0
H	Volunteer Bureau	4
I	Scouts/Guides/Cubs/Brownies	6
J	Church group	9
	Other (WRITE IN AND CODE `X')	3
	None of these	54
	Don't know	2

THANK RESPONDENT. GO TO DEMOGRAPHICS.

MORI/9101/10 (1-6)

NOTTINGHAMSHIRE
REVIEW: RUSHCLIFFE

Serial No ....
OUO (7-10)

TOPLINE FINDINGS

Gender

	%
Male	48
Female	52

Age

	%
18-24	12
25-34	18
35-44	17
45-54	19
55-64	16
65-74	12
75+	6

WRITE IN AGE [ ][ ]

Work Status

	%
Full-time (30 hrs/wk+)	48
Part-time (8-29 hrs/wk)	11
Not working (under 8 hrs)	1
Looking after home/children	10
Retired	23
Registered unemployed	4
Unemployed but not registered	1
Student	3
Other	0

Occupation of Chief Income Earner (CIE)
Position/rank/grade

....

Industry/type of company

....

Qualifications/degrees/apprenticeship

....

No of Staff Responsible for

....

PROBE FOR PENSION

	%
AB	26
C1	34
C2	19
D	12
E	9

Number in Household
Adults aged 18+ (inc. respondent)

1 2 3 4 5+

Children (17 or under)

0 1 2 3 4+

QA **Are you or other members of your household employed by a council?** IF YES: **Is this a Borough/District Council or a County Council?**
CODE FOR BOTH RESPONDENT AND OTHER HOUSEHOLD MEMBERS

	Respondent %	Other %
Yes:		
Borough/District	1	2
County	10	7
Don't know which	*	0
No	89	84
Don't know	*	7

Tenure

	%
Owned outright	28
Buying on mortgage	50
Rented from Council	10
Rented from Housing Association	1
Rented from private landlord	8
Other	3

QB **Is this your main permanent home, or is it a second or holiday home?**

	%
Main/permanent	99
Second/holiday	1

Car in Household
CIRCLE NUMBER

0 1 2 3+

Showcard Version

	%
A-M	1
A1-M1	2

INTERVIEWER DECLARATION: I confirm that I have conducted this interview face-to-face with the above named person and that I have asked all the relevant questions fully and recorded the answers in conformance with the survey specification and the MRS Code of Conduct.

Interviewer Name .... Signature ....

Interviewer Number					/	

	Month		Date	
DATE OF INTERVIEW				

NB INTERVIEWER: ALL SHOWCARDS HAVE BEEN REVERSED. PLEASE BE CAREFUL TO CODE THE CORRECT RESPONSE.

Good morning/afternoon/evening. I'm from MORI, the market research and polling organisation. We are doing a survey about local issues, and I would like to ask you a few questions.

ASK ALL

Q1 **Firstly, how long have you lived in this area?** (WITHIN FIVE MILES)

	%
Less than 1 year	6
1-2 years	5
3-5 years	11
6-10 years	16
11-20 years	20
Over 20 years/all my life	41
Don't know/can't remember	1

Q2 SHOWCARD A (R) **From this card, how much would you say you know about local councils and the services they provide?**

	%
A great deal	4
A fair amount	38
Not very much	50
Nothing at all	8
Don't know	1

Q3 SHOWCARD B (R) **Which of the statements on this card comes closest to your own view of the Councils in this area?**

		%
A)	I'm not interested in what the Council does, or whether they do their job	1
B)	I'm not interested in what the Council does, as long as they do their job	17
C)	I like to know what the Council is doing, but I'm happy to let them get on with their job	60
D)	I would like to have more of a say in what the Council does and the services it provides	19
E)	I already work for, or am involved with the Council and the services it provides	4
	Don't know	0

Q4 **From what you know, how many councils provide the main services in this neighbourhood?** (INTERVIEWER - NOT INCLUDING PARISH COUNCILS)

	%
One	25
Two	52
Three+	4
Don't know	19

In fact there are two main councils that provide, or are responsible for most services in this area: Rushcliffe Borough and Nottinghamshire County Council.

ROTATE ORDER OF Q5/6

☐ Q5 SHOWCARD C (R) **From this list, what services do you think are the responsibility of Rushcliffe Borough Council? Just read out the letter(s) that apply**

☐ Q6 SHOWCARD C AGAIN (R) **And which services on this list do you think are the responsibility of Nottinghamshire County Council? Again, just read out the letters that apply.**

Q7 SHOWCARD D (R) **Which, if any, of these services do you or members of your family use?** INCLUDE ONLY LOCAL USE

		Q5 "Borough" %	Q6 County %	Q7 Use %
A	Bus Services	15	48	56
B	Car Parks	47	28	69
C	Council Housing	54	21	10
D	Council Tax Benefit/Housing benefit	46	27	18
E	Fire service	17	56	21
F	Food safety	21	37	12
G	Household waste sites/dumps	58	19	63
H	Libraries	30	47	67
I	Parks, playgrounds and open spaces	60	19	60
J	Planning service	45	29	18
K	Public conveniences	47	19	40
L	Recycling/bottle banks	56	16	65
M	Refuse collection	72	10	84
N	Road maintenance	31	52	42
O	Schools/education	25	57	34
P	Social services	22	55	10
Q	Street sweeping	57	16	50
R	Swimming pools/sports facilities	54	18	56
	Other	2	1	1
	None of these	1	1	0
	Don't know	11	14	1

Q8 SHOWCARD E (R) **As you may know, there is currently a review being undertaken by the Local Government Commission on the future local government structure in the county. How much, if anything, would you say you know about this?**

	%
A great deal	2
A fair amount	16
Just a little	31
Heard of but know nothing about	20
Never heard of	30

PREFERENCES

HAND OVER MAP SHOWING AREAS UNDER REVIEW AND "CURRENT SERVICES" CARD

The Local Government Commission is considering options for the future structure of local government in parts of Nottinghamshire. Could you please read through this card, (SHOW OPTIONS CARD) **which outlines the options.**

Q9 **Please tell me which of the options, if either, you would prefer for each of Gedling, Broxtowe and Rushcliffe?**

CODE ONE ONLY FOR EACH DISTRICT

For Gedling	%
Option A (stay the same/status quo)	27
Option B (single all purpose council)	15
Some other option	1
Neither of these	0
Either of these/don't mind	10
Don't care	15
Don't know	32

For Broxtowe	%
Option A (stay the same/status quo)	26
Option B (single all purpose council)	16
Some other option	1
Neither of these	0
Either of these/don't mind	10
Don't care	15
Don't know	32

For Rushcliffe	%
Option A (stay the same/status quo)	45
Option B (single all purpose council)	39
Some other option	1
Neither of these	*
Either of these/don't mind	4
Don't care	3
Don't know	9

ASK IF "OTHER" NAMED FOR Rushcliffe AT Q9 (CODE 3)

Q10 **What other option is that for Rushcliffe?**

PROBE FULLY - DO NOT PROMPT.

....

....

....

....

ASK ALL PREFERRING AN OPTION (1, 2 OR 3 AT Q9). OTHERS GO TO Q13

Q11 SHOWCARD F (R) **You say that the option you would prefer for Rushcliffe is . . .** (INSERT OPTION PREFERRED). **How strongly would you say you feel about this?**

	%
Very strongly	23
Fairly strongly	55
Not very strongly	17
Not at all strongly	3
Don't know	2

Q12 **What do you think would be the main advantages of . . .**(OPTION PREFERRED)
PROBE FULLY FOR DETAILS

....

....

....

....

Nothing..
Don't know/can't think of anything..................................

ATTITUDES TO PROPOSALS

SHOWCARD G (R) **Imagine that there was one council in Rushcliffe providing all services. I am going to read out some statements that people have made about this proposal. To what extent do you agree or disagree that . . . .?** READ OUT, ROTATE ORDER OF ASKING Q13-22. TICK START

READ OUT:

			Strongly agree	Tend to agree	Neither/ Nor	Tend to disagree	Strongly disagree	Don't know
☐ Q13	**It would cost more overall**	%	9	27	13	32	8	12
Q14	**It would be more in touch with local people's needs**	%	19	40	13	20	4	4
Q15	**The single Council would be more efficient than the current system of two Councils**	%	16	35	11	26	6	7
☐ Q16	**The single council would not be big enough to manage services such as Education and Social Services effectively**	%	15	28	9	31	6	10
Q17	**It would better reflect the sense of community in Rushcliffe**	%	15	39	17	18	5	5
Q18	**We need a County Council to represent us nationally**	%	15	42	16	18	4	4
☐ Q19	**Services would suffer if the County Council no longer provides services in Rushcliffe%**	%	11	36	11	28	5	8
Q20	**It won't affect me whether there is a single Council in Rushcliffe or not**	%	4	21	12	41	16	7
Q21	**The change to a single Council for Rushcliffe would be too disruptive**	%	11	26	13	33	6	11
☐ Q22	**With a single Council it would be clearer who is responsible for local services**	%	28	49	8	10	3	2
ASK LAST Q23	**I would like to have more information on the proposals before making up my mind**	%	24	36	7	25	5	3

Q24 **On balance, which would you say is more in touch with local people and issues, ...** (ROTATE ORDER OF "DISTRICT" AND COUNTY)
Rushcliffe Borough Council, or
Nottinghamshire County Council, or would you say that they are both about the same?

	%
Rushcliffe Borough Council	62
Nottinghamshire County Council	3
Both about the same	25
Don't know	10

REFER BACK TO Q8. ASK ALL WHO HAVE HEARD OF REVIEW AT Q8 (IE CODES 1/2/3/4). OTHERS TO Q28

Q25 SHOWCARD H **Earlier in the interview, you said that you had heard of the Review of local government structure. From which, if any, of the sources shown on this card have you recently heard about the Review?** INTERVIEWER NOTE: "RECENTLY" = IN PAST 3 MONTHS
Base: 235

		%
A	Leaflet from County Council delivered to your door	36
B	Leaflet from County Council in library/ offices, etc	5
C	Advertisement from County Council in local newspaper	7
D	Advertisement from County Council on local radio/TV	2
E	Leaflet from Borough Council delivered to your door	25
F	Leaflet from Borough Council in library/ offices, etc	3
G	Borough Council newspaper	6
H	County Council newspaper	2
I	Advertisement from Borough Council in local newspaper	3
J	Advertisement from Borough Council on local radio/TV	1
K	Advertisement by the Commission on local radio	*
L	Local Government Commission advertisement in local newspaper	3
M	Local newspaper	31
N	National newspaper	7
O	TV	12
P	Local radio	14
Q	National radio	3
R	Friends/neighbours/family	10
S	Conversation with Borough Councillor	6
T	Conversation with County Councillor	4
U	Conversation with Borough Council staff	1
V	Conversation with County Council staff	3
W	Parish/community council	3
X	Residents' Association	2
	Other	7
	None of these	12
	Don't know	3

ASK ALL NAMING A SOURCE AT Q25. OTHERS GO TO Q28

Q26 **Would you say that the information you have received has influenced your opinion, or not?**
Base: 195

	%
Yes	24
No	71
Don't know	5

Q27 **What information in particular has influenced your opinion?**

....

....

....

....

ASK ALL

Q28 SHOWCARD I (R) **Assuming you receive the same level of services, how important is it to you, if at all, what the final decision is on the future local government structure in Rushcliffe?**

	%
Very important	22
Fairly important	47
Not very important	23
Not at all important	4
Don't know	4

ACTIVISM

Q29 SHOWCARD J **Which of the things on this list, if any, have you done in the last three years? Just read out the letter(s) that apply.**

		%
A	Voted in Local Council elections	80
B	Spoken or written to a local Councillor	29
C	Responded to the earlier Review of local government	10
D	Been to a meeting of a local committee or organisation (WRITE IN NAME OF ORGANISATION)	15
E	Spoken on a radio phone-in about a local issue	1
F	Written to a local newspaper about a local issue	2
G	Been to a meeting of a local branch of a political party	6
H	Written to your MP about a local issue	11
I	Been to a Council Committee meeting	3
J	Been to a Council meeting	3
K	Attended a public meeting run by the Council	4
	None of these	16
	Don't know/refused	1

Q30 SHOWCARD K **Which, if any, of these apply to you? Just read out the letter(s) that apply.**

		%
I am a member of a:		
A	Residents' Association	5
B	Community Association	2
C	Tenants' Association	*
D	Neighbourhood Watch	31
E	PTA/school governors	5
I do unpaid work for:		
F	A school	6
G	Citizens Advice Bureau	*
H	Volunteer Bureau	3
I	Scouts/Guides/Cubs/Brownies	4
J	Church group	8
	Other	6
	None of these	51
	Don't know	1

THANK RESPONDENT. GO TO DEMOGRAPHICS.

CHAPTER 4

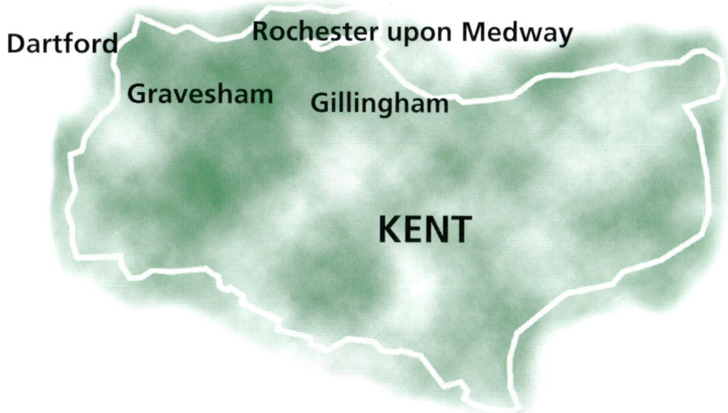

DARTFORD AND GRAVESHAM, GILLINGHAM AND ROCHESTER UPON MEDWAY IN THE COUNTY OF KENT

Draft Recommendations

4.1 The Commission's report *Draft Recommendations on the Future Local Government of Dartford, Gillingham, Gravesham and Rochester upon Medway in the County of Kent* summarised the evidence taken into account by the Commission in reaching its draft recommendations.

Figure 4.1

Draft Recommendations for Dartford, Gravesham, Gillingham and Rochester upon Medway in the County of Kent

Structure

- Dartford and Gravesham should be amalgamated and a new local government area of North West Kent constituted. The existing two-tier structure of local government in the area should be replaced by a unitary authority to be responsible for the broad range of local government functions currently carried out by both county and district councils.

- Gillingham and Rochester upon Medway should be amalgamated and a new local government area of the Medway Towns constituted. The existing two-tier structure of local government in the area should be replaced by a unitary authority to be responsible for the broad range of local government functions currently carried out by both county and district councils.

Ceremonial Arrangements

- The county of Kent should be retained for ceremonial and related purposes, and the areas of North West Kent (Dartford and Gravesham) and the Medway Towns (Gillingham and Rochester upon Medway) should be associated with the county for such purposes.

Public Protection

- There should be a combined authority established in the present county area for the fire service, on which representatives of the new unitary authorities and Kent County Council would serve. Similarly, representatives of the new unitary authorities should also serve on a joint committee with representatives of the County Council to select the local authority membership of the Kent Police Authority. No changes are proposed to the area covered by the Kent Police Authority, or to the probation and magistrates' courts services.

Strategic Planning

- The new unitary authority for North West Kent (Dartford and Gravesham) should be authorised to prepare a unitary development plan for its area, which will include policies for minerals and waste. The new unitary authority for the Medway Towns (Gillingham and Rochester upon Medway) should become a structure planning authority, with a view to that function being exercised jointly with Kent County Council so as to maintain a single structure plan across the whole of their combined area. The unitary authority for the Medway Towns will also be the minerals planning authority for its area, and should maintain a joint minerals plan with Kent County Council for the whole of their combined areas

Electoral Arrangements

- The unitary authority for North West Kent (Dartford combined with Gravesham) should have a total of 44 members, with 12 two-member wards and 20 single-member wards. Elections for the whole council should be held every four years.

- The unitary authority for the Medway Towns (Gillingham combined with Rochester upon Medway) should have a total of 68 members, with 34 two-member wards. Elections for the whole council should be held every four years.

- The continuing Kent County Council should have 73 members, with one member being returned from each of the Kent county divisions outside the current local government administrative areas of Dartford, Gillingham, Gravesham and Rochester upon Medway.

Views Expressed to the Commission

4.2 The Commission received a wide range of direct representations on its draft recommendations, from local authorities, residents, Members of Parliament, business and voluntary groups, parish and town councils, and from other public and private sector organisations. Over 5,000 representations were received from individuals and organisations, including over 3,500 from respondents within the four review districts (Figure 4.2). The Commission also received over 5,400 representations in the form of standard letters, response slips and petitions which were recorded separately (Figures 4.3). These all favoured no change or expressed concern about implications of the draft recommendations. Figures 4.2 and 4.3 exclude representations from the local authorities; these are summarised separately (Figure 4.4).

4.3 In addition, 91 representations were received from outside the county, of which 48 supported no change, 18 opposed either one or both of the draft recommendations without stating a preference and eight supported one or both of the draft recommendations. A more detailed tabulation of the written representations from individuals and interest groups, produced by NOP on behalf of the Commission, can be found towards the end of this Chapter.

Figure 4.2

Views of Respondents

Preferred structure	Dartford	Gravesham	Gillingham	Rochester upon Medway	Outside review areas
From Individuals					
Two unitary authorities (Dartford/Gravesham, Gillingham/Rochester)	0	2	2	1	13
Unitary Dartford/Gravesham	0	21	0	0	0
Unitary Medway Towns	0	2	54	45	2
Unitary districts	11	0	0	0	1
No change	283	867	874	513	1,081
Opposition to one or both draft recommendations	62	239	208	168	248
Other/no preference	13	12	12	11	24
From Organisations					
Two unitary authorities (Dartford/Gravesham, Gillingham/Rochester)	1	1	0	0	1
Unitary Dartford/Gravesham	1	2	0	0	0
Unitary Medway Towns	0	0	3	8	1
Unitary districts	0	1	0	1	0
No change	16	15	16	19	245
Opposition to one or both draft recommendations	5	5	12	9	39
Other/no preference	4	0	0	1	11

Source: Local Government Commission for England and NOP
Note: Excludes out of county representations

Figure 4.3
Views of Respondents: Standard Letters and Petition Signatures

Preferred structure	From Dartford and Gravesham	From Gillingham Rochester upon Medway	From wider area
Opposition to one or both draft recommendations	1,289	733	316
Concern about implications of a unitary Medway	0	617	0
No change	330	1,406	723

Source: Local Government Commission for England

Figure 4.4
Preferences of Kent Local Authorities at Stage Three

Authority	Preference
Ashford Borough Council	No view expressed.
Canterbury City Council	No view expressed.
Dartford Borough Council	Acknowledged "...the force of the Commission's arguments in favour of a merged authority". However, "...as long as Gravesham Borough Council continues to oppose any form of unitary local government in north west Kent, Dartford Council wishes to restate that its preferred option remains a unitary authority on its own boundaries".
Dover District Council	No change.
Gillingham Borough Council	No change, taking into account "...the clearly expressed opposition of the people of Gillingham and of the business community; and because no clear and convincing case for change has been made by the Commission".
Gravesham Borough Council	No change: "The Commission's own report makes many of the arguments for status quo and the only substantial factor quoted against a status quo recommendation is the Thames Gateway proposals. These were well-known when the Commission formed its view in favour of status quo during the previous review".

continued/

/continued

Authority	Preference
Maidstone Borough Council	Support for two unitaries in north Kent, conditional upon there being no boundary changes (other than the merging of the districts), and to further work being undertaken on costs.
Rochester upon Medway City Council	"The City Council fully supports...the creation of a unitary Medway authority". Should this prove unacceptable then "...a unitary City of Rochester upon Medway could effectively realise for this area the benefits of the unitary system of local government".
Sevenoaks District Council	Opposed to "...the piecemeal dismemberment of Kent".
Shepway District Council	No change: "It is clear there will be ongoing costs...which will fall on residents throughout the ten remaining districts".
Swale Borough Council	"Unitary authorities are to be preferred to the present two-tier system. However, the Council does not favour the hybrid option and is concerned about the proposal to remove the economic heartland of Kent with 27 per cent of its population while leaving the remainder of the County Council area with none of the benefits and opportunities which unitary status can bring".
Thanet District Council	No view expressed.
Tonbridge & Malling Borough Council	No view expressed.
Tunbridge Wells Borough Council	No change: "This Council believes that the benefits that are suggested that will flow from the Commission's recommended solution will prove illusory... The supposed benefits are insufficient to justify the high level of disruption and cost to the remainder of the county".
Kent County Council	No change: "All the evidence shows that the existing structure of local authorities in north-west Kent provides very good local government. We contend that it is also best equipped to continue the provision of good local government in the foreseeable future".

The Views of Local Authorities

4.4 The Commission received submissions from 11 of the 15 principal local authorities in Kent during Stage Three (Figure 4.4).

4.5 Local authorities who expressed a view generally maintained the views they had expressed at the initial stage of the review although, in Stage One, Tonbridge & Malling Borough Council expressed support for no change, while Sevenoaks District Council supported the principle of unitary authorities. The Kent Branch of the Association of District Councils did not make representations; the Association of District Councils' national submission is referred to in the Summary of National Representations. The Association of County Councils preferred the retention of the existing two-tier structure for the whole of Kent.

4.6 In relation to electoral arrangements in Dartford and Gravesham, Dartford Borough Council proposed an alternative membership of 66 councillors, as did the minority groups of both district councils. In the Medway Towns, Rochester upon Medway City Council accepted the Commission's draft recommendation but noted that it would result in some councillor:elector imbalances.

The Views of Others

4.7 A range of other interest groups made representations on the Commission's draft recommendations as summarised in the following paragraphs. These are in addition to those made in Stage One.

Businesses and Business Groups

4.8 Representations were received from 61 individual businesses and from 14 representative business groups. Of these, the majority (85 per cent) favoured no change while 12 per cent favoured unitary structures and 3 per cent did not express a preference. The Kent Chamber of Commerce and Industry, which incorporates ten individual chambers representing 3,000 Kent companies, argued for no change. It had canvassed its members and received responses from 148 companies: overall, just under 14 per cent preferred unitary authorities in north Kent, while over 85 per cent preferred no change. Of the 40 respondents from within north Kent, just over 32 per cent preferred unitary authorities while around 67 per cent preferred no change. It argued: "The need for strategy, for cohesion, for critical mass and the avoidance of a serious and costly upheaval all underline the severe dangers of proceeding with the proposed reorganisation".

4.9 Other organisations representing business interests across parts of the county also tended to favour a two-tier structure, often expressing the need for a strategic body in Kent. The Southern and South Eastern Regions of the Confederation of British Industry expressed particular concern about the need for a strategic authority to co-ordinate development pressures, strategic planning, the prospects for economic and employment growth, and costs. The Kent Training and Enterprise Council (TEC) argued: "There needs to be a democratically elected authority for the whole of the current county with relevant powers to promote and implement (principally through partnerships with organisations like the TEC) a shared single economic vision and strategy for the county".

4.10 Two major organisations much involved with development in the Kent Thames-side expressed their views: Lend Lease Global Investment plc, which is undertaking the new £500 million Bluewater shopping centre development in Dartford, supported a unitary authority for the area; Blue Circle Properties Limited argued that commitment and enthusiasm could be more important than local government structure in taking forward business interests, but "...if there is to be change to unitary status then it would be better for Gravesham and Dartford to be combined into one authority", rather than a unitary Dartford on its own boundaries; it also argued for co-ordination in areas such as the Medway Valley.

4.11 The Commission heard from two local chambers of commerce in north Kent. The Gravesham Chamber argued for no change while the Medway Chamber, covering the combined areas of Rochester upon Medway and Gillingham, argued for a unitary authority for the area. Four chambers elsewhere in Kent - Ashford, Birchington-on-Sea, Maidstone and Mid-Kent, and Tonbridge - preferred no change.

County, Regional and National Interests (including the Voluntary Sector)

4.12 The Commission received a relatively large number of representations from county, regional and national interests, and the clear overall preference was for no change. Some organisations expressed concerns about particular services provided by the County Council, for example the Library Association, the Public Record Office, the Museums and Galleries Commission, the Kent Branch of the British Red Cross (about emergency planning), the Royal Commission on Historical Manuscripts, the Royal Commission on Historical Monuments, the Institute of Archaeology (which referred to the County Council's Heritage Conservation Unit as being a "model of its kind"), the South East Museums Service and the Association of County Archive Officers. Many respondents, including the Country Landowners' Association, the National Trust, the Council for the Preservation of Rural England and the Royal Town Planning Institute, were concerned about the need for a strategic overview, particularly in land-use planning and the protection of rural or agricultural interests.

4.13 Various other county groups also opposed the draft recommendations, including the Kent Federation of Amenity Services, the Kent Trust for Nature Conservation, the Kent Council for Voluntary Youth Services and the Kent Association of Volunteer Bureaux. Such groups often expressed particular concerns about county council services or about the need for a Kent-wide strategic authority. The Kent Rural Community Council was concerned with a variety of issues, including the effect of the proposals on the rural parts of the county not included in the unitary authorities.

Education Groups

4.14 Representations from the National Union of Teachers' Kent Division and from the Dartford and Swanley District Teachers' Association, the Kent Adult Education Service, the National Association of Youth and Community Education Officers and the Rochester Diocesan Board of Education, all argued for no change. The Dartford group of the National Union of Teachers was concerned at the risk of increased costs and service disruption, and viewed the prospect of education being linked with leisure services as "derisory".

Health Interests

4.15 The Kent Family Health Services Authority, together with the East Kent and West Kent Health Authorities, are to be reconfigured from April 1996 to create two new health authorities. The Health Services Authority expressed concern that progress towards a primary care led health service would not be helped by restructuring local government, noting the "excellent relationship" with the County Council Social Services Department. The Mid-Kent Healthcare NHS Trust also argued for no change, but the North Kent Healthcare NHS Trust favoured a unitary authority for the Medway Towns.

4.16 The Chief Inspector, Social Services Inspectorate (Department of Health), indicated that Kent "...would remain viable" as a county should Dartford, Gravesham, Rochester and Gillingham become unitary authorities. However, he commented that "...some care will be necessary to ensure that the personal social services are adequately resourced".

Law, Order and Emergency Services

4.17 The Kent Police Authority expressed concern that unitary authorities in north Kent "...would not assist the effective policing of the county and would weaken the democratic accountability of the Authority to residents of Kent." It added: "Kent is possibly unique in England in that all major criminal justice organisations operate on an identical boundary - police, probation, courts, prisons and social and education services. This congruity greatly helps joint planning and co-operation." No change was also supported by the Kent Magistrates' Courts Committee, the Kent Probation Committee and the Kent County Constabulary. HM Fire Inspectorate brought to the Commission's attention the view of the County Fire Officer who pointed to the danger of "...potential conflict of interests between the partners in each unitary authority and a lack of willingness to co-operate with each other which is likely to have a detrimental effect on the efficient running of the combined fire authority". He expressed a particular concern about how such a combined authority would handle the "...disproportionate amount of resources that will be channelled into areas covered by the two unitary authorities". He also argued against fragmentation of the emergency planning function.

Local Groups

4.18 Most local groups also favoured no change. The St John's Centre for Deaf People in Gillingham, for example, was opposed to the prospect of merged unitary authorities for north west Kent and the Medway Towns, considering that the proposals would "...create considerable unjustified upheaval and confusion" and would "pose a financial threat to small charities...working hard to provide services on limited income". The Gillingham Branch of UNISON was also opposed to change, pointing to the threat of job losses in support services, increased costs and service reductions.

4.19 The Vigo Residents' Association wrote opposing a Dartford and Gravesham unitary authority, fearing the concept of a "...Thames Corridor urban area". The Association also reiterated its request for a new parished area for Vigo, currently in the Meopham Parish. Opposition to the merger was also received from the New Barn (Dartford) and Windmill Hill (Gravesham) Residents' Associations.

Parliamentary Interests

4.20 Two Members of Parliament from north Kent wrote during the consultation period. Mr Robert Dunn, MP for Dartford, favoured unitary status for Dartford on its existing boundaries; failing that, he favoured no change. He opposed a merger of Dartford and Gravesham, stating: "I am opposed to this on a number of grounds, not least putting together two communities with quite different tensions and impulses". Mr Jacques Arnold, MP for Gravesham, on the other hand, agreed with the draft recommendation for a single unitary authority to serve Dartford and Gravesham, pointing to the organisation of education and social services and other services, based in Gravesend, and the need for "...properly controlled and planned development of Ebbsfleet and Bluewater...[and]... coherence would also be given to the local implementation of the vision of the Thames Gateway". He also made specific comments about unparished areas in Dartford and Gravesham, in particular the possibility of Gravesend, Northfleet and Dartford being considered for Charter Trustee status, to reflect specific civic concerns. Outside north Kent, the Commission heard from three further Members of Parliament: Mr Roger Gale, MP for North Thanet, Sir Keith Speed, MP for Ashford, and Sir John Stanley, MP for Tonbridge and Malling, all opposed the draft recommendations.

Parish and Town Councils

4.21 During the consultation period, 125 town and parish councils wrote to the Commission out of a total of nearly 300 in the county, together with two area committees of the Kent Association of Parish Councils. Of the 17 local councils from north Kent, eight favoured no change; Gillingham has no parish councils. Of those from the rest of Kent, virtually all favoured no change. The Kent Association of Parish Councils commented: "Notwithstanding some support for the concept of unitary authorities from parish and town councils in Dartford, Gravesham and in Rochester upon Medway - the area under review - the Association is opposed to unitary authorities in north Kent". It also asked for a full parish review of Kent as early as possible.

NOP Tabulations of Written Representations

1 The following tabulations summarise the views expressed by members of the public and other interested parties during the consultation on the Local Government Commission's draft recommendations for Dartford, Gravesham, Gillingham and Rochester upon Medway.

2 The tabulations include only letters sent directly to NOP at its Chelmsford offices and to the Commission's offices in London. Where more than one person's view has been expressed in a letter, the comments from each individual have been recorded separately. Staff from the Commission and NOP have worked closely in ensuring that care has been taken in the interpretation of comments, and that a consistent approach has been adopted.

3 While many people expressed support for one or other of the draft options presented by the Commission, other responses were coded by NOP after further discussion. The pattern of views expressed has been carefully examined, and where a number of respondents supported an option not included in those put forward by the Commission, those views have been separately coded and reported by NOP.

4 The Commission has advertised through the local media, encouraging people to make their views known. All responses received up to two days after the end of the Stage Three consultation period have been included. Returns from campaigns organised by local authorities or other groups (for example, standardised postcards and letters, questionnaires and petitions) have not been included in the tabulations. These, and submissions written and dated before the commencement of the consultation process, have been considered separately by the Commission.

The following definitions have been applied by NOP in compiling the tabulations:

(i) Type of Respondent

Individuals:	includes individual members of the public, local councillors and Members of the Westminster and European Parliaments.
Businesses and Business Groups:	includes organisations which represent businesses, such as local Chambers of Commerce.
County, Regional and National Interests:	any organisation which covers an area which is the size of a county or larger is included here, for example, a county-wide voluntary organisation or a regional association. This classification includes most of the statutory consultees.
Education (and Church) Groups:	this group includes schools, religious organisations and teaching unions.
Local Groups:	this includes organisations smaller than a county area, for example, a district-level voluntary sector body. The group could be voluntary, sporting, political or cultural but does not include organisations from the education or religious sectors (included above). It also includes constituency parties and political groups on local authorities.
Parish and Town Councils:	this also includes district-level associations of town and parish councils. County level associations are classified as County, Regional and National interests.

(ii) Structural Options (Reports A and D)

No change in own district:	this code is used where there is more than one review district in the county. It indicates where respondents from a review district have expressed support for no change for that district and have not made reference to the other review district(s) in that county.
District/county-level authorities:	represents support for either a district or county-level authority although it is not clear whether this is for a unitary or a two-tier structure.
Opposition to structural preferences:	represents responses where a negative, but unspecified, structural preference has been expressed.
Rejects:	rejects are those responses with unclear comments/interpretation.

(iii) Other

Other issues (Report B):	these illustrate preferences in relation to boundary and electoral changes and (where applicable) the restoration of historic counties.
Parishing issues (Report C):	these illustrate preferences in relation to parishing issues, for example, the creation of new parishes or the enhancement of the role of parish and town councils.
Services (Report E):	these illustrate concerns expressed about the impact of proposed changes on particular service areas where the respondent has not additionally expressed a positive structural preference.

NOP Analysis of Responses to Local Government Commission Draft Recommendations - KENT

Report A: Opinions on the structural options, by authority of respondent
Base: all

	Review districts				Other districts in county												
	Dartford	Gilling -ham	Grave -sham	Rochester -upon-Medway	Ashford	Canter -bury	Dover	Maid-stone	Seven -oaks	Shepway	Swale	Thanet	Tonbridge & Malling	Tunbridge Wells	Rest of county total	County total	Out of county total
Status quo/two tier	177	457	466	411	139	89	43	395	182	46	103	41	174	97	1309	2820	47
	45%	*39%*	*40%*	*53%*	*82%*	*81%*	*78%*	*82%*	*74%*	*71%*	*77%*	*82%*	*79%*	*73%*	*79%*	*54%*	*52%*
Two unitary authorities (Dartford/Gravesham, Gillingham/Rochester)	1	2	3	1	-	1	-	8	-	-	-	-	4	1	14	21	3
	*	*	*	*	-	*1%*	-	*2%*	-	-	-	-	*2%*	*1%*	*1%*	*	*3%*
Unitary Dartford/Gravesham	1	-	23	-	-	-	-	-	-	-	-	-	-	-	-	24	3
	*	-	*2%*	-	-	-	-	-	-	-	-	-	-	-	-	*	*3%*
Unitary Medway Towns (Rochester/Gillingham)	-	57	2	53	1	-	-	-	-	-	1	-	1	-	3	115	2
	-	*5%*	*	*7%*	*1%*	-	-	-	-	-	*1%*	-	*	-	*	*2%*	*2%*
Unitary Dartford (on existing boundaries)	9	-	-	-	-	-	-	-	-	-	-	-	-	-	-	9	3
	2%	-	-	-	-	-	-	-	-	-	-	-	-	-	-	*	*3%*
Unitary Dartford (on extended boundaries)	2	-	-	-	-	-	-	-	-	-	-	-	-	-	-	2	-
	1%	-	-	-	-	-	-	-	-	-	-	-	-	-	-	*	-
Unitary Gravesham	-	-	1	-	-	-	-	-	-	-	-	-	-	-	-	1	-
	-	-	*	-	-	-	-	-	-	-	-	-	-	-	-	*	-
Unitary Rochester upon Medway	-	-	-	1	-	-	-	-	-	-	-	-	1	-	1	2	-
	-	-	-	*	-	-	-	-	-	-	-	-	*	-	*	*	-
No change to own district	122	433	416	121	1	-	-	1	10	-	1	-	3	1	17	1109	1
	31%	*37%*	*36%*	*16%*	*1%*	-	-	*	*4%*	-	*1%*	-	*1%*	*1%*	*1%*	*21%*	*1%*
County Level Authority (either two-tier or Unitary)	1	1	1	-	1	-	-	1	3	-	1	-	-	-	6	9	-
	*	*	*	-	*1%*	-	-	*	*1%*	-	*1%*	-	-	-	*	*	-
Opposition to structural options (where no positive preference is stated)	67	220	244	177	24	17	12	71	47	19	25	8	33	31	287	995	18
	17%	*19%*	*21%*	*23%*	*14%*	*15%*	*22%*	*15%*	*19%*	*29%*	*19%*	*16%*	*15%*	*23%*	*17%*	*19%*	*20%*
Others specified	1	-	1	4	-	-	-	2	1	-	-	-	2	-	5	11	3
	*	-	*	*1%*	-	-	-	*	*	-	-	-	*1%*	-	*	*	*3%*
No preference expressed/option defined	15	11	10	8	4	3	-	6	3	-	3	1	2	2	24	68	11
	4%	*1%*	*1%*	*1%*	*2%*	*3%*	-	*1%*	*1%*	-	*2%*	*2%*	*1%*	*2%*	*1%*	*1%*	*12%*
BASE TOTAL	396	1181	1167	776	170	110	55	484	246	65	134	50	220	132	1666	5186	91

* *Less than ½%*

NOP Analysis of Responses to Local Government Commission Draft Recommendations - KENT

Report B: Opinions on other issues, by authority of respondent
Base: all

	Review districts				Other districts in county												
	Dartford	Gilling -ham	Grave -sham	Rochester -upon-Medway	Ashford	Canter -bury	Dover	Maid-stone	Seven -oaks	Shepway	Swale	Thanet	Tonbridge & Malling	Tunbridge Wells	Rest of county total	County total	Out of county total
Electoral issues	- -	1 *	1 *	2 *	- -	- -	- -	- -	- -	- -	- -	- -	1 *	- -	1 *	5 *	- -
Opposition to unitary Dartford/Gravesham, Rochester/Gillingham	14 4%	21 2%	33 3%	22 3%	17 10%	16 15%	8 15%	39 8%	31 13%	13 20%	16 12%	6 12%	17 8%	22 17%	185 11%	275 5%	9 10%
Opposition to a merger of Dartford/Gravesham	36 9%	1 *	148 13%	2 *	- -	- -	- -	1 *	1 *	- -	- -	- -	- -	- -	2 *	189 4%	1 1%
Opposition to a merger of Rochester/Gillingham	- -	172 15%	10 1%	104 13%	- -	1 1%	1 2%	5 1%	- -	- -	1 1%	- -	3 1%	1 1%	12 1%	298 6%	- -
Other specified	2 1%	- -	- -	- -	- -	- -	- -	- -	- -	- -	- -	- -	- -	- -	- -	2 *	- -
BASE TOTAL	396	1181	1167	776	170	110	55	484	246	65	134	50	220	132	1666	5186	91

The figures in the table above do not sum to the base total/100% because undefined fields are not included, except as part of the base total.

* *Less than ½%*

NOP Analysis of Responses to Local Government Commission Draft Recommendations - KENT

Report C: Opinions on parishing issues, by authority of respondent
Base: all

	Review districts				Other districts in county												
	Dartford	Gilling -ham	Grave -sham	Rochester -upon-Medway	Ashford	Canter -bury	Dover	Maid-stone	Seven -oaks	Shepway	Swale	Thanet	Tonbricge & Malling	Tunbridge Wells	Rest of county total	County total	Out of county total
Enhanced Parish Powers	2 1%	- -	1 *	1 *	- -	- -	- -	- -	- -	- -	- -	- -	- -	- -	- -	4 *	- -
Create new parish councils	- -	- -	1 *	- -	- -	- -	- -	- -	- -	- -	- -	- -	- -	- -	- -	1 *	1 1%
BASE TOTAL	396	1181	1167	776	170	110	55	484	246	65	134	50	220	132	1666	5186	91

The figures in the table above do not sum to the base total/100% because undefined fields are not included, except as part of the base total.

* *Less than ½%*

NOP Analysis of Responses to Local Government Commission Draft Recommendations - KENT

Report D1: Opinions on the structural options, by respondent type (all respondents)
Base: all

	Respondent Type					
	Indiv-iduals	Business groups	County, regional & national interests	Education (& church) groups	Local groups	Parish and town councils
Status quo/two-tier	2543 *53%*	43 *57%*	54 *68%*	54 *66%*	63 *66%*	110 *86%*
Two unitary authorities (Dartford/Gravesham, Gillingham/Rochester)	20 *	1 *1%*	- -	1 *1%*	1 *1%*	1 *1%*
Unitary Dartford/Gravesham	23 *	1 *1%*	- -	1 *1%*	1 *1%*	1 *1%*
Unitary Medway Towns (Rochester/Gillingham)	104 *2%*	4 *5%*	- -	- -	7 *7%*	2 *2%*
Unitary Dartford (on existing boundaries)	11 *	1 *1%*	- -	- -	- -	- -
Unitary Dartford (on extended boundaries)	2 *	- -	- -	- -	- -	- -
Unitary Gravesham	- -	- -	- -	- -	- -	1 *1%*
Unitary Rochester upon Medway	1 *	- -	- -	- -	- -	1 *1%*
No change to own district	1101 *23%*	- -	- -	4 *5%*	2 *2%*	3 *2%*
County Level Authority (either two-tier or Unitary)	7 *	- -	1 *1%*	1 *1%*	- -	- -
Opposition to structural options (where no positive preference is stated)	938 *19%*	21 *28%*	12 *15%*	19 *23%*	17 *18%*	6 *5%*
Others specified	8 *	2 *3%*	1 *1%*	- -	2 *2%*	1 *1%*
No preference expressed/option defined	60 *1%*	2 *3%*	11 *14%*	2 *2%*	2 *2%*	2 *2%*
BASE TOTAL	4818	75	79	82	95	128

* *Less than ½%*

NOP Analysis of Responses to Local Government Commission Draft Recommendations - KENT

Report D2: Opinions on the structural options, by respondent type
Base: respondents in Dartford only

	Respondent Type					
	Indiv-iduals	Business groups	County, regional & national interests	Education (& church) groups	Local groups	Parish and town councils
Status quo/two-tier	161 *44%*	3 *43%*	2 *100%*	5 *56%*	4 *67%*	2 *67%*
Two unitary authorities (Dartford/Gravesham, Gillingham/Rochester)	- -	1 *14%*	- -	- -	- -	- -
Unitary Dartford/Gravesham	- -	- -	- -	1 *11%*	- -	- -
Unitary Dartford (on existing boundaries)	9 *2%*	- -	- -	- -	- -	- -
Unitary Dartford (on extended boundaries)	2 *1%*	- -	- -	- -	- -	- -
No change to own district	122 *33%*	- -	- -	- -	- -	- -
County Level Authority (Either two-tier or Unitary)	1 *	- -	- -	- -	- -	- -
Opposition to structural options (where no positive preference is stated)	62 *17%*	1 *14%*	- -	3 *33%*	1 *17%*	- -
Others specified	- -	1 *14%*	- -	- -	- -	- -
No preference expressed/option defined	12 *3%*	1 *14%*	- -	- -	1 *17%*	1 *33%*
BASE TOTAL	369	7	2	9	6	3

* *Less than ½%*

NOP Analysis of Responses to Local Government Commission Draft Recommendations - KENT

Report D3: Opinions on the structural options, by respondent type
Base: respondents in Gravesham only

	Respondent Type					
	Indiv-iduals	Business groups	County, regional & national interests	Education (& church) groups	Local groups	Parish and town councils
Status quo/two-tier	455 *40%*	3 *60%*	1 *50%*	1 *50%*	3 *38%*	3 *43%*
Two unitary authorities (Dartford/Gravesham, Gillingham/Rochester)	2 *	- -	- -	- -	- -	1 *14%*
Unitary Dartford/Gravesham	21 *2%*	- -	- -	- -	1 *13%*	1 *14%*
Unitary Medway Towns (Rochester/Gillingham)	2 *	- -	- -	- -	- -	- -
Unitary Gravesham	- -	- -	- -	- -	- -	1 *14%*
No change to own district	412 *36%*	- -	- -	1 *50%*	2 *25%*	1 *14%*
County Level Authority (either two-tier or Unitary)	1 *	- -	- -	- -	- -	- -
Opposition to structural options (where no positive preference is stated)	239 *21%*	2 *40%*	1 *50%*	- -	2 *25%*	- -
Others specified	1 *	- -	- -	- -	- -	- -
No preference expressed/option defined	10 *1%*	- -	- -	- -	- -	- -
BASE TOTAL	1143	5	2	2	8	7

* *Less than ½%*

NOP Analysis of Responses to Local Government Commission Draft Recommendations - KENT

Report D4: Opinions on the structural options, by respondent type
Base: respondents in Rochester upon Medway only

	Respondent Type					
	Indiv-iduals	Business groups	County, regional & national interests	Education (& church) groups	Local groups	Parish and town councils
Status quo/two-tier	394 *53%*	2 *25%*	- -	11 *73%*	2 *33%*	2 *29%*
Two unitary authorities (Dartford/Gravesham, Gillingham/Rochester)	1 *	- -	- -	- -	- -	- -
Unitary Medway Towns (Rochester/Gillingham)	45 *6%*	2 *25%*	- -	- -	4 *67%*	2 *29%*
Unitary Rochester upon Medway	- -	- -	- -	- -	- -	1 *14%*
No change to own district	119 *16%*	- -	- -	- -	- -	2 *29%*
Opposition to structural options (where no positive preference is stated)	168 *23%*	4 *50%*	1 *50%*	4 *27%*	- -	- -
Others specified	4 *1%*	- -	- -	- -	- -	- -
No preference expressed/option defined	7 *1%*	- -	1 *50%*	- -	- -	- -
BASE TOTAL	738	8	2	15	6	7

* *Less than ½%*

NOP Analysis of Responses to Local Government Commission Draft Recommendations - KENT

Report D5: Opinions on the structural options, by respondent type
Base : respondents in Gillingham only

	Respondent Type					
	Indiv-iduals	Business groups	County, regional & national interests	Education (& church) groups	Local groups	Parish and town councils
Status quo/two-tier	443 *39%*	5 *45%*	4 *80%*	4 *44%*	1 *17%*	- -
Two unitary authorities (Dartford/Gravesham, Gillingham/Rochester)	2 *	- -	- -	- -	- -	- -
Unitary Medway Towns (Rochester/Gillingham)	54 *5%*	1 *9%*	- -	- -	2 *33%*	- -
No change to own district	431 *37%*	- -	- -	2 *22%*	- -	- -
County Level Authority (either two-tier or Unitary)	1 *	- -	- -	- -	- -	- -
Opposition to structural options (where no positive preference is stated)	208 *18%*	5 *45%*	1 *20%*	3 *33%*	3 *50%*	- -
No preference expressed/option defined	11 *1%*	- -	- -	- -	- -	- -
BASE TOTAL	1150	11	5	9	6	-

* *Less than ½%*

NOP Analysis of Responses to Local Government Commission Draft Recommendations - KENT

Report D6: Opinions on the structural options, by respondent type
Base : respondents in rest of county only

	Respondent Type					
	Indiv-iduals	Business groups	County, regional & national interests	Education (& church) groups	Local groups	Parish and town councils
Status quo/two-tier	1065 *78%*	25 *76%*	33 *79%*	32 *70%*	52 *79%*	102 *93%*
Two unitary authorities (Dartford/Gravesham, Gillingham/Rochester)	13 *1%*	- -	- -	1 *2%*	- -	- -
Unitary Medway Towns (Rochester/Gillingham)	2 *	- -	- -	- -	1 *2%*	- -
Unitary Rochester upon Medway	1 *	- -	- -	- -	- -	- -
No change to own district	16 *1%*	- -	- -	1 *2%*	- -	- -
County Level Authority (either two-tier or Unitary)	4 *	- -	1 *2%*	1 *2%*	- -	- -
Opposition to structural options (where no positive preference is stated)	248 *18%*	8 *24%*	6 *14%*	9 *20%*	10 *15%*	6 *5%*
Others specified	2 *	- -	- -	- -	2 *3%*	1 *1%*
No preference expressed/option defined	18 *1%*	- -	2 *5%*	2 *4%*	1 *2%*	1 *1%*
BASE TOTAL	1369	33	42	46	66	110

* *Less than ½%*

NOP Analysis of Responses to Local Government Commission Draft Recommendations - KENT

Report E: Views on services, by authority of respondent
Base : all

	Review districts				Other districts in county												
	Dartford	Gilling -ham	Grave -sham	Rochester -upon-Medway	Ashford	Canter -bury	Dover	Maid-stone	Seven -oaks	Shepway	Swale	Thanet	Tonbridge & Malling	Tunbridge Wells	Rest of county total	County total	Out of county total
Archives	-	-	-	-	-	1	-	1	-	-	-	-	-	-	2	2	1
	-	-	-	-	-	*1%*	-	*	-	-	-	-	-	-	*	*	*1%*
Education	2	2	1	4	1	-	-	6	1	2	1	1	1	1	14	23	1
	1%	*	*	*1%*	*1%*	-	-	*1%*	*	*3%*	*1%*	*2%*	*	*1%*	*1%*	*	*1%*
Libraries	2	-	2	1	1	1	-	-	-	-	-	-	-	2	4	9	-
	1%	-	*	*	*1%*	*1%*	-	-	-	-	-	-	-	*2%*	*	*	-
Trading standards	-	1	-	-	-	-	-	-	-	-	-	-	-	-	-	1	-
	-	*	-	-	-	-	-	-	-	-	-	-	-	-	-	*	
Other specified services (or multiples of)	-	-	3	-	-	-	-	1	-	1	-	-	-	-	2	5	7
	-	-	*	-	-	-	-	*	-	*2%*	-	-	-	-	*	*	*8%*
BASE TOTAL	396	1181	1167	776	170	110	55	484	246	65	134	50	220	132	1666	5186	91

The figures in the table above do not sum to the base total/100% because undefined fields are not included, except as part of the base total.

* *Less than ½%*

NOP Analysis of Responses to Local Government Commission Draft Recommendations - KENT

Report F: Views on services, by respondent type
Base: all

	Respondent Type					
	Indiv-iduals	Business groups	County, regional & national interests	Education (& church) groups	Local groups	Parish and town councils
Archives	-	-	1	2	-	-
	-	-	*1%*	*2%*	-	-
Education	14	-	1	8	1	-
	*	-	*1%*	*10%*	*1%*	-
Libraries	7	-	1	-	1	-
	*	-	*1%*	-	*1%*	-
Trading standards	1	-	-	-	-	-
	*	-	-	-	-	-
Other specified services (or multiples of)	1	-	9	-	1	1
	*	-	*11%*	-	*1%*	*1%*
BASE TOTAL	4818	75	79	82	95	128

The figures in the table above do not sum to the base total/100% because undefined fields are not included, except as part of the base total.

* *Less than ½%*

NOP Analysis of Responses to Local Government Commission Draft Recommendations - KENT

Report G: Type of respondent, by authority of respondent
Base : all

	Review districts				Other districts in county												
	Dartford	Gilling -ham	Grave -sham	Rochester -upon-Medway	Ashford	Canter -bury	Dover	Maid-stone	Seven -oaks	Shepway	Swale	Thanet	Tonbridge & Malling	Tunbridge Wells	Rest of county total	County total	Out of county total
Individuals	369 93%	1150 97%	1143 98%	738 95%	139 82%	81 74%	38 69%	425 88%	202 82%	44 68%	110 82%	40 80%	184 84%	106 80%	1369 82%	4769 92%	49 54%
Business groups	7 2%	11 1%	5 *	8 1%	3 2%	3 3%	1 2%	4 1%	3 1%	3 5%	3 2%	3 6%	6 3%	4 3%	33 2%	64 1%	11 12%
County, regional and national interests	2 1%	5 *	2 *	2 *	4 2%	6 5%	- -	19 4%	3 1%	4 6%	3 2%	- -	1 *	2 2%	42 3%	53 1%	26 29%
Education (and church) groups	9 2%	9 1%	2 *	15 2%	3 2%	3 3%	2 4%	12 2%	11 4%	1 2%	5 4%	- -	6 3%	3 2%	46 3%	81 2%	1 1%
Local Groups	6 2%	6 1%	8 1%	6 1%	6 4%	8 7%	3 5%	12 2%	6 2%	5 8%	5 4%	5 10%	7 3%	9 7%	66 4%	92 2%	3 3%
Parish and town councils	3 1%	- -	7 1%	7 1%	15 9%	9 8%	11 20%	12 2%	21 9%	8 12%	8 6%	2 4%	16 7%	8 6%	110 7%	127 2%	1 1%
BASE TOTAL	396	1181	1167	776	170	110	55	484	246	65	134	50	220	132	1666	5186	91

* *Less than ½%*

MORI Research Study for the Local Government Commission

Introduction

Background

1 This summary report highlights the key findings from a survey of public opinion conducted in the Boroughs of Dartford, Gillingham and Gravesham, the City of Rochester upon Medway and across the rest of the County of Kent on behalf of the Local Government Commission for England. A copy of each of the marked-up questionnaires is appended. The computer tabulations are contained in a separate volume, which is available from MORI (32 Old Queen Street, London SW1H 9HP. Telephone 0171-222 0232. Price £15)

2 The survey was designed in close consultation with the Commission, following extensive qualitative research and pilot testing. All sampling, interviewing and analysis have been carried out independently by MORI, within the guidelines of the profession laid out by the Market Research Society.

3 In Dartford, all Census Enumeration Districts (EDs) were sorted by ward, and stratified according to social class. EDs were then sampled (32 in total) in proportion to the population size of each, and quotas set for sex, age and work status. A total of 332 interviews with adults aged 18+, conducted face-to-face and in-home, were carried out between 1 October and 7 November 1995. Data were weighted to match the population profile in the Borough. A similar approach was taken in Gillingham (where 325 interviews were conducted), Gravesham (323) and Rochester upon Medway (313).

4 In the remaining districts of Kent, all EDs were sorted into wards, and again were stratified according to social class. A total of 32 EDs across the whole area (that is, Kent excluding Dartford, Gillingham, Gravesham and Rochester upon Medway) were sampled, with quotas set by sex, age and work status. Face-to-face interviews, conducted in-home, were carried out with 325 adults aged 18+ between 1 October and 7 November 1995. Data were weighted to match the population profile of the area.

Publication of the Results

5 As with all our studies, these findings are subject to our Standard Terms and Conditions of Contract. Any press release or publication of the findings of this survey requires the advance approval of MORI. Such approval will only be refused on the grounds of inaccuracy or misinterpretation.

Objectives

6 This survey took place during Stage Three, the consultation period on the Commission's draft recommendations. It measures public preferences for the organisation of local government in the areas currently under review, as well as exploring strength of feeling, levels of knowledge about the review, involvement in, and broader perceptions of, local government in the area.

Statistical Reliability of the Data

7 Because we have interviewed a sample of residents, rather than the whole population, the results are subject to statistical tolerance limits, or "margins of error". These are expressed as our confidence that the true figure for the whole population falls within a given range. By convention this is expressed as a percentage, so our 95% confidence level means that in 95 times out of 100 the true figure would lie within this range.

8 The table below shows ranges of the 95% confidence level for a range of sample sizes. For each sample size, the table shows the tolerance limits for sample results close to 10%, 30% and 50%. Take, for example, the results of a survey of 300 residents showing that 50% are aware of the review. In 95 times out of 100 the true figure would lie between 44% and 56% (ie betweeen 50% ±6%).

Sample size	Sampling tolerances applicable to results at or near these percentages (based on 95% confidence level) 10/90% ±%	30/70% ±%	50% ±%
300	3	5	6
200	4	6	7
150	5	7	8
100	6	9	10
50	8	13	14

9 Clearly, 10% or 30% of the sample being aware of the review equate to 90% or 70% not being aware of it. So this table shows the ranges of 95% confidence for responses close to 10%, 30%, 50%, 70% and 90% of our sample. The figures for responses between can be obtained by extrapolation.

10 The true figure would only be known if all the residents of the area had been interviewed. It can be seen in the table, however, that large increases in the sample size do not greatly reduce the sampling tolerance. In addition, the true figure is more likely to lie at the midpoint of the range, rather than at either extreme.

11 When comparing results from separate groups within a sample we need to be sure that the differences are statistically significant. This would be important in comparing views expressed by different parts of a county. The table below shows how the statistical significance of the difference is determined by the size of the groups and the percentage result from the sample.

12 Assuming a 95% confidence level, the table shows the size of the differences required if different results are to be regarded as statistically significant. It can be seen that if 50% of a group of 300 were aware of the review, the result from another group of 300 would not become statistically significant until it became less than 42% or more than 58%.

Sample sizes	Differences required for significance at or near these percentage levels 10/90% ±	30/70% ±	50% ±
300 and 300	5	7	8
300 and 200	5	8	9
300 and 100	7	10	11
200 and 100	7	11	12
100 and 100	8	13	14

Survey Findings

Knowledge and Awareness

13 Residents within the four districts under review profess broadly similar levels of knowledge and interest in local government as those living in the rest of the County of Kent. In all five areas, three in five like to know what their council is doing, but want no greater involvement. Around one in five say they want a higher level of involvement, rising to one in four in Dartford.

14 Around two in five say they know at least a fair amount about what their council does. Nearly two in three admit to knowing, at best, not very much.

15 This is reflected in the number of residents who incorrectly ascribe services between the two tiers of local government. Thus, although four or five in ten recognise libraries as a county council service, three in ten allocate responsibility to their district/borough/city council. And although between six and eight in ten realise that refuse collection is a district service, as many as one in six thinks it is a county council service. Residents of Gravesham and Rochester upon Medway are less likely to be correct in the way that they allocate services across the two tiers than are those in other areas.

16 Awareness of the review itself is highest in Gravesham (where 78% claim to have heard of it); lowest awareness is in the rest of Kent (56%). Similarly, the proportion who say they know a fair amount or more is highest in Gravesham (at 24%); in Dartford, Rochester upon Medway and the rest of Kent, this level of knowledge is claimed by only one in ten.

Sources of Information

17 Local newspapers are the most common source of information about the review, by a considerable margin. Of those who have at least heard of the review, between five and seven in ten in the review areas (and four in ten in the rest of the County) name the local press as a recent source. Around two in three overall cite some media source as a recent source of information on the review.

18 Some local authorities appear to have been active in providing information to residents. In the rest of Kent, more cite a County Council source than cite a district source; the reverse is true in the review areas, except Dartford, where there is a balance. Of all the areas surveyed, those in Gillingham are most likely to specify local authority sources. Very few recognise receiving information directly from the Local Government Commission itself.

19 Although most of those aware of the review recognise one or more recent sources of information, few (around one in five, fewer still in Gravesham and Rochester upon Medway) say that this has influenced their opinion.

20 Furthermore, in spite of a relatively low level of knowledge and engagement with their local authority, most people say that the outcome of the review is either very important or fairly important to them. Even in the rest of Kent, the majority feel that it is important (52%), while perceived importance peaks in Dartford at 73%.

The Preferred Option

21 Majorities in both Dartford (56%) and Gravesham (71%) would prefer no change of two-tier local government in two separate authorities. Support for a single all-purpose council stands at 35% and 13% respectively. On balance, those in the rest of the County agree (25% would prefer a single all-purpose unitary, and 42% no change).

22 Similarly, majorities in both Gillingham (63%) and Rochester upon Medway (53%) say they would prefer no change, compared with 31% and 30% respectively, favouring an all-purpose unitary authority. Views in the non-review districts towards Gillingham and Rochester are similar to those towards Dartford and Gravesham: 41% would prefer no change, while 25% support the proposed combined unitary council.

23 More of those in the review areas who express a preference say that they feel strongly about it (three - quarters) than in the rest of Kent (68%). Those opting for no change feel most strongly.

Factors in Expressing a Preference

24 In questions 13 to 23, residents were asked to say to what extent they agreed or disagreed with a range of statements which related to a change to unitary local government. The statements were designed to cover the main issues raised by residents during the qualitative phase of research, and others that formed a part of the Commission's brief to take into consideration in making its recommendations.

25 The following charts summarise the results from these questions, with the full question wording presented in the questionnaires in the appendices. Values have been ascribed to the five attitudinal positions that people were offered (+2 for strongly agree, +1 for tend to agree, 0 for neither agree nor disagree, -1 for tend to disagree, and -2 for strongly disagree) and mean scores calculated across all respondents expressing a view. This has the combined benefit of distilling the range of opinion into one summary figure, while incorporating the varying intensity of feeling by ascribing values. Bars to the right indicate that the mean score value is positive, and thus that there is a balance of agreement with the statement. Bars to the left, conversely, indicate a balance of disagreement.

26 The first two charts, therefore, show how the views of people living in Dartford and Gravesham, and in Gillingham and Rochester upon Medway differ from those across the rest of Kent. In doing so, they illustrate the attitudes or perceptions that are, in relative terms, shared by different groups of residents (where the bars project in the same direction), and those where views differ markedly. Thus, in all five areas, there is a consensus on the need for County representation and that services would suffer; in all areas except Gravesham (whose residents are particularly negative about unitary authorities), there is a consensus that unitary authorities would clarify responsibility.

27 The subsequent charts take the results, separately, from each of the four review districts and the rest of Kent, and illustrate the difference in views between those within each area whose preference is for unitary status, and those who prefer no change. The chart therefore illustrates those attitudinal statements that most, or least, differentiate the residents of each area expressing the two opposing preferences. The perceived impact on efficiency is clearly a key determinant of opinion, as are reflecting the community, size, disruption and impact on services.

Attitudes to Change (Respondents in Dartford, Gravesham and rest of Kent)

Q To what extent do you agree or disagree that...?
(Figures represent 'mean scores' with *strong agreement* given a value of +2 through to *strong disagreement* given -2)

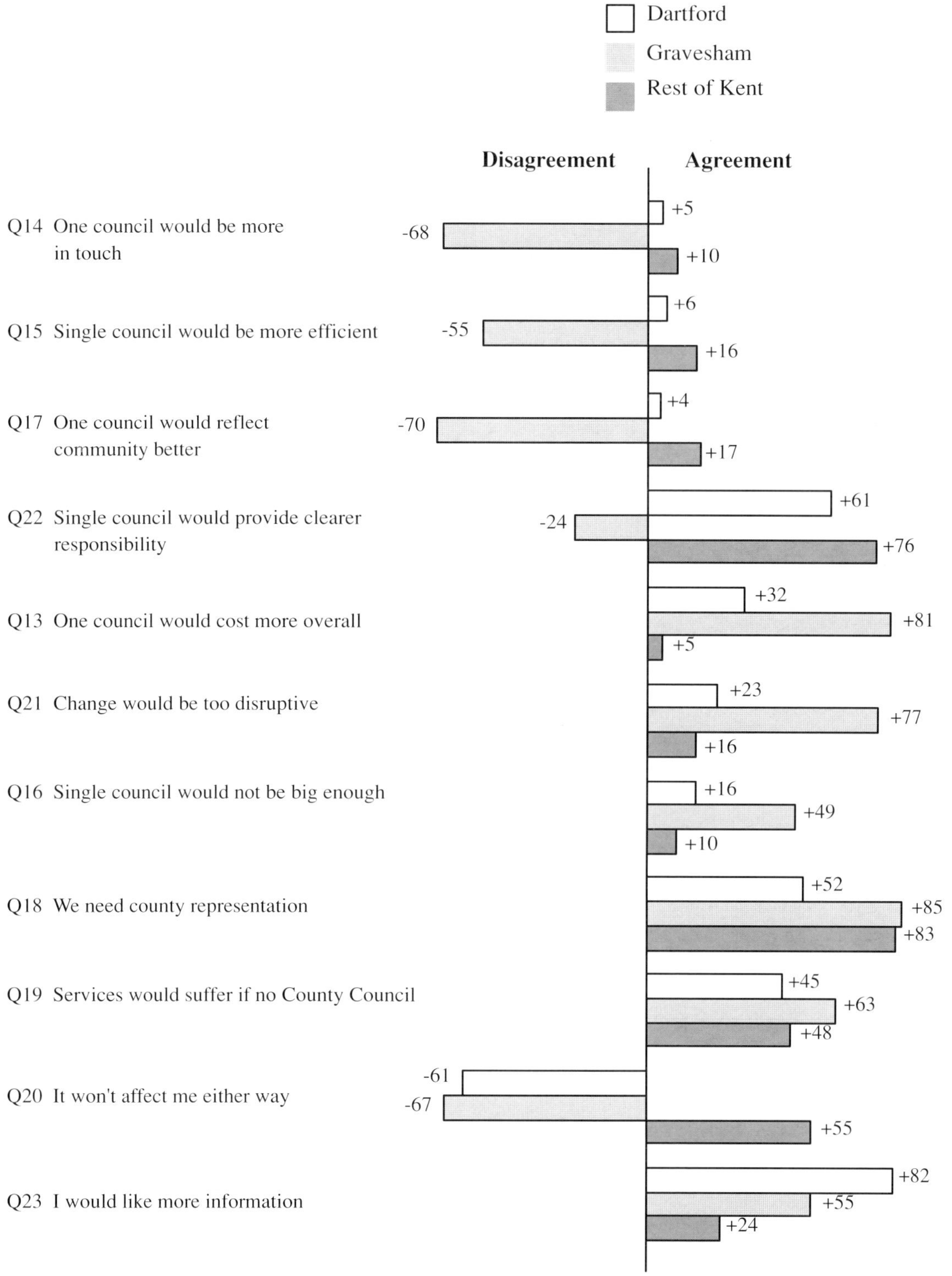

Attitudes to Change (Respondents in Gillingham, Rochester upon Medway and rest of Kent)

Q To what extent do you agree or disagree that...?
(Figures represent 'mean scores' with *strong agreement* given a value of +2 through to *strong disagreement* given -2)

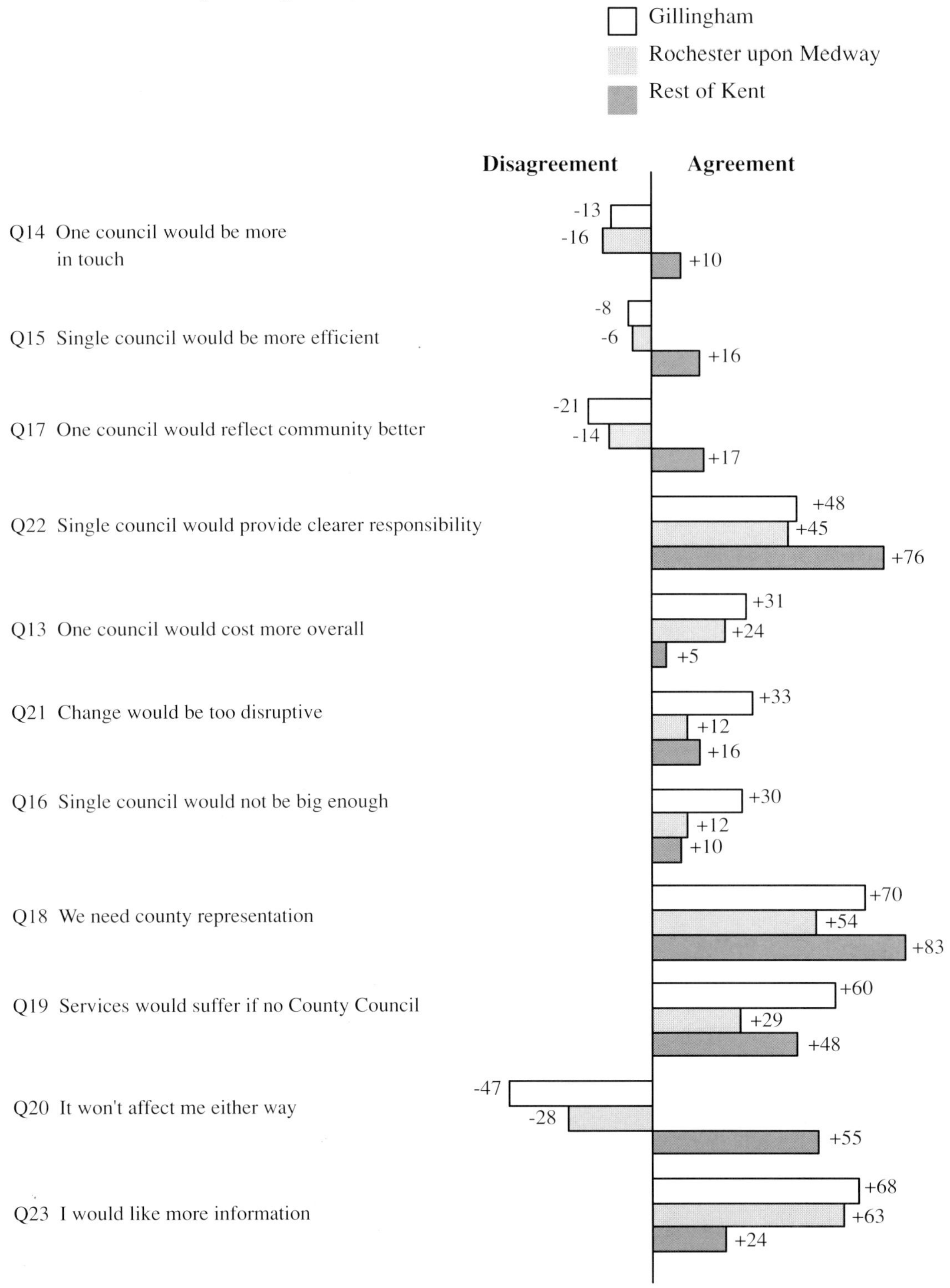

Attitudes to Change
(Respondents in Dartford)

Q To what extent do you agree or disagree that...?
(Figures represent 'mean scores' with *strong agreement* given a value of +2 through to *strong disagreement* given -2)

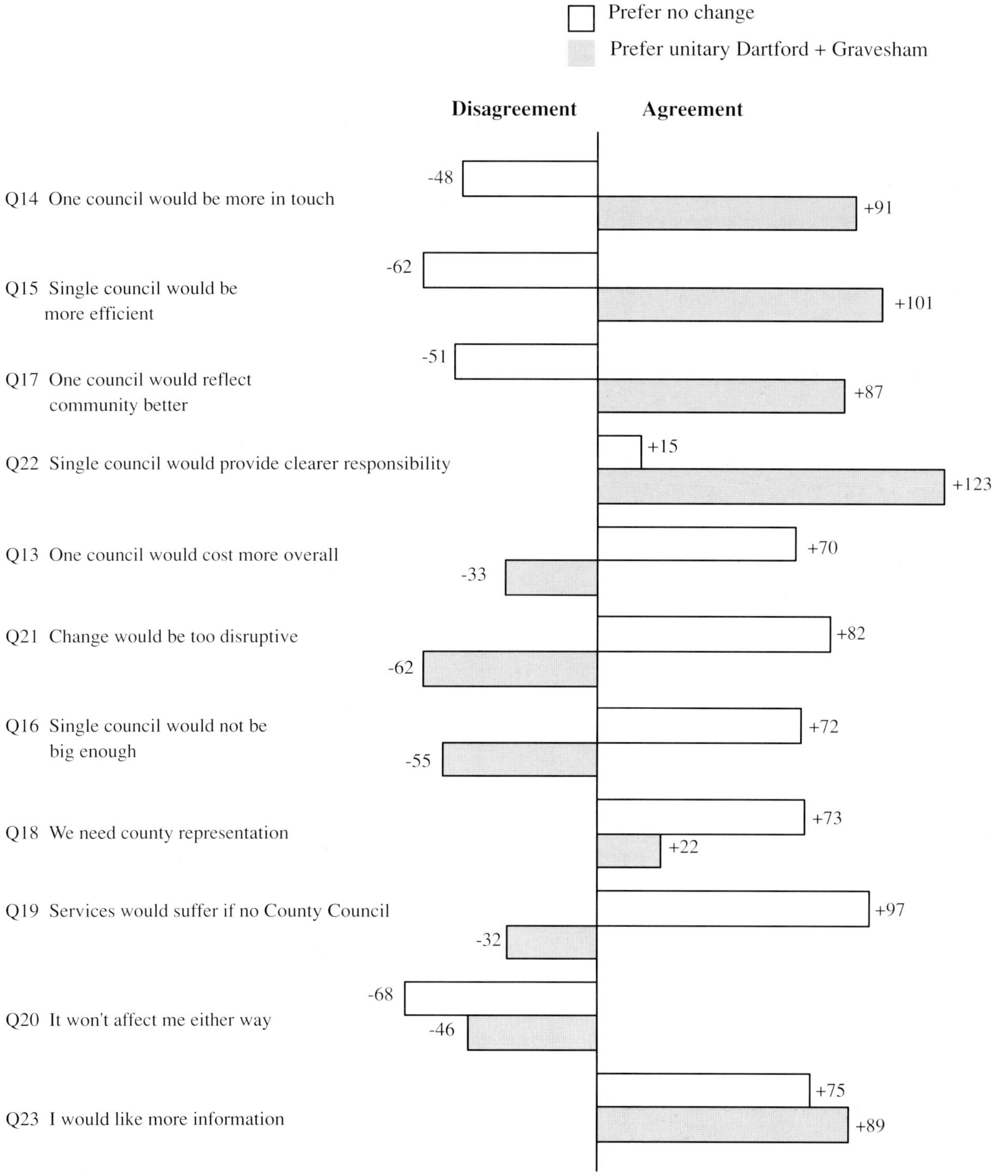

Attitudes to Change
(Respondents in Gillingham)

Q To what extent do you agree or disagree that...?
(Figures represent 'mean scores' with *strong agreement* given a value of +2 through to *strong disagreement* given -2)

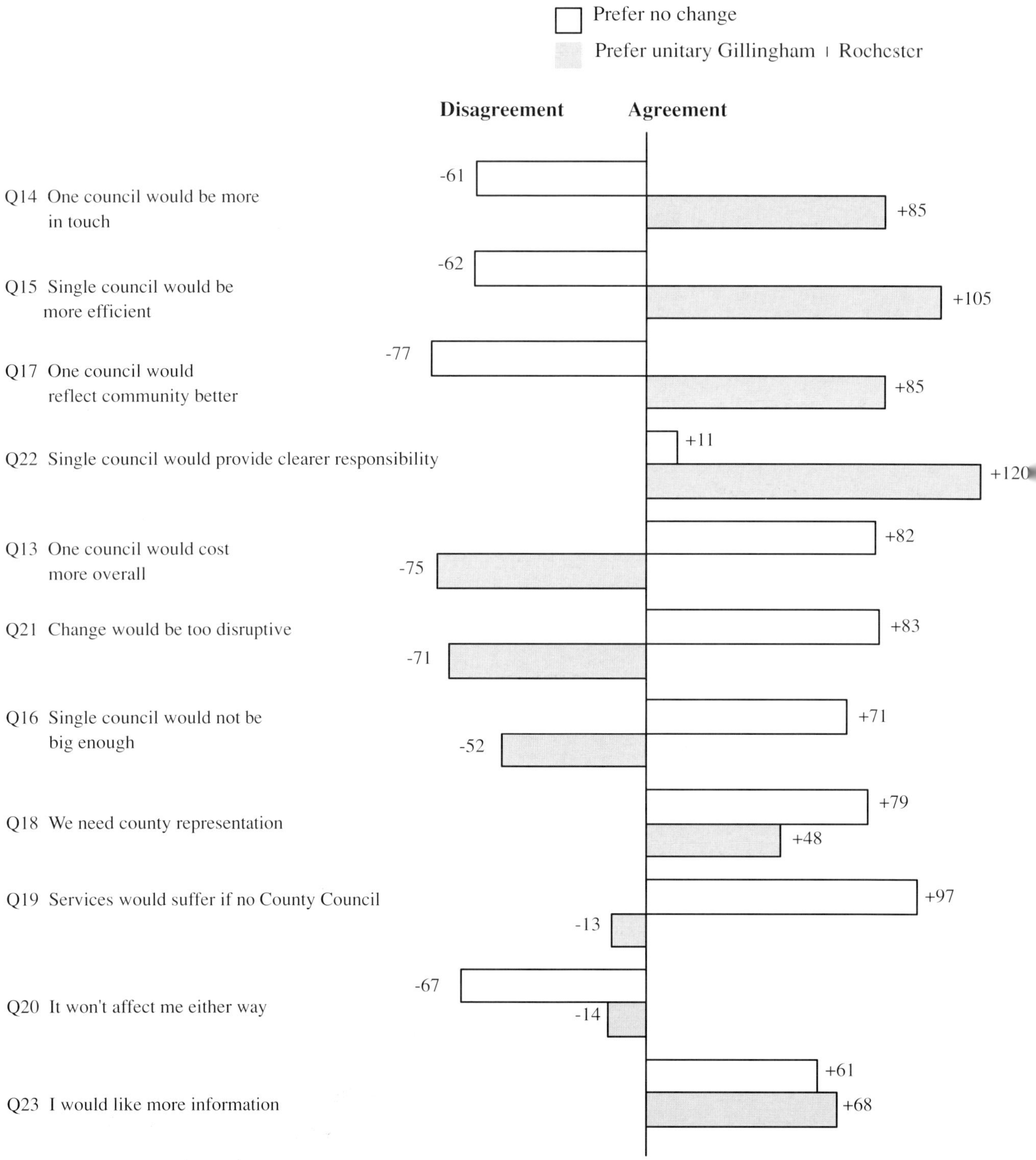

Attitudes to Change
(Respondents in Gravesham)

Q To what extent do you agree or disagree that...?
(Figures represent 'mean scores' with *strong agreement* given a value of +2 through to *strong disagreement* given -2)

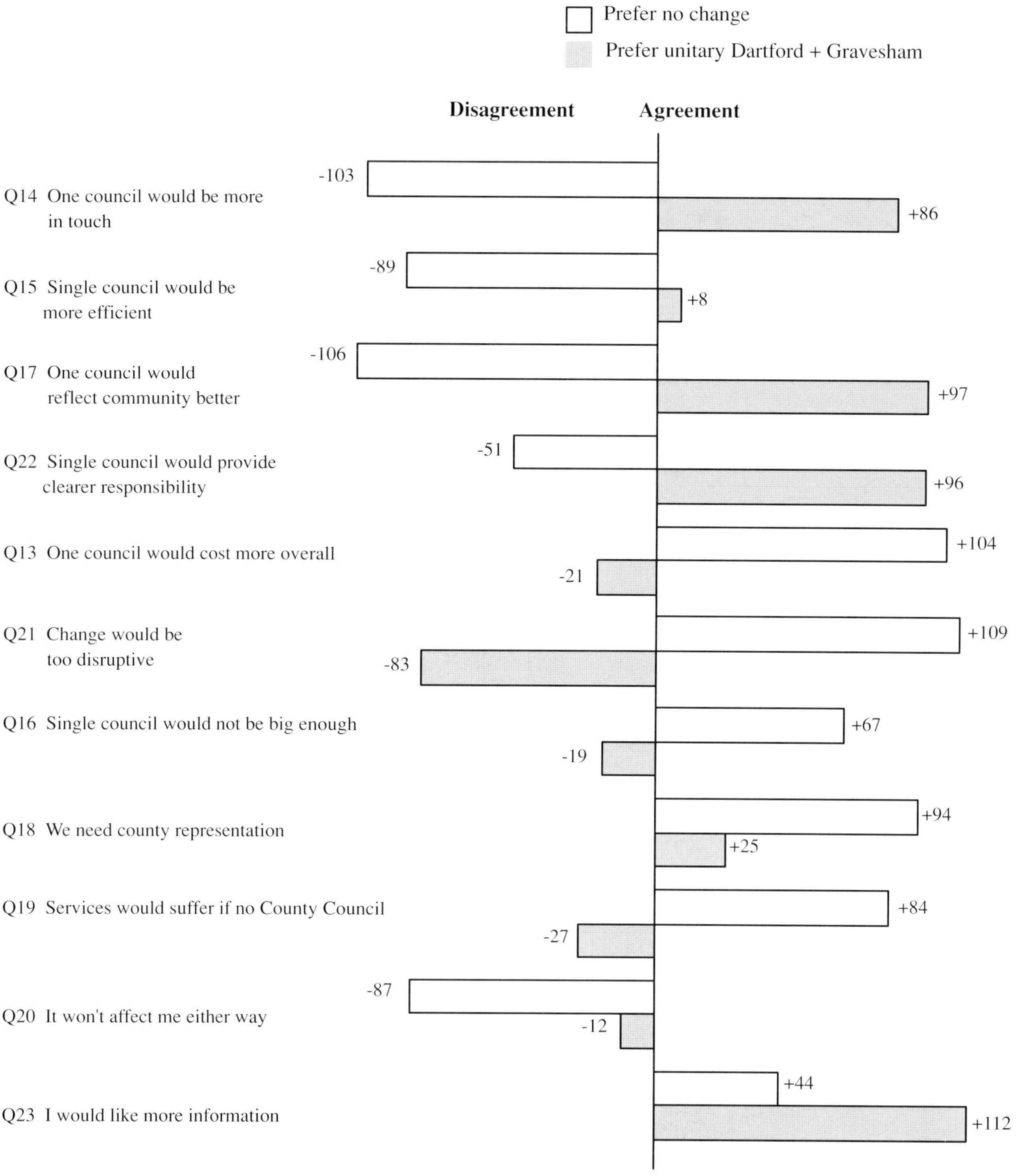

Attitudes to Change
(Respondents in Rochester upon Medway)

Q To what extent do you agree or disagree that...?
(Figures represent 'mean scores' with *strong agreement* given a value of +2 through to *strong disagreement* given -2)

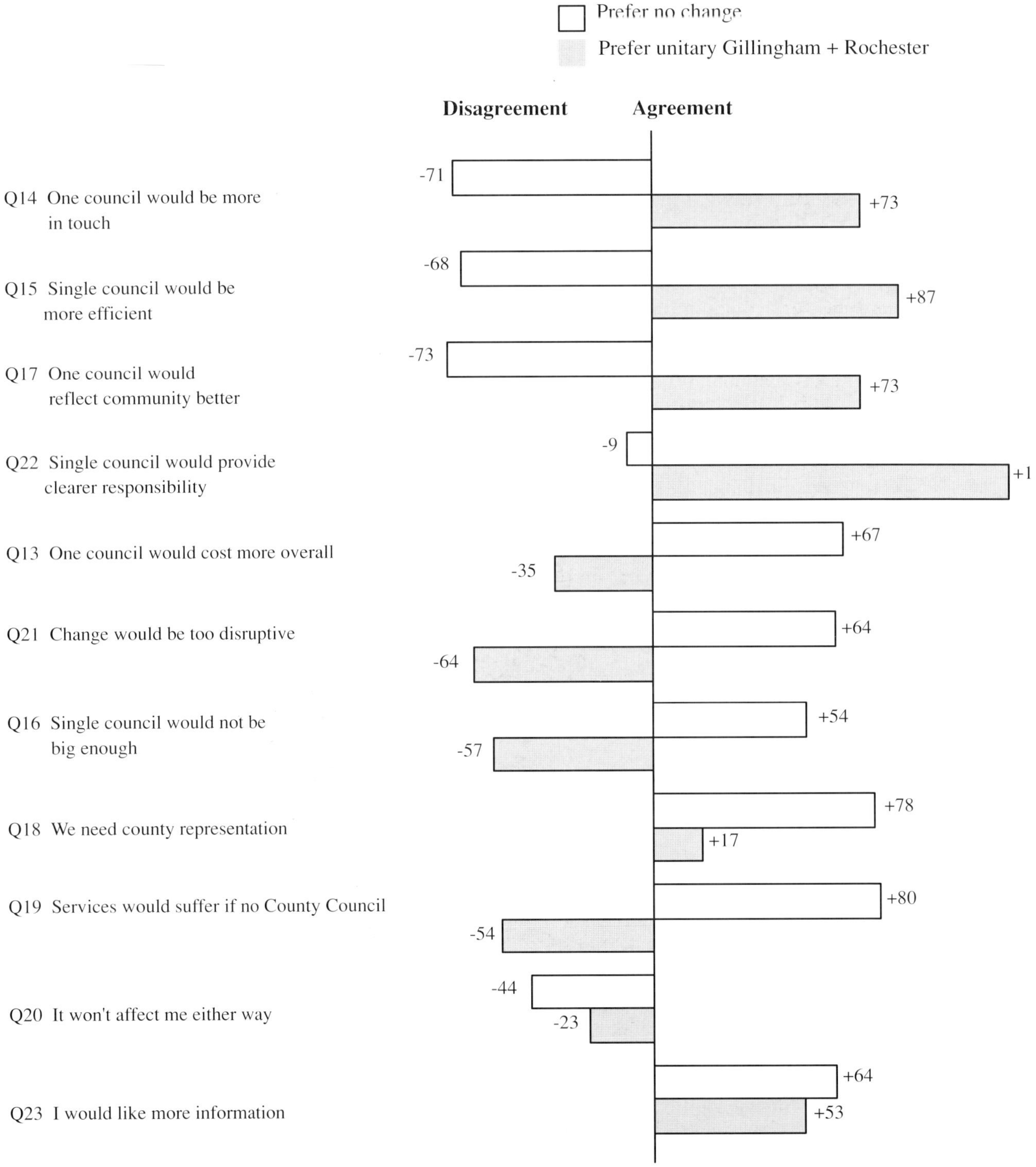

Attitudes to Change
(Respondents in the rest of Kent)

Q To what extent do you agree or disagree that...?
(Figures represent 'mean scores' with *strong agreement* given a value of +2 through to *strong disagreement* given -2)

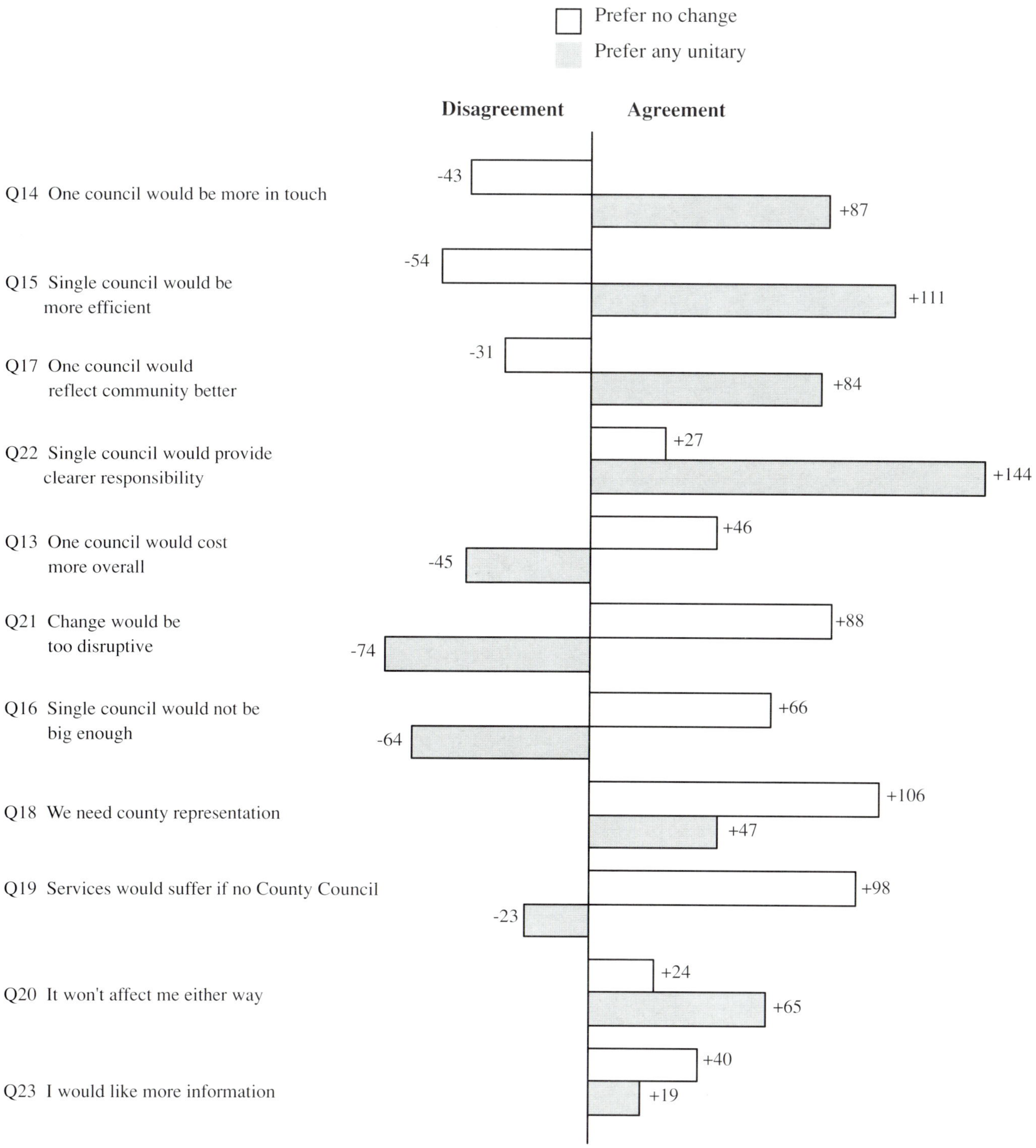

MORI/9101/06

KENT
REVIEW - REST OF COUNTY

Serial No ....

TOPLINE FINDINGS

Gender	%
Male	47
Female	53

Age	%
18-24	12
25-34	18
35-44	20
45-54	14
55-64	18
65-74	10
75+	8

WRITE IN AGE [|]

Work Status	%
Full-time (30 hrs/wk+)	45
Part-time (8-29 hrs/wk)	11
Not working (under 8 hrs)	2
Looking after home/children	13
Retired	19
Registered unemployed	5
Unemployed but not registered	*
Student	2
Other	1

Occupation of Chief Income Earner (CIE)
Position/rank/grade

....

Industry/type of company

....

Qualifications/degrees/apprenticeship

....

No of Staff Responsible for

....

PROBE FOR PENSION

	%
AB	20
C1	22
C2	24
D	19
E	15

* Less than 1/2%

Number in Household
Adults aged 18+ (inc. respondent)

1 2 3 4 5+

Children (17 or under)

0 1 2 3 4+

QA **Are you or other members of your household employed by a council?** IF YES: **Is this a Borough/District Council or a County Council?**
CODE FOR BOTH RESPONDENT AND OTHER HOUSEHOLD MEMBERS

	Respondent %	Other %
Yes:		
Borough/District	2	0
County	3	2
Don't know which	0	0
No	95	86
Don't know	1	11

Tenure	%
Owned outright	27
Buying on mortgage	45
Rented from Council	11
Rented from Housing Association	5
Rented from private landlord	8
Other	3

QB **Is this your main permanent home, or is it a second or holiday home?**

	%
Main/permanent	98
Second/holiday	2

Car in Household
CIRCLE NUMBER

0 1 2 3+

Showcard Version

A-K ....
A1-K ....

THIS FORM IS THE PROPERTY OF MARKET & OPINION RESEARCH INTERNATIONAL (MORI)
32 OLD QUEEN STREET, LONDON, SW1H 9HP

INTERVIEWER DECLARATION: I confirm that I have conducted this interview face-to-face with the above named person and that I have asked all the relevant questions fully and recorded the answers in conformance with the survey specification and the MRS Code of Conduct.

Interviewer Name .... Signature ....

Interviewer Number				/	

		Month		Date	
DATE OF INTERVIEW					

NB INTERVIEWER: ALL SHOWCARDS HAVE BEEN REVERSED. PLEASE BE CAREFUL TO CODE THE CORRECT RESPONSE.

Good morning/afternoon/evening. I'm from MORI, the market research and polling organisation. We are doing a survey about local issues, and I would like to ask you a few questions.

ASK ALL

Q1 **Firstly, how long have you lived in this area?** (WITHIN FIVE MILES)

	%
Less than 1 year	6
1-2 years	6
3-5 years	8
6-10 years	18
11-20 years	22
Over 20 years/all my life	41
Don't know/can't remember	*

Q2 SHOWCARD A (R) **From this card, how much would you say you know about local councils and the services they provide?**

	%
A great deal	3
A fair amount	32
Not very much	57
Nothing at all	8
Don't know	*

Q3 SHOWCARD B (R) **Which of the statements on this card comes closest to your own view of the Councils in this area?**

		%
A)	I'm not interested in what the Council does, or whether they do their job	2
B)	I'm not interested in what the Council does, as long as they do their job	14
C)	I like to know what the Council is doing, but I'm happy to let them get on with their job	59
D)	I would like to have more of a say in what the Council does and the services it provides	21
E)	I already work for, or am involved with the Council and the services it provides	3
	Don't know	1

Q4 **From what you know, how many councils provide the main services in this neighbourhood?** (INTERVIEWER - NOT INCLUDING PARISH COUNCILS)

	%
One	33
Two	35
Three+	5
Don't know	27

- 3 -

In fact there are two main councils that provide, or are responsible for, most services in this area:. . .district/borough/city and Kent County Council.

ROTATE ORDER OF Q5/6

☐ Q5 SHOWCARD C (R) **From this list, what services do you think are the responsibility of... district/borough/city council? Just read out the letter(s) that apply**

☐ Q6 SHOWCARD C AGAIN (R) **And which services on this list do you think are the responsibility of Kent County Council? Again, just read out the letters that apply.**

Q7 SHOWCARD D (R) **Which, if any, of these services do you or members of your family use?** INCLUDE ONLY LOCAL USE

		Q5 "Borough" %	Q6 County %	Q7 Use %
A	Bus Services	37	32	40
B	Car Parks	68	22	69
C	Council Housing	64	27	8
D	Council Tax Benefit/Housing benefit	54	28	19
E	Fire service	19	66	24
F	Food safety	28	40	16
G	Household waste sites/dumps	61	25	63
H	Libraries	33	55	62
I	Parks, playgrounds and open spaces	64	26	58
J	Planning service	51	40	16
K	Public conveniences	64	19	48
L	Recycling/bottle banks	61	18	53
M	Refuse collection	76	16	77
N	Road maintenance	34	66	40
O	Schools/education	23	66	39
P	Social services	22	62	14
Q	Street sweeping	75	15	37
R	Swimming pools/sports facilities	59	20	55
	Other	3	1	3*
	None of these	0	1	3
	Don't know	6	8	2

Q8 SHOWCARD E (R) **As you may know, there is currently a review being undertaken by the Local Government Commission on the future local government structure in the county. How much, if anything, would you say you know about this?**

	%
A great deal	2
A fair amount	4
Just a little	28
Heard of but know nothing about	22
Never heard of	44

PREFERENCES

HAND OVER MAP SHOWING AREAS UNDER REVIEW AND "CURRENT SERVICES" CARD
The Local Government Commission is considering options for the future structure of local government in parts of Kent. Could you please read through this card, (SHOW OPTIONS CARD) **which outlines the options.**

Q9 **Please tell me which of the options, if either, you would prefer for each of Dartford and Gravesham, Gillingham and Rochester upon Medway?**
CODE ONE ONLY FOR EACH DISTRICT

For Dartford and Gravesham	%
Option A (a single new all purpose council)	25
Option B (remain as now, separate councils with county services)	42
Some other option for Dartford	1
Some other option for Gravesham	0
Neither of these	*
Either of these/don't mind	8
Don't care	8
Don't know	17

For Gillingham and Rochester upon Medway	%
Option A (a single new all purpose council)	25
Option B (remain as now, separate councils with county services)	41
Some other option for Gillingham	1
Some other option for Rochester	0
Neither of these	*
Either of these/don't mind	8
Don't care	9
Don't know	16

ASK IF "OTHER" NAMED AT Q9 (CODE 3)
Q10 **What other option is that?**
PROBE FULLY - DO NOT PROMPT.

....

....

....

....

ASK ALL PREFERRING AN OPTION (1, 2 OR 3 AT Q9). OTHERS GO TO Q13
Q11 SHOWCARD F (R) **You say that the option you would prefer is . . . . .** (INSERT OPTION PREFERRED). **How strongly would you say you feel about this?**

	%
Very strongly	13
Fairly strongly	55
Not very strongly	27
Not at all strongly	3
Don't know	3

Q12 **What do you think would be the main advantages of . . .**(OPTION PREFERRED)
PROBE FULLY FOR DETAILS

....

....

....

....

Nothing..
Don't know/can't think of anything..................................

ATTITUDES TO PROPOSALS

SHOWCARD G (R) **Imagine that there was one council in any or all of Dartford with Gravesham or Rochester with Gillingham providing <u>all</u> services. I am going to read out some statements that people have made about this proposal. To what extent do you agree or disagree that . . .?** READ OUT, ROTATE ORDER OF ASKING Q13-22. TICK START

	READ OUT:	Strongly agree %	Tend to agree %	Neither/ Nor %	Tend to disagree %	Strongly disagree %	Don't know %
☐ Q13	**It would cost more overall**	8	28	14	29	5	16
Q14	**It would be more in touch with local people's needs**	11	32	12	23	12	10
Q15	**The single Council would be more efficient than the current system of two Councils**	8	34	13	22	8	14
☐ Q16	**The single council would not be big enough to manage services such as Education and Social Services effectively**	7	31	13	27	5	17
Q17	**It would better reflect the sense of community in those areas**	8	35	16	22	7	13
Q18	**We need a County Council to represent us nationally**	23	44	12	11	2	9
☐ Q19	**Services would suffer if the County Council no longer provides services in those areas**	14	41	9	21	3	12
Q20	**It won't affect me whether there is a single Council in those areas or not**	20	38	8	18	6	10
Q21	**The change to a single Council for those areas would be too disruptive**	11	26	18	26	5	14
☐ Q22	**With a single Council it would be clearer who is responsible for local services**	20	46	8	14	2	11
ASK LAST Q23	**I would like to have more information on the proposals before making up my mind**	18	31	12	19	13	7

Q24 **On balance, which would you say is more in touch with local people and issues, ...** (ROTATE ORDER OF "DISTRICT" AND COUNTY) (INSERT NAME OF "DISTRICT COUNCIL)**..district/borough/city council, or Kent County Council, or would you say that they are both about the same?**

	%
District/borough/city council	56
Kent County Council	3
Both about the same	30
Don't know	11

REFER BACK TO Q8. ASK ALL WHO HAVE HEARD OF REVIEW AT Q8 (IE CODES 1/2/3/4). OTHERS TO Q28

Q25 SHOWCARD H **Earlier in the interview, you said that you had heard of the Review of local government structure. From which, if any, of the sources shown on this card have you recently heard about the Review?** INTERVIEWER NOTE: "RECENTLY" = IN PAST 3 MONTHS
Base: All heard of Review (156)

		%
A	Leaflet from County Council delivered to your door	13
B	Leaflet from County Council in library/ offices, etc	2
C	Advertisement from County Council in local newspaper	8
D	Advertisement from County Council on local radio/TV	1
E	Leaflet from Borough Council delivered to your door	4
F	Leaflet from Borough Council in library/ offices, etc	1
G	Borough Council newspaper	3
H	County Council newspaper	2
I	Advertisement from Borough Council in local newspaper	3
J	Advertisement from Borough Council on local radio/TV	3
K	Advertisement by the Commission on local radio	0
L	Local Government Commission advertisement in local newspaper	2
M	Local newspaper	43
N	National newspaper	11
O	TV	28
P	Local radio	17
Q	National radio	5
R	Friends/neighbours/family	8
S	Conversation with Borough Councillor	2
T	Conversation with County Councillor	1
U	Conversation with Borough Council staff	2
V	Conversation with County Council staff	1
W	Parish/community council	1
X	Residents' Association	2
	Other	7
	None of these	5
	Don't know	7

ASK ALL NAMING A SOURCE AT Q25. OTHERS GO TO Q28

Q26 **Would you say that the information you have received has influenced your opinion, or not?**

	%
Yes	22
No	77
Don't know	1

Q27 **What information in particular has influenced your opinion?**

....

....

....

....

ASK ALL

Q28 SHOWCARD I (R) **Assuming you receive the same level of services, how important is it to you, if at all, what the final decision is on the future local government structure in the areas under review?**

	%
Very important	20
Fairly important	32
Not very important	30
Not at all important	14
Don't know	3

ACTIVISM

Q29 SHOWCARD J **Which of the things on this list, if any, have you done in the last three years? Just read out the letter(s) that apply.**

		%
A	Voted in Local Council elections	77
B	Spoken or written to a local Councillor	27
C	Responded to the earlier Review of local government	4
D	Been to a meeting of a local committee or organisation (WRITE IN NAME OF ORGANISATION)	14
E	Spoken on a radio phone-in about a local issue	1
F	Written to a local newspaper about a local issue	4
G	Been to a meeting of a local branch of a political party	4
H	Written to your MP about a local issue	10
I	Been to a Council Committee meeting	5
J	Been to a Council meeting	3
K	Attended a public meeting run by the Council	7
	None of these	17
	Don't know/refused	*

Q30 SHOWCARD K **Which, if any, of these apply to you? Just read out the letter(s) that apply.**

		%
I am a member of a:		
A	Residents' Association	11
B	Community Association	1
C	Tenants' Association	2
D	Neighbourhood Watch	27
E	PTA/school governors	6
I do unpaid work for:		
F	A school	8
G	Citizens Advice Bureau	1
H	Volunteer Bureau	3
I	Scouts/Guides/Cubs/Brownies	5
J	Church group	7
	Other	5
	None of these	53
	Don't know	0

THANK RESPONDENT. GO TO DEMOGRAPHICS.

.... Length of interview [|] minutes

MORI/9101/07

Kent
REVIEW - DARTFORD

Serial No ....
OUO (7-10)

TOPLINE FINDINGS

Gender %

	%
Male	49
Female	51

Age

	%
18-24	8
25-34	20
35-44	20
45-54	20
55-64	16
65-74	12
75+	4

WRITE IN AGE

Work Status

	%
Full-time (30 hrs/wk+)	45
Part-time (8-29 hrs/wk)	12
Not working (under 8 hrs)	1
Looking after home/children	12
Retired	23
Registered unemployed	4
Unemployed but not registered	*
Student	2
Other	2

Occupation of Chief Income Earner (CIE)

Position/rank/grade

....

Industry/type of company

....

Qualifications/degrees/apprenticeship

....

No of Staff Responsible for

....

PROBE FOR PENSION

	%
AB	18
C1	31
C2	26
D	16
E	28

Number in Household
Adults aged 18+ (inc. respondent)

1 2 3 4 5+

Children (17 or under)

0 1 2 3 4+

QA **Are you or other members of your household employed by a council?** IF YES: **Is this a Borough/District Council or a County Council?** CODE FOR BOTH RESPONDENT AND OTHER HOUSEHOLD MEMBERS

	Respondent %	Other %
Yes:		
Borough/District	4	3
County	3	2
Don't know which	0	*
No	93	91
Don't know	*	4

Tenure

	%
Owned outright	23
Buying on mortgage	54
Rented from Council	13
Rented from Housing Association	5
Rented from private landlord	5
Other	1

QB **Is this your main permanent home, or is it a second or holiday home?**

	%
Main/permanent	100
Second/holiday	*

Car in Household
CIRCLE NUMBER

0 1 2 3+

Showcard Version

A-K ....
A1-K ....

INTERVIEWER DECLARATION: I confirm that I have conducted this interview face-to-face with the above named person and that I have asked all the relevant questions fully and recorded the answers in conformance with the survey specification and the MRS Code of Conduct.

Interviewer Name .... Signature ....

Interviewer Number					/	

	Month		Date	
DATE OF INTERVIEW				

NB INTERVIEWER: ALL SHOWCARDS HAVE BEEN REVERSED. PLEASE BE CAREFUL TO CODE THE CORRECT RESPONSE.

Good morning/afternoon/evening. I'm from MORI, the market research and polling organisation. We are doing a survey about local issues, and I would like to ask you a few questions.

ASK ALL

Q1 **Firstly, how long have you lived in this area?** (WITHIN FIVE MILES)

	%
Less than 1 year	3
1-2 years	9
3-5 years	9
6-10 years	12
11-20 years	20
Over 20 years/all my life	48
Don't know/can't remember	0

Q2 SHOWCARD A (R) **From this card, how much would you say you know about local councils and the services they provide?**

	%
A great deal	3
A fair amount	34
Not very much	58
Nothing at all	5
Don't know	0

Q3 SHOWCARD B (R) **Which of the statements on this card comes closest to your own view of the Councils in this area?**

		%
A)	I'm not interested in what the Council does, or whether they do their job	1
B)	I'm not interested in what the Council does, as long as they do their job	11
C)	I like to know what the Council is doing, but I'm happy to let them get on with their job	60
D)	I would like to have more of a say in what the Council does and the services it provides	27
E)	I already work for, or am involved with the Council and the services it provides	2
	Don't know	*

Q4 **From what you know, how many councils provide the main services in this neighbourhood?** (INTERVIEWER - NOT INCLUDING PARISH COUNCILS)

	%
One	38
Two	37
Three+	3
Don't know	21

In fact there are two main councils that provide, or are responsible for most services in this area: Dartford Borough and Kent County Council.

ROTATE ORDER OF Q5/6

☐ Q5 SHOWCARD C (R) **From this list, what services do you think are the responsibility of Dartford Borough Council? Just read out the letter(s) that apply**

☐ Q6 SHOWCARD C AGAIN (R) **And which services on this list do you think are the responsibility of Kent County Council? Again, just read out the letters that apply.**

Q7 SHOWCARD D (R) **Which, if any, of these services do you or members of your family use?** INCLUDE ONLY LOCAL USE

		Q5 "Borough" %	Q6 County %	Q7 Use %
A	Bus Services	24	53	29
B	Car Parks	69	17	66
C	Council Housing	75	14	8
D	Council Tax Benefit/Housing benefit	70	20	19
E	Fire service	15	76	25
F	Food safety	34	38	10
G	Household waste sites/dumps	63	22	52
H	Libraries	38	56	58
I	Parks, playgrounds and open spaces	70	20	51
J	Planning service	54	36	11
K	Public conveniences	72	13	34
L	Recycling/bottle banks	64	19	45
M	Refuse collection	86	6	79
N	Road maintenance	38	62	30
O	Schools/education	19	76	33
P	Social services	31	53	8
Q	Street sweeping	81	8	37
R	Swimming pools/sports facilities	70	18	52
	Other	1	1	1
	None of these	0	*	1
	Don't know	2	5	3

Q8 SHOWCARD E (R) **As you may know, there is currently a review being undertaken by the Local Government Commission on the future local government structure in the county. How much, if anything, would you say you know about this?**

	%
A great deal	2
A fair amount	7
Just a little	27
Heard of but know nothing about	23
Never heard of	40

PREFERENCES

HAND OVER MAP SHOWING AREAS UNDER REVIEW AND "CURRENT SERVICES" CARD
The Local Government Commission is considering options for the future structure of local government in parts of Kent. Could you please read through this card, (SHOW OPTIONS CARD) **which outlines the options.**

Q9 **Please tell me which of the options, if either, you would prefer for each of Dartford and Gravesham, Gillingham and Rochester upon Medway?**
CODE ONE ONLY FOR EACH PAIR OF DISTRICT

	%
For Dartford and Gravesham	
Option A (a single new all purpose council)	35
Option B (remain as now, separate councils with county services)	56
Some other option for Dartford	5
Some other option for Gravesham	0
Neither of these	*
Either of these/don't mind	*
Don't care	1
Don't know	4
For Gillingham and Rochester upon Medway	%
Option A (single all purpose council)	13
Option B (remain as now, separate councils with county services)	24
Some other option for Gillingham	0
Some other option for Rochester	0
Neither of these	*
Either of these/don't mind	25
Don't care	29
Don't know	8

ASK IF "OTHER" NAMED FOR DARTFORD AT Q9 (CODE 3)
Q10 **What other option for Dartford is that?**
PROBE FULLY - DO NOT PROMPT.

....

....

....

....

ASK ALL PREFERRING AN OPTION (1, 2 OR 3 AT Q9). OTHERS GO TO Q13
Q11 SHOWCARD F (R) **You say that the option you would prefer for Dartford is . . . . .** (INSERT OPTION PREFERRED). **How strongly would you say you feel about this?**

	%
Very strongly	32
Fairly strongly	43
Not very strongly	21
Not at all strongly	4
Don't know	1

Q12 **What do you think would be the main advantages of . . .**(OPTION PREFERRED)
PROBE FULLY FOR DETAILS

....

....

....

....

Nothing..
Don't know/can't think of anything................................

ATTITUDES TO PROPOSALS

SHOWCARD G (R) **Imagine that there was one council in Dartford and Gravesham providing all services. I am going to read out some statements that people have made about this proposal. To what extent do you agree or disagree that . . . .?** READ OUT, ROTATE ORDER OF ASKING Q13-22. TICK START

READ OUT:	Strongly agree %	Tend to agree %	Neither/ Nor %	Tend to disagree %	Strongly disagree %	Don't know %
☐ Q13 **It would cost more overall**	13	39	13	26	4	5
Q14 **It would be more in touch with local people's needs**	11	39	7	30	12	1
Q15 **The single Council would be more efficient than the current system of two Councils**	11	36	13	26	12	3
☐ Q16 **The single council would not be big enough to manage services such as Education and Social Services effectively**	14	37	8	31	8	1
Q17 **It would better reflect the sense of community in Dartford and Gravesham**	10	36	13	30	11	1
Q18 **We need a County Council to represent us nationally**	13	48	20	14	4	1
☐ Q19 **Services would suffer if the County Council no longer provides services in Dartford and Gravesham**	18	42	9	23	6	2
Q20 **It won't affect me whether there is a single Council in Dartford and Gravesham or not**	1	24	9	39	23	3
Q21 **The change to a single Council for Dartford and Gravesham would be too disruptive**	16	35	12	27	8	2
☐ Q22 **With a single Council it would be clearer who is responsible for local services**	20	50	5	18	6	*
ASK LAST						
Q23 **I would like to have more information on the proposals before making up my mind**	32	43	6	10	8	1

Q24 **On balance, which would you say is more in touch with local people and issues, ...** (ROTATE ORDER OF "DISTRICT" AND COUNTY)
Dartford Borough Council, or
Kent County Council, or would you say that they are both about the same?

	%
Dartford Borough Council	57
Kent County Council	5
Both about the same	35
Don't know	2

REFER BACK TO Q8. ASK ALL WHO HAVE HEARD OF REVIEW AT Q8 (IE CODES 1/2/3/4). OTHERS TO Q28

Q25 SHOWCARD H **Earlier in the interview, you said that you had heard of the Review of local government structure. From which, if any, of the sources shown on this card have you recently heard about the Review?** INTERVIEWER NOTE: "RECENTLY" = IN PAST 3 MONTHS

		%
A	Leaflet from County Council delivered to your door	14
B	Leaflet from County Council in library/ offices, etc	2
C	Advertisement from County Council in local newspaper	9
D	Advertisement from County Council on local radio/TV	2
E	Leaflet from Borough Council delivered to your door	10
F	Leaflet from Borough Council in library/ offices, etc	3
G	Borough Council newspaper	7
H	County Council newspaper	2
I	Advertisement from Borough Council in local newspaper	6
J	Advertisement from Borough Council on local radio/TV	1
K	Advertisement by the Commission on local radio	0
L	Local Government Commission advertisement in local newspaper	2
M	Local newspaper	69
N	National newspaper	5
O	TV	16
P	Local radio	12
Q	National radio	4
R	Friends/neighbours/family	9
S	Conversation with Borough Councillor	4
T	Conversation with County Councillor	1
U	Conversation with Borough Council staff	4
V	Conversation with County Council staff	1
W	Parish/community council	0
X	Residents' Association	1
	Other	6
	None of these	2
	Don't know	1

ASK ALL NAMING A SOURCE AT Q25. OTHERS GO TO Q28

Q26 **Would you say that the information you have received has influenced your opinion, or not?**

	%
Yes	21
No	79
Don't know	1

Q27 **What information in particular has influenced your opinion?**

....

....

....

....

ASK ALL

Q28 SHOWCARD I (R) **Assuming you receive the same level of services, how important is it to you, if at all, what the final decision is on the future local government structure in Dartford?**

	%
Very important	34
Fairly important	39
Not very important	20
Not at all important	7
Don't know	1

ACTIVISM

Q29 SHOWCARD J **Which of the things on this list, if any, have you done in the last three years? Just read out the letter(s) that apply.**

		%
A	Voted in Local Council elections	77
B	Spoken or written to a local Councillor	27
C	Responded to the earlier Review of local government	7
D	Been to a meeting of a local committee or organisation (WRITE IN NAME OF ORGANISATION)	8
E	Spoken on a radio phone-in about a local issue	2
F	Written to a local newspaper about a local issue	5
G	Been to a meeting of a local branch of a political party	4
H	Written to your MP about a local issue	12
I	Been to a Council Committee meeting	4
J	Been to a Council meeting	4
K	Attended a public meeting run by the Council	8
	None of these	18
	Don't know/refused	0

Q30 SHOWCARD K **Which, if any, of these apply to you? Just read out the letter(s) that apply.**

		%
I am a member of a:		
A	Residents' Association	13
B	Community Association	4
C	Tenants' Association	4
D	Neighbourhood Watch	17
E	PTA/school governors	5
I do unpaid work for:		
F	A school	6
G	Citizens Advice Bureau	0
H	Volunteer Bureau	4
I	Scouts/Guides/Cubs/Brownies	3
J	Church group	6
	Other	7
	None of these	54
	Don't know	1

THANK RESPONDENT. GO TO DEMOGRAPHICS.

- 17 -

MORI/9101/07

Kent
REVIEW - GRAVESHAM

Serial No ....
OUO (7-10)

TOPLINE FINDINGS

Gender %
- Male ... 48
- Female ... 52

Age %
- 18-24 ... 14
- 25-34 ... 20
- 35-44 ... 16
- 45-54 ... 19
- 55-64 ... 12
- 65-74 ... 14
- 75+ ... 7

WRITE IN AGE ☐☐

Work Status %
- Full-time (30 hrs/wk+) ... 47
- Part-time (8-29 hrs/wk) ... 6
- Not working (under 8 hrs) ... 1
- Looking after home/children ... 17
- Retired ... 21
- Registered unemployed ... 4
- Unemployed but not registered ... 2
- Student ... 2
- Other ... 1

Occupation of Chief Income Earner (CIE)

Position/rank/grade

....

Industry/type of company

....

Qualifications/degrees/apprenticeship

....

No of Staff Responsible for

....

PROBE FOR PENSION

	%
AB	9
C1	29
C2	27
D	17
E	18

Number in Household
Adults aged 18+ (inc. respondent)

1 2 3 4 5+

Children (17 or under)

0 1 2 3 4+

QA **Are you or other members of your household employed by a council?** IF YES: **Is this a Borough/District Council or a County Council?**
CODE FOR BOTH RESPONDENT AND OTHER HOUSEHOLD MEMBERS

	Respondent %	Other %
Yes:		
Borough/District	2	2
County	3	2
Don't know which	1	0
No	94	81
Don't know	1	16

Tenure %
- Owned outright ... 24
- Buying on mortgage ... 46
- Rented from Council ... 22
- Rented from Housing Association ... 2
- Rented from private landlord ... 6
- Other ... 0

QB **Is this your main permanent home, or is it a second or holiday home?**

	%
Main/permanent	100
Second/holiday	0

Car in Household
CIRCLE NUMBER

0 1 2 3+

Showcard Version

A-K ....
A1-K ....

THIS FORM IS THE PROPERTY OF MARKET & OPINION RESEARCH INTERNATIONAL (MORI)
32 OLD QUEEN STREET, LONDON, SW1H 9HP

INTERVIEWER DECLARATION: I confirm that I have conducted this interview face-to-face with the above named person and that I have asked all the relevant questions fully and recorded the answers in conformance with the survey specification and the MRS Code of Conduct.

Interviewer Name .... Signature ....

Interviewer Number					/	

	Month		Date	
DATE OF INTERVIEW				

NB INTERVIEWER: ALL SHOWCARDS HAVE BEEN REVERSED. PLEASE BE CAREFUL TO CODE THE CORRECT RESPONSE.

Good morning/afternoon/evening. I'm from MORI, the market research and polling organisation. We are doing a survey about local issues, and I would like to ask you a few questions.

ASK ALL

Q1 **Firstly, how long have you lived in this area?** (WITHIN FIVE MILES)

	%
Less than 1 year	3
1-2 years	2
3-5 years	8
6-10 years	12
11-20 years	24
Over 20 years/all my life	50
Don't know/can't remember	0

Q2 SHOWCARD A (R) **From this card, how much would you say you know about local councils and the services they provide?**

	%
A great deal	2
A fair amount	40
Not very much	48
Nothing at all	9
Don't know	*

Q3 SHOWCARD B (R) **Which of the statements on this card comes closest to your own view of the Councils in this area?**

		%
A)	I'm not interested in what the Council does, or whether they do their job	2
B)	I'm not interested in what the Council does, as long as they do their job	17
C)	I like to know what the Council is doing, but I'm happy to let them get on with their job	59
D)	I would like to have more of a say in what the Council does and the services it provides	20
E)	I already work for, or am involved with the Council and the services it provides	1
	Don't know	2

Q4 **From what you know, how many councils provide the main services in this neighbourhood?** (INTERVIEWER - NOT INCLUDING PARISH COUNCILS)

	%
One	51
Two	21
Three+	3
Don't know	25

In fact there are two main councils that provide, or are responsible for most services in this area: Gravesham Borough and Kent County Council.

ROTATE ORDER OF Q5/6

☐ Q5 SHOWCARD C (R) **From this list, what services do you think are the responsibility of Gravesham Borough Council? Just read out the letter(s) that apply**

☐ Q6 SHOWCARD C AGAIN (R) **And which services on this list do you think are the responsibility of Kent County Council? Again, just read out the letters that apply.**

Q7 SHOWCARD D (R) **Which, if any, of these services do you or members of your family use?** INCLUDE ONLY LOCAL USE

		Q5 "Borough" %	Q6 County %	Q7 Use %
A	Bus Services	32	19	33
B	Car Parks	59	10	74
C	Council Housing	72	11	21
D	Council Tax Benefit/Housing benefit	49	17	16
E	Fire service	18	57	15
F	Food safety	26	20	6
G	Household waste sites/dumps	59	9	56
H	Libraries	38	36	53
I	Parks, playgrounds and open spaces	59	14	54
J	Planning service	37	21	7
K	Public conveniences	65	7	48
L	Recycling/bottle banks	54	11	45
M	Refuse collection	71	7	70
N	Road maintenance	34	33	21
O	Schools/education	21	53	32
P	Social services	27	39	9
Q	Street sweeping	72	7	37
R	Swimming pools/sports facilities	45	22	50
	Other	1	1	1
	None of these	*	1	1
	Don't know	15	20	1

Q8 SHOWCARD E (R) **As you may know, there is currently a review being undertaken by the Local Government Commission on the future local government structure in the county. How much, if anything, would you say you know about this?**

	%
A great deal	1
A fair amount	23
Just a little	38
Heard of but know nothing about	16
Never heard of	22

PREFERENCES

HAND OVER MAP SHOWING AREAS UNDER REVIEW AND "CURRENT SERVICES" CARD
The Local Government Commission is considering options for the future structure of local government in parts of Kent. Could you please read through this card, (SHOW OPTIONS CARD) **which outlines the options.**

Q9 **Please tell me which of the options, if either, you would prefer for each of Dartford and Gravesham, Gillingham and Rochester upon Medway?**
CODE ONE ONLY FOR EACH PAIR OF DISTRICT

For Dartford and Gravesham	%
Option A (a single new all purpose council)	13
Option B (remain as now, separate councils with county services)	71
Some other option for Dartford	0
Some other option for Gravesham	*
Neither of these	*
Either of these/don't mind	3
Don't care	4
Don't know	9

For Gillingham and Rochester upon Medway	%
Option A (single all purpose council)	7
Option B (remain as now, separate councils with county services)	35
Some other option for Gillingham	0
Some other option for Rochester	0
Neither of these	3
Either of these/don't mind	21
Don't care	6
Don't know	29

ASK IF "OTHER" NAMED FOR GRAVESHAM AT Q9 (CODE 3)
Q10 **What other option for Gravesham is that?**
PROBE FULLY - DO NOT PROMPT.

....

....

....

....

ASK ALL PREFERRING AN OPTION (1, 2 OR 3 AT Q9). OTHERS GO TO Q13
Q11 SHOWCARD F (R) **You say that the option you would prefer for Gravesham is . . .** (INSERT OPTION PREFERRED). **How strongly would you say you feel about this?**

	%
Very strongly	33
Fairly strongly	44
Not very strongly	19
Not at all strongly	3
Don't know	2

Q12 **What do you think would be the main advantages of . . .**(OPTION PREFERRED)
PROBE FULLY FOR DETAILS

....

....

....

....

Nothing...
Don't know/can't think of anything..................................

ATTITUDES TO PROPOSALS

SHOWCARD G (R) **Imagine that there was one council in Dartafod and Gravesham providing all services. I am going to read out some statements that people have made about this proposal. To what extent do you agree or disagree that . . . .?** READ OUT, ROTATE ORDER OF ASKING Q13-22. TICK START

READ OUT:	Strongly agree %	Tend to agree %	Neither/ Nor %	Tend to disagree %	Strongly disagree %	Don't know %
☐ Q13 **It would cost more overall**	19	28	6	10	2	35
Q14 **It would be more in touch with local people's needs**	5	14	5	28	23	27
Q15 **The single Council would be more efficient than the current system of two Councils**	5	14	7	18	21	34
☐ Q16 **The single council would not be big enough to manage services such as Education and Social Services effectively**	18	20	6	15	5	36
Q17 **It would better reflect the sense of community in Dartford and Gravesham**	4	14	6	26	25	25
Q18 **We need a County Council to represent us nationally**	23	35	3	8	5	26
☐ Q19 **Services would suffer if the County Council no longer provides services in Dartford and Gravesham**	19	28	8	10	6	29
Q20 **It won't affect me whether there is a single Council in Dartford and Gravesham or not**	4	18	3	24	27	24
Q21 **The change to a single Council for Dartford and Gravesham would be too disruptive**	22	36	5	8	6	23
☐ Q22 **With a single Council it would be clearer who is responsible for local services**	8	22	4	21	17	28
ASK LAST						
Q23 **I would like to have more information on the proposals before making up my mind**	20	29	12	6	10	24

Q24 **On balance, which would you say is more in touch with local people and issues, ...** (ROTATE ORDER OF "DISTRICT" AND COUNTY)
Gravesham Borough Council, or
Kent County Council, or would you say that they are both about the same?

	%
Gravesham Borough Council	50
Kent County Council	6
Both about the same	31
Don't know	13

REFER BACK TO Q8. ASK ALL WHO HAVE HEARD OF REVIEW AT Q8 (IE CODES 1/2/3/4). OTHERS TO Q28

Q25 SHOWCARD H **Earlier in the interview, you said that you had heard of the Review of local government structure. From which, if any, of the sources shown on this card have you recently heard about the Review?** INTERVIEWER NOTE: "RECENTLY" = IN PAST 3 MONTHS

		%
A	Leaflet from County Council delivered to your door	7
B	Leaflet from County Council in library/ offices, etc	1
C	Advertisement from County Council in local newspaper	6
D	Advertisement from County Council on local radio/TV	2
E	Leaflet from Borough Council delivered to your door	22
F	Leaflet from Borough Council in library/ offices, etc	3
G	Borough Council newspaper	2
H	County Council newspaper	1
I	Advertisement from Borough Council in local newspaper	4
J	Advertisement from Borough Council on local radio/TV	1
K	Advertisement by the Commission on local radio	1
L	Local Government Commission advertisement in local newspaper	1
M	Local newspaper	55
N	National newspaper	5
O	TV	22
P	Local radio	14
Q	National radio	3
R	Friends/neighbours/family	12
S	Conversation with Borough Councillor	1
T	Conversation with County Councillor	0
U	Conversation with Borough Council staff	2
V	Conversation with County Council staff	1
W	Parish/community council	1
X	Residents' Association	2
	Other	2
	None of these	12
	Don't know	3

ASK ALL NAMING A SOURCE AT Q25. OTHERS GO TO Q28

Q26 **Would you say that the information you have received has influenced your opinion, or not?**

	%
Yes	8
No	89
Don't know	4

Q27 **What information in particular has influenced your opinion?**

....

....

....

....

ASK ALL

Q28 SHOWCARD I (R) **Assuming you receive the same level of services, how important is it to you, if at all, what the final decision is on the future local government structure in Gravesham?**

	%
Very important	20
Fairly important	40
Not very important	25
Not at all important	9
Don't know	6

ACTIVISM

Q29 SHOWCARD J **Which of the things on this list, if any, have you done in the last three years? Just read out the letter(s) that apply.**

		%
A	Voted in Local Council elections	69
B	Spoken or written to a local Councillor	17
C	Responded to the earlier Review of local government	6
D	Been to a meeting of a local committee or organisation (WRITE IN NAME OF ORGANISATION)	6
E	Spoken on a radio phone-in about a local issue	1
F	Written to a local newspaper about a local issue	1
G	Been to a meeting of a local branch of a political party	1
H	Written to your MP about a local issue	3
I	Been to a Council Committee meeting	2
J	Been to a Council meeting	1
K	Attended a public meeting run by the Council	3
	None of these	20
	Don't know/refused	7

Q30 SHOWCARD K **Which, if any, of these apply to you? Just read out the letter(s) that apply.**

		%
I am a member of a:		
A	Residents' Association	4
B	Community Association	3
C	Tenants' Association	1
D	Neighbourhood Watch	13
E	PTA/school governors	2
I do unpaid work for:		
F	A school	2
G	Citizens Advice Bureau	*
H	Volunteer Bureau	4
I	Scouts/Guides/Cubs/Brownies	1
J	Church group	3
	Other	3
	None of these	71
	Don't know	1

THANK RESPONDENT. GO TO DEMOGRAPHICS.

MORI/9101/07

Kent
REVIEW - ROCHESTER-U-MEDWAY

Serial No ....
OUO (7-10)

TOPLINE FINDINGS

Gender %

Male 49
Female 51

Age %

18-24 15
25-34 23
35-44 20
45-54 14
55-64 14
65-74 10
75+ 5

WRITE IN AGE [|]

Work Status %

Full-time (30 hrs/wk+) 51
Part-time (8-29 hrs/wk) 8
Not working (under 8 hrs) 3
Looking after home/children 17
Retired 16
Registered unemployed 3
Unemployed but not registered 0
Student 2
Other 1

Occupation of Chief Income Earner (CIE)

Position/rank/grade

....

Industry/type of company

....

Qualifications/degrees/apprenticeship

....

No of Staff Responsible for

....

PROBE FOR PENSION

%

AB 13
C1 20
C2 38
D 18
E 10

Number in Household
Adults aged 18+ (inc. respondent)

1 2 3 4 5+

Children (17 or under)

0 1 2 3 4+

QA **Are you or other members of your household employed by a council?** IF YES: **Is this a Borough/District Council or a County Council?** CODE FOR BOTH RESPONDENT AND OTHER HOUSEHOLD MEMBERS

	Respondent %	Other %
Yes:		
Borough/District	1	1
County	3	6
Don't know which	0	0
No	96	83
Don't know	0	10

Tenure %

Owned outright 21
Buying on mortgage 55
Rented from Council 7
Rented from Housing Association 8
Rented from private landlord 7
Other 3

QB **Is this your main permanent home, or is it a second or holiday home?**

%

Main/permanent 97
Second/holiday 3

Car in Household
CIRCLE NUMBER

0 1 2 3+

Showcard Version

A-K ....
A1-K ....

INTERVIEWER DECLARATION: I confirm that I have conducted this interview face-to-face with the above named person and that I have asked all the relevant questions fully and recorded the answers in conformance with the survey specification and the MRS Code of Conduct.

Interviewer Name .... Signature ....

Interviewer Number				/	

	Month		Date	
DATE OF INTERVIEW				

NB INTERVIEWER: ALL SHOWCARDS HAVE BEEN REVERSED. PLEASE BE CAREFUL TO CODE THE CORRECT RESPONSE.

Good morning/afternoon/evening. I'm from MORI, the market research and polling organisation. We are doing a survey about local issues, and I would like to ask you a few questions.

ASK ALL

Q1 **Firstly, how long have you lived in this area?** (WITHIN FIVE MILES)

	%
Less than 1 year	4
1-2 years	5
3-5 years	12
6-10 years	19
11-20 years	21
Over 20 years/all my life	38
Don't know/can't remember	0

Q2 SHOWCARD A (R) **From this card, how much would you say you know about local councils and the services they provide?**

	%
A great deal	2
A fair amount	35
Not very much	54
Nothing at all	8
Don't know	0

Q3 SHOWCARD B (R) **Which of the statements on this card comes closest to your own view of the Councils in this area?**

		%
A)	I'm not interested in what the Council does, or whether they do their job	1
B)	I'm not interested in what the Council does, as long as they do their job	18
C)	I like to know what the Council is doing, but I'm happy to let them get on with their job	59
D)	I would like to have more of a say in what the Council does and the services it provides	20
E)	I already work for, or am involved with the Council and the services it provides	1
	Don't know	1

Q4 **From what you know, how many councils provide the main services in this neighbourhood?** (INTERVIEWER - NOT INCLUDING PARISH COUNCILS)

	%
One	33
Two	27
Three+	2
Don't know	37

In fact there are two main councils that provide, or are responsible for most services in this area: Rochester upon Medway City Council and Kent County Council.

ROTATE ORDER OF Q5/6

☐ Q5 SHOWCARD C (R) **From this list, what services do you think are the responsibility of Rochester upon Medway City Council? Just read out the letter(s) that apply**

☐ Q6 SHOWCARD C AGAIN (R) **And which services on this list do you think are the responsibility of Kent County Council? Again, just read out the letters that apply.**

Q7 SHOWCARD D (R) **Which, if any, of these services do you or members of your family use?** INCLUDE ONLY LOCAL USE

		Q5 "Borough" %	Q6 County %	Q7 Use %
A	Bus Services	27	24	35
B	Car Parks	52	16	73
C	Council Housing	48	16	9
D	Council Tax Benefit/Housing benefit	47	20	12
E	Fire service	19	53	24
F	Food safety	31	25	10
G	Household waste sites/dumps	50	21	60
H	Libraries	31	42	56
I	Parks, playgrounds and open spaces	51	21	49
J	Planning service	40	28	13
K	Public conveniences	48	15	43
L	Recycling/bottle banks	52	15	52
M	Refuse collection	61	8	82
N	Road maintenance	33	41	25
O	Schools/education	17	53	37
P	Social services	24	44	10
Q	Street sweeping	62	7	39
R	Swimming pools/sports facilities	50	17	57
	Other	1	*	*
	None of these	*	*	0
	Don't know	23	28	1

Q8 SHOWCARD E (R) **As you may know, there is currently a review being undertaken by the Local Government Commission on the future local government structure in the county. How much, if anything, would you say you know about this?**

	%
A great deal	1
A fair amount	10
Just a little	38
Heard of but know nothing about	23
Never heard of	28

PREFERENCES

HAND OVER MAP SHOWING AREAS UNDER REVIEW AND "CURRENT SERVICES" CARD
The Local Government Commission is considering options for the future structure of local government in parts of Kent. Could you please read through this card, (SHOW OPTIONS CARD) **which outlines the options.**

Q9 **Please tell me which of the options, if either, you would prefer for each of Dartford and Gravesham, Gillingham and Rochester upon Medway?**
CODE ONE ONLY FOR EACH PAIR OF DISTRICT

	%
For Dartford and Gravesham	
Option A (a single new all purpose council)	14
Option B (remain as now, separate councils with county services)	24
Some other option for Dartford	0
Some other option for Gravesham	0
Neither of these	0
Either of these/don't mind	12
Don't care	5
Don't know	45
For Gillingham and Rochester upon Medway	%
Option A (single all purpose council)	30
Option B (remain as now, separate councils with county services)	53
Some other option for Gillingham	0
Some other option for Rochester	1
Neither of these	0
Either of these/don't mind	4
Don't care	1
Don't know	10

ASK IF "OTHER" NAMED FOR ROCHESTER UPON MEDWAY AT Q9 (CODE 3)
Q10 **What other option for Rochester upon Medway is that?**
PROBE FULLY - DO NOT PROMPT.

....

....

....

....

ASK ALL PREFERRING AN OPTION (1, 2 OR 3 AT Q9). OTHERS GO TO Q13
Q11 SHOWCARD F (R) **You say that the option you would prefer for Rochester upon Medway is . . . . .** (INSERT OPTION PREFERRED). **How strongly would you say you feel about this?**

	%
Very strongly	19
Fairly strongly	57
Not very strongly	19
Not at all strongly	2
Don't know	2

Q12 **What do you think would be the main advantages of . . .**(OPTION PREFERRED)
PROBE FULLY FOR DETAILS

....

....

....

....

Nothing..
Don't know/can't think of anything.................................

ATTITUDES TO PROPOSALS

SHOWCARD G (R) **Imagine that there was one council in Rochester upon Medway and Gillingham providing <u>all</u> services. I am going to read out some statements that people have made about this proposal. To what extent do you agree or disagree that . . . .?**
READ OUT, ROTATE ORDER OF ASKING Q13-22. TICK START

	READ OUT:	Strongly agree %	Tend to agree %	Neither/ Nor %	Tend to disagree %	Strongly disagree %	Don't know %
☐	Q13 **It would cost more overall**	11	32	15	29	2	11
	Q14 **It would be more in touch with local people's needs**	8	29	10	40	10	3
	Q15 **The single Council would be more efficient than the current system of two Councils**	6	33	19	28	11	2
☐	Q16 **The single council would be big enough to manage services such as Education and Social Services effectively**	9	32	22	32	3	3
	Q17 **It would better reflect the sense of community in Rochester upon Medway and Gillingham**	5	31	17	32	12	2
	Q18 **We need a County Council to represent us nationally**	14	49	16	20	1	1
☐	Q19 **Services would suffer if the County Council no longer provides services in Rochester upon Medway and Gillingham**	11	40	16	26	3	3
	Q20 **It won't affect me whether there is a single Council in Rochester upon Medway and Gillingham or not**	3	29	17	37	13	2
	Q21 **The change to a single Council for Rochester upon Medway and Gillingham would be too disruptive**	10	34	18	34	3	1
☐	Q22 **With a single Council it would be clearer who is responsible for local services**	15	46	12	21	5	1
	ASK LAST Q23 **I would like to have more information on the proposals before making up my mind**	21	47	9	18	4	*

Q24 **On balance, which would you say is more in touch with local people and issues, ...** (ROTATE ORDER OF "DISTRICT" AND COUNTY)
Rochester upon Medway City Council, or
Kent County Council, or would you say that they are both about the same?

	%
Rochester upon Medway City Council	60
Kent County Council	2
Both about the same	27
Don't know	12

REFER BACK TO Q8. ASK ALL WHO HAVE HEARD OF REVIEW AT Q8 (IE CODES 1/2/3/4). OTHERS TO Q28

Q25 SHOWCARD H **Earlier in the interview, you said that you had heard of the Review of local government structure. From which, if any, of the sources shown on this card have you recently heard about the Review?** INTERVIEWER NOTE: "RECENTLY" = IN PAST 3 MONTHS

		%
A	Leaflet from County Council delivered to your door	8
B	Leaflet from County Council in library/ offices, etc	2
C	Advertisement from County Council in local newspaper	3
D	Advertisement from County Council on local radio/TV	4
E	Leaflet from Borough Council delivered to your door	6
F	Leaflet from Borough Council in library/ offices, etc	2
G	Borough Council newspaper	11
H	County Council newspaper	1
I	Advertisement from Borough Council in local newspaper	1
J	Advertisement from Borough Council on local radio/TV	3
K	Advertisement by the Commission on local radio	1
L	Local Government Commission advertisement in local newspaper	1
M	Local newspaper	58
N	National newspaper	4
O	TV	20
P	Local radio	21
Q	National radio	1
R	Friends/neighbours/family	15
S	Conversation with Borough Councillor	1
T	Conversation with County Councillor	0
U	Conversation with Borough Council staff	3
V	Conversation with County Council staff	1
W	Parish/community council	1
X	Residents' Association	0
	Other	9
	None of these	1
	Don't know	3

ASK ALL NAMING A SOURCE AT Q25. OTHERS GO TO Q28

Q26 **Would you say that the information you have received has influenced your opinion, or not?**

	%
Yes	12
No	80
Don't know	8

Q27 **What information in particular has influenced your opinion?**

....

....

....

....

ASK ALL

Q28 SHOWCARD I (R) **Assuming you receive the same level of services, how important is it to you, if at all, what the final decision is on the future local government structure in Rochester upon Medway?**

	%
Very important	28
Fairly important	36
Not very important	25
Not at all important	8
Don't know	2

ACTIVISM

Q29 SHOWCARD J **Which of the things on this list, if any, have you done in the last three years? Just read out the letter(s) that apply.**

		%
A	Voted in Local Council elections	74
B	Spoken or written to a local Councillor	26
C	Responded to the earlier Review of local government	4
D	Been to a meeting of a local committee or organisation (WRITE IN NAME OF ORGANISATION)	11
E	Spoken on a radio phone-in about a local issue	1
F	Written to a local newspaper about a local issue	3
G	Been to a meeting of a local branch of a political party	3
H	Written to your MP about a local issue	4
I	Been to a Council Committee meeting	2
J	Been to a Council meeting	2
K	Attended a public meeting run by the Council	9
	None of these	21
	Don't know/refused	1

Q30 SHOWCARD K **Which, if any, of these apply to you? Just read out the letter(s) that apply.**

		%
I am a member of a:		
A	Residents' Association	6
B	Community Association	1
C	Tenants' Association	2
D	Neighbourhood Watch	28
E	PTA/school governors	6
I do unpaid work for:		
F	A school	5
G	Citizens Advice Bureau	*
H	Volunteer Bureau	1
I	Scouts/Guides/Cubs/Brownies	3
J	Church group	4
	Other	2
	None of these	56
	Don't know	*

THANK RESPONDENT. GO TO DEMOGRAPHICS.

- 33 -

MORI/9101/07

Kent
REVIEW - GILLINGHAM

Serial No ....
OUO (7-10)

TOPLINE FINDINGS

Gender %

Male	48
Female	52

Age %

18-24	14
25-34	22
35-44	20
45-54	16
55-64	12
65-74	9
75+	7

WRITE IN AGE ☐☐

Work Status %

Full-time (30 hrs/wk+)	50
Part-time (8-29 hrs/wk)	9
Not working (under 8 hrs)	1
Looking after home/children	11
Retired	19
Registered unemployed	3
Unemployed but not registered	1
Student	5
Other	1

Occupation of Chief Income Earner (CIE)

Position/rank/grade

....

Industry/type of company

....

Qualifications/degrees/apprenticeship

....

No of Staff Responsible for

....

PROBE FOR PENSION

	%
AB	15
C1	38
C2	23
D	12
E	11

Number in Household
Adults aged 18+ (inc. respondent)

1 2 3 4 5+

Children (17 or under)

0 1 2 3 4+

QA **Are you or other members of your household employed by a council?** IF YES: **Is this a Borough/District Council or a County Council?** CODE FOR BOTH RESPONDENT AND OTHER HOUSEHOLD MEMBERS

	Respondent %	Other %
Yes:		
Borough/District	*	2
County	8	4
Don't know which	0	0
No	91	88
Don't know	*	7

Tenure %

Owned outright	25
Buying on mortgage	56
Rented from Council	10
Rented from Housing Association	1
Rented from private landlord	6
Other	2

QB **Is this your main permanent home, or is it a second or holiday home?**

	%
Main/permanent	99
Second/holiday	1

Car in Household
CIRCLE NUMBER

0 1 2 3+

Showcard Version

A-K ....
A1-K ....

THIS FORM IS THE PROPERTY OF MARKET & OPINION RESEARCH INTERNATIONAL (MORI)
32 OLD QUEEN STREET, LONDON, SW1H 9HP

INTERVIEWER DECLARATION: I confirm that I have conducted this interview face-to-face with the above named person and that I have asked all the relevant questions fully and recorded the answers in conformance with the survey specification and the MRS Code of Conduct.

Interviewer Name .... Signature ....

Interviewer Number					/	

		Month		Date	
DATE OF INTERVIEW					

NB INTERVIEWER: ALL SHOWCARDS HAVE BEEN REVERSED. PLEASE BE CAREFUL TO CODE THE CORRECT RESPONSE.

Good morning/afternoon/evening. I'm from MORI, the market research and polling organisation. We are doing a survey about local issues, and I would like to ask you a few questions.

ASK ALL

Q1 **Firstly, how long have you lived in this area?** (WITHIN FIVE MILES)

	%
Less than 1 year	8
1-2 years	3
3-5 years	9
6-10 years	15
11-20 years	19
Over 20 years/all my life	46
Don't know/can't remember	0

Q2 SHOWCARD A (R) **From this card, how much would you say you know about local councils and the services they provide?**

	%
A great deal	4
A fair amount	32
Not very much	52
Nothing at all	12
Don't know	*

Q3 SHOWCARD B (R) **Which of the statements on this card comes closest to your own view of the Councils in this area?**

		%
A)	I'm not interested in what the Council does, or whether they do their job	1
B)	I'm not interested in what the Council does, as long as they do their job	14
C)	I like to know what the Council is doing, but I'm happy to let them get on with their job	62
D)	I would like to have more of a say in what the Council does and the services it provides	19
E)	I already work for, or am involved with the Council and the services it provides	3
	Don't know	1

Q4 **From what you know, how many councils provide the main services in this neighbourhood?** (INTERVIEWER - NOT INCLUDING PARISH COUNCILS)

	%
One	36
Two	28
Three+	3
Don't know	32

In fact there are two main councils that provide, or are responsible for most services in this area: Gillingham Borough and Kent County Council.

ROTATE ORDER OF Q5/6

☐ Q5 SHOWCARD C (R) **From this list, what services do you think are the responsibility of Gillingham Borough Council? Just read out the letter(s) that apply**

☐ Q6 SHOWCARD C AGAIN (R) **And which services on this list do you think are the responsibility of Kent County Council? Again, just read out the letters that apply.**

Q7 SHOWCARD D (R) **Which, if any, of these services do you or members of your family use?** INCLUDE ONLY LOCAL USE

		Q5 "Borough" %	Q6 County %	Q7 Use %
A	Bus Services	37	26	34
B	Car Parks	65	14	75
C	Council Housing	64	17	11
D	Council Tax Benefit/Housing benefit	56	24	14
E	Fire service	22	63	20
F	Food safety	32	29	12
G	Household waste sites/dumps	55	28	57
H	Libraries	32	49	64
I	Parks, playgrounds and open spaces	70	16	60
J	Planning service	51	35	17
K	Public conveniences	63	14	43
L	Recycling/bottle banks	59	18	58
M	Refuse collection	74	10	84
N	Road maintenance	34	57	41
O	Schools/education	21	64	38
P	Social services	24	56	13
Q	Street sweeping	75	12	44
R	Swimming pools/sports facilities	63	15	65
	Other	1	1	*
	None of these	0	1	1
	Don't know	9	12	*

Q8 SHOWCARD E (R) **As you may know, there is currently a review being undertaken by the Local Government Commission on the future local government structure in the county. How much, if anything, would you say you know about this?**

	%
A great deal	4
A fair amount	16
Just a little	35
Heard of but know nothing about	17
Never heard of	28

PREFERENCES

HAND OVER MAP SHOWING AREAS UNDER REVIEW AND "CURRENT SERVICES" CARD
The Local Government Commission is considering options for the future structure of local government in parts of Kent. Could you please read through this card, (SHOW OPTIONS CARD) **which outlines the options.**

Q9 **Please tell me which of the options, if either, you would prefer for <u>each of</u> Dartford and Gravesham, Gillingham and Rochester upon Medway?**
CODE ONE ONLY FOR EACH PAIR OF DISTRICT

For Dartford and Gravesham	%
Option A (a single new all purpose council)	16
Option B (remain as now, separate councils with county services)	28
Some other option for Dartford	*
Some other option for Gravesham	0
Neither of these	0
Either of these/don't mind	20
Don't care	15
Don't know	21

For Gillingham and Rochester upon Medway	%
Option A (single all purpose council)	31
Option B (remain as now, separate councils with county services)	63
Some other option for Gillingham	0
Some other option for Rochester	*
Neither of these	0
Either of these/don't mind	1
Don't care	1
Don't know	4

ASK IF "OTHER" NAMED FOR GILLINGHAM AT Q9 (CODE 3)
Q10 **What other option for Gillingham is that?**
PROBE FULLY - DO NOT PROMPT.

....

....

....

....

ASK ALL PREFERRING AN OPTION (1, 2 OR 3 AT Q9). OTHERS GO TO Q13
Q11 SHOWCARD F (R) **You say that the option you would prefer for Gillingham is . . . . .** (INSERT OPTION PREFERRED). **How strongly would you say you feel about this?**

	%
Very strongly	29
Fairly strongly	45
Not very strongly	23
Not at all strongly	2
Don't know	1

Q12 **What do you think would be the main advantages of . . .**(OPTION PREFERRED)
PROBE FULLY FOR DETAILS

....

....

....

....

Nothing..

Don't know/can't think of anything..................................

ATTITUDES TO PROPOSALS

SHOWCARD G (R) **Imagine that there was one council in Rochester upon Medway with Gillingham providing all services. I am going to read out some statements that people have made about this proposal. To what extent do you agree or disagree that . . . ?**
READ OUT, ROTATE ORDER OF ASKING Q13-22. TICK START

READ OUT:	Strongly agree %	Tend to agree %	Neither/ Nor %	Tend to disagree %	Strongly disagree %	Don't know %
☐ Q13 **It would cost more overall**	17	33	15	22	7	7
Q14 **It would be more in touch with local people's needs**	11	29	12	29	18	2
Q15 **The single Council would be more efficient than the current system of two Councils**	10	28	17	30	13	2
☐ Q16 **The single council would be big enough to manage services such as Education and Social Services effectively**	18	28	20	25	5	3
Q17 **It would better reflect the sense of community in Rochester upon Medway and Gillingham**	7	29	13	32	16	4
Q18 **We need a County Council to represent us nationally**	24	41	16	14	3	2
☐ Q19 **Services would suffer if the County Council no longer provides services in Rochester upon Medway and Gillingham**	21	40	17	16	4	2
Q20 **It won't affect me whether there is a single Council in Rochester upon Medway and Gillingham or not**	4	22	17	34	20	3
Q21 **The change to a single Council for Rochester upon Medway and Gillingham would be too disruptive**	19	31	15	28	4	4
☐ Q22 **With a single Council it would be clearer who is responsible for local services**	19	44	9	21	7	*
ASK LAST Q23 **I would like to have more information on the proposals before making up my mind**	27	40	11	19	3	*

Q24 **On balance, which would you say is more in touch with local people and issues, ...** (ROTATE ORDER OF "DISTRICT" AND COUNTY)
Gillingham Borough Council, or
Kent County Council, or would you say that they are both about the same?

	%
Gillingham Borough Council	53
Kent County Council	4
Both about the same	35
Don't know	7

REFER BACK TO Q8. ASK ALL WHO HAVE HEARD OF REVIEW AT Q8 (IE CODES 1/2/3/4). OTHERS TO Q28

Q25 SHOWCARD H **Earlier in the interview, you said that you had heard of the Review of local government structure. From which, if any, of the sources shown on this card have you recently heard about the Review?** INTERVIEWER NOTE: "RECENTLY" = IN PAST 3 MONTHS

		%
A	Leaflet from County Council delivered to your door	20
B	Leaflet from County Council in library/ offices, etc	5
C	Advertisement from County Council in local newspaper	12
D	Advertisement from County Council on local radio/TV	4
E	Leaflet from Borough Council delivered to your door	30
F	Leaflet from Borough Council in library/ offices, etc	1
G	Borough Council newspaper	15
H	County Council newspaper	5
I	Advertisement from Borough Council in local newspaper	6
J	Advertisement from Borough Council on local radio/TV	2
K	Advertisement by the Commission on local radio	1
L	Local Government Commission advertisement in local newspaper	4
M	Local newspaper	61
N	National newspaper	6
O	TV	21
P	Local radio	21
Q	National radio	3
R	Friends/neighbours/family	20
S	Conversation with Borough Councillor	4
T	Conversation with County Councillor	1
U	Conversation with Borough Council staff	2
V	Conversation with County Council staff	3
W	Parish/community council	0
X	Residents' Association	1
	Other	8
	None of these	*
	Don't know	1

ASK ALL NAMING A SOURCE AT Q25. OTHERS GO TO Q28

Q26 **Would you say that the information you have received has influenced your opinion, or not?**

	%
Yes	21
No	77
Don't know	2

Q27 **What information in particular has influenced your opinion?**

....

....

....

....

ASK ALL

Q28 SHOWCARD I (R) **Assuming you receive the same level of services, how important is it to you, if at all, what the final decision is on the future local government structure in Gillingham?**

	%
Very important	28
Fairly important	38
Not very important	27
Not at all important	5
Don't know	3

ACTIVISM

Q29 SHOWCARD J **Which of the things on this list, if any, have you done in the last three years? Just read out the letter(s) that apply.**

		%
A	Voted in Local Council elections	77
B	Spoken or written to a local Councillor	28
C	Responded to the earlier Review of local government	8
D	Been to a meeting of a local committee or organisation (WRITE IN NAME OF ORGANISATION)	7
E	Spoken on a radio phone-in about a local issue	2
F	Written to a local newspaper about a local issue	3
G	Been to a meeting of a local branch of a political party	2
H	Written to your MP about a local issue	7
I	Been to a Council Committee meeting	2
J	Been to a Council meeting	2
K	Attended a public meeting run by the Council	5
	None of these	19
	Don't know/refused	1

Q30 SHOWCARD K **Which, if any, of these apply to you? Just read out the letter(s) that apply.**

		%
I am a member of a:		
A	Residents' Association	5
B	Community Association	1
C	Tenants' Association	1
D	Neighbourhood Watch	21
E	PTA/school governors	4
I do unpaid work for:		
F	A school	5
G	Citizens Advice Bureau	0
H	Volunteer Bureau	2
I	Scouts/Guides/Cubs/Brownies	3
J	Church group	5
	Other	5
	None of these	62
	Don't know	1

THANK RESPONDENT. GO TO DEMOGRAPHICS.

CHAPTER 5

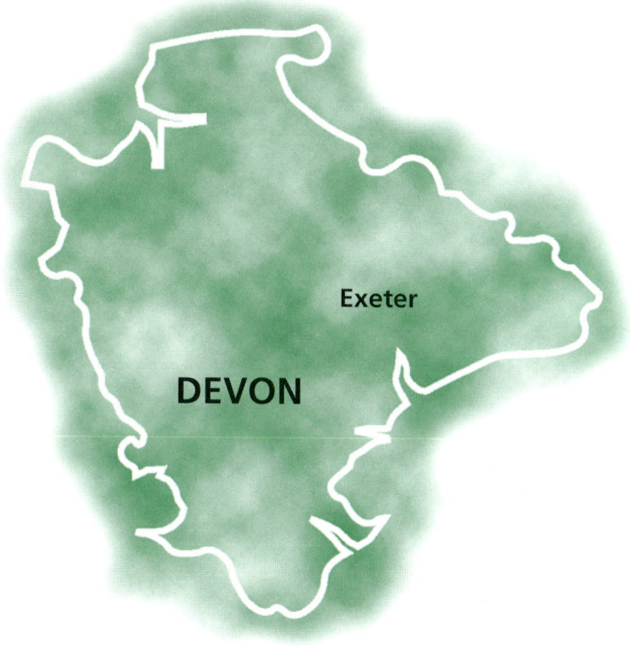

EXETER IN THE COUNTY OF DEVON

Draft Recommendations

5.1 The Commission's report *Draft Recommendations on the Future Local Government of Exeter in the County of Devon* summarised the evidence taken into account by the Commission in reaching its draft recommendations.

Figure 5.1
Draft Recommendation for Exeter in the County of Devon

Structure

- There should be no change to the existing two-tier structure of local government in Exeter.

Views Expressed to the Commission

5.2 The Commission received a wide range of direct representations on its draft recommendations, from local authorities, residents, Members of Parliament, business and voluntary groups, parish and town councils, and from other public and private sector organisations. Over 3,800 representations were received from individuals and organisations, including just under 2,000 from respondents within Exeter. The Commission also received over 1,600 representations in the form of standard letters, response slips and petitions (Figures 5.2 and 5.3). Figures 5.2 and 5.3 exclude representations from the local authorities; these are summarised separately (Figure 5.4).

5.3 In addition, 141 representations were received from outside the county, of which almost two-thirds supported the Commission's draft recommendation. A more detailed tabulation of the written representations from individuals and interest groups, produced by NOP on behalf of the Commission, can be found towards the end of this Chapter.

The Views of Local Authorities

5.4 The Commission received submissions from 10 of the 11 principal local authorities in Devon during Stage Three (Figure 5.4).

Figure 5.2
Views of Respondents Within Exeter

Preferred structure	Individuals	Organisations	Standard letters and petition signatures
Unitary Exeter	727	50	1,258
No change	1,105	66	139
Other	8	0	2
No preference	4	3	0

Source: Local Government Commission for England and NOP

Figure 5.3
Views of Respondents From Outside The Review District

Preferred structure	Individuals	Organisations	Standard letters and petition signatures
Unitary Exeter	201	14	121
No change	1,361	301	148
Other	9	5	3
No preference	7	1	0

Source: Local Government Commission for England and NOP
Note: Excludes out of county representations

Figure 5.4
Preferences of Devon Local Authorities at Stage Three

Authority	Preference
Exeter City Council	Reaffirmed support for unitary Exeter. Considered that, whilst there was recognition of the city's wider influence in the county, its functional centrality in terms of economic development would be best served by a strong Exeter with the focus provided by a unitary authority.
East Devon District Council	Supported retention of Exeter in a two-tier structure. Cited loss of benefits of scale in education and social services, affecting quality of delivered services.
Mid Devon District Council	Reiterated preference for the retention of the two-tier structure across Devon with the exceptions of Plymouth and Torbay.
North Devon District Council	Restated support for unitary authorities throughout Devon.
Plymouth City Council South Hams District Council	Confirmed support for unitary status for Exeter. Reaffirmed support for the establishment of unitary authorities in Devon.
Teignbridge District Council	Supported retention of Exeter in a two-tier structure. Considered that Exeter had important part to play in the two-tier structure of local government in Devon.
Torbay Borough Council	Reaffirmed support for unitary status for Exeter. Believed this would leave the County Council with an opportunity to draw up strategies and plans for an essentially rural county.
Torridge District Council	Expressed no views in Stage Three.
West Devon Borough Council	Supported retention of Exeter in a two-tier structure.
Devon County Council	Supported the retention of Exeter in a two-tier structure and highlighted the interdependence of Exeter and the rest of Devon, arguing that Devon's size, peripherality and sparsity of population meant that Exeter should remain central to Devon.

Source: Local authorities' submissions

5.5 These views are the same as those expressed in Stage One, except Teignbridge District Council supports the retention of a two-tier structure (no view expressed in Stage One), while South Hams District Council supports the principle of unitary authorities throughout the county (as against its previous support for unitary status for Exeter alone). The Devon Branch of the Association of District Councils did not make representations; the Association of District Councils' national submission is referred to in the Summary of National Representations. The Association of County Councils supported the draft recommendation.

The Views of Others

5.6 A range of other interest groups made representations on the Commission's draft recommendation as summarised in the following paragraphs. These are in addition to those made in Stage One.

Businesses and Business Groups

5.7 Over 175 businesses and business groups responded to the consultation. Seventy per cent of submissions supported no change in Exeter. However, many umbrella bodies within the city, such as the Exeter Branch of the Federation of Small Businesses, which represents 180 such businesses, the Exeter City Centre Consortium and the Exeter Business Forum, supported a unitary authority.

5.8 The Federation of Small Businesses argued that if Exeter remained under the two-tier structure then "...there is no question that the City will not be in a position to represent itself on major strategic issues, and will undoubtedly lose out to Plymouth and Torbay ...the argument that the hinterland is dependent on Exeter is, of course, perfectly true. That is why it is very important that Exeter should not be deprived of resources and certainly not of a seat at the strategic councils of the region".

5.9 The Exeter Business Forum concluded their submission with the statement that " ...it is a commonly held view that the creation of a unitary local authority would enhance the status of Exeter as a business and commercial centre and would facilitate the promotion of Exeter as a place for business and inward investment".

5.10 The South West Region of the Confederation of British Industry expressed support for the draft recommendation of no change and argued that "Exeter is too small an area on which to form a unitary authority ...damage would be caused to the economy of the area because of the resulting fragmentation of decision making on macro issues such as strategic and infrastructure planning". The Exeter Chamber of Commerce also supported no change for the city, following a ballot of their members. Outside Exeter, business groups and individual businesses were clearly opposed to a unitary solution. The Seaton Chamber of Commerce argued that "...the complexity of the operation and the chaos that will ensue are valid reasons to reject the proposal", and that view was generally held.

County, Regional and National Interests (including the Voluntary Sector)

5.11 There was strong support from county and regional bodies for the draft recommendation. Of over 50 submissions received, nearly three-quarters did not want a change in Exeter.

5.12 The Council for the Protection of Rural England stated that the "...essential local services at present provided by the County Council could not be adequately replaced by smaller authorities". The Devon County Branch of the National Farmers' Union was also of the view that Exeter should remain in a two-tier structure.

5.13 Views from the county-wide voluntary sector bodies were invariably in favour of the draft recommendation. For example, the Devon Voluntary Youth Services was typical in its view that "...it is important for a county-wide organisation to have the clear focus which is provided by having a county town. The continuation of Exeter in that role is seen as essential, particularly now that Plymouth and Torbay are to become unitary authorities".

5.14 However, the Exeter Council for Voluntary Service argued that the future prosperity of the city was likely to be enhanced by creating a unitary Exeter, rather than allowing important decisions to be taken by the County Council, which would inevitably be balancing the requirements of Exeter with the needs of other rural areas.

Education Groups

5.15 There was an overwhelming response from educational groups in favour of the recommendation for no change. Sixty-four responses were received, with over 90 per cent against a unitary Exeter. The majority of submissions were either from county groups or schools outside Exeter. The Devon Association of Governors stated that "...we are particularly concerned about the future provision of education services which we believe would suffer both in Exeter and in the rural areas were Exeter to become a unitary authority". The South West Region of the National Union of Teachers argued that costs would inevitably increase, while at the same time the lack of economies of scale would deny schools the services on which they rely.

Health Interests

5.16 There was a relatively limited response to the consultation from health bodies, including trusts and health authorities. Those that did respond were generally in favour of a unitary Exeter, albeit with some major concerns about cost and service delivery.

5.17 For example, the Exeter and North Devon Health Authority supported the "...general thrust of unitary status for Exeter", but went on to state that "...the Health Authority would wish to be reassured that the additional costs of delivering services to rural, sparsely populated areas have been fully recognised ...it is unclear whether the remainder of the county would remain viable if a further unitary council was established". This view - support for the unitary principle, but with concern over the viability of the remaining county - was echoed by the NHS Executive (South and West).

5.18 The South Devon Health Care NHS Trust argued that "three unitary councils [Plymouth, Torbay and Exeter] working in equal partnership with a rural based County Council would provide the greatest strength for all people of the county of Devon".

Law, Order and Emergency Services

5.19 As with health interests, there was a very small response from this sector. In all submissions received, the retention of the two-tier structure in Exeter was the preferred option.

5.20 The Devon Fire and Rescue Service stated that "...the implications of removing the city of Exeter would have a marked effect on the ability to provide for an integrated service for the whole of Devon". The Devon Probation Service was of a similar opinion and argued that "...without Exeter, what would be left of Devon would not only be a limbless torso but a headless one without any great sense of administrative integrity at all".

Local Groups

5.21 Over 60 submissions were received from local groups and voluntary organisations. More than half supported the draft recommendation, but there was also some significant support from within the city itself for a unitary Exeter.

5.22 For example, groups such as the Exeter Festival and the Exeter Canal and Quay Trust provided submissions in support of Exeter's case. It was argued that a unitary Exeter would be beneficial for both the city and east Devon generally.

5.23 The opposite perception was held by an equally diverse cross-section of local groups throughout the county. The East Devon Arts Association, Arundel Charity and Ottery St Mary Amenities Association were representative of many local groups in areas outside Exeter who expressed concern for the rest of Devon, should Exeter be given unitary status. "Exeter should remain in an adequately-resourced county system" was the view of the East Devon Arts Association, which was reflected in other submissions.

Parliamentary Interests

5.24 Mr Nick Harvey, MP for North Devon, expressed "...strong and full support for a unitary Exeter". He commented that: "I am acutely aware that the common concerns of the rural communities are in great contrast to those of the City of Exeter. It is possible to see rural issues and concerns forming unifying bonds between the various rural communities; it is not possible to see such a bond developing between the rural population and the City of Exeter". Two other Members of Parliament, Mrs Emma Nicholson, MP for Devon West and Torridge, and Mr David Jamieson, MP for Plymouth Devonport, also sent submissions supporting Exeter's case.

5.25 Sir Peter Emery, MP for Honiton, was of the opinion that no change was the correct decision and that there was "...a massive body of opinion within the county that supports Exeter's retention as an integral part of the County of Devon".

5.26 Mr Giles Chichester, MEP for Devon and East Plymouth, supported a unitary Exeter. Mr Graham Watson, MEP for Somerset and North Devon, and Mr Robin Teverson, MEP for Cornwall and West Plymouth, supported the draft recommendation of no change.

5.27 In addition, the Labour Party Environment Spokesman, Mr Frank Dobson, MP for Holborn and St Pancras, expressed his concern at the concept of centrality. He argued the case for Exeter to be granted unitary status. He commented that: "...the argument has to be confined to the question of whether taking from the counties their present responsibilities for education, social services and strategic planning and transport ... would remove the central keystone from those services county-wide". He felt that this was not the case in Exeter.

Parish And Town Councils

5.28 Over 150 of the parish and town councils throughout Devon responded during the public consultation. Exeter itself is not parished.

5.29 The vast majority of parish councils supported the retention of Exeter in the two-tier structure. Of the submissions received, over 95 per cent supported no change. This was also the view of the Devon Association of Parish Councils and the Devon Community Council.

NOP Tabulations of Written Representations

1 The following tabulations summarise the views expressed by members of the public and other interested parties during the consultation on the Local Government Commission's draft recommendations for Exeter.

2 The tabulations include only letters sent directly to NOP at its Chelmsford offices and to the Commission's offices in London. Where more than one person's view has been expressed in a letter, the comments from each individual have been recorded separately. Staff from the Commission and NOP have worked closely in ensuring that care has been taken in the interpretation of comments, and that a consistent approach has been adopted.

3 While many people expressed support for one or other of the draft options presented by the Commission, other responses were coded by NOP after further discussion. The pattern of views expressed has been carefully examined, and where a number of respondents supported an option not included in those put forward by the Commission, those views have been separately coded and reported by NOP.

4 The Commission has advertised through the local media, encouraging people to make their views known. All responses received up to two days after the end of the Stage Three consultation period have been included. Returns from campaigns organised by local authorities or other groups (for example, standardised postcards and letters, questionnaires and petitions) have not been included in the tabulations. These, and submissions written and dated before the commencement of the consultation process, have been considered separately by the Commission.

The following definitions have been applied by NOP in compiling the tabulations:

(i) Type of Respondent

Individuals:	includes individual members of the public, local councillors and Members of the Westminster and European Parliaments.
Businesses and Business Groups:	includes organisations which represent businesses, such as local Chambers of Commerce.
County, Regional and National Interests:	any organisation which covers an area which is the size of a county or larger is included here, for example, a county-wide voluntary organisation or a regional association. This classification includes most of the statutory consultees.
Education (and Church) Groups:	this group includes schools, religious organisations and teaching unions.
Local Groups:	this includes organisations smaller than a county area, for example, a district-level voluntary sector body. The group could be voluntary, sporting, political or cultural but does not include organisations from the education or religious sectors (included above). It also includes constituency parties and political groups on local authorities.
Parish and Town Councils:	this also includes district-level associations of town and parish councils. County level associations are classified as County, Regional and National interests.

(ii) Structural Options (Reports A and D)

No change in own district:	this code is used where there is more than one review district in the county. It indicates where respondents from a review district have expressed support for no change for that district and have not made reference to the other review district(s) in that county.
District/county-level authorities:	represents support for either a district or county-level authority although it is not clear whether this is for a unitary or a two-tier structure.
Opposition to structural preferences:	represents responses where a negative, but unspecified, structural preference has been expressed.
Rejects:	rejects are those responses with unclear comments/interpretation.

(iii) Other

Other issues (Report B):	these illustrate preferences in relation to boundary and electoral changes and (where applicable) the restoration of historic counties.
Parishing issues (Report C):	these illustrate preferences in relation to parishing issues, for example, the creation of new parishes or the enhancement of the role of parish and town councils.
Services (Report E):	these illustrate concerns expressed about the impact of proposed changes on particular service areas where the respondent has not additionally expressed a positive structural preference.

NOP Analysis of Responses to Local Government Commission Draft Recommendations - DEVON

Report A: Opinions on the structural options, by authority of respondent
Base: all

	Review district	Other districts in county											
	Exeter	East Devon	Mid Devon	North Devon	Plymouth	South Hams	Teign-bridge	Torbay	Torridge	West Devon	Rest of county total	County total	Out of county total
Status quo/two-tier	1171 *60%*	618 *91%*	238 *82%*	120 *97%*	51 *96%*	93 *89%*	351 *83%*	37 *71%*	60 *97%*	94 *90%*	1662 *88%*	2833 *73%*	92 *65%*
Unitary Exeter	777 *40%*	58 *9%*	50 *17%*	3 *2%*	2 *4%*	4 *4%*	71 *17%*	15 *29%*	2 *3%*	10 *10%*	215 *11%*	992 *26%*	44 *31%*
County-level authority (either two-tier or unitary)	1 *	2 *	- -	- -	- -	2 *2%*	- -	- -	- -	- -	4 *	5 *	- -
District-level authority (either two-tier or unitary)	2 *	- -	- -	- -	- -	1 *1%*	1 *	- -	- -	- -	2 *	4 *	- -
Pre-1974 structure	4 *	- -	1 *	- -	- -	- -	- -	- -	- -	- -	1 *	5 *	- -
County-wide unitary structure	1 *	- -	1 *	- -	- -	3 *3%*	- -	- -	- -	- -	4 *	5 *	- -
Reject	2 *	- -	- -	- -	- -	- -	- -	- -	- -	- -	- -	2 *	- -
Other specified	- -	1 *	- -	1 *1%*	- -	1 *1%*	- -	- -	- -	- -	3 *	3 *	- -
No preference expressed/option defined	5 *	3 *	2 *1%*	- -	- -	1 *1%*	1 *	- -	- -	1 *1%*	8 *	13 *	5 *4%*
BASE TOTAL	1963	682	292	124	53	105	424	52	62	105	1899	3862	141

* *Less than ½%*

Exeter

NOP Analysis of Responses to Local Government Commission Draft Recommendations - DEVON

Report B: Opinions on other issues, by authority of respondent
Base: all

	Review district	Other districts in county											
	Exeter	East Devon	Mid Devon	North Devon	Plymouth	South Hams	Teign-bridge	Torbay	Torridge	West Devon	Rest of county total	County total	Out of county total
Electoral issues	2	1	-	1	-	-	1	-	-	-	3	5	-
	*	*	-	*1%*	-	-	*	-	-	-	*	*	-
BASE TOTAL	1963	682	292	124	53	105	424	52	62	105	1899	3862	141

The figures in the table above do not sum to the base total/100% because undefined fields are not included, except as part of the base total.

* *Less than ½%*

NOP Analysis of Responses to Local Government Commission Draft Recommendations - DEVON

Report C: Opinions on parishing issues, by authority of respondent
Base: all

	Review district	Other districts in county											
	Exeter	East Devon	Mid Devon	North Devon	Plymouth	South Hams	Teign-bridge	Torbay	Torridge	West Devon	Rest of county total	County total	Out of county total
Enhanced parish powers	-	-	-	-	-	1	-	-	-	-	1	1	-
	-	-	-	-	-	*1%*	-	-	-	-	*	*	-
BASE TOTAL	1963	682	292	124	53	105	424	52	62	105	1899	3862	141

The figures in the table above do not sum to the base total/100% because undefined fields are not included, except as part of the base total.

* *Less than ½%*

NOP Analysis of Responses to Local Government Commission Draft Recommendations - DEVON

Report D1: Opinions on the structural options, by respondent type (all respondents)
Base: all

	Respondent Type					
	Indiv-iduals	Business groups	County, regional & national interests	Education (& church) groups	Local groups	Parish and town councils
Status quo/two-tier	2508 *72%*	130 *70%*	41 *75%*	61 *95%*	38 *58%*	147 *97%*
Unitary Exeter	945 *27%*	54 *29%*	10 *18%*	1 *2%*	24 *37%*	2 *1%*
County-level authority (either two-tier or unitary)	5 *	- -	- -	- -	- -	- -
District-level authority (either two-tier or unitary)	2 *	1 *1%*	- -	- -	- -	1 *1%*
Pre-1974 structure	5 *	- -	- -	- -	- -	- -
County-wide unitary structure	3 *	- -	- -	- -	1 *2%*	1 *1%*
Reject	2 *	- -	- -	- -	- -	- -
Other specified	2 *	- -	- -	- -	- -	1 *1%*
No preference expressed/option defined	9 *	1 *1%*	4 *7%*	2 *3%*	2 *3%*	- -
BASE TOTAL	3481	186	55	64	65	152

* *Less than ½%*

NOP Analysis of Responses to Local Government Commission Draft Recommendations - DEVON

Report D2: Opinions on the structural options, by respondent type
Base: respondents in Exeter only

	Respondent Type					
	Indiv-iduals	Business groups	County, regional & national interests	Education (& church) groups	Local groups	Parish and town councils
Status quo/two-tier	1105 *60%*	29 *50%*	20 *95%*	9 *82%*	8 *28%*	- -
Unitary Exeter	727 *39%*	28 *48%*	1 *5%*	1 *9%*	20 *69%*	- -
County-level authority (either two-tier or unitary)	1 *	- -	- -	- -	- -	- -
District-level authority (either two-tier or unitary)	2 *	- -	- -	- -	- -	- -
Pre-1974 structure	4 *	- -	- -	- -	- -	- -
County-wide unitary structure	1 *	- -	- -	- -	- -	- -
Reject	2 *	- -	- -	- -	- -	- -
No preference expressed/option defined	2 *	1 *2%*	- -	1 *9%*	1 *3%*	- -
BASE TOTAL	1844	58	21	11	29	-

* *Less than ½%*

Exeter

NOP Analysis of Responses to Local Government Commission Draft Recommendations - DEVON

Report D3: Opinions on the structural options, by respondent type
Base: respondents in rest of county only

	Respondent Type					
	Indiv-iduals	Business groups	County, regional & national interests	Education (& church) groups	Local groups	Parish and town councils
Status quo/two-tier	1361	60	13	52	30	146
	86%	*88%*	*93%*	*98%*	*86%*	*97%*
Unitary Exeter	201	7	1	-	4	2
	13%	*10%*	*7%*	-	*11%*	*1%*
County-level authority (either two-tier or unitary)	4	-	-	-	-	-
	*	-	-	-	-	-
District-level authority (either two-tier or unitary)	-	1	-	-	-	1
	-	*1%*	-	-	-	*1%*
Pre-1974 structure	1	-	-	-	-	-
	*	-	-	-	-	-
County-wide unitary structure	2	-	-	-	1	1
	*	-	-	-	*3%*	*1%*
Other specified	2	-	-	-	-	1
	*	-	-	-	-	*1%*
No preference expressed/option defined	7	-	-	1	-	-
	*	-	-	*2%*	-	-
BASE TOTAL	1578	68	14	53	35	151

* *Less than ½%*

NOP Analysis of Responses to Local Government Commission Draft Recommendations - DEVON

Report E: Views on services, by authority of respondent
Base: all

	Review district	Other districts in county											
	Exeter	East Devon	Mid Devon	North Devon	Plymouth	South Hams	Teign-bridge	Torbay	Torridge	West Devon	Rest of county total	County total	Out of county total
Archives	- -	- -	- -	1 *1%*	- -	- -	- -	- -	- -	- -	1 *	1 *	3 *2%*
Education	1 *	- -	- -	- -	- -	- -	- -	- -	- -	1 *1%*	1 *	2 *	- -
Libraries	- -	2 *	- -	- -	- -	- -	- -	- -	- -	- -	2 *	2 *	- -
Trading standards	- -	- -	- -	- -	- -	- -	- -	- -	- -	- -	- -	- -	1 *1%*
Other specified services (or multiples of)	1 *	- -	- -	- -	- -	- -	- -	- -	- -	- -	- -	1 *	1 *1%*
BASE TOTAL	1963	682	292	124	53	105	424	52	62	105	1899	3862	141

The figures in the table above do not sum to the base total/100% because undefined fields are not included, except as part of the base total.
* *Less than ½%*

NOP Analysis of Responses to Local Government Commission Draft Recommendations - DEVON

Report F: Views on services, by respondent type
Base: all

	Respondent Type					
	Indiv-iduals	Business groups	County, regional & national interests	Education (& church) groups	Local groups	Parish and town councils
Archives	1 *	- -	3 *5%*	- -	- -	- -
Education	1 *	- -	- -	1 *2%*	- -	- -
Libraries	2 *	- -	- -	- -	- -	- -
Trading standards	- -	- -	1 *2%*	- -	- -	- -
Other specified services (or multiples of)	- -	1 *1%*	- -	- -	1 *2%*	- -
BASE TOTAL	3481	186	55	64	65	152

The figures in the table above do not sum to the base total/100% because undefined fields are not included, except as part of the base total.
* *Less than ½%*

NOP Analysis of Responses to Local Government Commission Draft Recommendations - DEVON

Report G: Type of respondent, by authority of respondent
Base: all

	Review district	Other districts in county											
	Exeter	East Devon	Mid Devon	North Devon	Plymouth	South Hams	Teign-bridge	Torbay	Torridge	West Devon	Rest of county total	County total	Out of county total
Individuals	1844	597	240	101	38	70	379	48	42	63	1578	3422	59
	94%	*88%*	*82%*	*81%*	*72%*	*67%*	*89%*	*92%*	*68%*	*60%*	*83%*	*89%*	*42%*
Business groups	58	16	7	5	13	3	17	1	2	4	68	126	60
	3%	*2%*	*2%*	*4%*	*25%*	*3%*	*4%*	*2%*	*3%*	*4%*	*4%*	*3%*	*43%*
County, regional and national interests	21	3	4	-	-	-	3	1	2	1	14	35	20
	1%	*	*1%*	-	-	-	*1%*	*2%*	*3%*	*1%*	*1%*	*1%*	*14%*
Education (and church) groups	11	10	6	6	2	9	6	1	5	8	53	64	-
	1%	*1%*	*2%*	*5%*	*4%*	*9%*	*1%*	*2%*	*8%*	*8%*	*3%*	*2%*	-
Local Groups	29	13	6	4	-	6	2	1	-	3	35	64	1
	1%	*2%*	*2%*	*3%*	-	*6%*	*	*2%*	-	*3%*	*2%*	*2%*	*1%*
Parish and town councils	-	43	29	8	-	17	17	-	11	26	151	151	1
	-	*6%*	*10%*	*6%*	-	*16%*	*4%*	-	*18%*	*25%*	*8%*	*4%*	*1%*
BASE TOTAL	1963	682	292	124	53	105	424	52	62	105	1899	3862	141

* *Less than ½%*

MORI Research Study for the Local Government Commission

Introduction

Background

1 This summary report highlights the key findings from a survey of public opinion conducted in the City of Exeter and across the County of Devon on behalf of the Local Government Commission for England. A copy of each of the marked-up questionnaires is appended. The computer tabulations are contained in a separate volume, which is available from MORI (32 Old Queen Street, London SW1H 9HP. Telephone 0171-222 0232. Price £15)

2 The survey was designed in close consultation with the Commission, following extensive qualitative research and pilot testing. All sampling, interviewing and analysis have been carried out independently by MORI, within the guidelines of the profession laid out by the Market Research Society.

3 In Exeter, all Census Enumeration Districts (EDs) were sorted by ward, and stratified according to social class. EDs were then sampled (32 in total) in proportion to the population size of each, and quotas set for sex, age and work status. A total of 325 interviews with adults aged 18+, conducted face-to-face and in-home, were carried out between 29 September and 29 October 1995. Data were weighted to match the population profile in the City.

4 In the remaining districts of Devon, all EDs were sorted into ward, and again were stratified according to social class. A total of 32 EDs across the whole area (that is, Devon excluding Exeter) were sampled, with quotas set by sex, age and work status. Face-to-face interviews, conducted in-home, were carried out with 318 adults aged 18+ between 29 September and 29 October 1995. Data were weighted to match the population profile of the County excluding Exeter.

Publication of the Results

5 As with all our studies, these findings are subject to our Standard Terms and Conditions of Contract. Any press release or publication of the findings of this survey require the advance approval of MORI. Such approval will only be refused on the grounds of inaccuracy or misinterpretation.

Objectives

6 This survey took place during Stage Three, the consultation period on the Commission's draft recommendations. It measures public preferences for the organisation of local government in the area currently comprising the City of Exeter, as well as exploring strength of feeling, levels of knowledge about the review, involvement in, and broader perceptions of, local government in the area.

Statistical Reliability of the Data

7 Because we have interviewed a sample of residents, rather than the whole population, the results are subject to statistical tolerance limits, or "margins of error". These are expressed as our confidence that the true figure for the whole population falls within a given range. By convention this is expressed as a percentage, so our 95% confidence level means that in 95 times out of 100 the true figure would lie within this range

8 The table below shows ranges of the 95% confidence level for a range of sample sizes. For each sample size, the table shows the tolerance limits for sample results close to 10%, 30% and 50%. Take, for example, the results of a survey of 300 residents showing that 50% are aware of the review. In 95 times out of 100 the true figure would lie between 44% and 56% (ie 50% ±6%).

	Sampling tolerances applicable to results at or near these percentages (based on 95% confidence level)		
Sample size	10/90%	30/70%	50%
	±%	±%	±%
300	3	5	6
200	4	6	7
150	5	7	8
100	6	9	10
50	8	13	14

9 Clearly, 10% or 30% of the sample being aware of the review equate to 90% or 70% not being aware of it. So this table shows the ranges of 95% confidence for responses close to 10%, 30%, 50%, 70% and 90% of our sample. The figures for responses between can be obtained by extrapolation.

10 The true figure would only be known if all the residents of the area had been interviewed. It can be seen in the table, however, that large increases in the sample size do not greatly reduce the sampling tolerance. In addition, the true figure is more likely to lie at the midpoint of the range, rather than at either extreme.

11 When comparing results from separate groups within a sample we need to be sure that the differences are statistically significant. This would be important in comparing views expressed by different parts of a county. The table below shows how the statistical significance of the difference is determined by the size of the groups and the percentage result from the sample.

12 Assuming a 95% confidence level, the table shows the size of the differences required if different results are to be regarded as statistically significant. It can be seen that if 50% of a group of 300 were aware of the review, the result from another group of 300 would not become statistically significant until it became less than 42% or more than 58%.

	Differences required for significance at or near these percentage levels		
Sample sizes	10/90%	30/70%	50%
	±	±	±
300 and 300	5	7	8
300 and 200	5	8	9
300 and 100	7	10	11
200 and 100	7	11	12
100 and 100	8	13	14

Survey Findings

Knowledge and Awareness

13 Residents within the City of Exeter profess broadly similar levels of knowledge and interest in local government as those living in the rest of the County of Devon. In both, a clear majority like to know what their council is doing, but want no greater involvement. Around one in five in both areas say they want a higher level of involvement.

14 While around a third in the City and the County say they know at least a fair amount about what their council does, around six in ten admit to not knowing very much.

15 This is reflected in the number of residents who incorrectly ascribe services between the two tiers of local government. Thus, although between four and five in ten recognise libraries as a county council service, as many as two to three in ten allocate responsibility to their district/borough/city council. And although seven in ten realise that refuse collection is a district/borough/city service, around one in ten thinks it is a county council service. Residents of Exeter are slightly more likely to be correct in the way that they allocate services across the two tiers than are those living in the rest of the County.

16 Awareness of the review itself is fairly low, but is slightly higher in Exeter (where 79% have heard of it) than the rest of the Devon (where 70% have heard of it). Similarly, the proportions who say they know a fair amount or more are slightly higher in Exeter than in the rest of the County - 17% say they know at least a fair amount compared to 12% in the rest of Devon.

Sources of Information

17 Local newspapers are the most common source of information about the review, by a considerable margin. Of those who have at least heard of the review, between five and six in ten name the local press as a recent source. Around three-quarters cite some media source as a recent source of information on the review.

18 It would appear that the County has been fairly active in providing information to residents in Exeter - while 43% name a County Council source in Exeter, just 24% do so in the rest of Devon. By comparison, 33% in Exeter mention a City Council source, compared with 22% in the rest of Devon. Very few recognise receiving information directly from the Local Government Commission itself.

19 Although most of those aware of the review recognise one or more recent sources of information, few (around one in five) say that this has influenced their opinion.

20 Furthermore, in spite of a relatively low level of knowledge and engagement with their local authority, most people in Exeter say that the outcome of the review in the City is either very important to them (29%) or fairly important (40%). As one might expect, people in the rest of Devon perceive a lower level of importance (9% very important and 22% fairly important).

The Preferred Option

21 A majority in Exeter would prefer a unitary City Council (53%) to no change (32%), while in the rest of Devon rather more would prefer Exeter to retain two tier local government (42%) than opt for the unitary solution (32%). The rest, 15% and 26% respectively, had no views or were indifferent.

22 People in Exeter feel more strongly about the preference they express than do those living elsewhere in the County. In Exeter, 73% of those expressing a preference say they feel strongly (26% very strongly), while across the rest of Devon, 55% feel strongly (just 9% very strongly). There is little difference in the strength of feeling expressed in Exeter irrespective of which option they prefer. The same is also true across the rest of Devon.

Factors in Expressing a Preference

23 In questions 13 to 23, residents were asked to say to what extent they agreed or disagreed with a range.of statements which related to a change to unitary local government. The statements were designed to cover the main issues raised by residents during the qualitative phase of research, and others that formed a part of the Commission's brief to take into consideration in making its recommendations.

24 The following charts summarise the results from these questions, with the full question wording presented in the questionnaires in the appendices. Values have been ascribed to the five attitudinal positions that people were offered

(+2 for strongly agree, +1 for tend to agree, 0 for neither agree nor disagree, -1 for tend to disagree, and -2 for strongly disagree) and mean scores calculated across all respondents expressing a view. This has the combined benefit of distilling the range of opinion into one summary figure, while incorporating the varying intensity of feeling by ascribing values. Bars to the right indicate that the mean score value is positive, and thus that there is a balance of agreement with the statement. Bars to the left, conversely, indicate a balance of disagreement.

25 The first chart, therefore, shows how the views of people living in the City of Exeter differ from those across the rest of Devon. In doing so, it illustrates the attitudes or perceptions that are, in relative terms, shared by both groups of residents (where the bars project in the same direction), and those where views differ markedly. Thus there is broad agreement on many of the positive aspects of change, although residents in Exeter itself tend to feel more strongly, as one might expect. There is broad agreement that the County Council is needed for national representation (here, however, it is residents in the rest of Devon who feel more strongly). On the other hand, there is some divergence when it comes to whether change would be too disruptive, or whether a unitary Exeter would be too small to manage services like education and social services. There is also divergence on whether people feel that they will be affected by change; people in Exeter are more likely to agree that they would like more information before making up their minds.

26 The subsequent chart takes the results from just Exeter (and then from residents in the rest of Devon), and illustrates the difference in views between those within Exeter whose preference is for unitary status, and those who prefer no change. The chart therefore illustrates those attitudinal statements that most, or least, differentiate the residents of the City expressing the two opposing preferences. The perceived impact on efficiency is clearly a key determinant of opinion (in both Exeter and the rest of Devon), as are size, disruption and impact on services. People in Exeter who express a preference for no change are more likely to say they would like more information than are people who opt for a change to unitary status.

Attitudes to Change
(All respondents)

Q To what extent do you agree or disagree that...?
(Figures represent 'mean scores' with *strong agreement* given a value of +2 through to *strong disagreement* given -2)

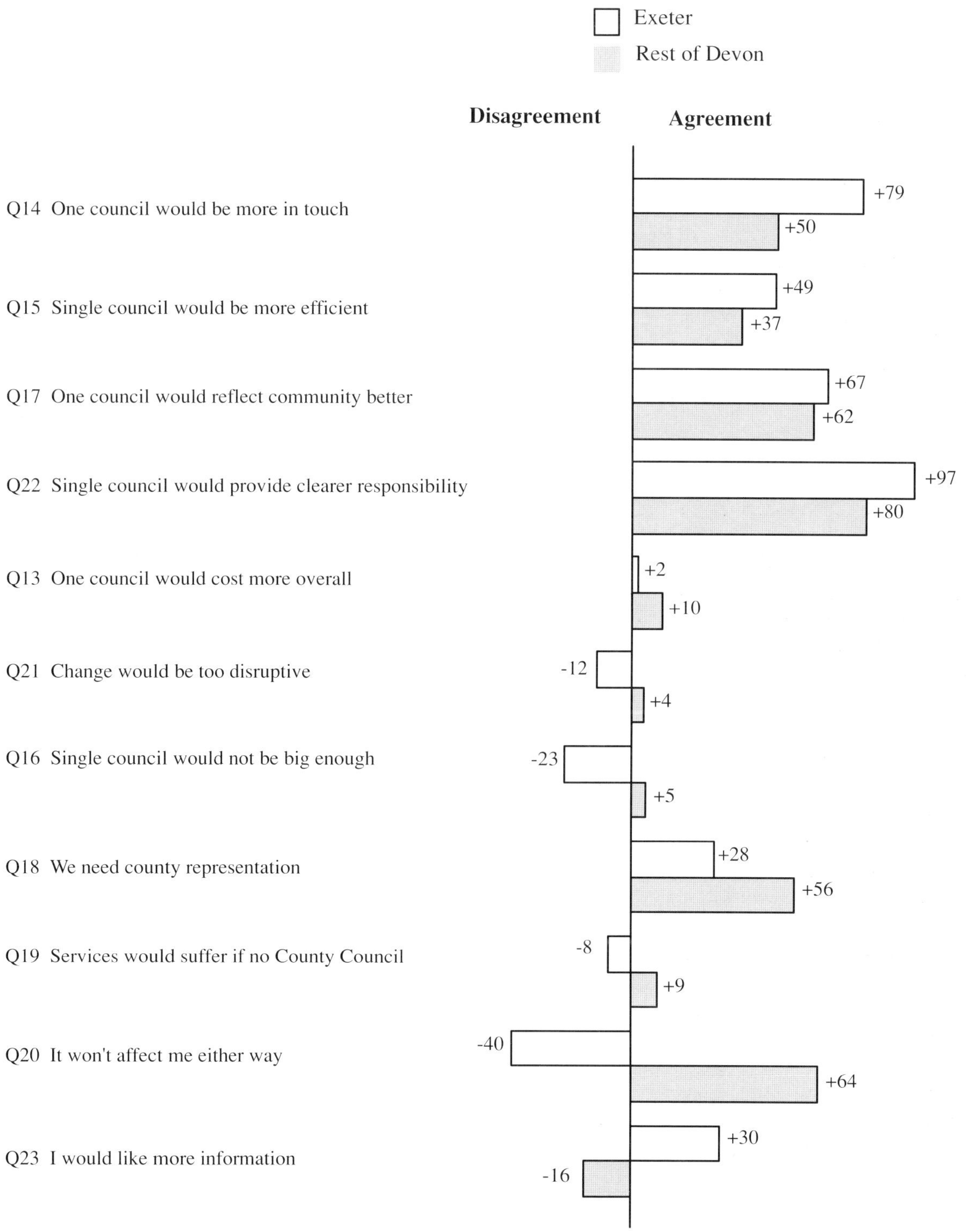

Attitudes to Change
(Respondents in Exeter)

Q To what extent do you agree or disagree that...?
(Figures represent 'mean scores' with *strong agreement* given a value of +2 through to *strong disagreement* given -2)

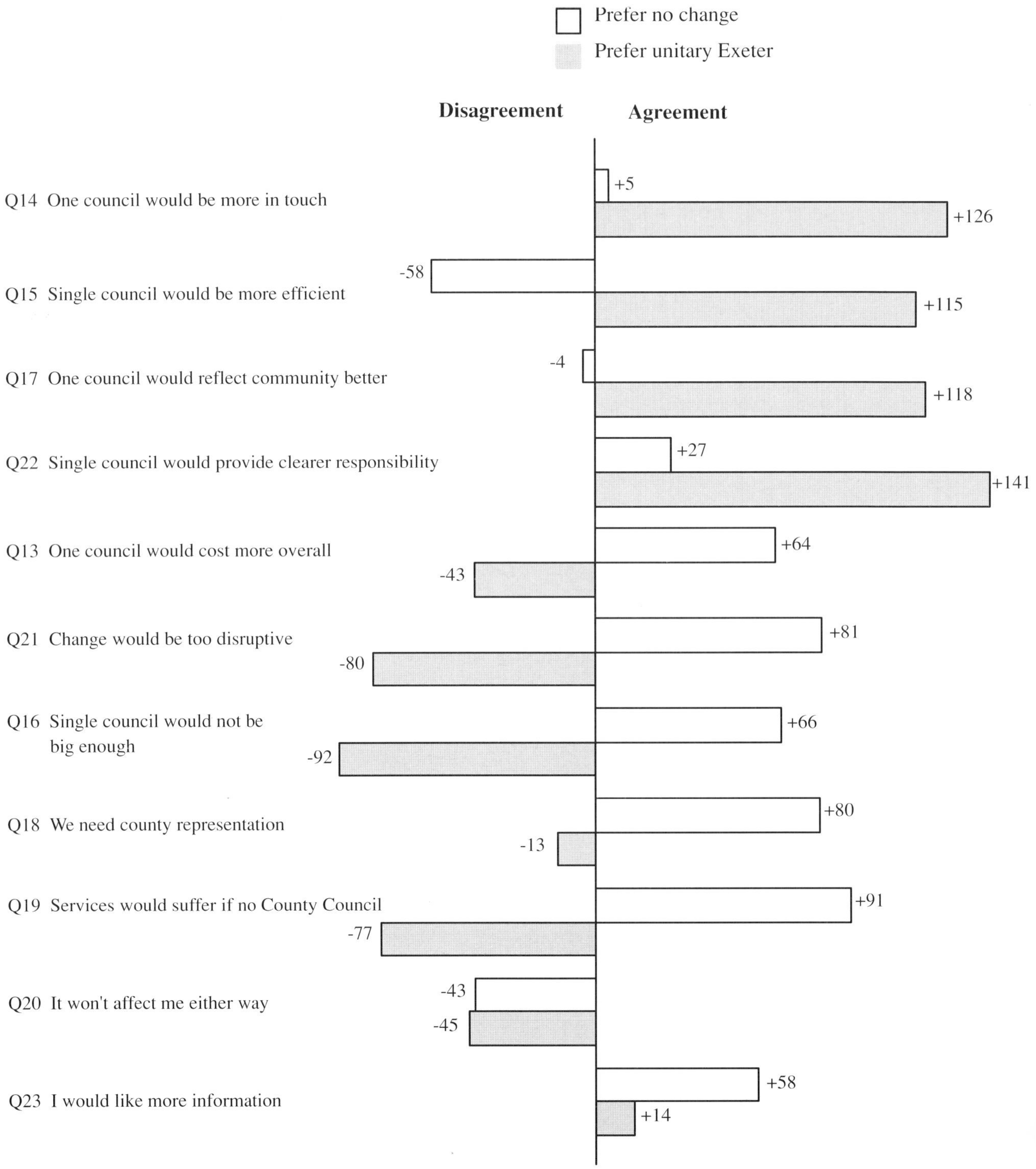

Attitudes to Change
(Respondents in the rest of Devon)

Q To what extent do you agree or disagree that...?
(Figures represent 'mean scores' with *strong agreement* given a value of +2 through to *strong disagreement* given -2)

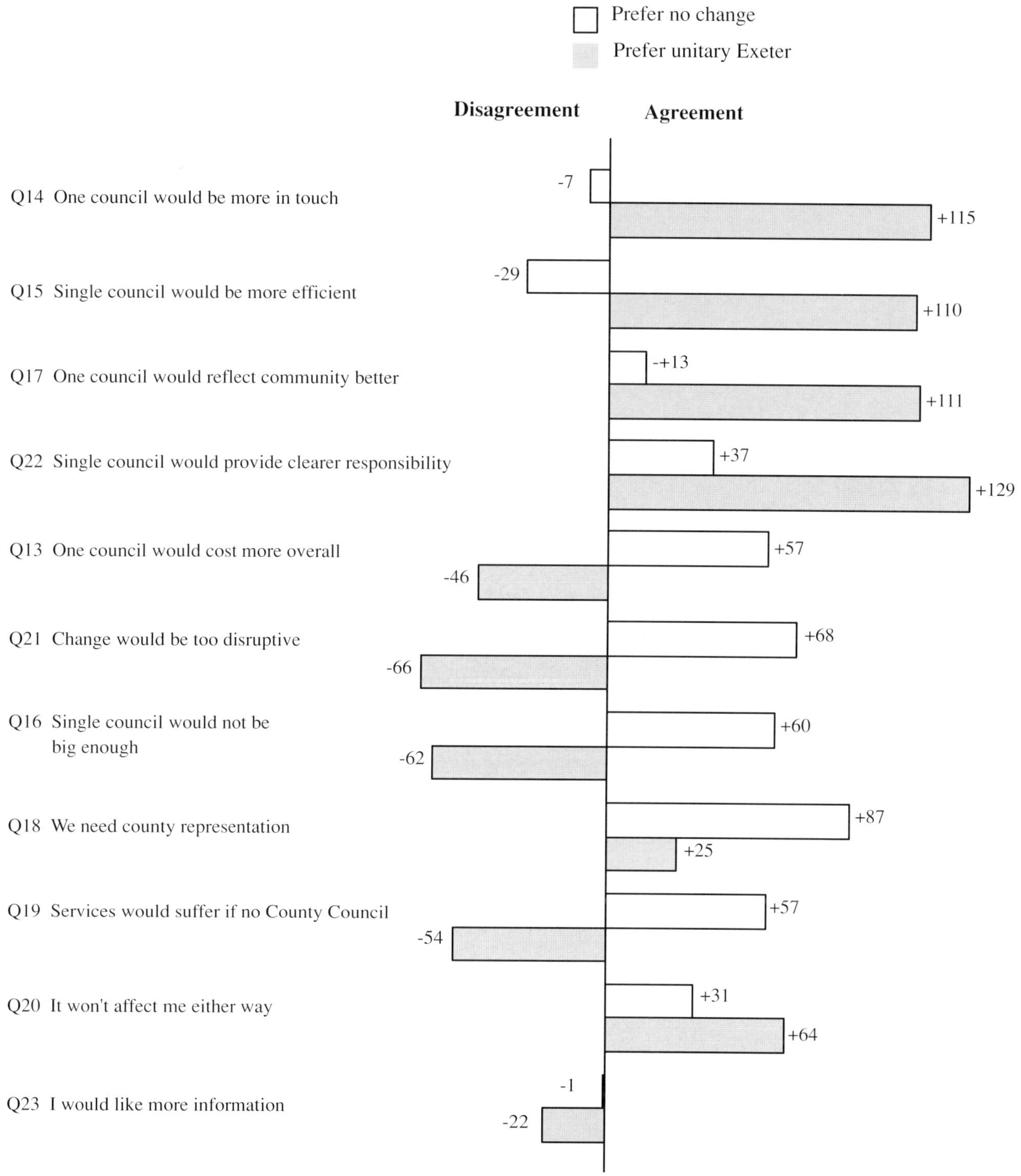

MORI/9101/03
(1-6)

DEVON
REVIEW - REST OF COUNTY

Serial No ....
OUO (7-10)

Name/Initials/Title ....

Address ....

.... **Postcode**..

Telephone: Yes.. 1 (11)
Number (inc STD code)
No 2

Sample Point
(12) (13) (14) (15) (16)

Gender %
Male 47
Female 53

Age %
18-24 12
25-34 17
35-44 16
45-54 16
55-64 13
65-74 17
75+.. 10

WRITE IN AGE

Work Status %
Full-time (30 hrs/wk+) 41
Part-time (8-29 hrs/wk) 7
Not working (under 8 hrs) 3
Looking after home/children........... 14
Retired 27
Registered unemployed................... 6
Unemployed but not registered 1
Student... 1
Other 0

Occupation of Chief Income Earner (CIE)
Position/rank/grade

....
Industry/type of company

....
Qualifications/degrees/apprenticeship

....
No of Staff Responsible for

....
PROBE FOR PENSION

	%
AB	18
C1	32
C2	23
D	12
E	15

* Less than $^1/_2$%

Number in Household
Adults aged 18+ (inc. respondent)

1 2 3 4 5+

Children (17 or under)

0 1 2 3 4+

QA **Are you or other members of your household employed by a council?** IF YES: **Is this a Borough/District Council or a County Council?** CODE FOR BOTH RESPONDENT AND OTHER HOUSEHOLD MEMBERS

	Respondent %	Other %
Yes:		
Borough/District	0	1
County	4	5
Don't know which	0	*
No	96	80
Don't know	0	14

Tenure %
Owned outright.. 32
Buying on mortgage 40
Rented from Council 13
Rented from Housing Association 2
Rented from private landlord 10
Other 3

QB **Is this your main permanent home, or is it a second or holiday home?**
%
Main/permanent...................................... 99
Second/holiday 1

Car in Household
CIRCLE NUMBER

0 1 2 3+

Showcard Version %
A-K ....
A1-K ....

THIS FORM IS THE PROPERTY OF MARKET & OPINION RESEARCH INTERNATIONAL (MORI)
32 OLD QUEEN STREET, LONDON, SW1H 9HP

INTERVIEWER DECLARATION: I confirm that I have conducted this interview face-to-face with the above named person and that I have asked all the relevant questions fully and recorded the answers in conformance with the survey specification and the MRS Code of Conduct.

Interviewer Name .... Signature ....

Interviewer Number					/	

	Month			Date	
DATE OF INTERVIEW					
	(29)	(30)		(30)	(32)

NB INTERVIEWER: ALL SHOWCARDS HAVE BEEN REVERSED. PLEASE BE CAREFUL TO CODE THE CORRECT RESPONSE.

Good morning/afternoon/evening. I'm from MORI, the market research and polling organisation. We are doing a survey about local issues, and I would like to ask you a few questions.

ASK ALL

Q1 **Firstly, how long have you lived in this area?** (WITHIN FIVE MILES)

	%
Less than 1 year	7
1-2 years	8
3-5 years	10
6-10 years	18
11-20 years	18
Over 20 years/all my life	39
Don't know/can't remember	0

Q2 SHOWCARD A (R) **From this card, how much would you say you know about local councils and the services they provide?**

	%
A great deal	2
A fair amount	36
Not very much	47
Nothing at all	15
Don't know	1

Q3 SHOWCARD B (R) **Which of the statements on this card comes closest to your own view of the Councils in this area?**

		%
A)	I'm not interested in what the Council does, or whether they do their job	3
B)	I'm not interested in what the Council does, as long as they do their job	17
C)	I like to know what the Council is doing, but I'm happy to let them get on with their job	57
D)	I would like to have more of a say in what the Council does and the services it provides	19
E)	I already work for, or am involved with the Council and the services it provides	3
	Don't know	1

Q4 **From what you know, how many councils provide the main services in this neighbourhood?** (INTERVIEWER - NOT INCLUDING PARISH COUNCILS)

	%
One	25
Two	31
Three+	5
Don't know	38

In fact there are two main councils that provide, or are responsible for most services in this area: . . .district/borough/city and Devon County Council.

ROTATE ORDER OF Q5/6

☐ Q5 SHOWCARD C (R) **From this list, what services do you think are the responsibility of... district/borough/city council? Just read out the letter(s) that apply**

☐ Q6 SHOWCARD C AGAIN (R) **And which services on this list do you think are the responsibility of Devon County Council? Again, just read out the letters that apply.**

Q7 SHOWCARD D (R) **Which, if any, of these services do you or members of your family use?** INCLUDE ONLY LOCAL USE

		Q5 "Borough" %	Q6 County %	Q7 Use %
A	Bus Services	36	24	44
B	Car Parks	63	15	66
C	Council Housing	55	24	14
D	Council Tax Benefit/Housing benefit	53	23	23
E	Fire service	20	58	37
F	Food safety	32	32	17
G	Household waste sites/dumps	53	18	48
H	Libraries	33	48	61
I	Parks, playgrounds and open spaces	58	16	54
J	Planning service	44	30	17
K	Public conveniences	63	10	54
L	Recycling/bottle banks	54	15	53
M	Refuse collection	69	13	87
N	Road maintenance	24	58	45
O	Schools/education	18	66	35
P	Social services	24	54	13
Q	Street sweeping	65	9	41
R	Swimming pools/sports facilities	54	16	54
	Other	2	1	0
	None of these	0	1	*
	Don't know	15	16	2

Q8 SHOWCARD E (R) **As you may know, there is currently a review being undertaken by the Local Government Commission on the future local government structure in the county. How much, if anything, would you say you know about this?**

	%
A great deal	1
A fair amount	11
Just a little	39
Heard of but know nothing about	19
Never heard of	30

PREFERENCES

HAND OVER MAP SHOWING AREAS UNDER REVIEW AND "CURRENT SERVICES" CARD
The Local Government Commission is considering options for the future structure of local government in Exeter. Could you please read through this card, (SHOW OPTIONS CARD) **which outlines the options.**

Q9 **Please tell me which of the options, if either, you would prefer for Exeter?**
SINGLE CODE ONLY

	%
For Exeter	
Option A (Stay the same/status quo)	42
Option B (Single all purpose council)	32
Some other option	2
Neither of these	*
Either of these/don't mind	10
Don't care	5
Don't know	8

ASK IF "OTHER" NAMED AT Q9 (CODE 3)
Q10 **What other option is that?**
PROBE FULLY - DO NOT PROMPT.

....

....

....

....

ASK ALL PREFERRING AN OPTION (1, 2 OR 3 AT Q9). OTHERS GO TO Q13
Q11 SHOWCARD F (R) **You say that the option you would prefer is . . . . .** (INSERT OPTION PREFERRED). **How strongly would you say you feel about this?**

	%
Very strongly	9
Fairly strongly	47
Not very strongly	31
Not at all strongly	8
Don't know	6

Q12 **What do you think would be the main advantages of . . .**(OPTION PREFERRED)
PROBE FULLY FOR DETAILS

....

....

....

....

....

Nothing..........
Don't know/can't think of anything..........

ATTITUDES TO PROPOSALS

SHOWCARD G (R) **Imagine that there was one council in Exeter providing all services. I am going to read out some statements that people have made about this proposal. To what extent do you agree or disagree that . . . .?**
READ OUT, ROTATE ORDER OF ASKING Q13-22. TICK START

READ OUT:	Strongly agree	Tend to agree	Neither/ Nor	Tend to disagree	Strongly disagree	Don't know
☐ Q13 **It would cost more overall**	9	30	15	32	4	11
Q14 **It would be more in touch with local people's needs**	12	50	9	20	4	5
Q15 **The single Council would be more efficient than the current system of two Councils**	13	39	13	23	4	9
☐ Q16 **The single council would not be big enough to manage services such as Education and Social Services effectively**	7	32	12	33	4	12
Q17 **It would better reflect the sense of community in Exeter**	11	52	13	15	1	8
Q18 **We need a County Council to represent us nationally**	14	48	12	20	2	5
☐ Q19 **Services would suffer if the County Council no longer provides services in Exeter**	7	34	12	29	5	12
Q20 **It won't affect me whether there is a single Council in Exeter or not**	23	44	7	19	4	3
Q21 **The change to a single Council for Exeter would be too disruptive**	6	31	18	31	4	10
☐ Q22 **With a single Council it would be clearer who is responsible for local services**	17	57	9	11	2	4
ASK LAST Q23 **I would like to have more information on the proposals before making up my mind**	12	24	10	35	15	4

Q24 **On balance, which would you say is more in touch with local people and issues, ...** (ROTATE ORDER OF "DISTRICT" AND COUNTY) (INSERT NAME OF "DISTRICT COUNCIL)..**district/borough/city council, or Devon County Council, or would you say that they are both about the same?**

	%
District/borough/city council	54
Devon County Council	7
Both about the same	28
Don't know	11

REFER BACK TO Q8. ASK ALL WHO HAVE HEARD OF REVIEW AT Q8 (IE CODES 1/2/3/4). OTHERS TO Q28

Q25 SHOWCARD H **Earlier in the interview, you said that you had heard of the Review of local government structure. From which, if any, of the sources shown on this card have you recently heard about the Review?** INTERVIEWER NOTE: "RECENTLY" = IN PAST 3 MONTHS

		%
A	Leaflet from County Council delivered to your door	16
B	Leaflet from County Council in library/ offices, etc	1
C	Advertisement from County Council in local newspaper	7
D	Advertisement from County Council on local radio/TV	2
E	Leaflet from Borough Council delivered to your door	11
F	Leaflet from Borough Council in library/ offices, etc	2
G	Borough Council newspaper	2
H	County Council newspaper	3
I	Advertisement from Borough Council in local newspaper	4
J	Advertisement from Borough Council on local radio/TV	3
K	Advertisement by the Commission on local radio	0
L	Local Government Commission advertisement in local newspaper	3
M	Local newspaper	46
N	National newspaper	12
O	TV	40
P	Local radio	20
Q	National radio	3
R	Friends/neighbours/family	12
S	Conversation with Borough Councillor	3
T	Conversation with County Councillor	2
U	Conversation with Borough Council staff	2
V	Conversation with County Council staff	2
W	Parish/community council	4
X	Residents' Association	*
	Other	4
	None of these	4
	Don't know	6

ASK ALL NAMING A SOURCE AT Q25. OTHERS GO TO Q28

Q26 **Would you say that the information you have received has influenced your opinion, or not?**

	%
Yes	17
No	78
Don't know	5

Q27 **What information in particular has influenced your opinion?**

....

....

....

....

ASK ALL

Q28 SHOWCARD I (R) **Assuming you receive the same level of services, how important is it to you, if at all, what the final decision is on the future local government structure in Exeter?**

	%
Very important	9
Fairly important	22
Not very important	35
Not at all important	32
Don't know	3

ACTIVISM

Q29 SHOWCARD J **Which of the things on this list, if any, have you done in the last three years? Just read out the letter(s) that apply.**

		%
A	Voted in Local Council elections	68
B	Spoken or written to a local Councillor	31
C	Responded to the earlier Review of local government	8
D	Been to a meeting of a local committee or organisation	12
E	Spoken on a radio phone-in about a local issue	2
F	Written to a local newspaper about a local issue	5
G	Been to a meeting of a local branch of a political party	3
H	Written to your MP about a local issue	8
I	Been to a Council Committee meeting	3
J	Been to a Council meeting	5
K	Attended a public meeting run by the Council	7
	None of these	25
	Don't know/refused	2

Q30 SHOWCARD K **Which, if any, of these apply to you? Just read out the letter(s) that apply.**

		%
	I am a member of a:	
A	Residents' Association	4
B	Community Association	2
C	Tenants' Association	1
D	Neighbourhood Watch	18
E	PTA/school governors	6
	I do unpaid work for:	
F	A school	9
G	Citizens Advice Bureau	0
H	Volunteer Bureau	3
I	Scouts/Guides/Cubs/Brownies	4
J	Church group	6
	Other	7
	None of these	61
	Don't know	1

THANK RESPONDENT. GO TO DEMOGRAPHICS.

- 8 -

MORI/9101/03 (1-6)

DEVON
REVIEW - EXETER

Serial No . . . . OUO (7-10)

Name/Initials/Title ....

Address ....

.... **Postcode**..

Telephone: Yes.. 1 (11)

Number (inc STD code)

No 2

Sample Point (12) (13) (14) (15) (16)

Gender

	%
Male	46
Female	54

Age

	%
18-24	14
25-34	20
35-44	14
45-54	17
55-64	14
65-74	11
75+	10

WRITE IN AGE

Work Status

	%
Full-time (30 hrs/wk+)	45
Part-time (8-29 hrs/wk)	10
Not working (under 8 hrs)	1
Looking after home/children	8
Retired	25
Registered unemployed	3
Unemployed but not registered	2
Student	5
Other	*

Occupation of Chief Income Earner (CIE)

Position/rank/grade

....

Industry/type of company

....

Qualifications/degrees/apprenticeship

....

No of Staff Responsible for

....

PROBE FOR PENSION

	%
AB	15
C1	32
C2	19
D	22
E	11

Number in Household
Adults aged 18+ (inc. respondent)

1 2 3 4 5+

Children (17 or under)

0 1 2 3 4+

QA **Are you or other members of your household employed by a council?** IF YES: **Is this a Borough/District Council or a County Council?** CODE FOR BOTH RESPONDENT AND OTHER HOUSEHOLD MEMBERS

	Respondent %	Other %
Yes:		
Borough/District	2	1
County	7	4
Don't know which	0	0
No	90	74
Don't know	1	21

Tenure

	%
Owned outright	24
Buying on mortgage	43
Rented from Council	16
Rented from Housing Association	5
Rented from private landlord	10
Other	2

QB **Is this your main permanent home, or is it a second or holiday home?**

	%
Main/permanent	98
Second/holiday	2

Car in Household
CIRCLE NUMBER

0 1 2 3+

Showcard Version

A-K ....

A1-K ....

THIS FORM IS THE PROPERTY OF MARKET & OPINION RESEARCH INTERNATIONAL (MORI)
32 OLD QUEEN STREET, LONDON, SW1H 9HP

INTERVIEWER DECLARATION: I confirm that I have conducted this interview face-to-face with the above named person and that I have asked all the relevant questions fully and recorded the answers in conformance with the survey specification and the MRS Code of Conduct.

Interviewer Name .... Signature ....

Interviewer Number					/	

	Month		Date		
DATE OF INTERVIEW					
	(29)	(30)		(30)	(32)

NB INTERVIEWER: ALL SHOWCARDS HAVE BEEN REVERSED. PLEASE BE CAREFUL TO CODE THE CORRECT RESPONSE.

Good morning/afternoon/evening. I'm from MORI, the market research and polling organisation. We are doing a survey about local issues, and I would like to ask you a few questions.

ASK ALL

Q1 **Firstly, how long have you lived in this area?** (WITHIN FIVE MILES)

	%
Less than 1 year	6
1-2 years	10
3-5 years	12
6-10 years	12
11-20 years	21
Over 20 years/all my life	38
Don't know/can't remember	-

Q2 SHOWCARD A (R) **From this card, how much would you say you know about local councils and the services they provide?**

	%
A great deal	5
A fair amount	37
Not very much	50
Nothing at all	7
Don't know	-

Q3 SHOWCARD B (R) **Which of the statements on this card comes closest to your own view of the Councils in this area?**

		%
A)	I'm not interested in what the Council does, or whether they do their job	2
B)	I'm not interested in what the Council does, as long as they do their job	14
C)	I like to know what the Council is doing, but I'm happy to let them get on with their job	57
D)	I would like to have more of a say in what the Council does and the services it provides	21
E)	I already work for, or am involved with the Council and the services it provides	5
	Don't know	1

Q4 **From what you know, how many councils provide the main services in this neighbourhood?** (INTERVIEWER - NOT INCLUDING PARISH COUNCILS)

	%
One	20
Two	44
Three+	2
Don't know	33

In fact there are two main councils that provide, or are responsible for most services in this area: Exeter City Council and Devon County Council.

ROTATE ORDER OF Q5/6

☐ Q5 SHOWCARD C (R) **From this list, what services do you think are the responsibility of Exeter City Council? Just read out the letter(s) that apply**

☐ Q6 SHOWCARD C AGAIN (R) **And which services on this list do you think are the responsibility of Devon County Council? Again, just read out the letters that apply.**

Q7 SHOWCARD D (R) **Which, if any, of these services do you or members of your family use?** INCLUDE ONLY LOCAL USE

		Q5 Exeter %	Q6 Devon %	Q7 Use %
A	Bus Services	39	22	63
B	Car Parks	62	17	61
C	Council Housing	61	17	13
D	Council Tax Benefit/Housing benefit	52	25	24
E	Fire service	16	63	36
F	Food safety	28	34	18
G	Household waste sites/dumps	50	25	50
H	Libraries	24	54	61
I	Parks, playgrounds and open spaces	62	17	57
J	Planning service	36	43	12
K	Public conveniences	64	11	57
L	Recycling/bottle banks	59	15	62
M	Refuse collection	68	9	84
N	Road maintenance	28	54	43
O	Schools/education	11	66	35
P	Social services	15	60	15
Q	Street sweeping	68	10	50
R	Swimming pools/sports facilities	57	12	51
	Other	2	2	2
	None of these	0	1	0
	Don't know	12	14	2

Q8 SHOWCARD E (R) **As you may know, there is currently a review being undertaken by the Local Government Commission on the future local government structure in the county. How much, if anything, would you say you know about this?**

	%
A great deal	3
A fair amount	14
Just a little	44
Heard of but know nothing about	19
Never heard of	21

PREFERENCES

HAND OVER MAP SHOWING AREAS UNDER REVIEW AND "CURRENT SERVICES" CARD
The Local Government Commission is considering options for the future structure of local government in Exeter. Could you please read through this card, (SHOW OPTIONS CARD) **which outlines the options.**

Q9 **Please tell me which of the options, if either, you would prefer for Exeter?**
SINGLE CODE ONLY

For Exeter

	%
Option A (Stay the same/status quo)	32
Option B (Single all purpose council)	53
Some other option	1
Neither of these	1
Either of these/don't mind	4
Don't care	2
Don't know	8

ASK IF "OTHER" NAMED AT Q9 (CODE 3)

Q10 **What other option is that?**
PROBE FULLY - DO NOT PROMPT.

....

....

....

....

ASK ALL PREFERRING AN OPTION (1, 2 OR 3 AT Q9). OTHERS GO TO Q13

Q11 SHOWCARD F (R) **You say that the option you would prefer is . . . . .** (INSERT OPTION PREFERRED). **How strongly would you say you feel about this?**

	%
Very strongly	26
Fairly strongly	48
Not very strongly	21
Not at all strongly	2
Don't know	3

Q12 **What do you think would be the main advantages of . . .**(OPTION PREFERRED)
PROBE FULLY FOR DETAILS

....

....

....

....

....

Nothing..
Don't know/can't think of anything..

ATTITUDES TO PROPOSALS

SHOWCARD G (R) **Imagine that there was one council in Exeter providing all services. I am going to read out some statements that people have made about this proposal. To what extent do you agree or disagree that . . . .?**
READ OUT, ROTATE ORDER OF ASKING Q13-22. TICK START

READ OUT:	Strongly agree	Tend to agree	Neither/ Nor	Tend to disagree	Strongly disagree	Don't know
☐ Q13 **It would cost more overall**	8	27	15	28	6	15
Q14 **It would be more in touch with local people's needs**	21	55	6	12	4	2
Q15 **The single Council would be more efficient than the current system of two Councils**	17	39	12	13	8	10
☐ Q16 **The single council would not be big enough to manage services such as Education and Social Services effectively**	12	21	9	37	15	7
Q17 **It would better reflect the sense of community in Exeter**	16	53	10	11	5	5
Q18 **We need a County Council to represent us nationally**	11	42	13	23	7	5
☐ Q19 **Services would suffer if the County Council no longer provides services in Exeter**	9	29	11	32	11	8
Q20 **It won't affect me whether there is a single Council in Exeter or not**	5	26	9	34	20	7
Q21 **The change to a single Council for Exeter would be too disruptive**	10	26	12	31	13	7
☐ Q22 **With a single Council it would be clearer who is responsible for local services**	26	54	5	9	2	4
ASK LAST Q23 **I would like to have more information on the proposals before making up my mind**	24	34	3	18	17	4

Q24 **On balance, which would you say is more in touch with local people and issues, ...** (ROTATE ORDER OF "DISTRICT" AND COUNTY)
Exeter City Council, or
Devon County Council, or would you say that they are both about the same?

	%
District/borough/city council	54
Devon County Council	3
Both about the same	32
Don't know	11

REFER BACK TO Q8. ASK ALL WHO HAVE HEARD OF REVIEW AT Q8 (IE CODES 1/2/3/4). OTHERS TO Q28

Q25 SHOWCARD H **Earlier in the interview, you said that you had heard of the Review of local government structure. From which, if any, of the sources shown on this card have you recently heard about the Review?** INTERVIEWER NOTE: "RECENTLY" = IN PAST 3 MONTHS

		%
A	Leaflet from County Council delivered to your door	30
B	Leaflet from County Council in library/ offices, etc	9
C	Advertisement from County Council in local newspaper	13
D	Advertisement from County Council on local radio/TV	5
E	Leaflet from Borough Council delivered to your door	17
F	Leaflet from Borough Council in library/ offices, etc	4
G	Borough Council newspaper	14
H	County Council newspaper	5
I	Advertisement from Borough Council in local newspaper	5
J	Advertisement from Borough Council on local radio/TV	5
K	Advertisement by the Commission on local radio	3
L	Local Government Commission advertisement in local newspaper	5
M	Local newspaper	58
N	National newspaper	9
O	TV	32
P	Local radio	21
Q	National radio	6
R	Friends/neighbours/family	15
S	Conversation with Borough Councillor	4
T	Conversation with County Councillor	1
U	Conversation with Borough Council staff	3
V	Conversation with County Council staff	4
W	Parish/community council	*
X	Residents' Association	1
	Other	6
	None of these	2
	Don't know	3

ASK ALL NAMING A SOURCE AT Q25. OTHERS GO TO Q28

Q26 **Would you say that the information you have received has influenced your opinion, or not?**

	%
Yes	23
No	74
Don't know	4

Q27 **What information in particular has influenced your opinion?**

....

....

....

....

ASK ALL

Q28 SHOWCARD I (R) **Assuming you receive the same level of services, how important is it to you, if at all, what the final decision is on the future local government structure in Exeter?**

	%
Very important	29
Fairly important	40
Not very important	23
Not at all important	5
Don't know	3

ACTIVISM

Q29 SHOWCARD J **Which of the things on this list, if any, have you done in the last three years? Just read out the letter(s) that apply.**

		%
A	Voted in Local Council elections	81
B	Spoken or written to a local Councillor	38
C	Responded to the earlier Review of local government	11
D	Been to a meeting of a local committee or organisation	6
E	Spoken on a radio phone-in about a local issue	2
F	Written to a local newspaper about a local issue	5
G	Been to a meeting of a local branch of a political party	3
H	Written to your MP about a local issue	10
I	Been to a Council Committee meeting	1
J	Been to a Council meeting	1
K	Attended a public meeting run by the Council	6
	None of these	15
	Don't know/refused	0

Q30 SHOWCARD K **Which, if any, of these apply to you? Just read out the letter(s) that apply.**

		%
	I am a member of a:	
A	Residents' Association	4
B	Community Association	2
C	Tenants' Association	2
D	Neighbourhood Watch	16
E	PTA/school governors	3
	I do unpaid work for:	
F	A school	4
G	Citizens Advice Bureau	*
H	Volunteer Bureau	3
I	Scouts/Guides/Cubs/Brownies	4
J	Church group	8
	Other	5
	None of these	65
	Don't know	0

THANK RESPONDENT. GO TO DEMOGRAPHICS

CHAPTER 6

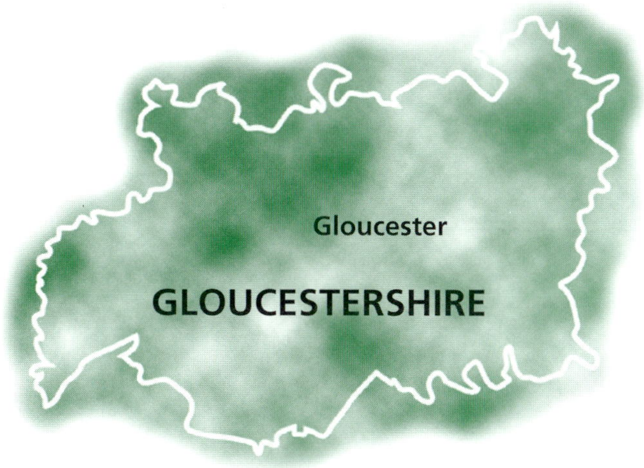

GLOUCESTER IN THE COUNTY OF GLOUCESTERSHIRE

Draft Recommendations

6.1 The Commission's report *Draft Recommendations on the Future Local Government of Gloucester in the County of Gloucestershire* summarised the evidence taken into account by the Commission in reaching its draft recommendations.

Figure 6.1
Draft Recommendations for Gloucester in the County of Gloucestershire

Structure
- There should be no change to the existing two-tier structure of local government in Gloucester.

Electoral Arrangements
- Gloucester City Council's warding arrangements should be amended such that the boundaries of the existing wards of Hucclecote and Barnwood are adjusted and a new ward of Abbeymead is created. All of these wards should have three councillors. The existing ward of Quedgeley should remain on its existing boundaries but have its democratic representation increased from two to three councillors.

Views Expressed to the Commission

6.2 The Commission received a wide range of direct representations on its draft recommendations, from local authorities, residents, Members of Parliament, business and voluntary groups, parish and town councils, and from other public and private sector organisations. Around 900 representations were received from individuals and organisations, including just over 600 from respondents within Gloucester. The Commission also received nearly 400 representations in the form of standard letters, response slips and petitions. (Figures 6.2 and 6.3). Figures 6.2 and 6.3 exclude representations from the local authorities; these are summarised separately (Figure 6.4).

Figure 6.2
Views of Respondents Within Gloucester

Preferred structure	Individuals	Organisations	Standard letters and petition signatures
Unitary Gloucester	479	31	252
No change	78	20	18
Other	8	0	0
No preference	4	0	0

Source: Local Government Commission for England and NOP

Figure 6.3
Views of Respondents From Outside the Review District

Preferred structure	Individuals	Organisations	Standard letters and petition signatures
Unitary Gloucester	16	6	0
No change	162	93	115
Other	1	2	0
No preference	1	0	0

Source: Local Government Commission for England and NOP
Note: Excludes out of county representations

6.3 In addition, 23 representations were received from outside the county, of which nearly three-quarters supported the Commission's draft recommendation. A more detailed tabulation of the written representations from individuals and interest groups, produced by NOP on behalf of the Commission, can be found towards the end of this Chapter.

The Views of Local Authorities

6.4 The Commission received submissions from four of the seven principal local authorities in Gloucestershire during Stage Three (Figure 6.4).

6.5 Of the authorities that responded to the draft recommendation, none had changed its position from that expressed in Stage One. Gloucester City Council supported the draft recommendation in relation to electoral changes within the City, as did Gloucestershire County Council, and no objections were received. However, the City Council proposed a minor ward boundary change in relation to the draft recommendation. The reasons for this change and the associated maps are set out in Volume I.

6.6 Unitary status for Gloucester was supported by Bristol City Council which stated that "...this Council sees that [unitary Gloucester] as essential in establishing a vigorous West of England region, apart from the other merits of the Gloucester case". Thamesdown Borough Council, which is based in Swindon, also supported a unitary Gloucester for similar reasons.

Figure 6.4
Preferences of Gloucestershire Local Authorities at Stage Three

Authority	Preference
Gloucester City Council	Reaffirmed its support for a unitary authority based on the present boundaries of Gloucester. Considered that the "...size, configuration and character" (of the City) are fully consistent with the criteria for unitary authorities.
Forest of Dean District Council	Continued to support the unitary principle. Recognised demand for unitary status from Gloucester City Council but pointed to their own case as being no less strong. Believed that County Council services would be weakened by the granting of unitary status for Gloucester alone.
Stroud District Council	The Council was content with the draft recommendations.
Cheltenham Borough Council	No opinion expressed in Stage Three.
Cotswold District Council	No opinion expressed in Stage Three.
Tewkesbury Borough Council	No opinion expressed in Stage Three.
Gloucestershire County Council	Reaffirmed its support for the retention of the existing two-tier structure throughout the county.

Source: Local authorities' submissions

6.7 The Gloucestershire Branch of the Association of District Councils did not make representations; the Association of District Councils' national submission is referred to in Summary of National Representations. The Association of County Councils supported the retention of the present structure.

The Views of Others

6.8 A range of other interest groups made representations on the Commission's draft recommendations as summarised in the following paragraphs. These are in addition to those made in Stage One.

Businesses and Business Groups

6.9 The Commission received nearly 40 submissions from individual businesses, business groups and Chambers of Commerce throughout the county. Overall, the views expressed were divided equally between support for the two-tier structure and support for unitary Gloucester.

6.10 There was particular support for Gloucester to be unitary from businesses based in the city. Three-quarters of those that responded had that view. The Gloucester Chamber of Trade and Commerce, which represents a major section of the business community, stated that: "The present two-tier system should now be abolished. Its very nature ensures an element of unnecessary duplication, provides confusion for residents and creates difficulty in establishing responsibility...a single council for Gloucester will be more focused in attracting the new investment, new jobs and funding from Europe that is needed at this time of major change in the regional structure". Similar views were expressed by individual businesses and smaller umbrella groups such as the Gloucestershire Ethnic Minority Business Association.

6.11 Views were also expressed from a number of major business groups calling for the retention of the existing two-tier structure in Gloucester. The Gloucestershire Chamber of Commerce and Industry, the Gloucestershire Training and Enterprise Council and the South West Region of the Confederation of British Industry (CBI) were of this mind. The CBI stated that "Gloucester is too small an area on which to form a unitary authority...a unitary Gloucester would produce increased costs and duplication of services".

6.12 Overall, opinion was polarised, with a picture of broad support for unitary status from within the city, and support for no change from county-wide business groups and individual businesses from elsewhere in the county.

County, Regional and National Interests (including the Voluntary Sector)

6.13 Apart from the county and regional business and commerce groups previously mentioned, the Commission received only a relatively limited response from this sector. In general, county-wide bodies supported the retention of the existing two-tier structure. Organisations such as Young Gloucestershire and the Gloucestershire Association for Mental Health held this view. The Gloucester City Society for the Mentally Handicapped argued that: "Gloucester City would not have the financial resources or the right calibre of professional staff to provide the education and social services responsibilities".

6.14 The two-tier structure was also generally favoured by regional bodies. For example, the Central Region of the National Farmers Union argued that: "The creation of a unitary authority for the City may seriously dilute these strategic services [trading standards, animal welfare enforcement]". The Town and Country Planning Association supported no change and said that: "Our particular concerns are the need to balance strategic planning with democratic control and community involvement". The submission from the Lord Lieutenant of Gloucestershire also supported the retention of the existing structure.

Education Groups

6.15 As with many other sectors of the community, the Commission received submissions on educational matters that were very polarised. From bodies within the city there was some support for unitary status, whilst from the rest of the county the view was that any change would damage services throughout. Overall, more than 85 per cent of responses were in support of the two-tier structure.

6.16 The Central Technology College in Gloucester argued that "...the City of Gloucester is a different entity from other areas of the county... Successive plans for reorganisation of the City schools have been 'blocked' by councillors from outside the City... lack of real direction for the City has caused middle class parents to seek the more stable environment of out of City schools". The Principal of the College went on to say that in his view: "The needs of education within the City can best be met by a more intimate and greater focused local authority which does not have to meet the conflicting needs of a diverse county".

6.17 The opposite view was put forward by county educational groups. The majority of respondents from outside the city supported the draft recommendation of no change. The Gloucestershire Branch of the Association of Teachers and Lecturers argued that "...a unitary council for Gloucester City is not viable and would cause both unnecessary waste of money and damage the provision of the education services in the rest of the county". This was strongly echoed in many other submissions.

Health Interests

6.18 In general, health authorities and trusts involved with local authorities in Gloucestershire did not respond with a firm opinion on the particular position of Gloucester. For example, the South and West NHS Executive voiced concerns regarding the "...quality of existing relationships with local government in areas that impact directly on the health, welfare and care of individuals, which might be compromised by the establishment of two separate social service authorities".

6.19 The Gloucestershire Royal NHS Trust was the one health body which supported the case for unitary status. In its submission, it stated that "...a unitary Gloucester authority would enable the Trust to negotiate community care, housing and related services with one organisation rather than two. for a substantial proportion of its patients". The Trust argued that: "Gloucester City is also unique within the county, in having a significant ethnic minority population" and that "Gloucester and Cheltenham, whilst in close proximity, are distinctive in character and independent of each other".

Law, Order and Emergency Services

6.20 The Commission received a small number of submissions from this sector. Bodies such as the Magistrates' Courts Service and the Probation Service were firmly in support of the Commission's draft recommendation for no change.

6.21 The Magistrates' Courts Service stated that "...arrangements for joint negotiations of budget and dealing with separate authorities in relation to the provision and maintenance of land and buildings would be cumbersome and wasteful".

Local Groups

6.22 Twenty local groups both within the city and from other parts of the county made representations. As with most other sectors, opinion tended to be divided, with support for a unitary authority coming from bodies within Gloucester and support for no change from those outside the city. The numbers who supported each option were broadly similar. Within Gloucester itself, there was a ratio of nearly four to one in favour of unitary status for the city.

6.23 From within Gloucester, groups such as the Barton Residents Association, Gloucestershire Housing Association, Oxbode Housing Association and the Hucclecote Community Association were of the view that Gloucester required unitary status for the city to go forward to the future. In particular, the submission from the Gloucestershire Housing Association argued that "...there is high unemployment, a concentration of poor quality, privately-owned housing, a high level of single parent families and evidence of poor educational attainment relative to the rest of the county. ...to accept therefore that the City has unique problems is also to acknowledge that the solutions must be unique". The Hucclecote Community Association expressed the view that "...from our experience the relationship with the City Council has been closer and more productive than was previously experienced with the County Council. ...this in turn is evident in the very positive attitude of local people to the City Council's record of effective local government, as opposed to the arm's length approach of the County Council".

6.24 Support for the retention of the two-tier structure from local groups was relatively strong, if limited in number. Bodies which made submissions supporting no change included the Diocese of Gloucester Board of Social Responsibility and the Society for Industrial Archaeology. In general, the main reasons given for this view were concerns about service delivery and provision, possible increased costs and the impact on the rest of the county.

Parliamentary Interests

6.25 Mr Douglas French, MP for Gloucester, supported unitary status for Gloucester and argued that "...it is clearly the case that the urban problems in the City differ sharply from those experienced in Cheltenham. Given this, the residents of Gloucester would be much better served by a unitary authority directly accountable to them".

6.26 Mr Nigel Jones, MP for Cheltenham, supported the draft recommendation for no change. He stated that: "Gloucester has been looked at by the Commission more than any other area in the country, and I welcome the decision of the Commission [to recommend] the status quo again".

6.27 In addition, the Labour Party Environment Spokesman, Mr Frank Dobson, MP for Holborn and St Pancras, expressed his concern at the concept of centrality. He argued the case for Gloucester to be granted unitary status. He commented that: "...the argument has to be confined to the question of whether taking from the counties their present responsibilities for education, social services and strategic planning and transport ... would remove the central keystone from those services county-wide". He felt that this was not the case in Gloucester.

Parish and Town Councils

6.28 Around fifty parish and town councils provided direct submissions to the Commission, of which 90 per cent supported the draft recommendation for no change. This included Quedgeley Parish Council which is the only parish within the boundaries of Gloucester. The Gloucestershire Association of Parish and Town Councils submitted details of a survey it had carried out among its members - this also came out strongly in favour of the present structure.

6.29 In general, the view from parish and town councils was that a unitary Gloucester authority would impair the delivery of services to rural areas. Many specialist services were based in Gloucester and parishes were concerned that a reorganisation of the County Council could lead to increased costs in providing services or a decrease in the quantity and quality of services delivered. Parish councils were also generally of the view that Gloucester was a vital part of the county and the needs of the county as a whole would best be met by retention of the two-tier structure.

NOP Tabulations of Written Representations

1 The following tabulations summarise the views expressed by members of the public and other interested parties during the consultation on the Local Government Commission's draft recommendations for Gloucester.

2 The tabulations include only letters sent directly to NOP at its Chelmsford offices and to the Commission's offices in London. Where more than one person's view has been expressed in a letter, the comments from each individual have been recorded separately. Staff from the Commission and NOP have worked closely in ensuring that care has been taken in the interpretation of comments, and that a consistent approach has been adopted.

3 While many people expressed support for one or other of the draft options presented by the Commission, other responses were coded by NOP after further discussion. The pattern of views expressed has been carefully examined, and where a number of respondents supported an option not included in those put forward by the Commission, those views have been separately coded and reported by NOP.

4 The Commission has advertised through the local media, encouraging people to make their views known. All responses received up to two days after the end of the Stage Three consultation period have been included. Returns from campaigns organised by local authorities or other groups (for example, standardised postcards and letters, questionnaires and petitions) have not been included in the tabulations. These, and submissions written and dated before the commencement of the consultation process, have been considered separately by the Commission.

The following definitions have been applied by NOP in compiling the tabulations:

(i) Type of Respondent

Individuals:	includes individual members of the public, local councillors and Members of the Westminster and European Parliaments.
Businesses and Business Groups:	includes organisations which represent businesses, such as local Chambers of Commerce.
County, Regional and National Interests:	any organisation which covers an area which is the size of a county or larger is included here, for example, a county-wide voluntary organisation or a regional association. This classification includes most of the statutory consultees.
Education (and Church) Groups:	this group includes schools, religious organisations and teaching unions.
Local Groups:	this includes organisations smaller than a county area, for example, a district-level voluntary sector body. The group could be voluntary, sporting, political or cultural but does not include organisations from the education or religious sectors (included above). It also includes constituency parties and political groups on local authorities.
Parish and Town Councils:	this also includes district-level associations of town and parish councils. County level associations are classified as County, Regional and National interests.

(ii) Structural Options (Reports A and D)

No change in own district:	this code is used where there is more than one review district in the county. It indicates where respondents from a review district have expressed support for no change for that district and have not made reference to the other review district(s) in that county.
District/county-level authorities:	represents support for either a district or county-level authority although it is not clear whether this is for a unitary or a two-tier structure.
Opposition to structural preferences:	represents responses where a negative, but unspecified, structural preference has been expressed.
Rejects:	rejects are those responses with unclear comments/interpretation.

(iii) Other

Other issues (Report B):	these illustrate preferences in relation to boundary and electoral changes and (where applicable) the restoration of historic counties.
Parishing issues (Report C):	these illustrate preferences in relation to parishing issues, for example, the creation of new parishes or the enhancement of the role of parish and town councils.
Services (Report E):	these illustrate concerns expressed about the impact of proposed changes on particular service areas where the respondent has not additionally expressed a positive structural preference.

NOP Analysis of Responses to Local Government Commission Draft Recommendations - GLOUCESTERSHIRE

Report A: Opinions on the structural options, by authority of respondent
Base: all

	Review district	Other districts in county							
	Gloucester	Cheltenham	Cotswold	Forest of Dean	Stroud	Tewkesbury	Rest of county total	County total	Out of county total
Status quo/two-tier	98 *16%*	40 *87%*	41 *93%*	38 *86%*	78 *94%*	58 *91%*	255 *91%*	353 *39%*	17 *74%*
Unitary Gloucester	510 *82%*	4 *9%*	2 *5%*	6 *14%*	5 *6%*	5 *8%*	22 *8%*	532 *59%*	2 *9%*
County-level authority (either two-tier or unitary)	1 *	- -	- -	- -	- -	- -	- -	1 *	- -
District-level authority (either two-tier or unitary)	3 *	- -	- -	- -	- -	- -	- -	3 *	- -
Pre-1974 structure	2 *	- -	- -	- -	- -	- -	- -	2 *	- -
County-wide unitary structure	1 *	1 *2%*	- -	- -	- -	1 *2%*	2 *1%*	3 *	- -
Other specified	1 *	- -	1 *2%*	- -	- -	- -	1 *	2 *	- -
No preference expressed/option defined	4 *1%*	1 *2%*	- -	- -	- -	- -	1 *	5 *1%*	4 *17%*
BASE TOTAL	620	46	44	44	83	64	281	901	23

* *Less than ½%*

Gloucester

NOP Analysis of Responses to Local Government Commission Draft Recommendations - GLOUCESTERSHIRE

Report B: Opinions on other issues, by authority of respondent
Base: all

	Review district	Other districts in county							
	Gloucester	Cheltenham	Cotswold	Forest of Dean	Stroud	Tewkesbury	Rest of county total	County total	Out of county total
Electoral issues	2 *	- -	- -	- -	- -	- -	- -	2 *	1 4%
BASE TOTAL	620	46	44	44	83	64	281	901	23

The figures in the table above do not sum to the base total/100% because undefined fields are not included, except as part of the base total.

* *Less than ½%*

NOP Analysis of Responses to Local Government Commission Draft Recommendations - GLOUCESTERSHIRE

Report C: Opinions on parishing issues, by authority of respondent
Base: all

	Review district	Other districts in county							
	Gloucester	Cheltenham	Cotswold	Forest of Dean	Stroud	Tewkesbury	Rest of county total	County total	Out of county total
BASE TOTAL	620	46	44	44	83	64	281	901	23

The figures in the table above do not sum to the base total/100% because undefined fields are not included, except as part of the base total.

NOP Analysis of Responses to Local Government Commission Draft Recommendations - GLOUCESTERSHIRE

Report D1: Opinions on the structural options, by respondent type (all respondents)
Base: all

	Respondent Type					
	Indiv-iduals	Business groups	County, regional & national interests	Education (& church) groups	Local groups	Parish and town councils
Status quo/two-tier	245 *32%*	20 *53%*	17 *68%*	34 *89%*	9 *45%*	45 *92%*
Unitary Gloucester	495 *66%*	18 *47%*	4 *16%*	4 *11%*	11 *55%*	2 *4%*
County-level authority (either two-tier or unitary)	1 *	- -	- -	- -	- -	- -
District-level authority (either two-tier or unitary)	3 *	- -	- -	- -	- -	- -
Pre-1974 structure	2 *	- -	- -	- -	- -	- -
County-wide unitary structure	2 *	- -	- -	- -	- -	1 *2%*
Other specified	1 *	- -	- -	- -	- -	1 *2%*
No preference expressed/option defined	5 *1%*	- -	4 *16%*	- -	- -	- -
BASE TOTAL	754	38	25	38	20	49

** Less than ½%*

NOP Analysis of Responses to Local Government Commission Draft Recommendations - GLOUCESTERSHIRE

Report D2: Opinions on the structural options, by respondent type
Base: respondents in Gloucester only

	Respondent Type					
	Indiv-iduals	Business groups	County, regional & national interests	Education (& church) groups	Local groups	Parish and town councils
Status quo/two-tier	78 *14%*	3 *16%*	7 *78%*	6 *75%*	2 *15%*	2 *100%*
Unitary Gloucester	479 *84%*	16 *84%*	2 *22%*	2 *25%*	11 *85%*	- -
County-level authority (either two-tier or unitary)	1 *	- -	- -	- -	- -	- -
District-level authority (either two-tier or unitary)	3 *1%*	- -	- -	- -	- -	- -
Pre-1974 structure	2 *	- -	- -	- -	- -	- -
County-wide unitary structure	1 *	- -	- -	- -	- -	- -
Other specified	1 *	- -	- -	- -	- -	- -
No preference expressed/option defined	4 *1%*	- -	- -	- -	- -	- -
BASE TOTAL	569	19	9	8	13	2

** Less than ½%*

Gloucester

NOP Analysis of Responses to Local Government Commission Draft Recommendations - GLOUCESTERSHIRE

Report D3: Opinions on the structural options, by respondent type
Base: respondents in rest of county only

	Respondent Type					
	Indiv-iduals	Business groups	County, regional & national interests	Education (& church) groups	Local groups	Parish and town councils
Status quo/two-tier	162 *90%*	9 *82%*	6 *100%*	28 *93%*	7 *100%*	43 *91%*
Unitary Gloucester	16 *9%*	2 *18%*	- -	2 *7%*	- -	2 *4%*
County-wide unitary structure	1 *1%*	- -	- -	- -	- -	1 *2%*
Other specified	- -	- -	- -	- -	- -	1 *2%*
No preference expressed/option defined	1 *1%*	- -	- -	- -	- -	- -
BASE TOTAL	180	11	6	30	7	47

NOP Analysis of Responses to Local Government Commission Draft Recommendations - GLOUCESTERSHIRE

Report E: Views on services, by authority of respondent
Base: all

	Review district	Other districts in county							
	Gloucester	Cheltenham	Cotswold	Forest of Dean	Stroud	Tewkesbury	Rest of county total	County total	Out of county total
Archives	- -	- -	- -	- -	- -	- -	- -	- -	1 *4%*
Education	1 *	- -	- -	- -	- -	- -	- -	1 *	- -
Trading standards	- -	- -	- -	- -	- -	- -	- -	- -	1 *4%*
Other specified services (or multiples of)	- -	- -	- -	- -	- -	- -	- -	- -	1 *4%*
BASE TOTAL	620	46	44	44	83	64	281	901	23

The figures in the table above do not sum to the base total/100% because undefined fields are not included, except as part of the base total.

* *Less than ½%*

NOP Analysis of Responses to Local Government Commission Draft Recommendations - GLOUCESTERSHIRE

Report F: Views on services, by respondent type
Base: all

	Respondent Type					
	Indiv-iduals	Business groups	County, regional & national interests	Education (& church) groups	Local groups	Parish and town councils
Archives	-	-	1	-	-	-
	-	-	*4%*	-	-	-
Education	1	-	-	-	-	-
	*	-	-	-	-	-
Trading standards	-	-	1	-	-	-
	-	-	*4%*	-	-	-
Other specified services (or multiples of)	-	-	1	-	-	-
	-	-	*4%*	-	-	-
BASE TOTAL	754	38	25	38	20	49

The figures in the table above do not sum to the base total/100% because undefined fields are not included, except as part of the base total.

* *Less than ½%*

Gloucester

NOP Analysis of Responses to Local Government Commission Draft Recommendations - GLOUCESTERSHIRE

Report G: Type of respondent, by authority of respondent
Base: all

	Review district	Other districts in county							
	Gloucester	Cheltenham	Cotswold	Forest of Dean	Stroud	Tewkesbury	Rest of county total	County total	Out of county total
Individuals	569 *92%*	29 *63%*	27 *61%*	26 *59%*	54 *65%*	44 *69%*	180 *64%*	749 *83%*	5 *22%*
Business groups	19 *3%*	7 *15%*	- -	1 *2%*	1 *1%*	2 *3%*	11 *4%*	30 *3%*	8 *35%*
County, regional and national interests	9 *1%*	3 *7%*	- -	1 *2%*	1 *1%*	1 *2%*	6 *2%*	15 *2%*	10 *43%*
Education (and church) groups	8 *1%*	5 *11%*	8 *18%*	6 *14%*	7 *8%*	4 *6%*	30 *11%*	38 *4%*	- -
Local Groups	13 *2%*	1 *2%*	- -	2 *5%*	4 *5%*	- -	7 *2%*	20 *2%*	- -
Parish and town councils	2 *	1 *2%*	9 *20%*	8 *18%*	16 *19%*	13 *20%*	47 *17%*	49 *5%*	- -
BASE TOTAL	620	46	44	44	83	64	281	901	23

MORI Research Study for the Local Government Commission

Introduction

Background

1 This summary report highlights the key findings from a survey of public opinion conducted in the City of Gloucester and across the County of Gloucestershire on behalf of the Local Government Commission for England. A copy of each marked-up questionnaire is appended. The computer tabulations are contained in a separate volume, which is available from MORI (32 Old Queen Street, London SW1H 9HP. Telephone 0171-222 0232. Price £15)

2 The survey was designed in close consultation with the Commission, following extensive qualitative research and pilot testing. All sampling, interviewing and analysis have been carried out independently by MORI, within the guidelines of the profession laid out by the Market Research Society.

3 In Gloucester, all Census Enumeration Districts (EDs) were sorted by ward, and stratified according to social class. EDs were then sampled (32 in total) in proportion to the population size of each, and quotas set for sex, age and work status. A total of 329 interviews with adults aged 18+, conducted face-to-face and in-home, were carried out between 7 and 29 October 1995. Data were weighted to match the population profile in the City.

4 In the remaining districts of Gloucestershire, all EDs were sorted into ward, and again were stratified according to social class. A total of 32 EDs across the whole area (that is, Gloucestershire excluding Gloucester) were sampled, with quotas set by sex, age and work status. Face-to-face interviews, conducted in-home, were carried out with 330 adults aged 18+ between 7 and 29 October 1995. Data were weighted to match the population profile of the County excluding Gloucester.

Publication of the Results

5 As with all our studies, these findings are subject to our Standard Terms and Conditions of Contract. Any press release or publication of the findings of this survey require the advance approval of MORI. Such approval will only be refused on the grounds of inaccuracy or misinterpretation.

Objectives

6 This survey took place during Stage Three, the consultation period on the Commission's draft recommendations. It measures public preferences for the organisation of local government in the area currently comprising the City of Gloucester, as well as exploring strength of feeling, levels of knowledge about the review, involvement in, and broader perceptions of, local government in the area.

Statistical Reliability of the Data

7 Because we have interviewed a sample of residents, rather than the whole population, the results are subject to statistical tolerance limits, or "margins of error". These are expressed as our confidence that the true figure for the whole population falls within a given range. By convention this is expressed as a percentage, so our 95% confidence level means that in 95 times out of 100 the true figure would lie within this range.

8 The table below shows ranges of the 95% confidence level for a range of sample sizes. For each sample size, the table shows the tolerance limits for sample results close to 10%, 30% and 50%. Take, for example, the results of a survey of 300 residents showing that 50% are aware of the review. In 95 times out of 100 the true figure would lie between 44% and 56% (ie between 50% ±6%).

Sample size	Sampling tolerances applicable to results at or near these percentages (based on 95% confidence level) 10/90% ±%	30/70% ±%	50% ±%
300	3	5	6
200	4	6	7
150	5	7	8
100	6	9	10
50	8	13	14

9 Clearly, 10% or 30% of the sample being aware of the review equate to 90% or 70% not being aware of it. So this table shows the ranges of 95% confidence for responses close to 10%, 30%, 50%, 70% and 90% of our sample. The figures for responses between can be obtained by extrapolation.

10 The true figure would only be known if all the residents of the area had been interviewed. It can be seen in the table, however, that large increases in the sample size do not greatly reduce the sampling tolerance. In addition, the true figure is more likely to lie at the midpoint of the range, rather than at either extreme.

11 When comparing results from separate groups within a sample we need to be sure that the differences are statistically significant. This would be important in comparing views expressed by different parts of a county. The table below shows how the statistical significance of the difference is determined by the size of the groups and the percentage result from the sample.

12 Assuming a 95% confidence level, the table shows the size of the differences required if different results are to be regarded as statistically significant. It can be seen that if 50% of a group of 300 were aware of the review, the result from another group of 300 would not become statistically significant until it became less than 42% or more than 58%.

Sample sizes	Differences required for significance at or near these percentage levels 10/90% ±	30/70% ±	50% ±
300 and 300	5	7	8
300 and 200	5	8	9
300 and 100	7	10	11
200 and 100	7	11	12
100 and 100	8	13	14

Survey Findings

Knowledge and Awareness

13 Residents within the City of Gloucester profess broadly similar levels of knowledge and interest in local government as those living in the rest of the County of Gloucestershire. In both, a clear majority like to know what their council is doing, but want no greater involvement. Around one in five in both areas say they want a higher level of involvement.

14 While around a third in the City and two in five in the rest of the County say they know at least a fair amount about what their council does, between three in five and two-thirds admit to not knowing very much.

15 This is reflected in the number of residents who incorrectly ascribe services between the two tiers of local government. Thus, although between four and six in ten recognise libraries as a county council service, as many as one third allocate responsibility to their district/borough/city council. And although two-thirds realise that refuse collection is a district/borough/city service, around one in six thinks it is a county council service.

16 Awareness of the review itself is equally low in Gloucester and the rest of the County. Slightly more than one half in each area have heard of it. Similarly, the proportions who say they know a fair amount or more are broadly equal in the City and the rest of the County, at just under one in ten.

Sources of Information

17 Local newspapers are the most common source of information about the review, by a considerable margin. Of those who have at least heard of the review, between five and six in ten name the local press as a recent source. Around seven in ten cite some media source as a recent source of information on the review.

18 It would appear that the County and City Councils have been fairly active in providing information to residents in Gloucester - while 38% name a County Council source in Gloucester, just 18% do so in the rest of Gloucestershire. Similarly, 38% in Gloucester mention a City Council source, compared with 16% in the rest of Gloucestershire. Very few recognise receiving information directly from the Local Government Commission itself.

19 Although most of those aware of the review recognise one or more recent sources of information, few (around one in five in Gloucester and one in seven in the rest of the County) say that this has influenced their opinion.

20 Furthermore, in spite of a relatively low level of knowledge and engagement with their local authority, most people in Gloucester say that the outcome of the review in the City is either very important to them (27%) or fairly important (43%). As one might expect, people in the rest of Gloucestershire tend to perceive a slightly lower level of importance (21% very important and 38% fairly important).

The Preferred Option

21 A majority in Gloucester would prefer a unitary City Council (56%) to no change (31%), while in the rest of Gloucestershire twice as many would prefer Gloucester to retain two tier local government (57%) as opt for the unitary solution (29%). Almost all others either had no views or were indifferent.

22 People in Gloucester tend to feel more strongly about the preference they express than do those living elsewhere in the County, although the proportions feeling very strongly are similar. In Gloucester, 74% of those expressing a preference say they feel strongly (18% very strongly), while across the rest of Gloucestershire, 66% feel strongly (20% very strongly). There is little difference in the strength of feeling expressed in Gloucester irrespective of which option they prefer. However, people in the rest of Gloucestershire tend to feel more strongly about maintaining the current structure.

Factors in Expressing a Preference

23 In questions 13 to 23, residents were asked to say to what extent they agreed or disagreed with a range of statements which related to a change to unitary local government. The statements were designed to cover the main issues raised by residents during the qualitative phase of research, and others that formed a part of the Commission's brief to take into consideration in making its recommendations.

24 The following charts summarise the results from these questions, with the full question wording presented in the questionnaires in the appendices. Values have been ascribed to the five attitudinal positions that people were offered (+2 for strongly agree, +1 for tend to agree, 0 for neither agree nor disagree, -1 for tend to disagree, and -2 for strongly disagree) and mean scores calculated across all respondents expressing a view. This has the combined benefit of distilling the range of opinion into one summary figure, while incorporating the varying intensity of feeling by ascribing values. Bars to the right indicate that the mean score value is positive, and thus that there is a balance of agreement with the statement. Bars to the left, conversely, indicate a balance of disagreement.

25 The first chart, therefore, shows how the views of people living in the City of Gloucester differ from those across the rest of Gloucestershire. In doing so, it illustrates the attitudes or perceptions that are, in relative terms, shared by both groups of residents (where the bars project in the same direction), and those where views differ markedly. Thus there is broad agreement that change would lead to clearer responsibility, whereas there is disagreement on the other positive aspects of change. The balance of opinion is more marked in Gloucester, than in the rest of the County. There is agreement in both areas that a County Council is needed for national representation and that services would suffer. On the other hand, there is some divergence when it comes to whether change would be too disruptive, would cost more, or whether a unitary Gloucester would be too small. There is also divergence on whether people feel that they will be affected by change. Residents across the County tend to agree equally that they would like more information before making up their minds.

26 The subsequent chart takes the results from just Gloucester (and then, from residents in the rest of Gloucestershire), and illustrates the difference in views between those within Gloucester whose preference is for unitary status, and those who prefer no change. The chart therefore illustrates those attitudinal statements that most, or least, differentiate the residents of the City expressing the two opposing preferences. The perceived impact on efficiency is clearly a key determinant of opinion (in both Gloucester and the rest of Gloucestershire), as are size, disruption, sense of community and impact on services.

Attitudes to Change
(All respondents)

Q To what extent do you agree or disagree that...?
(Figures represent 'mean scores' with *strong agreement* given a value of +2 through to *strong disagreement* given -2)

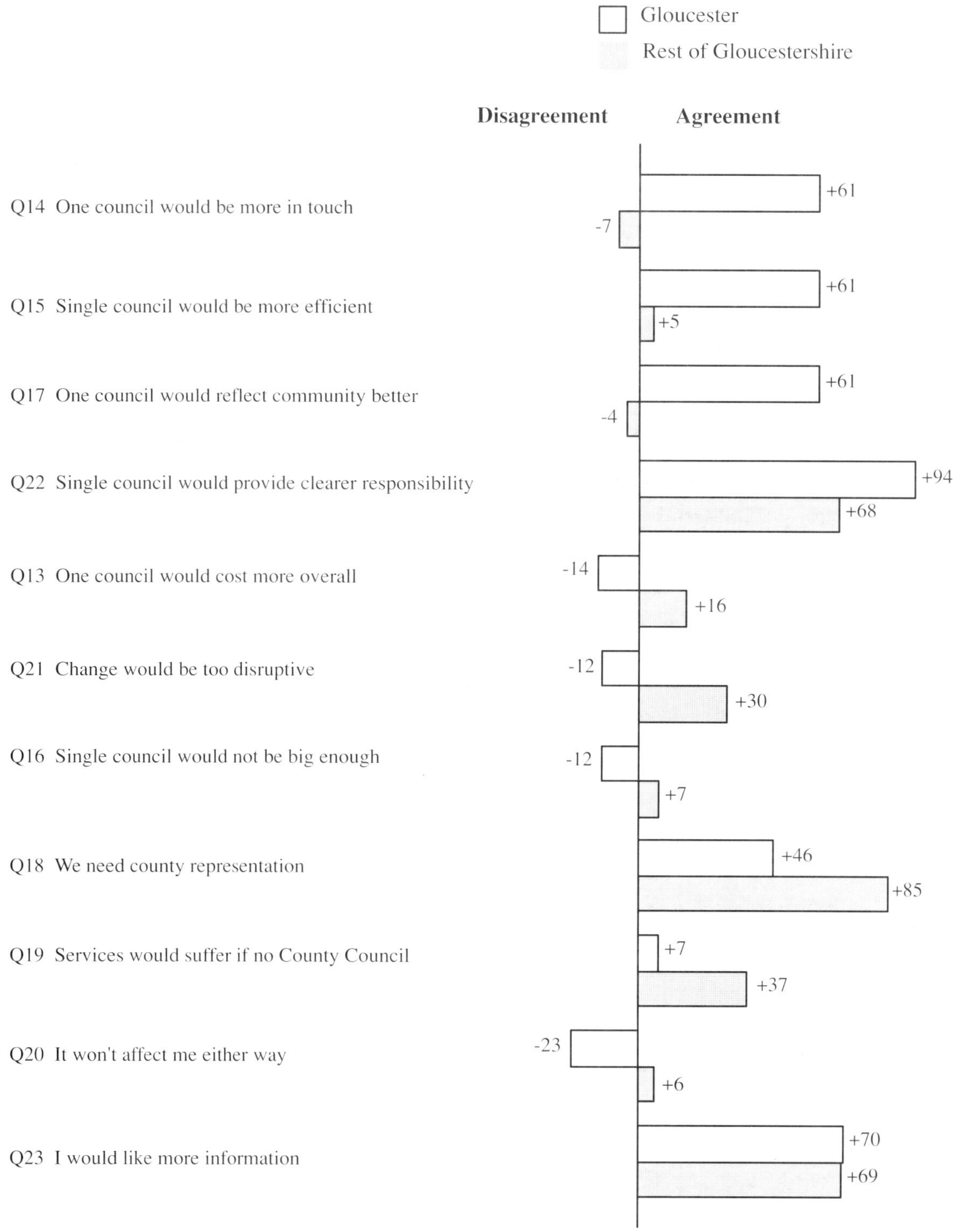

Attitudes to Change
(Respondents in Gloucester)

Q To what extent do you agree or disagree that...?
(Figures represent 'mean scores' with *strong agreement* given a value of +2 through to *strong disagreement* given -2)

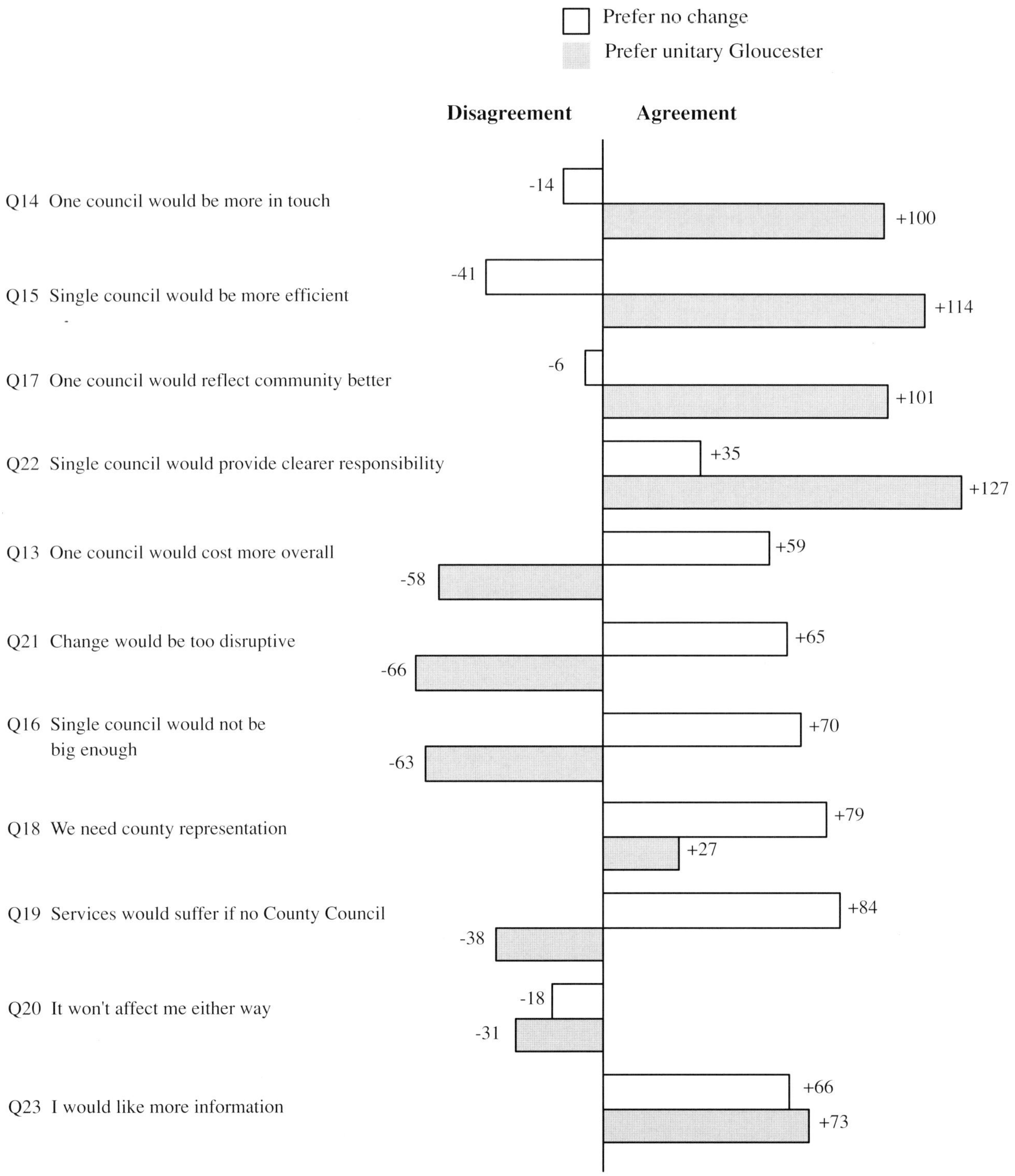

Attitudes to Change
(Respondents in the rest of Gloucestershire)

Q To what extent do you agree or disagree that...?
(Figures represent 'mean scores' with *strong agreement* given a value of +2 through to *strong disagreement* given -2)

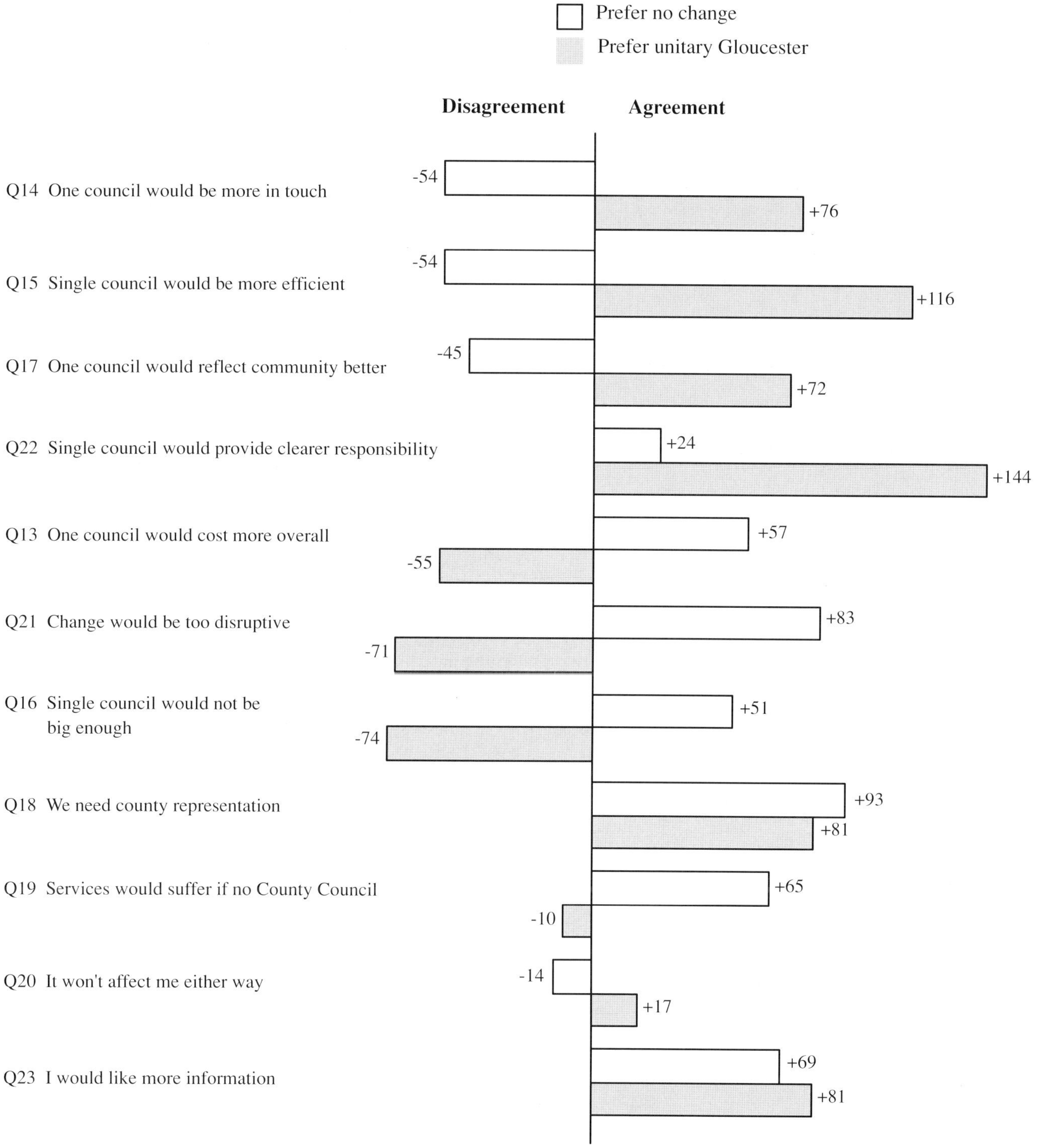

MORI/9101/05
(1-6)

Gloucestershire
REVIEW - REST OF COUNTY

Serial No ....
OUO (7-10)

Gender

	%
Male	48
Female	52

Age

	%
18-24	12
25-34	18
35-44	16
45-54	18
55-64	13
65-74	13
75+	11

WRITE IN AGE ☐☐

Work Status

	%
Full-time (30 hrs/wk+)	47
Part-time (8-29 hrs/wk)	8
Not working (under 8 hrs)	5
Looking after home/children	9
Retired	25
Registered unemployed	3
Unemployed but not registered	1
Student	2
Other	1

Occupation of Chief Income Earner (CIE)
Position/rank/grade

....

Industry/type of company

....

Qualifications/degrees/apprenticeship

....

No of Staff Responsible for

....

PROBE FOR PENSION

	%
AB	23
C1	25
C2	19
D	16
E	14

* Less than $^1/_2$%

Number in Household
Adults aged 18+ (inc. respondent)

1 2 3 4 5+

Children (17 or under)

0 1 2 3 4+

QA **Are you or other members of your household employed by a council?** IF YES: **Is this a Borough/District Council or a County Council?**
CODE FOR BOTH RESPONDENT AND OTHER HOUSEHOLD MEMBERS

	Respondent %	Other %
Yes:		
Borough/District	1	2
County	4	5
Don't know which	-	*
No	95	79
Don't know	-	14

Tenure

	%
Owned outright	29
Buying on mortgage	43
Rented from Council	15
Rented from Housing Association	2
Rented from private landlord	7
Other 7	4

QB **Is this your main permanent home, or is it a second or holiday home?**

	%
Main/permanent	100
Second/holiday	-

Car in Household
CIRCLE NUMBER

0 1 2 3+

Showcard Version
A-K ....
A1-K ....

THIS FORM IS THE PROPERTY OF MARKET & OPINION RESEARCH INTERNATIONAL (MORI)
32 OLD QUEEN STREET, LONDON, SW1H 9HP

- 2 -

INTERVIEWER DECLARATION: I confirm that I have conducted this interview face-to-face with the above named person and that I have asked all the relevant questions fully and recorded the answers in conformance with the survey specification and the MRS Code of Conduct.

Interviewer Name .... Signature ....

Interviewer Number					/	

	Month		Date		
DATE OF INTERVIEW					
	(29)	(30)		(30)	(32)

NB INTERVIEWER: ALL SHOWCARDS HAVE BEEN REVERSED. PLEASE BE CAREFUL TO CODE THE CORRECT RESPONSE.

Good morning/afternoon/evening. I'm from MORI, the market research and polling organisation. We are doing a survey about local issues, and I would like to ask you a few questions.

ASK ALL

Q1 **Firstly, how long have you lived in this area?** (WITHIN FIVE MILES)

	%
Less than 1 year	4
1-2 years	5
3-5 years	12
6-10 years	16
11-20 years	21
Over 20 years/all my life	42
Don't know/can't remember	1

Q2 SHOWCARD A (R) **From this card, how much would you say you know about local councils and the services they provide?**

	%
A great deal	3
A fair amount	37
Not very much	51
Nothing at all	8
Don't know	*

Q3 SHOWCARD B (R) **Which of the statements on this card comes closest to your own view of the Councils in this area?**

		%
A)	I'm not interested in what the Council does, or whether they do their job	1
B)	I'm not interested in what the Council does, as long as they do their job	15
C)	I like to know what the Council is doing, but I'm happy to let them get on with their job	59
D)	I would like to have more of a say in what the Council does and the services it provides	22
E)	I already work for, or am involved with the Council and the services it provides	2
	Don't know	1

Q4 **From what you know, how many councils provide the main services in this neighbourhood?** (INTERVIEWER - NOT INCLUDING PARISH COUNCILS)

	%
One	33
Two	38
Three+	6
Don't know	24

In fact there are two main councils that provide, or are responsible for most services in this area: . . .district/borough and Gloucestershire County Council.

ROTATE ORDER OF Q5/6

☐ Q5 SHOWCARD C (R) **From this list, what services do you think are the responsibility of... district/borough council? Just read out the letter(s) that apply**

☐ Q6 SHOWCARD C AGAIN (R) **And which services on this list do you think are the responsibility of Gloucestershire County Council? Again, just read out the letters that apply.**

Q7 SHOWCARD D (R) **Which, if any, of these services do you or members of your family use?** INCLUDE ONLY LOCAL USE

		Q5 "Borough" %	Q6 County %	Q7 Use %
A	Bus Services	36	32	37
B	Car Parks	58	20	61
C	Council Housing	59	24	12
D	Council Tax Benefit/Housing benefit	56	26	18
E	Fire service	18	63	34
F	Food safety	23	38	17
G	Household waste sites/dumps	46	31	52
H	Libraries	26	57	55
I	Parks, playgrounds and open spaces	58	21	46
J	Planning service	52	34	20
K	Public conveniences	59	16	41
L	Recycling/bottle banks	58	20	60
M	Refuse collection	68	17	80
N	Road maintenance	28	62	46
O	Schools/education	16	68	29
P	Social services	22	56	15
Q	Street sweeping	61	19	41
R	Swimming pools/sports facilities	52	24	45
	Other	4	3	1
	None of these	-	1	1
	Don't know	8	12	4

Q8 SHOWCARD E (R) **As you may know, there is currently a review being undertaken by the Local Government Commission on the future local government structure in the county. How much, if anything, would you say you know about this?**

	%
A great deal	1
A fair amount	7
Just a little	30
Heard of but know nothing about	16
Never heard of	45

PREFERENCES

HAND OVER MAP SHOWING AREAS UNDER REVIEW AND "CURRENT SERVICES" CARD
The Local Government Commission is considering options for the future structure of local government in Gloucester. Could you please read through this card, (SHOW OPTIONS CARD) **which outlines the options.**

Q9 **Please tell me which of the options, if either, you would prefer for Gloucester?**
SINGLE CODE ONLY

For Gloucester

	%
Option A (Remain the same/status quo)	57
Option B (Single all purpose council)	29
Some other option	1
Neither of these	-
Either of these/don't mind	3
Don't care	4
Don't know	6

ASK IF "OTHER" NAMED AT Q9 (CODE 3)

Q10 **What other option is that?**
PROBE FULLY - DO NOT PROMPT.

....

....

....

....

ASK ALL PREFERRING AN OPTION (1, 2 OR 3 AT Q9). OTHERS GO TO Q13

Q11 SHOWCARD F (R) **You say that the option you would prefer is . . . . .** (INSERT OPTION PREFERRED). **How strongly would you say you feel about this?**

	%
Very strongly	20
Fairly strongly	46
Not very strongly	26
Not at all strongly	3
Don't know	5

Q12 **What do you think would be the main advantages of . . .**(OPTION PREFERRED)
PROBE FULLY FOR DETAILS

....

....

....

....

....

Nothing..

Don't know/can't think of anything.................................

ATTITUDES TO PROPOSALS

SHOWCARD G (R) **Imagine that there was one council in Gloucester providing <u>all</u> services. I am going to read out some statements that people have made about this proposal. To what extent do you agree or disagree that . . . .?** READ OUT, ROTATE ORDER OF ASKING Q13-22. TICK START

READ OUT:	Strongly agree %	Tend to agree %	Neither/ Nor %	Tend to disagree %	Strongly disagree %	Don't know %
☐ Q13 **It would cost more overall**	13	29	12	29	6	11
Q14 **It would be more in touch with local people's needs**	7	35	8	31	13	6
Q15 **The single Council would be more efficient than the current system of two Councils**	11	32	14	28	10	5
☐ Q16 **The single council would not be big enough to manage services such as Education and Social Services effectively**	10	32	11	29	8	10
Q17 **It would better reflect the sense of community in Gloucester**	5	35	15	27	10	7
Q18 **We need a County Council to represent us nationally**	24	46	12	10	2	5
☐ Q19 **Services would suffer if the County Council no longer provides services in Gloucester**	11	41	12	24	3	9
Q20 **It won't affect me whether there is a single Council in Gloucester or not**	10	34	11	28	10	6
Q21 **The change to a single Council for Gloucester would be too disruptive**	13	37	12	25	5	7
☐ Q22 **With a single Council it would be clearer who is responsible for local services**	20	49	7	16	4	5
ASK LAST Q23 **I would like to have more information on the proposals before making up my mind**	25	42	10	14	5	4

Q24 **On balance, which would you say is more in touch with local people and issues, ...** (ROTATE ORDER OF "DISTRICT" AND COUNTY) (INSERT NAME OF "DISTRICT COUNCIL)..**district/borough counci', or Gloucestershire County Council, or would you say that they are both about the same?**

	%
District/borough council	71
Gloucestershire County Council	4
Both about the same	12
Don't know	13

<u>REFER BACK TO Q8. ASK ALL WHO HAVE HEARD OF REVIEW AT Q8 (IE CODES 1/2/3/4). OTHERS TO Q28</u>

Q25 SHOWCARD H **Earlier in the interview, you said that you had heard of the Review of local government structure. From which, if any, of the sources shown on this card have you recently heard about the Review?** INTERVIEWER NOTE: "RECENTLY" = IN PAST 3 MONTHS

		%
A	Leaflet from County Council delivered to your door	8
B	Leaflet from County Council in library/ offices, etc	2
C	Advertisement from County Council in local newspaper	7
D	Advertisement from County Council on local radio/TV	1
E	Leaflet from Borough Council delivered to your door	6
F	Leaflet from Borough Council in library/ offices, etc	1
G	Borough Council newspaper	5
H	County Council newspaper	3
I	Advertisement from Borough Council in local newspaper	3
J	Advertisement from Borough Council on local radio/TV	*
K	Advertisement by the Commission on local radio	*
L	Local Government Commission advertisement in local newspaper	1
M	Local newspaper	51
N	National newspaper	12
O	TV	22
P	Local radio	17
Q	National radio	6
R	Friends/neighbours/family	11
S	Conversation with Borough Councillor	3
T	Conversation with County Councillor	2
U	Conversation with Borough Council staff	1
V	Conversation with County Council staff	2
W	Parish/community council	4
X	Residents' Association	2
	Other	7
	None of these	12
	Don't know	9

<u>ASK ALL NAMING A SOURCE AT Q25. OTHERS GO TO Q28</u>

Q26 **Would you say that the information you have received has influenced your opinion, or not?**

	%
Yes	15
No	84
Don't know	1

Q27 **What information in particular has influenced your opinion?**

....

....

....

....

ASK ALL

Q28 SHOWCARD I (R) **Assuming you receive the same level of services, how important is it to you, if at all, what the final decision is on the future local government structure in Gloucester?**

	%
Very important	21
Fairly important	38
Not very important	28
Not at all important	10
Don't know	4

ACTIVISM

Q29 SHOWCARD J **Which of the things on this list, if any, have you done in the last three years? Just read out the letter(s) that apply.**

		%
A	Voted in Local Council elections	80
B	Spoken or written to a local Councillor	34
C	Responded to the earlier Review of local government	8
D	Been to a meeting of a local committee or organisation (WRITE IN NAME OF ORGANISATION)	15
E	Spoken on a radio phone-in about a local issue	1
F	Written to a local newspaper about a local issue	6
G	Been to a meeting of a local branch of a political party	4
H	Written to your MP about a local issue	12
I	Been to a Council Committee meeting	4
J	Been to a Council meeting	8
K	Attended a public meeting run by the Council	8
	None of these	14
	Don't know/refused	1

Q30 SHOWCARD K **Which, if any, of these apply to you? Just read out the letter(s) that apply.**

		%
I am a member of a:		
A	Residents' Association	5
B	Community Association	2
C	Tenants' Association	1
D	Neighbourhood Watch	24
E	PTA/school governors	4
I do unpaid work for:		
F	A school	6
G	Citizens Advice Bureau	1
H	Volunteer Bureau	2
I	Scouts/Guides/Cubs/Brownies	2
J	Church group	8
	Other	5
	None of these	58
	Don't know	1

THANK RESPONDENT. GO TO DEMOGRAPHICS.

Length of interview [ ][ ] minutes

MORI/9101/05
(1-6)

Gloucestershire
REVIEW - Gloucester

Serial No ....
OUO (7-10)

TOPLINE FINDINGS

Gender %
- Male 48
- Female 52

Age %
- 18-24 14
- 25-34 22
- 35-44 19
- 45-54 13
- 55-64 13
- 65-74 11
- 75+ 8

WRITE IN AGE [ ][ ]

Work Status %
- Full-time (30 hrs/wk+) 48
- Part-time (8-29 hrs/wk) 7
- Not working (under 8 hrs) 3
- Looking after home/children............. 9
- Retired 24
- Registered unemployed.................. 6
- Unemployed but not registered ....*
- Student.. 1
- Other 1

Occupation of Chief Income Earner (CIE)
Position/rank/grade

....

Industry/type of company

....

Qualifications/degrees/apprenticeship

....

No of Staff Responsible for

....

PROBE FOR PENSION

	%
AB	16
C1	27
C2	21
D	20
E	17

Number in Household
Adults aged 18+ (inc. respondent)

1 2 3 4 5+

Children 7 or under)

0 1 2 3 4+

QA **Are you or other members of your household employed by a council?** IF YES: **Is this a Borough/District Council or a County Council?**
CODE FOR BOTH RESPONDENT AND OTHER HOUSEHOLD MEMBERS

	Respondent %	Other %
Yes:		
Borough/District	*	1
County	3	3
Don't know which	-	-
No	96	91
Don't know	*	6

Tenure %
- Owned outright....................................... 25
- Buying on mortgage 50
- Rented from Council 14
- Rented from Housing Association 2
- Rented from private landlord 7
- Other 2

QB **Is this your main permanent home, or is it a second or holiday home?**

%
- Main/permanent.................................. 99
- Second/holiday 1

Car in Household
CIRCLE NUMBER

0 1 2 3+

Showcard Version
- A-K ....
- A1-K ....

INTERVIEWER DECLARATION: I confirm that I have conducted this interview face-to-face with the above named person and that I have asked all the relevant questions fully and recorded the answers in conformance with the survey specification and the MRS Code of Conduct.

Interviewer Name .... Signature ....

Interviewer Number					/	

	Month		Date			
DATE OF INTERVIEW						
	(29)	(30)		(30)	(32)	

NB INTERVIEWER: ALL SHOWCARDS HAVE BEEN REVERSED. PLEASE BE CAREFUL TO CODE THE CORRECT RESPONSE.

Good morning/afternoon/evening. I'm from MORI, the market research and polling organisation. We are doing a survey about local issues, and I would like to ask you a few questions.

ASK ALL

Q1 **Firstly, how long have you lived in this area?** (WITHIN FIVE MILES)

	%
Less than 1 year	6
1-2 years	10
3-5 years	15
6-10 years	20
11-20 years	19
Over 20 years/all my life	30
Don't know/can't remember	*

Q2 SHOWCARD A (R) **From this card, how much would you say you know about local councils and the services they provide?**

	%
A great deal	3
A fair amount	30
Not very much	49
Nothing at all	18
Don't know	*

Q3 SHOWCARD B (R) **Which of the statements on this card comes closest to your own view of the Councils in this area?**

		%
A)	I'm not interested in what the Council does, or whether they do their job	2
B)	I'm not interested in what the Council does, as long as they do their job	16
C)	I like to know what the Council is doing, but I'm happy to let them get on with their job	60
D)	I would like to have more of a say in what the Council does and the services it provides	18
E)	I already work for, or am involved with the Council and the services it provides	3
	Don't know	1

Q4 **From what you know, how many councils provide the main services in this neighbourhood?** (INTERVIEWER - NOT INCLUDING PARISH COUNCILS)

	%
One	21
Two	34
Three+	2
Don't know	43

In fact there are two main councils that provide, or are responsible for most services in this area: Gloucester City Council and Gloucestershire County Council.

ROTATE ORDER OF Q5/6

☐ Q5 SHOWCARD C (R) **From this list, what services do you think are the responsibility of Gloucester City Council? Just read out the letter(s) that apply**

☐ Q6 SHOWCARD C AGAIN (R) **And which services on this list do you think are the responsibility of Gloucestershire County Council? Again, just read out the letters that apply.**

Q7 SHOWCARD D (R) **Which, if any, of these services do you or members of your family use?** INCLUDE ONLY LOCAL USE

		Q5 Gloucester %	Q6 Gloucestershire %	Q7 Use %
A	Bus Services	47	24	47
B	Car Parks	45	26	60
C	Council Housing	51	26	11
D	Council Tax Benefit/Housing benefit	50	23	23
E	Fire service	18	53	33
F	Food safety	20	35	13
G	Household waste sites/dumps	42	32	46
H	Libraries	37	41	58
I	Parks, playgrounds and open spaces	45	32	53
J	Planning service	30	40	11
K	Public conveniences	55	13	35
L	Recycling/bottle banks	49	18	47
M	Refuse collection	66	15	77
N	Road maintenance	30	53	36
O	Schools/education	20	64	37
P	Social services	22	56	12
Q	Street sweeping	60	19	36
R	Swimming pools/sports facilities	37	26	53
	Other	1	*	1
	None of these	-	*	2
	Don't know	10	13	1

Q8 SHOWCARD E (R) **As you may know, there is currently a review being undertaken by the Local Government Commission on the future local government structure in the county. How much, if anything, would you say you know about this?**

	%
A great deal	1
A fair amount	8
Just a little	29
Heard of but know nothing about	16
Never heard of	46

PREFERENCES

HAND OVER MAP SHOWING AREAS UNDER REVIEW AND "CURRENT SERVICES" CARD

The Local Government Commission is considering options for the future structure of local government in Gloucester. Could you please read through this card, (SHOW OPTIONS CARD) **which outlines the options.**

Q9 **Please tell me which of the options, if either, you would prefer for Gloucester?**
SINGLE CODE ONLY

	%
For Gloucester	
Option A (Remain the same/status quo)	31
Option B (Single all purpose council)	56
Some other option	1
Neither of these	2
Either of these/don't mind	3
Don't care	1
Don't know	7

ASK IF "OTHER" NAMED AT Q9 (CODE 3)

Q10 **What other option is that?**
PROBE FULLY - DO NOT PROMPT.

....

....

....

....

ASK ALL PREFERRING AN OPTION (1, 2 OR 3 AT Q9). OTHERS GO TO Q13

Q11 SHOWCARD F (R) **You say that the option you would prefer is . . . . .** (INSERT OPTION PREFERRED). **How strongly would you say you feel about this?**

	%
Very strongly	18
Fairly strongly	55
Not very strongly	21
Not at all strongly	1
Don't know	4

Q12 **What do you think would be the main advantages of . . .**(OPTION PREFERRED)
PROBE FULLY FOR DETAILS

....

....

....

....

....

Nothing...

Don't know/can't think of anything.................................

ATTITUDES TO PROPOSALS

SHOWCARD G (R) **Imagine that there was one council in Gloucester providing all services. I am going to read out some statements that people have made about this proposal. To what extent do you agree or disagree that . . . .?** READ OUT, ROTATE ORDER OF ASKING Q13-22. TICK START

READ OUT:		Strongly agree %	Tend to agree %	Neither/ Nor %	Tend to disagree %	Strongly disagree %	Don't know %
☐ Q13	**It would cost more overall**	6	26	14	36	7	11
Q14	**It would be more in touch with local people's needs**	14	52	13	16	2	4
Q15	**The single Council would be more efficient than the current system of two Councils**	16	47	11	18	2	7
☐ Q16	**The single council would not be big enough to manage services such as Education and Social Services effectively**	8	23	17	37	7	9
Q17	**It would better reflect the sense of community in Gloucester**	11	52	13	15	1	8
Q18	**We need a County Council to represent us nationally**	12	46	18	20	2	2
☐ Q19	**Services would suffer if the County Council no longer provides services in Gloucester**	10	29	16	33	4	8
Q20	**It won't affect me whether there is a single Council in Gloucester or not**	4	24	20	38	8	6
Q21	**The change to a single Council for Gloucester would be too disruptive**	6	26	18	38	5	8
☐ Q22	**With a single Council it would be clearer who is responsible for local services**	23	58	4	8	2	4
ASK LAST Q23	**I would like to have more information on the proposals before making up my mind**	19	49	15	13	2	2

Q24 **On balance, which would you say is more in touch with local people and issues, ...**
(ROTATE ORDER OF "DISTRICT" AND COUNTY)
Gloucester City Council, or
Gloucestershire County Council, or would you say that they are both about the same?

	%
Gloucester City Council	51
Gloucestershire County Council	5
Both about the same	35
Don't know	9

REFER BACK TO Q8. ASK ALL WHO HAVE HEARD OF REVIEW AT Q8 (IE CODES 1/2/3/4). OTHERS TO Q28

Q25 SHOWCARD H **Earlier in the interview, you said that you had heard of the Review of local government structure. From which, if any, of the sources shown on this card have you recently heard about the Review?** INTERVIEWER NOTE: "RECENTLY" = IN PAST 3 MONTHS

		%
A	Leaflet from County Council delivered to your door	13
B	Leaflet from County Council in library/ offices, etc	3
C	Advertisement from County Council in local newspaper	15
D	Advertisement from County Council on local radio/TV	6
E	Leaflet from City Council delivered to your door	14
F	Leaflet from City Council in library/ offices, etc	3
G	City Council newspaper	21
H	County Council newspaper	6
I	Advertisement from City Council in local newspaper	7
J	Advertisement from City Council on local radio/TV	7
K	Advertisement by the Commission on local radio	1
L	Local Government Commission advertisement in local newspaper	5
M	Local newspaper	59
N	National newspaper	11
O	TV	14
P	Local radio	24
Q	National radio	3
R	Friends/neighbours/family	9
S	Conversation with City Councillor	5
T	Conversation with County Councillor	3
U	Conversation with City Council staff	7
V	Conversation with County Council staff	6
W	Parish/community council	2
X	Residents' Association	1
	Other	5
	None of these	-
	Don't know	4

ASK ALL NAMING A SOURCE AT Q25. OTHERS GO TO Q28

Q26 **Would you say that the information you have received has influenced your opinion, or not?**

	%
Yes	21
No	74
Don't know	5

Q27 **What information in particular has influenced your opinion?**

....

....

....

....

ASK ALL

Q28 SHOWCARD I (R) **Assuming you receive the same level of services, how important is it to you, if at all, what the final decision is on the future local government structure in Gloucester?**

	%
Very important	27
Fairly important	43
Not very important	25
Not at all important	5
Don't know	1

ACTIVISM

Q29 SHOWCARD J **Which of the things on this list, if any, have you done in the last three years? Just read out the letter(s) that apply.**

		%
A	Voted in Local Council elections	72
B	Spoken or written to a local Councillor	26
C	Responded to the earlier Review of local government	6
D	Been to a meeting of a local committee or organisation (WRITE IN NAME OF ORGANISATION)	6
	....	
E	Spoken on a radio phone-in about a local issue	1
F	Written to a local newspaper about a local issue	4
G	Been to a meeting of a local branch of a political party	3
H	Written to your MP about a local issue	7
I	Been to a Council Committee meeting	4
J	Been to a Council meeting	3
K	Attended a public meeting run by the Council	4
	None of these	20
	Don't know/refused	2

Q30 SHOWCARD K **Which, if any, of these apply to you? Just read out the letter(s) that apply.**

		%
	I am a member of a:	
A	Residents' Association	5
B	Community Association	2
C	Tenants' Association	*
D	Neighbourhood Watch	30
E	PTA/school governors	4
	I do unpaid work for:	
F	A school	8
G	Citizens Advice Bureau	1
H	Volunteer Bureau	2
I	Scouts/Guides/Cubs/Brownies	2
J	Church group	5
	Other	3
	None of these	56
	Don't know	*

THANK RESPONDENT. GO TO DEMOGRAPHICS.

CHAPTER 7

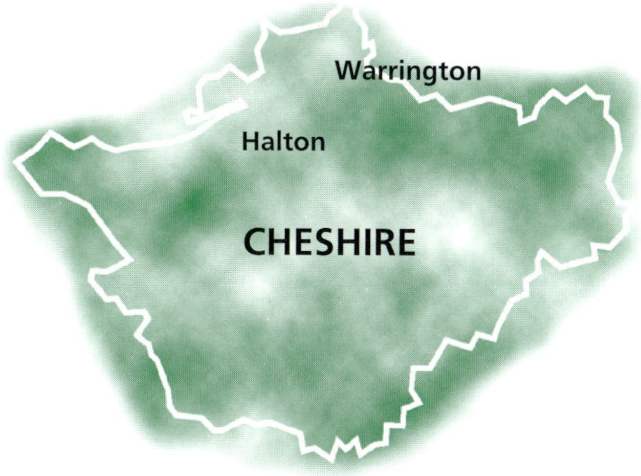

HALTON AND WARRINGTON IN THE COUNTY OF CHESHIRE

Draft Recommendations

7.1 The Commission's report *Draft Recommendations on the Future Local Government of Halton and Warrington in the County of Cheshire* summarised the evidence taken into account by the Commission in reaching its draft recommendations.

Figure 7.1
Draft Recommendations for Halton and Warrington in the County of Cheshire

Structure

- The existing two-tier structure of local government in Halton should be replaced. Halton should become a unitary authority responsible in its area for the broad range of local government functions currently carried out by both county and district councils.

- The existing two-tier structure of local government in Warrington should be replaced. Warrington should become a unitary authority responsible in its area for the broad range of local government functions currently carried out by both county and district councils.

Ceremonial Arrangements

- The county of Cheshire should be retained for ceremonial and related purposes, and the unitary authorities for Halton and Warrington should be associated with the county for such purposes.

Public Protection

- There should be a combined authority established in the present county area for the fire service, on which the representatives of the new unitary authorities should serve. Similarly, representatives of the new unitary authorities should also serve on a joint committee with representatives of the county council to select the local authority membership of the Cheshire Police Authority. No changes are proposed to the area covered by the Cheshire Police Authority, or to the probation and magistrates' courts services.

Strategic Planning

- The new unitary authorities for Halton and Warrington should become the structure planning authorities for their areas, with a view to this function being exercised in each case through joint arrangements with Cheshire County Council so as to maintain a single structure plan for their combined areas. The new authorities should also be mineral planning authorities, with a view to maintaining a county-wide minerals plan jointly with the County Council. However, the alternative option of including detailed policies for minerals and waste in their district-wide development plans should remain open to them, and the Commission so recommends.

Electoral Arrangements

- The Warrington unitary authority should retain the existing Warrington Borough Council electoral arrangements. The new authority should therefore have a total of 60 members with 15 three-member wards, seven two-member wards and one single-member ward. Elections should be held for the whole council every four years.

- The Halton unitary authority should retain the existing Halton Borough Council electoral arrangements. The new authority should therefore have a total of 53 members with 17 three-member wards and two single-member wards. Elections should be by thirds.

- The continuing Cheshire County Council should have 48 members with one member for each of the existing 48 county divisions outside the boroughs of Halton and Warrington.

Views Expressed to the Commission

7.2 The Commission received a large number, and a wide range, of direct representations on its draft recommendations, from local authorities, residents, Members of Parliament, business and voluntary groups, parish and town councils, and from other public and private sector organisations. Over 13,200 representations were received from individuals and organisations, including almost 9,000 from respondents within the two review districts. The Commission also received over 10,400 representations in the form of standard letters, response slips and petitions (Figures 7.2, 7.3 and 7.4). Figures 7.2, 7.3 and 7.4 exclude representations from the local authorities; these are summarised separately (Figure 7.5).

Figure 7.2

Views of Respondents Within Halton

Preferred structure	Individuals	Organisations	Standard letters and petition signatures
Unitary Halton	953	99	4,953
Unitary Warrington	13	1	0
Unitary Halton and Warrington	17	2	0
No change	2,481	53	995
Other	55	2	0
No preference	30	4	0

Source: Local Government Commission for England and NOP

Figure 7.3

Views of Respondents Within Warrington

Preferred structure	Individuals	Organisations	Standard letters and petition signatures
Unitary Warrington	1,236	58	363
Unitary Halton	9	4	0
Unitary Halton and Warrington	57	3	0
No change	3,696	86	2,387
Other	47	0	0
No preference	25	6	0

Source: Local Government Commission for England and NOP

Figure 7.4

Views of Respondents from Outside the Review Districts

Preferred structure	Individuals	Organisations	Standard letters and petition signatures
Unitary Halton	19	8	39
Unitary Warrington	22	1	22
Unitary Halton and Warrington	49	10	0
No change	3,288	141	1,709
Other	35	4	0
No preference	13	2	0

Source: Local Government Commission for England and NOP

Note: Excludes out of county representations

7.3 In addition, 686 representations were received from outside the county, of which 78 per cent supported no change, 11 per cent unitary status for Halton and 5 per cent unitary status for Warrington. A more detailed tabulation of the written representations from individuals and interest groups, produced by NOP on behalf of the Commission, can be found towards the end of this Chapter.

The Views of Local Authorities

7.4 The Commission received submissions from all nine principal local authorities in Cheshire during Stage Three (Figure 7.5).

Figure 7.5
Preferences of Cheshire Local Authorities at Stage Three

Authority	Preference
Halton Borough Council	Reiterated its support for separate unitary authorities for Halton and Warrington. It argued a unitary Halton would provide a more effective, responsive, convenient and accountable framework for local democracy and service provision and act as a catalyst for economic regeneration of the area.
Warrington Borough Council	Supported the creation of separate unitary authorities for Halton and Warrington. It argued that Warrington is a substantial and complex place that needs to find cross-functional solutions to local issues and problems that cannot come from services provided by different tiers of local government.
Chester City Council	Reaffirmed its support for the concept of unitary local government and welcomed the Commission's recommendation to create separate unitary authorities for Halton and Warrington.
Congleton Borough Council	Supported an improved two-tier structure in Cheshire, pointing to joint developments between the authority and the County Council. It argued that change would lead to increased cost both during transition and through the ongoing loss of economy of scale.
Crewe and Nantwich Borough Council	Reaffirmed its support for separate unitary authorities for Halton and Warrington, and for the concept of unitary local government. It also supported separate unitary development plans for Halton and Warrington.
Ellesmere Port and Neston Borough Council	Stated its support for the concept of unitary local government and for the creation of separate unitary authorities for Halton and Warrington, arguing that Warrington has a different focus, and Halton a different character from elsewhere in the county.

continued/

/continued

Authority	Preference
Macclesfield Borough Council	Confirmed its support for unitary local government and the recommendation to create separate unitary authorities for Halton and Warrington.
Vale Royal Borough Council	Reaffirmed its support for the concept of unitary local government and welcomed the recommendation to create separate unitary authorities for Halton and Warrington. It also supported separate unitary development plans for Halton and Warrington arguing that this would enable the Cheshire structure plan to more effectively recognise the interests of Cheshire's rural communities.
Cheshire County Council	Supported the retention of the two-tier structure in Cheshire, arguing the case for change had not been proved. It argued that the Commission had based its findings on a superficial and misleading picture of the county, had neglected to examine Warrington and Halton's role as a buffer between two major conurbations and had marginalised the importance of costs.

7.5 The views of local authorities have remained unaltered since Stage One of the review. The Cheshire Branch of the Association of District Councils supported separate unitary authorities for Halton and Warrington during Stage One, but did not make representations during Stage Three; the Association of District Councils' national submission is referred to in the Summary of National Representations. The Association of County Councils preferred the retention of the two-tier structure.

7.6 Support for a unitary authority for Halton was expressed by Knowsley Metropolitan Borough Council who stated, "...this Council as a unitary body recognises the many benefits to the people of Halton if such unitary status is attained and will endeavour to forge closer links with Halton in future provision of services". The Leaders of Liverpool City Council and St Helens Metropolitan Borough Council also stated a preference for a unitary Halton authority.

7.7 Wigan Metropolitan Borough Council preferred a unitary authority for Warrington and stressed particular support for the establishment of a Warrington Unitary Development Plan which, it believed, would improve liaison in respect of strategic planning issues.

The Views of Others

7.8 A range of other interest groups made representations on the Commission's draft recommendations as summarised in the following paragraphs. These are in addition to those made in Stage One.

Businesses and Business Groups

7.9 Over 250 businesses and business groups wrote to the Commission. Almost half supported a unitary Halton, while just over 10 per cent preferred a unitary Warrington with a further 4 per cent supporting a unitary authority for both. There was strong support (nearly 80 per cent) for a unitary authority for Halton from many businesses and business groups within the borough. The Halton Chamber of Commerce, with a membership of 325 local businesses, preferred a unitary authority as it considered this would remove the confusion within the business community as to which Council to approach, and enable the more effective development and implementation of regeneration policies and initiatives. The Manchester Ship Canal Company preferred a unitary Halton as it believed this would reduce duplication, increase efficiency and simplify relationships between public and private sectors.

7.10 The support for a unitary authority for Warrington was less strong, with many emphasising the strategic importance of the town. Manchester Airport plc, for example, was unconvinced that the benefits expected to flow from unitary status for Halton and Warrington are sufficient to outweigh the disadvantages. Locally, however, the Warrington Chamber of Commerce and Industry, with about 330 members, unanimously believed the borough would be better served by a unitary authority. Business groups outside the review districts tended to prefer no change, although there was some support for a unitary authority in Halton. The North West Region of the Confederation of British Industry preferred no change and stated that "...the proposed changes are unlikely to produce any noticeable benefits to local companies but with the clear implication that the local community will be faced with higher charges for no improvement in services".

County, Regional and National Interests (including the Voluntary Sector)

7.11 Groups with interests across the whole of Cheshire, or further, tended to prefer no change to the existing two-tier structure in the county. The Cheshire Wildlife Trust preferred the retention of the two-tier structure as it believed that unitary authorities may have an inadequate resource base for their needs and the collective needs of the county which may compromise strategic planning functions, levels of service provision and standards of property management. The Royal Commission on the Historical Monuments of England questioned whether the size of the proposed unitary authorities would be sufficient to maintain a cost effective conservation service.

Education Groups

7.12 Around 90 per cent of the responses from education groups, which included school governors, head teachers and education associations, preferred the retention of the two-tier structure in Cheshire. The Cheshire Association of Secondary Head Teachers stated that the current arrangements were working well and that there was no need to change them. The Association was concerned that reducing the size of local education authorities would mean a loss of economies of scale and a duplication of effort. The Cheshire Association of Special Head Teachers believed that unitary authorities for Halton and Warrington would be detrimental to the education of the most vulnerable children who have special needs. The Cheshire and Merseyside branch of the National Union of Teachers stated that a dismemberment of the education authority would result in significant disadvantage to services and to employees.

7.13 An alternative view was expressed by Halton College, which preferred a unitary authority for the borough. It considered that strong partnerships had been forged within the Halton area, with the Borough Council taking a leading role.

Health Groups

7.14 The North Cheshire Health Authority, which is coterminous with the review districts of Halton and Warrington, preferred no change to the structure of local government in Cheshire. It did, however, state that if two unitary authorities were created, good working relationships would be quickly established. It also expressed concern that if only one review district became a unitary authority this would probably lead to a further review of local health authorities.

7.15 The Halton General Hospital NHS Trust and the Halton Community Health Council preferred a unitary authority for the district. The Warrington Community Healthcare NHS Trust preferred a unitary authority for Warrington because it considered that it would be in the best interests of the Trust. The Warrington Hospital NHS Trust preferred to retain the two-tier structure as it has been satisfied with the level of co-operation and organisation of the County Council Social Services Department. Likewise, the Cheshire Community Healthcare NHS Trust preferred no change as it has recently entered into a contract with Cheshire County Council Social Services Department to provide domiciliary care services for the elderly and disabled. It argued that any division of the County Council would seriously disadvantage the work of the Trust and residents of the county.

Law, Order and Emergency Services

7.16 The Cheshire Police Authority was established on 1 April 1995 and, although it welcomed the recommendation to leave the area covered by the Police Authority unaltered, it considered that existing initiatives would be disrupted during any period of change. The Cheshire Fire Brigade preferred the retention of the two-tier structure and stated that the fewer the number of fire authorities forming any new combined fire authority the less expensive and more effective the new fire authority would be.

Local Groups

7.17 There was strong support from local groups within the review districts for unitary status. The Halton Tenants' Federation and Runcorn Residents' Federation preferred a unitary authority for Halton and considered it would strengthen the ties that bind the communities of Halton, create a locally accountable organisation better able to promote community and economic development and deliver a more effective, convenient and accessible local service. The Halton Carers' Action Group also expressed support for a unitary authority for the borough. It argued that local people use and pay for services and that they should be able to determine what form of local council is best suited to deliver the services required by that community.

7.18 The Warrington and Lymm Citizens' Advice Bureau stated that the interests of the voluntary bodies in Warrington would be best served by a unitary authority for the borough. The Warrington Civic Society preferred a unitary authority for the borough as it considered it would eliminate existing conflicts, facilitate greater accountability and "...provide a more appropriate system of local government for what is essentially an urban community". An alternative view was expressed by several local groups such as Relate, which wished to keep local government together within the two-tier structure, and was concerned that a change to unitary authorities would create disruption to its services and increase costs.

Parliamentary Interests

7.19 The two Warrington Members of Parliament, Mr Mike Hall, MP for Warrington South, and Mr Doug Hoyle, MP for Warrington North, wrote a joint submission outlining their support for a unitary Warrington. They argued that a unitary status would serve to make services for the area more accountable and strengthen democracy, and would lead to improvements through better coordination of interrelated services such as social services, housing, education and leisure. Mr Hall, whose Warrington South constituency includes part of Halton, also supported a unitary Halton, stressing the area's links with Merseyside. The MP for Halton, Mr Gordon Oakes, wrote in support of unitary status. Mr Nicholas Winterton, MP for Macclesfield, wrote in support of unitary authorities for Halton and Warrington. The MEP for Cheshire East, Mr Brian Simpson, also wrote in support of a unitary authority for Warrington.

7.20 The Duke of Westminster, The Marquess of Cholmondeley, The Earl Kitchenener of Khartoum and of Broome, Viscount Leverhulme, Lord Grey of Codnor, Lord Rochester, Lord Tordoff and Lord Carlisle of Bucklow submitted a joint response supporting the retention of the two-tier structure in Cheshire to avoid the disruption and costs of change.

Parish And Town Councils

7.21 Of the parish councils in Warrington that responded to the Commission's draft recommendations, opinion was split between those supporting a unitary authority for the district and those preferring to retain the two-tier structure. Burtonwood Parish Council argued that an all-purpose council based at the Warrington Town Hall would provide the most efficient, effective and economic form of local government. Lymm Parish Council, however, stated that Warrington was made up of two distinct populations. It expressed concern that the Borough Council had not always been sympathetic to the needs of the residents in the south of the borough and that, under a unitary authority, they would be even worse off than they are at present.

7.22 There are four parish councils in Halton Borough. Those south of the river preferred to retain the two-tier structure, arguing that the present system helps balance the representation between urban and rural communities. North of the river, Hale Parish Council indicated that it would prefer a unitary authority for Halton.

NOP Tabulations of Written Representations

1 The following tabulations summarise the views expressed by members of the public and other interested parties during the consultation on the Local Government Commission's draft recommendations for Halton and Warrington.

2 The tabulations include only letters sent directly to NOP at its Chelmsford offices and to the Commission's offices in London. Where more than one person's view has been expressed in a letter, the comments from each individual have been recorded separately. Staff from the Commission and NOP have worked closely in ensuring that care has been taken in the interpretation of comments, and that a consistent approach has been adopted.

3 While many people expressed support for one or other of the draft options presented by the Commission, other responses were coded by NOP after further discussion. The pattern of views expressed has been carefully examined, and where a number of respondents supported an option not included in those put forward by the Commission, those views have been separately coded and reported by NOP.

4 The Commission has advertised through the local media, encouraging people to make their views known. All responses received up to two days after the end of the Stage Three consultation period have been included. Returns from campaigns organised by local authorities or other groups (for example, standardised postcards and letters, questionnaires and petitions) have not been included in the tabulations. These, and submissions written and dated before the commencement of the consultation process, have been considered separately by the Commission.

The following definitions have been applied by NOP in compiling the tabulations:

(i) Type of Respondent

Individuals:	includes individual members of the public, local councillors and Members of the Westminster and European Parliaments.
Businesses and Business Groups:	includes organisations which represent businesses, such as local Chambers of Commerce.
County, Regional and National Interests:	any organisation which covers an area which is the size of a county or larger is included here, for example, a county-wide voluntary organisation or a regional association. This classification includes most of the statutory consultees.
Education (and Church) Groups:	this group includes schools, religious organisations and teaching unions.
Local Groups:	this includes organisations smaller than a county area, for example, a district-level voluntary sector body. The group could be voluntary, sporting, political or cultural but does not include organisations from the education or religious sectors (included above). It also includes constituency parties and political groups on local authorities.
Parish and Town Councils:	this also includes district-level associations of town and parish councils. County level associations are classified as County, Regional and National interests.

(ii) Structural Options (Reports A, D and H)

No change in own district:	this code is used where there is more than one review district in the county. It indicates where respondents from a review district have expressed support for no change for that district and have not made reference to the other review district(s) in that county.
District/county-level authorities:	represents support for either a district or county-level authority although it is not clear whether this is for a unitary or a two-tier structure.
Opposition to structural preferences:	represents responses where a negative, but unspecified, structural preference has been expressed.
Rejects:	rejects are those responses with unclear comments/interpretation.

(iii) Other

Other issues (Reports B and I):	these illustrate preferences in relation to boundary and electoral changes and (where applicable) the restoration of historic counties.
Parishing issues (Report C):	these illustrate preferences in relation to parishing issues, for example, the creation of new parishes or the enhancement of the role of parish and town councils.
Services (Report E):	these illustrate concerns expressed about the impact of proposed changes on particular service areas where the respondent has not additionally expressed a positive structural preference.

(iv) Ward/Area Level (Reports H and I)

These show analyses by local authority wards or specified areas and are designed to examine whether structural preferences vary across a particular local authority area.

NOP Analysis of Responses to Local Government Commission Draft Recommendations - CHESHIRE

Report A: Opinions on the structural options by authority of respondent
Base: all

	Review districts		Other districts in county								
	Halton	Warrington	Chester	Congleton	Crewe and Nantwich	Ellesmere Port and Neston	Macclesfield	Vale Royal	Rest of county total	County total	Out of county total
Status quo/two-tier	1254 *34%*	1648 *32%*	1257 *95%*	396 *98%*	294 *95%*	340 *98%*	384 *94%*	758 *95%*	3429 *95%*	6331 *51%*	535 *78%*
Unitary Warrington	14 *	1294 *25%*	5 *	- -	2 *1%*	2 *1%*	6 *1%*	8 *1%*	23 *1%*	1331 *11%*	34 *5%*
Unitary Halton	1052 *28%*	13 *	6 *	- -	1 *	1 *	1 *	18 *2%*	27 *1%*	1092 *9%*	75 *11%*
Two Unitary Districts (Warrington and Halton)	19 *1%*	60 *1%*	28 *2%*	4 *1%*	6 *2%*	2 *1%*	12 *3%*	7 *1%*	59 *2%*	138 *1%*	23 *3%*
No change in own district	1280 *35%*	2134 *41%*	- -	- -	- -	- -	- -	- -	- -	3414 *27%*	- -
County-level authority (either two-tier or unitary)	32 *1%*	16 *	- -	- -	- -	- -	- -	2 *	2 *	50 *	3 *
District-level authority (either two-tier or unitary)	8 *	19 *	- -	- -	- -	- -	- -	- -	- -	27 *	- -
Pre-1974 structure	- -	5 *	- -	1 *	2 *1%*	- -	- -	1 *	4 *	9 *	- -
County-wide unitary structure	- -	- -	7 *1%*	- -	1 *	1 *	- -	1 *	10 *	10 *	- -
Reject	4 *	4 *	1 *	- -	- -	- -	- -	3 *	4 *	12 *	- -
Other specified	13 *	3 *	13 *1%*	- -	- -	2 *1%*	4 *1%*	- -	19 *1%*	35 *	- -
No preference expressed/option defined	34 *1%*	31 *1%*	5 *	2 *	2 *1%*	- -	2 *	4 *	15 *	80 *1%*	16 *2%*
BASE TOTAL	3710	5227	1322	403	308	348	409	802	3592	12529	686

* *Less than ½%*

NOP Analysis of Responses to Local Government Commission Draft Recommendations - CHESHIRE

Report B: Opinions on other issues by authority of respondent
Base: all

	Review districts		Other districts in county								
	Halton	Warrington	Chester	Congleton	Crewe and Nantwich	Ellesmere Port and Neston	Macclesfield	Vale Royal	Rest of county total	County total	Out of county total
Electoral issues	- -	1 *	- -	- -	- -	- -	- -	1 *	1 *	2 *	1 *
Historic Lancashire	2 *	10 *	- -	- -	- -	- -	- -	- -	- -	12 *	- -
Historic Cheshire	- -	- -	- -	- -	- -	2 *1%*	- -	- -	2 *	2 *	- -
Historic Lancashire and Cheshire	2 *	- -	1 *	- -	- -	- -	- -	- -	1 *	3 *	- -
Other specified	- -	2 *	- -	- -	- -	- -	3 *1%*	- -	3 *	5 *	- -
BASE TOTAL	3710	5227	1322	403	308	348	409	802	3592	12529	686

The figures in the table above do not sum to the base total/100% because undefined fields are not included, except as part of the base total.
* *Less than ½%*

NOP Analysis of Responses to Local Government Commission Draft Recommendations - CHESHIRE

Report C: Opinions on parishing issues by authority of respondent
Base: all

	Review districts		Other districts in county								
	Halton	Warrington	Chester	Congleton	Crewe and Nantwich	Ellesmere Port and Neston	Macclesfield	Vale Royal	Rest of county total	County total	Out of county total
Westbrook parishing	- -	1 *	- -	- -	- -	- -	- -	- -	- -	1 *	- -
Other specified	- -	1 *	- -	- -	- -	- -	- -	- -	- -	1 *	- -
BASE TOTAL	3710	5227	1322	403	308	348	409	802	3592	12529	686

The figures in the table above do not sum to the base total/100% because undefined fields are not included, except as part of the base total.
* *Less than ½%*

NOP Analysis of Responses to Local Government Commission Draft Recommendations - CHESHIRE

Report D1: Opinions on the structural options by respondent type (all respondents)
Base: all

	Respondent Type					
	Indiv-iduals	Business groups	County, regional & national interests	Education (& church) groups	Local groups	Parish and town councils
Status quo/two-tier	6612 *52%*	73 *29%*	24 *51%*	87 *71%*	34 *35%*	36 *69%*
Unitary Warrington	1304 *10%*	27 *11%*	2 *4%*	2 *2%*	24 *25%*	6 *12%*
Unitary Halton	1016 *8%*	117 *46%*	7 *15%*	3 *2%*	24 *25%*	- -
Two Unitary Districts (Warrington and Halton)	143 *1%*	10 *4%*	2 *4%*	1 *1%*	1 *1%*	42 *8%*
No change in own district	3355 *27%*	22 *9%*	- -	23 *19%*	9 *9%*	5 *10%*
County-level authority (either two-tier or unitary)	53 *	- -	- -	- -	- -	- -
District-level authority (either two-tier or unitary)	27 *	- -	- -	- -	- -	- -
Pre-1974 structure	9 *	- -	- -	- -	- -	- -
County-wide unitary structure	7 *	1 *	- -	- -	1 *1%*	1 *2%*
Reject	11 *	1 *	- -	- -	- -	- -
Other specified	33 *	1 *	- -	1 *1%*	- -	- -
No preference expressed/option defined	72 *1%*	4 *2%*	12 *26%*	5 *4%*	3 *3%*	- -
BASE TOTAL	12642	256	47	122	96	52

* *Less than ½%*

NOP Analysis of Responses to Local Government Commission Draft Recommendations - CHESHIRE

Report D2: Opinions on the structural options, by respondent type
Base: respondents in Halton only

	Respondent Type					
	Indiv-iduals	Business groups	County, regional & national interests	Education (& church) groups	Local groups	Parish and town councils
Status quo/two-tier	1224 *34%*	10 *11%*	- -	14 *44%*	5 *16%*	1 *33%*
Unitary Warrington	13 *	- -	- -	- -	1 *3%*	- -
Unitary Halton	953 *27%*	71 *78%*	3 *75%*	3 *9%*	22 *71%*	- -
Two Unitary Districts (Warrington and Halton)	17 *	1 *1%*	- -	1 *3%*	- -	- -
No change in own district	1257 *35%*	7 *8%*	- -	12 *38%*	2 *6%*	2 *67%*
County-level authority (either two-tier or unitary)	32 *1%*	- -	- -	- -	- -	- -
District-level authority (either two-tier or unitary)	8 *	- -	- -	- -	- -	- -
Reject	3 *	1 *1%*	- -	- -	- -	- -
Other specified	12 *	- -	- -	1 *3%*	- -	- -
No preference expressed/option defined	30 *1%*	1 *1%*	1 *25%*	1 *3%*	1 *3%*	- -
BASE TOTAL	3549	91	4	32	31	3

* *Less than ½%*

NOP Analysis of Responses to Local Government Commission Draft Recommendations - CHESHIRE

Report D3: Opinions on the structural options, by respondent type
Base: respondents in Warrington only

	Respondent Type					
	Indiv-iduals	Business groups	County, regional & national interests	Education (& church) groups	Local groups	Parish and town councils
Status quo/two-tier	1598 *32%*	25 *34%*	1 *50%*	11 *41%*	9 *22%*	4 *31%*
Unitary Warrington	1236 *24%*	27 *36%*	- -	2 *7%*	23 *56%*	6 *46%*
Unitary Halton	9 *	4 *5%*	- -	- -	- -	- -
Two Unitary Districts (Warrington and Halton)	57 *1%*	2 *3%*	- -	- -	1 *2%*	- -
No change in own district	2098 *41%*	15 *20%*	- -	11 *41%*	7 *17%*	3 *23%*
County-level authority (either two-tier or unitary)	16 *	- -	- -	- -	- -	- -
District-level authority (either two-tier or unitary)	19 *	- -	- -	- -	- -	- -
Pre-1974 structure	5 *	- -	- -	- -	- -	- -
Reject	4 *	- -	- -	- -	- -	- -
Other specified	3 *	- -	- -	- -	- -	- -
No preference expressed/option defined	25 *	1 *1%*	1 *50%*	3 *11%*	1 *2%*	- -
BASE TOTAL	5070	74	2	27	41	13

* *Less than ½%*

NOP Analysis of Responses to Local Government Commission Draft Recommendations - CHESHIRE

Report D4: Opinions on the structural options, by respondent type
Base: respondents in rest of county only

	Respondent Type					
	Indiv-iduals	Business groups	County, regional & national interests	Education (& church) groups	Local groups	Parish and town councils
Status quo/two-tier	3288 *96%*	21 *55%*	16 *94%*	58 *98%*	15 *94%*	31 *86%*
Unitary Warrington	22 *1%*	- -	1 *6%*	- -	- -	- -
Unitary Halton	19 *1%*	8 *21%*	- -	- -	- -	- -
Two Unitary Districts (Warrington and Halton)	49 *1%*	6 *16%*	- -	- -	- -	4 *11%*
County-level authority (either two-tier or unitary)	2 *	- -	- -	- -	- -	- -
Pre-1974 structure	4 *	- -	- -	- -	- -	- -
County-wide unitary structure	7 *	1 *3%*	- -	- -	1 *6%*	1 *3%*
Reject	4 *	- -	- -	- -	- -	- -
Other specified	18 *1%*	1 *3%*	- -	- -	- -	- -
No preference expressed/option defined	13 *	1 *3%*	- -	1 *2%*	- -	- -
BASE TOTAL	3426	38	17	59	16	36

* *Less than ½%*

NOP Analysis of Responses to Local Government Commission Draft Recommendations - CHESHIRE

Report E: Views on services by authority of respondent
Base: all

	Review districts		Other districts in county								
	Halton	Warrington	Chester	Congleton	Crewe and Nantwich	Ellesmere Port and Neston	Macclesfield	Vale Royal	Rest of county total	County total	Out of county total
Archives	-	1	-	-	-	-	-	1	1	2	2
	-	*	-	-	-	-	-	*	*	*	*
Education	4	6	2	-	-	-	-	-	2	12	1
	*	*	*	-	-	-	-	-	*	*	*
Libraries	5	-	1	-	-	-	-	-	1	6	2
	*	-	*	-	-	-	-	-	*	*	*
Other specified services (or multiples of)	2	3	-	-	-	-	1	-	1	6	7
	*	*	-	-	-	-	*	-	*	*	1%
BASE TOTAL	3710	5227	1322	403	308	348	409	802	3592	12529	686

The figures in the table above do not sum to the base total/100% because undefined fields are not included, except as part of the base total.
* *Less than ½%*

NOP Analysis of Responses to Local Government Commission Draft Recommendations - CHESHIRE

Report F: Views on services by respondent type
Base: all

	Respondant Type							
	Individuals	Business groups	County, regional & national interests	Education (& church) groups	Local groups	Parliam-entary interests	Parish and town councils	Local councillors
Archives	1	-	2	1	-	-	-	-
	*	-	*4%*	*1%*	-	-	-	-
Education	10	-	-	3	-	-	-	-
	*	-	-	*2%*	-	-	-	-
Libraries	7	-	1	-	-	-	-	-
	*	-	*2%*	-	-	-	-	-
Other specified services (or multiples of)	4	1	5	-	3	-	-	-
	*	*	*11%*	-	*3%*	-	-	-
BASE TOTAL	12587	256	47	122	96	14	52	41

The figures in the table above do not sum to the base total/100% because undefined fields are not included, except as part of the base total.
* *Less than ½%*

Halton & Warrington

NOP Analysis of Responses to Local Government Commission Draft Recommendations - CHESHIRE

Report G: Type of respondent by authority of respondent
Base: all

	Review districts		Other districts in county								
	Halton	Warrington	Chester	Congleton	Crewe and Nantwich	Ellesmere Port and Neston	Macclesfield	Vale Royal	Rest of county total	County total	Out of county total
Individuals	3535 *95%*	5060 *97%*	1269 *96%*	379 *94%*	282 *92%*	336 *97%*	383 *94%*	760 *95%*	3409 *95%*	12004 *96%*	583 *85%*
Business groups	91 *2%*	74 *1%*	16 *1%*	5 *1%*	2 *1%*	3 *1%*	7 *2%*	5 *1%*	38 *1%*	203 *2%*	53 *8%*
County, regional and national interests	4 *	2 *	8 *1%*	1 *	3 *1%*	- -	1 *	4 *	17 *	23 *	24 *3%*
Education (and church) groups	32 *1%*	27 *1%*	12 *1%*	5 *1%*	15 *5%*	6 *2%*	5 *1%*	16 *2%*	59 *2%*	118 *1%*	4 *1%*
Local Groups	31 *1%*	41 *1%*	4 *	2 *	2 *1%*	1 *	2 *	5 *1%*	16 *	88 *1%*	8 *1%*
Parliamentary interests	- -	1 *	- -	- -	- -	- -	1 *	- -	1 *	2 *	12 *2%*
Parish and town councils	3 *	13 *	7 *1%*	7 *2%*	4 *1%*	- -	6 *1%*	12 *1%*	36 *1%*	52 *	- -
Local Councillors	14 *	9 *	6 *	4 *1%*	- -	2 *1%*	4 *1%*	- -	16 *	39 *	2 *
BASE TOTAL	3710	5227	1322	403	308	348	409	802	3592	12529	686

* *Less than ½%*

NOP Analysis of Responses to Local Government Commission Draft Recommendations - CHESHIRE

Report H: Opinions on the structural options by ward/area of respondent in Halton
Base: all

	Halton																		
	Apple-ton	Broad-heath	Brook-fields	Castle-fields	Clough	Dares-bury	Ditton	Farn-worth	Grange	Hale	Halton	Halton Brook	Heath	Hough Green	Kings-way	Mersey	Murdi-shaw	Norton	River-side
Status quo/two-tier	22	22	70	141	173	70	14	55	100	17	19	92	172	27	23	68	57	82	29
	19%	*22%*	*36%*	*36%*	*59%*	*45%*	*14%*	*26%*	*39%*	*19%*	*13%*	*42%*	*36%*	*21%*	*18%*	*33%*	*45%*	*37%*	*21%*
Unitary Warrington	1	4	1	-	1	-	-	-	1	-	3	-	-	1	-	1	-	1	-
	1%	*4%*	*1%*	-	*	-	-	-	*	-	*2%*	-	-	*1%*	-	*	-	*	-
Unitary Halton	62	46	58	42	38	8	58	93	47	56	99	36	35	62	74	73	20	67	77
	53%	*45%*	*29%*	*11%*	*13%*	*5%*	*59%*	*43%*	*18%*	*62%*	*69%*	*16%*	*7%*	*49%*	*58%*	*35%*	*16%*	*30%*	*55%*
Two Unitary Districts (Warrington and Halton)	1	2	-	2	-	1	-	3	-	-	3	-	1	2	-	1	-	2	1
	1%	*2%*	-	*1%*	-	*1%*	-	*1%*	-	-	*2%*	-	*	*2%*	-	*	-	*1%*	*1%*
No change in own district	25	27	68	190	77	74	20	57	101	14	19	87	257	32	30	56	49	64	27
	21%	*26%*	*35%*	*49%*	*26%*	*47%*	*20%*	*27%*	*39%*	*16%*	*13%*	*40%*	*54%*	*25%*	*23%*	*27%*	*39%*	*29%*	*19%*
County-level authority (either two-tier or unitary)	2	-	-	8	-	-	-	2	4	2	-	1	7	-	-	4	1	1	-
	2%	-	-	*2%*	-	-	-	*1%*	*2%*	*2%*	-	*	*1%*	-	-	*2%*	*1%*	*	-
District-level authority (either two-tier or unitary)	-	-	-	-	-	-	5	-	-	-	-	-	-	2	-	1	-	-	-
	-	-	-	-	-	-	*5%*	-	-	-	-	-	-	*2%*	-	*	-	-	-
Reject	-	-	-	1	-	-	-	-	-	-	-	-	2	-	-	-	-	-	1
	-	-	-	*	-	-	-	-	-	-	-	-	*	-	-	-	-	-	*1%*
Other specified	1	-	-	1	1	2	-	1	2	1	1	-	2	-	-	1	-	-	-
	1%	-	-	*	*	*1%*	-	*	*1%*	*1%*	*1%*	-	*	-	-	*	-	-	-
No preference expressed /option defined	3	1	-	5	2	2	1	3	1	-	-	3	1	1	1	2	-	4	4
	3%	*1%*	-	*1%*	*1%*	*1%*	*1%*	*1%*	*	-	-	*1%*	*	*1%*	*1%*	*1%*	-	*2%*	*3%*
BASE TOTAL	117	102	197	390	292	157	98	214	256	90	144	219	477	127	128	207	127	221	139

* *Less than ½%*

Halton & Warrington

NOP Analysis of Responses to Local Government Commission Draft Recommendations - CHESHIRE

Report H: Opinions on the structural options by ward/area of respondent in Warrington
Base: all

	Warrington												
	Appleton Stretton & Hatton	Bewsey	Burton -wood	Culcheth Glazebury & Croft	Fair-field	Grappen -hall & Thelwall	Great Sankey North	Great Sankey South	Howley & White -cross	Hulme	Latch -ford	Locking Stumps Gorse Covert & Risley	Lymm
Status quo/two-tier	190 *24%*	11 *10%*	50 *33%*	136 *60%*	19 *19%*	190 *33%*	71 *37%*	49 *37%*	26 *14%*	15 *16%*	42 *27%*	58 *50%*	318 *40%*
Unitary Warrington	30 *4%*	73 *69%*	62 *41%*	27 *12%*	57 *58%*	35 *6%*	67 *35%*	59 *44%*	117 *65%*	64 *67%*	77 *49%*	25 *21%*	27 *3%*
Unitary Halton	2 *	1 *1%*	1 *1%*	- -	1 *1%*	- -	1 *1%*	- -	2 *1%*	2 *2%*	- -	1 *1%*	- -
Two Unitary Districts (Warrington and Halton)	6 *1%*	1 *1%*	6 *4%*	1 *	3 *3%*	2 *	5 *3%*	1 *1%*	6 *3%*	3 *3%*	1 *1%*	3 *3%*	- -
No change in own district	566 *71%*	20 *19%*	32 *21%*	62 *27%*	14 *14%*	335 *59%*	47 *24%*	25 *19%*	20 *11%*	9 *9%*	34 *22%*	29 *25%*	446 *56%*
County-level authority (either two-tier or unitary)	2 *	- -	- -	- -	1 *1%*	1 *	1 *1%*	- -	1 *1%*	- -	- -	- -	3 *
District-level authority (either two-tier or unitary)	- -	- -	- -	- -	- -	1 *	- -	- -	2 *1%*	2 *2%*	3 *2%*	1 *1%*	- -
Pre-1974 structure	- -	- -	- -	- -	- -	- -	- -	- -	- -	- -	- -	- -	1 *
Reject	- -	- -	- -	- -	- -	- -	- -	- -	1 *1%*	- -	- -	- -	- -
Other specified	- -	- -	- -	- -	- -	1 *	- -	- -	- -	- -	- -	- -	1 *
No preference expressed/option defined	- -	- -	2 *1%*	2 *1%*	3 *3%*	3 *1%*	- -	- -	5 *3%*	- -	- -	- -	5 *1%*
BASE TOTAL	796	106	153	228	98	568	192	134	180	95	157	117	801

continued/

* *Less than ½%*

NOP Analysis of Responses to Local Government Commission Draft Recommendations - CHESHIRE

Report H: Opinions on the structural options by ward/area of respondent in Warrington
Base: all
/continued

	Warrington									
	Oakwood	Orford	Penketh & Cuerdley	Poplars	Poulton North	Poulton South	Rixton & Woolston	Stockton Heath & Walton	Westy	Winwick
Status quo/two-tier	13 *22%*	28 *18%*	73 *43%*	10 *14%*	40 *20%*	47 *35%*	50 *36%*	178 *33%*	19 *23%*	14 *27%*
Unitary Warrington	30 *52%*	101 *66%*	55 *32%*	52 *75%*	121 *61%*	67 *50%*	46 *33%*	38 *7%*	38 *46%*	23 *45%*
Unitary Halton	1 *2%*	- -	- -	- -	- -	- -	- -	- -	- -	1 *2%*
Two Unitary Districts (Warrington and Halton)	1 *2%*	4 *3%*	6 *4%*	- -	3 *2%*	- -	5 *4%*	1 *	- -	2 *4%*
No change in own district	10 *17%*	12 *8%*	36 *21%*	6 *9%*	31 *16%*	20 *15%*	31 *22%*	311 *58%*	23 *28%*	11 *22%*
County-level authority (either two-tier or unitary)	- -	- -	- -	1 *1%*	1 *1%*	- -	2 *1%*	3 *1%*	- -	- -
District-level authority (either two-tier or unitary)	- -	5 *3%*	- -	- -	2 *1%*	- -	- -	2 *	1 *1%*	- -
Pre-1974 structure	- -	2 *1%*	- -	- -	- -	- -	- -	2 *	- -	- -
Reject	- -	- -	- -	- -	- -	- -	2 *1%*	1 *	- -	- -
Other specified	- -	- -	- -	- -	- -	- -	- -	1 *	- -	- -
No preference expressed/option defined	3 *5%*	2 *1%*	1 *1%*	- -	1 *1%*	- -	2 *1%*	- -	1 *1%*	- -
BASE TOTAL	58	154	171	69	199	134	138	537	82	51

* *Less than ½%*

NOP Analysis of Responses to Local Government Commission Draft Recommendations - CHESHIRE

Report I: Opinions on other issues by ward/area of respondent in Halton
Base: all

	Halton																		
	Apple -ton	Broad-heath	Brook-fields	Castle -fields	Clough	Dares -bury	Ditton	Farn-worth	Grange	Hale	Halton	Halton Brook	Heath	Hough Green	Kings -way	Mersey	Murdi -shaw	Norton	River -side
Historic Lancashire	-	-	-	1	-	-	-	-	-	-	-	-	-	-	-	-	-	-	1
	-	-	-	*	-	-	-	-	-	-	-	-	-	-	-	-	-	-	1%
Historic Lancashire and Cheshire	-	-	-	1	-	-	-	-	1	-	-	-	-	-	-	-	-	-	-
	-	-	-	*	-	-	-	-	*	-	-	-	-	-	-	-	-	-	-
BASE TOTAL	117	102	197	390	292	157	98	214	256	90	144	219	477	127	128	207	127	221	139

The figures in the table above do not sum to the base total/100% because undefined fields are not included, except as part of the base total.
** Less than ½%*

NOP Analysis of Responses to Local Government Commission Draft Recommendations - CHESHIRE

Report I: Opinions on other issues by ward/area of respondent in Warrington
Base: all

	Warrington												
	Appleton Stretton & Hatton	Bewsey	Burton -wood	Culcheth Glazebury & Croft	Fair-field	Grappen -hall & Thelwall	Great Sankey North	Great Sankey South	Howley & White -cross	Hulme	Latch -ford	Locking Stumps Gorse Covert & Risley	Lymm
Historic Lancashire	-	-	1	-	-	1	-	-	-	1	-	-	2
	-	-	1%	-	-	*	-	-	-	1%	-	-	*
Other specified	1	-	1	-	-	-	-	-	-	-	-	-	-
	*	-	1%	-	-	-	-	-	-	-	-	-	-
BASE TOTAL	796	106	153	228	98	568	192	134	180	95	157	117	801

continued/

The figures in the table above do not sum to the base total/100% because undefined fields are not included, except as part of the base total.
** Less than ½%*

NOP Analysis of Responses to Local Government Commission Draft Recommendations - CHESHIRE

Report I: Opinions on other issues by ward/area of respondent in Warrington
Base: all
/continued

	Warrington									
	Oakwood	Orford	Penketh & Cuerdley	Poplars	Poulton North	Poulton South	Rixton & Woolston	Stockton Heath & Walton	Westy	Winwick
Historic Lancashire	-	2	-	-	2	-	-	-	1	-
	-	*1%*	-	-	*1%*	-	-	-	*1%*	-
BASE TOTAL	58	154	171	69	199	134	138	537	82	51

The figures in the table above do not sum to the base total/100% because undefined fields are not included, except as part of the base total.
* *Less than ½%*

MORI Research Study for the Local Government Commission

Introduction

Background

1 This summary report highlights the key findings from a survey of public opinion conducted in Boroughs of Halton and Warrington and across the County of Cheshire on behalf of the Local Government Commission for England. A copy of each of the marked-up questionnaires is appended. The computer tabulations are contained in a separate volume, which is available from MORI (32 Old Queen Street, London SW1H 9HP. Telephone 0171-222 0232. Price £15)

2 The survey was designed in close consultation with the Commission, following extensive qualitative research and pilot testing. All sampling, interviewing and analysis have been carried out independently by MORI, within the guidelines of the profession laid out by the Market Research Society.

3 In Halton and in Warrington, all Census Enumeration Districts (EDs) were sorted by ward, and stratified according to social class. EDs were then sampled (32 in total in each of Halton and Warrington) in proportion to the population size of each, and quotas set for sex, age and work status. In Halton, a total of 319 interviews with adults aged 18+, conducted face-to-face and in-home, were carried out between 9 October and 6 November 1995. In Warrington, 320 interviews were conducted. Data were weighted to match the population profile of each Borough.

4 In the remaining districts of Cheshire, all EDs were sorted into ward, and again were stratified according to social class. A total of 32 EDs across the whole area (that is, Cheshire excluding Halton and Warrington) were sampled, with quotas set by sex, age and work status. Face-to-face interviews, conducted in-home, were carried out with 311 adults aged 18+ between 9 October and 6 November 1995. Data were weighted to match the population profile of the County excluding Halton and Warrington.

Publication of the Results

5 As with all our studies, these findings are subject to our Standard Terms and Conditions of Contract. Any press release or publication of the findings of this survey require the advance approval of MORI. Such approval will only be refused on the grounds of inaccuracy or misinterpretation.

Objectives

6 This survey took place during Stage Three, the consultation period on the Commission's draft recommendations. It measures public preferences for the organisation of local government in the area currently comprising the Boroughs of Halton and Warrington, as well as exploring strength of feeling, levels of knowledge about the review, involvement in, and broader perceptions of, local government in the area.

Statistical Reliability of the Data

7 Because we have interviewed a sample of residents, rather than the whole population, the results are subject to statistical tolerance limits, or "margins of error". These are expressed as our confidence that the true figure for the whole population falls within a given range. By convention this is expressed as a percentage, so our 95% confidence level means that in 95 times out of 100 the true figure would lie within this range.

8 The table below shows ranges of the 95% confidence level for a range of sample sizes. For each sample size, the table shows the tolerance limits for sample results close to 10%, 30% and 50%. Take, for example, the results of a survey of 300 residents showing that 50% are aware of the review. In 95 times out of 100 the true figure would lie between 44% and 56% (ie between 50% ±6%).

Sample size	Sampling tolerances applicable to results at or near these percentages (based on 95% confidence level)		
	10/90% ±%	30/70% ±%	50% ±%
300	3	5	6
200	4	6	7
150	5	7	8
100	6	9	10
50	8	13	14

9 Clearly, 10% or 30% of the sample being aware of the review equate to 90% or 70% not being aware of it. So this table shows the ranges of 95% confidence for responses close to 10%, 30%, 50%, 70% and 90% of our sample. The figures for responses between can be obtained by extrapolation.

10 The true figure would only be known if all the residents of the area had been interviewed. It can be seen in the table, however, that large increases in the sample size do not greatly reduce the sampling tolerance. In addition, the true figure is more likely to lie at the midpoint of the range, rather than at either extreme.

11 When comparing results from separate groups within a sample we need to be sure that the differences are statistically significant. This would be important in comparing views expressed by different parts of a county. The table below shows how the statistical significance of the difference is determined by the size of the groups and the percentage result from the sample.

12 Assuming a 95% confidence level, the table shows the size of the differences required if different results are to be regarded as statistically significant. It can be seen that if 50% of a group of 300 were aware of the review, the result from another group of 300 would not become statistically significant until it became less than 42% or more than 58%.

Sample sizes	Differences required for significance at or near these percentage levels		
	10/90% ±	30/70% ±	50% ±
300 and 300	5	7	8
300 and 200	5	8	9
300 and 100	7	10	11
200 and 100	7	11	12
100 and 100	8	13	14

Survey Findings

Knowledge and Awareness

13 Residents in Halton and Warrington profess broadly similar levels of knowledge and interest in local government as those living in the rest of the County of Cheshire. A clear majority like to know what their council is doing, but want no greater involvement. Just under one in five say that they want a higher level of involvement.

14 Halton and Warrington residents are a little less likely than residents of the Rest of Cheshire to claim to be knowledgeable about what their council does (34% and 30%, respectively, claim to know a great deal or fair amount, compared with 40% in the Rest of Cheshire). In all areas, a clear majority admit not knowing, at best, not very much.

15 This is reflected in the number of residents who incorrectly ascribe services between the two tiers of local government. Thus, although between four and five in ten recognise libraries as a county council service, as many as one in three allocate responsibility to their district/borough/city council. And although nearly two-thirds realise that refuse collection is a district/borough/city service, more than one in ten thinks it is a county council service. Residents of Warrington are slightly less likely to be correct in the way that they allocate services across the two tiers than are those of Halton and those living in the rest of the County.

16 Awareness of the review itself is higher in Halton and Warrington (where 81% and 74%, respectively, have heard of it) than in the rest of Cheshire (61%). The proportions who say they know a fair amount or more are slightly (but not statistically significantly) higher in Halton and Warrington (14% and 16% respectively) than in the rest of the County (11%).

Sources of Information

17 Local newspapers are the most common source of information about the review. Of those who have at least heard of the review, around five in ten name the local press as a recent source. Up to six in ten cite some media source as a recent source of information on the review.

18 It would appear that both the County and Borough councils have been fairly active in providing information to residents in the review areas. In both Halton and Warrington, 45% name a Borough Council source, while 46% and 59% respectively cite a County source. The figures are lower in the rest of the County: 30% select a County source, and 23% a Borough source. Very few recognise receiving information directly from the Local Government Commission itself.

19 Although most of those aware of the review recognise one or more recent sources of information, only one in six say that this has influenced their opinion.

20 Furthermore, in spite of a relatively low level of knowledge of, and engagement with, their local authority, most people in Halton and Warrington say that the outcome of the review is either very important to them (20% and 28% respectively) or fairly important (42% and 31% respectively). As one might expect, people in the rest of Cheshire perceive a lower level of importance (16% very important and 34% fairly important).

The Preferred Option

21 In both Halton and Warrington, opinion is divided. In Halton, the balance of opinion is marginally in favour of a unitary council (preferred by 39%), rather than no change (34%); the balance is the opposite in Warrington, where 41% would prefer no change, and 33% a unitary council. Residents in the rest of the County are more inclined to no change; half would prefer to see no change in both Halton and Warrington, while, in both cases, two in five favour unitary solutions. Other residents have no view either way, or are indifferent.

22 People in Halton and Warrington feel more strongly about the preference they express than do those living elsewhere in the County. By a ratio of four-to-one, residents here feel very or fairly strongly about this, rather than not very or not at all strongly. The ratio in the rest of the County is two-to-one. The option selected has little influence on how strongly residents feel.

Factors in Expressing a Preference

23 In questions 13 to 23, residents were asked to say to what extent they agreed or disagreed with a range of statements which related to a change to unitary local government. The statements were designed to cover the main issues raised by residents during the qualitative phase of research, and others that formed a part of the

Commission's brief to take into consideration in making its recommendations.

24 The following charts summarise the results from these questions, with the full question wording presented in the questionnaires in the appendices. Values have been ascribed to the five attitudinal positions that people were offered (+2 for strongly agree, +1 for tend to agree, 0 for neither agree nor disagree, -1 for tend to disagree, and -2 for strongly disagree) and mean scores calculated across all respondents expressing a view. This has the combined benefit of distilling the range of opinion into one summary figure, while incorporating the varying intensity of feeling by ascribing values. Bars to the right indicate that the mean score value is positive, and thus that there is a balance of agreement with the statement. Bars to the left, conversely, indicate a balance of disagreement.

25 The first chart, therefore, shows how the views of people living in the review areas of Halton and Warrington differ from those across the rest of Cheshire. In doing so, it illustrates the attitudes or perceptions that are, in relative terms, shared by both groups of residents (where the bars project in the same direction), and those where views differ markedly. Thus there is broad agreement on the positive aspects of change, although the balance of opinion tends to be more marked in Halton and Warrington than in the rest of the County. On the other hand, there is broad agreement that a County Council is needed for national representation and that change would increase costs. On the need for national representation, it is in the rest of Cheshire that the balance of opinion is most marked. The only issue on which there is a clear divergence of opinion is on whether people feel that they will be affected by change; Halton and Warrington residents disagree, on balance, that they would not be affected. Residents of the two review districts are also considerably more likely to want more information before making up their minds than are those in the rest of the County.

26 The subsequent charts take the results, separately, from Halton, Warrington and the rest of Cheshire, and illustrate the difference in views between those within each area whose preference is for unitary status, and those who prefer no change. The perceived impact on efficiency is clearly a key determinant of opinion in Halton and Warrington, as this is the statement on which there is most differentiation between the two groups. Also important are: perceptions of how unitaries would reflect the community and be in touch with residents; the level of disruption, the impact on services and the perceived need for County representation. On the whole, differentiation between the two groups is less marked in the rest of the County.

Attitudes to Change
(All respondents)

Q To what extent do you agree or disagree that...?
(Figures represent 'mean scores' with *strong agreement* given a value of +2 through to *strong disagreement* given -2)

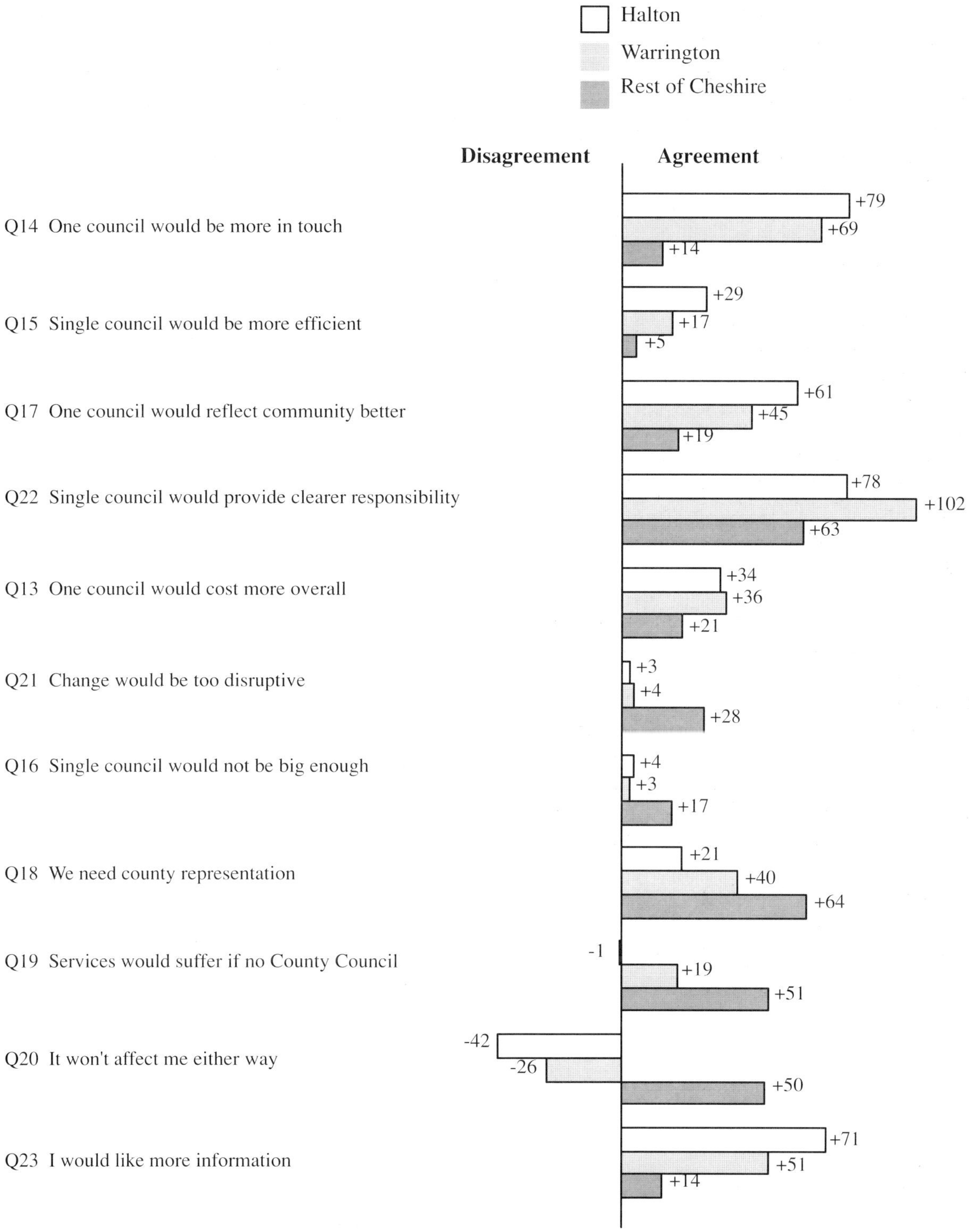

Attitudes to Change
(Respondents in Halton)

Q To what extent do you agree or disagree that...?
(Figures represent 'mean scores' with *strong agreement* given a value of +2 through to *strong disagreement* given -2)

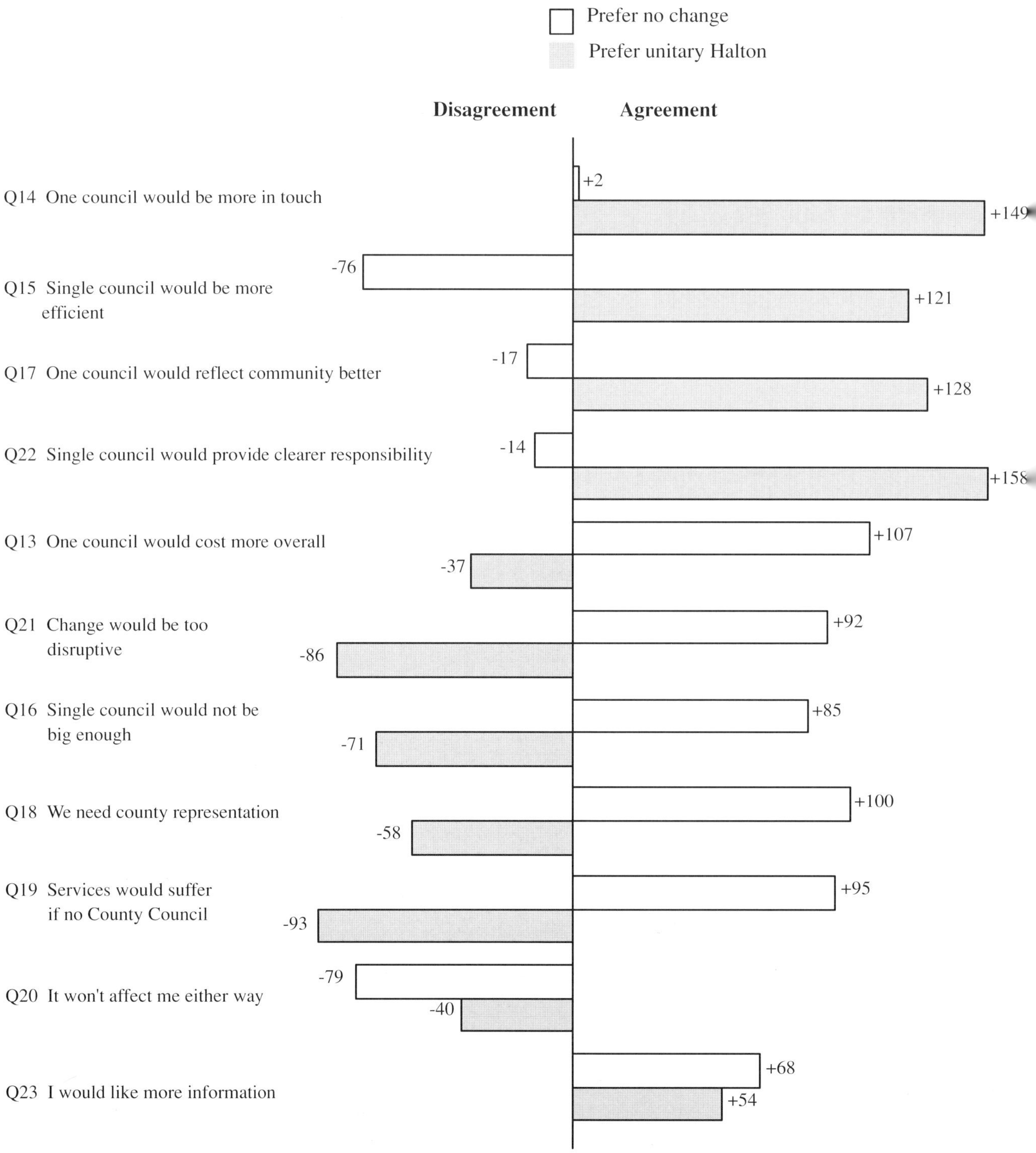

Attitudes to Change
(Respondents in Warrington)

Q To what extent do you agree or disagree that...?
(Figures represent 'mean scores' with *strong agreement* given a value of +2 through to *strong disagreement* given -2)

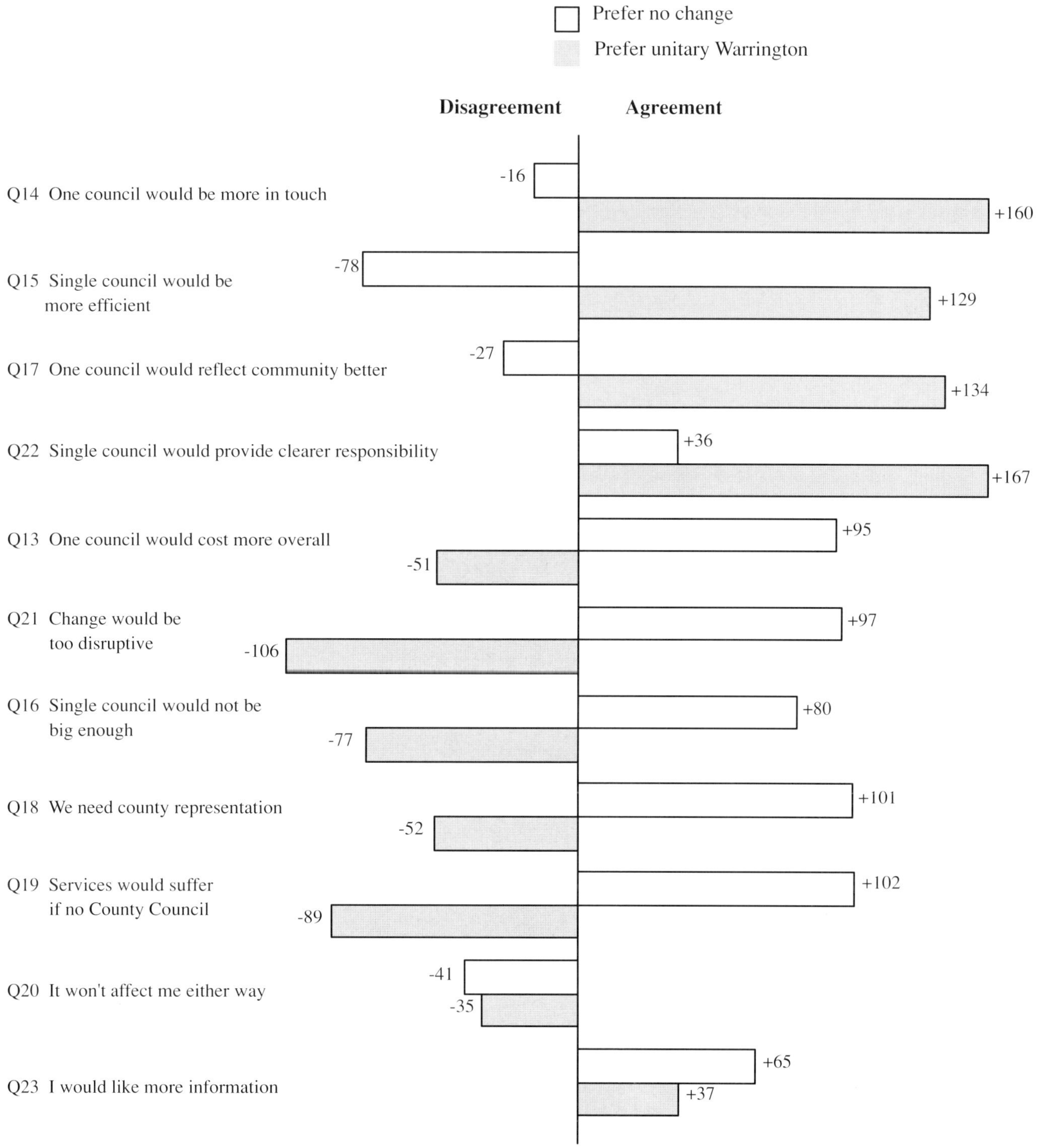

Halton & Warrington

Attitudes to Change
(Respondents in the rest of Cheshire)

Q To what extent do you agree or disagree that...?
(Figures represent 'mean scores' with *strong agreement* given a value of +2 through to *strong disagreement* given -2)

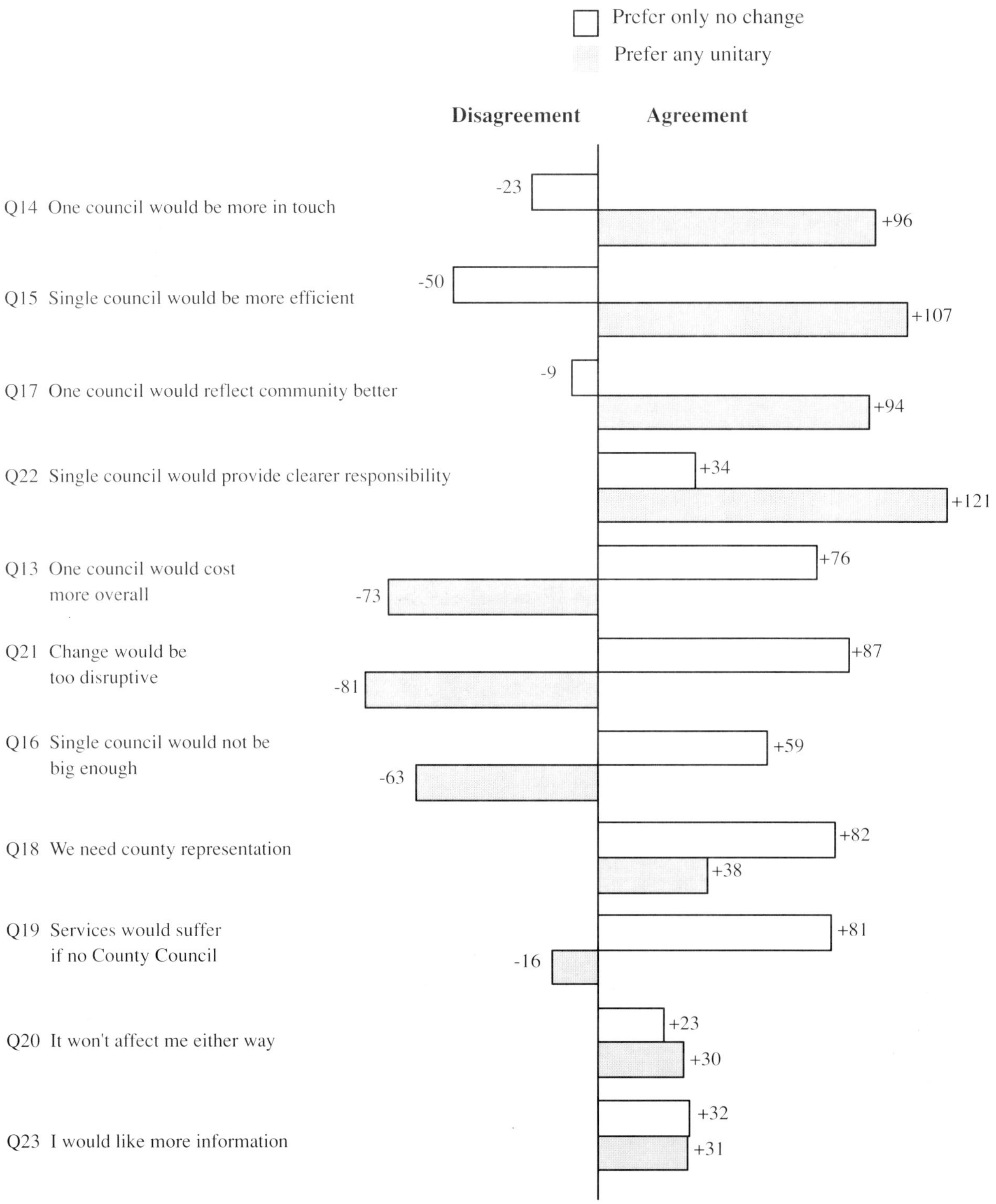

MORI/9101/02
(1-6)

CHESHIRE
REVIEW - REST OF COUNTY

Serial No ....
OUO (7-10)

TOPLINE FINDINGS

Gender %

	%
Male	48
Female	52

Age %

	%
18-24	13
25-34	18
35-44	21
45-54	14
55-64	15
65-74	13
75+	6

WRITE IN AGE [ ][ ]

Work Status %

	%
Full-time (30 hrs/wk+)	47
Part-time (8-29 hrs/wk)	11
Not working (under 8 hrs)	2
Looking after home/children	10
Retired	22
Registered unemployed	3
Unemployed but not registered	1
Student	2
Other	2

Occupation of Chief Income Earner (CIE)
Position/rank/grade

....

Industry/type of company

....

Qualifications/degrees/apprenticeship

....

No of Staff Responsible for

....

PROBE FOR PENSION

	%
AB	24
C1	25
C2	19
D	23
E	9

* Less than 1/2%

Number in Household
Adults aged 18+ (inc. respondent)

14	63	15	5	3	%
1	2	3	4	5+	

Children (17 or under)

61	12	19	6	2	%
0	1	2	3	4+	

QA **Are you or other members of your household employed by a council?** IF YES: **Is this a Borough/District Council or a County Council?** CODE FOR BOTH RESPONDENT AND OTHER HOUSEHOLD MEMBERS

	Respondent %	Other %
Yes:		
Borough/District	2	4
County	4	6
Don't know which	-	1
No	93	82
Don't know	*	8

Tenure %

	%
Owned outright	26
Buying on mortgage	48
Rented from Council	17
Rented from Housing Association	1
Rented from private landlord	5
Other	2

QB **Is this your main permanent home, or is it a second or holiday home?**

	%
Main/permanent	99
Second/holiday	*

Car in Household
CIRCLE NUMBER

15	50	29	6	%
0	1	2	+3	

THIS FORM IS THE PROPERTY OF MARKET & OPINION RESEARCH INTERNATIONAL (MORI)
32 OLD QUEEN STREET, LONDON, SW1H 9HP

INTERVIEWER DECLARATION: I confirm that I have conducted this interview face-to-face with the above named person and that I have asked all the relevant questions fully and recorded the answers in conformance with the survey specification and the MRS Code of Conduct.

Interviewer Name .... Signature ....

Interviewer Number					/	

	Month		Date	
DATE OF INTERVIEW				
	(29)	(30)	(31)	(32)

NB INTERVIEWER: ALL SHOWCARDS HAVE BEEN REVERSED. PLEASE BE CAREFUL TO CODE THE CORRECT RESPONSE.

Good morning/afternoon/evening. I'm from MORI, the market research and polling organisation. We are doing a survey about local issues, and I would like to ask you a few questions.

ASK ALL

Q1 **Firstly, how long have you lived in this area?** (WITHIN FIVE MILES)

	%
Less than 1 year	5
1-2 years	4
3-5 years	8
6-10 years	12
11-20 years	19
Over 20 years/all my life	51

Q2 SHOWCARD A (R) **From this card, how much would you say you know about local councils and the services they provide?**

	%
A great deal	3
A fair amount	37
Not very much	47
Nothing at all	12

Q3 SHOWCARD B (R) **Which of the statements on this card comes closest to your own view of the Councils in this area?**

		%
A)	I'm not interested in what the Council does, or whether they do their job	2
B)	I'm not interested in what the Council does, as long as they do their job	16
C)	I like to know what the Council is doing, but I'm happy to let them get on with their job	59
D)	I would like to have more of a say in what the Council does and the services it provides	18
E)	I already work for, or am involved with the Council and the services it provides	5
	Don't know	1

Q4 **From what you know, how many councils provide the main services in this neighbourhood?** (INTERVIEWER - NOT INCLUDING PARISH COUNCILS)

	%
One	31
Two	36
Three+	6
Don't know	26

In fact there are two main councils that provide, or are responsible for, most services in this area:. . .district/borough/city and Cheshire County Council.

ROTATE ORDER OF Q5/6

☐ Q5 SHOWCARD C (R) **From this list, what services do you think are the responsibility of... district/borough/city council? Just read out the letter(s) that apply**

☐ Q6 SHOWCARD C AGAIN (R) **And which services on this list do you think are the responsibility of Cheshire County Council? Again, just read out the letters that apply.**

Q7 SHOWCARD D (R) **Which, if any, of these services do you or members of your family use?** INCLUDE ONLY LOCAL USE

		Q5 "Borough" %	Q6 County %	Q7 Use %
A	Bus Services	36	32	37
B	Car Parks	64	14	69
C	Council Housing	66	16	11
D	Council Tax Benefit/Housing benefit	55	20	20
E	Fire service	19	64	26
F	Food safety	32	33	14
G	Household waste sites/dumps	53	26	65
H	Libraries	33	49	64
I	Parks, playgrounds and open spaces	59	23	53
J	Planning service	49	27	11
K	Public conveniences	62	11	43
L	Recycling/bottle banks	47	19	50
M	Refuse collection	63	16	80
N	Road maintenance	34	52	38
O	Schools/education	20	62	36
P	Social services	26	47	11
Q	Street sweeping	65	14	38
R	Swimming pools/sports facilities	54	20	54
	Other	2	2	3
	None of these	1	1	*
	Don't know	12	16	6

Q8 SHOWCARD E (R) **As you may know, there is currently a review being undertaken by the Local Government Commission on the future local government structure in the county. How much, if anything, would you say you know about this?**

	%
A great deal	2
A fair amount	9
Just a little	30
Heard of but know nothing about	20
Never heard of	39

PREFERENCES

HAND OVER MAP SHOWING AREAS UNDER REVIEW AND "CURRENT SERVICES" CARD
The Local Government Commission is considering options for the future structure of local government in parts of Cheshire. Could you please read through this card, (SHOW OPTIONS CARD) **which outlines the options.**

Q9 **Please tell me which of the options, if either, you would prefer for <u>each of</u> Warrington and Halton?**
CODE ONE ONLY FOR <u>EACH</u> DISTRICT

For Warrington

	%
Option A (single all purpose council)	21
Option B (stay the same/status quo)	51
Some other option	1
Neither of these	1
Either of these/don't mind	12
Don't care	7
Don't know	7

For Halton

	%
Option A (single all purpose council)	20
Option B (stay the same/status quo)	51
Some other option	2
Neither of these	1
Either of these/don't mind	12
Don't care	7
Don't know	7

<u>ASK IF "OTHER" NAMED AT Q9 (CODE 3)</u>
Q10 **What other option is that?**
PROBE FULLY - DO NOT PROMPT.

....

....

....

....

<u>ASK ALL PREFERRING AN OPTION (1, 2 OR 3 AT Q9). OTHERS GO TO Q13</u>
Q11 SHOWCARD F (R) **You say that the option you would prefer is . . . . .** (INSERT OPTION PREFERRED). **How strongly would you say you feel about this?**
(Base: 229)

	%
Very strongly	20
Fairly strongly	45
Not very strongly	27
Not at all strongly	5
Don't know	3

Q12 **What do you think would be the main advantages of . . .**(OPTION PREFERRED)
PROBE FULLY FOR DETAILS

....

....

....

....

Nothing...
Don't know/can't think of anything.................................

ATTITUDES TO PROPOSALS

SHOWCARD G (R) **Imagine that there was one council in any or both of Warrington and Halton, providing all services. I am going to read out some statements that people have made about this proposal. To what extent do you agree or disagree that . . . .?**
READ OUT, ROTATE ORDER OF ASKING Q13-22. TICK START

READ OUT:	Strongly agree	Tend to agree	Neither/ Nor	Tend to disagree	Strongly disagree	Don't know	
☐ Q13 **It would cost more overall**	16	26	14	30	4	9	%
Q14 **It would be more in touch with local people's needs**	9	38	12	27	8	5	%
Q15 **The single Council would be more efficient than the current system of two Councils**	9	33	15	30	8	5	%
☐ Q16 **The single council would not be big enough to manage services such as Education and Social Services effectively**	12	31	13	30	5	8	%
Q17 **It would better reflect the sense of community in those areas**	7	40	16	26	5	6	%
Q18 **We need a County Council to represent us nationally**	15	52	12	12	5	4	%
☐ Q19 **Services would suffer if the County Council no longer provides services in those areas**	12	50	13	16	4	6	%
Q20 **It won't affect me whether there is a single Council in those areas or not**	18	45	8	20	6	3	%
Q21 **The change to a single Council for those areas would be too disruptive**	10	39	15	24	4	7	%
☐ Q22 **With a single Council it would be clearer who is responsible for local services**	15	54	8	15	4	4	%
ASK LAST Q23 **I would like to have more information on the proposals before making up my mind**	12	35	16	25	10	3	%

Q24 **On balance, which would you say is more in touch with local people and issues,** .... (ROTATE ORDER OF "DISTRICT" AND COUNTY) (INSERT NAME OF "DISTRICT COUNCIL)..**district/borough/city council, or Cheshire County Council, or would you say that they are both about the same?**

	%
District/borough/city council	59
Cheshire County Council	6
Both about the same	26
Don't know	9

<u>REFER BACK TO Q8. ASK ALL WHO HAVE HEARD OF REVIEW AT Q8 (IE CODES 1/2/3/4). OTHERS TO Q28</u>

Q25 SHOWCARD H **Earlier in the interview, you said that you had heard of the Review of local government structure. From which, if any, of the sources shown on this card have you recently heard about the Review?** INTERVIEWER NOTE: "RECENTLY" = IN PAST 3 MONTHS
(Base: 195)

		%
A	Leaflet from County Council delivered to your door	16
B	Leaflet from County Council in library/ offices, etc	10
C	Advertisement from County Council in local newspaper	5
D	Advertisement from County Council on local radio/TV	1
E	Leaflet from Borough Council delivered to your door	14
F	Leaflet from Borough Council in library/ offices, etc	2
G	Borough Council newspaper	5
H	County Council newspaper	5
I	Advertisement from Borough Council in local newspaper	3
J	Advertisement from Borough Council on local radio/TV	1
K	Advertisement by the Commission on local radio	1
L	Local Government Commission advertisement in local newspaper	2
M	Local newspaper	46
N	National newspaper	7
O	TV	19
P	Local radio	8
Q	National radio	5
R	Friends/neighbours/family	9
S	Conversation with Borough Councillor	3
T	Conversation with County Councillor	3
U	Conversation with Borough Council staff	5
V	Conversation with County Council staff	2
W	Parish/community council	3
X	Residents' Association	-
	Other	12
	None of these	*
	Don't know	9

ASK ALL NAMING A SOURCE AT Q25. OTHERS GO TO Q28

Q26 **Would you say that the information you have received has influenced your opinion, or not?**
(Base: 177)

	%
Yes	17
No	78
Don't know	5

Q27 **What information in particular has influenced your opinion?**

....

....

....

....

ASK ALL

Q28 SHOWCARD I (R) **Assuming you receive the same level of services, how important is it to you, if at all, what the final decision is on the future local government structure in the areas under review?**

	%
Very important	16
Fairly important	34
Not very important	28
Not at all important	19
Don't know	3

ACTIVISM

Q29 SHOWCARD J **Which of the things on this list, if any, have you done in the last three years? Just read out the letter(s) that apply.**

		%
A	Voted in Local Council elections	81
B	Spoken or written to a local Councillor	30
C	Responded to the earlier Review of local government	12
D	Been to a meeting of a local committee or organisation (WRITE IN NAME OF ORGANISATION)	11
E	Spoken on a radio phone-in about a local issue	1
F	Written to a local newspaper about a local issue	3
G	Been to a meeting of a local branch of a political party	3
H	Written to your MP about a local issue	8
I	Been to a Council Committee meeting	3
J	Been to a Council meeting	3
K	Attended a public meeting run by the Council	6
	None of these	16
	Don't know/refused	*

Q30 SHOWCARD K **Which, if any, of these apply to you? Just read out the letter(s) that apply.**

		%
	I am a member of a:	
A	Residents' Association	3
B	Community Association	1
C	Tenants' Association	2
D	Neighbourhood Watch	26
E	PTA/school governors	7
	I do unpaid work for:	
F	A school	8
G	Citizens Advice Bureau	1
H	Volunteer Bureau	4
I	Scouts/Guides/Cubs/Brownies	5
J	Church group	12
	Other	4
	None of these	52
	Don't know	*

THANK RESPONDENT. GO TO DEMOGRAPHICS.

MORI/9101/02 (1-6)

CHESHIRE
REVIEW: Halton

Serial No ....
OUO (7-10)

TOPLINE FINDINGS

Gender %
- Male 48
- Female 52

Age %
- 18-24 14
- 25-34 21
- 35-44 21
- 45-54 14
- 55-64 12
- 65-74 13
- 75+.. 5

WRITE IN AGE [ ][ ]

Work Status %
- Full-time (30 hrs/wk+) 43
- Part-time (8-29 hrs/wk) 7
- Not working (under 8 hrs) 2
- Looking after home/children........... 17
- Retired 21
- Registered unemployed.................. 8
- Unemployed but not registered .... -
- Student.. 2
- Other 1

Occupation of Chief Income Earner (CIE)

Position/rank/grade

....

Industry/type of company

....

Qualifications/degrees/apprenticeship

....

No of Staff Responsible for

....

PROBE FOR PENSION

	%
AB	11
C1	22
C2	21
D	22
E	24

Number in Household
Adults aged 18+ (inc. respondent)

23	58	13	5	1	%
1	2	3	4	5+	

Children (17 or under)

56	15	19	7	3	%
0	1	2	3	4+	

QA **Are you or other members of your household employed by a council?** IF YES: **Is this a Borough/District Council or a County Council?** CODE FOR BOTH RESPONDENT AND OTHER HOUSEHOLD MEMBERS

	Respondent %	Other %
Yes:		
Borough/District	2	-
County	5	4
Don't know which	-	-
No	93	93
Don't know	*	3

Tenure %
- Owned outright.. 17
- Buying on mortgage 45
- Rented from Council 25
- Rented from Housing Association 8
- Rented from private landlord 3
- Other 1

QB **Is this your main permanent home, or is it a second or holiday home?**

	%
Main/permanent	98
Second/holiday	1
Not stated	1

Car in Household
CIRCLE NUMBER

28	53	17	1	%
0	1	2	3+	

INTERVIEWER DECLARATION: I confirm that I have conducted this interview face-to-face with the above named person and that I have asked all the relevant questions fully and recorded the answers in conformance with the survey specification and the MRS Code of Conduct.

Interviewer Name .... Signature ....

Interviewer Number					/	

	Month		Date	
DATE OF INTERVIEW				
	(29)	(30)	(31)	(32)

NB INTERVIEWER: ALL SHOWCARDS HAVE BEEN REVERSED. PLEASE BE CAREFUL TO CODE THE CORRECT RESPONSE.

Good morning/afternoon/evening. I'm from MORI, the market research and polling organisation. We are doing a survey about local issues, and I would like to ask you a few questions.

ASK ALL

Q1 **Firstly, how long have you lived in this area?** (WITHIN FIVE MILES)

	%
Less than 1 year	2
1-2 years	3
3-5 years	4
6-10 years	10
11-20 years	18
Over 20 years/all my life	62
Don't know/can't remember	*

Q2 SHOWCARD A (R) **From this card, how much would you say you know about local councils and the services they provide?**

	%
A great deal	4
A fair amount	30
Not very much	54
Nothing at all	12

Q3 SHOWCARD B (R) **Which of the statements on this card comes closest to your own view of the Councils in this area?**

		%
A)	I'm not interested in what the Council does, or whether they do their job	3
B)	I'm not interested in what the Council does, as long as they do their job	19
C)	I like to know what the Council is doing, but I'm happy to let them get on with their job	57
D)	I would like to have more of a say in what the Council does and the services it provides	19
E)	I already work for, or am involved with the Council and the services it provides	2
	Don't know	*

Q4 **From what you know, how many councils provide the main services in this neighbourhood?** (INTERVIEWER - NOT INCLUDING PARISH COUNCILS)

	%
One	24
Two	52
Three+	1
Don't know	23

In fact there are two main councils that provide, or are responsible for most services in this area: Halton Borough and Cheshire County Council.

ROTATE ORDER OF Q5/6

☐ Q5 SHOWCARD C (R) **From this list, what services do you think are the responsibility of Halton Borough Council? Just read out the letter(s) that apply**

☐ Q6 SHOWCARD C AGAIN (R) **And which services on this list do you think are the responsibility of Cheshire County Council? Again, just read out the letters that apply.**

Q7 SHOWCARD D (R) **Which, if any, of these services do you or members of your family use?** INCLUDE ONLY LOCAL USE

		Q5 Halton %	Q6 County %	Q7 Use %
A	Bus Services	55	15	54
B	Car Parks	55	14	65
C	Council Housing	62	13	25
D	Council Tax Benefit/Housing benefit	58	16	26
E	Fire service	15	58	23
F	Food safety	37	28	12
G	Household waste sites/dumps	53	19	48
H	Libraries	31	42	57
I	Parks, playgrounds and open spaces	56	19	63
J	Planning service	42	30	9
K	Public conveniences	55	11	46
L	Recycling/bottle banks	55	12	34
M	Refuse collection	60	15	91
N	Road maintenance	20	54	25
O	Schools/education	13	63	43
P	Social services	19	53	15
Q	Street sweeping	63	10	35
R	Swimming pools/sports facilities	51	19	62
	Other	2	*	1
	None of these	2	3	-
	Don't know	20	25	1

Q8 SHOWCARD E (R) **As you may know, there is currently a review being undertaken by the Local Government Commission on the future local government structure in the county. How much, if anything, would you say you know about this?**

	%
A great deal	2
A fair amount	12
Just a little	46
Heard of but know nothing about	20
Never heard of	18

PREFERENCES

HAND OVER MAP SHOWING AREAS UNDER REVIEW AND "CURRENT SERVICES" CARD
The Local Government Commission is considering options for the future structure of local government in parts of Cheshire. Could you please read through this card, (SHOW OPTIONS CARD) **which outlines the options.**

Q9 **Please tell me which of the options, if either, you would prefer for each of Warrington and Halton?**
CODE ONE ONLY FOR EACH DISTRICT

For Warrington	%
Option A (single all purpose council)	20
Option B (stay the same/status quo)	18
Some other option	1
Neither of these	*
Either of these/don't mind	8
Don't care	19
Don't know	34

For Halton	%
Option A (single all purpose council)	39
Option B (stay the same/status quo)	34
Some other option	1
Neither of these	*
Either of these/don't mind	3
Don't care	5
Don't know	18

ASK IF "OTHER" NAMED AT Q9 (CODE 3)

Q10 **What other option is that Halton?**
PROBE FULLY - DO NOT PROMPT.

....

....

....

....

ASK ALL PREFERRING AN OPTION (1, 2 OR 3 AT Q9). OTHERS GO TO Q13

Q11 SHOWCARD F (R) **You say that the option you would prefer is . . . . .** (INSERT OPTION PREFERRED). **How strongly would you say you feel about this?**
(Base: 241)

	%
Very strongly	20
Fairly strongly	58
Not very strongly	15
Not at all strongly	2
Don't know	6

Q12 **What do you think would be the main advantages of . . .**(OPTION PREFERRED)
PROBE FULLY FOR DETAILS

....

....

....

....

Nothing..
Don't know/can't think of anything..................................

ATTITUDES TO PROPOSALS

SHOWCARD G (R) **Imagine that there was one council in Halton, providing all services. I am going to read out some statements that people have made about this proposal. To what extent do you agree or disagree that . . . .?** READ OUT, ROTATE ORDER OF ASKING Q13-22. TICK START

READ OUT:

		Strongly agree	Tend to agree	Neither/ Nor	Tend to disagree	Strongly disagree	Don't know	
☐ Q13	**It would cost more overall**	11	31	14	20	3	20	%
Q14	**It would be more in touch with local people's needs**	23	43	10	13	2	9	%
Q15	**The single Council would be more efficient than the current system of two Councils**	12	28	14	20	4	22	%
☐ Q16	**The single council would not be big enough to manage services such as Education and Social Services effectively**	10	24	14	8	20	34	%
Q17	**It would better reflect the sense of community in Halton**	16	41	16	12	3	13	%
Q18	**We need a County Council to represent us nationally**	10	31	11	21	7	21	%
☐ Q19	**Services would suffer if the County Council no longer provides services in Halton**	11	22	10	29	8	20	%
Q20	**It won't affect me whether there is a single Council in Halton or not**	2	17	24	29	14	15	%
Q21	**The change to a single Council for Halton would be too disruptive**	9	27	13	29	7	15	%
☐ Q22	**With a single Council it would be clearer who is responsible for local services**	25	32	14	10	4	14	%
ASK LAST Q23	**I would like to have more information on the proposals before making up my mind**	33	30	12	16	6	4	%

Q24 **On balance, which would you say is more in touch with local people and issues, ...** (ROTATE ORDER OF "DISTRICT" AND COUNTY)
Halton Borough Council, or
Cheshire County Council, or would you say that they are both about the same?

	%
Halton Borough Council	53
Cheshire County Council	3
Both about the same	34

REFER BACK TO Q8. ASK ALL WHO HAVE HEARD OF REVIEW AT Q8 (IE CODES 1/2/3/4). OTHERS TO Q28

Q25 SHOWCARD H **Earlier in the interview, you said that you had heard of the Review of local government structure. From which, if any, of the sources shown on this card have you recently heard about the Review?** INTERVIEWER NOTE: "RECENTLY" = IN PAST 3 MONTHS

		%
A	Leaflet from County Council delivered to your door	41
B	Leaflet from County Council in library/ offices, etc	6
C	Advertisement from County Council in local newspaper	12
D	Advertisement from County Council on local radio/TV	6
E	Leaflet from Borough Council delivered to your door	39
F	Leaflet from Borough Council in library/ offices, etc	5
G	Borough Council newspaper	12
H	County Council newspaper	4
I	Advertisement from Borough Council in local newspaper	9
J	Advertisement from Borough Council on local radio/TV	2
K	Advertisement by the Commission on local radio	1
L	Local Government Commission advertisement in local newspaper	3
M	Local newspaper	53
N	National newspaper	4
O	TV	5
P	Local radio	7
Q	National radio	2
R	Friends/neighbours/family	9
S	Conversation with Borough Councillor	3
T	Conversation with County Councillor	*
U	Conversation with Borough Council staff	2
V	Conversation with County Council staff	1
W	Parish/community council	*
X	Residents' Association	1
	Other	9
	None of these	3
	Don't know	1

ASK ALL NAMING A SOURCE AT Q25. OTHERS GO TO Q28

Q26 **Would you say that the information you have received has influenced your opinion, or not?**
(Base: 257)

	%
Yes	16
No	80
Don't know	4

Q27 **What information in particular has influenced your opinion?**

....

....

....

....

ASK ALL

Q28 SHOWCARD I (R) **Assuming you receive the same level of services, how important is it to you, if at all, what the final decision is on the future local government structure in the areas under review?**

	%
Very important	20
Fairly important	42
Not very important	28
Not at all important	4
Don't know	6

ACTIVISM

Q29 SHOWCARD J **Which of the things on this list, if any, have you done in the last three years? Just read out the letter(s) that apply.**

		%
A	Voted in Local Council elections	77
B	Spoken or written to a local Councillor	19
C	Responded to the earlier Review of local government	
D	Been to a meeting of a local committee or	6
	organisation (WRITE IN NAME OF ORGANISATION)	9
E	Spoken on a radio phone-in about a local issue	-
F	Written to a local newspaper about a local issue	2
G	Been to a meeting of a local branch of a political party	1
H	Written to your MP about a local issue	4
I	Been to a Council Committee meeting	2
J	Been to a Council meeting	2
K	Attended a public meeting run by the Council	5
	None of these	19

Q30 SHOWCARD K **Which, if any, of these apply to you? Just read out the letter(s) that apply.**

		%
I am a member of a:		
A	Residents' Association	2
B	Community Association	1
C	Tenants' Association	1
D	Neighbourhood Watch	19
E	PTA/school governors	5
I do unpaid work for:		
F	A school	6
G	Citizens Advice Bureau	-
H	Volunteer Bureau	1
I	Scouts/Guides/Cubs/Brownies	3
J	Church group	5
	Other	3
	None of these	67
	Don't know	2

THANK RESPONDENT. GO TO DEMOGRAPHICS

MORI/9101/02
(1-6)

CHESHIRE
REVIEW: Warrington

Serial No ....
OUO (7-10)

TOPLINE FINDINGS

Gender

	%
Male	48
Female	52

Age

	%
18-24	13
25-34	21
35-44	20
45-54	15
55-64	11
65-74	11
75+	9

WRITE IN AGE [|]

Work Status

	%
Full-time (30 hrs/wk+)	47
Part-time (8-29 hrs/wk)	10
Not working (under 8 hrs)	3
Looking after home/children	9
Retired	23
Registered unemployed	4
Unemployed but not registered	1
Student	2
Other	2

Occupation of Chief Income Earner (CIE)
Position/rank/grade

....

Industry/type of company

....

Qualifications/degrees/apprenticeship

....

No of Staff Responsible for

....

PROBE FOR PENSION

	%
AB	20
C1	27
C2	18
D	23
E	13

Number in Household
Adults aged 18+ (inc. respondent)

1	2	3	4	5+	
15	64	14	5	2	%

Children (17 or under)

0	1	2	3	4+	
59	16	15	9	1	%

QA **Are you or other members of your household employed by a council?** IF YES: **Is this a Borough/District Council or a County Council?** CODE FOR BOTH RESPONDENT AND OTHER HOUSEHOLD MEMBERS

	Respondent %	Other %
Yes:		
Borough/District	2	2
County	8	2
Don't know which	*	*
No	89	90
Don't know	*	6

Tenure

	%
Owned outright	24
Buying on mortgage	50
Rented from Council	19
Rented from Housing Association	3
Rented from private landlord	3
Other	1

QB **Is this your main permanent home, or is it a second or holiday home?**

	%
Main/permanent	99
Second/holiday	-
Not stated	1

Car in Household
CIRCLE NUMBER

0	1	2	3+	
18	50	28	4	%

INTERVIEWER DECLARATION: I confirm that I have conducted this interview face-to-face with the above named person and that I have asked all the relevant questions fully and recorded the answers in conformance with the survey specification and the MRS Code of Conduct.

Interviewer Name .... Signature ....

Interviewer Number				/	

	Month		Date	
DATE OF INTERVIEW				
	(29)	(30)	(31)	(32)

NB INTERVIEWER: ALL SHOWCARDS HAVE BEEN REVERSED. PLEASE BE CAREFUL TO CODE THE CORRECT RESPONSE.

Good morning/afternoon/evening. I'm from MORI, the market research and polling organisation. We are doing a survey about local issues, and I would like to ask you a few questions.

ASK ALL

Q1 **Firstly, how long have you lived in this area?** (WITHIN FIVE MILES)

	%
Less than 1 year	5
1-2 years	4
3-5 years	9
6-10 years	15
11-20 years	27
Over 20 years/all my life	39

Q2 SHOWCARD A (R) **From this card, how much would you say you know about local councils and the services they provide?**

	%
A great deal	2
A fair amount	28
Not very much	57
Nothing at all	13

Q3 SHOWCARD B (R) **Which of the statements on this card comes closest to your own view of the Councils in this area?**

		%
A)	I'm not interested in what the Council does, or whether they do their job	1
B)	I'm not interested in what the Council does, as long as they do their job	18
C)	I like to know what the Council is doing, but I'm happy to let them get on with their job	61
D)	I would like to have more of a say in what the Council does and the services it provides	15
E)	I already work for, or am involved with the Council and the services it provides	4
	Don't know	1

Q4 **From what you know, how many councils provide the main services in this neighbourhood?** (INTERVIEWER - NOT INCLUDING PARISH COUNCILS)

	%
One	24
Two	31
Three+	2
Don't know	43

In fact there are two main councils that provide, or are responsible for most services in this area: Warrington Borough and Cheshire County Council.

ROTATE ORDER OF Q5/6

☐ Q5 SHOWCARD C (R) **From this list, what services do you think are the responsibility of Warrington Borough Council? Just read out the letter(s) that apply**

☐ Q6 SHOWCARD C AGAIN (R) **And which services on this list do you think are the responsibility of Cheshire County Council? Again, just read out the letters that apply.**

Q7 SHOWCARD D (R) **Which, if any, of these services do you or members of your family use?** INCLUDE ONLY LOCAL USE

		Q5 Warrington %	Q6 County %	Q7 Use %
A	Bus Services	63	11	56
B	Car Parks	60	10	69
C	Council Housing	56	16	17
D	Council Tax Benefit/Housing benefit	43	23	19
E	Fire service	17	51	24
F	Food safety	17	29	9
G	Household waste sites/dumps	46	23	59
H	Libraries	25	49	61
I	Parks, playgrounds and open spaces	47	21	58
J	Planning service	32	27	11
K	Public conveniences	48	11	30
L	Recycling/bottle banks	42	13	38
M	Refuse collection	64	13	87
N	Road maintenance	29	38	40
O	Schools/education	18	59	42
P	Social services	23	39	12
Q	Street sweeping	56	13	34
R	Swimming pools/sports facilities	48	20	57
	Other	2	2	2
	None of these	1	1	*
	Don't know	17	25	1

Q8 SHOWCARD E (R) **As you may know, there is currently a review being undertaken by the Local Government Commission on the future local government structure in the county. How much, if anything, would you say you know about this?**

	%
A great deal	2
A fair amount	14
Just a little	31
Heard of but know nothing about	27
Never heard of	25
Don't know	1

PREFERENCES

HAND OVER MAP SHOWING AREAS UNDER REVIEW AND "CURRENT SERVICES" CARD
The Local Government Commission is considering options for the future structure of local government in parts of Cheshire. Could you please read through this card, (SHOW OPTIONS CARD) **which outlines the options.**

Q9 **Please tell me which of the options, if either, you would prefer for each of Warrington and Halton?**
CODE ONE ONLY FOR EACH DISTRICT

For Warrington

	%
Option A (single all purpose council)	33
Option B (stay the same/status quo)	41
Some other option	*
Neither of these	-
Either of these/don't mind	2
Don't care	3
Don't know	20

For Halton

	%
Option A (single all purpose council)	19
Option B (stay the same/status quo)	23
Some other option	-
Neither of these	*
Either of these/don't mind	8
Don't care	8
Don't know	42

ASK IF "OTHER" NAMED AT Q9 (CODE 3)
Q10 **What other option is that for Warrington?**
PROBE FULLY - DO NOT PROMPT.

....

....

....

....

ASK ALL PREFERRING AN OPTION (1, 2 OR 3 AT Q9). OTHERS GO TO Q13
Q11 SHOWCARD F (R) **You say that the option you would prefer is . . . . .** (INSERT OPTION PREFERRED). **How strongly would you say you feel about this?**
(Base: 241)

	%
Very strongly	29
Fairly strongly	50
Not very strongly	18
Not at all strongly	2
Don't know	2

Q12 **What do you think would be the main advantages of . . .**(OPTION PREFERRED)
PROBE FULLY FOR DETAILS

....

....

....

....

Nothing..
Don't know/can't think of anything................................

ATTITUDES TO PROPOSALS

SHOWCARD G (R) **Imagine that there was one council in Warrington providing all services. I am going to read out some statements that people have made about this proposal. To what extent do you agree or disagree that . . . .?** READ OUT, ROTATE ORDER OF ASKING Q13-22. TICK START

READ OUT:

		Strongly agree	Tend to agree	Neither/ Nor	Tend to disagree	Strongly disagree	Don't know	
☐	Q13 **It would cost more overall**	21	25	10	20	8	15	%
	Q14 **It would be more in touch with local people's needs**	28	34	12	13	6	7	%
	Q15 **The single Council would be more efficient than the current system of two Councils**	16	22	13	20	11	18	%
☐	Q16 **The single council would not be big enough to manage services such as Education and Social Services effectively**	14	23	10	25	12	16	%
	Q17 **It would better reflect the sense of community in Warrington**	21	31	14	15	9	11	%
	Q18 **We need a County Council to represent us nationally**	18	32	9	15	10	16	%
☐	Q19 **Services would suffer if the County Council no longer provides services in Warrington**	16	27	9	21	11	16	%
	Q20 **It won't affect me whether there is a single Council in Warrington or not**	7	30	7	29	20	6	%
	Q21 **The change to a single Council for Warrington would be too disruptive**	14	22	13	20	14	17	%
☐	Q22 **With a single Council it would be clearer who is responsible for local services**	32	42	8	6	3	8	%
	ASK LAST Q23 **I would like to have more information on the proposals before making up my mind**	28	32	9	18	10	3	%

Q24 **On balance, which would you say is more in touch with local people and issues, ...** (ROTATE ORDER OF "DISTRICT" AND COUNTY)
Warrington Borough Council, or
Cheshire County Council, or would you say that they are both about the same?

	%
Warrington Borough Council	42
Cheshire County Council	5
Both about the same	40
Don't know	13

REFER BACK TO Q8. ASK ALL WHO HAVE HEARD OF REVIEW AT Q8 (IE CODES 1/2/3/4). OTHERS TO Q28

Q25 SHOWCARD H **Earlier in the interview, you said that you had heard of the Review of local government structure. From which, if any, of the sources shown on this card have you recently heard about the Review?** INTERVIEWER NOTE: "RECENTLY" = IN PAST 3 MONTHS

(Base: 241)

		%
A	Leaflet from County Council delivered to your door	55
B	Leaflet from County Council in library/ offices, etc	4
C	Advertisement from County Council in local newspaper	8
D	Advertisement from County Council on local radio/TV	1
E	Leaflet from Borough Council delivered to your door	33
F	Leaflet from Borough Council in library/ offices, etc	6
G	Borough Council newspaper	13
H	County Council newspaper	5
I	Advertisement from Borough Council in local newspaper	8
J	Advertisement from Borough Council on local radio/TV	2
K	Advertisement by the Commission on local radio	1
L	Local Government Commission advertisement in local newspaper	3
M	Local newspaper	46
N	National newspaper	4
O	TV	10
P	Local radio	7
Q	National radio	3
R	Friends/neighbours/family	18
S	Conversation with Borough Councillor	4
T	Conversation with County Councillor	2
U	Conversation with Borough Council staff	2
V	Conversation with County Council staff	3
W	Parish/community council	3
X	Residents' Association	*
	Other	14
	None of these	4
	Don't know	1

ASK ALL NAMING A SOURCE AT Q25. OTHERS GO TO Q28

Q26 **Would you say that the information you have received has influenced your opinion, or not?**
(Base: 228)

	%
Yes	17
No	80
Don't know	3

Q27 **What information in particular has influenced your opinion?**

....

....

....

....

ASK ALL

Q28 SHOWCARD I (R) **Assuming you receive the same level of services, how important is it to you, if at all, what the final decision is on the future local government structure in Warrington?**

	%
Very important	28
Fairly important	31
Not very important	23
Not at all important	16
Don't know	2

ACTIVISM

Q29 SHOWCARD J **Which of the things on this list, if any, have you done in the last three years? Just read out the letter(s) that apply.**

		%
A	Voted in Local Council elections	81
B	Spoken or written to a local Councillor	24
C	Responded to the earlier Review of local government	10
D	Been to a meeting of a local committee or organisation (WRITE IN NAME OF ORGANISATION)	8
E	Spoken on a radio phone-in about a local issue	1
F	Written to a local newspaper about a local issue	3
G	Been to a meeting of a local branch of a political party	2
H	Written to your MP about a local issue	7
I	Been to a Council Committee meeting	3
J	Been to a Council meeting	2
K	Attended a public meeting run by the Council	5
	None of these	17
	Don't know/refused	2

Q30 SHOWCARD K **Which, if any, of these apply to you? Just read out the letter(s) that apply.**

		%
A	Residents' Association	3
B	Community Association	1
C	Tenants' Association	*
D	Neighbourhood Watch	28
E	PTA/school governors	3
I do unpaid work for:		
F	A school	5
G	Citizens Advice Bureau	*
H	Volunteer Bureau	1
I	Scouts/Guides/Cubs/Brownies	3
J	Church group	8
	Other	5
	None of these	57
	Don't know	2

THANK RESPONDENT. GO TO DEMOGRAPHICS.

CHAPTER 8

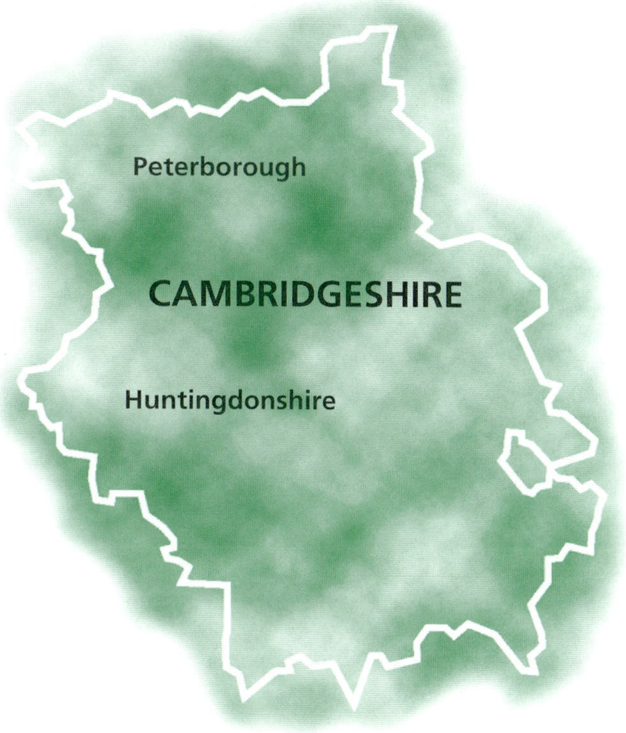

HUNTINGDONSHIRE AND PETERBOROUGH IN THE COUNTY OF CAMBRIDGESHIRE

Draft Recommendations

8.1 The Commission's report *Draft Recommendations on the Future Local Government of Huntingdonshire and Peterborough in the County of Cambridgeshire* summarised the evidence taken into account by the Commission in reaching its draft recommendations.

Figure 8.1

Draft Recommendations for Huntingdonshire and Peterborough in the County of Cambridgeshire

Structure

- The existing two-tier structure of local government in Peterborough should be replaced. Peterborough should become a unitary authority, responsible in its area for the broad range of local government functions carried out by both county and district councils.

- There should be no change to the existing two-tier structure of local government in Huntingdonshire.

Ceremonial Arrangements

- The County of Cambridgeshire should be retained for ceremonial and related purposes, and the City Council area of Peterborough should be associated with the county for such purposes.

Public Protection

- There should be a combined authority established in the present county area for the fire service, on which the representatives of the new unitary authority and the County Council should serve. Similarly, representatives of the new unitary authority should also serve on a joint committee with representatives of the County Council to select the local authority membership of the Cambridgeshire Police Authority. No changes are proposed to the area covered by the Cambridgeshire Police Authority, or to the probation and magistrates' courts services.

Strategic Planning

- For strategic planning, the new unitary authority of Peterborough should become the structure planning authority for its area, with a view to this function being exercised through joint arrangements with Cambridgeshire County Council so as to retain a single structure plan. The new authority should also be a mineral and waste planning authority with strategic minerals and waste policies being included in the joint structure plan. Peterborough should individually have responsibility for formulating detailed minerals and waste policies for its area in general conformity with the policy framework established by the structure plan, and it should be authorised to include such policies in its local plans. Responsibility for the local plans should rest with the new authority and it should also exercise development control functions in its area for all purposes.

Electoral Arrangements

- The Commission reaffirms its previous recommendation that:

  'There should be a modification to the boundary between the districts of Peterborough and Huntingdonshire around the area of the proposed Southern Township development. The proposed Southern Township area plus adjacent parts of the parishes of Yaxley and Alwalton should be transferred from Huntingdonshire to form part of Peterborough. This area should form part of the Fletton ward and should cease to be parished. That part of Farcet village which is currently in Peterborough should be transferred to Huntingdonshire. This area should form part of the Farcet district ward, the Norman Cross county division and the parish area of Farcet. Part of the present parish of Orton Waterville in Peterborough should be transferred to Huntingdonshire. This area should form part of the Elton district ward, the Norman Cross county division and the parish area of Alwalton'.

- The Peterborough unitary authority should have a total of 54 members, with 18 three-member wards based on the existing county divisions within the city council area. Elections should be held by thirds.

- The continuing Cambridgeshire County Council should have 59 members with one councillor being returned for each of the 59 county divisions outside the proposed local government administrative area of Peterborough.

Views Expressed to the Commission

8.2 The Commission received a wide range of direct representations on its draft recommendations, from local authorities, residents, Members of Parliament, business and voluntary groups, parish and town councils, and from other public and private sector organisations. Just over 3,000 representations were received from individuals and organisations, including nearly 1,600 from respondents within the two review districts. The Commission also received over 1,400 representations in the form of standard letters, response slips and petitions (Figures 8.2, 8.3 and 8.4).

8.3 Cambridgeshire County Council also conducted a survey in Peterborough and commissioned the Electoral Reform Society to analyse the returns. The County Council produced a leaflet setting out the options with its own commentary, together with a freepost questionnaire. It aimed to distribute the leaflet to all 64,000 households in Peterborough. Over 2,500 forms were returned (a 4.1 per cent response rate) representing the views of 4,103 people, of which 81 per cent supported no change.

8.4 A small number of representations addressed the Commission's draft recommendation in relation to the boundary between Peterborough and Huntingdonshire. Similarly, representations were received in relation to the draft recommendation for the electoral arrangements in Peterborough. These are also included in the tables and the larger petitions are referred to under "Local Groups". Figures 8.2, 8.3 and 8.4 exclude representations from the local authorities; these are summarised separately (Figure 8.5).

Figure 8.2
Views of Respondents Within Peterborough

Preferred structure	Individuals	Organisations	Standard letters and petition signatures
Unitary Peterborough[1]	132	47	35
Unitary Huntingdonshire[2]	2	0	0
No change in Peterborough	549	89	61
Other	14	9	356
No preference	50	9	0

Source: Local Government Commission for England and NOP

Note 1: Excludes four representations in support of an expanded unitary Peterborough, categorised under'other', and includes two representations in favour of separate unitary authorities for both Huntingdonshire and Peterborough

Note 2: Includes two representations in favour of separate unitary authorities for both Huntingdonshire and Peterborough

Figure 8.3
Views of Respondents Within Huntingdonshire

Preferred structure	Individuals	Organisations	Standard letters and petition signatures
Unitary Huntingdonshire[1]	88	6	336
Unitary Peterborough[2]	19	3	0
No change in Huntingdonshire	516	46	131
Other	11	0	49
No preference	13	1	0

Source: Local Government Commission for England and NOP

Note 1: Excludes one representation in support of an expanded unitary Peterborough, categorised under 'other', and includes five representations in favour of separate unitary authorities for both Huntingdonshire and Peterborough

Note 2: Includes six representations in favour of separate unitary authorities for both Huntingdonshire andPeterborough

Figure 8.4

Views of Respondents From Outside The Review Districts[1]

Preferred structure	Individuals	Organisations	Standard letters and petition signatures
Unitary Huntingdonshire	0	0	0
Unitary Peterborough[2]	11	2	0
No change	1,076	115	430
Other	33	5	19
No preference	64	10	0

Source: Local Government Commission for England and NOP

Note 1: Excludes out of county representations

Note 2: Excludes two representations in favour of an expanded unitary Peterborough, categorised under 'other'.

8.5 In addition, 96 representations were received from outside the county, of which just over three-quarters supported no change to the existing two-tier structure. A more detailed tabulation of the written representations from individuals and interest groups, produced by NOP on behalf of the Commission, can be found towards the end of this Chapter.

The Views of Local Authorities

8.6 The Commission received submissions from all seven of the principal local authorities in Cambridgeshire during Stage Three (Figure 8.5).

Figure 8.5
Preferences of Cambridgeshire Local Authorities at Stage Three

Authority	Preference
Cambridge City Council	Was content with a unitary authority for Peterborough and no change in Huntingdonshire but objected to the fact that some of the costs of change will fall on Cambridge residents. This was "...not acceptable to the City Council".
East Cambridgeshire District Council	Considered that if Peterborough is confirmed as a unitary authority, no proportion of the costs should be borne by residents of East Cambridgeshire. It would be seriously concerned if the Commission also recommended that Huntingdonshire should be unitary.
Fenland District Council	Opposed unitary authorities for Peterborough and/or Huntingdonshire. Considered transitional and ongoing costs should not be met by Fenland District's taxpayers.
Huntingdonshire District Council	Supported a unitary authority for Huntingdonshire. It put forward a number of pertinent factors to suggest that the balance of arguments should point to a unitary option. It felt that these factors together with evidence in its earlier submissions strongly underscored the distinctiveness of Huntingdonshire relative to the other districts in Cambridgeshire.
Peterborough City Council	Supported a unitary authority for Peterborough. Considered that it was distinctive from its county and capable of administering its own local government services effectively.
South Cambridgeshire District Council	Was content with the recommendation that Peterborough should become a unitary authority but would have very serious concerns should the Commission now propose a unitary authority for Huntingdonshire as well. Concerned about the impact on the remaining two-tier county and argued that costs arising from change should be borne by those authorities who stand to benefit from the change.
Cambridgeshire County Council	Supported no change in Peterborough and Huntingdonshire. Urged the Commission to reconsider the potential and the promise of a renewed two-tier structure throughout Cambridgeshire.

Source: Local authorities' submissions

8.7 The Cambridgeshire Branch of the Association of District Councils did not make representations; the Association of District Councils' national submission is referred to in the Summary of National Representations. The Association of County Councils supported the recommendation for the continuation of the two-tier structure in Huntingdonshire but rejected the recommendation for a unitary authority for Peterborough.

8.8 Peterborough City Council supported the Commission's draft recommendations for changes to its electoral arrangements, commenting that they would be "...the most appropriate short term arrangement". It also supported the Commission's draft recommendation for the proposed boundary change to accommodate the Southern Township within Peterborough. Huntingdonshire District Council considered that this area should only include "...that part of the Southern Township covered by approved planning permissions". Cambridgeshire County Council suggested that irrespective of the unitary/two-tier conclusions, such tightly drawn boundaries were unstable and did not provide good local government.

The Views of Others

8.9 A range of other interest groups made representations on the Commission's draft recommendations, as summarised in the following paragraphs. These are in addition to those made in Stage One.

Businesses and Business Groups

8.10 The Commission received submissions from the business community both from within each of the review districts and from the rest of the county. There were both supporters and opponents of the Commission's draft recommendations for Peterborough. In the case of Huntingdonshire there were few comments and little support for a change to a unitary structure for the district.

8.11 The Greater Peterborough Training and Enterprise Council continued to support unitary status for the northern part of the county, that is for the whole of Fenland and Peterborough together. In relation to a unitary authority for Peterborough alone, it saw advantages and disadvantages from the city's viewpoint. However, it remained concerned that this could have adverse effects on Fenland District which it considered "...is so dependent on Peterborough economically" and that "...both Cambridgeshire County Council and Peterborough City Council should be specifically charged to remove the possibility of marginalisation of Fenland". The Fens Business Enterprise Trust (FenBET) also expressed concern that a unitary authority for Peterborough "...will tend to weaken the residual parts of Cambridgeshire and in particular Fenland District". It "...wish[ed] to be assured that existing and future links between FenBET and Peterborough based organisations would be fully supported by the new authority".

8.12 The Eastern Region of the Confederation of British Industry did not support a unitary authority for the City of Peterborough. It considered that Peterborough's influence extended into adjacent counties and stated "Unitary status that failed to recognise such economic links would achieve nothing - other than extra expense". It also considered that unitary status in one part of the county and two-tier for the rest "...would be opening Pandora's box for years of uncertainty...". The Greater Peterborough Chamber of Commerce and Industry, which covers Peterborough, the Stamford area of South Lincolnshire and Fenland, stated that its preference was for a unitary Peterborough based on the area of the Greater Peterborough Training and Enterprise Council, while not commenting specifically on the draft recommendation.

8.13 A number of Peterborough-based business groups expressed support for a unitary authority for Peterborough. These included the Thomas Cook Group which stated that Peterborough had become a major city in its own right and "...the management of the city and its future is best controlled and dealt with by the change of status into that of a unitary authority". The East of England Agricultural Society welcomed the draft recommendation for a unitary Peterborough. It considered that it allowed "...a proper sense of ownership with the decision-making process". Furthermore they believed "...the dynamics of a city with development status surely requires a single-minded and dedicated approach if there is to be a totally successful outcome to its endeavours".

8.14 The Norwich and Peterborough Building Society considered that "For a conurbation of this size clear planning policies are essential and [that] these can be best achieved by granting unitary status" which the Society strongly supported. On the other hand, the Viscount Bus and Coach Company did not support unitary status for Peterborough or Huntingdonshire. It considered

"...the arguments in favour of a unitary Huntingdonshire too feeble to need any opposition from us", and a unitary authority for Peterborough would "...be a change sharply for the worse..."

8.15 In relation to Huntingdonshire, the Cambridgeshire Training and Enterprise Council argued that there should be no change. It considered that it "...does not have the critical size necessary for a unitary authority". It preferred to maintain the existing structure throughout the county. St Neots and District Chamber of Commerce confined its comments to Huntingdonshire, where it felt "...services are more effectively delivered to businesses and residents of St Neots and District by the current structure".

County, Regional and National Interests (including the Voluntary Sector)

8.16 The Sports Council (Eastern Region) stated that "...it does not foresee any problems within Peterborough itself, should unitary status be confirmed". It added, in relation to the draft recommendation, that "...as Huntingdonshire is not now being considered for unitary status, the delivery and co-ordination of sport at a county level is strengthened [relative to the position with two unitary authorities]". UNISON (Eastern Region) stated that its "...concerns about the financing of change and the consequent effect on staff and services have led us to form the view that the present system should be retained". Transport 2000 (Cambridgeshire and West Suffolk Branch) also opposed a unitary authority for Peterborough. If it was set up, it "...calls for a Passenger Transport Executive, with precepting powers to be set up, covering [at least] the whole of Cambridgeshire". The Cambridgeshire Tenants and Small Farmers Committee of the National Farmers Union opposed the draft recommendation. It was concerned about the impact on the 50 tenants of the Cambridgeshire County Farms Estate which would be incorporated within the city area of Peterborough.

8.17 A number of organisations expressed concern for particular areas of service delivery. The County Planning Officers Society stated that: "We are very concerned that your proposals in respect of Cambridgeshire...would seriously undermine the effective operation of strategic planning, and indeed County Planning services more generally", and asked the Commission to reconsider its proposals in the light of these concerns. The Council for the Protection of Rural England (Cambridgeshire Branch) was primarily concerned with the preservation of the integrity and effectiveness of planning. It expressed doubt, "...about the practicality of purely voluntary joint arrangements..." for the preparation of a single Structure Plan. The Cambridgeshire Action with Communities in Rural England "...remains concerned that within a unitary Peterborough the rural areas will command a lower priority in terms of policies and service programmes". The group pointed to parishes in Fenland and Huntingdonshire that have a service focus on Peterborough and was concerned that they would have "...a poorer quality service unless additional problems of the costs and practical delivery of those services is recognised".

8.18 The Museums and Galleries Commission recommended that Peterborough should remain in membership of the Cambridgeshire Museums Advisory Committee, and have the resources to maintain present levels of service. The Royal Commission on the Historical Monuments of England questioned whether the size of the proposed new authority for Peterborough would be sufficient to maintain a cost-effective conservation service. On the other hand the Social Services Inspectorate expressed the view that "Peterborough would be a viable unitary authority as would the remaining Cambridgeshire".

Education Groups

8.19 There was widespread support for no change throughout the county from education groups. Among these were the Cambridgeshire Teachers' Consultative Committee, the Cambridgeshire Local Education Authority Secondary Heads, the Cambridgeshire Special School Heads Association and the Cambridgeshire Federation of the National Association of Schoolmasters and Union of Women Teachers. All expressed their concern over the transitional and ongoing costs of change, and did not want to break up the existing educational system.

8.20 The Peterborough Regional College, an incorporated organisation and the largest provider of further and higher education in the north of the county, supported a unitary authority for Peterborough stating that: "...almost all of our decisions are based upon the needs identified within Peterborough and its immediate environs". Consequently they welcomed the opportunity to have a more focused administration and decision making authority with which to work.

Health Interests

8.21 There was support generally for a unitary Peterborough among those in the health care sector. The North West Anglia Health Commission supported a unitary authority for the City of Peterborough including the Southern Township. It believed that it would bring "...significant benefits for the residents of Peterborough..." including "...even stronger partnership working between health and local government at both the strategic and multi-agency community development levels". However, it did have major concerns about the implications for Fenland and additionally proposed that the unitary authority should cover Fenland as well. It believed it probable that Fenland's "...isolation will be exacerbated with a two-tier county based in Cambridge". Peterborough Hospitals NHS Trust continued to favour a unitary authority for Peterborough. It stated that "Against a background of rising demand for joint planning across the health, social care, housing and transport boundaries this can only help". North West Anglia Healthcare Trust also considered "...the excellent relationships which currently exist between the Trust and Peterborough City Council should be considerably strengthened..." and expressed strong support for unitary status for Peterborough.

8.22 Hinchingbrooke Healthcare NHS Trust covering most of Huntingdonshire, reiterated its support for a unitary Huntingdonshire. However, the Papworth Hospital Trust preferred no change, on efficiency and financial grounds. It urged the Commission to retain the present structure in Huntingdonshire.

Law, Order and Emergency Services

8.23 Cambridgeshire Fire and Rescue Service considered that, from a fire service perspective, the "...creation of a unitary Peterborough (or Huntingdonshire) would hold no operational advantages and would undermine effective decision making and control". Cambridgeshire Police Authority also supported no change, considering effective policing would be more difficult. It considered that the "...funding for multi-agency initiatives...could be squeezed..." and that electors in the unitary authority would have a greater say in the make-up of the Police Authority than those in the two-tier areas.

8.24 The Cambridgeshire Probation Service was "pleased" with the recommendation for no change in Huntingdonshire but disappointed that the Commission was "...recommending the creation of a unitary authority in the Peterborough area". It considered this would "...require more joint negotiations and arrangements which will result in increased costs and potential less effectiveness".

Local Groups

8.25 The majority of local groups in Peterborough that submitted representations supported a unitary authority for Peterborough. For example, the Peterborough and District Citizens' Advice Bureau considered that "Unitary status is likely to provide a good base for future development of the bureau". The Peterborough Federation of Tenants' and Residents' Association considered that "...unitary status is essential for the future growth and prosperity of Peterborough, its businesses, ...and all its citizens". There was also support from organisations representing minority ethnic groups including the Pakistan Community Association of Peterborough, the Bharat Hindu Samaj (Hindu Community Centre), the Marcus Garvey International Community Association & the Caribbean Golden Age Association. In addition, Peterborough and Fenland MIND also expressed support for a unitary Peterborough believing "...it would be able to make its voice heard more effectively with a Peterborough authority than as at present with a Cambridge based/centred county council". The Peterborough Council for Voluntary Service stated that it "...welcomes any proposal that brings local government into more direct, accountable and flexible partnership with local people" but raised a number of factors that needed to be considered. These included concerns as to whether the authority would have sufficient resources.

8.26 Huntingdon Area Victim Support said that it was "...very pleased that the Commission recommended that Cambridgeshire County Council and Huntingdonshire District Council should be retained" and Huntingdon Charter 88 Group considered that it would not in the best interest of the people of that area to form a new council. In the rest of Cambridgeshire, nearly all the representations supported no change throughout the county.

8.27 The Commission also received a petition of 56 signatures from residents of Farcet village currently in Peterborough. The petition opposed the transfer of part of Farcet village to Huntingdonshire. Councillor Miners, a ward councillor for Dogsthorpe, also wrote in opposing the division of the local Dogsthorpe community between the proposed Dogsthorpe and

Peterborough North wards, and arguing that the Dogsthorpe Ward should continue to cover the existing city ward of Dogsthorpe to retain local community identity. The Commission had previously received a 300 signature petition from residents in the Dogsthorpe area, expressing the same views, which was resubmitted.

Parliamentary Interests

8.28 The Commission heard further from Dr Brian Mawhinney, MP for Peterborough, and from three other Members of Parliament. Dr Mawhinney reiterated his wish for unitary status for Peterborough. However, he stated that he found the proposals for electoral arrangements unacceptable, and considered there to be a major democratic deficit in his constituency that needed to be addressed. He considered that ward boundaries needed to be addressed to enhance the fairness of the system.

8.29 Mr William Powell, MP for Corby, whose constituency shares a boundary with Peterborough and Huntingdonshire, expressed support for the draft recommendation for Peterborough. Mr James Paice, MP for South East Cambridgeshire, stated that "Whilst not objecting in principle to Peterborough becoming a unitary authority ...the Commission should ensure that the costs of that change should be borne by the Peterborough taxpayers rather than the rest of Cambridgeshire..." Mr Malcolm Moss, MP for North East Cambridgeshire, stated that his preference was to retain the two-tier structure. He said that "...allowing Peterborough to become a separate entity will further isolate the Fens area, yield a much lower expenditure base for the remaining county council and undo a lot of the very useful work that has been done...".

Parish And Town Councils

8.30 The Commission received 79 submissions from parish and town councils in Cambridgeshire, with 53 supporting the continuation of the current structure of local government throughout the county. In Huntingdonshire, a clear majority of parish and town councils continued to favour no change. However, within Peterborough, of the 11 parish and town councils who responded individually, seven supported the unitary authority proposed for Peterborough.

8.31 The Chairmen of sixteen of the 28 parishes in Peterborough also made a joint submission with the Mayor of Peterborough to advise "...of the very considerable progress that has been made...to establish the basis for a constructive and fruitful relationship between the proposed... [authority]...and the local councils operating within its boundaries". The parishes laid out six major issues on which agreement had been reached with the existing City Council.

8.32 The Cambridgeshire Association of Local Councils Executive Committee stated that it strongly supported the draft recommendation for no change in Huntingdonshire and for the replacement of the two-tier structure in Peterborough. However, it felt as a condition of its unitary status Peterborough should be required to assist in the new arrangements for county services to neighbouring districts, to minimise disruption and concerns of local councils particularly in Fenland and Huntingdonshire.

8.33 Yaxley Parish Council expressed the wish that the transfer of land to Peterborough be restricted to the bare minimum necessary for the development of the Southern Township. Northborough Parish Council stated that the area to be represented by a councillor for Northborough was geographically large and this would make representation difficult.

NOP Tabulations of Written Representations

1 The following tabulations summarise the views expressed by members of the public and other interested parties during the consultation on the Local Government Commission's draft recommendations for Huntingdonshire and Peterborough.

2 The tabulations include only letters sent directly to NOP at its Chelmsford offices and to the Commission's offices in London. Where more than one person's view has been expressed in a letter, the comments from each individual have been recorded separately. Staff from the Commission and NOP have worked closely in ensuring that care has been taken in the interpretation of comments, and that a consistent approach has been adopted.

3 While many people expressed support for one or other of the draft options presented by the Commission, other responses were coded by NOP after further discussion. The pattern of views expressed has been carefully examined, and where a number of respondents supported an option not included in those put forward by the Commission, those views have been separately coded and reported by NOP.

4 The Commission has advertised through the local media, encouraging people to make their views known. All responses received up to two days after the end of the Stage Three consultation period have been included. Returns from campaigns organised by local authorities or other groups (for example, standardised postcards and letters, questionnaires and petitions) have not been included in the tabulations. These, and submissions written and dated before the commencement of the consultation process, have been considered separately by the Commission.

The following definitions have been applied by NOP in compiling the tabulations:

(i) Type of Respondent

Individuals:	includes individual members of the public, local councillors and Members of the Westminster and European Parliaments.
Businesses and Business Groups:	includes organisations which represent businesses, such as local Chambers of Commerce.
County, Regional and National Interests:	any organisation which covers an area which is the size of a county or larger is included here, for example, a county-wide voluntary organisation or a regional association. This classification includes most of the statutory consultees.
Education (and Church) Groups:	this group includes schools, religious organisations and teaching unions.
Local Groups:	this includes organisations smaller than a county area, for example, a district-level voluntary sector body. The group could be voluntary, sporting, political or cultural but does not include organisations from the education or religious sectors (included above). It also includes constituency parties and political groups on local authorities.
Parish and Town Councils:	this also includes district-level associations of town and parish councils. County level associations are classified as County, Regional and National interests.

(ii) Structural Options (Reports A and D)

No change in own district:	this code is used where there is more than one review district in the county. It indicates where respondents from a review district have expressed support for no change for that district and have not made reference to the other review district(s) in that county.
District/county-level authorities:	represents support for either a district or county-level authority although it is not clear whether this is for a unitary or a two-tier structure.
Opposition to structural preferences:	represents responses where a negative, but unspecified, structural preference has been expressed.
Rejects:	rejects are those responses with unclear comments/interpretation.

(iii) Other

Other issues (Report B):	these illustrate preferences in relation to boundary and electoral changes and (where applicable) the restoration of historic counties.
Parishing issues (Report C):	these illustrate preferences in relation to parishing issues, for example, the creation of new parishes or the enhancement of the role of parish and town councils.
Services (Report E):	these illustrate concerns expressed about the impact of proposed changes on particular service areas where the respondent has not additionally expressed a positive structural preference.

NOP Analysis of Responses to Local Government Commission Draft Recommendations - CAMBRIDGESHIRE

Report A: Opinions on the structural options, by authority of respondent
Base: all

	Review districts		Other districts in county						
	Huntingdonshire	Peterborough	Cambridge	East Cambridgeshire	Fenland	South Cambridgeshire	Rest of county total	County total	Out of county total
No change	438 *63%*	246 *27%*	277 *92%*	207 *88%*	258 *88%*	449 *92%*	1191 *91%*	1875 *64%*	75 *78%*
Unitary Peterborough	3 *	175 *19%*	- -	- -	6 *2%*	2 *	8 *1%*	186 *6%*	10 *10%*
Unitary Huntingdonshire	89 *13%*	- -	- -	- -	- -	- -	- -	89 *3%*	- -
Two UAs for Peterborough & Huntingdonshire	5 *1%*	2 *	- -	- -	- -	- -	- -	7 *	- -
Unitary Peterborough/two-tier rest (LGC proposal)	14 *2%*	2 *	1 *	1 *	- -	3 *1%*	5 *	21 *1%*	2 *2%*
Unitary expanded Peterborough	1 *	4 *	- -	1 *	1 *	- -	2 *	7 *	- -
No change in own district	124 *18%*	392 *44%*	- -	- -	- -	- -	- -	516 *18%*	- -
County-level authority (either two-tier or unitary)	2 *	6 *1%*	2 *1%*	4 *2%*	4 *1%*	2 *	12 *1%*	20 *1%*	1 *1%*
District-level authority (either two-tier or unitary)	2 *	3 *	- -	- -	1 *	- -	1 *	6 *	- -
Pre-1974 structure	1 *	- -	- -	- -	- -	- -	- -	1 *	- -
County-wide unitary structure	- -	- -	- -	- -	1 *	- -	1 *	1 *	1 *1%*
Opposition to structural options (where no positive preference is stated)	2 *	1 *	2 *1%*	3 *1%*	3 *1%*	8 *2%*	16 *1%*	19 *1%*	- -
Other specified	3 *	9 *1%*	2 *1%*	- -	- -	4 *1%*	6 *	18 *1%*	- -
No preference expressed/ option defined	14 *2%*	59 *7%*	16 *5%*	18 *8%*	18 *6%*	22 *4%*	74 *6%*	147 *5%*	7 *7%*
BASE TOTAL	698	899	300	234	292	490	1316	2913	96

* *Less than ½%*

NOP Analysis of Responses to Local Government Commission Draft Recommendations - CAMBRIDGESHIRE

Report B: Opinions on other issues, by authority of respondent
Base: all

	Review districts		Other districts in county						
	Huntingdonshire	Peterborough	Cambridge	East Cambridgeshire	Fenland	South Cambridgeshire	Rest of county total	County total	Out of county total
Electoral issues	-	6	-	-	2	-	2	8	1
	-	*1%*	-	-	*1%*	-	*	*	*1%*
Don't transfer us to Peterborough	4	-	-	-	-	-	-	4	-
	1%	-	-	-	-	-	-	*	-
Concern over costs (no preference expressed)	1	9	3	13	3	8	27	37	2
	*	*1%*	*1%*	*6%*	*1%*	*2%*	*2%*	*1%*	*2%*
Don't transfer us to Huntingdonshire	1	12	-	-	-	-	-	13	-
	*	*1%*	-	-	-	-	-	*	-
BASE TOTAL	698	899	300	234	292	490	1316	2913	96

The figures in the table above do not sum to the base total/100% because undefined fields are not included, except as part of the base total.

** Less than ½%*

NOP Analysis of Responses to Local Government Commission Draft Recommendations - CAMBRIDGESHIRE

Report C: Opinions on parishing issues, by authority of respondent
Base: all

	Review districts		Other districts in county						
	Huntingdonshire	Peterborough	Cambridge	East Cambridgeshire	Fenland	South Cambridgeshire	Rest of county total	County total	Out of county total
Enhanced parish powers	-	2	-	-	-	-	-	2	1
	-	*	-	-	-	-	-	*	*1%*
BASE TOTAL	698	899	300	234	292	490	1316	2913	96

The figures in the table above do not sum to the base total/100% because undefined fields are not included, except as part of the base total.

** Less than ½%*

NOP Analysis of Responses to Local Government Commission Draft Recommendations - CAMBRIDGESHIRE

Report D1: Opinions on the structural options, by respondent type (all respondents)
Base: all

	Respondent Type					
	Indiv-iduals	Business groups	County, regional & national interests	Education (& church) groups	Local groups	Parish and town councils
No change	1737 *66%*	25 *32%*	17 *50%*	95 *74%*	23 *43%*	53 *68%*
Unitary Peterborough	142 *5%*	20 *26%*	5 *15%*	1 *1%*	19 *35%*	9 *12%*
Unitary Huntingdonshire	85 *3%*	- -	- -	- -	- -	4 *5%*
Two UAs for Peterborough & Huntingdonshire	5 *	1 *1%*	- -	- -	- -	1 *1%*
Unitary Peterborough/two-tier rest (LGC proposal)	21 *1%*	- -	2 *6%*	- -	- -	- -
Unitary expanded Peterborough	3 *	2 *3%*	- -	- -	1 *2%*	1 *1%*
No change in own district	459 *17%*	22 *29%*	1 *3%*	24 *19%*	4 *7%*	6 *8%*
County-level authority (either two-tier or unitary)	18 *1%*	- -	- -	2 *2%*	1 *2%*	- -
District-level authority (either two-tier or unitary)	5 *	1 *1%*	- -	- -	- -	- -
Pre-1974 structure	1 *	- -	- -	- -	- -	- -
County-wide unitary structure	1 *	1 *1%*	- -	- -	- -	- -
Opposition to structural options (where no positive preference is stated)	19 *1%*	- -	- -	- -	- -	- -
Other specified	11 *	3 *4%*	1 *3%*	- -	2 *4%*	1 *1%*
No preference expressed/ option defined	130 *5%*	2 *3%*	8 *24%*	7 *5%*	4 *7%*	3 *4%*
BASE TOTAL	2637	77	34	129	54	78

* *Less than ½%*

NOP Analysis of Responses to Local Government Commission Draft Recommendations - CAMBRIDGESHIRE

Report D2: Opinions on the structural options, by respondent type
Base: respondents in Huntingdonshire only

	Respondent Type					
	Indiv-iduals	Business groups	County, regional & national interests	Education (& church) groups	Local groups	Parish and town councils
No change	403 *63%*	1 *33%*	1 *50%*	21 *84%*	3 *50%*	9 *50%*
Unitary Peterborough	2 *	- -	- -	- -	- -	1 *6%*
Unitary Huntingdonshire	85 *13%*	- -	- -	- -	- -	4 *22%*
Two UAs for Peterborough & Huntingdonshire	3 *	1 *33%*	- -	- -	- -	1 *6%*
Unitary Peterborough/two-tier rest (LGC proposal)	14 *2%*	- -	- -	- -	- -	- -
Unitary expanded Peterborough	1 *	- -	- -	- -	- -	- -
No change in own district	113 *18%*	1 *33%*	1 *50%*	3 *12%*	3 *50%*	3 *17%*
County-level authority (either two-tier or unitary)	2 *	- -	- -	- -	- -	- -
District-level authority (either two-tier or unitary)	2 *	- -	- -	- -	- -	- -
Pre-1974 structure	1 *	- -	- -	- -	- -	- -
Opposition to structural options (where no positive preference is stated)	2 *	- -	- -	- -	- -	- -
Other specified	3 *	- -	- -	- -	- -	- -
No preference expressed/ option defined	13 *2%*	- -	- -	1 *4%*	- -	- -
BASE TOTAL	644	3	2	25	6	18

* *Less than ½%*

NOP Analysis of Responses to Local Government Commission Draft Recommendations - CAMBRIDGESHIRE

Report D3: Opinions on the structural options, by respondent type
Base: respondents in Peterborough only

	Respondent Type					
	Indiv-iduals	Business groups	County, regional & national interests	Education (& church) groups	Local groups	Parish and town councils
No change	203 *27%*	14 *25%*	3 *30%*	21 *44%*	5 *18%*	- -
Unitary Peterborough	128 *17%*	17 *30%*	4 *40%*	1 *2%*	18 *64%*	7 *64%*
Two UAs for Peterborough & Huntingdonshire	2 *	- -	- -	- -	- -	- -
Unitary Peterborough/two-tier rest (LGC proposal)	2 *	- -	- -	- -	- -	- -
Unitary expanded Peterborough	- -	2 *4%*	- -	- -	1 *4%*	1 *9%*
No change in own district	346 *46%*	21 *37%*	- -	21 *44%*	1 *4%*	3 *27%*
County-level authority (either two-tier or unitary)	5 *1%*	- -	- -	- -	1 *4%*	- -
District-level authority (either two-tier or unitary)	3 *	- -	- -	- -	- -	- -
Opposition to structural options (where no positive preference is stated)	1 *	- -	- -	- -	- -	- -
Other specified	5 *1%*	2 *4%*	1 *10%*	- -	1 *4%*	- -
No preference expressed/ option defined	50 *7%*	1 *2%*	2 *20%*	5 *10%*	1 *4%*	- -
BASE TOTAL	745	57	10	48	28	11

* *Less than ½%*

NOP Analysis of Responses to Local Government Commission Draft Recommendations - CAMBRIDGESHIRE

Report D4: Opinions on the structural options, by respondent type
Base: respondents in rest of county only

	Respondent Type					
	Indiv-iduals	Business groups	County, regional & national interests	Education (& church) groups	Local groups	Parish and town councils
No change	1076 *91%*	4 *57%*	7 *70%*	51 *96%*	12 *75%*	41 *89%*
Unitary Peterborough	7 *1%*	- -	- -	- -	- -	1 *2%*
Unitary Peterborough/two-tier rest (LGC proposal)	4 *	- -	1 *10%*	- -	- -	- -
Unitary expanded Peterborough	2 *	- -	- -	- -	- -	- -
County-level authority (either two-tier or unitary)	11 *1%*	- -	- -	1 *2%*	- -	- -
District-level authority (either two-tier or unitary)	- -	1 *14%*	- -	- -	- -	- -
County-wide unitary structure	1 *	- -	- -	- -	- -	- -
Opposition to structural options (where no positive preference is stated)	16 *1%*	- -	- -	- -	- -	- -
Other specified	3 *	1 *14%*	- -	- -	1 *6%*	1 *2%*
No preference expressed/ option defined	64 *5%*	1 *14%*	2 *20%*	1 *2%*	3 *19%*	3 *7%*
BASE TOTAL	1184	7	10	53	16	46

* *Less than ½%*

NOP Analysis of Responses to Local Government Commission Draft Recommendations - CAMBRIDGESHIRE

Report E: Views on services, by authority of respondent
Base: all

	Review districts		Other districts in county						
	Huntingdonshire	Peterborough	Cambridge	East Cambridgeshire	Fenland	South Cambridgeshire	Rest of county total	County total	Out of county total
Archives	-	-	-	-	-	-	-	-	1
	-	-	-	-	-	-	-	-	*1%*
Education	15	33	9	6	14	17	46	94	-
	2%	*4%*	*3%*	*3%*	*5%*	*3%*	*3%*	*3%*	-
Other specified services (or multiples of)	-	1	3	-	-	-	3	4	2
	-	*	*1%*	-	-	-	*	*	*2%*
BASE TOTAL	698	899	300	234	292	490	1316	2913	96

The figures in the table above do not sum to the base total/100% because undefined fields are not included, except as part of the base total.

* *Less than ½%*

NOP Analysis of Responses to Local Government Commission Draft Recommendations - CAMBRIDGESHIRE

Report F: Views on services, by respondent type
Base: all

	Respondent Type					
	Indiv-iduals	Business groups	County, regional & national interests	Education (& church) groups	Local groups	Parish and town councils
Archives	-	-	1	-	-	-
	-	-	*3%*	-	-	-
Education	86	-	-	8	-	-
	3%	-	-	*6%*	-	-
Other specified services (or multiples of)	-	1	5	-	-	-
	-	*1%*	*15%*	-	-	-
BASE TOTAL	2637	77	34	129	54	78

The figures in the table above do not sum to the base total/100% because undefined fields are not included, except as part of the base total.

NOP Analysis of Responses to Local Government Commission Draft Recommendations - CAMBRIDGESHIRE

Report G: Type of respondent, by authority of respondent
Base: all

	Review districts		Other districts in county						
	Huntingdonshire	Peterborough	Cambridge	East Cambridgeshire	Fenland	South Cambridgeshire	Rest of county total	County total	Out of county total
Individuals	644 *92%*	745 *83%*	275 *92%*	213 *91%*	261 *89%*	435 *89%*	1184 *90%*	2573 *88%*	64 *67%*
Business groups	3 *	57 *6%*	2 *1%*	- -	4 *1%*	1 *	7 *1%*	67 *2%*	10 *10%*
County, regional and national interests	2 *	10 *1%*	6 *2%*	- -	- -	4 *1%*	10 *1%*	22 *1%*	12 *13%*
Education (and church) groups	25 *4%*	48 *5%*	9 *3%*	9 *4%*	16 *5%*	19 *4%*	53 *4%*	126 *4%*	3 *3%*
Local Groups	6 *1%*	28 *3%*	8 *3%*	2 *1%*	4 *1%*	2 *	16 *1%*	50 *2%*	4 *4%*
Parish and town councils	18 *3%*	11 *1%*	- -	10 *4%*	7 *2%*	29 *6%*	46 *3%*	75 *3%*	3 *3%*
BASE TOTAL	698	899	300	234	292	490	1316	2913	96

* *Less than ½%*

MORI Research Study for the Local Government Commission

Introduction

Background

1 This summary report highlights the key findings from a survey of public opinion conducted in the district of Huntingdonshire, the City of Peterborough and across the County of Cambridgeshire on behalf of the Local Government Commission for England. A copy of each of the marked-up questionnaires is appended. The computer tabulations are contained in a separate volume, which is available from MORI (32 Old Queen Street, London SW1H 9HP. Telephone 0171-222 0232. Price £15)

2 The survey was designed in close consultation with the Commission, following extensive qualitative research and pilot testing. All sampling, interviewing and analysis have been carried out independently by MORI, within the guidelines of the profession laid out by the Market Research Society.

3 In Peterborough, all Census Enumeration Districts (EDs) were sorted by ward, and stratified according to social class. EDs were then sampled (32 in total) in proportion to the population size of each, and quotas set for sex, age and work status. A total of 311 interviews with adults aged 18+, conducted face-to-face and in-home, were carried out between 1 October and 2 November 1995. Data were weighted to match the population profile in the City. The same procedure was followed in Huntingdonshire, where 317 interviews were conducted.

4 In the remaining districts of Cambridgeshire, all EDs were sorted into wards, and again stratified according to social class. A total of 32 EDs across the whole area (that is, Cambridgeshire excluding Huntingdonshire and Peterborough) were sampled, with quotas set by sex, age and work status. Face-to-face interviews, conducted in-home, were carried out with 309 adults aged 18+ between 1 October and 2 November 1995. Data were weighted to match the population profile of the County excluding Peterborough and Huntingdonshire.

Publication of the Results

5 As with all our studies, these findings are subject to our Standard Terms and Conditions of Contract. Any press release or publication of the findings of this survey require the advance approval of MORI. Such approval will only be refused on the grounds of inaccuracy or misinterpretation.

Objectives

6 This survey took place during Stage Three, the consultation period on the Commission's draft recommendations. It measures public preferences for the organisation of local government in the area currently comprising the City of Peterborough and the district of Huntingdonshire, as well as exploring strength of feeling, levels of knowledge about the review, involvement in, and broader perceptions of, local government in the area.

Statistical Reliability of the Data

7 Because we have interviewed a sample of residents, rather than the whole population, the results are subject to statistical tolerance limits, or "margins of error". These are expressed as our confidence that the true figure for the whole population falls within a given range. By convention this is expressed as a percentage, so our 95% confidence level means that in 95 times out of 100 the true figure would lie within this range.

8 The table below shows ranges of the 95% confidence level for a range of sample sizes. For each sample size, the table shows the tolerance limits for sample results close to 10%, 30% and 50%. Take, for example, the results of a survey of 300 residents showing that 50% are aware of the review. In 95 times out of 100 the true figure would lie between 44% and 56% (ie between 50% ±6%).

Sample size	Sampling tolerances applicable to results at or near these percentages (based on 95% confidence level) 10/90% ±%	30/70% ±%	50% ±%
300	3	5	6
200	4	6	7
150	5	7	8
100	6	9	10
50	8	13	14

9 Clearly, 10% or 30% of the sample being aware of the review equate to 90% or 70% not being aware of it. So this table shows the ranges of 95% confidence for responses close to 10%, 30%, 50%, 70% and 90% of our sample. The figures for responses between can be obtained by extrapolation.

10 The true figure would only be known if all the residents of the area had been interviewed. It can be seen in the table, however, that large increases in the sample size do not greatly reduce the sampling tolerance. In addition, the true figure is more likely to lie at the midpoint of the range, rather than at either extreme.

11 When comparing results from separate groups within a sample we need to be sure that the differences are statistically significant. This would be important in comparing views expressed by different parts of a county. The table below shows how the statistical significance of the difference is determined by the size of the groups and the percentage result from the sample.

12 Assuming a 95% confidence level, the table shows the size of the differences required if different results are to be regarded as statistically significant. It can be seen that if 50% of a group of 300 were aware of the review, the result from another group of 300 would not become statistically significant until it became less than 42% or more than 58%.

Sample sizes	Differences required for significance at or near these percentage levels 10/90% ±	30/70% ±	50% ±
300 and 300	5	7	8
300 and 200	5	8	9
300 and 100	7	10	11
200 and 100	7	11	12
100 and 100	8	13	14

Survey Findings

Knowledge and Awareness

13 Residents within Peterborough and Huntingdonshire profess broadly similar levels of knowledge and interest in local government to those living in the rest of the County of Cambridgeshire. In both, a clear majority like to know what their council is doing, but want no greater involvement. Around one in five in all three areas say they want a higher level of involvement.

14 While between two and four in ten in Peterborough, Huntingdonshire and the rest of the County say they know at least a fair amount about what their council does, between six and seven in ten admit to not knowing very much.

15 This is reflected in the number of residents who incorrectly ascribe services between the two tiers of local government. Thus, although up to half recognise libraries as a county council service, as many as two to three in ten allocate responsibility to their district/borough/city council. And although majorities realise that refuse collection is a district/borough/city service, between one and two in ten thinks it is a county council service.

16 Awareness of the review itself is slightly higher in Huntingdonshire (where 75% have heard of it) than in Peterborough and the rest of the Cambridgeshire (where 57% and 62% respectively have heard of it). The proportions who say they know a fair amount or more are slightly higher in Huntingdonshire and Peterborough than in the rest of the County - 14% and 13% respectively, compared to 8% in the rest of Cambridgeshire.

Sources of Information

17 Local newspapers are the most common source of information about the review, by a considerable margin. Of those who have at least heard of the review, just under half in Cambridgeshire, around six in ten in Huntingdonshire and around seven in ten in Peterborough name the local press as a recent source. Between two-thirds (in Huntingdonshire and the rest of Cambridgeshire) and three-quarters (in Peterborough) cite some media source as a recent source of information on the review.

18 It would appear that the County has been fairly active in providing information to residents in Huntingdonshire - while 42% name a County Council source in Huntingdonshire, just 28% do so in the rest of Cambridgeshire and only 22% in Peterborough. By comparison, 24% in Peterborough mention a City Council source, compared to 16% in Huntingdonshire mentioning the district, and six per cent in the rest of Cambridgeshire. Very few recognise receiving information directly from the Local Government Commission itself. Although most of those aware of the review recognise one or more recent sources of information, few (between two and three in ten) say that this has influenced their opinion.

19 Furthermore, in spite of a relatively low level of knowledge and engagement with their local authority, most people in Peterborough say that the outcome of the review in the City is either very important to them (24%) or fairly important (43%). People in Huntingdonshire tend to share this view (19% very important and 46% fairly important). As one might expect, people in the rest of Cambridgeshire perceive a lower level of importance (12% very important and 30% fairly important).

The Preferred Option

20 People in Peterborough are equally divided over whether they would prefer a unitary authority to no change (40% select each). In Huntingdonshire, there is a slim balance in favour of no change (47%) rather than a unitary authority (40%). The balance of opinion in the rest of Cambridgeshire is towards retaining two-tier local authorities for both Peterborough and Huntingdonshire. Around three in ten would prefer unitary authorities for each of Peterborough and Huntingdonshire, while over four in ten opt for no change.

21 People in Peterborough and Huntingdonshire feel more strongly about the preference they express than do those living elsewhere in the County. In Peterborough, 72% of those expressing a preference say they feel strongly (including 22% very strongly). Similarly, in Huntingdonshire, 69%, say they feel strongly (including 22% very strongly). In contrast, across the rest of Cambridgeshire, 55% feel strongly (including 14% very strongly). There is little difference in the strength of feeling expressed in Peterborough or Huntingdonshire, irrespective of which option is preferred. In the rest of the County, those preferring no change are most likely to feel strongly.

Factors in Expressing a Preference

22 In questions 13 to 23, residents were asked to say to what extent they agreed or disagreed with a range of statements which related to a change to unitary local government. The statements were designed to cover the main issues raised by residents during the qualitative phase of research, and others that formed a part of the Commission's brief to take into consideration in making its recommendations.

23 The following charts summarise the results from these questions, with the full question wording presented in the questionnaires in the appendices. Values have been ascribed to the five attitudinal positions that people were offered (+2 for strongly agree, +1 for tend to agree, 0 for neither agree nor disagree, -1 for tend to disagree, and -2 for strongly disagree) and mean scores calculated across all respondents expressing a view. This has the combined benefit of distilling the range of opinion into one summary figure, while incorporating the varying intensity of feeling by ascribing values. Bars to the right indicate that the mean score value is positive, and thus that there is a balance of agreement with the statement. Bars to the left, conversely, indicate a balance of disagreement.

24 The chart opposite, therefore, shows how the views of people living in Peterborough and Huntingdonshire differ from those across the rest of Cambridgeshire and between one another. In doing so, it illustrates the attitudes or perceptions that are, in relative terms, shared by different groups of residents (where the bars project in the same direction), and those where views differ markedly. Thus there is broad agreement on the positive aspects of change, although the balance of opinion is more marked among residents in Peterborough and Huntingdonshire, as one might expect. There is even broad agreement that a County Council is needed for national representation, that services would suffer (on both of these, however, opinion is more marked among residents in the rest of Cambridgeshire) and that a unitary Peterborough or Huntingdonshire would be too small to manage services like education and social services. On the other hand, there is some divergence when it comes to whether change would be too disruptive or cost more. There is also divergence on whether people feel that they will be affected by change. People in Peterborough and Huntingdonshire are most likely to want more information.

25 The subsequent chart takes the results separately from Huntingdonshire, Peterborough and the rest of Cambridgeshire, and illustrates the difference in views between those within each area whose preference is for unitary status, and those who prefer no change. The chart therefore illustrates those attitudinal statements that most, or least, differentiate residents expressing two opposing preferences. The perceived impact on efficiency is clearly a key determinant of opinion across the County, as are reflecting community identity, size, cost, disruption and impact on services.

Attitudes to Change
(All respondents)

Q To what extent do you agree or disagree that...?
(Figures represent 'mean scores' with *strong agreement* given a value of +2 through to *strong disagreement* given -2)

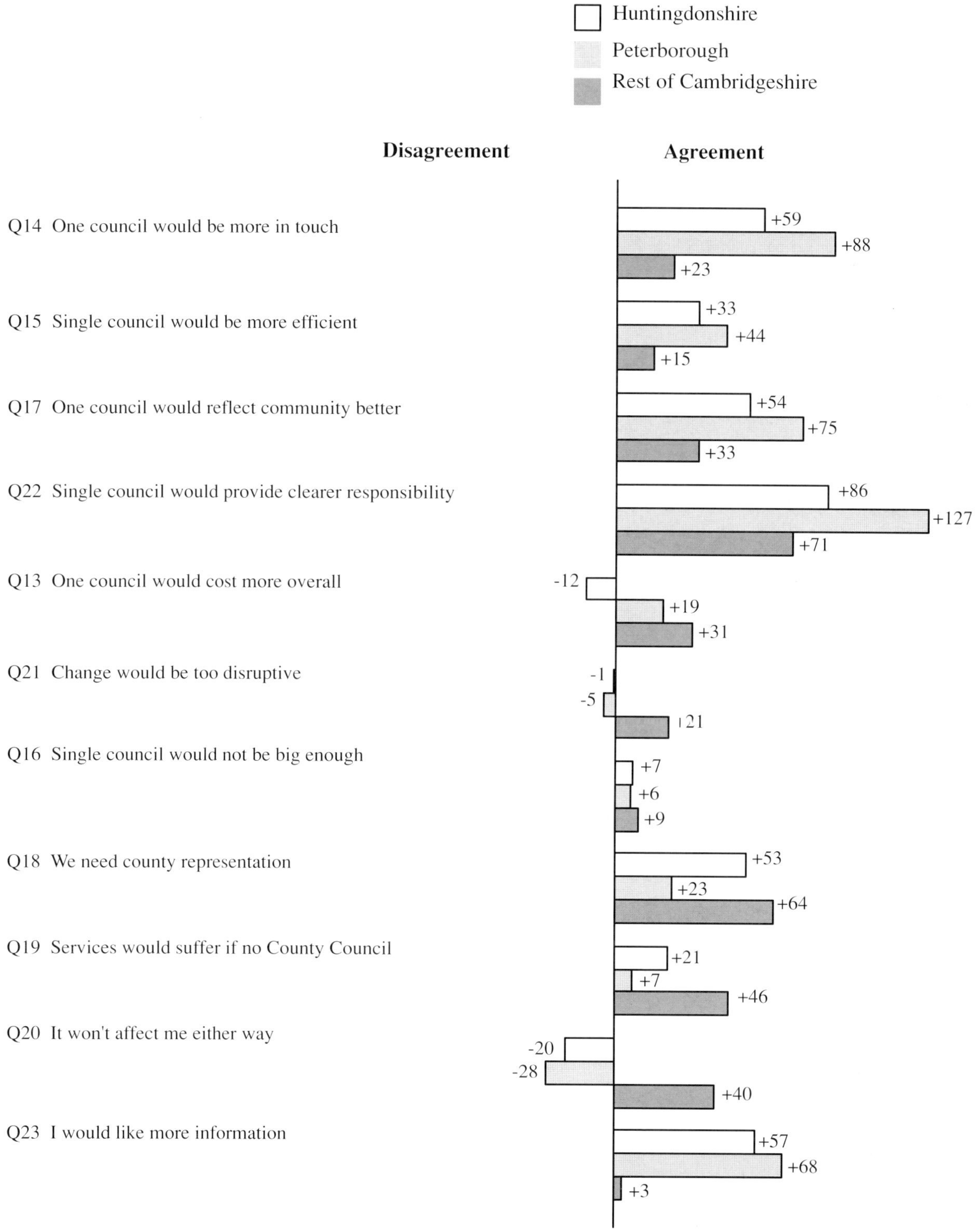

Attitudes to Change
(Respondents in Huntingdonshire)

Q To what extent do you agree or disagree that...?
(Figures represent 'mean scores' with *strong agreement* given a value of +2 through to *strong disagreement* given -2)

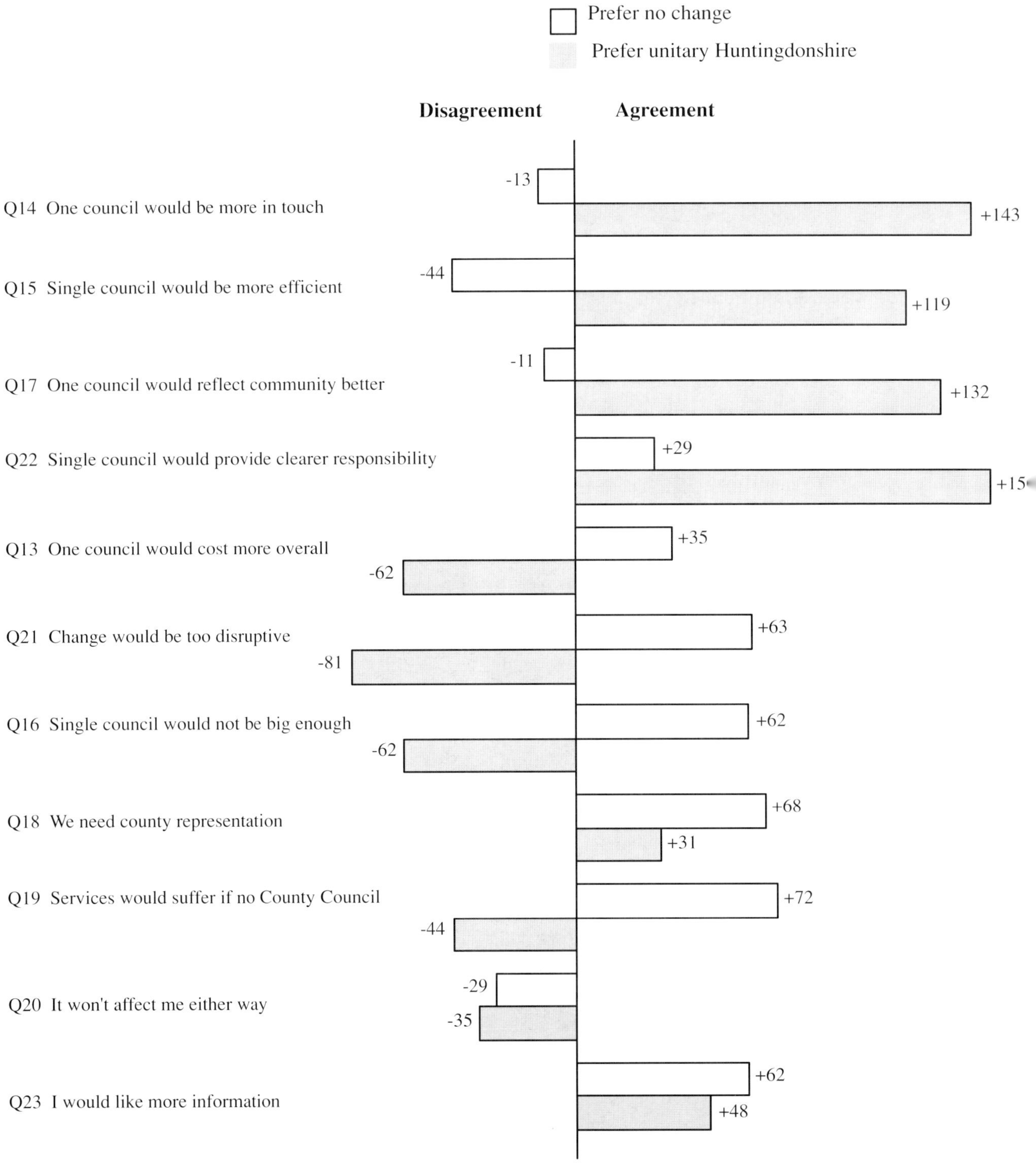

Attitudes to Change
(Respondents in Peterborough)

Q To what extent do you agree or disagree that...?
(Figures represent 'mean scores' with *strong agreement* given a value of +2 through to *strong disagreement* given -2)

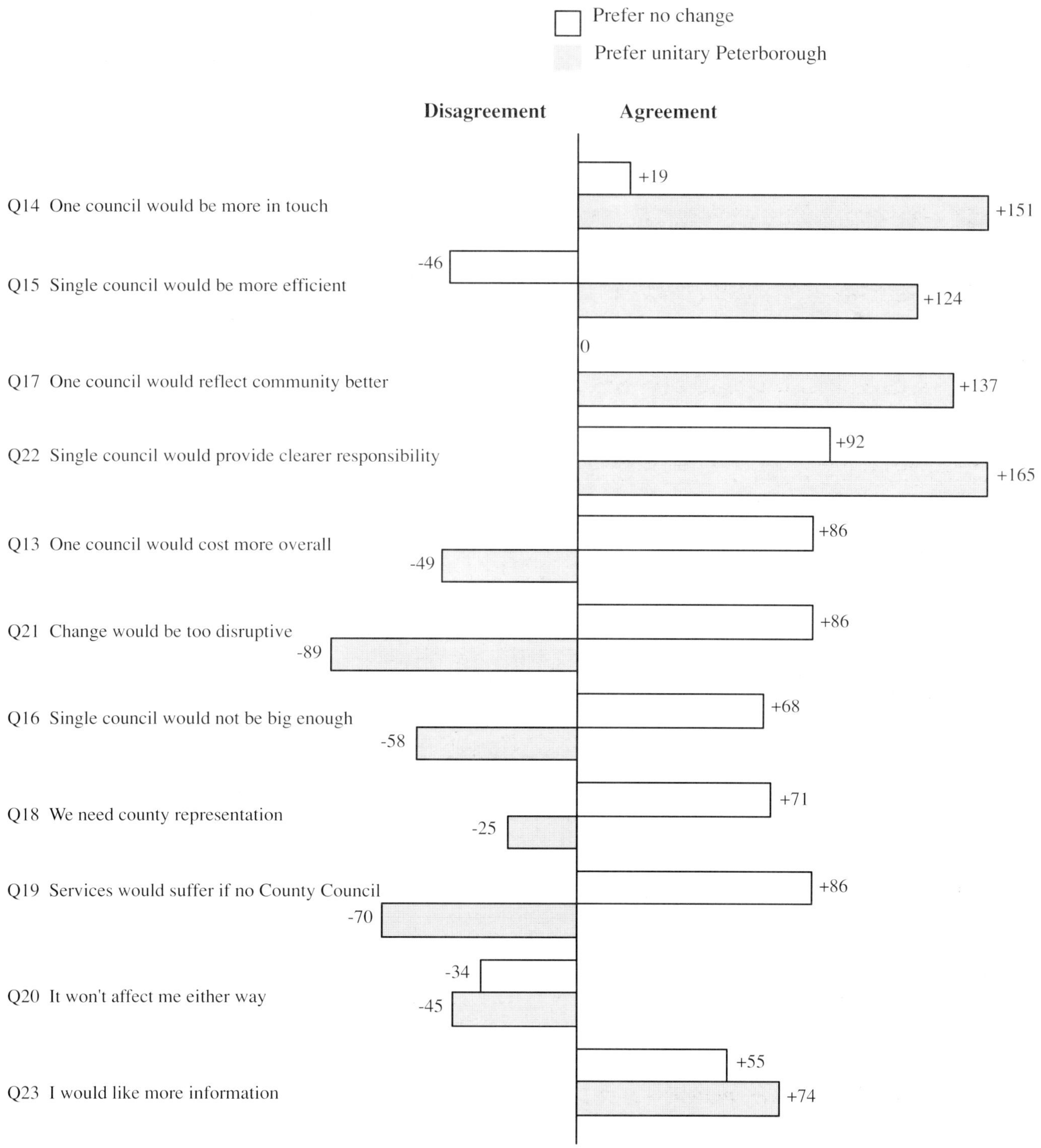

Attitudes to Change
(Respondents in the rest of Cambridgeshire)

Q To what extent do you agree or disagree that...?
(Figures represent 'mean scores' with *strong agreement* given a value of +2 through to *strong disagreement* given -2)

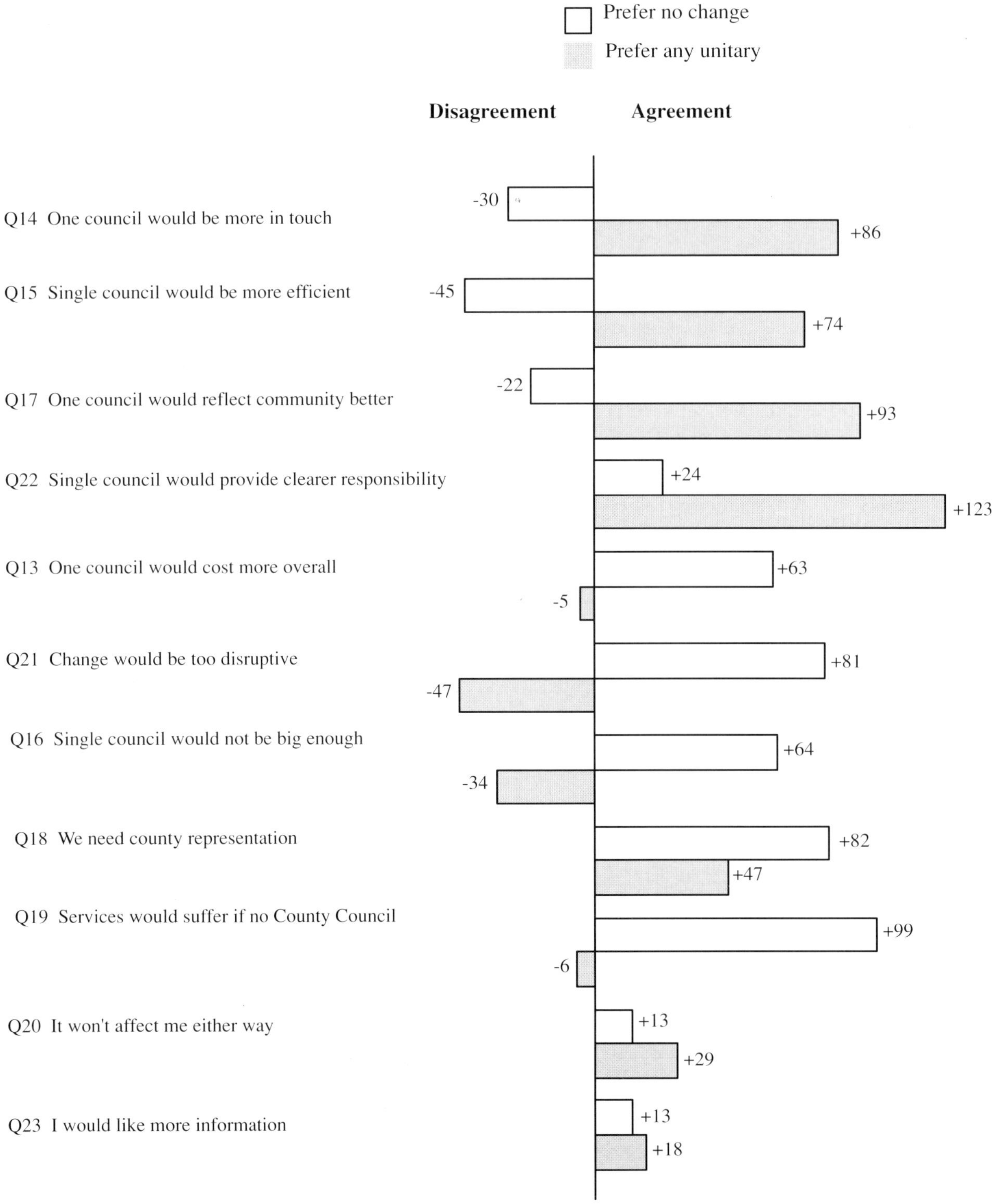

MORI/9101/01
(1-6)

CAMBRIDGESHIRE
REVIEW - REST OF COUNTY

Serial No ....
OUO (7-10)

Name/Initials/Title ....

Address ....

.... **Postcode**..

Telephone: Yes....................................... 1 (11)

Number (inc STD code)

No 2

Sample Point

(12) (13) (14) (15) (16)

Gender %
- Male 49
- Female 51

Age %
- 18-24 13
- 25-34 20
- 35-44 20
- 45-54 14
- 55-64 10
- 65-74 13
- 75+.. 10

WRITE IN AGE

Work Status %
- Full-time (30 hrs/wk+) 49
- Part-time (8-29 hrs/wk) 8
- Not working (under 8 hrs) 2
- Looking after home/children............ 6
- Retired 25
- Registered unemployed.................. 4
- Unemployed but not registered ....*
- Student... 4
- Other 2

Occupation of Chief Income Earner (CIE)
Position/rank/grade

....

Industry/type of company

....

Qualifications/degrees/apprenticeship

....

No of Staff Responsible for

....

PROBE FOR PENSION %
- AB 19
- C1... 24
- C2... 21
- D.. 16
- E.. 21

* Less than 1/2%

Number in Household
Adults aged 18+ (inc. respondent)

1 2 3 4 5+ ______ 21

Children (17 or under)

0 1 2 3 4+ ______ 22

QA **Are you or other members of your household employed by a council?** IF YES: **Is this a Borough/District Council or a County Council?** CODE FOR BOTH RESPONDENT AND OTHER HOUSEHOLD MEMBERS

	Respondent %	Other %
Yes:		
Borough/District	*	-
County	3	4
Don't know which	-	*
No	97	86
Don't know	*	10

Tenure %
- Owned outright...................................... 25
- Buying on mortgage 42
- Rented from Council 18
- Rented from Housing Association 2
- Rented from private landlord 9
- Other 4

QB **Is this your main permanent home, or is it a second or holiday home?**

%
- Main/permanent.................................. 99
- Second/holiday 1

Car in Household
CIRCLE NUMBER

0 1 2 3+

Showcard Version

%
- A-K 1
- A1-K1 2

THIS FORM IS THE PROPERTY OF MARKET & OPINION RESEARCH INTERNATIONAL (MORI)
32 OLD QUEEN STREET, LONDON, SW1H 9HP

INTERVIEWER DECLARATION: I confirm that I have conducted this interview face-to-face with the above named person and that I have asked all the relevant questions fully and recorded the answers in conformance with the survey specification and the MRS Code of Conduct.

Interviewer Name .... Signature ....

Interviewer Number					/	

	Month		Date	
DATE OF INTERVIEW				
	(29)	(30)	(31)	(32)

29/32

NB INTERVIEWER: ALL SHOWCARDS HAVE BEEN REVERSED. PLEASE BE CAREFUL TO CODE THE CORRECT RESPONSE.

Good morning/afternoon/evening. I'm from MORI, the market research and polling organisation. We are doing a survey about local issues, and I would like to ask you a few questions.

ASK ALL

Q1 **Firstly, how long have you lived in this area?** (WITHIN FIVE MILES)

	%
Less than 1 year	6
1-2 years	5
3-5 years	10
6-10 years	15
11-20 years	17
Over 20 years/all my life	47
Don't know/can't remember	-

Q2 SHOWCARD A (R) **From this card, how much would you say you know about local councils and the services they provide?**

	%
A great deal	3
A fair amount	34
Not very much	53
Nothing at all	9
Don't know	1

Q3 SHOWCARD B (R) **Which of the statements on this card comes closest to your own view of the Councils in this area?**

		%
A)	I'm not interested in what the Council does, or whether they do their job	1
B)	I'm not interested in what the Council does, as long as they do their job	14
C)	I like to know what the Council is doing, but I'm happy to let them get on with their job	59
D)	I would like to have more of a say in what the Council does and the services it provides	22
E)	I already work for, or am involved with the Council and the services it provides	2
	Don't know	2

Q4 **From what you know, how many councils provide the main services in this neighbourhood?** (INTERVIEWER - NOT INCLUDING PARISH COUNCILS)

	%
One	24
Two	33
Three+	5
Don't know	37

In fact there are two main councils that provide, or are responsible for, most services in this area:. . .district/borough/city and Cambridgeshire County Council.

ROTATE ORDER OF Q5/6

☐ Q5 SHOWCARD C (R) **From this list, what services do you think are the responsibility of... district/borough/city council? Just read out the letter(s) that apply**

☐ Q6 SHOWCARD C AGAIN (R) **And which services on this list do you think are the responsibility of Cambridgeshire County Council? Again, just read out the letters that apply.**

Q7 SHOWCARD D (R) **Which, if any, of these services do you or members of your family use?** INCLUDE ONLY LOCAL USE

		Q5 "Borough" %	Q6 County %	Q7 Use %
A	Bus Services	31	26	45
B	Car Parks	46	20	61
C	Council Housing	48	21	18
D	Council Tax Benefit/Housing benefit	43	28	30
E	Fire service	25	44	39
F	Food safety	26	28	19
G	Household waste sites/dumps	44	25	55
H	Libraries	29	40	60
I	Parks, playgrounds and open spaces	48	25	59
J	Planning service	41	30	18
K	Public conveniences	45	21	45
L	Recycling/bottle banks	45	17	59
M	Refuse collection	55	20	90
N	Road maintenance	28	48	50
O	Schools/education	20	55	40
P	Social services	25	43	16
Q	Street sweeping	51	17	42
R	Swimming pools/sports facilities	40	26	53
	Other (WRITE IN AND CODE "7")	1	1	1
	....			
	None of these	1	1	-
	Don't know	25	26	1

Q8 SHOWCARD E (R) **As you may know, there is currently a review being undertaken by the Local Government Commission on the future local government structure in the county. How much, if anything, would you say you know about this?**

	%
A great deal	2
A fair amount	6
Just a little	35
Heard of but know nothing about	19
Never heard of	37

PREFERENCES

HAND OVER MAP SHOWING AREAS UNDER REVIEW AND "CURRENT SERVICES" CARD
The Local Government Commission is considering options for the future structure of local government in parts of Cambridgeshire. Could you please read through this card, (SHOW OPTIONS CARD) **which outlines the options.**

Q9 **Please tell me which of the options, if either, you would prefer for each of Peterborough and Huntingdonshire?**
CODE ONE ONLY FOR EACH DISTRICT

For Peterborough

	%
Option A (single all purpose council)	30
Option B (stay the same/status quo)	42
Some other option	1
Neither of these	*
Either of these/don't mind	4
Don't care	6
Don't know	16

For Huntingdonshire

	%
Option A (stay the same/status quo)	45
Option B (single all purpose council)	27
Some other option	1
Neither of these	*
Either of these/don't mind	4
Don't care	6
Don't know	18

ASK IF "OTHER" NAMED AT Q9 (CODE 3)
Q10 **What other option is that?**
PROBE FULLY - DO NOT PROMPT.

....

....

....

....

ASK ALL PREFERRING AN OPTION (1, 2 OR 3 AT Q9). OTHERS GO TO Q13
Q11 SHOWCARD F (R) **You say that the option you would prefer is . . . . .** (INSERT OPTION PREFERRED). **How strongly would you say you feel about this?**

	%
Very strongly	14
Fairly strongly	41
Not very strongly	32
Not at all strongly	7
Don't know	5

Q12 **What do you think would be the main advantages of . . .**(OPTION PREFERRED) PROBE FULLY FOR DETAILS

....

....

....

....

Nothing...

Don't know/can't think of anything.................................

ATTITUDES TO PROPOSALS

SHOWCARD G (R) **Imagine that there was one council in any or both of Peterborough and Huntingdonshire, providing <u>all</u> services. I am going to read out some statements that people have made about this proposal. To what extent do you agree or disagree that . . . .?** READ OUT, ROTATE ORDER OF ASKING Q13-22. TICK START

	READ OUT:	Strongly agree %	Tend to agree %	Neither/ Nor %	Tend to disagree %	Strongly disagree %	Don't know %
☐ Q13	**It would cost more overall**	15	24	12	21	5	22
Q14	**It would be more in touch with local people's needs**	12	36	7	20	11	14
Q15	**The single Council would be more efficient than the current system of two Councils**	12	26	15	16	11	19
☐ Q16	**The single council would not be big enough to manage services such as Education and Social Services effectively**	13	22	10	24	8	22
Q17	**It would better reflect the sense of community in those areas**	11	39	10	17	8	15
Q18	**We need a County Council to represent us nationally**	19	38	12	14	3	14
☐ Q19	**Services would suffer if the County Council no longer provides services in those areas**	18	29	13	18	5	17
Q20	**It won't affect me whether there is a single Council in those areas or not**	21	33	9	22	8	8
Q21	**The change to a single Council for those areas would be too disruptive**	14	25	14	25	5	17
☐ Q22	**With a single Council it would be clearer who is responsible for local services**	25	37	9	12	6	11

ASK LAST

Q23 **I would like to have more information on the proposals before making up my mind** ....19.............26............ 11............ 19 ....22 4

Q24 **On balance, which would you say is more in touch with local people and issues,** .... (ROTATE ORDER OF "DISTRICT" AND COUNTY) (INSERT NAME OF "DISTRICT COUNCIL)..**district/borough/city council, or Cambridgeshire County Council, or would you say that they are both about the same?**

	%
District/borough/city council	44
Cambridgeshire County Council	9
Both about the same	32
Don't know	15

<u>REFER BACK TO Q8. ASK ALL WHO HAVE HEARD OF REVIEW AT Q8 (IE CODES 1/2/3/4). OTHERS TO Q28</u>

Q25 SHOWCARD H **Earlier in the interview, you said that you had heard of the Review of local government structure. From which, if any, of the sources shown on this card have you recently heard about the Review?** INTERVIEWER NOTE: "RECENTLY" = IN PAST 3 MONTHS

		%
A	Leaflet from County Council delivered to your door	18
B	Leaflet from County Council in library/ offices, etc	2
C	Advertisement from County Council in local newspaper	6
D	Advertisement from County Council on local radio/TV	4
E	Leaflet from Borough Council delivered to your door	1
F	Leaflet from Borough Council in library/ offices, etc	*
G	Borough Council newspaper	2
H	County Council newspaper	1
I	Advertisement from Borough Council in local newspaper	*
J	Advertisement from Borough Council on local radio/TV	2
K	Advertisement by the Commission on local radio	1
L	Local Government Commission advertisement in local newspaper	3
M	Local newspaper	45
N	National newspaper	6
O	TV	22
P	Local radio	17
Q	National radio	4
R	Friends/neighbours/family	10
S	Conversation with Borough Councillor	*
T	Conversation with County Councillor	*
U	Conversation with Borough Council staff	1
V	Conversation with County Council staff	1
W	Parish/community council	2
X	Residents' Association	2
	Other	12
	None of these	4
	Don't know	4

ASK ALL NAMING A SOURCE AT Q25. OTHERS GO TO Q28

Q26 **Would you say that the information you have received has influenced your opinion, or not?**

Base: 168	%
Yes	21
No	71
Don't know	7

Q27 **What information in particular has influenced your opinion?**

....

....

....

....

ASK ALL

Q28 SHOWCARD I (R) **Assuming you receive the same level of services, how important is it to you, if at all, what the final decision is on the future local government structure in the areas under review?**

	%
Very important	12
Fairly important	30
Not very important	37
Not at all important	14
Don't know	8

ACTIVISM

Q29 SHOWCARD J **Which of the things on this list, if any, have you done in the last three years? Just read out the letter(s) that apply.**

		%
A	Voted in Local Council elections	73
B	Spoken or written to a local Councillor	29
C	Responded to the earlier Review of local government	7
D	Been to a meeting of a local committee or organisation (WRITE IN NAME OF ORGANISATION)	13
E	Spoken on a radio phone-in about a local issue	1
F	Written to a local newspaper about a local issue	6
G	Been to a meeting of a local branch of a political party	4
H	Written to your MP about a local issue	12
I	Been to a Council Committee meeting	2
J	Been to a Council meeting	4
K	Attended a public meeting run by the Council	10
	None of these	22
	Don't know/refused	1

Q30 SHOWCARD K **Which, if any, of these apply to you? Just read out the letter(s) that apply.**

		%
	I am a member of a:	
A	Residents' Association	4
B	Community Association	1
C	Tenants' Association	1
D	Neighbourhood Watch	22
E	PTA/school governors	6
	I do unpaid work for:	
F	A school	4
G	Citizens Advice Bureau	-
H	Volunteer Bureau	3
I	Scouts/Guides/Cubs/Brownies	2
J	Church group	7
	Other	4
	None of these	60
	Don't know	2

THANK RESPONDENT. GO TO DEMOGRAPHICS.

MORI/9101/01
(1-6)

CAMBRIDGESHIRE
REVIEW: Huntingdonshire

Serial No ....
OUO (7-10)

Name/Initials/Title ....

Address ....

.... **Postcode**..

(11)
Telephone: Yes.. 1

Number (inc STD code)

No 2

Sample Point

(12) (13) (14) (15) (16)

Gender %
- Male 49
- Female 51

Age %
- 18-24 14
- 25-34 22
- 35-44 21
- 45-54 16
- 55-64 14
- 65-74 8
- 75+ 5

WRITE IN AGE

Work Status %
- Full-time (30 hrs/wk+) 54
- Part-time (8-29 hrs/wk) 10
- Not working (under 8 hrs) 1
- Looking after home/children........... 12
- Retired 18
- Registered unemployed.................. 1
- Unemployed but not registered 1
- Student.. 2
- Other 1

Occupation of Chief Income Earner (CIE)
Position/rank/grade

....

Industry/type of company

....

Qualifications/degrees/apprenticeship

....

No of Staff Responsible for

....

PROBE FOR PENSION

	%
AB	21
C1	38
C2	19
D	16
E	7

Number in Household
Adults aged 18+ (inc. respondent)

1 2 3 4 5+

Children (17 or under)

0 1 2 3 4+

QA **Are you or other members of your household employed by a council?** IF YES: **Is this a Borough/District Council or a County Council?** CODE FOR BOTH RESPONDENT AND OTHER HOUSEHOLD MEMBERS

	Respondent %	Other %
Yes:		
Borough/District	-	*
County	4	4
Don't know which	-	-
No	95	90
Don't know	1	6

Tenure %
- Owned outright.. 19
- Buying on mortgage 52
- Rented from Council 14
- Rented from Housing Association 2
- Rented from private landlord 8
- Other 5

QB **Is this your main permanent home, or is it a second or holiday home?**

	%
Main/permanent	99
Second/holiday	1

Car in Household
CIRCLE NUMBER

0 1 2 3+

Showcard Version
- A-K ....
- A1-K1 ....

THIS FORM IS THE PROPERTY OF MARKET & OPINION RESEARCH INTERNATIONAL (MORI)
32 OLD QUEEN STREET, LONDON, SW1H 9HP

INTERVIEWER DECLARATION: I confirm that I have conducted this interview face-to-face with the above named person and that I have asked all the relevant questions fully and recorded the answers in conformance with the survey specification and the MRS Code of Conduct.

Interviewer Name .... Signature ....

Interviewer Number					/	

	Month		Date	
DATE OF INTERVIEW				
	(29)	(30)	(31)	(32)

29/32

NB INTERVIEWER: ALL SHOWCARDS HAVE BEEN REVERSED. PLEASE BE CAREFUL TO CODE THE CORRECT RESPONSE.

Good morning/afternoon/evening. I'm from MORI, the market research and polling organisation. We are doing a survey about local issues, and I would like to ask you a few questions.

ASK ALL

Q1 **Firstly, how long have you lived in this area?** (WITHIN FIVE MILES)

	%
Less than 1 year	5
1-2 years	4
3-5 years	7
6-10 years	25
11-20 years	22
Over 20 years/all my life	36
Don't know/can't remember	1

Q2 SHOWCARD A (R) **From this card, how much would you say you know about local councils and the services they provide?**

	%
A great deal	3
A fair amount	31
Not very much	57
Nothing at all	9
Don't know	1

Q3 SHOWCARD B (R) **Which of the statements on this card comes closest to your own view of the Councils in this area?**

		%
A)	I'm not interested in what the Council does, or whether they do their job	2
B)	I'm not interested in what the Council does, as long as they do their job	19
C)	I like to know what the Council is doing, but I'm happy to let them get on with their job	58
D)	I would like to have more of a say in what the Council does and the services it provides	18
E)	I already work for, or am involved with the Council and the services it provides	3
	Don't know	*

Q4 **From what you know, how many councils provide the main services in this neighbourhood?** (INTERVIEWER - NOT INCLUDING PARISH COUNCILS)

	%
One	18
Two	49
Three+	5
Don't know	28

In fact there are two main councils that provide, or are responsible for most services in this area: Huntingdonshire District and Cambridgeshire County Council.

ROTATE ORDER OF Q5/6

☐ Q5 SHOWCARD C (R) **From this list, what services do you think are the responsibility of Huntingdonshire District Council? Just read out the letter(s) that apply**

☐ Q6 SHOWCARD C AGAIN (R) **And which services on this list do you think are the responsibility of Cambridgeshire County Council? Again, just read out the letters that apply.**

Q7 SHOWCARD D (R) **Which, if any, of these services do you or members of your family use?** INCLUDE ONLY LOCAL USE

		Q5 Huntingdonshire %	Q6 County %	Q7 Use %
A	Bus Services	35	36	33
B	Car Parks	61	20	71
C	Council Housing	69	17	12
D	Council Tax Benefit/Housing benefit	50	32	17
E	Fire service	23	52	41
F	Food safety	20	36	15
G	Household waste sites/dumps	61	19	62
H	Libraries	25	55	66
I	Parks, playgrounds and open spaces	53	20	52
J	Planning service	48	33	21
K	Public conveniences	56	12	31
L	Recycling/bottle banks	55	13	59
M	Refuse collection	70	13	76
N	Road maintenance	37	55	36
O	Schools/education	17	66	35
P	Social services	21	57	19
Q	Street sweeping	70	12	37
R	Swimming pools/sports facilities	47	27	50
	Other	1	1	3
	None of these	*	1	*
	Don't know	11	15	10

Q8 SHOWCARD E (R) **As you may know, there is currently a review being undertaken by the Local Government Commission on the future local government structure in the county. How much, if anything, would you say you know about this?**

	%
A great deal	2
A fair amount	12
Just a little	42
Heard of but know nothing about	19
Never heard of	25

PREFERENCES

HAND OVER MAP SHOWING AREAS UNDER REVIEW AND "CURRENT SERVICES" CARD
The Local Government Commission is considering options for the future structure of local government in parts of Cambridgeshire. Could you please read through this card, (SHOW OPTIONS CARD) **which outlines the options.**

Q9 **Please tell me which of the options, if either, you would prefer for each of Peterborough and Huntingdonshire?**
CODE ONE ONLY FOR EACH DISTRICT

For Peterborough	%
Option A (single all purpose council)	28
Option B (stay the same/status quo)	28
Some other option	1
Neither of these	1
Either of these/don't mind	8
Don't care	13
Don't know	22

For Huntingdonshire	%
Option A (stay the same/status quo)	47
Option B (single all purpose council)	40
Some other option	1
Neither of these	*
Either of these/don't mind	2
Don't care	2
Don't know	8

ASK IF "OTHER" NAMED FOR Huntingdonshire AT Q9 (CODE 3)

Q10 **What other option is that for Huntingdonshire?**
PROBE FULLY - DO NOT PROMPT.

....

....

....

....

ASK ALL PREFERRING AN OPTION (1, 2 OR 3 AT Q9). OTHERS GO TO Q13

Q11 SHOWCARD F (R) **You say that the option you would prefer for Huntingdonshire is . . . . .** (INSERT OPTION PREFERRED). **How strongly would you say you feel about this?**

	%
Very strongly	22
Fairly strongly	47
Not very strongly	24
Not at all strongly	3
Don't know	4

Q12 **What do you think would be the main advantages of . . .**(OPTION PREFERRED)
PROBE FULLY FOR DETAILS

....

....

....

....

Nothing...
Don't know/can't think of anything.................................

ATTITUDES TO PROPOSALS

SHOWCARD G (R) **Imagine that there was one council in Huntingdonshire, providing all services. I am going to read out some statements that people have made about this proposal. To what extent do you agree or disagree that . . . .?** READ OUT, ROTATE ORDER OF ASKING Q13-22. TICK START

READ OUT:	Strongly agree %	Tend to agree %	Neither/ Nor %	Tend to disagree %	Strongly disagree %	Don't know %
☐ Q13 **It would cost more overall**	4	25	11	37	3	20
Q14 **It would be more in touch with local people's needs**	23	41	8	21	4	4
Q15 **The single Council would be more efficient than the current system of two Councils**	15	35	10	29	3	8
☐ Q16 **The single council would not be big enough to manage services such as Education and Social Services effectively**	9	34	8	34	5	9
Q17 **It would better reflect the sense of community in Huntingdonshire**	18	45	9	22	3	4
Q18 **We need a County Council to represent us nationally**	10	48	14	15	2	10
☐ Q19 **Services would suffer if the County Council no longer provides services in Huntingdonshire**	6	43	10	27	5	9
Q20 **It won't affect me whether there is a single Council in Huntingdonshire or not**	4	32	14	33	13	4
Q21 **The change to a single Council for Huntingdonshire would be too disruptive**	8	30	12	35	6	9
☐ Q22 **With a single Council it would be clearer who is responsible for local services**	29	45	8	16	1	2

ASK LAST

Q23 **I would like to have more information on the proposals before making up my mind** ....25 .... 35............ 12............ 17 ....7 5

Q24 **On balance, which would you say is more in touch with local people and issues, ...** (ROTATE ORDER OF "DISTRICT" AND COUNTY) **Huntingdonshire District Council, or Cambridgeshire County Council, or would you say that they are both about the same?**

	%
Huntingdonshire District Council	57
Cambridgeshire County Council	6
Both about the same	26
Don't know	11

<u>REFER BACK TO Q8. ASK ALL WHO HAVE HEARD OF REVIEW AT Q8 (IE CODES 1/2/3/4). OTHERS TO Q28</u>

Q25 SHOWCARD H **Earlier in the interview, you said that you had heard of the Review of local government structure. From which, if any, of the sources shown on this card have you recently heard about the Review?** INTERVIEWER NOTE: "RECENTLY" = IN PAST 3 MONTHS

Base: 234

		%
A	Leaflet from County Council delivered to your door	26
B	Leaflet from County Council in library/ offices, etc	10
C	Advertisement from County Council in local newspaper	12
D	Advertisement from County Council on local radio/TV	3
E	Leaflet from Borough Council delivered to your door	7
F	Leaflet from Borough Council in library/ offices, etc	1
G	Borough Council newspaper	1
H	County Council newspaper	1
I	Advertisement from Borough Council in local newspaper	6
J	Advertisement from Borough Council on local radio/TV	2
K	Advertisement by the Commission on local radio	1
L	Local Government Commission advertisement in local newspaper	3
M	Local newspaper	57
N	National newspaper	8
O	TV	14
P	Local radio	13
Q	National radio	4
R	Friends/neighbours/family	7
S	Conversation with Borough Councillor	3
T	Conversation with County Councillor	3
U	Conversation with Borough Council staff	-
V	Conversation with County Council staff	2
W	Parish/community council	5
X	Residents' Association	1
	Other	7
	None of these	9
	Don't know	5

ASK ALL NAMING A SOURCE AT Q25. OTHERS GO TO Q28

Q26 **Would you say that the information you have received has influenced your opinion, or not?**

Base: 202

	%
Yes	30
No	68
Don't know	2

Q27 **What information in particular has influenced your opinion?**

....

....

....

....

ASK ALL

Q28 SHOWCARD I (R) **Assuming you receive the same level of services, how important is it to you, if at all, what the final decision is on the future local government structure in Huntingdonshire?**

	%
Very important	19
Fairly important	46
Not very important	26
Not at all important	7
Don't know	1

ACTIVISM

Q29 SHOWCARD J **Which of the things on this list, if any, have you done in the last three years? Just read out the letter(s) that apply.**

		%
A	Voted in Local Council elections	75
B	Spoken or written to a local Councillor	35
C	Responded to the earlier Review of local government	10
D	Been to a meeting of a local committee or organisation (WRITE IN NAME OF ORGANISATION)	20
E	Spoken on a radio phone-in about a local issue	1
F	Written to a local newspaper about a local issue	4
G	Been to a meeting of a local branch of a political party	5
H	Written to your MP about a local issue	16
I	Been to a Council Committee meeting	4
J	Been to a Council meeting	4
K	Attended a public meeting run by the Council	16
	None of these	19
	Don't know/refused	-

Q30 SHOWCARD K **Which, if any, of these apply to you? Just read out the letter(s) that apply.**

		%
	I am a member of a:	
A	Residents' Association	4
B	Community Association	7
C	Tenants' Association	1
D	Neighbourhood Watch	30
E	PTA/school governors	8
	I do unpaid work for:	
F	A school	15
G	Citizens Advice Bureau	*
H	Volunteer Bureau	3
I	Scouts/Guides/Cubs/Brownies	5
J	Church group	8
	Other	3
	None of these	53
	Don't know	1

THANK RESPONDENT. GO TO DEMOGRAPHICS.

- 17 -

MORI/9101/01 (1-6)

CAMBRIDGESHIRE
REVIEW: Peterborough

Serial No ....
OUO (7-10)

Name/Initials/Title ....

Address ....

.... **Postcode** ....

(11)

Telephone: Yes 1

Number (inc STD code)

No 2

Sample Point

(12) (13) (14) (15) (16)

Gender	%
Male	48
Female	52

Age	%
18-24	15
25-34	22
35-44	17
45-54	16
55-64	14
65-74	10
75+	7

WRITE IN AGE

Work Status	%
Full-time (30 hrs/wk+)	48
Part-time (8-29 hrs/wk)	13
Not working (under 8 hrs)	2
Looking after home/children	7
Retired	19
Registered unemployed	6
Unemployed but not registered	2
Student	1
Other	1

Occupation of Chief Income Earner (CIE)
Position/rank/grade

....

Industry/type of company

....

Qualifications/degrees/apprenticeship

....

No of Staff Responsible for

....

PROBE FOR PENSION

	%
AB	17
C1	25
C2	18
D	19
E	20

Number in Household
Adults aged 18+ (inc. respondent)

1 2 3 4 5+

Children (17 or under)

0 1 2 3 4+

QA **Are you or other members of your household employed by a council?** IF YES: **Is this a Borough/District Council or a County Council?** CODE FOR BOTH RESPONDENT AND OTHER HOUSEHOLD MEMBERS

	Respondent %	Other %
Yes:		
Borough/District	1	2
County	5	3
Don't know which	*	*
No	92	84
Don't know	1	11

Tenure	%
Owned outright	19
Buying on mortgage	45
Rented from Council	21
Rented from Housing Association	5
Rented from private landlord	7
Other	3

QB **Is this your main permanent home, or is it a second or holiday home?**

	%
Main/permanent	99
Second/holiday	1

Car in Household
CIRCLE NUMBER

0 1 2 3+

Showcard Version
A-K ....
A1-K1 ....

INTERVIEWER DECLARATION: I confirm that I have conducted this interview face-to-face with the above named person and that I have asked all the relevant questions fully and recorded the answers in conformance with the survey specification and the MRS Code of Conduct.

Interviewer Name .... Signature ....

Interviewer Number					/	

	Month		Date	
DATE OF INTERVIEW				
	(29)	(30)	(31)	(32)

29/32

NB INTERVIEWER: ALL SHOWCARDS HAVE BEEN REVERSED. PLEASE BE CAREFUL TO CODE THE CORRECT RESPONSE.

Good morning/afternoon/evening. I'm from MORI, the market research and polling organisation. We are doing a survey about local issues, and I would like to ask you a few questions.

ASK ALL

Q1 **Firstly, how long have you lived in this area?** (WITHIN FIVE MILES)

	%
Less than 1 year	2
1-2 years	7
3-5 years	12
6-10 years	17
11-20 years	22
Over 20 years/all my life	40
Don't know/can't remember	-

Q2 SHOWCARD A (R) **From this card, how much would you say you know about local councils and the services they provide?**

	%
A great deal	1
A fair amount	27
Not very much	51
Nothing at all	18
Don't know	3

Q3 SHOWCARD B (R) **Which of the statements on this card comes closest to your own view of the Councils in this area?**

		%
A)	I'm not interested in what the Council does, or whether they do their job	4
B)	I'm not interested in what the Council does, as long as they do their job	16
C)	I like to know what the Council is doing, but I'm happy to let them get on with their job	60
D)	I would like to have more of a say in what the Council does and the services it provides	16
E)	I already work for, or am involved with the Council and the services it provides	2
	Don't know	1

Q4 **From what you know, how many councils provide the main services in this neighbourhood?** (INTERVIEWER - NOT INCLUDING PARISH COUNCILS)

	%
One	29
Two	26
Three+	5
Don't know	40

In fact there are two main councils that provide, or are responsible for most services in this area: Peterborough City and Cambridgeshire County Council.

ROTATE ORDER OF Q5/6

☐ Q5 SHOWCARD C (R) **From this list, what services do you think are the responsibility of Peterborough City Council? Just read out the letter(s) that apply**

☐ Q6 SHOWCARD C AGAIN (R) **And which services on this list do you think are the responsibility of Cambridgeshire County Council? Again, just read out the letters that apply.**

Q7 SHOWCARD D (R) **Which, if any, of these services do you or members of your family use?** INCLUDE ONLY LOCAL USE

		Q5 Peterborough %	Q6 County %	Q7 Use %
A	Bus Services	41	15	48
B	Car Parks	57	11	62
C	Council Housing	60	15	19
D	Council Tax Benefit/Housing benefit	48	22	23
E	Fire service	17	50	24
F	Food safety	32	27	10
G	Household waste sites/dumps	52	16	46
H	Libraries	24	48	59
I	Parks, playgrounds and open spaces	52	19	61
J	Planning service	33	33	6
K	Public conveniences	52	13	39
L	Recycling/bottle banks	49	11	40
M	Refuse collection	60	11	87
N	Road maintenance	29	42	30
O	Schools/education	15	56	39
P	Social services	18	50	9
Q	Street sweeping	58	13	34
R	Swimming pools/sports facilities	47	20	48
	Other	1	1	3
	None of these	1	2	*
	Don't know	19	27	1

Q8 SHOWCARD E (R) **As you may know, there is currently a review being undertaken by the Local Government Commission on the future local government structure in the county. How much, if anything, would you say you know about this?**

	%
A great deal	2
A fair amount	11
Just a little	27
Heard of but know nothing about	17
Never heard of	43

PREFERENCES

HAND OVER MAP SHOWING AREAS UNDER REVIEW AND "CURRENT SERVICES" CARD
The Local Government Commission is considering options for the future structure of local government in parts of Cambridgeshire. Could you please read through this card, (SHOW OPTIONS CARD) **which outlines the options.**

Q9 **Please tell me which of the options, if either, you would prefer for each of Peterborough and Huntingdonshire?**
CODE ONE ONLY FOR EACH DISTRICT

For Peterborough

	%
Option A (single all purpose council)	40
Option B (stay the same/status quo)	40
Some other option	*
Neither of these	*
Either of these/don't mind	5
Don't care	2
Don't know	12

For Huntingdonshire

	%
Option A (stay the same/status quo)	27
Option B (single all purpose council)	21
Some other option	1
Neither of these	1
Either of these/don't mind	15
Don't care	6
Don't know	28

ASK IF "OTHER" NAMED FOR Peterborough AT Q9 (CODE 3)

Q10 **What other option is that for Peterborough?**
PROBE FULLY - DO NOT PROMPT.

....

....

....

....

ASK ALL PREFERRING AN OPTION (1, 2 OR 3 AT Q9). OTHERS GO TO Q13

Q11 SHOWCARD F (R) **You say that the option you would prefer for Peterborough is .....** (INSERT OPTION PREFERRED). **How strongly would you say you feel about this?**

	%
Very strongly	22
Fairly strongly	50
Not very strongly	23
Not at all strongly	4
Don't know	1

Q12 **What do you think would be the main advantages of . . .**(OPTION PREFERRED)
PROBE FULLY FOR DETAILS

....

....

....

....

Nothing...
Don't know/can't think of anything..................................

ATTITUDES TO PROPOSALS

SHOWCARD G (R) **Imagine that there was one council in Peterborough providing <u>all</u> services. I am going to read out some statements that people have made about this proposal. To what extent do you agree or disagree that . . . .?** READ OUT, ROTATE ORDER OF ASKING Q13-22. TICK START

READ OUT:

		Strongly agree %	Tend to agree %	Neither/ Nor %	Tend to disagree %	Strongly disagree %	Don't know %
Q13	**It would cost more overall**	15	24	11	24	7	19
Q14	**It would be more in touch with local people's needs**	30	41	6	12	4	7
Q15	**The single Council would be more efficient than the current system of two Councils**	19	31	13	17	7	13
Q16	**The single council would not be big enough to manage services such as Education and Social Services effectively**	12	23	11	26	8	19
Q17	**It would better reflect the sense of community in Peterborough**	27	39	6	16	4	7
Q18	**We need a County Council to represent us nationally**	10	32	14	22	5	16
Q19	**Services would suffer if the County Council no longer provides services in Peterborough**	12	26	11	31	7	13
Q20	**It won't affect me whether there is a single Council in Peterborough or not**	9	23	9	36	15	8
Q21	**The change to a single Council for Peterborough would be too disruptive**	11	23	11	33	8	13
Q22	**With a single Council it would be clearer who is responsible for local services**	45	41	5	6	*	3

ASK LAST

Q23 **I would like to have more information on the proposals before making up my mind** ....35 ....33 .... 7.... 10 ....13 2

Q24 **On balance, which would you say is more in touch with local people and issues, ...** (ROTATE ORDER OF "DISTRICT" AND COUNTY)
Peterborough City Council, or
Cambridgeshire County Council, or would you say that they are both about the same?

	%
Peterborough City Council	52
Cambridgeshire County Council	1
Both about the same	29
Don't know	18

REFER BACK TO Q8. ASK ALL WHO HAVE HEARD OF REVIEW AT Q8 (IE CODES 1/2/3/4). OTHERS TO Q28

Q25 SHOWCARD H **Earlier in the interview, you said that you had heard of the Review of local government structure. From which, if any, of the sources shown on this card have you recently heard about the Review?** INTERVIEWER NOTE: "RECENTLY" = IN PAST 3 MONTHS

Base: 181

		%
A	Leaflet from County Council delivered to your door	16
B	Leaflet from County Council in library/ offices, etc	3
C	Advertisement from County Council in local newspaper	7
D	Advertisement from County Council on local radio/TV	2
E	Leaflet from City Council delivered to your door	12
F	Leaflet from City Council in library/ offices, etc	2
G	City Council newspaper	5
H	County Council newspaper	-
I	Advertisement from City Council in local newspaper	5
J	Advertisement from City Council on local radio/TV	1
K	Advertisement by the Commission on local radio	1
L	Local Government Commission advertisement in local newspaper	3
M	Local newspaper	68
N	National newspaper	8
O	TV	18
P	Local radio	15
Q	National radio	5
R	Friends/neighbours/family	20
S	Conversation with City Councillor	2
T	Conversation with County Councillor	-
U	Conversation with City Council staff	1
V	Conversation with County Council staff	1
W	Parish/community council	1
X	Residents' Association	1
	Other	8
	None of these	1
	Don't know	4

ASK ALL NAMING A SOURCE AT Q25. OTHERS GO TO Q28

Q26 **Would you say that the information you have received has influenced your opinion, or not?**

Base: 172

	%
Yes	25
No	62
Don't know	13

Q27 **What information in particular has influenced your opinion?**

....

....

....

....

ASK ALL

Q28 SHOWCARD I (R) **Assuming you receive the same level of services, how important is it to you, if at all, what the final decision is on the future local government structure in Peterborough?**

	%
Very important	24
Fairly important	43
Not very important	19
Not at all important	6
Don't know	8

ACTIVISM

Q29 SHOWCARD J **Which of the things on this list, if any, have you done in the last three years? Just read out the letter(s) that apply.**

		%
A	Voted in Local Council elections	68
B	Spoken or written to a local Councillor	28
C	Responded to the earlier Review of local government	6
D	Been to a meeting of a local committee or organisation (WRITE IN NAME OF ORGANISATION)	7
E	Spoken on a radio phone-in about a local issue	2
F	Written to a local newspaper about a local issue	5
G	Been to a meeting of a local branch of a political party	3
H	Written to your MP about a local issue	6
I	Been to a Council Committee meeting	2
J	Been to a Council meeting	2
K	Attended a public meeting run by the Council	5
	None of these	25
	Don't know/refused	1

Q30 SHOWCARD K **Which, if any, of these apply to you? Just read out the letter(s) that apply.**

		%
	I am a member of a:	
A	Residents' Association	5
B	Community Association	2
C	Tenants' Association	2
D	Neighbourhood Watch	16
E	PTA/school governors	3
	I do unpaid work for:	
F	A school	8
G	Citizens Advice Bureau	1
H	Volunteer Bureau	2
I	Scouts/Guides/Cubs/Brownies	2
J	Church group	5
	Other	4
	None of these	64
	Don't know	1

THANK RESPONDENT. GO TO DEMOGRAPHICS.

CHAPTER 9

NORTHAMPTON IN THE COUNTY OF NORTHAMPTONSHIRE

Draft Recommendations

9.1 The Commission's report *Draft Recommendations on the Future Local Government of Northampton in the County of Northamptonshire* summarised the evidence taken into account by the Commission in reaching its draft recommendations.

Figure 9.1

Draft Recommendations for Northampton in the County of Northamptonshire

Structure

- The existing two-tier structure of local government in Northampton should be replaced. Northampton should become a unitary authority, responsible in its area for the broad range of local government functions currently carried out by both county council and district councils.

Ceremonial Arrangements

- The county of Northamptonshire should be retained for ceremonial and related purposes, and the unitary authority of Northampton should be associated with the county for such purposes.

Public Protection

- There should be a combined authority established in the present county area for the fire service, on which the representatives of the new unitary authority should serve. Similarly, representatives of the new unitary authority should serve on a joint committee with representatives of the county council to select the local authority membership of the Northamptonshire Police Authority. No changes are proposed to the area covered by the Northamptonshire Police Authority, or to the probation and magistrates' courts services.

Strategic Planning

- For strategic planning, the new unitary authority of Northampton should become a structure planning authority for its area, with a view to this function being exercised through joint arrangements with Northamptonshire County Council so as to retain a single structure plan. The new authority should individually have responsibility for formulating detailed minerals and waste policies for its area in general conformity with the policy framework established by the structure plan, and it should be authorised to include such policies in its local plans. Responsibility for the local plans should rest with the new authority and it should also exercise development control functions for its area for all purposes.

Electoral Arrangements

- The Northampton unitary authority should retain the existing Northampton Borough Council electoral arrangements. The council should therefore have a total of 43 members with 20 two-member wards and one three-member ward. Elections for the whole council should be held every four years.

Views Expressed to the Commission

9.2 The Commission received a wide range of direct representations on its draft recommendations, from local authorities, residents, Members of Parliament, business and voluntary groups, parish and town councils, and from other public and private sector organisations. Over 1,500 representations were received from individuals and organisations, including just under 600 from respondents within Nothampton. The Commission also received over 800 standard letters, completed questionnaires and petitions (Figures 9.2 and 9.3). Figures 9.2 and 9.3 exclude representations from the local authorities; these are summarised separately (Figure 9.4).

9.3 Northamptonshire County Council also distributed a leaflet with a tear-off questionnaire to every household in the county. In Northampton itself there was a response rate of 11 per cent, of which 81 per cent favoured no change and 19 per cent supported a unitary Northampton. Outside the borough, support for no change was over 95 per cent in each of the six districts.

Figure 9.2
Views of Respondents Within Northampton

Preferred structure	Individuals	Organisations	Standard letters and petition signatures
Unitary Northampton	148	42	527
No change	307	81	131
Other	8	2	0
No preference	3	2	0

Source: *Local Government Commission for England and NOP*
Note: *Northampton Borough Council also sent a number of submissions to the Commission from representatives of the business community in Northampton. These submissions were dated before the commencement of Stage Three and therefore have not been included in this table but have been considered by the Commission in reaching its final recommendation*

Figure 9.3
Views of Respondents from Outside Northampton

Preferred structure	Individuals	Organisations	Standard letters and petition signatures
Unitary Northampton	33	9	3
No change	626	247	180
Other	14	2	0
No preference	5	1	0

Source: *Local Government Commission for England and NOP*
Note: *Excludes out of county representations*

9.4 In addition, 87 representations were received from outside the county, of which 63 per cent supported no change and 18 per cent a unitary Northampton. A more detailed tabulation of the written representations from individuals and interest groups, produced by NOP on behalf of the Commission, can be found towards the end of this Chapter.

The Views of Local Authorities

9.5 The Commission received submissions from all eight principal local authorities in Northamptonshire during Stage Three (Figure 9.4).

Figure 9.4
Preferences of Northamptonshire Local Authorities During Stage Three

Authority	Preference
Corby Borough Council	Supported no change on the grounds of public opinion, costs and anticipated deterioration of county services.
Daventry District Council	During the first review of Northamptonshire the Council supported a unitary authority for the districts of South Northamptonshire and Daventry combined and remains fundamentally opposed to other options. It considered that the case for a unitary Northampton was not proven and urged the Commission to recommend no change.
East Northamptonshire District Council	Supported no change and considered that the case for a unitary Northampton was insufficiently strong to justify the upheaval which would result.
Kettering Borough Council	Contended that no case for change in Northampton had been made on the grounds of either local identities or effective and convenient local government.
Northampton Borough Council	Considered that Northampton had a strong and compelling case for unitary local government which had been widely accepted. Given the large population of the town and its growing influence as a sub-regional centre it argued that Northampton needs unitary status to make the most of its opportunities. The Council also believed that there was strong local support for the creation of a unitary Northampton.
South Northamptonshire District Council	Considered that the proposal for a unitary Northampton was totally lacking in public support, both from the populace at large and from those businesses and representative bodies that would be required to work with the new authority. The Council unanimously supported no change.
Wellingborough Borough Council	Opposed a unitary Northampton primarily due to its grave concerns regarding the effect on the provision of local government services and the level of council tax.
Northamptonshire County Council	Considered that the Commission's draft recommendation to create a hybrid local government structure in Northamptonshire would fail to provide effective or convenient local government for the county as a whole or even for Northampton if viewed in isolation.

Source: Local authorities' submissions

9.6 The Northamptonshire Branch of the Association of District Councils, with the exception of Northampton Borough Council, favoured no change. The Association of County Councils expressed support for no change. It argued that the creation of a unitary Northampton would be costly in financial terms, impair service delivery in the county and lack sufficient local champions. The Commission also received submissions from three local authorities outside the county of Northamptonshire. Milton Keynes Borough Council, Luton Borough Council and Derby City Council all expressed support for the creation of a Northampton unitary authority.

The Views of Others

9.7 A range of other interest groups made representations on the Commission's draft recommendations and these are summarised in the following paragraphs. These are in addition to, or in some cases a revision of, those made during Stage One.

Businesses and Business Groups

9.8 In Northamptonshire as a whole a significant majority of respondents from the business community favoured no change. Representations from Northampton-based companies were, however, more evenly distributed between support for a unitary Northampton and no change.

9.9 The Northamptonshire Chamber of Commerce Training and Enterprise, a body representing some 800 businesses in the county, indicated that it had been particularly active in informing the county-wide business community about the review process and the Commission's draft recommendations. An in-depth survey of its members conducted by the Chamber resulted in over 100 companies expressing a preference, and giving detailed reasons for their choice. Overall, 74 per cent of respondents preferred the current two-tier structure with 76 per cent of the Northampton-based firms supporting no change. A majority of respondents tended to agree that "...Northampton and the rest of the county are inextricably linked", "...the costs of change will lead to cuts in services" and "...the majority of residents do not support change". In a separate submission the Board of the Chamber itself also expressed support for no change.

9.10 In the context of the present review, the Northamptonshire Confederation of British Industry Group expressed support for the retention of the present two-tier structure of local government in the county. Scottish and Newcastle Retail Limited argued in favour of the retention of the present structure from the perspective of service delivery and costs. The National Farmers Union East Midlands Region and the Wellingborough Chamber of Trade and Commerce expressed similar sentiments. Among national business organisations the British Aggregate Construction Materials Industries supported the retention of the two-tier system and the Anti-Counterfeiting Group expressed particular concern about the potential fragmentation of the Trading Standards Service.

9.11 Of the submissions received from the business community supporting a unitary Northampton there was a common emphasis on the strong economic development work of the Borough Council and a belief that this would be enhanced by the creation of a unitary Northampton. Barclaycard, which had favoured no change during Stage One of the review, expressed support during Stage Three for a unitary Northampton. It believed that this structure would be the right long-term option to secure the prosperity of the town. The Northampton Chamber of Trade stated that when the subject of local government reorganisation was discussed at its recent meeting, a majority of those present favoured a unitary Northampton. Additionally, East Midlands Electricity favoured the logic of unitary status for Northampton but considered that the current proposals "...seem to be a half way house and would appear to have cost disadvantages in not seeing through a complete change [for the whole county] to unitary status".

9.12 The Commission also received a submission from the East Midlands Development Company (EMDC) which argued that the creation of a unitary Northampton was "...eminently sensible". In particular, it considered that: "Unitary status applied to all the major urban centres along the M1 Corridor will enable the EMDC to promote with equal force the county areas of Northamptonshire, Nottinghamshire, Derbyshire and Leicestershire".

County, Regional and National Interests (including the Voluntary Sector)

9.13 The Royal Commission on Historical Manuscripts stated that the creation of a unitary authority for Northampton would place further pressure on the local heritage records service. The Northamptonshire Branch of the Council for the

Protection of Rural England, which favoured no change, considered that it was of the greatest importance that there should be one county-wide body responsible for strategic planning in Northamptonshire and were concerned that the proposal might lead to a smaller budget being allocated to environmental concerns.

9.14 The Midlands Regional Office of the Countryside Commission was concerned to ensure that in the event of change the existing funding and quality of the landscape conservation and countryside recreation services in Northamptonshire would continue. English Nature expressed similar sentiments in relation to nature conservation. The Commission also received a number of submissions from local branches of the Ramblers' Association arguing for no change.

9.15 The Chief Inspector of the Social Services Inspectorate (Department of Health) expressed the view that: "Northampton is of sufficient size and population density to function as a unitary authority. The remainder of the county would also be viable". The Commission for the New Towns argued in its national submission that "...on balance, and assuming the continuation of the growth culture...greater benefits could be derived from dealing with a single authority...(in Northampton). This could simplify arrangements, avoid any danger of duplication and thus help to attract investment". In its national submission, the County Planning Officers Society, expressed concerns that "...your proposals in respect of...Northamptonshire... would seriously undermine the effective operation of strategic planning...". Similar concerns were expressed by the East Midlands Branch of the Royal Town Planning Institute. In the light of these concerns, and the Institute's belief that the proposal for a unitary Northampton lacked local support, it considered that the present structure should be retained. The Town and Country Planning Association expressed similar sentiments.

9.16 The Council for Voluntary Services for Northampton and County (CVS) said that, since Stage One, the voluntary sector had received assurances from Northampton Borough Council concerning specialist services, consultation and funding. The CVS said that if these assurances were substantiated it "...would remove its reservations to the establishment of Northampton as a unitary authority". Opposition to change, however, was expressed by the majority of local organisations including Northamptonshire Age Concern and the Northamptonshire Council for the Disabled. The Northamptonshire Council for Voluntary Youth Services also remained opposed to the creation of a unitary Northampton and expressed particular worries in relation to grant applications and inter-agency links.

9.17 The Northamptonshire Action for Communities in Rural England (ACRE) remained opposed to the creation of a unitary Northampton. It considered that this option had little local support and was concerned about the costs of change. Northamptonshire's Rural Voice raised concerns about the impact of change on the rural areas of the county and favoured no change.

9.18 The East Midlands Arts Board (EMAB) considered that there were strong opportunities and threats presented by a unitary Northampton. While it recognised that a new Northampton unitary authority might be well placed to exploit the importance of cities in economic, social and cultural development across Europe, EMAB remained concerned about the effectiveness of the continuing county. The Royal Commission on the Historical Monuments of England considered that the Commission's "...proposals will also inevitably place further pressure on the existing conservation service..." in relation to sites and monuments records.

Education Groups

9.19 The Commission received over 90 submissions from the education sector, of which the overwhelming majority favoured the retention of the present structure. The Northamptonshire Branch of the National Association of Schoolmasters and Union of Women Teachers expressed a number of concerns over change, including its impact on the cost and viability of services, particularly in relation to the youth service, sports development and Special Educational Needs. It fully endorsed the concept of no change. Similarly, the Association of Northamptonshire School Governing Bodies argued in favour of no change, as did the county branch of the Association of Teachers and Lecturers.

Health Interests

9.20 The Northamptonshire Family Health Services Authority and Northamptonshire Health Authority believed that "...the balance of advantage lies in retaining the present local government arrangements in Northamptonshire". They also stated that: "Having carefully examined the submission of the [Northampton] Borough Council and the Commission's recommendations, we believe that Northampton is not sufficiently different in its health and social care needs from the rest of the county as to be able to offer significant benefits to its citizens from unitary status". The Northamptonshire South Community Health Council also supported no change.

9.21 The Northampton General Hospital NHS Trust considered that "...nothing would be gained by establishing a new Northampton unitary council". It was specifically concerned about the likely effectiveness of inter-agency working under a new structure, which was particularly important in relation to community care and education.

Law, Order and Emergency Services

9.22 The Northamptonshire Police Authority, whilst recognising that there "...may be some short term difficulties to overcome...", was confident that present levels of good relationships and goodwill would carry through to succeeding councils, and maintained a neutral position on the question of change. The Northamptonshire County Fire Officer was convinced that "...things really should be left structurally as they are" arguing that the creation of a unitary Northampton might hamper the efforts of his service to maintain the necessary strategic overview of the fire defence needs of the county as a whole. The Northamptonshire Probation Committee and Northamptonshire Magistrates' Courts Committee were also opposed to the creation of a unitary Northampton.

Local Groups

9.23 A number of local organisations within the voluntary sector in particular made valuable contributions to the debate. The Northampton Citizens' Advice Bureau saw advantages in the creation of a unitary Northampton but was concerned to ensure that whichever structure emerged the partnership arrangements which existed between the Bureau and local authorities would be retained. Some local organisations based in the Northampton area, such as the Old Northamptonians Association, the Pakistan Welfare Association and the Polish Roman Catholic Association, did express support for the creation of a unitary Northampton, while Northampton Women's Aid expressed opposition to change.

Parliamentary Interests

9.24 Five of the six Northamptonshire Members of Parliament made their views known to the Commission. Mr William Powell, MP for Corby, Mr Tony Marlow, MP for Northampton North, and Mr Michael Morris, MP for Northampton South, each expressed support for a unitary Northampton. Mr Tim Boswell, MP for Daventry, said that he could accept the recommendation if a real effort were made to secure co-operation among the local authorities. Sir Peter Fry, MP for Wellingborough, expressed opposition to the draft recommendations, feeling that a Northampton unitary authority could only be a disadvantage to his constituents and all residents outside the Borough of Northampton.

9.25 The Earl Spencer expressed support for a unitary Northampton, believing that only a unitary authority would be able to grasp the economic opportunities which Northampton's geographic position brought.

Parish And Town Councils

9.26 Around 100 of the 267 parish and town councils in Northamptonshire made their views known at Stage Three. Of these, over 95 per cent expressed support for no change. The Commission also heard directly from five of the seven parish councils within Northampton, all of which expressed opposition to the creation of a unitary authority. The prevalent view was that the proposed change would involve costs without any attendant benefit accruing to local councils and would have a detrimental effect on key services. The submissions from the Northamptonshire Association of Local Councils and the Mid Northamptonshire Parishes Group also supported no change.

NOP Tabulations of Written Representations

1 The following tabulations summarise the views expressed by members of the public and other interested parties during the consultation on the Local Government Commission's draft recommendations for Northampton.

2 The tabulations include only letters sent directly to NOP at its Chelmsford offices and to the Commission's offices in London. Where more than one person's view has been expressed in a letter, the comments from each individual have been recorded separately. Staff from the Commission and NOP have worked closely in ensuring that care has been taken in the interpretation of comments, and that a consistent approach has been adopted.

3 While many people expressed support for one or other of the draft options presented by the Commission, other responses were coded by NOP after further discussion. The pattern of views expressed has been carefully examined, and where a number of respondents supported an option not included in those put forward by the Commission, those views have been separately coded and reported by NOP.

4 The Commission has advertised through the local media, encouraging people to make their views known. All responses received up to two days after the end of the Stage Three consultation period have been included. Returns from campaigns organised by local authorities or other groups (for example, standardised postcards and letters, questionnaires and petitions) have not been included in the tabulations. These, and submissions written and dated before the commencement of the consultation process, have been considered separately by the Commission.

The following definitions have been applied by NOP in compiling the tabulations:

(i) Type of Respondent

Individuals:	includes individual members of the public, local councillors and Members of the Westminster and European Parliaments.
Businesses and Business Groups:	includes organisations which represent businesses, such as local Chambers of Commerce.
County, Regional and National Interests:	any organisation which covers an area which is the size of a county or larger is included here, for example, a county-wide voluntary organisation or a regional association. This classification includes most of the statutory consultees.
Education (and Church) Groups:	this group includes schools, religious organisations and teaching unions.
Local Groups:	this includes organisations smaller than a county area, for example, a district-level voluntary sector body. The group could be voluntary, sporting, political or cultural but does not include organisations from the education or religious sectors (included above). It also includes constituency parties and political groups on local authorities.
Parish and Town Councils:	this also includes district-level associations of town and parish councils. County level associations are classified as County, Regional and National interests.

(ii) Structural Options (Reports A and D)

No change in own district:	this code is used where there is more than one review district in the county. It indicates where respondents from a review district have expressed support for no change for that district and have not made reference to the other review district(s) in that county.
District/county-level authorities:	represents support for either a district or county-level authority although it is not clear whether this is for a unitary or a two-tier structure.
Opposition to structural preferences:	represents responses where a negative, but unspecified, structural preference has been expressed.
Rejects:	rejects are those responses with unclear comments/interpretation.

(iii) Other

Other issues (Report B):	these illustrate preferences in relation to boundary and electoral changes and (where applicable) the restoration of historic counties.
Parishing issues (Report C):	these illustrate preferences in relation to parishing issues, for example, the creation of new parishes or the enhancement of the role of parish and town councils.
Services (Report E):	these illustrate concerns expressed about the impact of proposed changes on particular service areas where the respondent has not additionally expressed a positive structural preference.

NOP Analysis of Responses to Local Government Commission Draft Recommendations - NORTHAMPTONSHIRE

Report A: Opinions on the structural options, by authority of respondent
Base: all

	Review district	Other districts in county								
	Northampton	Corby	Daventry	East Northants	Kettering	South Northants	Welling-borough	Rest of county total	County total	Out of county total
No change	388 *65%*	50 *94%*	121 *85%*	108 *95%*	81 *95%*	239 *93%*	274 *96%*	873 *93%*	1261 *82%*	55 *63%*
Unitary Northampton	190 *32%*	1 *2%*	18 *13%*	5 *4%*	3 *4%*	12 *5%*	3 *1%*	42 *4%*	232 *15%*	16 *18%*
County-level authority (either two-tier or unitary)	- -	1 *2%*	- -	- -	- -	- -	- -	1 *	1 *	- -
District-level authority (either two-tier or unitary)	- -	- -	- -	- -	- -	1 *	5 *2%*	6 *1%*	6 *	- -
Pre-1974 structure	- -	- -	- -	- -	- -	- -	- -	- -	- -	2 *2%*
Opposition to structural options (where no positive preference is stated)	- -	- -	- -	- -	- -	2 *1%*	- -	2 *	2 *	1 *1%*
Other specified	1 *	- -	- -	- -	- -	1 *	-	1 *	2 *	- -
Reject	9 *2%*	- -	2 *1%*	1 *1%*	1 *1%*	- -	2 *1%*	6 *1%*	15 *1%*	1 *1%*
No preference expressed/option defined	5 *1%*	1 *2%*	2 *1%*	- -	- -	1 *	2 *1%*	6 *1%*	11 *1%*	12 *14%*
BASE TOTAL	593	53	143	114	85	256	286	937	1530	87

* *Less than ½%*

Northampton

NOP Analysis of Responses to Local Government Commission Draft Recommendations - NORTHAMPTONSHIRE

Report B: Opinions on other issues, by authority of respondent
Base: all

	Review district	Other districts in county								
	Northampton	Corby	Daventry	East Northants	Kettering	South Northants	Welling-borough	Rest of county total	County total	Out of county total
BASE TOTAL	593	53	143	114	85	256	286	937	1530	87

The figures in the table above do not sum to the base total/100% because undefined fields are not included, except as part of the base total.

NOP Analysis of Responses to Local Government Commission Draft Recommendations - NORTHAMPTONSHIRE

Report C: Opinions on parishing issues, by authority of respondent
Base: all

	Review district	Other districts in county								
	Northampton	Corby	Daventry	East Northants	Kettering	South Northants	Welling-borough	Rest of county total	County total	Out of county total
Enhanced parish powers	-	-	-	-	-	-	-	-	-	1
	-	-	-	-	-	-	-	-	-	1%
Abolish all parish/town councils	-	-	-	-	-	1	-	1	1	-
	-	-	-	-	-	*	-	*	*	-
BASE TOTAL	593	53	143	114	85	256	286	937	1530	87

The figures in the table above do not sum to the base total/100% because undefined fields are not included, except as part of the base total.

* *Less than ½%*

NOP Analysis of Responses to Local Government Commission Draft Recommendations - NORTHAMPTONSHIRE

Report D1: Opinions on the structural options, by respondent type (all respondents)
Base: all

	Respondent Type					
	Indiv-iduals	Business groups	County, regional & national interests	Education (& church) groups	Local groups	Parish and town councils
No change	948	103	38	86	45	96
	81%	*71%*	*83%*	*93%*	*68%*	*97%*
Unitary Northampton	185	38	2	4	16	3
	16%	*26%*	*4%*	*4%*	*24%*	*3%*
County-level authority (either two-tier or unitary)	1	-	-	-	-	-
	*	-	-	-	-	-
District-level authority (either two-tier or unitary)	5	-	-	-	1	-
	*	-	-	-	*2%*	-
Pre-1974 structure	2	-	-	-	-	-
	*	-	-	-	-	-
Opposition to structural options (where no positive preference is stated)	2	-	1	-	-	-
	*	-	*2%*	-	-	-
Other specified	-	2	-	-	-	-
	-	*1%*	-	-	-	-
Reject	14	-	1	-	1	-
	1%	-	*2%*	-	*2%*	-
No preference expressed/option defined	11	3	4	2	3	-
	1%	*2%*	*9%*	*2%*	*5%*	-
BASE TOTAL	1168	146	46	92	66	99

* *Less than ½%*

NOP Analysis of Responses to Local Government Commission Draft Recommendations - NORTHAMPTONSHIRE

Report D2: Opinions on the structural options, by respondent type
Base : respondents in Northampton only

	Respondent Type					
	Indiv-iduals	Business groups	County, regional & national interests	Education (& church) groups	Local groups	Parish and town councils
No change	307	19	19	24	14	5
	66%	*40%*	*90%*	*92%*	*50%*	*100%*
Unitary Northampton	148	27	1	1	13	-
	32%	*57%*	*5%*	*4%*	*46%*	-
District-level authority (either two-tier or unitary)	-	-	-	-	-	-
	-	-	-	-	-	-
Pre-1974 structure	-	-	-	-	-	-
	-	-	-	-	-	-
Opposition to structural options (where no positive preference is stated)	-	-	-	-	-	-
	-	-	-	-	-	-
Other specified	-	1	-	-	-	-
	-	*2%*	-	-	-	-
Reject	8	-	1	-	-	-
	2%	-	*5%*	-	-	-
No preference expressed/option defined	3	-	-	1	1	-
	1%	-	-	*4%*	*4%*	-
BASE TOTAL	466	47	21	26	28	5

NOP Analysis of Responses to Local Government Commission Draft Recommendations - NORTHAMPTONSHIRE

Report D3: Opinions on the structural options, by respondent type
Base : respondents in rest of county only

	Respondent Type					
	Indiv-iduals	Business groups	County, regional & national interests	Education (& church) groups	Local groups	Parish and town councils
No change	626 *92%*	61 *94%*	9 *100%*	60 *94%*	28 *97%*	89 *97%*
Unitary Northampton	33 *5%*	3 *5%*	- -	3 *5%*	- -	3 *3%*
County-level authority (either two-tier or unitary)	1 *	- -	- -	- -	- -	- -
District-level authority (either two-tier or unitary)	5 *1%*	- -	- -	- -	1 *3%*	- -
Pre-1974 structure	- -	- -	- -	- -	- -	- -
Opposition to structural options (where no positive preference is stated)	2 *	- -	- -	- -	- -	- -
Other specified	- -	1 *2%*	- -	- -	- -	- -
Reject	6 *1%*	- -	- -	- -	- -	- -
No preference expressed/option defined	5 *1%*	- -	- -	1 *2%*	- -	- -
BASE TOTAL	678	65	9	64	29	92

* *Less than ½%*

NOP Analysis of Responses to Local Government Commission Draft Recommendations - NORTHAMPTONSHIRE

Report E: Views on services, by authority of respondent
Base: all

	Review district	Other districts in county								
	Northampton	Corby	Daventry	East Northants	Kettering	South Northants	Wellingborough	Rest of county total	County total	Out of county total
Archives	-	-	-	-	-	1	-	1	1	1
	-	-	-	-	-	*	-	*	*	*1%*
Education	17	3	4	1	1	11	3	23	40	1
	3%	*6%*	*3%*	*1%*	*1%*	*4%*	*1%*	*2%*	*3%*	*1%*
Libraries	2	-	-	-	-	-	1	1	3	1
	*	-	-	-	-	-	*	*	*	*1%*
Trading standards	-	-	-	-	-	-	-	-	-	1
	-	-	-	-	-	-	-	-	-	*1%*
Other specified services (or multiples of)	3	-	-	-	2	2	1	5	8	1
	1%	-	-	-	*2%*	*1%*	*	*1%*	*1%*	*1%*
BASE TOTAL	593	53	143	114	85	256	286	937	1530	87

The figures in the table above do not sum to the base total/100% because undefined fields are not included, except as part of the base total.

* *Less than ½%*

Northampton

NOP Analysis of Responses to Local Government Commission Draft Recommendations - NORTHAMPTONSHIRE

Report F: Views on services, by respondent type
Base: all

	Respondent Type					
	Indiv-iduals	Business groups	County, regional & national interests	Education (& church) groups	Local groups	Parish and town councils
Archives	1	-	1	-	-	-
	*	-	*2%*	-	-	-
Education	31	-	-	9	-	1
	3%	-	-	*10%*	-	*1%*
Libraries	3	-	-	-	1	-
	*	-	-	-	*2%*	-
Trading standards	-	1	-	-	-	-
	-	*1%*	-	-	-	-
Other specified services (or multiples of)	5	-	1	-	1	2
	*	-	*2%*	-	*2%*	*2%*
BASE TOTAL	1168	146	46	92	66	99

The figures in the table above do not sum to the base total/100% because undefined fields are not included, except as part of the base total.

* Less than ½%

NOP Analysis of Responses to Local Government Commission Draft Recommendations - NORTHAMPTONSHIRE

Report G: Type of respondent, by authority of respondent
Base: all

	Review district	Other districts in county								
	Northampton	Corby	Daventry	East Northants	Kettering	South Northants	Welling-borough	Rest of county total	County total	Out of county total
Individuals	466 *79%*	38 *72%*	93 *65%*	79 *69%*	50 *59%*	174 *68%*	244 *85%*	678 *72%*	1144 *75%*	24 *28%*
Business groups	47 *8%*	5 *9%*	10 *7%*	7 *6%*	13 *15%*	12 *5%*	18 *6%*	65 *7%*	112 *7%*	34 *39%*
County, regional and national interests	21 *4%*	- -	3 *2%*	1 *1%*	3 *4%*	1 *	1 *	9 *1%*	30 *2%*	16 *18%*
Education (and church) groups	26 *4%*	9 *17%*	11 *8%*	8 *7%*	8 *9%*	19 *7%*	9 *3%*	64 *7%*	90 *6%*	2 *2%*
Local Groups	28 *5%*	- -	5 *3%*	5 *4%*	4 *5%*	8 *3%*	7 *2%*	29 *3%*	57 *4%*	9 *10%*
Parish and town councils	5 *1%*	1 *2%*	21 *15%*	14 *12%*	7 *8%*	42 *16%*	7 *2%*	92 *10%*	97 *6%*	2 *2%*
BASE TOTAL	593	53	143	114	85	256	286	937	1530	87

* *Less than ½%*

Northampton

MORI Research Study for the Local Government Commission

Introduction

Background

1 This summary report highlights the key findings from a survey of public opinion conducted in the Borough of Northampton and across the County of Northamptonshire on behalf of the Local Government Commission for England. A copy of each of the marked-up questionnaires is appended. The computer tabulations are contained in a separate volume, which is available from MORI (32 Old Queen Street, London SW1H 9HP. Telephone 0171-222 0232. Price £15)

2 The survey was designed in close consultation with the Commission, following extensive qualitative research and pilot testing. All sampling, interviewing and analysis have been carried out independently by MORI, within the guidelines of the profession laid out by the Market Research Society.

3 In Northampton, all Census Enumeration Districts (EDs) were sorted by ward, and stratified according to social class. EDs were then sampled (32 in total) in proportion to the population size of each, and quotas set for sex, age and work status. A total of 320 interviews with adults aged 18+, conducted face-to-face and in-home, were carried out between 7 and 29 October 1995. Data were weighted to match the population profile in the Borough.

4 In the remaining districts of Northamptonshire, all EDs were sorted by ward, and again were stratified according to social class. A total of 32 EDs across the whole area (that is, Northamptonshire excluding Northampton) were sampled, with quotas set by sex, age and work status. Face-to-face interviews, conducted in-home, were carried out with 323 adults aged 18+ between 7 and 29 October 1995. Data were weighted to match the population profile of the County excluding Northampton.

Publication of the Results

5 As with all our studies, these findings are subject to our Standard Terms and Conditions of Contract. Any press release or publication of the findings of this survey require the advance approval of MORI. Such approval will only be refused on the grounds of inaccuracy or misinterpretation.

Objectives

6 This survey took place during Stage Three, the consultation period on the Commission's draft recommendations. It measures public preferences for the organisation of local government in the area currently comprising the Borough of Northampton, as well as exploring strength of feeling, levels of knowledge about the review, involvement in, and broader perceptions of, local government in the area.

Statistical Reliability of the Data

7 Because we have interviewed a sample of residents, rather than the whole population, the results are subject to statistical tolerance limits, or "margins of error". These are expressed as our confidence that the true figure for the whole population falls within a given range. By convention this is expressed as a percentage, so our 95% confidence level means that in 95 times out of 100 the true figure would lie within this range.

8 The table below shows ranges of the 95% confidence level for a range of sample sizes. For each sample size, the table shows the tolerance limits for sample results close to 10%, 30% and 50%. Take, for example, the results of a survey of 300 residents showing that 50% are aware of the review. In 95 times out of 100 the true figure would lie between 44% and 56% (ie 50% ±6%).

Sample size	Sampling tolerances applicable to results at or near these percentages (based on 95% confidence level)		
	10/90% ±%	30/70% ±%	50% ±%
300	3	5	6
200	4	6	7
150	5	7	8
100	6	9	10
50	8	13	14

9 Clearly, 10% or 30% of the sample being aware of the review equate to 90% or 70% not being aware of it. So this table shows the ranges of 95% confidence for responses close to 10%, 30%, 50%, 70% and 90% of our sample. The figures for responses between can be obtained by extrapolation.

10 The true figure would only be known if all the residents of the area had been interviewed. It can be seen in the table, however, that large increases in the sample size do not greatly reduce the sampling tolerance. In addition, the true figure is more likely to lie at the midpoint of the range, rather than at either extreme.

11 When comparing results from separate groups within a sample we need to be sure that the differences are statistically significant. This would be important in comparing views expressed by different parts of a county. The table below shows how the statistical significance of the difference is determined by the size of the groups and the percentage result from the sample.

12 Assuming a 95% confidence level, the table shows the size of the differences required if different results are to be regarded as statistically significant. It can be seen that if 50% of a group of 300 were aware of the review, the result from another group of 300 would not become statistically significant until it became less than 42% or more than 58%.

Sample sizes	Differences required for significance at or near these percentage levels		
	10/90% ±	30/70% ±	50% ±
300 and 300	5	7	8
300 and 200	5	8	9
300 and 100	7	10	11
200 and 100	7	11	12
100 and 100	8	13	14

Survey Findings

Knowledge and Awareness

13 Residents within the Borough of Northampton say that they know rather less about what their local council does than do those living elsewhere in the County, but they also express less interest in being informed. In Northamptonshire outside the Borough, two thirds like to know what their council is doing, but want no greater involvement, in Northampton this falls to just half. Around one in six in both areas say they want a higher level of involvement.

14 While around a third in the Borough (31%) and the County (38%) say they know at least a fair amount about what their council does, at least six in ten admit to not knowing very much.

15 This is reflected in the number of residents who incorrectly ascribe services between the two tiers of local government. Thus, although between four and five in ten recognise libraries as a county council service, as many as two to three in ten allocate responsibility to their district/borough council. And although between five and six in ten realise that refuse collection is a district/borough service, around one in seven thinks it is a county council service. Residents of Northampton are less likely to be correct in the way that they allocate services across the two tiers than are those living in the rest of the County.

16 Awareness of the review itself is fairly low, and there is no real difference between Northampton (where 59% have heard of it) and the rest of Northamptonshire (where 60% have heard of it). Similarly, the proportions who say they know a fair amount or more are the same in Northampton and in the rest of the County (12%).

Sources of Information

17 Leaflets from the County Council form a significant source of information to those who have heard of the review. In Northampton, 46% say these are recent sources, and in the rest of the County, 57% say the same. On the other hand, local newspapers are also a significant source, mentioned by 53% in Northampton and 41% in the rest of the County.

18 By comparison, 35% in Northampton mention a Borough Council source, compared with 19% in the rest of Northamptonshire. Very few recognise receiving information directly from the Local Government Commission itself.

19 Although most of those aware of the review recognise one or more recent sources of information, few (around one in five) say that this has influenced their opinion.

20 Furthermore, in spite of a relatively low level of knowledge and engagement with their local authority, many people in Northampton say that the outcome of the review in the Borough is either very important to them (22%) or fairly important (36%). Interestingly, people in the rest of Northamptonshire perceive a similar level of importance (23% very important and 37% fairly important).

The Preferred Option

21 More people in Northampton would prefer no change (44%) to a unitary council (28%), and in the rest of Northamptonshire the verdict is more clear-cut - 65% opt for no change and just 15% for a unitary Northampton. Out of the whole sample, 28% in Northampton and 19% in the rest of the County had no views or were indifferent.

22 There is no difference in the strength of feeling expressed between Northampton and the rest of the County. In Northampton, 65% of those expressing a preference say they feel strongly (16% very strongly), while across the rest of Northamptonshire, 69% feel strongly (19% very strongly). There is little difference in the strength of feeling expressed in Northampton irrespective of which option they prefer. However, in the rest of the County, it is those who prefer no change who feel most strongly about it (72% feel strongly compared with 53%).

Factors in Expressing a Preference

23 In questions 13 to 23, residents were asked to say to what extent they agreed or disagreed with a range of statements which related to a change to unitary local government. The statements were designed to cover the main issues raised by residents during the qualitative phase of research, and others that formed a part of the Commission's brief to take into consideration in making its recommendations.

24 The following charts summarise the results from these questions, with the full question wording presented in the questionnaires in the appendices. Values have been ascribed to the five

attitudinal positions that people were offered (+2 for strongly agree, +1 for tend to agree, 0 for neither agree nor disagree, -1 for tend to disagree, and -2 for strongly disagree) and mean scores calculated across all respondents expressing a view. This has the combined benefit of distilling the range of opinion into one summary figure, while incorporating the varying intensity of feeling by ascribing values. Bars to the right indicate that the mean score value is positive, and thus that there is a balance of agreement with the statement. Bars to the left, conversely, indicate a balance of disagreement.

25 The first chart, therefore, shows how the views of people living in the Borough of Northampton differ from those across the rest of Northamptonshire. In doing so, it illustrates the attitudes or perceptions that are, in relative terms, shared by both groups of residents (where the bars project in the same direction), and those where views differ markedly. Thus there is broad agreement on several items, but apart from the issue of a unitary authority making service responsibility more transparent, the other points of agreement are on the negative outcomes of changing to a unitary authority. The issues over which people diverge in their opinions are on whether a unitary Northampton would be more in touch with local people's needs, more efficient and better reflect the community. People in Northampton are more likely to agree that they would like more information before making up their minds. People in the County outside Northampton are more likely to feel they will be affected by a shift to a unitary Northampton than are those who live within the Borough itself.

26 The subsequent chart takes the results from just Northampton (and then from residents in the rest of Northamptonshire), and illustrates the difference in views between those within Northampton whose preference is for unitary status, and those who prefer no change. The chart therefore illustrates those attitudinal statements that most, or least, differentiate the residents of the Borough expressing the two opposing preferences. The perceived impact on efficiency is clearly a key determinant of opinion (in both Northampton and the rest of Northamptonshire), as are the issues of being in touch with local people, disruption and impact on services.

Attitudes to Change
(All respondents)

Q To what extent do you agree or disagree that...?
(Figures represent 'mean scores' with *strong agreement* given a value of +2 through to *strong disagreement* given -2)

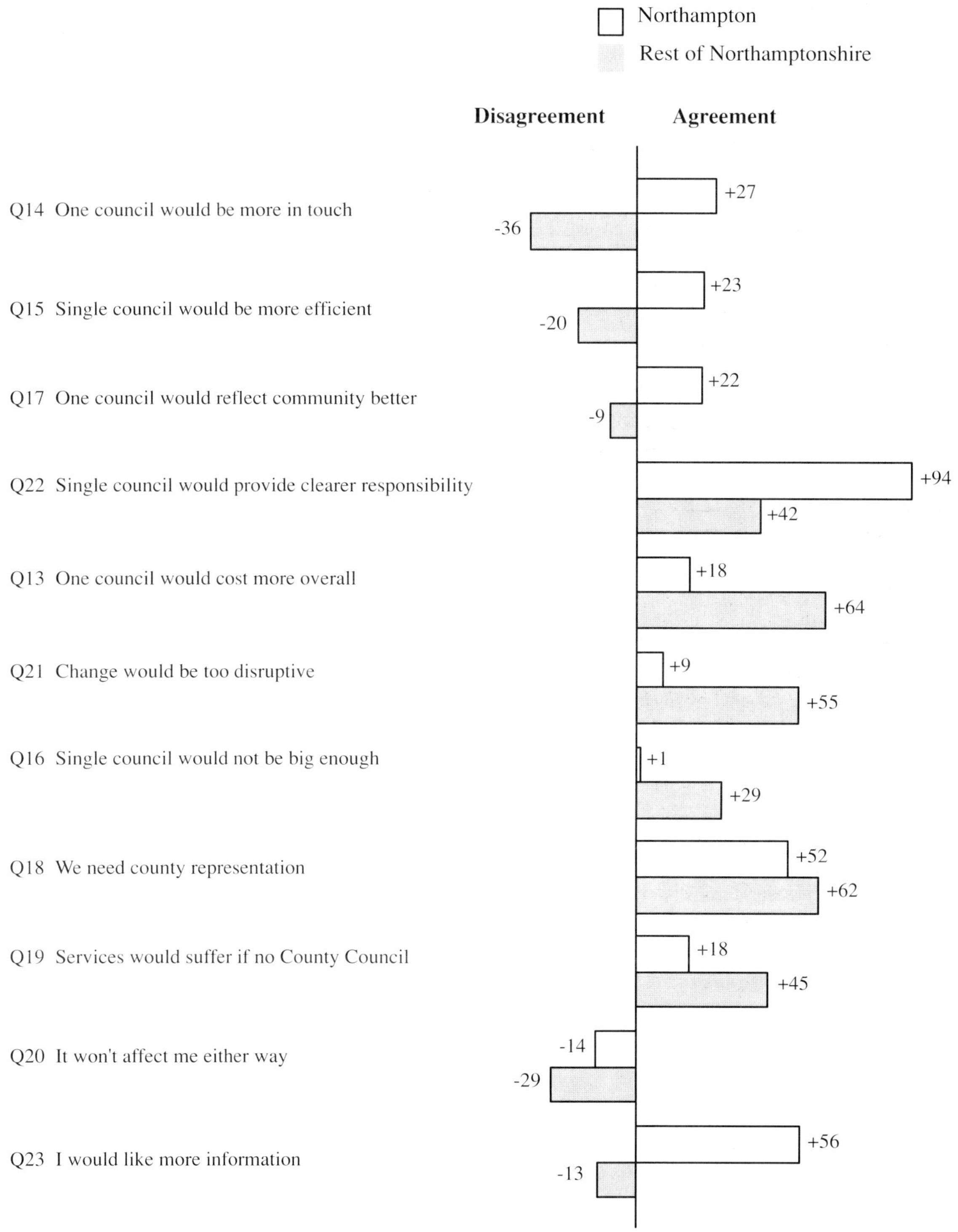

Attitudes to Change
(Respondents in Northampton)

Q To what extent do you agree or disagree that...?
(Figures represent 'mean scores' with *strong agreement* given a value of +2 through to *strong disagreement* given -2)

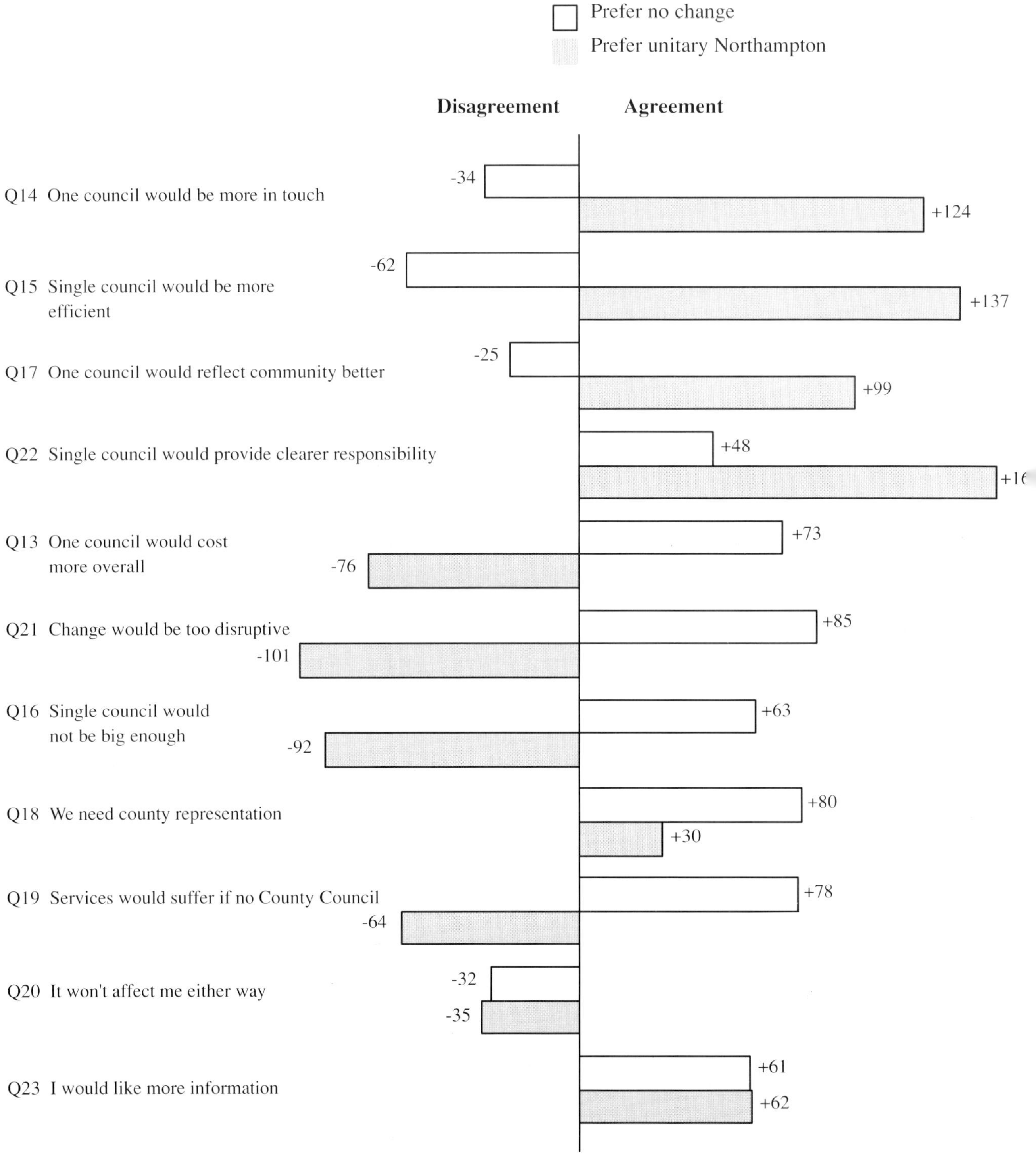

Attitudes to Change
(Respondents in the rest of Northamptonshire)

Q To what extent do you agree or disagree that...?
(Figures represent 'mean scores' with *strong agreement* given a value of +2 through to *strong disagreement* given -2)

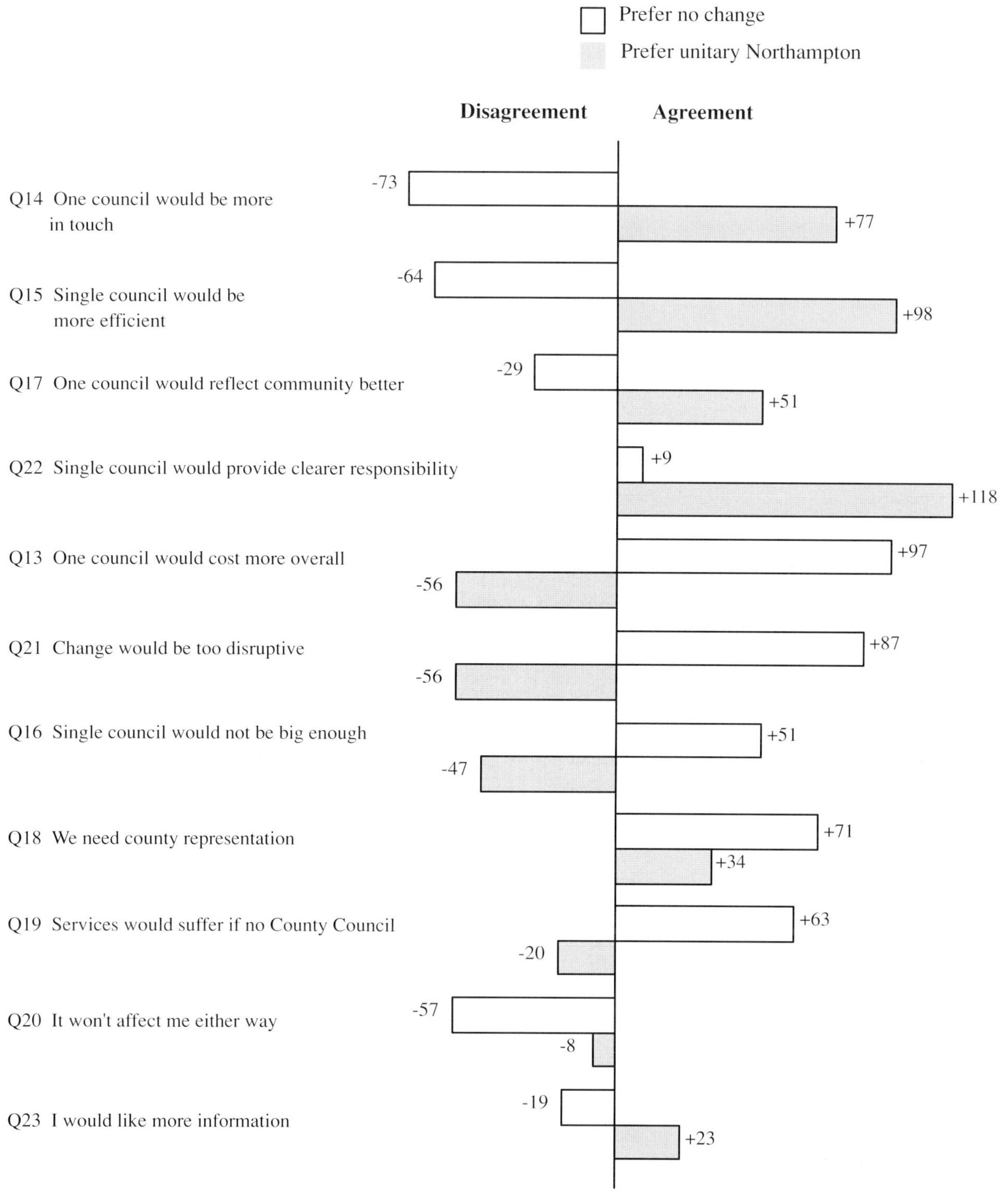

Northampton

MORI/9101/09
(1-6)

NORTHAMPTONSHIRE
REVIEW - REST OF COUNTY

Serial No . . . .
OUO (7-10)

TOPLINE RESULTS
N = 323
7-28 October 1995
Main sample data only
Base: All, unless stated

Gender %

	%
Male	49
Female	51

Age

	%
18-24	13
25-34	19
35-44	20
45-54	16
55-64	12
65-74	12
75+	8

WRITE IN AGE [|]

Work Status

	%
Full-time (30 hrs/wk+)	51
Part-time (8-29 hrs/wk)	8
Not working (under 8 hrs)	1
Looking after home/children	8
Retired	22
Registered unemployed	7
Unemployed but not registered	1
Student	2
Other	*

Occupation of Chief Income Earner (CIE)
Position/rank/grade

....

Industry/type of company

....

Qualifications/degrees/apprenticeship

....

No of Staff Responsible for

....

PROBE FOR PENSION

	%
AB	13
C1	24
C2	30
D	17
E	15

* Less than $^1/_2$%

Number in Household
Adults aged 18+ (inc. respondent)

1	2	3	4	5+	
17	58	17	7	1	%

Children (17 or under)

0	1	2	3	4+	
57	16	17	8	2	%

QA **Are you or other members of your household employed by a council?** IF YES: **Is this a Borough/District Council or a County Council?**
CODE FOR BOTH RESPONDENT AND OTHER HOUSEHOLD MEMBERS

	Respondent %	Other %
Yes:		
Borough/District	2	2
County	3	4
Don't know which	0	0
No	94	90
Don't know	*	4

Tenure

	%
Owned outright	22
Buying on mortgage	49
Rented from Council	20
Rented from Housing Association	1
Rented from private landlord	5
Other	2

QB **Is this your main permanent home, or is it a second or holiday home?**

	%
Main/permanent	100
Second/holiday	*

Car in Household
CIRCLE NUMBER

0	1	2	3+	
17	44	30	9	%

THIS FORM IS THE PROPERTY OF MARKET & OPINION RESEARCH INTERNATIONAL (MORI)
32 OLD QUEEN STREET, LONDON, SW1H 9HP

INTERVIEWER DECLARATION: I confirm that I have conducted this interview face-to-face with the above named person and that I have asked all the relevant questions fully and recorded the answers in conformance with the survey specification and the MRS Code of Conduct.

Interviewer Name .... Signature ....

Interviewer Number				/	

	Month			Date	
DATE OF INTERVIEW					
	(29)	(30)		(30)	(32)

NB INTERVIEWER: ALL SHOWCARDS HAVE BEEN REVERSED. PLEASE BE CAREFUL TO CODE THE CORRECT RESPONSE.

Good morning/afternoon/evening. I'm from MORI, the market research and polling organisation. We are doing a survey about local issues, and I would like to ask you a few questions.

ASK ALL

Q1 **Firstly, how long have you lived in this area?** (WITHIN FIVE MILES)

	%
Less than 1 year	4
1-2 years	2
3-5 years	8
6-10 years	13
11-20 years	23
Over 20 years/all my life	50
Don't know/can't remember	0

Q2 SHOWCARD A (R) **From this card, how much would you say you know about local councils and the services they provide?**

	%
A great deal	2
A fair amount	36
Not very much	50
Nothing at all	12
Don't know	*

Q3 SHOWCARD B (R) **Which of the statements on this card comes closest to your own view of the Councils in this area?**

		%
A)	I'm not interested in what the Council does, or whether they do their job	4
B)	I'm not interested in what the Council does, as long as they do their job	15
C)	I like to know what the Council is doing, but I'm happy to let them get on with their job	64
D)	I would like to have more of a say in what the Council does and the services it provides	13
E)	I already work for, or am involved with the Council and the services it provides	4
	Don't know	*

Q4 **From what you know, how many councils provide the main services in this neighbourhood?** (INTERVIEWER - NOT INCLUDING PARISH COUNCILS)

	%
One	25
Two	44
Three+	3
Don't know	28

In fact there are two main councils that provide, or are responsible for most services in this area: . . .district/borough/city and Northamptonshire County Council.

ROTATE ORDER OF Q5/6

☐ Q5 SHOWCARD C (R) **From this list, what services do you think are the responsibility of... district/borough council? Just read out the letter(s) that apply**

☐ Q6 SHOWCARD C AGAIN (R) **And which services on this list do you think are the responsibility of Northamptonshire County Council? Again, just read out the letters that apply.**

Q7 SHOWCARD D (R) **Which, if any, of these services do you or members of your family use?** INCLUDE ONLY LOCAL USE

		Q5 "Borough" %	Q6 County %	Q7 Use %
A	Bus Services	32	28	38
B	Car Parks	52	17	69
C	Council Housing	52	20	16
D	Council Tax Benefit/Housing benefit	46	24	19
E	Fire service	16	58	24
F	Food safety	23	32	14
G	Household waste sites/dumps	48	20	59
H	Libraries	26	50	63
I	Parks, playgrounds and open spaces	51	20	56
J	Planning service	47	23	13
K	Public conveniences	51	14	36
L	Recycling/bottle banks	52	15	47
M	Refuse collection	61	16	80
N	Road maintenance	28	47	34
O	Schools/education	16	59	40
P	Social services	18	51	15
Q	Street sweeping	58	15	50
R	Swimming pools/sports facilities	49	19	54
	Other	1	2	2
	None of these	1	1	1
	Don't know	19	20	2

Q8 SHOWCARD E (R) **As you may know, there is currently a review being undertaken by the Local Government Commission on the future local government structure in the county. How much, if anything, would you say you know about this?**

	%
A great deal	1
A fair amount	11
Just a little	30
Heard of but know nothing about	17
Never heard of	40

PREFERENCES

HAND OVER MAP SHOWING AREAS UNDER REVIEW AND "CURRENT SERVICES" CARD
The Local Government Commission is considering options for the future structure of local government in Northampton. Could you please read through this card, (SHOW OPTIONS CARD) **which outlines the options.**

Q9 **Please tell me which of the options, if either, you would prefer for Northampton?**
SINGLE CODE ONLY

For Northampton

	%
Option A (Single all purpose council)	15
Option B (Stay the same/status quo)	65
Some other option	1
Neither of these	0
Either of these/don't mind	4
Don't care	3
Don't know	12

ASK IF "OTHER" NAMED AT Q9 (CODE 3)
Q10 **What other option is that?**
PROBE FULLY - DO NOT PROMPT.

....

....

....

....

ASK ALL PREFERRING AN OPTION (1, 2 OR 3 AT Q9). OTHERS GO TO Q13
Q11 SHOWCARD F (R) **You say that the option you would prefer is . . . . .** (INSERT OPTION PREFERRED). **How strongly would you say you feel about this?**

	%
Very strongly	19
Fairly strongly	50
Not very strongly	19
Not at all strongly	2
Don't know	10

Q12 **What do you think would be the main advantages of . . .**(OPTION PREFERRED)
PROBE FULLY FOR DETAILS

....

....

....

....

....

Nothing..
Don't know/can't think of anything..................................

ATTITUDES TO PROPOSALS

SHOWCARD G (R) **Imagine that there was one council in Northampton providing all services. I am going to read out some statements that people have made about this proposal. To what extent do you agree or disagree that . . . .?** READ OUT, ROTATE ORDER OF ASKING Q13-22. TICK START

	READ OUT:	Strongly agree %	Tend to agree %	Neither/ Nor %	Tend to disagree %	Strongly disagree %	Don't know
Q13	**It would cost more overall**	26	30	7	25	1	11
Q14	**It would be more in touch with local people's needs**	3	21	8	40	8	19
Q15	**The single Council would be more efficient than the current system of two Councils**	3	26	10	35	7	19
Q16	**The single council would not be big enough to manage services such as Education and Social Services effectively**	7	35	11	23	1	22
Q17	**It would better reflect the sense of community in Northampton**	1	28	21	27	5	18
Q18	**We need a County Council to represent us nationally**	11	54	19	12	2	3
Q19	**Services would suffer if the County Council no longer provides services in Northampton**	7	41	11	17	2	22
Q20	**It won't affect me whether there is a single Council in Northampton or not**	7	25	13	39	14	3
Q21	**The change to a single Council for Northampton would be too disruptive**	7	50	14	16	1	13
Q22	**With a single Council it would be clearer who is responsible for local services**	6	46	13	16	3	16
ASK LAST Q23	**I would like to have more information on the proposals before making up my mind**	9	29	6	45	7	5

Q24 **On balance, which would you say is more in touch with local people and issues, ...** (ROTATE ORDER OF "DISTRICT" AND COUNTY) (INSERT NAME OF "DISTRICT COUNCIL)..**district/borough council, or Northamptonshire County Council, or would you say that they are both about the same?**

	%
District/borough council	59
Northamptonshire County Council	3
Both about the same	23
Don't know	16

REFER BACK TO Q8. ASK ALL WHO HAVE HEARD OF REVIEW AT Q8 (IE CODES 1/2/3/4). OTHERS TO Q28

Q25 SHOWCARD H **Earlier in the interview, you said that you had heard of the Review of local government structure. From which, if any, of the sources shown on this card have you recently heard about the Review?** INTERVIEWER NOTE: "RECENTLY" = IN PAST 3 MONTHS

		%
A	Leaflet from County Council delivered to your door	57
B	Leaflet from County Council in library/ offices, etc	3
C	Advertisement from County Council in local newspaper	6
D	Advertisement from County Council on local radio/TV	1
E	Leaflet from Borough Council delivered to your door	9
F	Leaflet from Borough Council in library/ offices, etc	1
G	Borough Council newspaper	5
H	County Council newspaper	2
I	Advertisement from Borough Council in local newspaper	2
J	Advertisement from Borough Council on local radio/TV	2
K	Advertisement by the Commission on local radio	0
L	Local Government Commission advertisement in local newspaper	2
M	Local newspaper	41
N	National newspaper	2
O	TV	16
P	Local radio	14
Q	National radio	2
R	Friends/neighbours/family	10
S	Conversation with Borough Councillor	3
T	Conversation with County Councillor	1
U	Conversation with Borough Council staff	1
V	Conversation with County Council staff	1
W	Parish/community council	7
X	Residents' Association	1
	Other	3
	None of these	1
	Don't know	4

ASK ALL NAMING A SOURCE AT Q25. OTHERS GO TO Q28

Q26 **Would you say that the information you have received has influenced your opinion, or not?**

	%
Yes	17
No	75
Don't know	8

Q27 **What information in particular has influenced your opinion?**

....

....

....

....

ASK ALL

Q28 SHOWCARD I (R) **Assuming you receive the same level of services, how important is it to you, if at all, what the final decision is on the future local government structure in Northampton?**

	%
Very important	23
Fairly important	37
Not very important	24
Not at all important	9
Don't know	7

ACTIVISM

Q29 SHOWCARD J **Which of the things on this list, if any, have you done in the last three years? Just read out the letter(s) that apply.**

		%
A	Voted in Local Council elections	78
B	Spoken or written to a local Councillor	22
C	Responded to the earlier Review of local government	9
D	Been to a meeting of a local committee or organisation (WRITE IN NAME OF ORGANISATION)	9
E	Spoken on a radio phone-in about a local issue	1
F	Written to a local newspaper about a local issue	1
G	Been to a meeting of a local branch of a political party	2
H	Written to your MP about a local issue	7
I	Been to a Council Committee meeting	2
J	Been to a Council meeting	4
K	Attended a public meeting run by the Council	5
	None of these	20
	Don't know/refused	1

Q30 SHOWCARD K **Which, if any, of these apply to you? Just read out the letter(s) that apply.**

		%
	I am a member of a:	
A	Residents' Association	1
B	Community Association	1
C	Tenants' Association	1
D	Neighbourhood Watch	15
E	PTA/school governors	4
	I do unpaid work for:	
F	A school	4
G	Citizens Advice Bureau	0
H	Volunteer Bureau	2
I	Scouts/Guides/Cubs/Brownies	1
J	Church group	6
	Other	2
	None of these	72
	Don't know	3

THANK RESPONDENT. GO TO DEMOGRAPHICS.

Length of interview ☐☐ minutes

MORI/9101/09 (1-6)

NORTHAMPTONSHIRE
REVIEW - NORTHAMPTON

Serial No .... OUO (7-10)

TOPLINE RESULTS
N = 320
7 - 28 October 1995
Main sample data only
Base: All, unless stated

Gender %
- Male 48
- Female 52

Age %
- 18-24 14
- 25-34 22
- 35-44 21
- 45-54 12
- 55-64 13
- 65-74 13
- 75+... 4

WRITE IN AGE [ ][ ]

Work Status %
- Full-time (30 hrs/wk+) 50
- Part-time (8-29 hrs/wk) 12
- Not working (under 8 hrs) 3
- Looking after home/children............ 8
- Retired 22
- Registered unemployed.................. 3
- Unemployed but not registered 1
- Student... 2
- Other 0

Occupation of Chief Income Earner (CIE)
Position/rank/grade

....

Industry/type of company

....

Qualifications/degrees/apprenticeship

....

No of Staff Responsible for

....

PROBE FOR PENSION

	%
AB	11
C1	31
C2	24
D	19
E	16

Number in Household
Adults aged 18+ (inc. respondent)

1	2	3	4	5+	
11	31	24	19	16	%

Children (17 or under)

0	1	2	3	4+	
22	62	12	5	*	%

QA **Are you or other members of your household employed by a council?** IF YES: **Is this a Borough/District Council or a County Council?**
CODE FOR BOTH RESPONDENT AND OTHER HOUSEHOLD MEMBERS

	Respondent %	Other %
Yes:		
Borough/District	2	2
County	7	5
Don't know which	1	1
No	90	82
Don't know	1	10

Tenure %
- Owned outright.. 20
- Buying on mortgage 50
- Rented from Council 23
- Rented from Housing Association 2
- Rented from private landlord 5
- Other 0

QB **Is this your main permanent home, or is it a second or holiday home?**

	%
Main/permanent	99
Second/holiday	1

Car in Household
CIRCLE NUMBER

0	1	2	3+	
17	44	30	9	%

INTERVIEWER DECLARATION: I confirm that I have conducted this interview face-to-face with the above named person and that I have asked all the relevant questions fully and recorded the answers in conformance with the survey specification and the MRS Code of Conduct.

Interviewer Name .... Signature ....

Interviewer Number					/	

	Month			Date	
DATE OF INTERVIEW					
	(29)	(30)		(30)	(32)

NB INTERVIEWER: ALL SHOWCARDS HAVE BEEN REVERSED. PLEASE BE CAREFUL TO CODE THE CORRECT RESPONSE.

Good morning/afternoon/evening. I'm from MORI, the market research and polling organisation. We are doing a survey about local issues, and I would like to ask you a few questions.

ASK ALL

Q1 **Firstly, how long have you lived in this area?** (WITHIN FIVE MILES)

	%
Less than 1 year	5
1-2 years	5
3-5 years	11
6-10 years	23
11-20 years	15
Over 20 years/all my life	41
Don't know/can't remember	0

Q2 SHOWCARD A (R) **From this card, how much would you say you know about local councils and the services they provide?**

	%
A great deal	4
A fair amount	27
Not very much	55
Nothing at all	14
Don't know	1

Q3 SHOWCARD B (R) **Which of the statements on this card comes closest to your own view of the Councils in this area?**

		%
A)	I'm not interested in what the Council does, or whether they do their job	1
B)	I'm not interested in what the Council does, as long as they do their job	25
C)	I like to know what the Council is doing, but I'm happy to let them get on with their job	50
D)	I would like to have more of a say in what the Council does and the services it provides	17
E)	I already work for, or am involved with the Council and the services it provides	6
	Don't know	1

Q4 **From what you know, how many councils provide the main services in this neighbourhood?** (INTERVIEWER - NOT INCLUDING PARISH COUNCILS)

	%
One	20
Two	36
Three+	4
Don't know	40

In fact there are two main councils that provide, or are responsible for most services in this area: Northampton Borough Council and Northamptonshire County Council.

ROTATE ORDER OF Q5/6

☐ Q5 SHOWCARD C (R) **From this list, what services do you think are the responsibility of Northampton Borough Council? Just read out the letter(s) that apply**

☐ Q6 SHOWCARD C AGAIN (R) **And which services on this list do you think are the responsibility of Northamptonshire County Council? Again, just read out the letters that apply.**

Q7 SHOWCARD D (R) **Which, if any, of these services do you or members of your family use?** INCLUDE ONLY LOCAL USE

		Q5 Northampton %	Q6 Northamptonshire %	Q7 Use %
A	Bus Services	32	16	59
B	Car Parks	42	11	61
C	Council Housing	46	14	20
D	Council Tax Benefit/Housing benefit	36	19	20
E	Fire service	17	35	31
F	Food safety	19	23	12
G	Household waste sites/dumps	40	15	57
H	Libraries	19	37	55
I	Parks, playgrounds and open spaces	39	20	64
J	Planning service	22	28	8
K	Public conveniences	40	12	46
L	Recycling/bottle banks	37	15	53
M	Refuse collection	49	11	86
N	Road maintenance	28	30	39
O	Schools/education	15	44	39
P	Social services	19	33	13
Q	Street sweeping	50	8	43
R	Swimming pools/sports facilities	33	19	52
	Other	1	1	1
	None of these	1	3	1
	Don't know	31	37	3

Q8 SHOWCARD E (R) **As you may know, there is currently a review being undertaken by the Local Government Commission on the future local government structure in the county. How much, if anything, would you say you know about this?**

	%
A great deal	2
A fair amount	10
Just a little	27
Heard of but know nothing about	20
Never heard of	41

PREFERENCES

HAND OVER MAP SHOWING AREAS UNDER REVIEW AND "CURRENT SERVICES" CARD
The Local Government Commission is considering options for the future structure of local government in Northampton. Could you please read through this card, (SHOW OPTIONS CARD) **which outlines the options.**

Q9 **Please tell me which of the options, if either, you would prefer for Northampton?**
SINGLE CODE ONLY

For Northampton

	%
Option A (Single all purpose council)	28
Option B (Remain the same/status quo)	44
Some other option	*
Neither of these	1
Either of these/don't mind	3
Don't care	4
Don't know	20

ASK IF "OTHER" NAMED AT Q9 (CODE 3)
Q10 **What other option is that?**
PROBE FULLY - DO NOT PROMPT.

....

....

....

....

ASK ALL PREFERRING AN OPTION (1, 2 OR 3 AT Q9). OTHERS GO TO Q13
Q11 SHOWCARD F (R) **You say that the option you would prefer is . . . . .** (INSERT OPTION PREFERRED). **How strongly would you say you feel about this?**

	%
Very strongly	16
Fairly strongly	49
Not very strongly	28
Not at all strongly	2
Don't know	5

Q12 **What do you think would be the main advantages of . . .**(OPTION PREFERRED)
PROBE FULLY FOR DETAILS

....

....

....

....

....

Nothing..............................
Don't know/can't think of anything..............................

ATTITUDES TO PROPOSALS

SHOWCARD G (R) **Imagine that there was one council in Northampton providing <u>all</u> services. I am going to read out some statements that people have made about this proposal. To what extent do you agree or disagree that . . . .?** READ OUT, ROTATE ORDER OF ASKING Q13-22. TICK START

READ OUT:	Strongly agree %	Tend to agree %	Neither/ Nor %	Tend to disagree %	Strongly disagree %	Don't know %
☐ Q13 **It would cost more overall**	16	26	18	19	11	9
Q14 **It would be more in touch with local people's needs**	18	31	12	24	9	5
Q15 **The single Council would be more efficient than the current system of two Councils**	17	28	19	20	10	5
☐ Q16 **The single council would not be big enough to manage services such as Education and Social Services effectively**	12	24	19	23	13	10
Q17 **It would better reflect the sense of community in Northampton**	11	35	21	20	8	4
Q18 **We need a County Council to represent us nationally**	16	40	23	13	5	4
☐ Q19 **Services would suffer if the County Council no longer provides services in Northampton**	13	32	18	24	8	6
Q20 **It won't affect me whether there is a single Council in Northampton or not**	9	25	16	33	12	6
Q21 **The change to a single Council for Northampton would be too disruptive**	13	27	18	24	10	7
☐ Q22 **With a single Council it would be clearer who is responsible for local services**	32	43	12	8	4	2
ASK LAST Q23 **I would like to have more information on the proposals before making up my mind**	26	36	10	16	9	4

Q24 **On balance, which would you say is more in touch with local people and issues, ...** (ROTATE ORDER OF "DISTRICT" AND COUNTY) **Northampton Borough Council, or Northamptonshire County Council, or would you say that they are both about the same?**

	%
Northampton Borough Council	35
Northamptonshire County Council	6
Both about the same	37
Don't know	23

REFER BACK TO Q8. ASK ALL WHO HAVE HEARD OF REVIEW AT Q8 (IE CODES 1/2/3/4). OTHERS TO Q28

Q25 SHOWCARD H **Earlier in the interview, you said that you had heard of the Review of local government structure. From which, if any, of the sources shown on this card have you recently heard about the Review?** INTERVIEWER NOTE: "RECENTLY" = IN PAST 3 MONTHS

		%
A	Leaflet from County Council delivered to your door	46
B	Leaflet from County Council in library/ offices, etc	4
C	Advertisement from County Council in local newspaper	9
D	Advertisement from County Council on local radio/TV	1
E	Leaflet from Borough Council delivered to your door	22
F	Leaflet from Borough Council in library/ offices, etc	3
G	Borough Council newspaper	4
H	County Council newspaper	2
I	Advertisement from Borough Council in local newspaper	5
J	Advertisement from Borough Council on local radio/TV	1
K	Advertisement by the Commission on local radio	0
L	Local Government Commission advertisement in local newspaper	3
M	Local newspaper	53
N	National newspaper	6
O	TV	12
P	Local radio	15
Q	National radio	3
R	Friends/neighbours/family	11
S	Conversation with Borough Councillor	3
T	Conversation with County Councillor	4
U	Conversation with Borough Council staff	2
V	Conversation with County Council staff	5
W	Parish/community council	1
X	Residents' Association	1
	Other	8
	None of these	*
	Don't know	3

ASK ALL NAMING A SOURCE AT Q25. OTHERS GO TO Q28

Q26 **Would you say that the information you have received has influenced your opinion, or not?**

	%
Yes	20
No	77
Don't know	3

Q27 **What information in particular has influenced your opinion?**

....

....

....

....

ASK ALL

Q28 SHOWCARD I (R) **Assuming you receive the same level of services, how important is it to you, if at all, what the final decision is on the future local government structure in Northampton?**

	%
Very important	22
Fairly important	36
Not very important	30
Not at all important	10
Don't know	2

ACTIVISM

Q29 SHOWCARD J **Which of the things on this list, if any, have you done in the last three years? Just read out the letter(s) that apply.**

		%
A	Voted in Local Council elections	73
B	Spoken or written to a local Councillor	22
C	Responded to the earlier Review of local government	9
D	Been to a meeting of a local committee or organisation (WRITE IN NAME OF ORGANISATION)	9
E	Spoken on a radio phone-in about a local issue	3
F	Written to a local newspaper about a local issue	4
G	Been to a meeting of a local branch of a political party	2
H	Written to your MP about a local issue	7
I	Been to a Council Committee meeting	2
J	Been to a Council meeting	2
K	Attended a public meeting run by the Council	4
	None of these	21
	Don't know/refused	1

Q30 SHOWCARD K **Which, if any, of these apply to you? Just read out the letter(s) that apply**

		%
I am a member of a:		
A	Residents' Association	2
B	Community Association	2
C	Tenants' Association	0
D	Neighbourhood Watch	19
E	PTA/school governors	5
I do unpaid work for:		
F	A school	7
G	Citizens Advice Bureau	0
H	Volunteer Bureau	2
I	Scouts/Guides/Cubs/Brownies	5
J	Church group	7
	Other 3	3
	None of these	66
	Don't know	1

THANK RESPONDENT. GO TO DEMOGRAPHICS.

Length of interview [|] minutes

CHAPTER 10

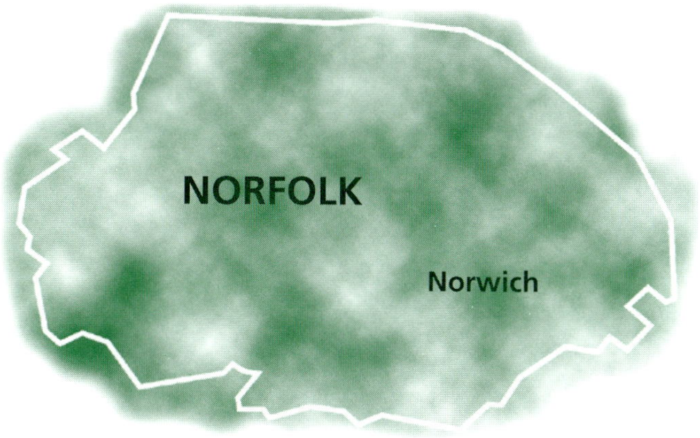

NORWICH IN THE COUNTY OF NORFOLK

Draft Recommendations

10.1 The Commission's report *Draft Recommendations on the Future Local Government of Norwich in the County of Norfolk* summarised the evidence taken into account by the Commission in reaching its draft recommendations.

Figure 10.1
Draft Recommendation for Norwich in the County of Norfolk

Structure
- There should be no change to the existing two-tier structure of local government in Norwich.

Views Expressed to the Commission

10.2 The Commission received a wide range of direct representations on its draft recommendations, from local authorities, residents, Members of Parliament, business and voluntary groups, parish and town councils, and from other public and private sector organisations. Just under 3,000 representations were received from individuals and organisations, including over 650 from respondents within Norwich. The Commission also received almost 1,300 standard letters and standardised postcards. Over 150 of the responses from outside Norwich came from Costessey Parish residents (in the urban fringe), stating that Norwich City should not be given unitary status (Figure 10.2 and 10.3). Figures 10.2 and 10.3 exclude representations from the local authorities; these are summarised separately (Figure 10.4).

Figure 10.2
Views of Respondents From Norwich

Preferred structure	Individuals	Organisations	Standard letters and petition signatures
Unitary Norwich	219	17	1,201
Unitary Norwich on expanded boundaries	19	4	0
No change	369	30	82
Other	12	2	0
No preference	6	2	12

Source: Local Government Commission for England and NOP

Figure 10.3
Views of Respondents From Outside Norwich

Preferred structure	Individuals	Organisations	Standard letters and petition signatures
Unitary Norwich	47	4	0
Unitary Norwich on expanded boundaries	11	1	0
No change	1,767	359	241
Other	51	5	0
No preference	19	3	0

Source: Local Government Commission for England and NOP
Note: Excludes out of county representations

10.3 In addition, 33 representations were received from outside the county, of which about two-thirds supported the Commission's draft recommendation. A more detailed tabulation of the written representations from individuals and interest groups, produced by NOP on behalf of the Commission, can be found towards the end of this Chapter.

The Views of Local Authorities

10.4 The Commission received submissions from seven of the eight principal local authorities in Norfolk during Stage Three (Figure 10.4).

Figure 10.4
Preferences of Norfolk Local Authorities at Stage Three

Authority	Preference
Breckland District Council	Supported the continuation of the two-tier structure. Supported the retention of the existing boundaries and status of Norwich.
Broadland District Council	Supported no change in Norwich. Considered that a unitary authority for the City of Norwich based on existing boundaries would not be viable. Urged the Commission not to recommend a further review of the case for unitary status on extended boundaries.
Great Yarmouth Borough Council	Supported a unitary authority for Norwich. The Council saw no reason to change its opinion in the light of the Commission's view that "...the County Council would remain a large authority in territory, resources and population and would continue to provide effective and convenient local government in its area".
King's Lynn and West Norfolk Borough Council	No submission at Stage Three.
North Norfolk District Council	Supported the Commission's draft recommendation and "...considers the boundary of the area administered by Norwich City Council to be correct".
Norwich City Council	Supported a unitary authority for the present City of Norwich and considered that the Commission should recommend that the Secretary of State instigate a review of the boundary of Norwich at the earliest possibility.
South Norfolk District Council	Supported no change in Norwich. Considered that any further review of the boundary between the City of Norwich and the District of South Norfolk should not be pursued for a substantial number of years.
Norfolk County Council	Supported no change in Norwich. Considered that in the absence of a clear case for change the arguments in favour of no change were decisive and that the boundary issue presented such difficulties and uncertainties that change should not be contemplated.

Source: Local authorities' submissions

10.5 None of these local authorities which expressed a view in Stage One has changed its view since. There was no submission from King's Lynn and West Norfolk Borough Council. A joint submission was also received from Breckland, Broadland and South Norfolk District Councils which considered that any further review of the boundary between the City of Norwich and the districts of Broadland and South Norfolk should not be pursued for a substantial number of years. The Norfolk Branch of the Association of District Councils did not make representations; the Association of District Councils' national submission is referred to in the Summary of National Representations. The Association of County Councils also supported the continuation of the existing two-tier structure in Norwich. Waveney District Council (in Suffolk) wrote to reiterate its support for a unitary authority for Norwich.

The Views of Others

10.6 A range of other interest groups made representations on the Commission's draft recommendations, as summarised in the following paragraphs. These are in addition to those made in Stage One.

Businesses and Business Groups

10.7 The Commission heard from 53 individual businesses and business organisations. Of these, two-thirds preferred no change, including the Great Yarmouth Chamber of Commerce, Great Yarmouth Port Authority, Anglia Railways and many businesses. Barclays Bank plc (East Anglia) had "...no strong views on the relative merits of unitary versus two-tier structures" but considered that: "What we really need is effective people in local government and a good partnership between local government and business". Norfolk and Waveney Business Link also considered that the issue of partnerships should be the thrust of the debate, not extended boundaries. The Norfolk and Waveney Training and Enterprise Council felt that while it supported the concept of unitary authorities the creation of a unitary authority on the existing boundary was not viable.

10.8 However, about a fifth of those businesses which made their views known to the Commission supported a unitary Norwich, including Norwich Union, Ernst and Young (Norwich), Eversheds and Property Partnerships, a major local property investment company. Among those supporting change, the generally held view was that Norwich should become a unitary authority on its existing boundary, with a boundary review to follow. Ernst and Young, for example stated "...to deny Norwich unitary status because of this anomaly [the boundary] means that the City is not being looked at in its entirety and [this] will only serve to perpetuate the problem".

County, Regional and National Interests (including the Voluntary Sector)

10.9 The majority of these groups, including the Norwich and Norfolk Voluntary Services, the Norfolk Rural Community Council, the Norfolk Society, the Norfolk Branch of the Council for the Protection of Rural England and the Norfolk Playing Fields Association, opposed change in Norwich. Age Concern Norfolk supported no change and said its members felt that "...given the important arguments to have coterminous health and social services boundaries in order to deliver quality community care, it is totally inappropriate to be establishing two social service departments in the County of Norfolk". The British Red Cross (Norfolk Branch) also expressed "...grave concern as to the continued efficiency and cost of our service to the community should the City of Norwich achieve unitary status".

10.10 A number of groups addressed particular service delivery issues. The Eastern Counties Omnibus Company argued "...we do not believe that Norwich City is a meaningful area for transport planning purposes" and concluded that no structural change was necessary. The Museums and Galleries Commission emphasised the value of the Norfolk Joint Museums Committee. The Broads Authority reiterated earlier comments that the implementation of a new structure would disturb the existing joint working arrangements between the authority and existing district and county councils, and that similar arrangements should be sought with a new authority. The Chief Inspector of the Social Services Inspectorate supported the recommendation for no change and considered that this would avoid disruption to existing services.

10.11 Sir James Cleminson, Deputy Lord Lieutenant of Norfolk, considered the city with its present boundaries to be clearly non-viable as a unitary authority.

Education Groups

10.12 Almost all the submissions from this group opposed change to the current structure. For example, Easton College considered that: "The benefits of unitary status for Norwich are outweighed in our view by the financial costs and the complexity of having to deal with two separate education authorities". The Norfolk Pre-School Learning Alliance (Norfolk Sub-Committee) in supporting the existing structure argued that change, from its perspective, would: "Require more time and resources" and put "...pressure on staff and volunteers, with no guarantee of improved services to our members". The Norwich City Association of the National Union of Teachers welcomed the draft recommendation for no change.

10.13 The University of East Anglia considered there should be a unitary authority for the built-up area of Norwich. However it felt that if this could not "...be achieved in or immediately following the present exercise, [it]...reluctantly agrees that retention of the status quo is the best solution".

Health Interests

10.14 Norfolk Health (the East Norfolk Health Commission) supported the Commission's draft recommendations. It stated that "...we believe the wider urban area is the main focus for services and that the hinterland population would be a significant loser if Norwich services were only planned for the current city population". While it considered that a boundary review would address the immediate service delivery problems, it would still leave the issue of a natural base for central Norfolk services.

Law, Order and Emergency Services

10.15 The Norfolk Fire Service welcomed the recommendation for no change, believing a unitary Norwich would cause concern on the grounds of funding, disruption, operational joint arrangements and the implications for support services. The Norfolk Magistrates' Courts Committee reiterated its support for no change.

Local Groups

10.16 The large majority of local groups which submitted representations supported no change. For example, the Norwich and District Carers' Forum felt that: "Splitting the responsibility for social services between two authorities would probably double the time which we have to spend on discussion and the corresponding administrative load". Similarly, Breckland Crossroads Care Attendant Scheme argued that this "...would require us to plan, negotiate and develop relationships with two authorities rather than one...".

10.17 On the other hand a minority of groups including The Norwich Society, Norwich and District Citizens' Advice Bureau, Age Concern Norwich and the Norwich and Norfolk Asian Society considered that Norwich should be an all-purpose authority. The Norwich Society argued that Norwich "...should not be punished for its centrality, nor for having a large suburban population on its periphery...".

Parliamentary Interests

10.18 The Commission received written submissions from five of the eight Norfolk Members of Parliament. Mrs Gillian Shephard, MP for South West Norfolk, Sir Ralph Howell, MP for North Norfolk, Mr Henry Bellingham, MP for North West Norfolk, Mr John MacGregor, MP for South Norfolk, and Mr Richard Ryder, MP for Mid Norfolk, all opposed a change of structure. Mr Bellingham was concerned at the costs and disruption of change and that "...such a change could isolate the non-city residents". Mr MacGregor considered that the existing structure worked well and expressed his concern at the costs of change. He added that it would "...cause considerable difficulties for a number of services but most notably strategic planning and transport". He also considered that "...if one is thinking of economic development it is imperative that one thinks well beyond Norwich City boundaries" but that to " ...take into account the economic activity area as a whole would involve a massive restructuring of local government..." because the "...issues would be fundamental to the whole of Norfolk". He strongly supported no change. Mr Clive Needle, MEP for Norfolk, expressed his support for a unitary Norwich, albeit with reservations in relation to cross-county co-ordination.

10.19 Baroness Hollis of Heigham asked: "Why should the city not be an effective unitary authority on existing boundaries?". She considered that: "A unitary authority has the standing, the political weight and the economic resource that business wants". She also said that: "To tie the boundary review with a change to unitary status doubles, not halves, the disturbance on the ground". Lady Hollis disputed the arguments used against it on the grounds of physical centrality stating that "...the unitary city brings added economic value to its county" and that there would be "...a coherent logic and symmetry to a review process which gave the same status to Plymouth, Nottingham, Leicester, York, Peterborough, Hull and Norwich". Lord and Lady Walpole, however, both supported the retention of the present structure.

10.20 In addition, the Labour Party Environment Spokesman, Mr Frank Dobson, MP for Holborn and St Pancras, considered that Norwich's "...capacity to deliver these services [economic, social and cultural] to the rest of the county would be enhanced if it had an all-purpose council with a primary concern to promote these functions so as to add to the prosperity of the city". He expressed his concern at the concept of centrality. He could not "...see why it should weigh against separating local government functions". He stated that Norwich would "...most-likely always be the religious, judicial, legal, financial and business centre in Norfolk".

Parish And Town Councils

10.21 The Commission heard directly from 179 parish and town councils, of which only three supported a unitary Norwich. Most of the remainder specifically expressed a preference for no change. The Norfolk County Association of Parish and Town Councils urged the Commission to recommend that the current structure be retained in Norwich. Typical of these views expressed by individual parishes was Hempnall Parish Council, which considered that there would be no proven organisational benefit; that it was likely that administration costs would increase; and that it would lead to further pressure for an expanded Greater Norwich. Amongst parish councils in the immediate hinterland of Norwich, Thorpe St Andrew expressed the commonly held opposition to "...any suggestion of another review of Norwich City to take account of any boundary changes".

NOP Tabulations of Written Representations

1 The following tabulations summarise the views expressed by members of the public and other interested parties during the consultation on the Local Government Commission's draft recommendations for Norwich.

2 The tabulations include only letters sent directly to NOP at its Chelmsford offices and to the Commission's offices in London. Where more than one person's view has been expressed in a letter, the comments from each individual have been recorded separately. Staff from the Commission and NOP have worked closely in ensuring that care has been taken in the interpretation of comments, and that a consistent approach has been adopted.

3 While many people expressed support for one or other of the draft options presented by the Commission, other responses were coded by NOP after further discussion. The pattern of views expressed has been carefully examined, and where a number of respondents supported an option not included in those put forward by the Commission, those views have been separately coded and reported by NOP.

4 The Commission has advertised through the local media, encouraging people to make their views known. All responses received up to two days after the end of the Stage Three consultation period have been included. Returns from campaigns organised by local authorities or other groups (for example, standardised postcards and letters, questionnaires and petitions) have not been included in the tabulations. These, and submissions written and dated before the commencement of the consultation process, have been considered separately by the Commission.

The following definitions have been applied by NOP in compiling the tabulations:

(i) Type of Respondent

Individuals:	includes individual members of the public, local councillors and Members of the Westminster and European Parliaments.
Businesses and Business Groups:	includes organisations which represent businesses, such as local Chambers of Commerce.
County, Regional and National Interests:	any organisation which covers an area which is the size of a county or larger is included here, for example, a county-wide voluntary organisation or a regional association. This classification includes most of the statutory consultees.
Education (and Church) Groups:	this group includes schools, religious organisations and teaching unions.
Local Groups:	this includes organisations smaller than a county area, for example, a district-level voluntary sector body. The group could be voluntary, sporting, political or cultural but does not include organisations from the education or religious sectors (included above). It also includes constituency parties and political groups on local authorities.
Parish and Town Councils:	this also includes district-level associations of town and parish councils. County level associations are classified as County, Regional and National interests.

(ii) Structural Options (Reports A, D and H)

No change in own district:	this code is used where there is more than one review district in the county. It indicates where respondents from a review district have expressed support for no change for that district and have not made reference to the other review district(s) in that county.
District/county-level authorities:	represents support for either a district or county-level authority although it is not clear whether this is for a unitary or a two-tier structure.
Opposition to structural preferences:	represents responses where a negative, but unspecified, structural preference has been expressed.
Rejects:	rejects are those responses with unclear comments/interpretation.

(iii) Other

Other issues (Reports B and I):	these illustrate preferences in relation to boundary and electoral changes and (where applicable) the restoration of historic counties.
Parishing issues (Report C):	these illustrate preferences in relation to parishing issues, for example, the creation of new parishes or the enhancement of the role of parish and town councils.
Services (Report E):	these illustrate concerns expressed about the impact of proposed changes on particular service areas where the respondent has not additionally expressed a positive structural preference.

(iv) Ward/Area Level (Reports H and I)

These show analyses by local authority wards or specified areas and are designed to examine whether structural preferences vary across a particular local authority area. The areas specified are defined in the table below. These areas broadly correspond to those parts of the districts of Broadland and South Norfolk which fall within the Norwich urban area.

Broadland District

Area	Comprising district wards of
Sprowston	Sprowston Central Sprowston South Sprowston West Sprowston East
Thorpe	Thorpe North East Thorpe North West Thorpe South
Catton	Catton
Hellesdon	Hellesdon South East Hellesdon North Hellesdon West
Drayton	Drayton
Taverham	Taverham

South Norfolk District

Area	Comprising district wards of
New Costessey	New Costessey
Old Costessey	Old Costessey
Cringleford and Colney	Cringleford and Colney

NOP Analysis of Responses to Local Government Commission Draft Recommendations - NORFOLK

Report A: Opinions on the structural options, by authority of respondent
Base: all

	Review district	Other districts in county								
	Norwich	Breckland	Broadland	Great Yarmouth	King's Lynn & West Norfolk	North Norfolk	South Norfolk	Rest of county total	County total	Out of county total
No change	399 *59%*	207 *95%*	701 *93%*	42 *93%*	177 *96%*	274 *97%*	725 *92%*	2126 *94%*	2525 *86%*	22 *67%*
Unitary Norwich	236 *35%*	6 *3%*	15 *2%*	3 *7%*	2 *1%*	5 *2%*	20 *3%*	51 *2%*	287 *10%*	7 *21%*
Unitary expanded Norwich (boundary not specified)	23 *3%*	- -	2 *	- -	2 *1%*	1 *	7 *1%*	12 *1%*	35 *1%*	- -
Expanded Norwich (Unitary or two-tier)	1 *	- -	- -	- -	- -	- -	1 *	1 *	2 *	- -
County-level authority (either two-tier or unitary)	4 *1%*	1 *	2 *	- -	- -	1 *	2 *	6 *	10 *	- -
District-level authority (either two-tier or unitary)	3 *	- -	6 *1%*	- -	2 *1%*	- -	4 *1%*	12 *1%*	15 *1%*	- -
County-wide unitary structure	1 *	1 *	- -	- -	- -	- -	- -	1 *	2 *	- -
Opposition to structural options (where no positive preference is stated)	1 *	1 *	16 *2%*	- -	- -	- -	18 *2%*	35 *2%*	36 *1%*	- -
Reject	1 *	- -	- -	- -	- -	- -	- -	- -	1 *	- -
Other specified	3 *	- -	- -	- -	- -	1 *	- -	1 *	4 *	- -
No preference expressed/option defined	8 *1%*	2 *1%*	9 *1%*	- -	2 *1%*	1 *	8 *1%*	22 *1%*	30 *1%*	4 *12%*
BASE TOTAL	680	218	751	45	185	283	785	2267	2947	33

* *Less than ½%*

NOP Analysis of Responses to Local Government Commission Draft Recommendations - NORFOLK

Report B: Opinions on other issues, by authority of respondent
Base: all

	Review district	Other districts in county								
	Norwich	Breckland	Broadland	Great Yarmouth	King's Lynn & West Norfolk	North Norfolk	South Norfolk	Rest of county total	County total	Out of county total
Don't put us in Norwich	-	-	24	-	1	-	18	43	43	-
	-	-	*3%*	-	*1%*	-	*2%*	*2%*	*1%*	-
Opposition to/Anti unitary expanded Norwich	1	-	13	-	-	-	17	31	32	-
	*	-	*2%*	-	-	-	*2%*	*1%*	*1%*	-
BASE TOTAL	680	218	751	45	185	283	785	2267	2947	33

The figures in the table above do not sum to the base total/100% because undefined fields are not included, except as part of the base total.

* *Less than ½%*

NOP Analysis of Responses to Local Government Commission Draft Recommendations - NORFOLK

Report C: Opinions on parishing issues, by authority of respondent
Base: all

	Review district	Other districts in county								
	Norwich	Breckland	Broadland	Great Yarmouth	King's Lynn & West Norfolk	North Norfolk	South Norfolk	Rest of county total	County total	Out of county total
BASE TOTAL	680	218	751	45	185	283	785	2267	2947	33

The figures in the table above do not sum to the base total/100% because undefined fields are not included, except as part of the base total.

NOP Analysis of Responses to Local Government Commission Draft Recommendations - NORFOLK

Report D1: Opinions on the structural options, by respondent type (all respondents)
Base: all

	Respondent Type					
	Indiv-iduals	Business groups	County, regional & national interests	Education (& church) groups	Local groups	Parish and town councils
No change	2149 *85%*	35 *66%*	21 *72%*	117 *98%*	52 *85%*	173 *97%*
Unitary Norwich	272 *11%*	9 *17%*	2 *7%*	- -	8 *13%*	3 *2%*
Unitary expanded Norwich (boundary not specified)	30 *1%*	3 *6%*	1 *3%*	1 *1%*	- -	- -
Expanded Norwich (Unitary or two-tier)	2 *	- -	- -	- -	- -	- -
County-level authority (either two-tier or unitary)	10 *	- -	- -	- -	- -	- -
District-level authority (either two-tier or unitary)	13 *1%*	2 *4%*	- -	- -	- -	- -
County-wide unitary structure	1 *	1 *2%*	- -	- -	- -	- -
Opposition to structural options (where no positive preference is stated)	33 *1%*	- -	- -	1 *1%*	- -	2 *1%*
Reject	1 *	- -	- -	- -	- -	- -
Other specified	3 *	- -	- -	- -	1 *2%*	- -
No preference expressed/option defined	25 *1%*	3 *6%*	5 *17%*	- -	- -	1 *1%*
BASE TOTAL	2539	53	29	119	61	179

* *Less than ½%*

NOP Analysis of Responses to Local Government Commission Draft Recommendations - NORFOLK

Report D2: Opinions on the structural options, by respondent type
Base: respondents in Norwich only

	Respondent Type					
	Indiv-iduals	Business groups	County, regional & national interests	Education (& church) groups	Local groups	Parish and town councils
No change	369 *59%*	7 *33%*	12 *80%*	6 *86%*	5 *42%*	- -
Unitary Norwich	219 *35%*	9 *43%*	1 *7%*	- -	7 *58%*	- -
Unitary expanded Norwich (boundary not specified)	19 *3%*	2 *10%*	1 *7%*	1 *14%*	- -	- -
Expanded Norwich (Unitary or two-tier)	1 *	- -	- -	- -	- -	- -
County-level authority (either two-tier or unitary)	4 *1%*	- -	- -	- -	- -	- -
District-level authority (either two-tier or unitary)	1 *	2 *10%*	- -	- -	- -	- -
County-wide unitary structure	1 *	- -	- -	- -	- -	- -
Opposition to structural options (where no positive preference is stated)	1 *	- -	- -	- -	- -	- -
Reject	1 *	- -	- -	- -	- -	- -
Other specified	3 *	- -	- -	- -	- -	- -
No preference expressed/option defined	6 *1%*	1 *5%*	1 *7%*	- -	- -	- -
BASE TOTAL	625	21	15	7	12	-

* *Less than ½%*

NOP Analysis of Responses to Local Government Commission Draft Recommendations - NORFOLK

Report D3: Opinions on the structural options, by respondent type
Base: respondents in rest of county only

	Respondent Type					
	Indiv-iduals	Business groups	County, regional & national interests	Education (& church) groups	Local groups	Parish and town councils
No change	1767 *93%*	25 *93%*	6 *75%*	109 *99%*	47 *96%*	172 *97%*
Unitary Norwich	47 *2%*	- -	- -	- -	1 *2%*	3 *2%*
Unitary expanded Norwich (boundary not specified)	11 *1%*	1 *4%*	- -	- -	- -	- -
Expanded Norwich (Unitary or two-tier)	1 *	- -	- -	- -	- -	- -
County-level authority (either two-tier or unitary)	6 *	- -	- -	- -	- -	- -
District-level authority (either two-tier or unitary)	12 *1%*	- -	- -	- -	- -	- -
County-wide unitary structure	- -	1 *4%*	- -	- -	- -	- -
Opposition to structural options (where no positive preference is stated)	32 *2%*	- -	- -	1 *1%*	- -	2 *1%*
Other specified	- -	- -	- -	- -	1 *2%*	- -
No preference expressed/option defined	19 *1%*	- -	2 *25%*	- -	- -	1 *1%*
BASE TOTAL	1895	27	8	110	49	178

** Less than ½%*

Norwich

NOP Analysis of Responses to Local Government Commission Draft Recommendations - NORFOLK

Report E: Views on services, by authority of respondent
Base: all

	Review district	Other districts in county								
	Norwich	Breckland	Broadland	Great Yarmouth	King's Lynn & West Norfolk	North Norfolk	South Norfolk	Rest of county total	County total	Out of county total
Archives	1	-	-	-	-	-	-	-	1	1
	*	-	-	-	-	-	-	-	*	*3%*
Education	-	-	-	-	1	-	-	1	1	-
	-	-	-	-	*1%*	-	-	*	*	-
Libraries	-	-	-	-	1	-	-	1	1	-
	-	-	-	-	*1%*	-	-	*	*	-
Other specified services (or multiples of)	-	-	3	-	-	1	-	4	4	-
	-	-	*	-	-	*	-	*	*	-
BASE TOTAL	680	218	751	45	185	283	785	2267	2947	33

The figures in the table above do not sum to the base total/100% becauseundefined fields are not included, except as part of the base total.

* *Less than ½%*

NOP Analysis of Responses to Local Government Commission Draft Recommendations - NORFOLK

Report F: Views on services, by respondent type
Base: all

	Respondent Type					
	Indiv-iduals	Business groups	County, regional & national interests	Education (& church) groups	Local groups	Parish and town councils
Archives	1	-	1	-	-	-
	*	-	3%	-	-	-
Education	1	-	-	-	-	-
	*	-	-	-	-	-
Libraries	1	-	-	-	-	-
	*	-	-	-	-	-
Other specified services (or multiples of)	3	-	1	-	-	-
	*	-	3%	-	-	-
BASE TOTAL	2539	53	29	119	61	179

The figures in the table above do not sum to the base total/100% because undefined fields are not included, except as part of the base total.

* *Less than ½%*

NOP Analysis of Responses to Local Government Commission Draft Recommendations - NORFOLK

Report G: Type of respondent, by authority of respondent
Base: all

	Review district	Other districts in county								
	Norwich	Breckland	Broadland	Great Yarmouth	King's Lynn & West Norfolk	North Norfolk	South Norfolk	Rest of county total	County total	Out of county total
Individuals	625 *92%*	159 *73%*	679 *90%*	32 *71%*	132 *71%*	228 *81%*	665 *85%*	1895 *84%*	2520 *86%*	19 *58%*
Business groups	21 *3%*	7 *3%*	8 *1%*	1 *2%*	6 *3%*	- -	5 *1%*	27 *1%*	48 *2%*	5 *15%*
County, regional and national interests	15 *2%*	- -	3 *	- -	- -	- -	5 *1%*	8 *	23 *1%*	6 *18%*
Education (and church) groups	7 *1%*	15 *7%*	24 *3%*	7 *16%*	16 *9%*	16 *6%*	32 *4%*	110 *5%*	117 *4%*	2 *6%*
Local Groups	12 *2%*	8 *4%*	11 *1%*	2 *4%*	5 *3%*	5 *2%*	18 *2%*	49 *2%*	61 *2%*	- -
Parish and town councils	- -	29 *13%*	26 *3%*	3 *7%*	26 *14%*	34 *12%*	60 *8%*	178 *8%*	178 *6%*	1 *3%*
BASE TOTAL	680	218	751	45	185	283	785	2267	2947	33

* *Less than ½%*

NOP Analysis of Responses to Local Government Commission Draft Recommendations - NORFOLK

Report H: Opinions on the structural options, by ward/area of respondent
Base: all

	Broadland						South Norfolk		
	Sprowston	Thorpe	Catton	Hellesdon	Drayton	Taverham	Cringleford & Colney	Old Costessey	New Costessey
No change	109 *95%*	153 *93%*	41 *85%*	126 *92%*	16 *100%*	34 *97%*	242 *91%*	24 *89%*	27 *90%*
Unitary Norwich	- -	5 *3%*	4 *8%*	1 *1%*	- -	- -	5 *2%*	1 *4%*	1 *3%*
Unitary expanded Norwich (boundary not specified)	- -	1 *1%*	- -	1 *1%*	- -	- -	1 *	- -	- -
Expanded Norwich (Unitary or two-tier)	- -	- -	- -	- -	- -	- -	- -	1 *4%*	- -
District-level authority (either two-tier or unitary)	- -	2 *1%*	- -	2 *1%*	- -	1 *3%*	3 *1%*	- -	1 *3%*
Opposition to structural options (where no positive preference is stated)	5 *4%*	1 *1%*	1 *2%*	6 *4%*	- -	- -	9 *3%*	- -	- -
No preference expressed/option defined	1 *1%*	2 *1%*	2 *4%*	1 *1%*	- -	- -	5 *2%*	1 *4%*	1 *3%*
BASE TOTAL	115	164	48	137	16	35	265	27	30

* *Less than ½%*

NOP Analysis of Responses to Local Government Commission Draft Recommendations - NORFOLK

Report I: Opinions on other issues, by ward/area of respondent
Base: all

	Broadland						South Norfolk		
	Sprowston	Thorpe	Catton	Hellesdon	Drayton	Taverham	Cringleford & Colney	Old Costessey	New Costessey
Don't put us in Norwich	9 *8%*	5 *3%*	1 *2%*	6 *4%*	- -	1 *3%*	8 *3%*	2 *7%*	2 *7%*
Opposition to/Anti unitary expanded Norwich	2 *2%*	1 *1%*	1 *2%*	6 *4%*	- -	- -	9 *3%*	- -	- -
BASE TOTAL	115	164	48	137	16	35	265	27	30

The figures in the table above do not sum to the base total/100% because undefined fields are not included, except as part of the base total.

Norwich

MORI Research Study for the Local Government Commission

Introduction

Background

1 This summary report highlights the key findings from a survey of public opinion conducted in the City of Norwich and across the County of Norfolk on behalf of the Local Government Commission for England. A copy of each of the marked-up questionnaires is appended. The computer tabulations are contained in a separate volume, which is available from MORI (32 Old Queen Street, London SW1H 9HP. Telephone 0171-222 0232. Price £15).

2 The survey was designed in close consultation with the Commission, following extensive qualitative research and pilot testing. All sampling, interviewing and analysis have been carried out independently by MORI, within the guidelines of the profession laid out by the Market Research Society.

3 In Norwich, all Census Enumeration Districts (EDs) were sorted by ward, and stratified according to social class. EDs were then sampled (32 in total) in proportion to the population size of each, and quotas set for sex, age and work status. A total of 324 interviews with adults aged 18+, conducted face-to-face and in-home, were carried out between 9 and 31 October 1995. Data were weighted to match the population profile in the City.

4 In the remaining districts of Norfolk, all EDs were sorted into wards, and again were stratified according to social class. A total of 32 EDs across the whole area (that is, Norfolk excluding Norwich) were sampled, with quotas set by sex, age and work status. Face-to-face interviews, conducted in-home, were carried out with 326 adults aged 18+ between 9 and 31 October 1995. Data were weighted to match the population profile of the County excluding Norwich. In addition, a special booster sample was interviewed in the fringe area around Norwich, to form a total sample in the area of 140 interviews. Booster interviews have not been included in the county-wide analysis, in order not to over-represent this area in the total analysis.

Publication of the Results

5 As with all our studies, these findings are subject to our Standard Terms and Conditions of Contract. Any press release or publication of the findings of this survey require the advance approval of MORI. Such approval will only be refused on the grounds of inaccuracy or misinterpretation.

Objectives

6 This survey took place during Stage Three, the consultation period on the Commission's draft recommendations. It measures public preferences for the organisation of local government in the area currently comprising the City of Norwich, as well as exploring strength of feeling, levels of knowledge about the review, involvement in, and broader perceptions of, local government in the area.

Statistical Reliability of the Data

7 Because we have interviewed a sample of residents, rather than the whole population, the results are subject to statistical tolerance limits, or "margins of error". These are expressed as our confidence that the true figure for the whole population falls within a given range. By convention this is expressed as a percentage, so our 95% confidence level means that in 95 times out of 100 the true figure would lie within this range

8 The table below shows ranges of the 95% confidence level for a range of sample sizes. For each sample size, the table shows the tolerance limits for sample results close to 10%, 30% and 50%. Take, for example, the results of a survey of 300 residents showing that 50% are aware of the review. In 95 times out of 100 the true figure would lie between 44% and 56% (ie between 50% ±6%).

	Sampling tolerances applicable to results at or near these percentages (based on 95% confidence level)		
Sample size	10/90% ±%	30/70% ±%	50% ±%
300	3	5	6
200	4	6	7
150	5	7	8
100	6	9	10
50	8	13	14

9 Clearly, 10% or 30% of the sample being aware of the review equate to 90% or 70% not being aware of it. So this table shows the ranges of 95% confidence for responses close to 10%, 30%, 50%, 70% and 90% of our sample. The figures for responses between can be obtained by extrapolation.

10 The true figure would only be known if all the residents of the area had been interviewed. It can be seen in the table, however, that large increases in the sample size do not greatly reduce the sampling tolerance. In addition, the true figure is more likely to lie at the midpoint of the range, rather than at either extreme.

11 When comparing results from separate groups within a sample we need to be sure that the differences are statistically significant. This would be important in comparing views expressed by different parts of a county. The table below shows how the statistical significance of the difference is determined by the size of the groups and the percentage result from the sample.

12 Assuming a 95% confidence level, the table shows the size of the differences required if different results are to be regarded as statistically significant. It can be seen that if 50% of a group of 300 were aware of the review, the result from another group of 300 would not become statistically significant until it became less than 42% or more than 58%.

	Differences required for significance at or near these percentage levels		
Sample sizes	10/90% ±	30/70% ±	50% ±
300 and 300	5	7	8
300 and 200	5	8	9
300 and 100	7	10	11
200 and 100	7	11	12
100 and 100	8	13	14

Survey Findings

Knowledge and Awareness

13 Residents within the City of Norwich profess broadly similar levels of knowledge and interest in local government as those living in the rest of the County of Norfolk. In both, a clear majority like to know what their council is doing, but want no greater involvement. Around one in five in both areas say they want a higher level of involvement.

14 While around two in five in the City and three in ten in the rest of the County say they know at least a fair amount about what their council does, over half admit to not knowing very much.

15 This is reflected in the number of residents who incorrectly ascribe services between the two tiers of local government. Thus, although between four and five in ten recognise libraries as a county council service, as many as two in five (in Norwich) allocate responsibility to the City Council. And although five to seven in ten realise that refuse collection is a district/borough/city service, around one in five (in the rest of Norfolk) thinks it is a county council service.

16 Awareness of the review itself is similar in Norwich and the rest of the County (73% and 70% respectively). Similarly, the proportions who say they know a fair amount or more are broadly equal in the City and the rest of the County, at around one in eight.

Sources of Information

17 Local newspapers are the most common source of information about the review. Of those who have at least heard of the review, between four and five in ten name the local press as a recent source. Around six to seven in ten cite some media source as a recent source of information on the review.

18 It would appear that the City Council has been particularly active in providing information to residents in Norwich, whereas the County Council has been fairly active in providing information to residents throughout the County. Three in five (62%) in Norwich mention a City Council source, compared to 30% in the rest of Norfolk. By comparison, 38% name a County Council source in Norwich, while 45% do so in the rest of Norfolk. Few recognise receiving information directly from the Local Government Commission itself.

19 Although most of those aware of the review recognise one or more recent sources of information, only around one in five say that this has influenced their opinion.

20 Furthermore, in spite of a relatively low level of knowledge and engagement with their local authority, the majority of people in Norwich say that the outcome of the review in the City is either very important to them (19%) or fairly important (43%). As one might expect, people in the rest of Norfolk perceive a lower level of importance (12% very important and 27% fairly important). Over half in the rest of the County say the outcome is not very or not at all important to them.

The Preferred Option

21 Residents in Norwich are divided over whether they would prefer no change (45%) to a unitary City Council (43%), while in the rest of Norfolk over twice as many would prefer Norwich to retain two tier local government (51%) as opt for the unitary solution (22%). Almost all others had no views or were indifferent.

22 More people in Norwich feel strongly about the preference they express than elsewhere in the County. In Norwich, 64% of those expressing a preference say they feel strongly (including 12% very strongly), while across the rest of Norfolk, 58% feel strongly (15% very strongly). There is no difference in the strength of feeling expressed in Norwich irrespective of which option they prefer. However, people in the rest of Norfolk who express support for no change are more likely to feel strongly about it (of whom 61% say that they feel strongly) than are those preferring a unitary Norwich (50%).

Factors in Expressing a Preference

23 In questions 13 to 23, residents were asked to say to what extent they agreed or disagreed with a range of statements which related to a change to unitary local government. The statements were designed to cover the main issues raised by residents during the qualitative phase of research, and others that formed a part of the Commission's brief to take into consideration in making its recommendations.

24 The following charts summarise the results from these questions, with the full question wording presented in the questionnaires in the appendices. Values have been ascribed to the five

attitudinal positions that people were offered (+2 for strongly agree, +1 for tend to agree, 0 for neither agree nor disagree, -1 for tend to disagree, and -2 for strongly disagree) and mean scores calculated across all respondents expressing a view. This has the combined benefit of distilling the range of opinion into one summary figure, while incorporating the varying intensity of feeling by ascribing values. Bars to the right indicate that the mean score value is positive, and thus that there is a balance of agreement with the statement. Bars to the left, conversely, indicate a balance of disagreement.

25 The first chart, therefore, shows how the views of people living in the City of Norwich differ from those across the rest of Norfolk. In doing so, it illustrates the attitudes or perceptions that are, in relative terms, shared by both groups of residents (where the bars project in the same direction), and those where views differ markedly. Thus there is broad agreement that change would lead to clearer responsibility, whereas there is more disagreement on the other positive aspects of change. The balance of opinion is more marked in Norwich than in the rest of the County. There is even broad agreement that a County Council is needed for national representation (here, however, it is residents in the rest of Norfolk who feel more strongly). On the other hand, there is some divergence when it comes to whether a unitary Norwich would be too small, or whether services would suffer. There is also divergence on whether people feel that they will be affected by change; people in Norwich are especially likely to agree that they would like more information before making up their minds.

26 The subsequent chart takes the results from just Norwich (and then from residents in the rest of Norfolk), and illustrates the difference in views between those within Norwich whose preference is for unitary status, and those who prefer no change. The chart therefore illustrates those attitudinal statements that most, or least, differentiate the residents of the City expressing the two opposing preferences. The perceived impact on efficiency is clearly a key determinant of opinion (in both Norwich and the rest of Norfolk), as are size, cost, whether a unitary authority would be in touch, sense of community, disruption and impact on services.

Attitudes to Change
(All respondents)

Q To what extent do you agree or disagree that...?
(Figures represent 'mean scores' with *strong agreement* given a value of +2 through to *strong disagreement* given -2)

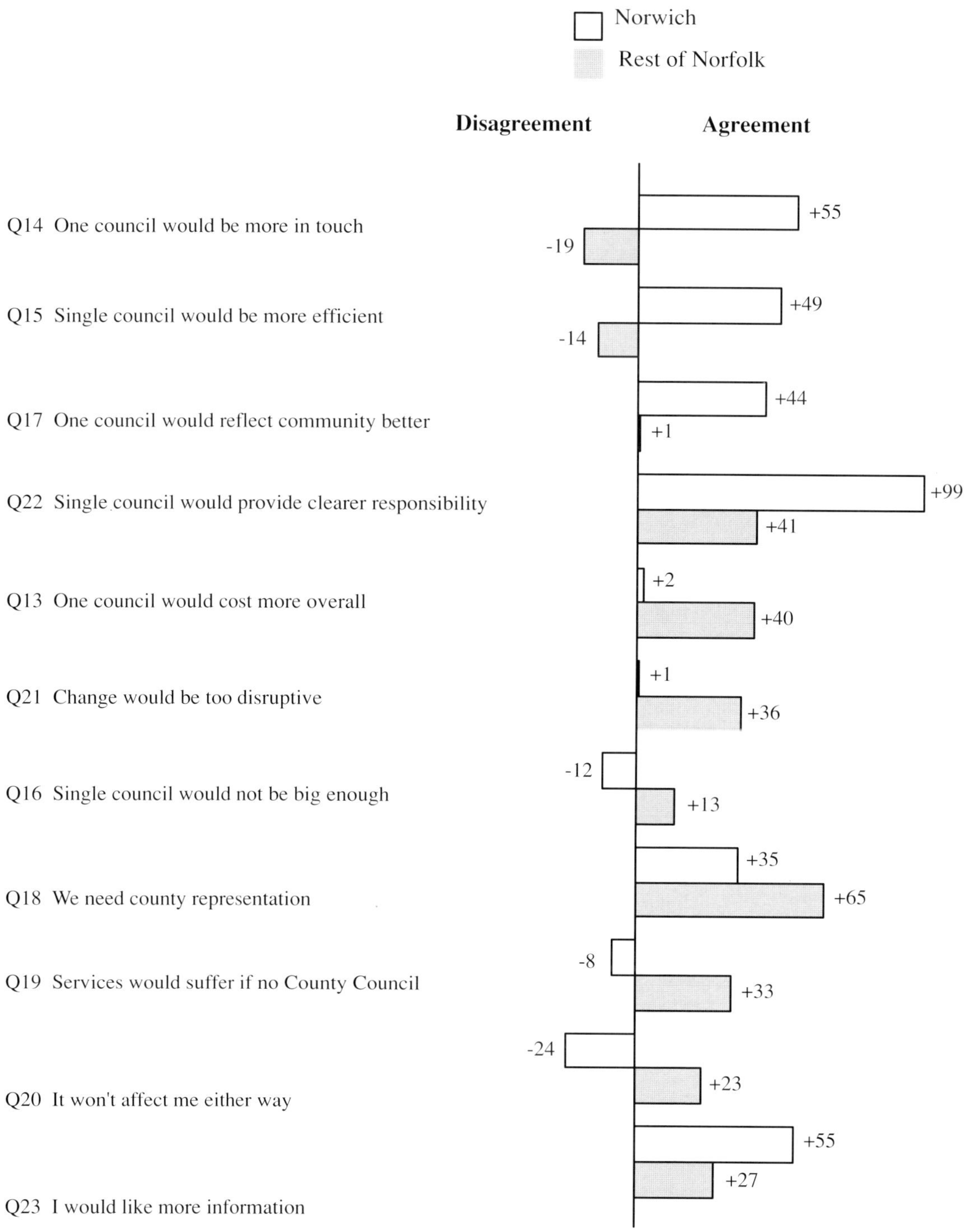

Attitudes to Change
(Respondents in Norwich)

Q To what extent do you agree or disagree that...?
(Figures represent 'mean scores' with *strong agreement* given a value of +2 through to *strong disagreement* given -2)

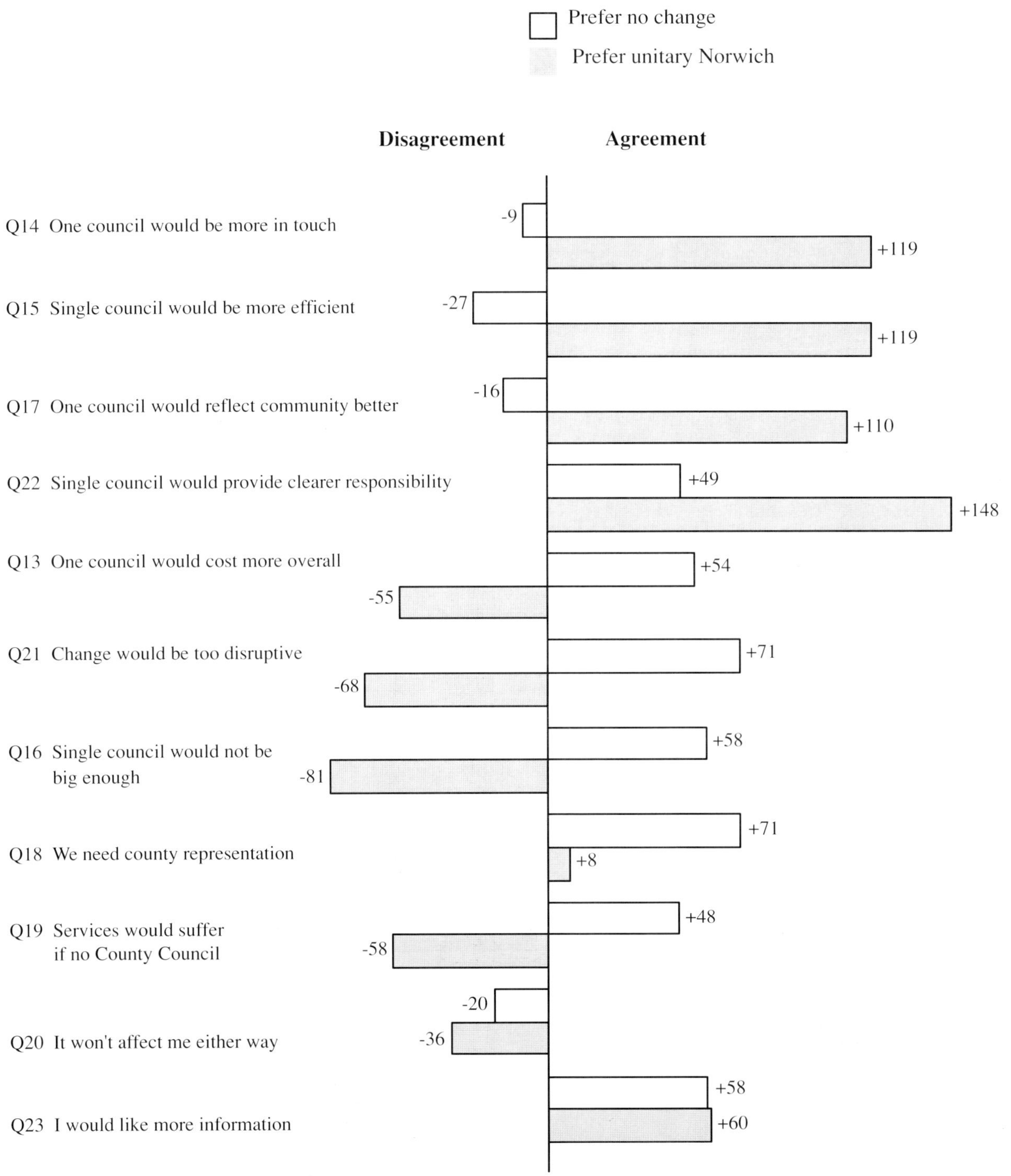

Attitudes to Change
(Respondents in the rest of Norfolk)

Q To what extent do you agree or disagree that...?
(Figures represent 'mean scores' with *strong agreement* given a value of +2 through to *strong disagreement* given -2)

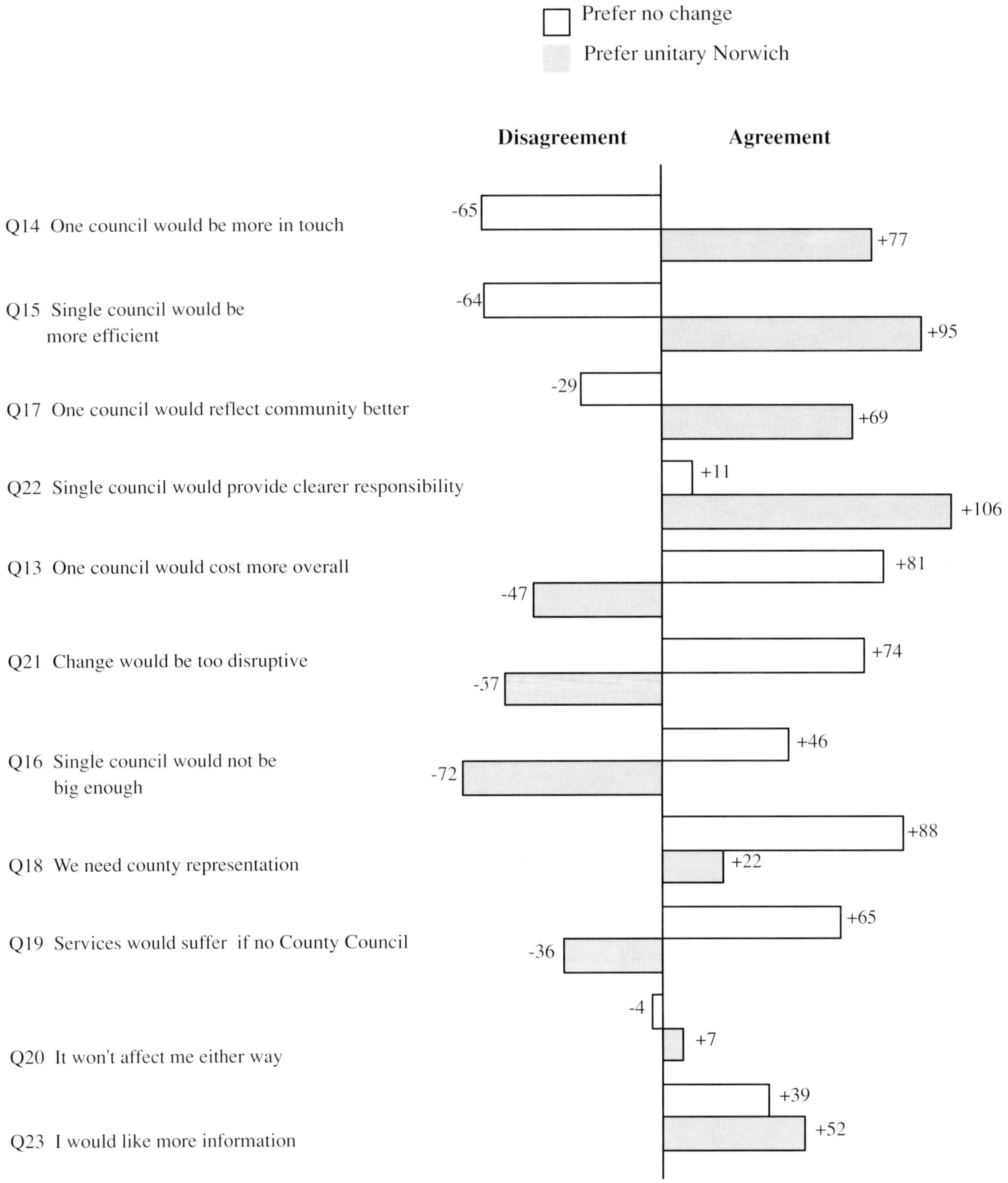

MORI/9101/08
(1-6)

NORFOLK
REVIEW - REST OF COUNTY
TOPLINE RESULTS

Serial No ....
OUO (7-10)

N = 326
9 - 31 October 1995
Main sample data only
Base: All, unless stated

Gender %
Male 48
Female 52

Age %
18-24 11
25-34 16
35-44 20
45-54 14
55-64 15
65-74 15
75+ 9

WRITE IN AGE ☐☐

Work Status %
Full-time (30 hrs/wk+) 44
Part-time (8-29 hrs/wk) 9
Not working (under 8 hrs) 1
Looking after home/children 16
Retired 25
Registered unemployed 2
Unemployed but not registered ....*
Student 1
Other 1

Occupation of Chief Income Earner (CIE)
Position/rank/grade

....

Industry/type of company

....

Qualifications/degrees/apprenticeship

....

No of Staff Responsible for

....

PROBE FOR PENSION

	%
AB	16
C1	34
C2	19
D	17
E	13

* Less than $^1/_2$%

Number in Household
Adults aged 18+ (inc. respondent)

16%	71%	9%	2%	*%
1	2	3	4	5+

Children (17 or under)

58%	16%	17%	7%	3%
0	1	2	3	4+

QA **Are you or other members of your household employed by a council?** IF YES: **Is this a Borough/District Council or a County Council?** CODE FOR BOTH RESPONDENT AND OTHER HOUSEHOLD MEMBERS

	Respondent %	Other %
Yes:		
Borough/District	2	1
County	8	5
Don't know which	0	*
No	89	80
Don't know	1	14

Tenure %
Owned outright 33
Buying on mortgage 40
Rented from Council 14
Rented from Housing Association 2
Rented from private landlord 7
Other 4

QB **Is this your main permanent home, or is it a second or holiday home?**

	%
Main/permanent	97
Second/holiday	2

Car in Household
CIRCLE NUMBER

15%	52%	29%	3%
0	1	2	3+

INTERVIEWER DECLARATION: I confirm that I have conducted this interview face-to-face with the above named person and that I have asked all the relevant questions fully and recorded the answers in conformance with the survey specification and the MRS Code of Conduct.

Interviewer Name .... Signature ....

Interviewer Number				/	

	Month		Date		
DATE OF INTERVIEW					
	(29)	(30)		(30)	(32)

NB INTERVIEWER: ALL SHOWCARDS HAVE BEEN REVERSED. PLEASE BE CAREFUL TO CODE THE CORRECT RESPONSE.

Good morning/afternoon/evening. I'm from MORI, the market research and polling organisation. We are doing a survey about local issues, and I would like to ask you a few questions.

ASK ALL

Q1 **Firstly, how long have you lived in this area?** (WITHIN FIVE MILES)

	%
Less than 1 year	5
1-2 years	8
3-5 years	16
6-10 years	18
11-20 years	20
Over 20 years/all my life	33
Don't know/can't remember	0

Q2 SHOWCARD A (R) **From this card, how much would you say you know about local councils and the services they provide?**

	%
A great deal	3
A fair amount	26
Not very much	59
Nothing at all	11
Don't know	0

Q3 SHOWCARD B (R) **Which of the statements on this card comes closest to your own view of the Councils in this area?**

		%
A)	I'm not interested in what the Council does, or whether they do their job	1
B)	I'm not interested in what the Council does, as long as they do their job	17
C)	I like to know what the Council is doing, but I'm happy to let them get on with their job	59
D)	I would like to have more of a say in what the Council does and the services it provides	19
E)	I already work for, or am involved with the Council and the services it provides	2
	Don't know	1

Q4 **From what you know, how many councils provide the main services in this neighbourhood?** (INTERVIEWER - NOT INCLUDING PARISH COUNCILS)

	%
One	24
Two	32
Three+	5
Don't know	39

In fact there are two main councils that provide, or are responsible for most services in this area: . . .district/borough/city and Norfolk County Council.

ROTATE ORDER OF Q5/6

☐ Q5 SHOWCARD C (R) **From this list, what services do you think are the responsibility of... district/borough/city council? Just read out the letter(s) that apply**

☐ Q6 SHOWCARD C AGAIN (R) **And which services on this list do you think are the responsibility of Norfolk County Council? Again, just read out the letters that apply.**

Q7 SHOWCARD D (R) **Which, if any, of these services do you or members of your family use?** INCLUDE ONLY LOCAL USE

		Q5 "District" %	Q6 County %	Q7 Use %
A	Bus Services	28	31	39
B	Car Parks	44	23	72
C	Council Housing	43	27	11
D	Council Tax Benefit/Housing benefit	34	31	16
E	Fire service	16	52	32
F	Food safety	18	28	15
G	Household waste sites/dumps	45	25	61
H	Libraries	20	50	60
I	Parks, playgrounds and open spaces	46	23	50
J	Planning service	38	33	13
K	Public conveniences	45	22	47
L	Recycling/bottle banks	44	19	54
M	Refuse collection	49	22	81
N	Road maintenance	26	50	41
O	Schools/education	14	56	41
P	Social services	17	50	14
Q	Street sweeping	47	18	35
R	Swimming pools/sports facilities	38	20	45
	Other	2	5	1
	None of these	0	0	1
	Don't know	25	25	2

Q8 SHOWCARD E (R) **As you may know, there is currently a review being undertaken by the Local Government Commission on the future local government structure in the county. How much, if anything, would you say you know about this?**

	%
A great deal	2
A fair amount	10
Just a little	37
Heard of but know nothing about	21
Never heard of	30

PREFERENCES

HAND OVER MAP SHOWING AREAS UNDER REVIEW AND "CURRENT SERVICES" CARD
The Local Government Commission is considering options for the future structure of local government in Norwich. Could you please read through this card, (SHOW OPTIONS CARD) **which outlines the options.**

Q9 **Please tell me which of the options, if either, you would prefer for Norwich?**
SINGLE CODE ONLY

For Norwich	%
Option A (Remain the same/status quo)	51
Option B (Single all purpose council)	22
Some other option	*
Neither of these	*
Either of these/don't mind	11
Don't care	2
Don't know	14

ASK IF "OTHER" NAMED AT Q9 (CODE 3)
Q10 **What other option is that?**
PROBE FULLY - DO NOT PROMPT.

....

....

....

....

ASK ALL PREFERRING AN OPTION (1, 2 OR 3 AT Q9). OTHERS GO TO Q13
Q11 SHOWCARD F (R) **You say that the option you would prefer is . . . . .** (INSERT OPTION PREFERRED). **How strongly would you say you feel about this?**

	%
Very strongly	15
Fairly strongly	43
Not very strongly	28
Not at all strongly	4
Don't know	9

Q12 **What do you think would be the main advantages of . . .**(OPTION PREFERRED)
PROBE FULLY FOR DETAILS

....

....

....

....

....

Nothing...
Don't know/can't think of anything..................................

ATTITUDES TO PROPOSALS

SHOWCARD G (R) **Imagine that there was one council in Norwich providing <u>all</u> services. I am going to read out some statements that people have made about this proposal. To what extent do you agree or disagree that . . . .?** READ OUT, ROTATE ORDER OF ASKING Q13-22. TICK START

READ OUT:		Strongly agree %	Tend to agree %	Neither/ Nor %	Tend to disagree %	Strongly disagree %	Don't know %
☐ Q13	**It would cost more overall**	11	36	9	19	3	22
Q14	**It would be more in touch with local people's needs**	4	25	11	30	9	21
Q15	**The single Council would be more efficient than the current system of two Councils**	3	25	12	29	7	24
☐ Q16	**The single council would not be big enough to manage services such as Education and Social Services effectively**	7	28	14	25	3	24
Q17	**It would better reflect the sense of community in Norwich**	3	27	19	20	6	26
Q18	**We need a County Council to represent us nationally**	13	46	15	12	2	13
☐ Q19	**Services would suffer if the County Council no longer provides services in Norwich**	8	32	13	19	2	25
Q20	**It won't affect me whether there is a single Council in Norwich or not**	12	34	15	22	8	10
Q21	**The change to a single Council for Norwich would be too disruptive**	10	34	14	21	2	19
☐ Q22	**With a single Council it would be clearer who is responsible for local services**	7	41	12	15	4	21
ASK LAST Q23	**I would like to have more information on the proposals before making up my mind**	14	37	18	14	12	6

Q24 **On balance, which would you say is more in touch with local people and issues, ...** (ROTATE ORDER OF "DISTRICT" AND COUNTY) (INSERT NAME OF "DISTRICT COUNCIL)**..district/borough/city council, or Norfolk County Council, or would you say that they are both about the same?**

	%
District/borough/city council	51
Norfolk County Council	8
Both about the same	21
Don't know	20

REFER BACK TO Q8. ASK ALL WHO HAVE HEARD OF REVIEW AT Q8 (IE CODES 1/2/3/4). OTHERS TO Q28

Q25 SHOWCARD H **Earlier in the interview, you said that you had heard of the Review of local government structure. From which, if any, of the sources shown on this card have you recently heard about the Review?** INTERVIEWER NOTE: "RECENTLY" = IN PAST 3 MONTHS

		%
A	Leaflet from County Council delivered to your door	32
B	Leaflet from County Council in library/ offices, etc	5
C	Advertisement from County Council in local newspaper	17
D	Advertisement from County Council on local radio/TV	3
E	Leaflet from Borough Council delivered to your door	15
F	Leaflet from Borough Council in library/ offices, etc	3
G	Borough Council newspaper	13
H	County Council newspaper	11
I	Advertisement from Borough Council in local newspaper	6
J	Advertisement from Borough Council on local radio/TV	2
K	Advertisement by the Commission on local radio	2
L	Local Government Commission advertisement in local newspaper	4
M	Local newspaper	44
N	National newspaper	5
O	TV	19
P	Local radio	18
Q	National radio	2
R	Friends/neighbours/family	10
S	Conversation with Borough Councillor	3
T	Conversation with County Councillor	1
U	Conversation with Borough Council staff	3
V	Conversation with County Council staff	1
W	Parish/community council	4
X	Residents' Association	1
	Other	5
	None of these	12
	Don't know	3

ASK ALL NAMING A SOURCE AT Q25. OTHERS GO TO Q28

Q26 **Would you say that the information you have received has influenced your opinion, or not?**

	%
Yes	20
No	74
Don't know	6

Q27 **What information in particular has influenced your opinion?**

....

....

....

....

ASK ALL

Q28 SHOWCARD I (R) **Assuming you receive the same level of services, how important is it to you, if at all, what the final decision is on the future local government structure in Norwich?**

	%
Very important	12
Fairly important	27
Not very important	34
Not at all important	19
Don't know	8

ACTIVISM

Q29 SHOWCARD J **Which of the things on this list, if any, have you done in the last three years? Just read out the letter(s) that apply.**

		%
A	Voted in Local Council elections	72
B	Spoken or written to a local Councillor	29
C	Responded to the earlier Review of local government	13
D	Been to a meeting of a local committee or organisation (WRITE IN NAME OF ORGANISATION)	17
E	Spoken on a radio phone-in about a local issue	2
F	Written to a local newspaper about a local issue	3
G	Been to a meeting of a local branch of a political party	2
H	Written to your MP about a local issue	8
I	Been to a Council Committee meeting	3
J	Been to a Council meeting	3
K	Attended a public meeting run by the Council	7
	None of these	23
	Don't know/refused	2

Q30 SHOWCARD K **Which, if any, of these apply to you? Just read out the letter(s) that apply.**

	I am a member of a:	%
A	Residents' Association	2
B	Community Association	2
C	Tenants' Association	1
D	Neighbourhood Watch	20
E	PTA/school governors	5
	I do unpaid work for:	
F	A school	7
G	Citizens Advice Bureau	1
H	Volunteer Bureau	1
I	Scouts/Guides/Cubs/Brownies	3
J	Church group	8
	Other	4
	None of these	64
	Don't know	2

THANK RESPONDENT. GO TO DEMOGRAPHICS.

Length of interview [|] minutes

MORI/9101/08
(1-6)

NORFOLK
REVIEW - NORWICH
TOPLINE RESULTS

Serial No ....
OUO (7-10)

N = 324
9 - 31 October 1995
Main sample data only
Base: All, unless stated

Gender %

	%
Male	48
Female	52

Age %

	%
18-24	15
25-34	21
35-44	14
45-54	16
55-64	14
65-74	13
75+	8

WRITE IN AGE [ ][ ]

Work Status

	%
Full-time (30 hrs/wk+)	43
Part-time (8-29 hrs/wk)	10
Not working (under 8 hrs)	1
Looking after home/children	9
Retired	23
Registered unemployed	6
Unemployed but not registered	1
Student	4
Other	2

Occupation of Chief Income Earner (CIE)
Position/rank/grade

....

Industry/type of company

....

Qualifications/degrees/apprenticeship

....

No of Staff Responsible for

....

PROBE FOR PENSION

	%
AB	11
C1	29
C2	22
D	21
E	18

Number in Household
Adults aged 18+ (inc. respondent)

1	2	3	4	5+	
26	58	12	3	1	%

Children (17 or under)

0	1	2	3	4+	
70	12	11	6	2	%

QA **Are you or other members of your household employed by a council?** IF YES: **Is this a Borough/District Council or a County Council?** CODE FOR BOTH RESPONDENT AND OTHER HOUSEHOLD MEMBERS

	Respondent %	Other %
Yes:		
Borough/District	3	4
County	4	3
Don't know which	0	0
No	93	75
Don't know	*	18

Tenure

	%
Owned outright	16
Buying on mortgage	31
Rented from Council	37
Rented from Housing Association	4
Rented from private landlord	10
Other	2

QB **Is this your main permanent home, or is it a second or holiday home?**

	%
Main/permanent	97
Second/holiday	2

Car in Household
CIRCLE NUMBER

0	1	2	3+	
31	49	17	2	%

INTERVIEWER DECLARATION: I confirm that I have conducted this interview face-to-face with the above named person and that I have asked all the relevant questions fully and recorded the answers in conformance with the survey specification and the MRS Code of Conduct.

Interviewer Name .... Signature ....

Interviewer Number				/	

	Month		Date		
DATE OF INTERVIEW					
	(29)	(30)		(30)	(32)

NB INTERVIEWER: ALL SHOWCARDS HAVE BEEN REVERSED. PLEASE BE CAREFUL TO CODE THE CORRECT RESPONSE.

Good morning/afternoon/evening. I'm from MORI, the market research and polling organisation. We are doing a survey about local issues, and I would like to ask you a few questions.

ASK ALL

Q1 **Firstly, how long have you lived in this area?** (WITHIN FIVE MILES)

	%
Less than 1 year	7
1-2 years	7
3-5 years	9
6-10 years	15
11-20 years	22
Over 20 years/all my life	40
Don't know/can't remember	1

Q2 SHOWCARD A (R) **From this card, how much would you say you know about local councils and the services they provide?**

	%
A great deal	2
A fair amount	36
Not very much	53
Nothing at all	8
Don't know	1

Q3 SHOWCARD B (R) **Which of the statements on this card comes closest to your own view of the Councils in this area?**

		%
A)	I'm not interested in what the Council does, or whether they do their job	1
B)	I'm not interested in what the Council does, as long as they do their job	15
C)	I like to know what the Council is doing, but I'm happy to let them get on with their job	59
D)	I would like to have more of a say in what the Council does and the services it provides	20
E)	I already work for, or am involved with the Council and the services it provides	5
	Don't know	1

Q4 **From what you know, how many councils provide the main services in this neighbourhood?** (INTERVIEWER - NOT INCLUDING PARISH COUNCILS)

	%
One	33
Two	34
Three+	3
Don't know	29

In fact there are two main councils that provide, or are responsible for most services in this area: Norwich City Council and Norfolk County Council.

ROTATE ORDER OF Q5/6

☐ Q5 SHOWCARD C (R) **From this list, what services do you think are the responsibility of Norwich City Council? Just read out the letter(s) that apply**

☐ Q6 SHOWCARD C AGAIN (R) **And which services on this list do you think are the responsibility of Norfolk County Council? Again, just read out the letters that apply.**

Q7 SHOWCARD D (R) **Which, if any, of these services do you or members of your family use?** INCLUDE ONLY LOCAL USE

		Q5 Norwich %	Q6 Norfolk %	Q7 Use %
A	Bus Services	44	29	55
B	Car Parks	64	14	57
C	Council Housing	78	14	35
D	Council Tax Benefit/Housing benefit	69	16	27
E	Fire service	33	46	27
F	Food safety	34	30	16
G	Household waste sites/dumps	61	22	56
H	Libraries	43	41	57
I	Parks, playgrounds and open spaces	67	20	62
J	Planning service	49	32	9
K	Public conveniences	66	12	42
L	Recycling/bottle banks	55	17	49
M	Refuse collection	73	16	82
N	Road maintenance	37	50	31
O	Schools/education	32	54	35
P	Social services	35	44	13
Q	Street sweeping	73	13	32
R	Swimming pools/sports facilities	67	20	47
	Other	1	1	1
	None of these	0	2	*
	Don't know	8	19	4

Q8 SHOWCARD E (R) **As you may know, there is currently a review being undertaken by the Local Government Commission on the future local government structure in the county. How much, if anything, would you say you know about this?**

	%
A great deal	1
A fair amount	13
Just a little	33
Heard of but know nothing about	26
Never heard of	27

PREFERENCES

HAND OVER MAP SHOWING AREAS UNDER REVIEW AND "CURRENT SERVICES" CARD
The Local Government Commission is considering options for the future structure of local government in Norwich. Could you please read through this card, (SHOW OPTIONS CARD) **which outlines the options.**

Q9 **Please tell me which of the options, if either, you would prefer for Norwich?**
SINGLE CODE ONLY

	%
For Norwich	
Option A (Remain the same/status quo)	45
Option B (Single all purpose council)	43
Some other option	1
Neither of these	*
Either of these/don't mind	3
Don't care	2
Don't know	5

ASK IF "OTHER" NAMED AT Q9 (CODE 3)
Q10 **What other option is that?**
PROBE FULLY - DO NOT PROMPT.

....

....

....

....

ASK ALL PREFERRING AN OPTION (1, 2 OR 3 AT Q9). OTHERS GO TO Q13
Q11 SHOWCARD F (R) **You say that the option you would prefer is . . . . .** (INSERT OPTION PREFERRED). **How strongly would you say you feel about this?**

	%
Very strongly	12
Fairly strongly	52
Not very strongly	29
Not at all strongly	6
Don't know	1

Q12 **What do you think would be the main advantages of . . .**(OPTION PREFERRED)
PROBE FULLY FOR DETAILS

....

....

....

....

....

Nothing..
Don't know/can't think of anything..

ATTITUDES TO PROPOSALS

SHOWCARD G (R) **Imagine that there was one council in Norwich providing <u>all</u> services. I am going to read out some statements that people have made about this proposal. To what extent do you agree or disagree that . . . .?** READ OUT, ROTATE ORDER OF ASKING Q13-22. TICK START

READ OUT:

		Strongly agree %	Tend to agree %	Neither/ Nor %	Tend to disagree %	Strongly disagree %	Don't know %
☐ Q13	**It would cost more overall**	8	25	16	29	6	15
Q14	**It would be more in touch with local people's needs**	20	39	15	16	5	6
Q15	**The single Council would be more efficient than the current system of two Councils**	15	40	14	18	4	8
☐ Q16	**The single council would not be big enough to manage services such as Education and Social Services effectively**	5	30	10	33	9	13
Q17	**It would better reflect the sense of community in Norwich**	13	43	14	23	2	5
Q18	**We need a County Council to represent us nationally**	10	43	17	19	5	7
☐ Q19	**Services would suffer if the County Council no longer provides services in Norwich**	7	28	13	35	7	10
Q20	**It won't affect me whether there is a single Council in Norwich or not**	2	32	14	36	11	6
Q21	**The change to a single Council for Norwich would be too disruptive**	8	31	12	36	6	8
☐ Q22	**With a single Council it would be clearer who is responsible for local services**	29	48	7	9	1	5
ASK LAST Q23	**I would like to have more information on the proposals before making up my mind**	17	42	12	17	4	8

Q24 **On balance, which would you say is more in touch with local people and issues, ...** (ROTATE ORDER OF "DISTRICT" AND COUNTY)
Norwich City Council, or
Norfolk County Council, or would you say that they are both about the same?

	%
Norwich City Council	50
Norfolk County Council	4
Both about the same	38
Don't know	8

REFER BACK TO Q8. ASK ALL WHO HAVE HEARD OF REVIEW AT Q8 (IE CODES 1/2/3/4). OTHERS TO Q28

Q25 SHOWCARD H **Earlier in the interview, you said that you had heard of the Review of local government structure. From which, if any, of the sources shown on this card have you recently heard about the Review?** INTERVIEWER NOTE: "RECENTLY" = IN PAST 3 MONTHS

		%
A	Leaflet from County Council delivered to your door	25
B	Leaflet from County Council in library/ offices, etc	7
C	Advertisement from County Council in local newspaper	13
D	Advertisement from County Council on local radio/TV	3
E	Leaflet from City Council delivered to your door	50
F	Leaflet from City Council in library/ offices, etc	7
G	City Council newspaper	21
H	County Council newspaper	5
I	Advertisement from City Council in local newspaper	11
J	Advertisement from City Council on local radio/TV	1
K	Advertisement by the Commission on local radio	2
L	Local Government Commission advertisement in local newspaper	6
M	Local newspaper	52
N	National newspaper	7
O	TV	23
P	Local radio	22
Q	National radio	4
R	Friends/neighbours/family	11
S	Conversation with City Councillor	3
T	Conversation with County Councillor	1
U	Conversation with City Council staff	3
V	Conversation with County Council staff	4
W	Parish/community council	1
X	Residents' Association	0
	Other	5
	None of these	2
	Don't know	4

ASK ALL NAMING A SOURCE AT Q25. OTHERS GO TO Q28

Q26 **Would you say that the information you have received has influenced your opinion, or not?**

	%
Yes	22
No	75
Don't know	4

Q27 **What information in particular has influenced your opinion?**

....

....

....

....

ASK ALL

Q28 SHOWCARD I (R) **Assuming you receive the same level of services, how important is it to you, if at all, what the final decision is on the future local government structure in Norwich?**

	%
Very important	19
Fairly important	43
Not very important	24
Not at all important	12
Don't know	2

ACTIVISM

Q29 SHOWCARD J **Which of the things on this list, if any, have you done in the last three years? Just read out the letter(s) that apply.**

		%
A	Voted in Local Council elections	72
B	Spoken or written to a local Councillor	21
C	Responded to the earlier Review of local government	10
D	Been to a meeting of a local committee or organisation (WRITE IN NAME OF ORGANISATION)	8
E	Spoken on a radio phone-in about a local issue	1
F	Written to a local newspaper about a local issue	4
G	Been to a meeting of a local branch of a political party	5
H	Written to your MP about a local issue	9
I	Been to a Council Committee meeting	1
J	Been to a Council meeting	2
K	Attended a public meeting run by the Council	5
	None of these	25
	Don't know/refused	1

Q30 SHOWCARD K **Which, if any, of these apply to you? Just read out the letter(s) that apply.**

		%
	I am a member of a:	
A	Residents' Association	9
B	Community Association	*
C	Tenants' Association	2
D	Neighbourhood Watch	6
E	PTA/school governors	2
	I do unpaid work for:	
F	A school	4
G	Citizens Advice Bureau	0
H	Volunteer Bureau	1
I	Scouts/Guides/Cubs/Brownies	2
J	Church group	5
	Other	4
	None of these	72
	Don't know	1

THANK RESPONDENT. GO TO DEMOGRAPHICS.

Length of interview [|] minutes

CHAPTER 11

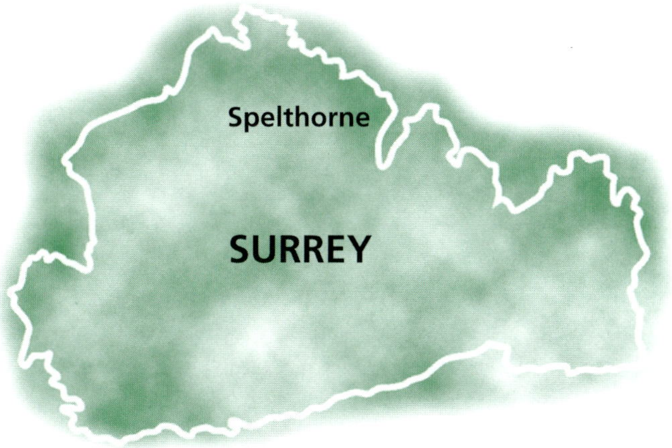

SPELTHORNE IN THE COUNTY OF SURREY

Draft Recommendations

11.1 The Commission's report *Draft Recommendations on the Future Local Government of Spelthorne in the County of Surrey* summarised the evidence taken into account by the Commission in reaching its draft recommendation.

Figure 11.1
Draft Recommendation for Spelthorne in the County of Surrey

Structure
- There should be no change to the existing two-tier structure of local government in Spelthorne.

Boundary Issues

11.2 The Commission also consulted, at draft recommendation stage, on four minor boundary and consequential electoral changes between the areas of Spelthorne and Runnymede Borough Councils which would bring the boundary in line with the River Thames. Full details are contained in Volume 1.

Views Expressed to the Commission

11.3 The Commission received a wide range of direct representations on its draft recommendations, from local authorities, residents, Members of Parliament, business and voluntary groups, parish and town councils, and from other public and private sector organisations. Over 1,500 representations were received from individuals and organisations, including over 1,300 from respondents within Spelthorne. The Commission also received a small number of representations in the form of standard letters, response slips and petitions. (Figures 11.2 and 11.3). Figures 11.2 and 11.3 exclude representations from the local authorities; these are summarised separately (Figure 11.4).

Figure 11.2
Views of Respondents Within Spelthorne

Preferred structure	Individuals	Organisations	Standard letters and petition signatures
Unitary Spelthorne	917	22	15
No change	384	13	0
Other	4	0	0
No preference	27	2	0

Source: Local Government Commission for England and NOP

Figure 11.3
Views of Respondents From Outside The Review District

Preferred structure	Individuals	Organisations	Standard letters and petition signatures
Unitary Spelthorne	30	1	0
No change	43	35	0
Other	2	0	0
No preference	14	0	0

Source: Local Government Commission for England and NOP
Note: Excludes out of county representations

11.4 In addition, 62 representations were received from outside the county, of which 34 supported a unitary Spelthorne and 24 supported no change, with the remainder favouring another option or not expressing a preference. A more detailed tabulation of the written representations from individuals and interest groups, produced by NOP on behalf of the Commission, can be found towards the end of this Chapter.

11.5 Just over 20 representations were received in response to the proposals for boundary changes between Spelthorne and Runnymede. The views expressed were evenly balanced.

The Views of Local Authorities

11.6 The Commission received submissions from all of the 12 principal local authorities in Surrey during Stage Three (Figure 11.4).

11.7 Spelthorne Borough Council and Surrey County Council maintained their positions throughout the present review. A majority of the other Surrey district councils maintained their support for a unitary Spelthorne. Four district councils, who had not expressed a preference during the initial stage of the review, wrote during Stage Three: Elmbridge, Mole Valley and Waverley accepted the Commission's draft recommendation for no change, while Woking pointed to the need to reflect the views of local residents. The Surrey District Councils' Association remained supportive of a Spelthorne unitary authority. The Association of County Councils favoured the retention of the two-tier structure.

11.8 The London Boroughs of Hillingdon and Hounslow both submitted representations in favour of a unitary authority for Spelthorne. Hillingdon highlighted its common interests and concerns with Spelthorne, with which it shares a substantial land border. The two areas, having formed part of the former County of Middlesex, also have a shared history, culture and heritage. Hillingdon noted that Spelthorne co-operated with both it and Hounslow on several areas of importance, such as Heathrow Airport and "...the development of the strategic and integrated transport plan for West London and its hinterland". Hounslow's support for a unitary Spelthorne was based on the proposition that it would "...bring local government in the area closer to the people who receive its services, and will give a much more consistent pattern of local government arrangements across this outer London fringe".

Figure 11.4
Preferences of Surrey Local Authorities at Stage Three

Authority	Preference
Elmbridge Borough Council	Retention of the two-tier structure.
Epsom & Ewell Borough Council	Unitary Spelthorne.
Guildford Borough Council	Unitary Spelthorne.
Mole Valley District Council	Content with no change.
Reigate & Banstead Borough Council	Unitary Spelthorne.
Runnymede Borough Council	A majority of members supported a unitary Spelthorne. All political groups on the Council saw no difficulty in the "...tidying up of the various boundary anomalies".
Spelthorne Borough Council	Unitary Spelthorne; continued support for minor boundary changes with Runnymede borough.
Surrey Heath Borough Council	Unitary Spelthorne.
Tandridge District Council	Unitary Spelthorne.
Waverley Borough Council	The Council accepted the draft recommendation for no change. It requested that the Commission "...endorse the need for legislative change to ensure that lasting improvements to the present structure of local government in Surrey can be achieved".
Woking Borough Council	Asked that the final recommendations be framed "...on the basis of the views of the local people and organisations in Spelthorne, recognising that there is no reason...why the benefits of unitary local government could not be achieved".
Surrey County Council	Retention and continuing improvement to the two-tier structure.

Source: Local authorities' submissions

The Views of Others

11.9 A range of other interest groups made representations on the Commission's draft recommendations as summarised in the following paragraphs. These are in addition to those made in Stage One.

Businesses and Business Groups

11.10 Representations from business interests, both individual firms and the organisations that represent them, reflected considerable support for Spelthorne's case. This included the Spelthorne Chamber of Commerce, representing over 400 businesses in the area, which considered that "...a unitary council would be better able...to promote a local 'focus' and point of contact for businesses...ensuring policies were developed to maximise the economic potential of Spelthorne, rather than having to take a more balanced and diluted 'across the county' view". The Surrey Business Enterprise, a county-wide group which provides advice to people looking to establish their own businesses, commented: "It is clear from our experience that the nature and needs of the business community in Spelthorne is unique relative to the rest of Surrey". The Ashford Chamber of Commerce also supported a unitary Spelthorne, although the Haslemere Chamber of Trade preferred no change.

11.11 Significant local business interests such as Shepperton Studios, Heathrow Airport Limited (HAL) and British Airways all wrote in support of a unitary Spelthorne, the latter two organisations disagreeing with the view that the County Council was a more substantial advocate for local people on strategic issues such as Heathrow. HAL commented: "Apart from a major proposal such as Terminal 5, Surrey has very little contact or involvement with the running, development or operation of the Airport and therefore gains little experience of the issues involved". It added that Spelthorne was "...more likely to achieve a well reasoned conclusion...given the benefit of a more in-depth knowledge of the subject". Support for a unitary Spelthorne was also given by Middlesex Radio Limited.

11.12 Some concerns were expressed on behalf of groups in the rest of the county, where the focus was on worries over increased costs for other districts or possible implications for county council services. The West Thames Branch of the Institute of Directors, with some 1,700 members in the area, referred to "...the current satisfactory working relationships with, and the provision of services by, the two-tier structure". In relation to strategic issues, the Sand and Gravel Association Limited felt that the two-tier structure "...allows a strategic perspective to be maintained which is vital in the execution of many local government services, in particular mineral and waste planning".

County, Regional and National Interests (including the Voluntary Sector)

11.13 Most county-wide and national interests were concerned about the prospect of reorganisation, in particular with regard to the costs and the strategic role of the County Council. The Surrey Branch of UNISON commented that Spelthorne in its submission had shown little understanding of some county-wide services , "...nor is there any real acknowledgement of the specialist expertise provided by our members where such expertise is thinly spread but economically used and not readily provided in any one, relatively small, local authority". Other professional groups such as the Royal Town Planning Institute, the Town and Country Planning Association and the South East Counties Trading Standards Officers' Group were also concerned about the strategic role of the County Council, particularly in planning and other specialist services. Other organisations supporting no change were also concerned about specific services, such as the Museums and Galleries Commission, the Library Association and the Surrey County Council Playing Fields Association.

11.14 The Surrey Branch of the British Red Cross Society was concerned at an increase in the workload of various organisations such as its own in having to deal with two authorities rather than just Surrey County Council. It also felt that "...the people of Spelthorne would be isolated from the rest of the county".

11.15 The Spelthorne Victims Support Scheme felt that the support, both financial and physical given by Spelthorne to the Scheme, and many other voluntary agencies in the borough "...is second to none and is indicative of their dedication to the community". Along with other groups, the Scheme felt that a unitary authority would be able "...to promote a local 'focus' and point of contact for both business and voluntary services".

Education Groups

11.16 Teachers' representative groups in the county were opposed to any change in structure, with the Surrey Division of the National Union of Teachers and the Teachers' Panel both commenting: "We have consistently opposed any reorganisation that would lead to the break-up of Surrey County Council as the Local Education Authority for the area and have expressed our grave concerns for the future of education if a larger number of smaller unitary authorities were to be established". There was also support for no change in separate submissions from the Surrey Federation of the Professional Association of Teachers and the Surrey Branch of the Association of Teachers and Lecturers.

Health Interests

11.17 The West Surrey Health Commission (with caveats concerning development of social care policies) and the Hounslow and Spelthorne NHS Trust both favoured a unitary outcome. The Health Commission reflected that the Health Authorities which had preceded it had, during the county-wide review, strongly supported the concept of unitary authorities which would bring together responsibilities for social care, housing and joint planning, all "...key to the development and success of Care in the Community...Spelthorne's track record in contributing positively to health and social care provision is impressive and puts it in a good position to exploit the benefits of unitary status". The Chief Inspector, Social Services Inspectorate (Department of Health) supported no change so as to "...avoid disruption of existing services".

Law, Order and Emergency Services

11.18 The Assistant Commissioner of the Metropolitan Police at the South West Headquarters in Kingston-upon-Thames wrote in support of a unitary Spelthorne. HM Fire Service Inspectorate expressed concerns about transitional costs, adding: "Fire authorities do not stand to benefit from any long-term savings from the reorganisation process".

Local Groups

11.19 A variety of local groups made representations in support of a unitary Spelthorne, including the Stanwell Village Hall Council, and the Parkland Neighbourhood Society. A number of Middlesex-related groups including the Middlesex Geographical Society, the Middlesex Young Peoples' Club, the Friends of the County of Middlesex, the County of Middlesex Trust, the Federation of Middlesex Sports - also argued for a unitary Spelthorne as well as, in some cases, for a return to historic Middlesex.

11.20 Some concerns were expressed locally, however, at the prospect of change. The Shepperton Residents' Association felt that no change was necessary as the majority of people during the county-wide review, both in Spelthorne and Surrey as a whole, had expressed a wish for no change. Concerns were also expressed about costs and possible effects to county council services. Support for no change was also shared by the Staines Town Society and the Kempton Residents' Association.

Parliamentary Interests

11.21 The local Member of Parliament, Mr David Wilshire, supported a unitary authority and sent the Commission over 1,100 representations which he had received, mainly from constituents, including completed response slips from his newsletter which was delivered to households in the district. The great majority of these responses were in support of his own views. Mr John Stevens, MEP for the Thames Valley, also wrote in support of a unitary Spelthorne. The only other Surrey Member of Parliament to make formal comments during Stage Three was Mr Kenneth Baker, MP for Mole Valley, who was opposed to any change to the current structure in the county.

Parish and Town Councils

11.22 There are no parishes in Spelthorne, but seven parish councils from elsewhere in Surrey made representations to the Commission: all supported no change.

NOP Tabulations of Written Representations

1 The following tabulations summarise the views expressed by members of the public and other interested parties during the consultation on the Local Government Commission's draft recommendations for Spelthorne.

2 The tabulations include only letters sent directly to NOP at its Chelmsford offices and to the Commission's offices in London. Where more than one person's view has been expressed in a letter, the comments from each individual have been recorded separately. Staff from the Commission and NOP have worked closely in ensuring that care has been taken in the interpretation of comments, and that a consistent approach has been adopted.

3 While many people expressed support for one or other of the draft options presented by the Commission, other responses were coded by NOP after further discussion. The pattern of views expressed has been carefully examined, and where a number of respondents supported an option not included in those put forward by the Commission, those views have been separately coded and reported by NOP.

4 The Commission has advertised through the local media, encouraging people to make their views known. All responses received up to two days after the end of the Stage Three consultation period have been included. Returns from campaigns organised by local authorities or other groups (for example, standardised postcards and letters, questionnaires and petitions) have not been included in the tabulations. These, and submissions written and dated before the commencement of the consultation process, have been considered separately by the Commission.

The following definitions have been applied by NOP in compiling the tabulations:

(i) Type of Respondent

Individuals:	includes individual members of the public, local councillors and Members of the Westminster and European Parliaments.
Businesses and Business Groups:	includes organisations which represent businesses, such as local Chambers of Commerce.
County, Regional and National Interests:	any organisation which covers an area which is the size of a county or larger is included here, for example, a county-wide voluntary organisation or a regional association. This classification includes most of the statutory consultees.
Education (and Church) Groups:	this group includes schools, religious organisations and teaching unions.
Local Groups:	this includes organisations smaller than a county area, for example, a district-level voluntary sector body. The group could be voluntary, sporting, political or cultural but does not include organisations from the education or religious sectors (included above). It also includes constituency parties and political groups on local authorities.
Parish and Town Councils:	this also includes district-level associations of town and parish councils. County level associations are classified as County, Regional and National interests.

(ii) Structural Options (Reports A and D)

No change in own district:	this code is used where there is more than one review district in the county. It indicates where respondents from a review district have expressed support for no change for that district and have not made reference to the other review district(s) in that county.
District/county-level authorities:	represents support for either a district or county-level authority although it is not clear whether this is for a unitary or a two-tier structure.
Opposition to structural preferences:	represents responses where a negative, but unspecified, structural preference has been expressed.
Rejects:	rejects are those responses with unclear comments/interpretation.

(iii) Other

Other issues (Report B):	these illustrate preferences in relation to boundary and electoral changes and (where applicable) the restoration of historic counties.
Parishing issues (Report C):	these illustrate preferences in relation to parishing issues, for example, the creation of new parishes or the enhancement of the role of parish and town councils.
Services (Report E):	these illustrate concerns expressed about the impact of proposed changes on particular service areas where the respondent has not additionally expressed a positive structural preference.

NOP Analysis of Responses to Local Government Commission Draft Recommendations - SURREY

Report A: Opinions on the structural options, by authority of respondent
Base: all

	Review district	Other districts in county												
	Spelthorne	Elmbridge	Epsom & Ewell	Guild -ford	Mole Valley	Reigate & Banstead	Runny -mede	Surrey Heath	Tandridge	Waverley	Woking	Rest of county total	County total	Out of county
Status quo/two-tier	397 *29%*	8 *47%*	12 *92%*	5 *71%*	17 *94%*	11 *92%*	10 *30%*	1 *33%*	3 *100%*	5 *83%*	6 *46%*	78 *62%*	475 *32%*	24 *39%*
Unitary Spelthorne	939 *69%*	9 *53%*	1 *8%*	2 *29%*	- -	- -	9 *27%*	2 *67%*	- -	1 *17%*	7 *54%*	31 *25%*	970 *65%*	34 *55%*
County-level authority (either two-tier or unitary)	4 *	- -	- -	- -	- -	- -	- -	- -	- -	- -	- -	- -	4 *	- -
District-level authority (either two-tier or unitary)	- -	- -	- -	- -	1 *6%*	- -	- -	- -	- -	- -	- -	1 *1%*	1 *	- -
Other specified	- -	- -	- -	- -	- -	1 *8%*	- -	- -	- -	- -	- -	1 *1%*	1 *	- -
No preference expressed/option defined	29 *2%*	- -	- -	- -	- -	- -	14 *42%*	- -	- -	- -	- -	14 *11%*	43 *3%*	4 *6%*
BASE TOTAL	1369	17	13	7	18	12	33	3	3	6	13	125	1494	62

**Less than* ½%

NOP Analysis of Responses to Local Government Commission Draft Recommendations - SURREY

Report B: Opinions on other issues, by authority of respondent
Base: all

	Review district	Other districts in county												
	Spelthorne	Elmbridge	Epsom & Ewell	Guild -ford	Mole Valley	Reigate & Banstead	Runny -mede	Surrey Heath	Tandridge	Waverley	Woking	Rest of county total	County total	Out of county
Return to Middlesex	12 *1%*	- -	- -	- -	- -	- -	- -	- -	- -	- -	- -	- -	12 *1%*	- -
Support for changes to Runnymede/Spelthorne boundary	8 *1%*	1 *6%*	- -	- -	- -	- -	1 *3%*	- -	- -	- -	- -	2 *2%*	10 *1%*	2 *3%*
Opposition to changes to Runnymede/Spelthorne boundary	1 *	- -	- -	- -	- -	- -	10 *30%*	- -	- -	- -	- -	10 *8%*	11 *1%*	- -
Other specified	2 *	- -	- -	- -	- -	- -	2 *6%*	- -	- -	- -	- -	2 *2%*	4 *	- -
BASE TOTAL	1369	17	13	7	18	12	33	3	3	6	13	125	1494	62

The figures in the table above do not sum to the base total/100% because undefined fields are not included, except as part of the base total.
**Less than* ½%

NOP Analysis of Responses to Local Government Commission Draft Recommendations - SURREY

Report C: Opinions on parishing issues, by authority of respondent
Base: all

	Review district	Other districts in county												
	Spelthorne	Elmbridge	Epsom & Ewell	Guild -ford	Mole Valley	Reigate & Banstead	Runny -mede	Surrey Heath	Tandridge	Waverley	Woking	Rest of county total	County total	Out of county
BASE TOTAL	1369	17	13	7	18	12	33	3	3	6	13	125	1494	62

The figures in the table above do not sum to the base total/100% because undefined fields are not included, except as part of the base total.

NOP Analysis of Responses to Local Government Commission Draft Recommendations - SURREY

Report D1: Opinions on the structural options, by respondent type (all respondents)
Base: all

	Respondent Type					
	Indiv-iduals	Business groups	County, regional & national interests	Education (& church) groups	Local groups	Parish and town councils
Status quo/two-tier	434 *30%*	3 *13%*	18 *56%*	10 *71%*	27 *79%*	7 *100%*
Unitary Spelthorne	964 *67%*	21 *88%*	10 *31%*	4 *29%*	5 *15%*	- -
County-level authority (either two-tier or unitary)	4 *	- -	- -	- -	- -	- -
District-level authority (either two-tier or unitary)	1 *	- -	- -	- -	- -	- -
Other specified	1 *	- -	- -	- -	- -	- -
No preference expressed/option defined	41 *3%*	- -	4 *13%*	- -	2 *6%*	- -
BASE TOTAL	1445	24	32	14	34	7

* *Less than ½%*

NOP Analysis of Responses to Local Government Commission Draft Recommendations - SURREY

Report D2: Opinions on the structural options, by respondent type
Base : respondents in Spelthorne only

	Respondent Type					
	Indiv-iduals	Business groups	County, regional & national interests	Education (& church) groups	Local groups	Parish and town councils
Status quo/two-tier	384 *29%*	- -	1 *25%*	6 *60%*	6 *50%*	- -
Unitary Spelthorne	917 *69%*	11 *100%*	3 *75%*	4 *40%*	4 *33%*	- -
County-level authority (either two-tier or unitary)	4 *	- -	- -	- -	- -	- -
No preference expressed/option defined	27 *2%*	- -	- -	- -	2 *17%*	- -
BASE TOTAL	1332	11	4	10	12	-

* *Less than ½%*

NOP Analysis of Responses to Local Government Commission Draft Recommendations - SURREY

Report D3: Opinions on the structural options, by respondent type
Base : respondents in rest of county only

	Respondent Type					
	Indiv-iduals	Business groups	County, regional & national interests	Education (& church) groups	Local groups	Parish and town councils
Status quo/two-tier	43 *48%*	1 *50%*	6 *100%*	2 *100%*	19 *100%*	7 *100%*
Unitary Spelthorne	30 *34%*	1 *50%*	- -	- -	- -	- -
District-level authority (either two-tier or unitary)	1 *1%*	- -	- -	- -	- -	- -
Other specified	1 *1%*	- -	- -	- -	- -	- -
No preference expressed/option defined	14 *16%*	- -	- -	- -	- -	- -
BASE TOTAL	89	2	6	2	19	7

NOP Analysis of Responses to Local Government Commission Draft Recommendations - SURREY

Report E: Views on services, by authority of respondent
Base: all

	Review district	Other districts in county												
	Spelthorne	Elmbridge	Epsom & Ewell	Guild -ford	Mole Valley	Reigate & Banstead	Runny -mede	Surrey Heath	Tandridge	Waverley	Woking	Rest of county total	County total	Out of county
Archives	1 *	- -	- -	- -	- -	- -	- -	- -	- -	- -	- -	- -	1 *	1 *2%*
Education	1 *	- -	- -	- -	- -	- -	- -	- -	- -	- -	- -	- -	1 *	- -
Libraries	- -	- -	- -	- -	- -	- -	- -	- -	- -	- -	- -	- -	- -	1 *2%*
Other specified services (or multiples of)	2 *	- -	- -	- -	- -	- -	- -	- -	- -	- -	- -	- -	2 *	2 *3%*
BASE TOTAL	1369	17	13	7	18	12	33	3	3	6	13	125	1494	62

The figures in the table above do not sum to the base total/100% because undefined fields are not included, except as part of the base total.
* *Less than ½%*

NOP Analysis of Responses to Local Government Commission Draft Recommendations - SURREY

Report F: Views on services, by respondent type
Base: all

	Respondent Type					
	Indiv-iduals	Business groups	County, regional & national interests	Education (& church) groups	Local groups	Parish and town councils
Archives	1	-	1	-	-	-
	*	-	*3%*	-	-	-
Education	1	-	-	-	-	-
	*	-	-	-	-	-
Libraries	-	-	1	-	-	-
	-	-	*3%*	-	-	-
Other specified services (or multiples of)	1	-	2	-	1	-
	*	-	*6%*	-	*3%*	-
BASE TOTAL	1445	24	32	14	34	7

The figures in the table above do not sum to the base total/100% because undefined fields are not included, except as part of the base total.
* *Less than ½%*

NOP Analysis of Responses to Local Government Commission Draft Recommendations - SURREY

Report G: Type of respondent, by authority of respondent
Base: all

	Review district	Other districts in county												
	Spelthorne	Elmbridge	Epsom & Ewell	Guild -ford	Mole Valley	Reigate & Banstead	Runny -mede	Surrey Heath	Tandridge	Waverley	Woking	Rest of county total	County total	Out of county
Individuals	1332 *97%*	14 *82%*	7 *54%*	4 *57%*	8 *44%*	9 *75%*	32 *97%*	2 *67%*	2 *67%*	2 *33%*	9 *69%*	89 *71%*	1421 *95%*	24 *39%*
Business groups	11 *1%*	- -	- -	- -	- -	- -	- -	- -	- -	1 *17%*	1 *8%*	2 *2%*	13 *1%*	11 *18%*
County, regional and national interests	4 *	- -	1 *8%*	2 *29%*	3 *17%*	- -	- -	- -	- -	- -	- -	6 *5%*	10 *1%*	22 *35%*
Education (and church) groups	10 1%	- -	- -	- -	- -	1 8%	- -	- -	- -	1 17%	- -	2 2%	12 1%	2 3%
Local Groups	12 *1%*	3 *18%*	5 *38%*	1 *14%*	4 *22%*	1 *8%*	1 *3%*	1 *33%*	- -	- -	3 *23%*	19 *15%*	31 *2%*	3 *5%*
Parish and town councils	- -	- -	- -	- -	3 *17%*	1 *8%*	- -	- -	1 *33%*	2 *33%*	- -	7 *6%*	7 *	- -
BASE TOTAL	1369	17	13	7	18	12	33	3	3	6	13	125	1494	62

* *Less than ½%*

MORI Research Study for the Local Government Commission

Introduction

Background

1 This summary report highlights the key findings from a survey of public opinion conducted in the Borough of Spelthorne and across the County of Surrey on behalf of the Local Government Commission for England. A copy of each of the marked-up questionnaires is appended. The computer tabulations are contained in a separate volume, which is available from MORI (32 Old Queen Street, London SW1H 9HP. Telephone 0171-222 0232. Price £15)

2 The survey was designed in close consultation with the Commission, following extensive qualitative research and pilot testing. All sampling, interviewing and analysis have been carried out independently by MORI, within the guidelines of the profession laid out by the Market Research Society.

3 In Spelthorne, all Census Enumeration Districts (EDs) were sorted by ward, and stratified according to social class. EDs were then sampled (32 in total) in proportion to the population size of each, and quotas set for sex, age and work status. A total of 324 interviews with adults aged 18+, conducted face-to-face and in-home, were carried out between 6 and 29 October 1995. Data were weighted to match the population profile in the Borough.

4 In the remaining districts of Surrey, all EDs were sorted into ward, and again were stratified according to social class. A total of 32 EDs across the whole area (that is, Surrey excluding Spelthorne) were sampled, with quotas set by sex, age and work status. Face-to-face interviews, conducted in-home, were carried out with 283 adults aged 18+ between 6 and 29 October 1995. Data were weighted to match the population profile of the County excluding Spelthorne.

Publication of the Results

5 As with all our studies, these findings are subject to our Standard Terms and Conditions of Contract. Any press release or publication of the findings of this survey require the advance approval of MORI. Such approval will only be refused on the grounds of inaccuracy or misinterpretation.

Objectives

6 This survey took place during Stage Three, the consultation period on the Commission's draft recommendations. It measures public preferences for the organisation of local government in the area currently comprising the Borough of Spelthorne, as well as exploring strength of feeling, levels of knowledge about the review, involvement in, and broader perceptions of, local government in the area.

Statistical Reliability of the Data

7 Because we have interviewed a sample of residents, rather than the whole population, the results are subject to statistical tolerance limits, or "margins of error". These are expressed as our confidence that the true figure for the whole population falls within a given range. By convention this is expressed as a percentage, so our 95% confidence level means that in 95 times out of 100 the true figure would lie within this range.

8 The table below shows ranges of the 95% confidence level for a range of sample sizes. For each sample size, the table shows the tolerance limits for sample results close to 10%, 30% and 50%. Take, for example, the results of a survey of 300 residents showing that 50% are aware of the review. In 95 times out of 100 the true figure would lie between 44% and 56% (ie between 50% ±6%).

Sample size	Sampling tolerances applicable to results at or near these percentages (based on 95% confidence level) 10/90% ±%	30/70% ±%	50% ±%
300	3	5	6
200	4	6	7
150	5	7	8
100	6	9	10
50	8	13	14

9 Clearly, 10% or 30% of the sample being aware of the review equate to 90% or 70% not being aware of it. So this table shows the ranges of 95% confidence for responses close to 10%, 30%, 50%, 70% and 90% of our sample. The figures for responses between can be obtained by extrapolation.

10 The true figure would only be known if all the residents of the area had been interviewed. It can be seen in the table, however, that large increases in the sample size do not greatly reduce the sampling tolerance. In addition, the true figure is more likely to lie at the midpoint of the range, rather than at either extreme.

11 When comparing results from separate groups within a sample we need to be sure that the differences are statistically significant. This would be important in comparing views expressed by different parts of a county. The table below shows how the statistical significance of the difference is determined by the size of the groups and the percentage result from the sample.

12 Assuming a 95% confidence level, the table shows the size of the differences required if different results are to be regarded as statistically significant. It can be seen that if 50% of a group of 300 were aware of the review, the result from another group of 300 would not become statistically significant until it became less than 42% or more than 58%.

Sample sizes	Differences required for significance at or near these percentage levels 10/90% ±	30/70% ±	50% ±
300 and 300	5	7	8
300 and 200	5	8	9
300 and 100	7	10	11
200 and 100	7	11	12
100 and 100	8	13	14

Survey Findings

Knowledge and Awareness

13 Residents within the Borough of Spelthorne profess broadly similar levels of knowledge and interest in local government as those living in the rest of the County of Surrey. In both, a clear majority like to know what their council is doing, but want no greater involvement. Around one in six in both areas say they want a higher level of involvement.

14 While around four in ten in the Borough (36%) and the County (44%) say they know at least a fair amount about what their council does, around six in ten admit to not knowing very much.

15 This is reflected in the number of residents who incorrectly ascribe services between the two tiers of local government. Thus, although between four and five in ten recognise libraries as a county council service, as many as a third in the County, and half in Spelthorne allocate responsibility to their district/borough council. And although three-quarters realise that refuse collection is a district/borough service, around one in seven thinks it is a county council service.

16 Awareness of the review itself is fairly low, but is slightly lower in Spelthorne (where 64% have heard of it) than the rest of the Surrey (where 73% have heard of it). However, of those who have heard of the review, depth of knowledge is similar. Seventeen per cent in Spelthorne say they know at least a fair amount compared to 13% in the rest of Surrey.

Sources of Information

17 Local newspapers are the most common source of information about the review, by some margin. Of those who have at least heard of the review, four in ten (in Surrey) and six in ten (in Spelthorne) name the local press as a recent source.

18 Both the County and Borough Councils have been active in Spelthorne, it would appear. Similar numbers say that they have recently heard about the review from Borough (39%) and County (35%) leaflets delivered to their door. Around one in five say they have heard about it in a Borough newspaper. By comparison, in the rest of Surrey, one in six (17%) say that they have heard about the review through County Council leaflets, and one in ten (11%) say they have seen Borough leaflets. As many as one in six in Spelthorne (18%) say they have seen County Council advertisements in local newspapers. Very few recognise receiving information directly from the Local Government Commission itself.

19 Although most of those aware of the review recognise one or more recent sources of information, relatively few (around one in four) say that this has influenced their opinion.

20 Furthermore, in spite of a relatively low level of knowledge and engagement with their local authority, most people in Spelthorne say that the outcome of the review in the Borough is either very important to them (39%) or fairly important (33%). As one might expect, people in the rest of Surrey perceive a lower level of importance (15% very important and 23% fairly important).

The Preferred Option

21 Marginally more people in Spelthorne would prefer a unitary Council (46%) to no change (41%), although this difference is not statistically significant, given the sample size (see introductory notes). In the rest of Surrey, however rather more would prefer Spelthorne to retain two tier local government (38%) than opt for the unitary solution (27%). The rest, 13% and 34% respectively had no views or were indifferent.

22 People in Spelthorne feel more strongly about the preference they express than do those living elsewhere in the County. In Spelthorne, 81% of those expressing a preference say they feel strongly (29% very strongly), while across the rest of Surrey, 64% feel strongly (just 15% very strongly). There is a slight difference in the strength of feeling expressed in Spelthorne according to which option people prefer - of those who prefer the unitary option, one in three say they feel very strongly about it, while of those opting for no change, a quarter say they feel very strongly. In the rest of Surrey, however, it is those who prefer no change who feel more strongly.

Factors in Expressing a Preference

23 In questions 13 to 23, residents were asked to say to what extent they agreed or disagreed with a range of statements which related to a change to unitary local government. The statements were designed to cover the main issues raised by residents during the qualitative phase of research, and others that formed a part of the Commission's brief to take into consideration in making its recommendations.

24 The following charts summarise the results from these questions, with the full question wording presented in the questionnaires in the appendices. Values have been ascribed to the five attitudinal positions that people were offered (+2 for strongly agree, +1 for tend to agree, 0 for neither agree nor disagree, -1 for tend to disagree, and -2 for strongly disagree) and mean scores calculated across all respondents expressing a view. This has the combined benefit of distilling the range of opinion into one summary figure, while incorporating the varying intensity of feeling by ascribing values. Bars to the right indicate that the mean score value is positive, and thus that there is a balance of agreement with the statement. Bars to the left, conversely, indicate a balance of disagreement.

25 The first chart, therefore, shows how the views of people living in the Borough of Spelthorne differ from those across the rest of Surrey. In doing so, it illustrates the attitudes or perceptions that are, in relative terms, shared by both groups of residents (where the bars project in the same direction), and those where views differ markedly. Thus there is broad agreement on many of the positive aspects of change, although residents in Spelthorne itself tend to feel more strongly, as one might expect. There is broad agreement that a county council is needed for national representation (here, however, it is residents in the rest of Surrey who feel more strongly). On the other hand, there is some divergence when it comes to whether change would be too disruptive, whether it would cost more, or whether a unitary Spelthorne would be too small to manage services like education and social services. There is also divergence on whether people feel that they will be affected by change.

26 The subsequent chart takes the results from just Spelthorne (and then from residents in the rest of Surrey), and illustrates the difference in views between those within Spelthorne whose preference is for unitary status, and those who prefer no change. The chart therefore illustrates those attitudinal statements that most, or least, differentiate the residents of the Borough expressing the two opposing preferences. The perceived impact on efficiency is clearly a key determinant of opinion (in both Spelthorne and the rest of Surrey), as are size, disruption, cost and impact on services. In Spelthorne, both those who express a preference for unitary status and those who opt for no change are likely to agree that a unitary Spelthorne would be more in touch with local needs.

Attitudes to Change
(All respondents)

Q To what extent do you agree or disagree that...?
(Figures represent 'mean scores' with *strong agreement* given a value of +2 through to *strong disagreement* given -2)

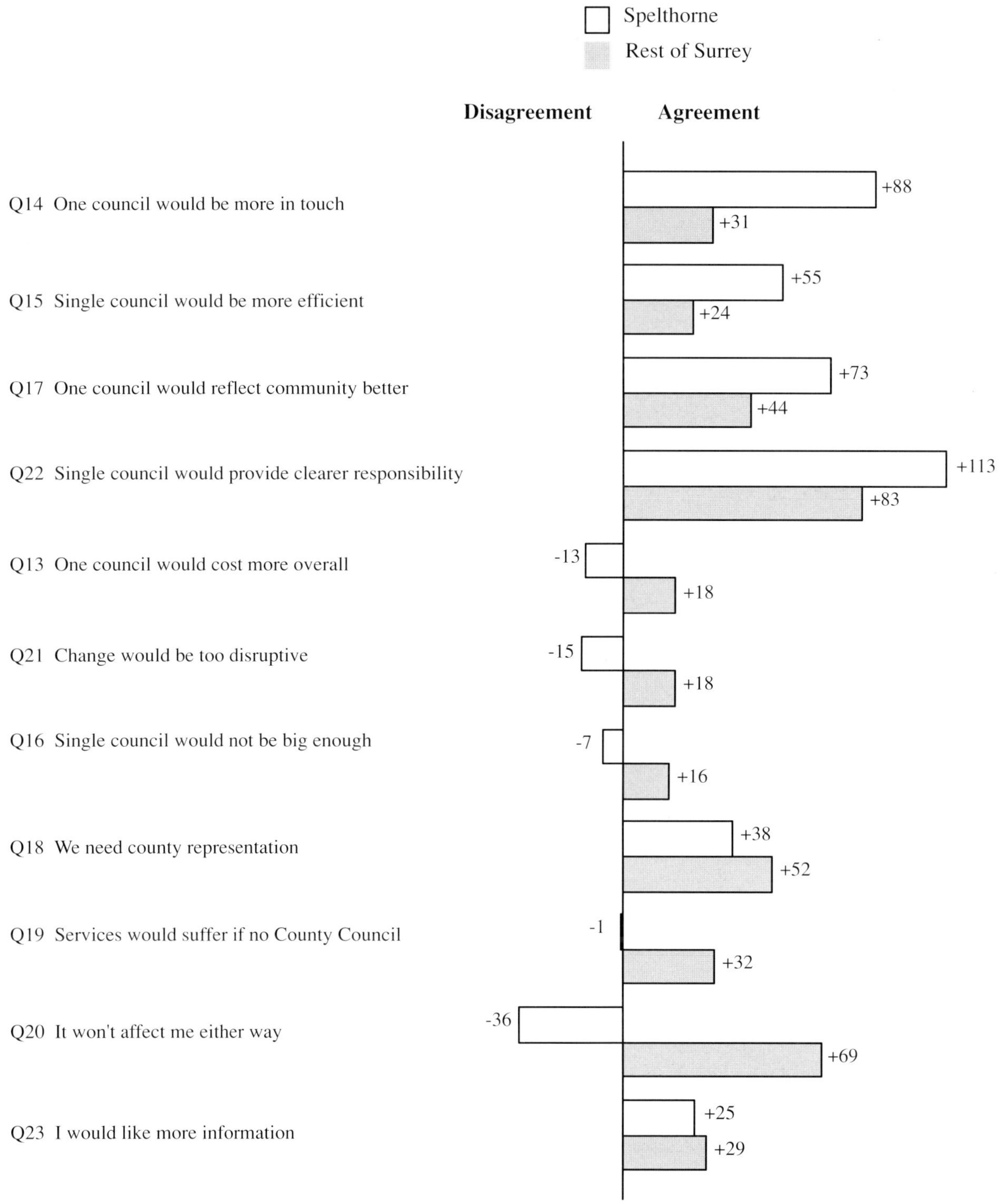

Attitudes to Change
(Respondents in Spelthorne)

Q To what extent do you agree or disagree that...?
(Figures represent 'mean scores' with *strong agreement* given a value of +2 through to *strong disagreement* given -2)

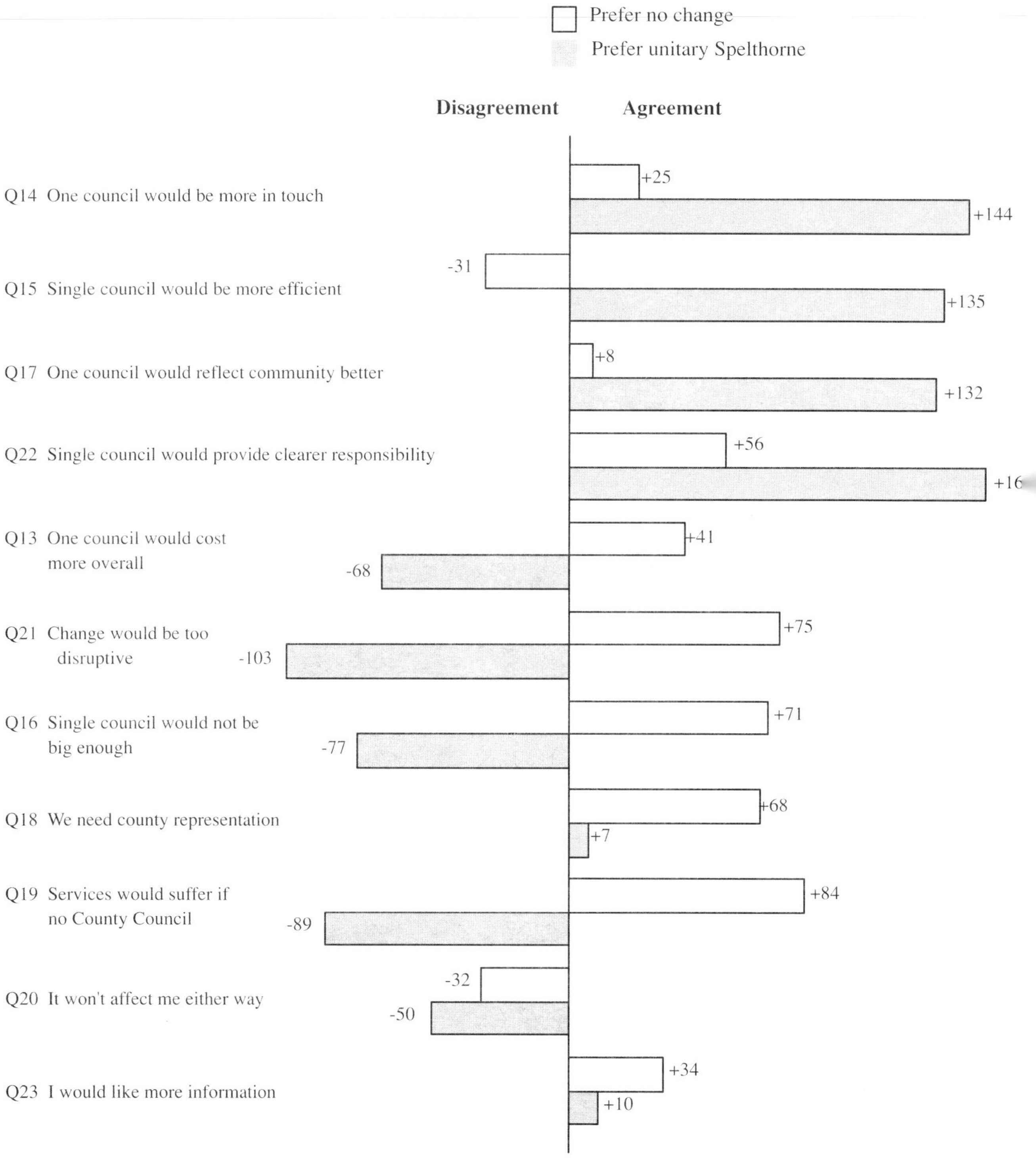

Attitudes to Change
(Respondents in the rest of Surrey)

Q To what extent do you agree or disagree that...?
(Figures represent 'mean scores' with *strong agreement* given a value of +2 through to *strong disagreement* given -2)

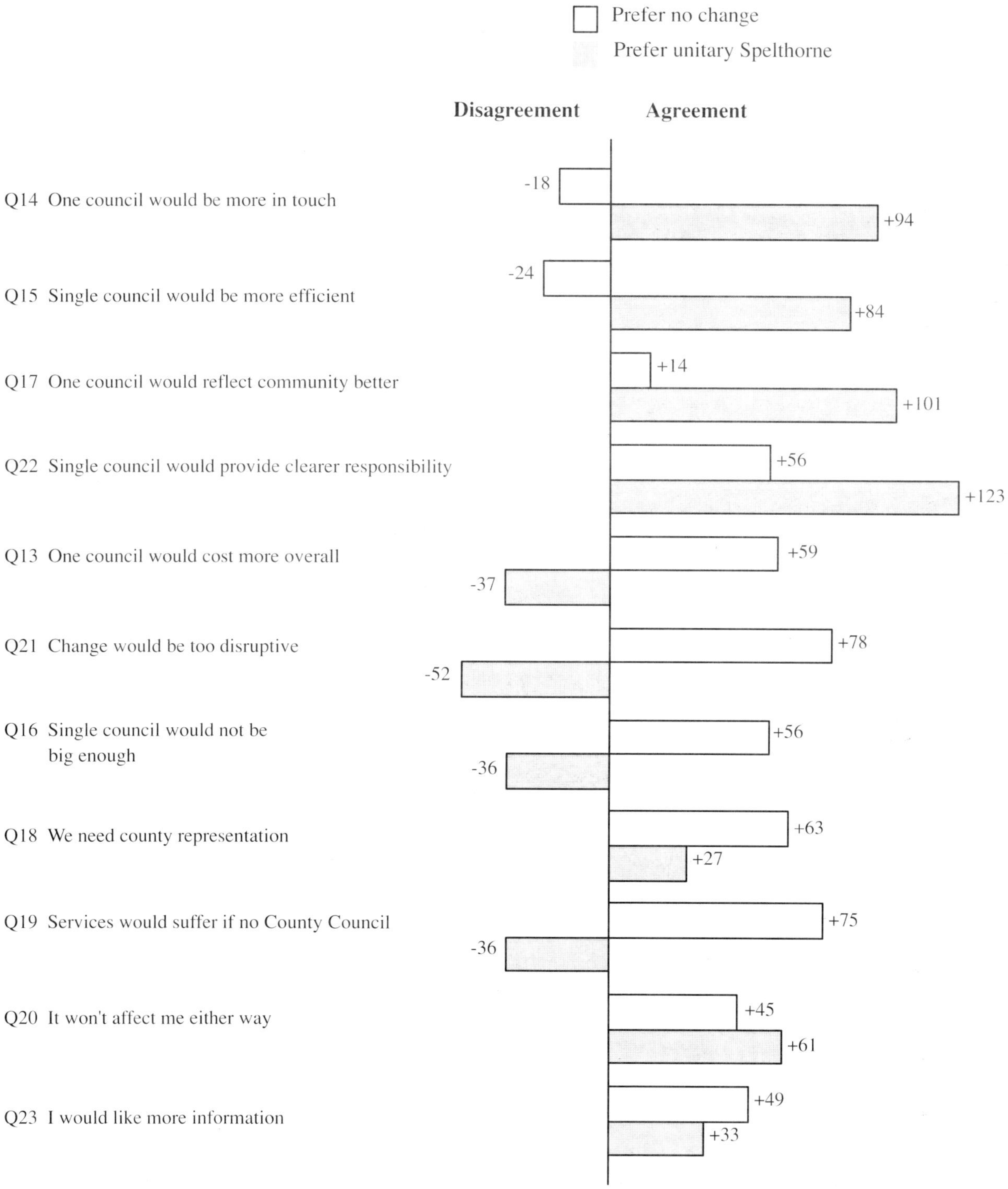

MORI/9101/12
(1-6)

SURREY
REVIEW - REST OF COUNTY

Serial No ....
OUO (7-10)

Name/Initials/Title ....

Address ....

.... **Postcode**..

Telephone: Yes.......................................(11) 1
Number (inc STD code)
No 2

Sample Point (12) (13) (14) (15) (16)

Gender %
Male 48
Female 52

Age %
18-24 12
25-34 18
35-44 16
45-54 19
55-64 15
65-74 11
75+.. 8

WRITE IN AGE

Work Status %
Full-time (30 hrs/wk+) 50
Part-time (8-29 hrs/wk) 12
Not working (under 8 hrs) 1
Looking after home/children............. 8
Retired 22
Registered unemployed.................. 3
Unemployed but not registered 2
Student.. 2
Other 1

Occupation of Chief Income Earner (CIE)
Position/rank/grade

....

Industry/type of company

....

Qualifications/degrees/apprenticeship

....

No of Staff Responsible for

....

PROBE FOR PENSION

	%
AB	38
C1	30
C2	12
D	11
E	8

* Less than $1/2$%

Number in Household
Adults aged 18+ (inc. respondent)

1 2 3 4 5+

Children (17 or under)

0 1 2 3 4+

QA **Are you or other members of your household employed by a council?** IF YES: **Is this a Borough/District Council or a County Council?** CODE FOR BOTH RESPONDENT AND OTHER HOUSEHOLD MEMBERS

	Respondent %	Other %
Yes:		
Borough/District	1	*
County	6	2
Don't know which	0	0
No	93	77
Don't know	1	21

Tenure %
Owned outright.. 26
Buying on mortgage 50
Rented from Council 12
Rented from Housing Association 2
Rented from private landlord 6
Other 3

QB **Is this your main permanent home, or is it a second or holiday home?**
%
Main/permanent................................... 99
Second/holiday ....*

Car in Household
CIRCLE NUMBER

0 1 2 3+

Showcard Version
A-K ....
A1-K ....

THIS FORM IS THE PROPERTY OF MARKET & OPINION RESEARCH INTERNATIONAL (MORI)
32 OLD QUEEN STREET, LONDON, SW1H 9HP

- 2 -

INTERVIEWER DECLARATION: I confirm that I have conducted this interview face-to-face with the above named person and that I have asked all the relevant questions fully and recorded the answers in conformance with the survey specification and the MRS Code of Conduct.

Interviewer Name .... Signature ....

Interviewer Number				/	

	Month		Date		
DATE OF INTERVIEW					
	(29)	(30)		(30)	(32)

NB INTERVIEWER: ALL SHOWCARDS HAVE BEEN REVERSED. PLEASE BE CAREFUL TO CODE THE CORRECT RESPONSE.

Good morning/afternoon/evening. I'm from MORI, the market research and polling organisation. We are doing a survey about local issues, and I would like to ask you a few questions.

ASK ALL

Q1 **Firstly, how long have you lived in this area?** (WITHIN FIVE MILES)

	%
Less than 1 year	6
1-2 years	8
3-5 years	13
6-10 years	18
11-20 years	17
Over 20 years/all my life	37
Don't know/can't remember	0

Q2 SHOWCARD A (R) **From this card, how much would you say you know about local councils and the services they provide?**

	%
A great deal	5
A fair amount	39
Not very much	50
Nothing at all	5
Don't know	1

Q3 SHOWCARD B (R) **Which of the statements on this card comes closest to your own view of the Councils in this area?**

		%
A)	I'm not interested in what the Council does, or whether they do their job	1
B)	I'm not interested in what the Council does, as long as they do their job	15
C)	I like to know what the Council is doing, but I'm happy to let them get on with their job	63
D)	I would like to have more of a say in what the Council does and the services it provides	18
E)	I already work for, or am involved with the Council and the services it provides	2
	Don't know	*

Q4 **From what you know, how many councils provide the main services in this neighbourhood?** (INTERVIEWER - NOT INCLUDING PARISH COUNCILS)

	%
One	35
Two	38
Three+	7
Don't know	20

In fact there are two main councils that provide, or are responsible for most services in this area: . . .district/borough and Surrey County Council.

ROTATE ORDER OF Q5/6

☐ Q5 SHOWCARD C (R) **From this list, what services do you think are the responsibility of... district/borough council? Just read out the letter(s) that apply**

☐ Q6 SHOWCARD C AGAIN (R) **And which services on this list do you think are the responsibility of Surrey County Council? Again, just read out the letters that apply.**

Q7 SHOWCARD D (R) **Which, if any, of these services do you or members of your family use?** INCLUDE ONLY LOCAL USE

		Q5 "Borough" %	Q6 County %	Q7 Use %
A	Bus Services	28	41	25
B	Car Parks	66	19	79
C	Council Housing	57	34	10
D	Council Tax Benefit/Housing benefit	50	33	19
E	Fire service	19	64	28
F	Food safety	27	40	15
G	Household waste sites/dumps	57	26	61
H	Libraries	33	52	63
I	Parks, playgrounds and open spaces	60	22	64
J	Planning service	53	31	18
K	Public conveniences	60	19	41
L	Recycling/bottle banks	65	16	63
M	Refuse collection	73	14	84
N	Road maintenance	37	52	45
O	Schools/education	20	66	32
P	Social services	27	55	13
Q	Street sweeping	68	16	40
R	Swimming pools/sports facilities	58	18	60
	Other	1	4	2
	None of these	0	0	0
	Don't know	10	12	2

Q8 SHOWCARD E (R) **As you may know, there is currently a review being undertaken by the Local Government Commission on the future local government structure in the county. How much, if anything, would you say you know about this?**

	%
A great deal	3
A fair amount	10
Just a little	31
Heard of but know nothing about	29
Never heard of	27

PREFERENCES

HAND OVER MAP SHOWING AREAS UNDER REVIEW AND "CURRENT SERVICES" CARD
The Local Government Commission is considering options for the future structure of local government in Spelthorne. Could you please read through this card, (SHOW OPTIONS CARD) **which outlines the options.**

Q9 **Please tell me which of the options, if either, you would prefer for Spelthorne?**
SINGLE CODE ONLY
For Spelthorne

	%
Option A (Stay the same/status quo)	38
Option B (Single all purpose council)	27
Some other option	1
Neither of these	3
Either of these/don't mind	11
Don't care	10
Don't know	10

ASK IF "OTHER" NAMED AT Q9 (CODE 3)
Q10 **What other option is that?**
PROBE FULLY - DO NOT PROMPT.

....

....

....

....

ASK ALL PREFERRING AN OPTION (1, 2 OR 3 AT Q9). OTHERS GO TO Q13
Q11 SHOWCARD F (R) **You say that the option you would prefer is . . . . .** (INSERT OPTION PREFERRED). **How strongly would you say you feel about this?**

	%
Very strongly	15
Fairly strongly	49
Not very strongly	28
Not at all strongly	6
Don't know	2

Q12 **What do you think would be the main advantages of . . .**(OPTION PREFERRED)
PROBE FULLY FOR DETAILS

....

....

....

....

....

Nothing..
Don't know/can't think of anything..

ATTITUDES TO PROPOSALS

SHOWCARD G (R) **Imagine that there was one council in Spelthorne providing all services. I am going to read out some statements that people have made about this proposal. To what extent do you agree or disagree that . . . .?**
READ OUT, ROTATE ORDER OF ASKING Q13-22. TICK START

READ OUT:		Strongly agree %	Tend to agree %	Neither/ Nor %	Tend to disagree %	Strongly disagree %	Don't know %
☐ Q13	**It would cost more overall**	9	28	22	22	4	15
Q14	**It would be more in touch with local people's needs**	9	45	15	21	5	5
Q15	**The single Council would be more efficient than the current system of two Councils**	11	31	22	26	3	7
☐ Q16	**The single council would not be big enough to manage services such as Education and Social Services effectively**	10	26	22	29	2	11
Q17	**It would better reflect the sense of community in Spelthorne**	10	40	20	14	4	11
Q18	**We need a County Council to represent us nationally**	14	48	16	14	6	1
☐ Q19	**Services would suffer if the County Council no longer provides services in Spelthorne**	9	38	18	21	3	11
Q20	**It won't affect me whether there is a single Council in Spelthorne or not**	28	34	10	20	2	5
Q21	**The change to a single Council for Spelthorne would be too disruptive**	7	30	20	23	3	16
☐ Q22	**With a single Council it would be clearer who is responsible for local services**	20	52	11	11	1	5
ASK LAST Q23	**I would like to have more information on the proposals before making up my mind**	21	26	20	14	13	6

Q24 **On balance, which would you say is more in touch with local people and issues, . . .** (ROTATE ORDER OF "DISTRICT" AND COUNTY) (INSERT NAME OF "DISTRICT COUNCIL)..**district/borough council, or Surrey County Council, or would you say that they are both about the same?**

	%
District/borough council	52
Surrey County Council	8
Both about the same	27
Don't know	12

REFER BACK TO Q8. ASK ALL WHO HAVE HEARD OF REVIEW AT Q8 (IE CODES 1/2/3/4). OTHERS TO Q28

Q25 SHOWCARD H **Earlier in the interview, you said that you had heard of the Review of local government structure. From which, if any, of the sources shown on this card have you recently heard about the Review?** INTERVIEWER NOTE: "RECENTLY" = IN PAST 3 MONTHS

		%
A	Leaflet from County Council delivered to your door	17
B	Leaflet from County Council in library/ offices, etc	5
C	Advertisement from County Council in local newspaper	10
D	Advertisement from County Council on local radio/TV	2
E	Leaflet from Borough Council delivered to your door	11
F	Leaflet from Borough Council in library/ offices, etc	3
G	Borough Council newspaper	7
H	County Council newspaper	3
I	Advertisement from Borough Council in local newspaper	5
J	Advertisement from Borough Council on local radio/TV	1
K	Advertisement by the Commission on local radio	2
L	Local Government Commission advertisement in local newspaper	6
M	Local newspaper	42
N	National newspaper	12
O	TV	10
P	Local radio	7
Q	National radio	4
R	Friends/neighbours/family	9
S	Conversation with Borough Councillor	3
T	Conversation with County Councillor	3
U	Conversation with Borough Council staff	3
V	Conversation with County Council staff	2
W	Parish/community council	1
X	Residents' Association	6
	Other	4
	None of these	0
	Don't know	11

ASK ALL NAMING A SOURCE AT Q25. OTHERS GO TO Q28

Q26 **Would you say that the information you have received has influenced your opinion, or not?**

	%
Yes	23
No	75
Don't know	2

Q27 **What information in particular has influenced your opinion?**

....

....

....

....

ASK ALL

Q28 SHOWCARD I (R) **Assuming you receive the same level of services, how important is it to you, if at all, what the final decision is on the future local government structure in Spelthorne?**

	%
Very important	15
Fairly important	23
Not very important	35
Not at all important	21
Don't know	5

ACTIVISM

Q29 SHOWCARD J **Which of the things on this list, if any, have you done in the last three years? Just read out the letter(s) that apply.**

		%
A	Voted in Local Council elections	76
B	Spoken or written to a local Councillor	38
C	Responded to the earlier Review of local government	12
D	Been to a meeting of a local committee or organisation	17
E	Spoken on a radio phone-in about a local issue	3
F	Written to a local newspaper about a local issue	7
G	Been to a meeting of a local branch of a political party	5
H	Written to your MP about a local issue	14
I	Been to a Council Committee meeting	4
J	Been to a Council meeting	4
K	Attended a public meeting run by the Council	12
	None of these	17
	Don't know/refused	1

Q30 SHOWCARD K **Which, if any, of these apply to you? Just read out the letter(s) that apply.**

		%
	I am a member of a:	
A	Residents' Association	24
B	Community Association	2
C	Tenants' Association	1
D	Neighbourhood Watch	31
E	PTA/school governors	9
	I do unpaid work for:	
F	A school	10
G	Citizens Advice Bureau	*
H	Volunteer Bureau	4
I	Scouts/Guides/Cubs/Brownies	3
J	Church group	9
	Other	4
	None of these	43
	Don't know	1

THANK RESPONDENT. GO TO DEMOGRAPHICS

- 8 -

MORI/9101/12 SURREY Serial No . . . .
(1-6) **REVIEW - Spelthorne** OUO (7-10)

Name/Initials/Title ....

Address ....

.... **Postcode**..........................

Telephone: Yes.. (11) 1

Number (inc STD code)
No 2

Sample Point

(12)	(13)	(14)	(15)	(16)

Gender

	%
Male	49
Female	51

Age

	%
18-24	13
25-34	21
35-44	20
45-54	14
55-64	13
65-74	16
75+	5

WRITE IN AGE

Work Status

	%
Full-time (30 hrs/wk+)	54
Part-time (8-29 hrs/wk)	7
Not working (under 8 hrs)	2
Looking after home/children	11
Retired	20
Registered unemployed	1
Unemployed but not registered	1
Student	3
Other	*

Occupation of Chief Income Earner (CIE)
Position/rank/grade

....

Industry/type of company

....

Qualifications/degrees/apprenticeship

....

No of Staff Responsible for

....

PROBE FOR PENSION

	%
AB	19
C1	34
C2	24
D	10
E	13

Number in Household
Adults aged 18+ (inc. respondent)

1 2 3 4 5+

Children (17 or under)

0 1 2 3 4+

QA **Are you or other members of your household employed by a council?** IF YES: **Is this a Borough/District Council or a County Council?** CODE FOR BOTH RESPONDENT AND OTHER HOUSEHOLD MEMBERS

	Respondent %	Other %
Yes:		
Borough/District	2	3
County	3	2
Don't know which	0	1
No	94	92
Don't know	*	3

Tenure

	%
Owned outright	26
Buying on mortgage	54
Rented from Council	10
Rented from Housing Association	2
Rented from private landlord	6
Other	2

QB **Is this your main permanent home, or is it a second or holiday home?**

	%
Main/permanent	98
Second/holiday	2

Car in Household
CIRCLE NUMBER

0 1 2 3+

Showcard Version
A-K ....
A1-K ....

INTERVIEWER DECLARATION: I confirm that I have conducted this interview face-to-face with the above named person and that I have asked all the relevant questions fully and recorded the answers in conformance with the survey specification and the MRS Code of Conduct.

Interviewer Name .... Signature ....

Interviewer Number					/	

	Month		Date		
DATE OF INTERVIEW					
	(29)	(30)		(30)	(32)

NB INTERVIEWER: ALL SHOWCARDS HAVE BEEN REVERSED. PLEASE BE CAREFUL TO CODE THE CORRECT RESPONSE.

Good morning/afternoon/evening. I'm from MORI, the market research and polling organisation. We are doing a survey about local issues, and I would like to ask you a few questions.

ASK ALL

Q1 **Firstly, how long have you lived in this area?** (WITHIN FIVE MILES)

	%
Less than 1 year	5
1-2 years	6
3-5 years	10
6-10 years	17
11-20 years	18
Over 20 years/all my life	43
Don't know/can't remember	*

Q2 SHOWCARD A (R) **From this card, how much would you say you know about local councils and the services they provide?**

	%
A great deal	3
A fair amount	33
Not very much	55
Nothing at all	8
Don't know	*

Q3 SHOWCARD B (R) **Which of the statements on this card comes closest to your own view of the Councils in this area?**

		%
A)	I'm not interested in what the Council does, or whether they do their job	3
B)	I'm not interested in what the Council does, as long as they do their job	17
C)	I like to know what the Council is doing, but I'm happy to let them get on with their job	60
D)	I would like to have more of a say in what the Council does and the services it provides	17
E)	I already work for, or am involved with the Council and the services it provides	2
	Don't know	1

Q4 **From what you know, how many councils provide the main services in this neighbourhood?** (INTERVIEWER - NOT INCLUDING PARISH COUNCILS)

	%
One	42
Two	32
Three+	3
Don't know	24

In fact there are two main councils that provide, or are responsible for most services in this area: Spelthorne Borough Council and Surrey County Council.

ROTATE ORDER OF Q5/6

☐ Q5 SHOWCARD C (R) **From this list, what services do you think are the responsibility of Spelthorne Borough Council? Just read out the letter(s) that apply**

☐ Q6 SHOWCARD C AGAIN (R) **And which services on this list do you think are the responsibility of Surrey County Council? Again, just read out the letters that apply.**

Q7 SHOWCARD D (R) **Which, if any, of these services do you or members of your family use?** INCLUDE ONLY LOCAL USE

		Q5 Spelthorne	Q6 Surrey	Q7 Use
		%	%	%
A	Bus Services	28	41	27
B	Car Parks	57	26	70
C	Council Housing	67	17	7
D	Council Tax Benefit/Housing benefit	69	16	15
E	Fire service	28	54	36
F	Food safety	32	40	13
G	Household waste sites/dumps	55	27	56
H	Libraries	46	39	62
I	Parks, playgrounds and open spaces	63	23	65
J	Planning service	48	33	14
K	Public conveniences	59	21	33
L	Recycling/bottle banks	59	20	52
M	Refuse collection	73	13	86
N	Road maintenance	40	45	46
O	Schools/education	38	48	35
P	Social services	40	38	9
Q	Street sweeping	66	17	50
R	Swimming pools/sports facilities	63	18	55
	Other	2	1	2
	None of these	0	3	1
	Don't know	6	15	*

Q8 SHOWCARD E (R) **As you may know, there is currently a review being undertaken by the Local Government Commission on the future local government structure in the county. How much, if anything, would you say you know about this?**

	%
A great deal	4
A fair amount	13
Just a little	32
Heard of but know nothing about	15
Never heard of	36

PREFERENCES

HAND OVER MAP SHOWING AREAS UNDER REVIEW AND "CURRENT SERVICES" CARD
The Local Government Commission is considering options for the future structure of local government in Spelthorne. Could you please read through this card, (SHOW OPTIONS CARD) **which outlines the options.**

Q9 **Please tell me which of the options, if either, you would prefer for Spelthorne?**
SINGLE CODE ONLY

For Spelthorne

	%
Option A (Stay the same/status quo)	41
Option B (Single all purpose council)	46
Some other option	1
Neither of these	1
Either of these/don't mind	7
Don't care	2
Don't know	3

ASK IF "OTHER" NAMED AT Q9 (CODE 3)

Q10 **What other option is that?**
PROBE FULLY - DO NOT PROMPT.

....

....

....

....

ASK ALL PREFERRING AN OPTION (1, 2 OR 3 AT Q9). OTHERS GO TO Q13

Q11 SHOWCARD F (R) **You say that the option you would prefer is . . . . .** (INSERT OPTION PREFERRED). **How strongly would you say you feel about this?**

	%
Very strongly	29
Fairly strongly	52
Not very strongly	16
Not at all strongly	1
Don't know	2

Q12 **What do you think would be the main advantages of . . .**(OPTION PREFERRED)
PROBE FULLY FOR DETAILS

....

....

....

....

....

Nothing...

Don't know/can't think of anything................................

ATTITUDES TO PROPOSALS

SHOWCARD G (R) **Imagine that there was one council in Spelthorne providing <u>all</u> services. I am going to read out some statements that people have made about this proposal. To what extent do you agree or disagree that . . . .?**
READ OUT, ROTATE ORDER OF ASKING Q13-22. TICK START

	READ OUT:	Strongly agree %	Tend to agree %	Neither/ Nor %	Tend to disagree %	Strongly disagree %	Don't know %
☐ Q13	**It would cost more overall**	8	22	23	36	7	5
Q14	**It would be more in touch with local people's needs**	27	47	12	12	1	1
Q15	**The single Council would be more efficient than the current system of two Councils**	24	32	18	16	5	5
☐ Q16	**The single council would not be big enough to manage services such as Education and Social Services effectively**	11	23	19	35	8	4
Q17	**It would better reflect the sense of community in Spelthorne**	21	46	15	16	*	2
Q18	**We need a County Council to represent us nationally**	13	40	21	19	6	1
☐ Q19	**Services would suffer if the County Council no longer provides services in Spelthorne**	11	29	15	32	10	3
Q20	**It won't affect me whether there is a single Council in Spelthorne or not**	5	19	18	49	8	1
Q21	**The change to a single Council for Spelthorne would be too disruptive**	8	27	19	31	13	2
☐ Q22	**With a single Council it would be clearer who is responsible for local services**	40	43	7	9	1	1
ASK LAST Q23	**I would like to have more information on the proposals before making up my mind**	17	32	18	25	8	0

Q24 **On balance, which would you say is more in touch with local people and issues,** .... (ROTATE ORDER OF "DISTRICT" AND COUNTY)
Spelthorne Borough Council, or
Surrey County Council, or would you say that they are both about the same?

	%
Spelthorne Borough Council	57
Surrey County Council	4
Both about the same	30
Don't know	9

REFER BACK TO Q8. ASK ALL WHO HAVE HEARD OF REVIEW AT Q8 (IE CODES 1/2/3/4). OTHERS TO Q28

Q25 SHOWCARD H **Earlier in the interview, you said that you had heard of the Review of local government structure. From which, if any, of the sources shown on this card have you recently heard about the Review?** INTERVIEWER NOTE: "RECENTLY" = IN PAST 3 MONTHS

		%
A	Leaflet from County Council delivered to your door	35
B	Leaflet from County Council in library/ offices, etc	10
C	Advertisement from County Council in local newspaper	18
D	Advertisement from County Council on local radio/TV	1
E	Leaflet from Borough Council delivered to your door	39
F	Leaflet from Borough Council in library/ offices, etc	11
G	Borough Council newspaper	21
H	County Council newspaper	5
I	Advertisement from Borough Council in local newspaper	6
J	Advertisement from Borough Council on local radio/TV	1
K	Advertisement by the Commission on local radio	0
L	Local Government Commission advertisement in local newspaper	4
M	Local newspaper	62
N	National newspaper	5
O	TV	7
P	Local radio	14
Q	National radio	2
R	Friends/neighbours/family	6
S	Conversation with Borough Councillor	4
T	Conversation with County Councillor	2
U	Conversation with Borough Council staff	4
V	Conversation with County Council staff	2
W	Parish/community council	1
X	Residents' Association	7
	Other	16
	None of these	1
	Don't know	1

ASK ALL NAMING A SOURCE AT Q25. OTHERS GO TO Q28

Q26 **Would you say that the information you have received has influenced your opinion, or not?**

	%
Yes	23
No	74
Don't know	3

Q27 **What information in particular has influenced your opinion?**

....

....

....

....

ASK ALL

Q28 SHOWCARD I (R) **Assuming you receive the same level of services, how important is it to you, if at all, what the final decision is on the future local government structure in Spelthorne?**

	%
Very important	39
Fairly important	33
Not very important	15
Not at all important	11
Don't know	2

ACTIVISM

Q29 SHOWCARD J **Which of the things on this list, if any, have you done in the last three years? Just read out the letter(s) that apply.**

		%
A	Voted in Local Council elections	76
B	Spoken or written to a local Councillor	26
C	Responded to the earlier Review of local government	9
D	Been to a meeting of a local committee or organisation	7
E	Spoken on a radio phone-in about a local issue	*
F	Written to a local newspaper about a local issue	2
G	Been to a meeting of a local branch of a political party	2
H	Written to your MP about a local issue	11
I	Been to a Council Committee meeting	3
J	Been to a Council meeting	4
K	Attended a public meeting run by the Council	7
	None of these	16
	Don't know/refused	1

Q30 SHOWCARD K **Which, if any, of these apply to you? Just read out the letter(s) that apply.**

	I am a member of a:	%
A	Residents' Association	22
B	Community Association	1
C	Tenants' Association	1
D	Neighbourhood Watch	26
E	PTA/school governors	6
	I do unpaid work for:	
F	A school	4
G	Citizens Advice Bureau	*
H	Volunteer Bureau	1
I	Scouts/Guides/Cubs/Brownies	4
J	Church group	7
	Other	3
	None of these	48
	Don't know	2

THANK RESPONDENT. GO TO DEMOGRAPHICS

CHAPTER 12

THE WREKIN IN THE COUNTY OF SHROPSHIRE

Draft Recommendations

12.1 The Commission's report *Draft Recommendations on the Future Local Government of The Wrekin in the County of Shropshire* summarised the evidence taken into account by the Commission in reaching its draft recommendations.

Figure 12.1
Draft Recommendations for The Wrekin in the County of Shropshire

Structure

- The existing two-tier structure of local government in The Wrekin should be replaced. The Wrekin should become a unitary authority, responsible in its area for the broad range of local government functions currently carried out by both county and district councils.

Ceremonial Arrangements

- The county of Shropshire should be retained for ceremonial and related purposes, and the unitary authority of The Wrekin should be associated with the county for such purposes.

Strategic Planning

- The new unitary authority for The Wrekin should be a structure planning authority for its area, with a view to that function being exercised jointly with Shropshire County Council, so as to maintain a single structure plan across the whole of their combined area. The new unitary authority should also be a minerals and waste planning authority, with a view to maintaining a county-wide minerals plan jointly with the County Council. If, however, local circumstances are such that adequate strategic policies for minerals and waste for The Wrekin are capable of being formulated through the joint structure plan, the new unitary authority should be authorised to include detailed minerals and waste policies in its district wide development plan.

Electoral Arrangements

- The Wrekin unitary authority should retain the existing district council electoral arrangements. The new authority should therefore have a total of 46 members, with 13 two-member wards and 20 single-member wards. Elections should be held for the whole council every four years.

- The continuing Shropshire County Council should have 44 councillors with one councillor being returned from each of the 44 county divisions outside The Wrekin.

Views Expressed to the Commission

12.2 The Commission received a wide range of direct representations on its draft recommendations, from local authorities, residents, Members of Parliament, business and voluntary groups, parish and town councils, and from other public and private sector organisations. Just over 5,000 representations were received from individuals and organisations, including just under 2,000 from respondents within The Wrekin. The Commission also received over 5,000 representations in the form of standard letters, response slips, pre-printed postcards and petitions (Figures 12.2 and 12.3). Figures 12.2 and 12.3 exclude representations from the local authorities; these are summarised separately (Figure 12.4).

Figure 12.2
Views of Respondents Within The Wrekin

Preferred structure	Individuals	Organisations	Standard letters and petition signatures
Unitary Wrekin	724	129	3076
No change	897	74	112
Other	59	3	1
No preference	25	3	0

Source: Local Government Commission for England and NOP

Figure 12.3
Views of Respondents From Outside The Wrekin

Preferred structure	Individuals	Organisations	Standard letters and petition signatures
Unitary Wrekin	110	12	62
No change	2519	263	1905
Other	111	4	0
No preference	65	8	0

Source: Local Government Commission for England and NOP
Note: Excludes out of county representations

12.3 In addition, 126 representations were received from outside the county, of which 60 per cent supported the retention of the existing two-tier structure. A more detailed tabulation of the written representations from individuals and interest groups, produced by NOP on behalf of the Commission, can be found towards the end of this Chapter.

The Views of Local Authorities

12.4 The Commission received submissions from all seven principal local authorities in Shropshire during Stage Three (Figure 12.4). Five authorities (Bridgnorth, North Shropshire, Oswestry, South Shropshire and the County Council) produced a joint submission *Shropshire Together*.

Figure 12.4
Preferences of Shropshire Local Authorities at Stage Three

Authority	Preference
Bridgnorth District Council North Shropshire District Council Oswestry Borough Council South Shropshire District Council Shropshire County Council	Joint submission supporting the retention of the two-tier structure. Considered there is no logic behind separating The Wrekin from the rest of Shropshire. Pointed to the importance of the interdependence of The Wrekin and Shropshire and the probable impact on the rest of Shropshire. Remained firmly of the view that the present structure best suits the needs of the county.
Shrewsbury and Atcham Borough Council	Reaffirmed support for the establishment of unitary councils throughout Shropshire. Considered the "hybrid solution" (of the draft recommendation) was a significantly inferior system to the "...already discredited" two-tier system in Shropshire.
The Wrekin District Council	Reaffirmed support for a unitary authority for The Wrekin. Considered it essential for the area to develop and prosper. Believed that, on all criteria, there was a powerful case for change. Stated that no solution except a unitary Wrekin would provide a stable basis for the future.

Source: Local authorities' submissions

12.5 None of the local authorities has changed its position regarding the outcome of The Wrekin review since Stage One. Stafford Borough Council submitted a response in support of a unitary authority for The Wrekin. The Shropshire Branch of the Association of District Councils did not make representations; the Association of District Councils' national submission is referred to in the Summary of National Representations. The Association of County Councils supported the retention of the two-tier structure.

The Views of Others

12.6 A range of other interest groups made representations on the Commission's draft recommendation as summarised in the following paragraphs. These are in addition to those made in Stage One.

Businesses and Business Groups

12.7 The Commission received over 150 responses from the business sector throughout Shropshire. Overall, there was a two to one majority supporting the draft recommendation including significant support for a unitary Wrekin authority from Chambers of Commerce and business forums, both county-wide and within The Wrekin district.

12.8 The Shropshire Chamber of Industry and Commerce stated that "...the primary reason for adopting unitary status...is that of economic development". The Chamber also stated that "...there are clearly different needs and priorities between the rural west and the urbanised east of the county, which separate authorities could each focus upon within an agreed overall strategic and regional framework".

12.9 Within The Wrekin, there was strong support for the draft recommendation from some smaller and more local business groups such as the Wellington Chamber of Commerce and the Newport Chamber of Commerce. Many local businesses also indicated their support. Overall, over 75 per cent of businesses within The Wrekin who responded endorsed the draft recommendation.

12.10 The opinion of businesses in the rest of the county was three to one against a unitary Wrekin. The Shrewsbury Business Club supported a single unitary authority for the county, although this is beyond the Commission's remit to recommend. In addition, it stated that if the Commission decided in favour of a separate authority for The Wrekin, the effect on the remainder of the county would be "devastating": "...We would have the smallest county in England in terms of population, and one of the most sparsely populated without a major industrial centre and without assisted area status, having to support and contend with six local authorities". This view was supported by groups such as the Ludlow Chamber of Trade and Commerce and many individual business employers.

County, Regional and National Interests (including the Voluntary Sector)

12.11 Submissions were received from a broad range of public bodies and other organisations. A majority of nearly seven to one was against the draft recommendation on structure.

12.12 The Agricultural Advisory Services (Shropshire) was firmly against the proposal. It stated that: "The effects on the rest of the county will be very serious indeed. Shropshire does not benefit like the counties in the south east from generous area cost adjustments and as such two lots of overheads will be created from one".

12.13 County groups such as the Federation of Women's Institutes, the Shropshire Playing Fields Association and the West Midlands Branch of the Library Association were against the draft recommendation. The Shropshire Voluntary Association of the Blind said that "by far the best solution for voluntary organisations...is the status quo". There was general concern about the ongoing quality and provision of county services in the rest of Shropshire should The Wrekin become a unitary authority.

12.14 Support for a unitary Wrekin came from groups such as the Union of Construction Allied Trades and Technicians, Relate (Shropshire and North Powys) and the Lilleshall Sports and Conference Centre. Relate stated that: "Families living in The Wrekin area have very different needs - needs which are not being met by the current local government structure". This view, and the opinion that The Wrekin was a distinct area different from the rest of the county with an identity of its own, was shared by many respondents who supported the unitary recommendation.

12.15 However, the Lord Lieutenant of Shropshire, the Viscount Boyne, was strongly against the proposed change. He argued that "I am especially concerned about education and social services, which will be severely damaged if divided". He also stated his concern that "...the remainder of the county will have to function at a much reduced level... and with no guarantees from a unitary authority that purchase of services will continue...I cannot see any merit in taking out The Wrekin and artificially creating a Shropshire with the smallest population [of a county] in England".

12.16 The Royal Commission on the Historical Monuments of England drew the Commission's attention to the "...integrated nature of the existing service", commenting that this service had been very effective but risked becoming diluted "...in the present proposals".

Education Groups

12.17 Submissions from interested parties involved in education were very much polarised in opinion In particular, views from the rest of the county were strongly against any change. A typical response was that from the Shropshire Branch of the National Association of Head Teachers. It said that: "The break up of Shropshire as an education authority will devastate the provision of education in both newly proposed authorities". This view was also evident in responses from school governors and teachers throughout the county. Overall, support for the retention of the two-tier structure from educational groups was shown by 90 per cent of the representations from this sector.

12.18 There was, however, support for unitary status from some schools, governors and teachers within The Wrekin. Additionally, the University of Wolverhampton (Telford Campus) wrote that "...the present Wrekin District Council was an able partner [who] involve themselves so actively in the projects...undertaken. These projects have ensured that a new dimension in higher education and training is available to the people of this part of the West Midlands".

Health Interests

12.19 As with other interest groups, there was a balance of views from health bodies. Support for both structural options was received from this sector.

12.20 At county level, Shropshire Health Authority made a detailed submission recommending no change. It stated that: "The county needs to be looked at as a whole and services planned in a dovetailed and complementary way between the west and east of the county. To increase the separation between the two parts by creating a Wrekin authority [we believe] would lead to increased expenditure on acute hospital services because of the pressure for duplication, and lead to less funds being available for those areas...presently underfunded". This view was reiterated by the Robert Jones and Agnes Hunt Orthopaedic and District Hospital NHS Trust.

12.21 The NHS Trust hospital within The Wrekin district area, the Princess Royal, firmly supported unitary status. It said that: "The boundary of The Wrekin unitary authority would encompass the majority of people served by this hospital,...it will enhance the integration of all forms of social care locally whilst having no real material operational effect on the provision of county based services such as mental health or children's services".

Law, Order and Emergency Services

12.22 There were few responses from these services. One submission came from the Shropshire Magistrates' Court Committee. In opposing the draft recommendation, the Committee argued that: "The present system whereby [the Committee] consults with one local authority for the purpose of funding is regarded as very satisfactory...it is very much feared that divisiveness in local government in Shropshire will be the result of the creation of a separate unitary authority in The Wrekin". The Shropshire Branch of the National Association of Fire Officers also supported the retention of the two-tier structure.

Local Groups

12.23 Over 80 local groups responded to the consultation. A majority (58 per cent to 37 per cent) supported no change in Shropshire. However, groups within The Wrekin were six to one in favour of a unitary district as recommended.

12.24 Groups such as The Wrekin Tourism Association, the Coalbrookdale Society, Sanctuary Housing and the Rotary Club of Telford Centre supported the unitary proposal. The Rotary Club stated that "...it is quite clear that a unitary council would allow a more focused delivery of local services to local residents". The Madeley Citizens Advice Bureau echoed many submissions from local groups within The Wrekin by stating that: "The needs in The Wrekin are essentially those of an urban population; Shropshire functioned as a county prior to the new town and is comparable in size to other existing counties".

12.25 Ninety five per cent of local groups from the remainder of Shropshire who responded were against the draft recommendation. Shrewsbury Friends of the Earth argued that "...such a division will lead to an erosion of services for the main area of the county". Many other groups such as the Women's Royal Voluntary Service, Multiple Sclerosis (Oswestry), and the Service for Visually Impaired Children responded with serious concerns for the ongoing provision of services in the remainder of the county should The Wrekin be given unitary status.

Parliamentary Interests

12.26 Mr Bruce Grocott, MP for The Wrekin, reiterating his support from Stage One, said that: "The huge growth of Telford means that the present county council structure, which has been in operation for 107 years, is now simply out of date. I believe that the Commission's draft recommendations establish a structure which will be viable well into the 21st century".

12.27 Lord Northfield of Telford echoed that view, and argued further that: "The influx of new modern industry - hundreds of companies, including over one hundred from all parts of the world - and well over 50,000 residents from other counties, has created a community with interests and loyalties that diverge from those in the remaining traditional part of Shropshire".

Parish and Town Councils

12.28 The Commission received over 90 submissions from both parish associations and individual parish and town councils. From the rest of the county there was almost universal rejection of the draft recommendation, whilst within The Wrekin there was a slight majority (53 per cent to 47 per cent) in favour of unitary status. Overall, the retention of the present structure was the majority opinion by a factor of seven.

12.29 Oswestry Town Council argued strongly for no change and stated that: "Grave concern is expressed at the inevitable consequence...creating additional and unnecessary expense, continuing uncertainty and long-terms damage to the core services, with particular reference to educational standards". Bridgnorth Town Council echoed those concerns and considered that grave problems would be faced by both the remainder of the county and The Wrekin itself if the "...splitting of control was allowed to proceed". Similar views were expressed by other parishes and town councils outside The Wrekin district.

12.30 The Shropshire Association of Parish and Town Councils, reiterated its Stage One view that no change was the best solution for the county as a whole.

12.31 In support of the draft recommendation, The Wrekin Association of Parish and Town Councils also reiterated its previous position. Wellington Town Council and Oakengates Town Council were representative of those parish and town councils who sent individual submissions of support. Oakengates Town Council argued that there were "...distinct advantages..., leading to improvement in the quality and co-ordination of services, with clear objectives and policies, with no competition and overlap... Unitary status will also be a distinct advantage in attracting and keeping overseas development, which is so very important to Telford".

NOP Tabulations of Written Representations

1 The following tabulations summarise the views expressed by members of the public and other interested parties during the consultation on the Local Government Commission's draft recommendations for The Wrekin.

2 The tabulations include only letters sent directly to NOP at its Chelmsford offices and to the Commission's offices in London. Where more than one person's view has been expressed in a letter, the comments from each individual have been recorded separately. Staff from the Commission and NOP have worked closely in ensuring that care has been taken in the interpretation of comments, and that a consistent approach has been adopted.

3 While many people expressed support for one or other of the draft options presented by the Commission, other responses were coded by NOP after further discussion. The pattern of views expressed has been carefully examined, and where a number of respondents supported an option not included in those put forward by the Commission, those views have been separately coded and reported by NOP.

4 The Commission has advertised through the local media, encouraging people to make their views known. All responses received up to two days after the end of the Stage Three consultation period have been included. Returns from campaigns organised by local authorities or other groups (for example, standardised postcards and letters, questionnaires and petitions) have not been included in the tabulations. These, and submissions written and dated before the commencement of the consultation process, have been considered separately by the Commission.

The following definitions have been applied by NOP in compiling the tabulations:

(i) Type of Respondent

Individuals:	includes individual members of the public, local councillors and Members of the Westminster and European Parliaments.
Businesses and Business Groups:	includes organisations which represent businesses, such as local Chambers of Commerce.
County, Regional and National Interests:	any organisation which covers an area which is the size of a county or larger is included here, for example, a county-wide voluntary organisation or a regional association. This classification includes most of the statutory consultees.
Education (and Church) Groups:	this group includes schools, religious organisations and teaching unions.
Local Groups:	this includes organisations smaller than a county area, for example, a district-level voluntary sector body. The group could be voluntary, sporting, political or cultural but does not include organisations from the education or religious sectors (included above). It also includes constituency parties and political groups on local authorities.
Parish and Town Councils:	this also includes district-level associations of town and parish councils. County level associations are classified as County, Regional and National interests.

(ii) Structural Options (Reports A, D and H)

No change in own district:	this code is used where there is more than one review district in the county. It indicates where respondents from a review district have expressed support for no change for that district and have not made reference to the other review district(s) in that county.
District/county-level authorities:	represents support for either a district or county-level authority although it is not clear whether this is for a unitary or a two-tier structure.
Opposition to structural preferences:	represents responses where a negative, but unspecified, structural preference has been expressed.
Rejects:	rejects are those responses with unclear comments/interpretation.

(iii) Other

Other issues (Reports B and I):	these illustrate preferences in relation to boundary and electoral changes and (where applicable) the restoration of historic counties.
Parishing issues (Report C):	these illustrate preferences in relation to parishing issues, for example, the creation of new parishes or the enhancement of the role of parish and town councils.
Services (Report E):	these illustrate concerns expressed about the impact of proposed changes on particular service areas where the respondent has not additionally expressed a positive structural preference.

(iv) Ward/Area Level (Reports H and I)

These show analyses by local authority wards or specified areas and are designed to examine whether structural preferences vary across a particular local authority area.

NOP Analysis of Responses to Local Government Commission Draft Recommendations - SHROPSHIRE

Report A: Opinions on the structural options, by authority of respondent
Base: all

	Review district	Other districts in county							
	The Wrekin	Bridgnorth	North Shropshire	Oswestry	Shrewsbury & Atcham	South Shropshire	Rest of county total	County total	Out of county total
Status quo/two-tier	971 *51%*	469 *87%*	488 *92%*	281 *92%*	1160 *90%*	384 *89%*	2782 *90%*	3753 *75%*	76 *60%*
Unitary Wrekin	853 *45%*	36 *7%*	15 *3%*	8 *3%*	47 *4%*	16 *4%*	122 *4%*	975 *19%*	39 *31%*
Two unitary authorities (Wrekin and rest of Shropshire)	6 *	- -	1 *	- -	3 *	- -	4 *	10 *	- -
County Level Authority (Either two-tier or Unitary)	52 *3%*	15 *3%*	17 *3%*	8 *3%*	40 *3%*	21 *5%*	101 *3%*	153 *3%*	2 *2%*
County-wide unitary structure	- -	2 *	- -	- -	4 *	- -	6 *	6 *	- -
Reject	1 *	- -	- -	2 *1%*	- -	- -	2 *	3 *	- -
Others specified	4 *	2 *	- -	- -	2 *	- -	4 *	8 *	- -
No preference expressed/option defined	27 *1%*	15 *3%*	9 *2%*	5 *2%*	31 *2%*	11 *3%*	71 *2%*	98 *2%*	9 *7%*
BASE TOTAL	1914	539	530	304	1287	432	3092	5006	126

* *Less than ½%*

The Wrekin

NOP Analysis of Responses to Local Government Commission Draft Recommendations - SHROPSHIRE

Report B: Opinions on other issues, by authority of respondent
Base: all

	Review district	Other districts in county							
	The Wrekin	Bridgnorth	North Shropshire	Oswestry	Shrewsbury & Atcham	South Shropshire	Rest of county total	County total	Out of county total
Other specified	-	1	-	-	-	-	1	1	-
	-	*	-	-	-	-	*	*	-
BASE TOTAL	1914	539	530	304	1287	432	3092	5006	126

The figures in the table above do not sum to the base total/100% because undefined fields are not included, except as part of the base total.

* *Less than ½%*

NOP Analysis of Responses to Local Government Commission Draft Recommendations - SHROPSHIRE

Report C: Opinions on parishing issues, by authority of respondent
Base: all

	Review district	Other districts in county							
	The Wrekin	Bridgnorth	North Shropshire	Oswestry	Shrewsbury & Atcham	South Shropshire	Rest of county total	County total	Out of county total
BASE TOTAL	1914	539	530	304	1287	432	3092	5006	126

The figures in the table above do not sum to the base total/100% because undefined fields are not included, except as part of the base total.

NOP Analysis of Responses to Local Government Commission Draft Recommendations - SHROPSHIRE

Report D1: Opinions on the structural options, by respondent type (all respondents)
Base: all

	Respondent Type					
	Indiv-iduals	Business groups	County, regional & national interests	Education (& church) groups	Local groups	Parish and town councils
Status quo/two-tier	3479 *76%*	49 *31%*	34 *76%*	135 *91%*	49 *58%*	83 *87%*
Unitary Wrekin	860 *19%*	101 *65%*	5 *11%*	6 *4%*	31 *37%*	11 *12%*
Two unitary authorities (Wrekin and rest of Shropshire)	5 *	4 *3%*	- -	- -	- -	1 *1%*
County Level Authority (Either two-tier or Unitary)	154 *3%*	1 *1%*	- -	- -	- -	- -
County-wide unitary structure	5 *	1 *1%*	- -	- -	- -	- -
Reject	3 *	- -	- -	- -	- -	- -
Others specified	7 *	- -	- -	- -	1 *1%*	- -
No preference expressed/option defined	91 *2%*	- -	6 *13%*	7 *5%*	3 *4%*	- -
BASE TOTAL	4604	156	45	148	84	95

* *Less than ½%*

NOP Analysis of Responses to Local Government Commission Draft Recommendations - SHROPSHIRE

Report D2: Opinions on the structural options, by respondent type
Base: respondents in The Wrekin only

	Respondent Type					
	Indiv-iduals	Business groups	County, regional & national interests	Education (& church) groups	Local groups	Parish and town councils
Status quo/two-tier	897 *53%*	22 *20%*	3 *75%*	35 *83%*	5 *14%*	9 *47%*
Unitary Wrekin	724 *42%*	83 *77%*	1 *25%*	5 *12%*	30 *83%*	10 *53%*
Two unitary authorities (Wrekin and rest of Shropshire)	3 *	3 *3%*	- -	- -	- -	- -
County Level Authority (Either two-tier or Unitary)	52 *3%*	- -	- -	- -	- -	- -
Reject	1 *	- -	- -	- -	- -	- -
Others specified	4 *	- -	- -	- -	- -	- -
No preference expressed/option defined	24 *1%*	- -	- -	2 *5%*	1 *3%*	- -
BASE TOTAL	1705	108	4	42	36	19

* *Less than ½%*

NOP Analysis of Responses to Local Government Commission Draft Recommendations - SHROPSHIRE

Report D3: Opinions on the structural options, by respondent type
Base: respondents in rest of county only

	Respondent Type					
	Indiv-iduals	Business groups	County, regional & national interests	Education (& church) groups	Local groups	Parish and town councils
Status quo/two-tier	2519 *90%*	23 *68%*	29 *91%*	98 *94%*	39 *95%*	74 *97%*
Unitary Wrekin	110 *4%*	9 *26%*	1 *3%*	1 *1%*	- -	1 *1%*
Two unitary authorities (Wrekin and rest of Shropshire)	2 *	1 *3%*	- -	- -	- -	1 *1%*
County Level Authority (Either two-tier or Unitary)	101 *4%*	- -	- -	- -	- -	- -
County-wide unitary structure	5 *	1 *3%*	- -	- -	- -	- -
Reject	2 *	- -	- -	- -	- -	- -
Others specified	3 *	- -	- -	- -	1 *2%*	- -
No preference expressed/option defined	63 *2%*	- -	2 *6%*	5 *5%*	1 *2%*	- -
BASE TOTAL	2805	34	32	104	41	76

* *Less than ½%*

NOP Analysis of Responses to Local Government Commission Draft Recommendations - SHROPSHIRE

Report E: Views on services, by authority of respondent
Base: all

	Review district	Other districts in county							
	The Wrekin	Bridgnorth	North Shropshire	Oswestry	Shrewsbury & Atcham	South Shropshire	Rest of county total	County total	Out of county total
Archives	-	-	-	-	2	-	2	2	1
	-	-	-	-	*	-	*	*	*1%*
Education	21	12	7	4	21	5	49	70	4
	1%	*2%*	*1%*	*1%*	*2%*	*1%*	*2%*	*1%*	*3%*
Libraries	-	-	1	1	-	-	2	2	-
	-	-	*	*	-	-	*	*	-
Trading standards	-	-	-	-	-	-	-	-	1
	-	-	-	-	-	-	-	-	*1%*
Other specified services (or multiples of)	3	-	1	-	4	2	7	10	3
	*	-	*	-	*	*	*	*	*2%*
BASE TOTAL	1914	539	530	304	1287	432	3092	5006	126

The figures in the table above do not sum to the base total/100% because undefined fields are not included, except as part of the base total.

* *Less than* ½%

NOP Analysis of Responses to Local Government Commission Draft Recommendations - SHROPSHIRE

Report F: Views on services, by respondent type
Base: all

	Respondent Type					
	Indiv-iduals	Business groups	County, regional & national interests	Education (& church) groups	Local groups	Parish and town councils
Archives	1	-	1	-	1	-
	*	-	*2%*	-	*1%*	-
Education	67	-	-	7	-	-
	1%	-	-	*5%*	-	-
Libraries	2	-	-	-	-	-
	*	-	-	-	-	-
Trading standards	-	-	1	-	-	-
	-	-	*2%*	-	-	-
Other specified services (or multiples of)	7	-	4	-	2	-
	*	-	*9%*	-	*2%*	-
BASE TOTAL	4604	156	45	148	84	95

The figures in the table above do not sum to the base total/100% because undefined fields are not included, except as part of the base total.

* *Less than* ½%

NOP Analysis of Responses to Local Government Commission Draft Recommendations - SHROPSHIRE

Report G: Type of respondent, by authority of respondent
Base: all

	Review district	Other districts in county							
	The Wrekin	Bridgnorth	North Shropshire	Oswestry	Shrewsbury & Atcham	South Shropshire	Rest of county total	County total	Out of county total
Individuals	1705 *89%*	481 *89%*	480 *91%*	270 *89%*	1182 *92%*	392 *91%*	2805 *91%*	4510 *90%*	94 *75%*
Business groups	108 *6%*	12 *2%*	4 *1%*	3 *1%*	10 *1%*	5 *1%*	34 *1%*	142 *3%*	14 *11%*
County, regional and national interests	4 *	- -	1 *	- -	28 *2%*	3 *1%*	32 *1%*	36 *1%*	9 *7%*
Education (and church) groups	42 2%	22 4%	22 4%	12 4%	37 3%	11 3%	104 3%	146 3%	2 2%
Local Groups	36 *2%*	6 *1%*	7 *1%*	10 *3%*	14 *1%*	4 *1%*	41 *1%*	77 *2%*	7 *6%*
Parish and town councils	19 *1%*	18 *3%*	16 *3%*	9 *3%*	16 *1%*	17 *4%*	76 *2%*	95 *2%*	- -
BASE TOTAL	1914	539	530	304	1287	432	3092	5006	126

* *Less than ½%*

NOP Analysis of Responses to Local Government Commission Draft Recommendations - SHROPSHIRE

Report H: Opinions on the structural options, by ward/area of respondent
Base: all

	The Wrekin															
	Arleston	Brook-side	Church Aston	College	Cuckoo Oak	Dawley Magna	Donning-ton	Donning-ton Wood	Dothill & Park	Edgmond	Ercall	Ercall Magna	Hadley	Haygate	Hollins-wood & Randlay	Iron-bridge
Status quo/two-tier	8 *31%*	18 *41%*	33 *60%*	16 *41%*	16 *39%*	34 *41%*	11 *42%*	11 *55%*	61 *54%*	64 *76%*	47 *65%*	57 *75%*	18 *31%*	31 *51%*	19 *28%*	56 *64%*
Unitary Wrekin	17 *65%*	25 *57%*	19 *35%*	21 *54%*	25 *61%*	48 *58%*	15 *58%*	8 *40%*	50 *44%*	13 *15%*	25 *35%*	13 *17%*	39 *67%*	24 *39%*	41 *61%*	29 *33%*
Two unitary authorities (Wrekin and rest of Shropshire)	1 *4%*	1 *2%*	-	-	-	-	-	-	-	-	-	-	-	1 *2%*	1 *1%*	1 *1%*
County Level Authority (Either two-tier or Unitary)	-	-	3 *5%*	2 *5%*	-	-	-	-	1 *1%*	6 *7%*	-	3 *4%*	-	3 *5%*	4 *6%*	-
Reject	-	-	-	-	-	-	-	1 *5%*	-	-	-	-	-	-	-	-
Others specified	-	-	-	-	-	-	-	-	-	-	-	1 *1%*	-	-	-	-
No preference expressed/option defined	-	-	-	-	-	1 *1%*	-	-	1 *1%*	1 *1%*	-	2 *3%*	1 *2%*	2 *3%*	2 *3%*	1 *1%*
BASE TOTAL	26	44	55	39	41	83	26	20	113	84	72	76	58	61	67	87

continued/

NOP Analysis of Responses to Local Government Commission Draft Recommendations - SHROPSHIRE

Report H: Opinions on the structural options, by ward/area of respondent
Base: all
/continued

	The Wrekin																
	Ketley	Ketley Bank	Langley	Lawley	Lee-gomery	Lille-shall	Madeley	Malin-slee	Newport East	Newport North	Newport West	Prior-slee	Stirch-ley	Wom-bridge	Wood-side	Wrock-wardine	Wrock-wardine Wood
Status quo/two-tier	26 *60%*	8 *42%*	8 *31%*	21 *46%*	23 *38%*	29 *58%*	32 *41%*	10 *29%*	33 *49%*	55 *77%*	29 *57%*	39 *42%*	39 *66%*	24 *38%*	21 *45%*	54 *59%*	18 *31%*
Unitary Wrekin	14 *33%*	11 *58%*	18 *69%*	24 *52%*	30 *50%*	21 *42%*	39 *50%*	23 *66%*	32 *48%*	13 *18%*	22 *43%*	49 *53%*	20 *34%*	38 *60%*	14 *30%*	32 *35%*	39 *66%*
Two unitary authorities (Wrekin and rest of Shropshire)	-	-	-	-	-	-	-	-	-	1 *1%*	-	-	-	-	-	-	-
County Level Authority (Either two-tier or Unitary)	2 *5%*	-	-	1 *2%*	6 *10%*	-	4 *5%*	2 *6%*	-	-	-	4 *4%*	-	-	5 *11%*	4 *4%*	2 *3%*
Others specified	-	-	-	-	-	-	-	-	2 *3%*	1 *1%*	-	-	-	-	-	-	-
No preference expressed/option defined	1 *2%*	-	-	-	1 *2%*	-	3 *4%*	-	-	1 *1%*	-	-	-	1 *2%*	7 *15%*	2 *2%*	-
BASE TOTAL	43	19	26	46	60	50	78	35	67	71	51	92	59	63	47	92	59

NOP Analysis of Responses to Local Government Commission Draft Recommendations - SHROPSHIRE

Report I: Opinions on other issues, by ward/area of respondent
Base: all

	The Wrekin															
	Arleston	Brook-side	Church Aston	College	Cuckoo Oak	Dawley Magna	Donning-ton	Donning-ton Wood	Dothill & Park	Edgmond	Ercall	Ercall Magna	Hadley	Haygate	Hollins-wood & Randlay	Iron-bridge
BASE TOTAL	26	44	55	39	41	83	26	20	113	84	72	76	58	61	67	87

The figures in the table above do not sum to the base total/100% because undefined fields are not included, except as part of the base total.

continued/

NOP Analysis of Responses to Local Government Commission Draft Recommendations - SHROPSHIRE

Base: all
/continued

	The Wrekin																
	Ketley	Ketley Bank	Langley	Lawley	Lee-gomery	Lille-shall	Madeley	Malin-slee	Newport East	Newport North	Newport West	Prior-slee	Stirch-ley	Wom-bridge	Wood-side	Wrock-wardine	Wrock-wardine Wood
BASE TOTAL	43	19	26	46	60	50	78	35	67	71	51	92	59	63	47	92	59

The figures in the table above do not sum to the base total/100% because undefined fields are not included, except as part of the base total.

MORI Research Study for the Local Government Commission

Introduction

Background

1 This summary report highlights the key findings from a survey of public opinion conducted in the district of the Wrekin and across the County of Shropshire on behalf of the Local Government Commission for England. A copy of each of the marked-up questionnaires is appended. The computer tabulations are contained in a separate volume, which is available from MORI (32 Old Queen Street, London SW1H 9HP. Telephone 0171-222 0232. Price £15)

2 The survey was designed in close consultation with the Commission, following extensive qualitative research and pilot testing. All sampling, interviewing and analysis have been carried out independently by MORI, within the guidelines of the profession laid out by the Market Research Society.

3 In The Wrekin, all Census Enumeration Districts (EDs) were sorted by ward, and stratified according to social class. EDs were then sampled (32 in total) in proportion to the population size of each, and quotas set for sex, age and work status. A total of 324 interviews with adults aged 18+, were conducted face-to-face and in-home, between 4 and 29 October 1995. Data are weighted to match the population profile in the district.

4 In the remaining districts of Shropshire, all EDs were sorted into ward, and again were stratified according to social class. A total of 32 EDs across the whole area (that is, Shropshire excluding The Wrekin) were sampled, with quotas set by sex, age and work status. Face-to-face interviews, conducted in-home, were carried out with 326 adults aged 18+ between 9 and 31 October 1995. Data were weighted to match the population profile of the County excluding The Wrekin.

5 In addition, a special booster sample was conducted in the part of The Wrekin outside of Telford to form a total sample of 111 interviews in this area. The special booster interviews were not included in the District analysis in order not to over-represent the area in the total analysis.

Publication of the Results

6 As with all our studies, these findings are subject to our Standard Terms and Conditions of Contract. Any press release or publication of the findings of this survey require the advance approval of MORI. Such approval will only be refused on the grounds of inaccuracy or misinterpretation.

Objectives

7 This survey took place during Stage Three, the consultation period on the Commission's draft recommendations. It measures public preferences for the organisation of local government in the area currently comprising the district of the Wrekin, as well as exploring strength of feeling, levels of knowledge about the review, involvement in, and broader perceptions of, local government in the area.

Statistical Reliability of the Data

8 Because we have interviewed a sample of residents, rather than the whole population, the results are subject to statistical tolerance limits, or "margins of error". These are expressed as our confidence that the true figure for the whole population falls within a given range. By convention this is expressed as a percentage, so our 95% confidence level means that in 95 times out of 100 the true figure would lie within this range.

9 The table below shows ranges of the 95% confidence level for a range of sample sizes. For each sample size, the table shows the tolerance limits for sample results close to 10%, 30% and 50%. Take, for example, the results of a survey of 300 residents showing that 50% are aware of the review. In 95 times out of 100 the true figure would lie between 44% and 56% (ie 50% ±6%).

	Sampling tolerances applicable to results at or near these percentages (based on 95% confidence level)		
Sample size	10/90% ±%	30/70% ±%	50% ±%
300	3	5	6
200	4	6	7
150	5	7	8
100	6	9	10
50	8	13	14

10 Clearly, 10% or 30% of the sample being aware of the review equate to 90% or 70% not being aware of it. So this table shows the ranges of 95% confidence for responses close to 10%, 30%, 50%, 70% and 90% of our sample. The figures for responses between can be obtained by extrapolation.

11 The true figure would only be known if all the residents of the area had been interviewed. It can be seen in the table, however, that large increases in the sample size do not greatly reduce the sampling tolerance. In addition, the true figure is more likely to lie at the midpoint of the range, rather than at either extreme.

12 When comparing results from separate groups within a sample we need to be sure that the differences are statistically significant. This would be important in comparing views expressed by different parts of a county. The table below shows how the statistical significance of the difference is determined by the size of the groups and the percentage result from the sample.

13 Assuming a 95% confidence level, the table shows the size of the differences required if different results are to be regarded as statistically significant. It can be seen that if 50% of a group of 300 were aware of the review, the result from another group of 300 would not become statistically significant until it became less than 42% or more than 58%.

	Differences required for significance at or near these percentage levels		
Sample sizes	10/90% ±	30/70% ±	50% ±
300 and 300	5	7	8
300 and 200	5	8	9
300 and 100	7	10	11
200 and 100	7	11	12
100 and 100	8	13	14

Survey Findings

Knowledge and Awareness

14 Residents within the The Wrekin profess broadly similar levels of knowledge and interest in local government as those living in the rest of the County of Shropshire. In both, a clear majority like to know what their council is doing, but want no greater involvement. Around one in five in both areas say they want a higher level of involvement.

15 While around two in five in the District and the County say they know at least a fair amount about what their council does, over half admit to not knowing very much or nothing at all.

16 This is reflected in the number of residents who incorrectly ascribe services between the two tiers of local government. Thus, although over half recognise libraries as a county council service, as many as three in ten allocate responsibility to their district/borough/city council. And although seven to eight in ten realise that refuse collection is a district/borough/city service, around one to two in ten think it is a county council service. Residents in The Wrekin are slightly more likely to be correct in identifying district services than are those living in the rest of the County.

17 Awareness of the review itself stands at 77% in The Wrekin and 80% in the rest of Shropshire. The proportion who say they know a fair amount or more is slightly higher in The Wrekin than in the rest of the County - 20%, compared to 14% in the rest of Shropshire.

Sources of Information

18 Local newspapers are the most common source of information about the review, by a considerable margin. Of those who have at least heard of the review, between five and six in ten name the local press as a recent source. Around two in three cite some media source as a recent source of information on the review.

19 It would appear that the County and District Councils have been fairly active in providing information to residents. Of those who have heard of the review, 36% in The Wrekin name a County Council source, and 47% do so in the rest of Shropshire. By comparison, 34% in The Wrekin mention a District Council source, as do 27% in the rest of Shropshire. Very few recognise receiving information directly from the Local Government Commission itself.

20 Although most of those aware of the review recognise one or more recent sources of information, few (around one in five) say that this has influenced their opinion.

21 Furthermore, in spite of a relatively low level of knowledge and engagement with their local authority, most people in The Wrekin say that the outcome of the review is either very important to them (28%) or fairly important (41%). As one might expect, people in the rest of Shropshire perceive a lower level of importance (26% very important and 27% fairly important).

The Preferred Option

22 The most preferred option in The Wrekin is a unitary Council (45%) rather than no change (38%). Opinion is consistent throughout the District, including the rural areas outside of Telford. In the rest of Shropshire, rather more would prefer The Wrekin to retain two tier local government (60%) than opt for the unitary solution (21%). The rest, 17% and 19% respectively, had no views or were indifferent.

23 People in The Wrekin feel slightly more strongly about the preference they express than do those living elsewhere in the County. In The Wrekin, 75% of those expressing a preference say they feel strongly (including 26% very strongly), while across the rest of Shropshire, 69% feel strongly (including 27% who say they feel very strongly). There is no significant difference in the strength of feeling expressed in The Wrekin according to which option is preferred. However, in the rest of the County those preferring no change feel more strongly overall than those preferring unitary Wrekin.

Factors in Expressing a Preference

24 In questions 13 to 23, residents were asked to say to what extent they agreed or disagreed with a range of statements which related to a change to unitary local government. The statements were designed to cover the main issues raised by residents during the qualitative phase of research, and others that formed a part of the Commission's brief to take into consideration in making its recommendations.

25 The following charts summarise the results from these questions, with the full question wording presented in the questionnaires in the appendices. Values have been ascribed to the five attitudinal positions that people were offered (+2 for strongly agree, +1 for tend to agree, 0 for neither agree nor disagree, -1 for tend to disagree, and -2 for strongly disagree) and mean scores calculated across all respondents expressing a view. This has the combined benefit of distilling the range of opinion into one summary figure, while incorporating the varying intensity of feeling by ascribing values. Bars to the right indicate that the mean score value is positive, and thus that there is a balance of agreement with the statement. Bars to the left, conversely, indicate a balance of disagreement.

26 The first chart, therefore, shows how the views of people living in the district of The Wrekin differ from those across the rest of Shropshire. In doing so, it illustrates the attitudes or perceptions that are, in relative terms, shared by both groups of residents (where the bars project in the same direction), and those where views differ markedly. Thus there is broad agreement on many of the positive aspects of change, although the balance of opinion tends to be more marked among residents in The Wrekin as one might expect. There is broad agreement that a County Council is needed for national representation (here, however, it is among residents in the rest of Shropshire that opinion is most marked). On the other hand, there is some divergence when it comes to whether change would be too disruptive and whether a unitary Wrekin would cost more. There is also divergence on whether people feel that they will be affected by change. Both people in The Wrekin and people in the rest of Shropshire are likely to agree that they would like more information before making up their minds.

27 The subsequent chart takes the results from just The Wrekin (and then from residents in the rest of Shropshire), and illustrates the difference in views between those within The Wrekin whose preference is for unitary status, and those who prefer no change. The chart therefore illustrates those attitudinal statements that most, or least, differentiate the residents of the District expressing the two opposing preferences. The perceived impact on efficiency is clearly a key determinant of opinion (in both The Wrekin and the rest of Shropshire), as are size, disruption, impact on services and whether a unitary council would reflect the community and be more in touch with local needs. The only sources of agreement between those who prefer no change and those who want change in both the District and the County are that it would be clearer who is responsible for local services, that there is a need for County representation and that they would like more information (as mentioned above).

Attitudes to Change
(All respondents)

Q To what extent do you agree or disagree that...?
(Figures represent 'mean scores' with *strong agreement* given a value of +2 through to *strong disagreement* given -2)

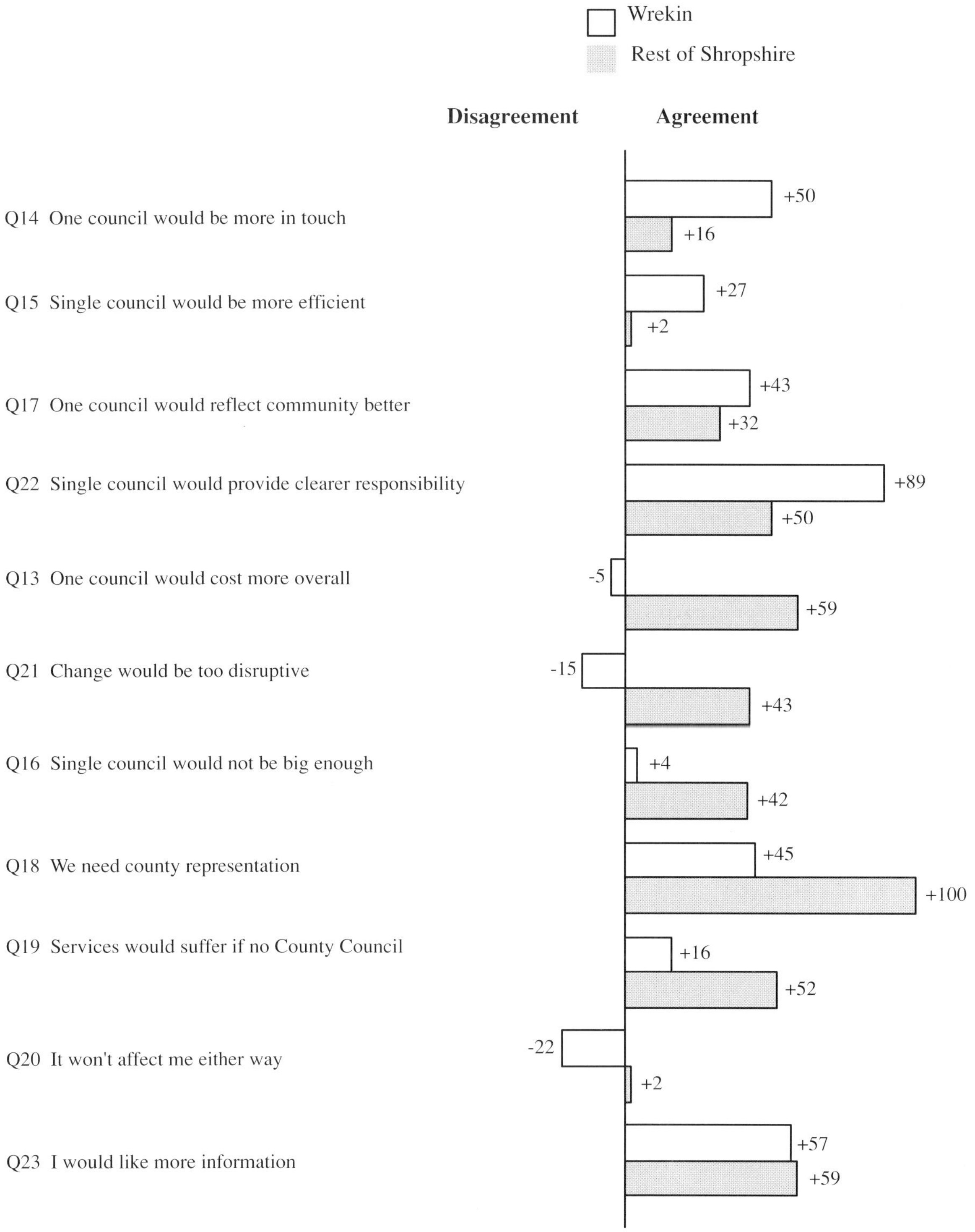

Attitudes to Change
(Respondents in The Wrekin)

Q To what extent do you agree or disagree that...?
(Figures represent 'mean scores' with *strong agreement* given a value of +2 through to *strong disagreement* given -2)

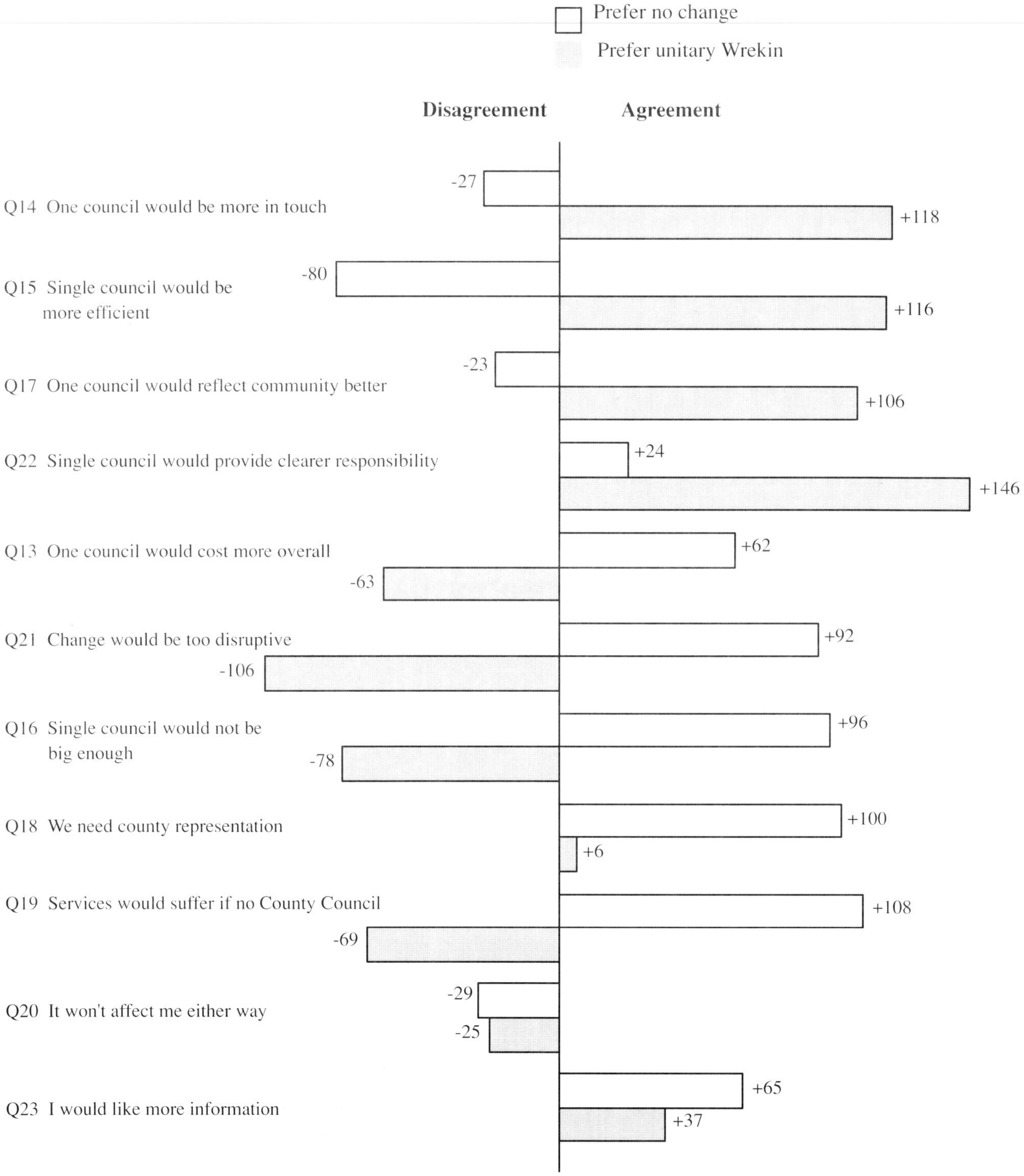

Attitudes to Change
(Respondents in the rest of Shropshire)

Q To what extent do you agree or disagree that...?
(Figures represent 'mean scores' with *strong agreement* given a value of +2 through to *strong disagreement* given -2)

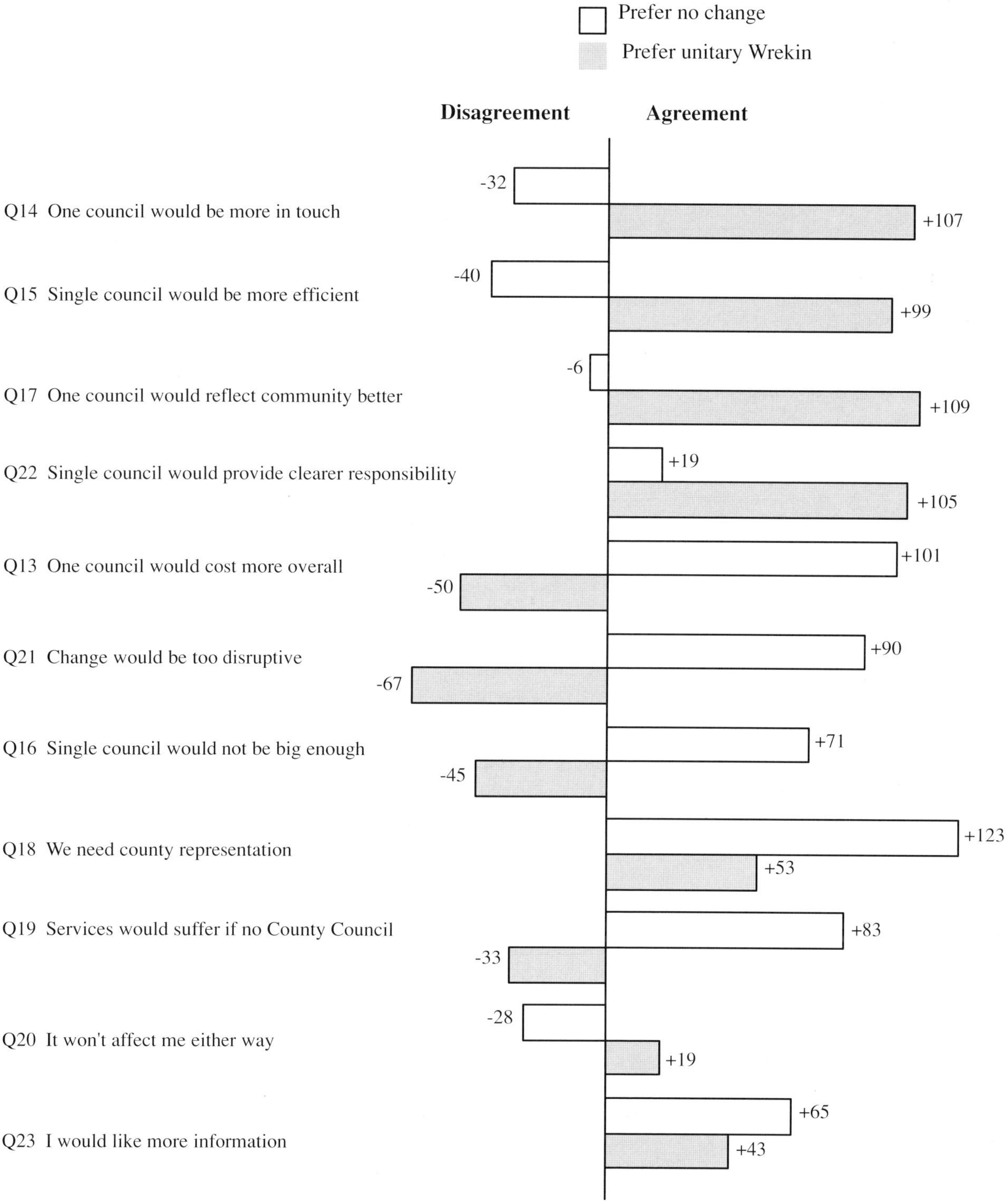

MORI/9101/11
(1-6)

SHROPSHIRE
REVIEW - REST OF COUNTY

Serial No . . . .
OUO (7-10)

TOPLINE FINDINGS

Gender %
Male 48
Female 52

Age %
18-24 12
25-34 17
35-44 13
45-54 21
55-64 15
65-74 12
75+.. 9

WRITE IN AGE [|]

Work Status %
Full-time (30 hrs/wk+) 46
Part-time (8-29 hrs/wk) 11
Not working (under 8 hrs) 2
Looking after home/children............ 7
Retired 26
Registered unemployed................... 2
Unemployed but not registered 1
Student... 2
Other 2

Occupation of Chief Income Earner (CIE)
Position/rank/grade

....
Industry/type of company

....
Qualifications/degrees/apprenticeship

....
No of Staff Responsible for

....
PROBE FOR PENSION

	%
AB	17
C1	36
C2	20
D	17
E	10

* Less than $^1/_2$%

Number in Household
Adults aged 18+ (inc. respondent)

18%	61%	13%	5%	2%
1	2	3	4	5+

Children (17 or under)

64%	13%	16%	5%	2%
0	1	2	3	4+

QA **Are you or other members of your household employed by a council?** IF YES: **Is this a Borough/District Council or a County Council?** CODE FOR BOTH RESPONDENT AND OTHER HOUSEHOLD MEMBERS

	Respondent %	Other %
Yes:		
Borough/District	3	2
County	4	6
Don't know which	*	*
No	93	78
Don't know	-	14

Tenure %
Owned outright.. 30
Buying on mortgage 41
Rented from Council 16
Rented from Housing Association 1
Rented from private landlord 8
Other 5

QB **Is this your main permanent home, or is it a second or holiday home?**
%
Main/permanent.................................. 99
Second/holiday .... *
Not stated .... *

Car in Household
CIRCLE NUMBER

17%	46%	28%	8%
0	1	2	3+

Showcard Version %
A-K 1
A1-K 2

THIS FORM IS THE PROPERTY OF MARKET & OPINION RESEARCH INTERNATIONAL (MORI)
32 OLD QUEEN STREET, LONDON, SW1H 9HP

INTERVIEWER DECLARATION: I confirm that I have conducted this interview face-to-face with the above named person and that I have asked all the relevant questions fully and recorded the answers in conformance with the survey specification and the MRS Code of Conduct.

Interviewer Name .... Signature ....

Interviewer Number					/	

	Month			Date	
DATE OF INTERVIEW					
	(29)	(30)		(30)	(32)

NB INTERVIEWER: ALL SHOWCARDS HAVE BEEN REVERSED. PLEASE BE CAREFUL TO CODE THE CORRECT RESPONSE.

Good morning/afternoon/evening. I'm from MORI, the market research and polling organisation. We are doing a survey about local issues, and I would like to ask you a few questions.

ASK ALL

Q1 **Firstly, how long have you lived in this area?** (WITHIN FIVE MILES)

	%
Less than 1 year	4
1-2 years	4
3-5 years	8
6-10 years	17
11-20 years	20
Over 20 years/all my life	46

Q2 SHOWCARD A (R) **From this card, how much would you say you know about local councils and the services they provide?**

	%
A great deal	4
A fair amount	36
Not very much	54
Nothing at all	7

Q3 SHOWCARD B (R) **Which of the statements on this card comes closest to your own view of the Councils in this area?**

		%
A)	I'm not interested in what the Council does, or whether they do their job	1
B)	I'm not interested in what the Council does, as long as they do their job	14
C)	I like to know what the Council is doing, but I'm happy to let them get on with their job	59
D)	I would like to have more of a say in what the Council does and the services it provides	21
E)	I already work for, or am involved with the Council and the services it provides	5
	Don't know	1

Q4 **From what you know, how many councils provide the main services in this neighbourhood?** (INTERVIEWER - NOT INCLUDING PARISH COUNCILS)

	%
One	27
Two	46
Three+	6
Don't know	20

In fact there are two main councils that provide, or are responsible for most services in this area: . . .district/borough/city and Shropshire County Council.

ROTATE ORDER OF Q5/6

☐ Q5 SHOWCARD C (R) **From this list, what services do you think are the responsibility of... district/borough/city council? Just read out the letter(s) that apply**

☐ Q6 SHOWCARD C AGAIN (R) **And which services on this list do you think are the responsibility of Shropshire County Council? Again, just read out the letters that apply.**

Q7 SHOWCARD D (R) **Which, if any, of these services do you or members of your family use?** INCLUDE ONLY LOCAL USE

		Q5 "Borough" %	Q6 County %	Q7 Use %
A	Bus Services	36	43	44
B	Car Parks	57	25	68
C	Council Housing	57	31	15
D	Council Tax Benefit/Housing benefit	52	31	19
E	Fire service	20	63	32
F	Food safety	29	38	16
G	Household waste sites/dumps	58	23	57
H	Libraries	29	53	58
I	Parks, playgrounds and open spaces	56	26	52
J	Planning service	52	33	18
K	Public conveniences	60	20	50
L	Recycling/bottle banks	56	18	63
M	Refuse collection	72	18	83
N	Road maintenance	32	58	46
O	Schools/education	17	72	34
P	Social services	17	60	16
Q	Street sweeping	64	21	45
R	Swimming pools/sports facilities	49	32	50
	Other	3	2	2
	None of these	-	1	1
	Don't know	8	10	3

Q8 SHOWCARD E (R) **As you may know, there is currently a review being undertaken by the Local Government Commission on the future local government structure in the county. How much, if anything, would you say you know about this?**

	%
A great deal	2
A fair amount	12
Just a little	43
Heard of but know nothing about	23
Never heard of	20

PREFERENCES

HAND OVER MAP SHOWING AREAS UNDER REVIEW AND "CURRENT SERVICES" CARD
The Local Government Commission is considering options for the future structure of local government in The Wrekin. Could you please read through this card, (SHOW OPTIONS CARD) **which outlines the options.**

Q9 **Please tell me which of the options, if either, you would prefer for The Wrekin?**
SINGLE CODE ONLY

For The Wrekin	%
Option A (Single all purpose council)	21
Option B (Stay the same/status quo)	60
Some other option	*
Neither of these	-
Either of these/don't mind	6
Don't care	3
Don't know	9

ASK IF "OTHER" NAMED AT Q9 (CODE 3)
Q10 **What other option is that?**
PROBE FULLY - DO NOT PROMPT.

....

....

....

....

ASK ALL PREFERRING AN OPTION (1, 2 OR 3 AT Q9). OTHERS GO TO Q13
Q11 SHOWCARD F (R) **You say that the option you would prefer is . . . . .** (INSERT OPTION PREFERRED). **How strongly would you say you feel about this?**
Base: (265)

	%
Very strongly	27
Fairly strongly	42
Not very strongly	20
Not at all strongly	3
Don't know	2

Q12 **What do you think would be the main advantages of . . .**(OPTION PREFERRED)
PROBE FULLY FOR DETAILS

....

....

....

....

....

Nothing...
Don't know/can't think of anything.................................

ATTITUDES TO PROPOSALS

SHOWCARD G (R) **Imagine that there was one council in the Wrekin providing all services. I am going to read out some statements that people have made about this proposal. To what extent do you agree or disagree that . . . .?** READ OUT, ROTATE ORDER OF ASKING Q13-22. TICK START

	READ OUT:		Strongly agree	Tend to agree	Neither/ Nor	Tend to disagree	Strongly disagree	Don't know	
☐	Q13	**It would cost more overall**	25	26	10	10	23	1	%
	Q14	**It would be more in touch with local people's needs**	8	42	11	22	11	5	%
	Q15	**The single Council would be more efficient than the current system of two Councils**	10	31	14	25	12	9	%
☐	Q16	**The single council would not be big enough to manage services such as Education and Social Services effectively**	15	39	9	21	5	11	%
	Q17	**It would better reflect the sense of community in the Wrekin**	8	41	14	16	7	15	%
	Q18	**We need a County Council to represent us nationally**	29	43	10	7	1	9	%
☐	Q19	**Services would suffer if the County Council no longer provides services in the Wrekin**	17	37	13	18	4	12	%
	Q20	**It won't affect me whether there is a single Council in the Wrekin or not**	9	36	9	24	14	8	%
	Q21	**The change to a single Council for the Wrekin would be too disruptive**	17	33	14	21	4	11	%
☐	Q22	**With a single Council it would be clearer who is responsible for local services**	12	51	10	16	6	4	%
	ASK LAST								
	Q23	**I would like to have more information on the proposals before making up my mind**	29	36	8	12	12	3	%

Q24 **On balance, which would you say is more in touch with local people and issues, ...** (ROTATE ORDER OF "DISTRICT" AND COUNTY) (INSERT NAME OF "DISTRICT COUNCIL)..**district/borough/city council, or Shropshire County Council, or would you say that they are both about the same?**

	%
District/borough/city council	61
Shropshire County Council	9
Both about the same	25
Don't know	5

REFER BACK TO Q8. ASK ALL WHO HAVE HEARD OF REVIEW AT Q8 (IE CODES 1/2/3/4). OTHERS TO Q28

Q25 SHOWCARD H **Earlier in the interview, you said that you had heard of the Review of local government structure. From which, if any, of the sources shown on this card have you recently heard about the Review?** INTERVIEWER NOTE: "RECENTLY" = IN PAST 3 MONTHS

		%
A	Leaflet from County Council delivered to your door	29
B	Leaflet from County Council in library/ offices, etc	4
C	Advertisement from County Council in local newspaper	20
D	Advertisement from County Council on local radio/TV	6
E	Leaflet from Borough Council delivered to your door	10
F	Leaflet from Borough Council in library/ offices, etc	1
G	Borough Council newspaper	3
H	County Council newspaper	2
I	Advertisement from Borough Council in local newspaper	10
J	Advertisement from Borough Council on local radio/TV	5
K	Advertisement by the Commission on local radio	1
L	Local Government Commission advertisement in local newspaper	5
M	Local newspaper	53
N	National newspaper	6
O	TV	11
P	Local radio	24
Q	National radio	2
R	Friends/neighbours/family	17
S	Conversation with Borough Councillor	5
T	Conversation with County Councillor	3
U	Conversation with Borough Council staff	3
V	Conversation with County Council staff	4
W	Parish/community council	6
X	Residents' Association	*
	Other	9
	None of these	4
	Don't know	4

ASK ALL NAMING A SOURCE AT Q25. OTHERS GO TO Q28

Q26 **Would you say that the information you have received has influenced your opinion, or not?**
Base: (237)

	%
Yes	23
No	72
Don't know	5

Q27 **What information in particular has influenced your opinion?**

....

....

....

....

ASK ALL

Q28 SHOWCARD I (R) **Assuming you receive the same level of services, how important is it to you, if at all, what the final decision is on the future local government structure in the Wrekin?**

	%
Very important	26
Fairly important	27
Not very important	29
Not at all important	13
Don't know	4

ACTIVISM

Q29 SHOWCARD J **Which of the things on this list, if any, have you done in the last three years? Just read out the letter(s) that apply.**

		%
A	Voted in Local Council elections	84
B	Spoken or written to a local Councillor	38
C	Responded to the earlier Review of local government	13
D	Been to a meeting of a local committee or organisation (WRITE IN NAME OF ORGANISATION)	20
E	Spoken on a radio phone-in about a local issue	1
F	Written to a local newspaper about a local issue	4
G	Been to a meeting of a local branch of a political party	2
H	Written to your MP about a local issue	13
I	Been to a Council Committee meeting	4
J	Been to a Council meeting	6
K	Attended a public meeting run by the Council	12
	None of these	12
	Don't know/refused	1

Q30 SHOWCARD K **Which, if any, of these apply to you? Just read out the letter(s) that apply.**

		%
	I am a member of a:	
A	Residents' Association	3
B	Community Association	1
C	Tenants' Association	2
D	Neighbourhood Watch	23
E	PTA/school governors	6
	I do unpaid work for:	
F	A school	10
G	Citizens Advice Bureau	*
H	Volunteer Bureau	1
I	Scouts/Guides/Cubs/Brownies	3
J	Church group	9
	Other (WRITE IN AND CODE `X')	7
	None of these	61
	Don't know	1

- 8 -

MORI/9101/11
(1-6)

SHROPSHIRE
REVIEW - THE WREKIN

Serial No . . . .
OUO (7-10)

TOPLINE FINDINGS

Gender

	%
Male	49
Female	51

Age

	%
18-24	15
25-34	20
35-44	20
45-54	16
55-64	13
65-74	8
75+	7

WRITE IN AGE [ ][ ]

Work Status

	%
Full-time (30 hrs/wk+)	49
Part-time (8-29 hrs/wk)	9
Not working (under 8 hrs)	3
Looking after home/children	9
Retired	20
Registered unemployed	3
Unemployed but not registered	1
Student	2
Other	2

Occupation of Chief Income Earner (CIE)

Position/rank/grade

....

Industry/type of company

....

Qualifications/degrees/apprenticeship

....

No of Staff Responsible for

....

PROBE FOR PENSION

	%
AB	11
C1	24
C2	26
D	22
E	17

Number in Household

Adults aged 18+ (inc. respondent)

17%	64%	13%	5%	*%
1	2	3	4	5+

Children (17 or under)

54%	20%	15%	8%	2%
0	1	2	3	4+

QA **Are you or other members of your household employed by a council?** IF YES: **Is this a Borough/District Council or a County Council?**
CODE FOR BOTH RESPONDENT AND OTHER HOUSEHOLD MEMBERS

	Respondent %	Other %
Yes:		
Borough/District	2	1
County	7	4
Don't know which	*	*
No	90	92
Don't know	1	3

Tenure

	%
Owned outright	18
Buying on mortgage	48
Rented from Council	27
Rented from Housing Association	2
Rented from private landlord	3
Other	2

QB **Is this your main permanent home, or is it a second or holiday home?**

	%
Main/permanent	98
Second/holiday	*
Not stated	1

Car in Household

CIRCLE NUMBER

19%	52%	24%	5%
0	1	2	3+

THIS FORM IS THE PROPERTY OF MARKET & OPINION RESEARCH INTERNATIONAL (MORI)
32 OLD QUEEN STREET, LONDON, SW1H 9HP

INTERVIEWER DECLARATION: I confirm that I have conducted this interview face-to-face with the above named person and that I have asked all the relevant questions fully and recorded the answers in conformance with the survey specification and the MRS Code of Conduct.

Interviewer Name .... Signature ....

Interviewer Number					/	

	Month		Date		
DATE OF INTERVIEW					
	(29)	(30)		(30)	(32)

NB INTERVIEWER: ALL SHOWCARDS HAVE BEEN REVERSED. PLEASE BE CAREFUL TO CODE THE CORRECT RESPONSE.

Good morning/afternoon/evening. I'm from MORI, the market research and polling organisation. We are doing a survey about local issues, and I would like to ask you a few questions.

ASK ALL

Q1 **Firstly, how long have you lived in this area?** (WITHIN FIVE MILES)

	%
Less than 1 year	5
1-2 years	6
3-5 years	9
6-10 years	15
11-20 years	24
Over 20 years/all my life	40
Don't know/can't remember	*

Q2 SHOWCARD A (R) **From this card, how much would you say you know about local councils and the services they provide?**

	%
A great deal	3
A fair amount	38
Not very much	46
Nothing at all	8
Don't know	5

Q3 SHOWCARD B (R) **Which of the statements on this card comes closest to your own view of the Councils in this area?**

		%
A)	I'm not interested in what the Council does, or whether they do their job	1
B)	I'm not interested in what the Council does, as long as they do their job	14
C)	I like to know what the Council is doing, but I'm happy to let them get on with their job	59
D)	I would like to have more of a say in what the Council does and the services it provides	19
E)	I already work for, or am involved with the Council and the services it provides	4
	Don't know	2

Q4 **From what you know, how many councils provide the main services in this neighbourhood?** (INTERVIEWER - NOT INCLUDING PARISH COUNCILS)

	%
One	40
Two	35
Three+	3
Don't know	23

In fact there are two main councils that provide, or are responsible for most services in this area: The Wrekin District Council and Shropshire County Council.

ROTATE ORDER OF Q5/6

☐ Q5 SHOWCARD C (R) **From this list, what services do you think are the responsibility of the Wrekin District Council? Just read out the letter(s) that apply**

☐ Q6 SHOWCARD C AGAIN (R) **And which services on this list do you think are the responsibility of Shropshire County Council? Again, just read out the letters that apply.**

Q7 SHOWCARD D (R) **Which, if any, of these services do you or members of your family use?** INCLUDE ONLY LOCAL USE

		Q5 Wrekin %	Q6 Shropshire %	Q7 Use %
A	Bus Services	43	35	40
B	Car Parks	62	19	70
C	Council Housing	75	14	24
D	Council Tax Benefit/Housing benefit	63	23	34
E	Fire service	17	66	35
F	Food safety	26	49	35
G	Household waste sites/dumps	63	23	53
H	Libraries	25	58	58
I	Parks, playgrounds and open spaces	64	25	53
J	Planning service	51	38	9
K	Public conveniences	63	20	41
L	Recycling/bottle banks	64	21	50
M	Refuse collection	79	11	83
N	Road maintenance	38	56	47
O	Schools/education	19	68	42
P	Social services	24	61	20
Q	Street sweeping	64	22	38
R	Swimming pools/sports facilities	61	25	58
	Other	4	5	4
	None of these	-	*	1
	Don't know	8	14	1

Q8 SHOWCARD E (R) **As you may know, there is currently a review being undertaken by the Local Government Commission on the future local government structure in the county. How much, if anything, would you say you know about this?**

	%
A great deal	4
A fair amount	16
Just a little	38
Heard of but know nothing about	19
Never heard of	23

PREFERENCES

HAND OVER MAP SHOWING AREAS UNDER REVIEW AND "CURRENT SERVICES" CARD
The Local Government Commission is considering options for the future structure of local government in the Wrekin. Could you please read through this card, (SHOW OPTIONS CARD) **which outlines the options.**

Q9 **Please tell me which of the options, if either, you would prefer for The Wrekin?**
SINGLE CODE ONLY

For The Wrekin

	%
Option A (Single all purpose council)	45
Option B (Remain the same/status quo)	38
Some other option	1
Neither of these	1
Either of these/don't mind	6
Don't care	2
Don't know	7

ASK IF "OTHER" NAMED AT Q9 (CODE 3)

Q10 **What other option is that?**
PROBE FULLY - DO NOT PROMPT.

....

....

....

....

ASK ALL PREFERRING AN OPTION (1, 2 OR 3 AT Q9). OTHERS GO TO Q13

Q11 SHOWCARD F (R) **You say that the option you would prefer is . . . . .** (INSERT OPTION PREFERRED). **How strongly would you say you feel about this?**
Base: (269)

	%
Very strongly	26
Fairly strongly	49
Not very strongly	19
Not at all strongly	3
Don't know	4

Q12 **What do you think would be the main advantages of . . .**(OPTION PREFERRED)
PROBE FULLY FOR DETAILS

....

....

....

....

....

Nothing..........
Don't know/can't think of anything..........

ATTITUDES TO PROPOSALS

SHOWCARD G (R) **Imagine that there was one council in the Wrekin providing all services. I am going to read out some statements that people have made about this proposal. To what extent do you agree or disagree that . . . .?** READ OUT, ROTATE ORDER OF ASKING Q13-22. TICK START

READ OUT:		Strongly agree	Tend to agree	Neither/ Nor	Tend to disagree	Strongly disagree	Don't know	
Q13	**It would cost more overall**	10	25	8	32	9	16	%
Q14	**It would be more in touch with local people's needs**	19	38	8	17	7	10	%
Q15	**The single Council would be more efficient than the current system of two Councils**	15	34	11	16	12	12	%
Q16	**The single council would not be big enough to manage services such as Education and Social Services effectively**	17	20	12	29	11	12	%
Q17	**It would better reflect the sense of community in the Wrekin**	14	41	12	13	9	12	%
Q18	**We need a County Council to represent us nationally**	21	33	14	19	7	7	%
Q19	**Services would suffer if the County Council no longer provides services in the Wrekin**	15	28	11	20	12	14	%
Q20	**It won't affect me whether there is a single Council in the Wrekin or not**	7	24	12	26	15	16	%
Q21	**The change to a single Council for the Wrekin would be too disruptive**	12	22	11	29	15	12	%
Q22	**With a single Council it would be clearer who is responsible for local services**	32	35	10	10	4	10	%
ASK LAST Q23	**I would like to have more information on the proposals before making up my mind**	27	33	13	10	12	5	%

Q24 **On balance, which would you say is more in touch with local people and issues, ...** (ROTATE ORDER OF "DISTRICT" AND COUNTY)
The Wrekin District Council, or **Shropshire County Council, or would you say that they are both about the same?**

	%
The Wrekin district council	53
Shropshire County Council	6
Both about the same	32
Don't know	9

REFER BACK TO Q8. ASK ALL WHO HAVE HEARD OF REVIEW AT Q8 (IE CODES 1/2/3/4). OTHERS TO Q28

Q25 SHOWCARD H **Earlier in the interview, you said that you had heard of the Review of local government structure. From which, if any, of the sources shown on this card have you recently heard about the Review?** INTERVIEWER NOTE: "RECENTLY" = IN PAST 3 MONTHS

		%
A	Leaflet from County Council delivered to your door	24
B	Leaflet from County Council in library/ offices, etc	3
C	Advertisement from County Council in local newspaper	16
D	Advertisement from County Council on local radio/TV	3
E	Leaflet from Borough Council delivered to your door	23
F	Leaflet from Borough Council in library/ offices, etc	4
G	Borough Council newspaper	9
H	County Council newspaper	5
I	Advertisement from Borough Council in local newspaper	6
J	Advertisement from Borough Council on local radio/TV	4
K	Advertisement by the Commission on local radio	1
L	Local Government Commission advertisement in local newspaper	3
M	Local newspaper	59
N	National newspaper	3
O	TV	9
P	Local radio	18
Q	National radio	4
R	Friends/neighbours/family	11
S	Conversation with Borough Councillor	2
T	Conversation with County Councillor	1
U	Conversation with Borough Council staff	2
V	Conversation with County Council staff	1
W	Parish/community council	3
X	Residents' Association	1
	Other	10
	None of these	1
	Don't know	5

ASK ALL NAMING A SOURCE AT Q25. OTHERS GO TO Q28

Q26 **Would you say that the information you have received has influenced your opinion, or not?**
Base: (222)

	%
Yes	21
No	71
Don't know	9

Q27 **What information in particular has influenced your opinion?**

....

....

....

....

ASK ALL

Q28 SHOWCARD I (R) **Assuming you receive the same level of services, how important is it to you, if at all, what the final decision is on the future local government structure in the Wrekin?**

	%
Very important	28
Fairly important	41
Not very important	21
Not at all important	8
Don't know	2

ACTIVISM

Q29 SHOWCARD J **Which of the things on this list, if any, have you done in the last three years? Just read out the letter(s) that apply.**

		%
A	Voted in Local Council elections	75
B	Spoken or written to a local Councillor	22
C	Responded to the earlier Review of local government	12
D	Been to a meeting of a local committee or organisation (WRITE IN NAME OF ORGANISATION)	11
E	Spoken on a radio phone-in about a local issue	2
F	Written to a local newspaper about a local issue	4
G	Been to a meeting of a local branch of a political party	2
H	Written to your MP about a local issue	8
I	Been to a Council Committee meeting	2
J	Been to a Council meeting	6
K	Attended a public meeting run by the Council	8
	None of these	19
	Don't know/refused	1

Q30 SHOWCARD K **Which, if any, of these apply to you? Just read out the letter(s) that apply.**

		%
	I am a member of a:	
A	Residents' Association	2
B	Community Association	3
C	Tenants' Association	2
D	Neighbourhood Watch	11
E	PTA/school governors	3
	I do unpaid work for:	
F	A school	4
G	Citizens Advice Bureau	-
H	Volunteer Bureau	-
I	Scouts/Guides/Cubs/Brownies	2
J	Church group	6
	Other	3
	None of these	72
	Don't know	1

THANK RESPONDENT. GO TO DEMOGRAPHICS.

SUMMARY OF NATIONAL REPRESENTATIONS

Archives

1 The Commission received representations over the effect which structural change might have on the provision of local authority archive services from four national organisations: the Lord Chancellor's Advisory Council on Public Records, the National Council on Archives, the Public Record Office (PRO) and the Royal Commission on Historical Manuscripts.

2 The Lord Chancellor's Advisory Council explained that about one-fifth of all public records were stored in local places of deposit throughout the country, many of them local authority archive centres. It was therefore concerned about the impact of local government reorganisation on the provision of local authority archive services, which might in turn affect public records.

3 The Advisory Council emphasised that the Public Record Office would need to be consulted over the arrangements for archive services before new unitary authorities were established. It also expressed concern over the lack of reserve powers to establish joint authorities where voluntary arrangements between unitary authorities and county councils do not prove possible.

4 The Advisory Council reinforced its concerns during Stage Three, commenting that the provision of archive services was "...a question of vital significance to the nation's heritage".

5 Similar concerns were expressed by the National Council on Archives, which felt that the retention of the existing two-tier structure would be the best outcome for the archive service. It also felt that the absence of reserve powers to establish joint authorities for the service could result in its financial base being eroded, since there was no certainty that the new unitary authorities would contribute towards a county councils' costs in maintaining archives.

6 In Stage Three, the National Council reiterated its concerns, expressing the view that "...the collections themselves are in very many cases county-wide and cannot be split. The need to maintain county-wide services derives from this strategic coverage of the whole county as much as from the small and specialist nature of most local authority archive services".

7 The PRO commented that "...any changes in the structure of local government should, at the very least, safeguard existing standards of preservation for locally held public records. We believe that reorganisation should not be allowed to have any adverse impact on the county record office network". It also expressed the view that the present county-wide archive services would be most effectively maintained in the existing structure of local government in all the areas under review and that, in its experience, local government units smaller than the current counties would find it difficult to find the resources required to provide a satisfactory local archive service.

8 The PRO also drew attention to the lack of reserve powers to establish joint authorities in hybrid counties. In its view, this emphasised the need for binding agreements to secure the long-term future of existing archive services.

9 In addition to commenting on individual review areas, the Royal Commission on Historical Manuscripts argued that the costs of meeting today's standards of building and service provision meant that the archive service was best delivered from a few large centres. In its view, fragmentation meant sacrificing economies of scale and shared expertise, leading to a lowering of standards. There was therefore a need for a commitment to joint funding, where necessary, to maintain services at their present levels.

10 As the districts subject to review were central to county-wide archive provision, if not the home to the headquarters of the counties' archive services, the Royal Commission indicated that it would not support any of the districts bidding to run an independent archive service.

11 The Royal Commission expressed its concerns again during Stage Three of the review. It commented that the archive service, predominantly provided at the county level at present, was potentially vulnerable to change to the two-tier structure. These dangers would not only be present if a unitary authority chose to set up its own archive service, but also if a new unitary authority accepted the need for a county-wide service but was unwilling to give sufficient financial support.

National Heritage

12 The Museums and Galleries Commission commented specifically on the reviews of Exeter, Gloucester and The Wrekin. It also resubmitted representations, both general and specific, made during the course of the 1994 county-wide structural reviews. In addition, the Commission drew attention to and endorsed the sentiments in the Secretary of State's *Guidance* about the future maintenance of archive and museum functions, and the possible need for joint strategies and co-operative funding arrangements.

13 In the interests of overall efficiency, the preference of the Royal Commission on the Historical Monuments of England was for the retention of the specialist information systems provided by county sites and monuments records. The Royal Commission commented that these provide an essential archaeological information and advisory service to the development control process within constituent district authorities, and that it would urge the Secretary of State to require all new authorities to discuss their proposals for the support and delivery of heritage services with them and English Heritage.

14 In Stage Three the Royal Commission reinforced the arguments that it had submitted earlier in the review, and made specific comments on a number of the Commission's draft recommendations.

Trading Standards

15 The Commission received a total of 27 national submissions in respect of trading standards from a wide range of leading businesses, business groups and other organisations. They included the Association of Public Analysts, the British Bankers' Association, the British Retail Association, the Finance and Leasing Association, Levi Strauss & Co, Marks & Spencer Limited, the Ministry of Agriculture, Fisheries and Food (MAFF), Proctor & Gamble Limited, The Assay Office, The Boots Company plc, and Unilever UK Limited.

16 Virtually all respondents expressed concern that changes in the structure of local government might lead to the fragmentation of the trading standards service. They felt that this in turn might result in a loss of expertise, specialist knowledge and consistency in the service. Many argued that such an outcome would be to the detriment not only of consumers, but also business and commerce.

17 In addition to these concerns, the Association of British Chambers of Commerce expressed doubts over the effectiveness and durability of voluntary arrangements between authorities on the trading standards service, a view which was shared by a number of respondents. The Association commented that it would prefer to see statutory arrangements, which would ensure the consistent delivery of the service to its current high quality, or better.

18 MAFF highlighted the need for the adequate resourcing of trading standards departments. The Ministry explained the 'Home Authority' principle, under which the local authority in whose area a major company had its operational base undertook responsibility for assisting and advising that company on compliance with food laws. It commented that this could be a considerable commitment for the authority if the headquarters of one of the large national or international companies was located in their area.

19 A number of firms and organisations also drew attention to the role trading standards departments play in combatting counterfeiting a wide range of products, again expressing concern over the possible fragmentation of the service. The Anti-Counterfeiting Group commented "...we fear that any fragmentation of the service in the local government review would mean a resulting diminution of effectiveness in the fight against counterfeiting as economies of scale, strategic planning and close co-ordination all become more difficult".

Planning

20 The County Planning Officers' Society, which represents the chief planning advisers to the shire counties, considered that the Commission's draft recommendations for the creation of unitary authorities would have an unsatisfactory effect on planning services. It argued that the resultant voluntary joint working between the unitary authorities and the residual county councils on structure planning and associated development programmes would be too fragile to survive the "robust debate" which takes place on such matters. Accordingly, it considered that the viability of the strategic planning process would be threatened in the medium term.

21 The Society also commented that the removal of part of a county area would impact adversely on the financial resources available to structure planning teams. While the teams would still have to plan on a county-wide basis, the resources available to a county council under the present Standard Spending Assessment arrangements would be substantially reduced.

Public Protection

22 HM Chief Inspector of Fire Services indicated that the Central Fire Brigades Advisory Council's Sub-Committee on the Local Government Review (which advises the Home Secretary on the implications for the fire service of the local government review process) had been consulted over the Commission's draft recommendations. The Chief Inspector reported that the Advisory Council's Sub-Committee had endorsed the proposal that, where there is structural change, combined fire authorities should be established for each existing county, in order to avoid unnecessary upheaval for the service.

23 However, the Chief Inspector expressed concern about the transitional costs which could arise for the fire service as a result of local government reorganisation. He commented that fire authorities would not stand to benefit from any long term savings emerging from the review process.

Social Services

24 The Association of Directors of Social Services acknowledged that personal social services could be organised and delivered effectively in both two-tier and unitary authorities. However, it expressed the view that, with the increasing focus on planning, commissioning and regulation, social services departments must have sufficient economies of scale to perform their role effectively and efficiently. These economies of scale were lessened by the creation of new unitary authorities. While it was open to unitary authorities to combine their resources, experience had shown that they were likely to resist joint arrangements with continuing county councils, except for specific services.

25 The Association felt that there was a risk to the quality of some services if an effective network and partnership approach with other agencies were to be fragmented. This could lessen the protection currently afforded to the most vulnerable.

26 The Chief Inspector of the Social Services Inspectorate at the Department of Health commented on the Commission's draft recommendations for individual review areas. However, more generally, he urged the Commission to take account of the complexity of personal social services, the need for good co-ordination with the NHS and, when necessary, the need for joint arrangements. He commented that the various specialised social services should be safeguarded and where personal social services were combined with other local government service departments, there should be clear lines of accountability to the Director of Social Services and the Social Services Committee.

Voluntary Sector

27 The National Association of Councils for Voluntary Service (NACVS) commented that it was primarily concerned with strategic issues and policy, and therefore had an interest in a local authority structure that could operate adequately at a strategic level. Having said that, it felt that it was the nature of relationships with local authorities that was of importance, rather than the size of the authorities' area.

28 It considered that the voluntary sector needed to be assured that the nature of its relationship with new authorities would enable the voluntary organisations to be effective partners. It would be essential that the review resulted in a clear policy and strategy for maintaining voluntary sector funding to at least existing levels. This would need to be combined with clear structures for liaison between statutory bodies, for example health authorities, and arrangements to secure good practices.

29 Voluntary sector access to resources and goods in kind, such as premises, was a vital addition to the funding support of voluntary groups. However, NACVS considered that they were harder to make available in a small authority due to the less flexible use of resources. In its view, small authorities were unlikely to have budgets large enough to maintain a full range of specialist services. These would have to be bought from the county council or other supplier, creating the need for joint arrangements and increasing bureaucracy at the expense of services.

30 The Royal Society for Mentally Handicapped Children and Adults (MENCAP) expressed the view there were enough changes already taking place within health and social services, and further change was not helpful. Arrangements should be made for maintaining existing working relationships, commitments and expertise.

Environment and Conservation

31 The Rural Development Commission referred specifically in its Stage One submission to the districts of Broxtowe, Gedling, Rushcliffe, Gloucester, Exeter, Huntingdonshire, Norwich and The Wrekin. More generally, it expressed the view that the Commission should take account of "...the needs and dispositions of rural communities and their focus for work, and [the] provision of services should be reflected in any future local government structure". It drew attention to the need to strengthen the economies of the needier rural areas, and to ensure that development was not restricted in the more prosperous areas.

32 The Commission felt that due consideration should be given to the need for joint arrangements in the event of a hybrid structure, since some issues affecting the countryside, such as population growth, development pressures and the need strategic planning, required co-operation across wider areas than most current district boundaries.

Other

33 The Association of District Councils (ADC) did not submit representations specific to individual review areas. Rather, it restricted its comments to the Commission's report *The 1995 Review of 21 Districts in England - Overview Report.*

34 In general, the ADC welcomed the approach set out in that report, which it considered to be "deliberative and rational". However, it drew attention to a number of issues, such as size of authorities, service provision, boundaries, community identity and centrality, on which it felt the Commission should either have adopted a different approach or to which it should give further reflection and examination.

35 The Association of County Councils submitted individual representations for each of the counties in which reviews took place; its views are referred to in the relevant chapter of this volume.

36 The Automobile Association (AA) emphasised the need that for new unitary authorities and their continuing county councils to be able to deliver transport services. How this was to be achieved, either at the unitary or joint arrangement level, needed to be fully assessed and agreed before decisions to fragment existing counties were taken. The AA felt that, unless formalised now, the new unitary and remaining two-tier authorities would be unable to deliver acceptable transportation services.

37 The Local Identity Agency commented that while it strongly supported unitary status for the big cities and free-standing county boroughs, it believed that many solutions to two-tier problems lay within the two-tier structure itself. The Agency considered that there was a danger of exaggerating these problems and assuming that unitary government provided automatic solutions. In its view, the biggest obstacle to the success of measures to improve the two-tier structure was the lack of goodwill between authorities still competing over unitary status.

38 The Commission also received two submissions from private individuals which it treated as national submissions. One was written in support of maintaining current library service standards; the other expressed concern about the disruption caused by reorganisation.

APPENDIX

The Commision's Draft Recommendation Reports

Available from HMSO

Review Area	Issued	ISBN	Price
Basildon and Thurrock	September 1995	0-11-780113-5	£14.50
Blackburn and Blackpool	September 1995	0-11-780120-8	£15.00
Broxtowe, Gedling and Rushcliffe	September 1995	0-11-780121-6	£13.75
Dartford, Gillingham, Gravesham and Rochester upon Medway	September 1995	0-11-780114-3	£15.75
Exeter	September 1995	0-11-780118-6	£11.25
Gloucester	September 1995	0-11-780116-X	£12.00
Halton and Warrington	September 1995	0-11-780119-4	£15.00
Huntingdonshire and Peterborough	September 1995	0-11-780123-2	£15.00
Northampton	September 1995	0-11-780122-4	£12.00
Norwich	September 1995	0-11-780115-1	£12.00
Spelthorne	September 1995	0-11-780124-0	£12.75
The Wrekin	September 1995	0-11-780117-8	£12.00
The 1995 Review of 21 Districts in England - Overview Report	September 1995	0-11-780125-9	£10.25

HMSO Telephone Hot Line: 24 hour Orders - 0171 873 9090
HMSO General Enquiries - 0171 873 0011

Printed in the UK for HMSO. Dd. 301832 C105 12/95 9385 3533